THE PSALMS AS CHRISTIAN WORSHIP

The Psalms as Christian Worship

A Historical Commentary

Bruce K. Waltke & James M. Houston

With

Erika Moore

William B. Eerdmans Publishing Company
Grand Rapids, Michigan / Cambridge, U.K.

Published 2010 by
Wm. B. Eerdmans Publishing Co.
2140 Oak Industrial Drive N.E., Grand Rapids, Michigan 49505 /
P.O. Box 163, Cambridge CB3 9PU U.K.

Printed in the United States of America

15 14 13 12 11 10 7 6 5 4 3 2 1

Library of Congress Cataloging-in-Publication Data

Waltke, Bruce K.
The Psalms as Christian worship: a historical commentary /
Bruce K. Waltke & James M. Houston; with Erika Moore.
p. cm.
ISBN 978-0-8028-6374-4 (pbk.: alk. paper)
1. Bible. O.T. Psalms — Criticism, interpretation, etc.
I. Houston, J. M. (James Macintosh), 1922- II. Moore, Erika. III. Title.

BS1430.52.W36 2010
223'.2067 — dc22

2010008909

www.eerdmans.com

Contents

PROLOGUE

I. Commentary's History 1
II. Commentary's Objective: An Apologia 2
III. Commentary's Scholarly Context 11
IV. Commentary's Arrangement 15

SECTION I
SURVEY OF HISTORY OF INTERPRETATION OF THE BOOK OF PSALMS

1. Survey of Second Temple Period Interpretation of the Psalms 19
I. Diversity in Judaism and the Psalter 19
II. The Composition and Shape of the Psalter 21
III. Common Features of Second Temple Interpretation of the Psalms 24
IV. Distinctive Features of the Major Extant Witnesses to Second Temple Interpretation of the Psalms 28
V. Summary 36

2. Historical Introduction to the Interpretation of the Psalms in Church Orthodoxy **37**

I. Interpretive Principles of Pre-Nicene and Post-Nicene Fathers 39

II. Augustine and Medieval Monastic Exegesis 48

III. Christian Hebraism and Scholasticism in the High to Late Middle Ages 54

IV. "The Plain Text" of the Reformers 60

V. The Beginnings of Biblical Criticism During the Seventeenth and Eighteenth Centuries 65

VI. Separation of the "Literal" from the "Historical" in Biblical Studies During the Eighteenth Century 70

VII. Conservative German and British Scholars of the Nineteenth Century 73

VIII. Contemporary Form-Criticism 75

IX. Contemporary Trends 77

3. History of Interpretation Since the Reformation: "Accredited Exegesis" **80**

I. The Approach of Historical Biblical Criticism 81

II. An Evaluation of HBC 82

III. Nineteenth-Century Division of Orthodox and Biblical Critics 86

IV. 1900: Form-Critical Approach 93

V. 1920: Cult-Functional Approach 98

VI. The Canonical-Messianic Approach 100

VII. Conclusion: Accredited Exegesis 112

SECTION II
COMMENTARY ON SELECTED PSALMS

4. Psalm 1: The Rewarded Life **115**

Part I. Voice of the Church **115**

I. Seeking the Presence of *I AM* 115
II. Psalms as the Microcosm of the Bible 117
III. Divisions of the Psalter 117
IV. Psalm 1 as the Preface to the Psalter 118
V. A Wisdom Psalm 120
VI. Hilary of Poitiers' Commentary on Psalm 1 121
VII. Later Latin Fathers 122
VIII. Renaissance and Reformation Commentators 124
IX. John Calvin's Commentary on Psalm 1 125
Part II. Voice of the Psalmist: Translation **128**
Part III. Commentary **129**
I. Introduction 129
II. Exegesis 132
Part IV. Conclusion **143**

5. Psalm 2: Ask of Me, My Son **145**
Part I. Voice of the Church **145**
I. Unity of Psalms 1 and 2 145
II. Prosopopoeia of Psalm 2 146
III. Origen on the Awesome Realism of God's Rule 147
IV. Augustine on God's Continual Wrath Against Evil 149
V. Eastern Fathers' Use of Typology 149
VI. Changing Contexts of Medieval Commentaries 151
VII. Commentaries in the Political Turbulence of the Sixteenth Century 154
Part II. Voice of the Psalmist: Translation **157**
Part III. Commentary **160**
I. Introduction 160
II. Exegesis 163
Part IV. Theology **179**

6. Psalm 3: Living in the Borderland: Morning Prayer After a Dark Night **182**

Part I. Voice of the Church **182**

I. Messianic Character of the Psalm 182

II. Monastic Liturgy of the Night 184

III. Expansion and Changes in Western Monasticism 186

IV. Medieval Monastic Commentaries 187

V. Living Paraphrase of Erasmus 190

Part II. Voice of the Psalmist: Translation **192**

Part III. Commentary **193**

I. Introduction 193

II. Exegesis 195

Part IV. Conclusion **208**

7. Psalm 4: An Evening Prayer in Crisis **210**

Part I. Voice of the Church **210**

I. Indirect Messianic Psalm 210

II. Antiochene Commentators 210

III. Augustine's "Liturgical Eschatology" 212

IV. Liturgical Role of Psalm 4 in the Middle Ages 215

V. Erasmus, a Renaissance Sermon 219

VI. Reformation Commentaries 220

Part II. Voice of the Psalmist: Translation **223**

Part III. Commentary **225**

I. Introduction 225

II. Exegesis 228

Part IV. Conclusion **242**

8. Psalm 8: *I AM* Rules Through "Infants" **244**

Part I: Voice of the Church **244**

I. Introduction 244

II. Francis of Assisi on Creation 244

III. Interpretations of Eastern Greek Fathers 245
IV. Augustine's Allegorical Heritage 248
V. Christian Hebraism in the High Middle Ages 250
VI. Reformers: Luther and Calvin 251
VII. Post-Reformation Commentators 253
Part II. Voice of the Psalmist: Translation **254**
Part III. Commentary **255**
I. Introduction 255
II. Exegesis 259
Part IV. Conclusion **272**
I. Genesis 1:26-28 272
II. Job 7:17-18; 15:14-15 273
III. Hebrews 2:8-9 274

9. Psalm 15: A Liturgical Decalogue **276**
Part I. Voice of the Church **276**
I. In the Early Fathers 276
II. In the Moral Reform of the Later Middle Ages 281
III. In the Reform Movements, Twelfth to Fifteenth Centuries 282
IV. In the Ongoing Reform of "Devotio Moderna" 286
V. In John Calvin's "Reformed" Summary 288
Part II. Voice of the Psalmist: Translation **289**
Part III. Commentary **290**
I. Introduction 290
II. Exegesis 295
Part IV. Conclusion **306**

10. Psalm 16: My Body Will Not Decay **307**
Part I. Voice of the Church **307**
I. Pre-Reformation Commentaries 308
II. Commentaries of the Reformers 315

III. Effects of Historical Critical Commentary 317
Part II. Voice of the Psalmist: Translation **321**
Part III. Commentary **324**
I. Introduction: Form, Structure, and Message 326
II. Exegesis 327
Part IV. Conclusion **338**

11. Psalm 19: A Royal Sage Praises and Petitions *I AM* **340**
Part I. Voice of the Church **340**
I. Modern Interpreters 341
II. Study in Contrast: The Reformers, Calvin and Luther 346
III. Aquinas 350
Part II. Voice of the Psalmist: Translation **351**
Part III. Commentary **353**
I. Introduction 353
II. Exegesis 357
Part IV. Conclusion **374**

12. Psalm 22: Prophetic Psalm of Christ's Passion **376**
Part I. Voice of the Church **376**
I. Apostolic Interpretation of Psalm 22 377
II. Early Christian Apologists 378
III. Polemical Interpretation of Psalm 22 in the Third to Sixth Centuries 382
IV. Jewish-Christian Dialogue in the Twelfth Century 385
V. Late Medieval Scholastic Commentaries 388
VI. Late Medieval Commentaries: Psalm 22 as "Prophetic" 390
Part II. Voice of the Psalmist: Translation **392**
Part III. Commentary **396**
I. Form, Structure, and Message 396
II. Exegesis 398
Part IV. Canonical Context **414**

13. **Psalm 23: The Good Shepherd** **416**

Part I. Voice of the Church **416**

I. Early Fathers' Use 416

II. Transition from Monastic to Scholastic Commentary 418

III. Fifteenth-Century Reforming Commentators 421

IV. Reformers' Reinstatement of Historical David 424

V. Cultural Popularization of Psalm 23 432

Part II. Voice of the Psalmist: Translation **434**

Part III. Commentary **435**

I. Introduction: Form and Structure 435

II. Exegesis 436

Part IV. Conclusion **445**

14. **Psalm 51: "The Psalm of All Psalms" in Penitential Devotion** **446**

Part I: Voice of the Church: Historical Regimes of Penance **446**

I. Public Confession in the Early Church 447

II. The Personal Devotion of "Compunction" 450

III. Rupture of Ancient Penance in the Early Middle Ages 452

IV. The Carolingian Personal Reforms Until the Lateran Council of 1215 452

V. Penance After the Lateran Council of 1215 456

Part II: Voice of the Psalmist: Translation **462**

Part III: Commentary **464**

I. Introduction 464

II. Exegesis 467

15. **Psalm 110: "Sit at My Right Hand"** **484**

Part I. Voice of the Church **484**

I. In the New Testament 484

II. Musical Heritage of the Early Christian Confessions 485

III. Messianic Polemics of Justin Martyr 487

IV. Augustine's Figurative Use of Psalm 110 488

V. Jerome's Prophetic Sense 489

VI. Luther's Revolt Against Medieval Exegesis 490

VII. Calvin's Plain Sense of the Text 493

VIII. Conclusion 496

Part II. Voice of the Psalmist: Translation **497**

Part III. Commentary **498**

I. Introduction 498

II. Exegesis 502

Part IV: Identification of "My Lord" **512**

Part V. Conclusion **518**

16. Psalm 139: Search Me, God **519**

Part I: Voice of the Church **519**

I. The Apologists 519

II. The Post-Nicene Fathers 521

III. Monastic Scholars of the Early Middle Ages 526

IV. Reformation Commentaries 529

V. Religious Confusion of the Seventeenth and Eighteenth Centuries 531

Part II: Voice of the Psalmist: Translation **534**

Part III: Commentary **541**

I. Introduction 541

II. Exegesis 544

Part IV: Conclusion **570**

Glossary 573

Index of Authors 583

Index of Subjects 589

Index of Scripture References 605

Prologue

I. Commentary's History

Professor Bruce Waltke has been teaching and preaching the book of Psalms throughout his teaching career, beginning in 1958. His career includes teaching courses on the book of Psalms as a whole and on the practice of exegesis, in which he uses selected psalms as textbook examples. At the end of his career he thought it fitting to put the fruit of his work into writing.

However, Bruce is not competent to empower the reader to hear the church's voice of response. To his great delight, Professor James M. Houston, formerly a lecturer of historical and cultural geography at Oxford, specialist in the history of ideas, and pioneer in spiritual theology among Evangelicals, volunteered to write that history.[1] We hope that our readers will be edified, at least to some extent, as we have by our interaction. Jim and Bruce respectively take responsibility for the history of Psalter interpretation and for its exegesis.

Erika Moore, Associate Professor of Old Testament at Trinity School for Ministry, volunteered her help to produce the commentary. Jim and Bruce gladly accepted her offer and asked her to write the Psalter's history during the Second Temple Period (chapter 1). She also graciously prepared the glossary and indices.

1. Jim commissioned fresh translations of numerous Latin and Middle English texts, and is indebted to Ken Pearson of Trinity Western University, British Columbia, Dr. Elizabeth Bongie, emeritus professor of classics at the University of British Columbia, and Dr. Ellie McCullough of York University England for these translations. He is also grateful to the trustees of the foundation, Institute for Religion and Culture, for the necessary funding. His granddaughter Jen Cairns generously helped to provide research materials.

II. Commentary's Objective: An Apologia

Our basic concerns in this book are to enrich the daily life of the contemporary Christian and to deepen the church's community worship in hearing God's voice both through an accredited exegesis of the Psalms and through the believing response of the church. The humanist Desiderius Erasmus of Rotterdam (1469-1536) once wrote, "Who indeed has not written on the Psalms?" Yet the two voices of the Holy Spirit, infallibly in Scripture and edifyingly in the church's response, are rarely combined.[2] This lack calls for a defense of our interdisciplinary approach. Jim and Bruce present apologias respectively for hearing the believing response of the church and for an accredited exegesis. Though presenting separately, the authors are in full agreement with each other's apologias.

A. Hearing the Voice of the Believing Church

Psalms were and are of key importance in the daily life of the Christian and in Christian community worship. Both were the basic features of early Christianity, since it was believed by the early Christians that Jesus Christ himself lived within the Psalms. The early fathers of the church, in contrast to much modern scholarship, rightly believed in the maxim that "Scripture interprets Scripture." The incident of the risen Christ asserting to the two disciples on the Emmaus way the hermeneutical principle that all the Scriptures, including the Psalms, speak of Christ set a basis for the early church thinkers to interpret the Bible as *the* book about Christ (Luke 24:13-49). The radical power of "the Spirit" over "the letter" introduced the centrality of Christ into apostolic exegesis of the Old Testament — especially in the Psalms — in a totally new way.

Around this new hermeneutical principle of "interpreting Scripture by Scripture" the early Fathers developed "The Rule of Faith," which now determined how exegesis should be done. Augustine in his *De doctrina christiana* demarcates clearly that the principles of theological enquiry and the claims for truth are distinctive, when they are "Christian." Christian scholarship is now

2. While D. H. Williams (*Tradition, Scripture, and Interpretation: A Sourcebook of the Ancient Church* [Grand Rapids: Baker Academic, 2006]), professor of religion in patristics and historical theology at Baylor University, on the one hand, wants to elevate the confessions of the early church to a canonical level equal with Scripture — and so presumably infallible — he acknowledges, on the other hand, that for the early church the canon of Scripture was the *norma normans* (the norm that sets the norm): "All the major creeds and works of theology acknowledge, implicitly or explicitly, the supremacy of the Bible" (p. 24).

contrasted with classical scholarship in important ways, even when classical procedures for rhetoric are still imitated, and then modified.

So we deplore the confessional reductionism in much contemporary Biblical scholarship, which overlooks two thousand years of Christian devotion and orthodoxy or "right worship," in the use of the Book of Psalms. It ignores the historical continuity of tradition in the communion of saints. It is like studying the activities of a seaport, and yet ignoring the existence of its hinterland. Such liberal scholarship is expressive of the skeptical culture of "postmodernism," which rejects all "absolutes" and denies "truth claims." It reinterprets "the historical" as a series of events subjectively selected according to the interest of the investigator, with no sense of a divinely ordered past or of any sovereign guidance and providence. Such randomness brings about "the death of the past," as J. H. Plumb warned us at the waning of modernism in 1969.[3]

With the loss of their continuity and "historical hinterland," the psalms then lose their spirituality, and the whole heritage of devotion becomes ignored for both Jews and Christians. As the Jewish scholar James L. Kugel, Harvard professor of Hebrew, has observed: "it would not be unfair to say that research into the Psalms in this century has had a largely negative effect on the Psalter's reputation as the natural focus of Israelite spirituality, and much that was heretofore prized in this domain has undergone a somewhat reluctant reevaluation." Rather than being inspired by the spirituality of the Psalter, critical "moderns" despiritualize the Psalms.[4] Scholarly questions about authorship, psalm classifications, pagan origins of Canaanite and Ugaritic sources, cultic or non-cultic sources of worship, the changing roles of the psalms, all tend to detract, indeed as Kugel argues, to "despiritualize" them for their use today, by secular scholars whether "Jews" or "Christians."

Yet, paradoxically, historical studies flourish more than ever, as ideologies wilt and worldviews change. For "the past" is now viewed as the source for multiplying differing perspectives, through the lens of receptor-commentary. Scholarly attention is now being given to "history" as a series of anthropological studies, of which "the history of Biblical commentaries" is traceable through its sequence of historical cultures and "paradigm shifts." "Historiography" then becomes more confused and complex in its usage. For there are multiple reasons for using "history" as a tool of scholarship, as well as using "commentary" for Biblical studies. Since both Judaism and Christianity have been faiths of

3. J. H. Plumb, *The Death of the Past* (New York: Columbia University Press, 1969).

4. James L. Kugel, "Topics in the History of the Spirituality of the Psalms," in Arthur Green, ed., *Jewish Spirituality from the Bible Through the Middle Ages* (New York: Crossroad, 1988), p. 113.

"the Book," secular literary criticism challenges them deeply. The history of doctrine is intertwined with the history of exegesis of the Scriptures, to make this the new battlefield for faith against skepticism.

Nevertheless, the increasing number of scholars who are now reviewing the history of previous commentaries is a welcome new trend in Biblical scholarship (see pp. 12-13).

B. Hearing the Voice of the Inspired Author

We also deplore the lack of authentic exegesis in the use of the psalms, as well as the lack of Christian commitment and orthodoxy in much contemporary Biblical scholarship. In chapter 3 an argument is made for an integrated threefold approach to the interpretation of Scripture: prayerful and devotional to hear the voice of God; trustful and sympathetic to hear the voice of the author; and scientific to hear the voice of the text. All three are necessary at one and the same time, we will argue, for an accredited exegesis. The confession that the interpreter needs spiritual illumination to understand the text differs radically from the Enlightenment confession that positivism is sufficient for accredited exegesis. In his still influential study, J. A. Ernesti pitted the scientific method against the spiritual method. He denied the proposition "that the Scriptures cannot be properly explained without prayer, and pious simplicity of mind." In Ernesti's view, "pious simplicity of mind is useless in the investigation of Scriptural truth." But the text's divine Author and his meaning in the text cannot be truly known or understood without a spiritual commitment to him. Ours is a sacred hermeneutic because the Author is spirit and known in the human spirit through the medium of the Holy Spirit (1 Cor. 2:11).[5] Martin Luther taught, "If God does not open and explain Holy Writ, no one can understand it; it will remain a closed book, enveloped in darkness." The Geneva Catechism (1541) put it this way: "Our mind is too weak to comprehend the spiritual wisdom of God which is revealed to us by faith, and our hearts are too prone either to defiance or to a perverse confidence in ourselves or creaturely things. But the Holy Spirit enlightens us to make us capable of understanding what would otherwise be incomprehensible to us, and fortifies us in certitude, sealing and imprinting the promises of salvation in our hearts."

5. Bruce K. Waltke with Charles Yu, *An Old Testament Theology: An Exegetical, Thematic and Canonical Approach* (Grand Rapids: Zondervan, 2007), p. 80.

1. *Empirical Text Demands a Scientific Approach*

On the other hand, a scientific investigation of the text's empirical data is also necessary for an accredited hermeneutic. By scientific we mean the grammatico-historical approach, interpreting words within the context of the speaker's world. The Bible itself uses this approach, explaining words not understood by the audience (cf. 1 Sam. 9:9) and explaining customs that had become otiose at the time of writing (cf. Ruth 4:7). Orthodox theology demands this approach, for it confesses the authors of the Bible were inspired by the Spirit of God to reveal the mind of God to his covenant people and that he did so in words that demanded faith and obedience.

2. *New Testament Validates Orthodoxy by Text's Plain Sense*

Before Jesus explained to the disciples on the Emmaus way what was said in all the Scriptures — beginning with Moses and all the prophets — concerning himself, he condemned them for failing to understand the text's plain sense:[6] "How foolish you are, and how slow to believe all that the prophets have spoken! Did not Messiah have to suffer these things and then enter his glory?" (Luke 24:25-26). Christ rebuked these disciples for not believing what should have been apparent upon a plain reading of the text. He did not rely upon the faulty *pesher* method of hermeneutics to validate his claims, as the Teacher of Righteousness at Qumran had done, or on the allegorical method of the Church Fathers. The failure to see Christ in the Psalms is not due to the grammatico-historical method of exegesis but to the slowness of the human heart to believe in the death of Christ for sin and in his resurrection from the dead. Indeed, it takes the Holy Spirit to remove this veil of unbelief. "The radical power of 'the Spirit' over 'the letter' that introduced the centrality of Christ into apostolic exegesis of the Old Testament in a totally new way in the history of interpretation," as Jim so well puts it, is due to God's grace that "has now been revealed through the appearing of our Savior, Christ Jesus, who has destroyed death and has brought life and immortality to light through the gospel" (2 Tim. 1:10), not to negating the plain sense of Scripture. Instead of focusing on the letter of the Law as the rabbis had done, they focused on the gospel of Jesus Christ: his death for the church's sins, his burial, his bodily resurrection and ascension, *according to the Scriptures' plain sense.* In sum, the veil of unbelief, not of philo-

6. "Plain sense," Calvin's description of his hermeneutics, means examining the text carefully and plainly within the broad context of all the Scriptures.

logical and historical ignorance, had to be lifted for the radical power of the Spirit to empower an accredited reading of Scripture.

Some allege that the apostles used allegory, but we disagree. As we shall see in the selected psalms, such as 2, 16, 22, 110, which we label as "typico-prophetic," the prophetic interpretation is derived from the texts' plain sense, from accredited exegesis, not from *pesher* or allegorical interpretation. In the one instance where Paul uses allegory he alerts his reader to this exception (Gal. 4:24; *allēgoreō* is never used elsewhere in the New Testament).

3. *Continuity of Faithful Extends to Inspired Authors*

Moreover, the continuum of the community of faith must begin with the acceptance of the inspired authors of the Old Testament, and then move to the apostolic authority of the New Testament writers. The reliability of the later Christian commentators, such as Origen, Hilary of Poitiers, Jerome, and John Chrysostom, is then twofold: their linguistic skills in exegeting the text, and their theological acumen in their "spiritual appreciation" of the message being communicated. It is this severance of textual scholarship from historical/theological studies of "the Biblical faith" that has created our contemporary crisis of credibility.

4. *To Protect the Church from False Teachers*

In late antiquity the early church had brought to maturity a helpful fourfold approach to interpretation: the literal, the tropological (from "trope," figurative), the eschatological, and the moral. That model is still useful in preaching. Gregory likened it to building a church: laying the foundation (literal), building its walls (tropological with reference to Christ), its roof (eschatological), and its decorations (moral). In practice, however, commentators outside of the Antiochene School, such as Origen, Jerome, Hilary of Poitiers, and Chrysostom, essentially started with its walls by using an allegorical approach apart from its plain sense foundation. The church they built was edifying but without a foundation, and as such it was unsteady and capable of being supplanted by false teachings using the same unaccredited approach. To be sure they thought they were doing Biblical interpretation by starting with Christ, but in truth they muffled the voice of the inspired writers who gave them their Bibles. A famous statue that symbolizes allegorizing the text depicts Gregory the Great seated with the Bible in hand and a dove — classic symbol of the Spirit — perched on his shoulders with its beak in his ear. In short, their theology was orthodox; their method was unorthodox.

5. *A Rapprochement Between Tropology and Plain Sense*

For too long contemporary exegesis has been at loggerheads with the church's historic commentators. What is needed in this dialogue is more understanding, sympathy, and an accredited hermeneutic.

a. Earlier Commentaries More Biblical Than Biblical Critics

Nevertheless, Pre-Reformation commentators who center on Christ with piety and passion are in fact more Biblical than academics who dispassionately and scientifically explain the text without considering its holistic context, including the New Testament, and without passion and devotion to Christ. The Christ-centered piety and devotion of commentators before the recovery of the plain sense should be treasured, not trashed. Although some of their interpretations seem to us to be ridiculous and silly, for the most part they stayed within the parameters of orthodoxy — that is to say, within the parameters of the apostolic traditions as they found later expression in the creeds of the early church, especially in the Nicene Creed. Nevertheless, they are to be faulted when they twisted the original author's interpretation and represented it as the meaning of the text, justifying their ignoring of the author's intention by claiming spiritual illumination of divine mysteries.

b. Allegory Is Not Postmodern Reader-Response

Let me segue here. The allegorical approach of Christian commentators cannot be used to defend postmodern interpretation, which gives priority to the reader's response to the text, not to the author's intention. To be sure, both the "allegorizers" and postmoderns impose meanings on a text not intended by the author, but postmoderns bastardize the Christian commentator's allegorical method. The church's commentators allegorized the text, but they were orthodox, pastoral, and above all Christ-centered, whereas postmoderns are, for the most part, apostate, anthropocentric, and self-serving, and so deconstruct the author's intention to foist their own political and/or social agenda on Scripture to validate their elitism, while accusing the Biblical writers of doing the same thing.

c. Earlier Commentators Lacked Modern Exegetical Tools

Christian commentators before the Reformation usually did not have a historical mindset, and even those who did lacked the modern tools both of archaeology to reconstruct the ancient world and of philology to interpret the text's complex linguistic phenomena. In the Providence of God those tools became available after the Reformers realized the necessity of having a historical mindset. If we believe in Providence, it is wrong to neglect the church's more developed mindset of history and of precision. Yearly the archaeologist's spade uncovers new artifacts and ancient texts to fill in the world of the Bible, and new, very sophisticated philological tools are being developed to advance the science of literary analysis, making the church's memory sharper as it ages and comes to its full maturity. To neglect these tools is irresponsible to Providence, to the church, and to the Christian's spiritual life.

Yet paradoxically, exegetical studies, like historical studies, flourish more than ever, while the devotional life of Christians and of corporate worship withers. An endless stream of commentary emerges from the press, reporting on new textual insights garnered from both recent archaeological discovery and advances in interpreting literature. These insights and advances should not be seen as a threat to orthodoxy.

Ironically, Providence allows historic Biblical critics — who use these tools to "de-theologize" the Bible in order to totally "humanize" it — unwittingly to sharpen the tools of faithful scholars to "theologize" the Word of God. In chapter 3 an accredited method of exegesis that uses these tools will be explored more thoroughly and, in that connection, the history of more recent commentaries will be presented and evaluated.

d. Rapprochement Found in Typological and Canonical Interpretation

Let us continue to hold fast to what is good both in the Christ-centered approach of church history and in the development of exegetical tools by Biblical scholars of all theological persuasions. Let us also continue to compare Scripture with Scripture, for in that hermeneutic we can integrate the church's earlier allegorical interpretations with Calvin's plain sense[7] (which included what today is known as "typological" interpretation). Let us defend the rapprochement by noting three points. First, both the allegorical and the typological hermeneutic assume that God has an eternal plan that is being worked out in salva-

7. Calvin's plain sense reads a text within the holistic context of canon, while showing respect to the Patristic contribution.

tion history. By this is meant that the linear history of the world, and more particularly of Israel — called today "salvation history" — exists eternally in the decree of God. This history includes both the "facts" of God's activity and his inspired interpretation of their meaning.[8]

Second, God revealed his rule over history both by fulfilling announced prophecies and by prefiguring through unwitting persons as well as through events and situations (i.e., "types") a greater fulfillment in their "antitypes" (see pp. 111-12). Whereas prophecies predict events in salvation history, types are recognized only in the light of fulfillment in their corresponding antitypes. In sum, the mind of Scripture's Author transcends the mind of its human authors (see pp. 199, 202, 208-9) and requires comparing and interpreting Scripture with and by the whole canon of Scripture.

Third, typology is a disciplined form of allegory, for both assume God's eternal design and look for correspondences within it. But allegory is unrestrained in imagining correspondences, for it neglects a careful, if any, exegesis of the historical reality, whereas typology demands keeping a precise exegetical eye on the type as well as the antitype to validate the plausibility of a divinely intended correspondence (see Jim, Psalm 110, p. 493).

e. Prosopological Hermeneutic

As we will see in the historical survey of Psalm 2, Origen and his followers used prosopological criticism — that is, he saw different speakers in the psalm speaking from different perspectives. His method was flawed, however, because he applied his hermeneutical principle arbitrarily and fancifully. However, there is some legitimacy in reading the psalm as two voices, from two perspectives. Allowing that David and his kingdom are types of Christ and his church, we can additionally read the Psalms as the voice of Christ and his church to the Father, and as the words of the church to their Lord and Savior, Jesus Christ. This is so be-

8. Scripture both implies and states clearly that God has an eternal, decreed plan; for example, through his foretelling of unanticipated future events (cf. Isa. 41:21-29); his decreeing the unborn's mission to fulfill his salvation history (cf. Isa. 49:1-2); and Paul's mysteries "which for ages past [were] kept hidden in God, who created all things," that are now "made known . . . according to his eternal purpose that he accomplished in Christ Jesus our Lord" (Eph. 3:1-13). The theology of salvation history, a sort of emanation of God's decreed plan, resembles somewhat the philosophy of neo-Platonism, which taught the existence of an ineffable and transcendent One, from which emanated the rest of the universe as a sequence of lesser beings. The synthesis of this thought of the Greek Plotinus, a follower of Plato, with Jewish thought through the Greek translation of the Old Testament exercised an immense influence on medieval mysticism and Renaissance Humanism.

cause Christ is as fully human as his father David and as his brothers. But he is also fully God. According to his human perspective, we hear his voice to God, and according to the latter we hear the voice of the church to him. Thus in Psalm 1 he is "the man" who delights in God's Torah, but as God he is the author of Torah and so the church delights in his teaching. For example: in Psalm 2 Christ asks God for his inheritance, but as God he has authority over all nations; in Psalm 3 he is himself surrounded by enemies, but he is also the one who delivers his church; in Psalm 4 he goes to sleep facing death but trusting God, and so does his church trusting the risen Christ. In other words, Jesus Christ is *I AM*, as he himself testified and as his apostles affirm. This dual perspective that informs the entire Psalter is a mystery that historical Biblical critics cannot handle.

C. Selection of the Psalter

We chose the Psalter for our "historico-exegetical" study for several reasons.

1. *To Restore the Unique Role of the Psalms in Worship*

The Psalms have occupied a unique role in both Israel and the Christian Church, as the prayer book and hymnal of both their worshiping communities. Unlike the other books of the Bible, the Psalms were always sung and recited, having deep musical and poetic roots in the religious life of devotion. However, since the eighteenth century, hymnody has replaced the centrality of the Psalter in the liturgy of evangelical churches. The uniqueness of the Psalms has thus gradually disappeared from our religious radar screen.

2. *To Restore the Role of the Psalms in Spiritual Formation*

For the early Christians the Psalms were also the unique emotional handbook for personal use of what might be termed "psalmno-therapy" — only eclipsed by modern psychology and the more recent "pop culture" of popular praise songs with their wearisome repetitions, substituting emotional enthusiasm apart from sober reflection. As Jonathan Edwards pointed out in his masterpiece, *the Religious Affections* (1746), the gospel provides us with appropriately responsive emotions.[9]

9. See Robert C. Roberts, *Spiritual Emotions: A Psychology of Christian Virtues* (Grand Rapids: Eerdmans, 2007).

3. *To Restore the Holistic Use of a Psalm*

Modern psychology and praise songs have replaced the holistic study and singing of the Psalms for nurturing the spiritual life and for enriching the church's worship. This has resulted in the loss of the church's deep musical and poetic roots in the religious life of devotion.

Our purpose, therefore, is to recover these losses through accredited exegesis and hearing afresh the rich devotional response of the true church. We are heirs of all the ages, and we are the poorer for our failure to hear and embrace that rich heritage.

We have selected only thirteen psalms, to give depth of study, as well as to illustrate the differing pastoral applications of the use of the Psalms generally. They reflect distinct genres, but also differ in their interrelated themes, as expressive of the whole Psalter. This is reflected in their differing historical treatments.

D. A Caveat

It is important to note that the book's objective is to write an interdisciplinary commentary, not a typical commentary. For lack of space, no attention is paid to some traditional concerns of a commentary, such as setting forth its texts and versions, the nature of Hebrew philology and poetry, and so forth. Overall, our desire is for thoughtful lay readers, as well as preachers and teachers, to reach into the pure gold of the Biblical text and into the hinterland of Christian history, to draw fresh renewal of spirit and thought from both, from what has become neglected in our secular society today.

The history of interpretation requires less propaedeutic than exegesis, which assumes a familiarity with the essentials of exegetical praxis. The footnotes in the exegesis sections are intended mostly for more advanced students.

III. Commentary's Scholarly Context

A. Survey of History of Commentary Writing

Under the influence of the Tractarian Movement in the latter nineteenth century, J. M. Neale pioneered *A Commentary on the Psalms: From Primitive and Medieval Writers.*[10] At the beginning of the twentieth century, Rowland E.

10. The Rev. J. M. Neale and the Rev. R. F. Littledale, *A Commentary on the Psalms: From Primitive and Medieval Writers . . .*, 4 vols. (London: Joseph Masters & Co., 1860-).

Prothero wrote about *The Psalms in Human Life*[11] and in the context of contemporary faith and scholarship; such is our objective for the beginning of the third millennium of the church. However, simply to quote how a verse of a psalm was significant to a particular Christian at one point of his or her life, as Prothero does, does not satisfy the contemporary reader who is now spoilt by many excellent biographies. We require much more cultural "depth" in the use of history.

Since the history of doctrine is intertwined with exegesis, it is a welcome new trend in Biblical scholarship to see the increasing number of scholars who are now reviewing the history of previous commentaries. Four such efforts are worthy of note. Regarding the Ancient Christian Commentary on Scripture series, editor Thomas C. Oden explains: "by the aid of computer technology, the vast array of writings from the church fathers — including much that is only available in the original languages — have been combed for their comments on Scripture."[12] This is being published in a twenty-eight-volume edition patristic commentary on Scripture. However, its span is limited to the era from Clement of Rome, c. 95, to John of Damascus, c. 645–c. 749. It is a source book of selected passages on the texts of the Biblical books, and as such is not critical of the ancient authors. Rather, they have been allowed to speak for themselves. Yet the contributors have worked with nine principles of selection in the authors and texts chosen, to guide their data. As an ecumenical venture it includes Apocryphal books that some Fathers accepted, and are still accepted by Roman Catholic and Greek Orthodox traditions.

Second, the more recent project edited by Robert Louis Wilken, The Church's Bible series, focuses on key texts that have been most influential in the course of church history. Short Bible passages, translated from the Septuagint and Vulgate versions, are followed with appropriate excerpts from selected ancient texts. The work is designed for use as a textual tool rather than as a contemporary commentary. As such there are neither editorial comments nor information to provide historical context for the selected passages. It includes later medieval commentators. But if the other volumes follow the format of the first volume on *The Song of Songs,* commentaries will cease before the Reformation since it is primarily for a Roman Catholic public.[13] No indication is given how many of the Biblical books will be covered in the series.

11. Rowland E. Prothero, *The Psalms in Human Life* (New York: E. P. Dutton, 1905). The first English edition was in 1903. Prothero was Fellow of New College, Oxford.

12. Gerald Bray, ed., *Romans,* The Ancient Christian Commentary on Scripture, ed. Thomas C. Oden, gen. ed., New Testament, vol. 6 (Downers Grove, IL: InterVarsity Press, 1998), pp. xi-xii.

13. Richard A. Norris, *The Song of Songs,* The Church's Bible, Robert Louis Wilken, gen. ed., vol. 1 (Grand Rapids: Eerdmans, 2003).

The third work, *Hebrew Bible/Old Testament,* edited by the Norwegian scholar Magne Saebo,[14] is composed of a series of essays written mostly by Jewish European scholars. Unlike the two American volumes, which highlight selected Biblical texts, these essays focus on the history of Biblical interpretation, somewhat analogous to *The Cambridge History of the Bible.* So far, three volumes (of four in the series) have appeared, covering the period from the Qumran literature to the end of the eighteenth century. It is broad in its approach, and focuses on selected Christian and Jewish commentators.

Finally, Susan Gillingham's two-volume work, *Psalms Through the Centuries,* provides us with another example of the new academic movement that we criticized above (i.e., "reception history" — how the Bible has been "received" anthropologically, by both Christians and Jews during the last two thousand years).[15] Her work, expressive of the postmodern culture that "reports" on history and culture, offers detailed scholarship without being confessional in commitment. It "informs" on the Bible, taking the history of religious practices further than "the Bible-and-culture" studies. Her work may be characterized as "the outsider's" approach to Biblical orthodoxy and orthopraxis. In intention, it is more historiographic than theological.

It is encouraging that an increasing number of doctoral students are now attentive to the history of particular commentaries. "History" and "historiography" always have been a complex subject, but when applied to the Bible the issues become intense. For the Bible as *the* sacred book has been part of our cultural heritage in Western society. It is inseparable from ecclesiastical history, cultural changes, issues of heresy and reform. As the *influential Subject,* indeed the Word of God, it has been "the dynamism" of Western history. As "the Bible in miniature," the Psalms have been uniquely central to the history of the church's devotion, right up until the eighteenth century. The other kind of history is of "texts," such as were studied by the classical world, or reintroduced in the Renaissance, or which have now dominated Western culture since the Enlightenment. This has turned the Bible into "an object of study" rather than remaining as "the two-edged sword" that the apostles used pastorally.

14. Magne Saebø, ed., *Hebrew Bible/Old Testament: The History of Its Interpretation,* vol. 1, part 1: *Antiquity* (Göttingen: Vandenhoeck & Ruprecht, 1996).

15. Susan Gillingham, *Psalms Through the Centuries,* vol. 1, Blackwell Bible Commentaries (Oxford: Blackwell Publishing, 2008).

B. Difficulties of Writing a Historical and Exegetical Commentary

The historical focus of contemporary scholarship encounters many roadblocks with regard to the Psalms.

First, not many key commentators of the past ever completed their commentaries. Or, for various reasons, all they did compile may not have survived.

Second, at various periods commentators have had differing perspectives and challenges in writing as they did. The history of doctrine, or the interpretation of "history" and its uses, has developed over time in diverse ways.[16]

Third, the understanding of what is "literal" and/or "historical," as well as what is "prophecy," has shifted through time, as we shall note.

Fourth, the interactions of "typology" and "allegory" have their own complex history. Suffice it to say that we applaud the typological use of the Psalms, for that approach grounds and unifies what the Spirit said in its historical incarnation and what it came to prefigure in the progressive history of salvation as recounted in the canon. We reject allegory as a method, for it arbitrarily imposes meaning apart from what the inspired poet intended. Though allegory seems heavily overused by the ancient commentators, we need to study and appreciate their mindset, for they thought of their work as "Biblical" — and they were, more so than many commentators who pride themselves on scholarly research.[17] For the most part, though their method is questionable, their allegorical interpretations are informed by sound doctrine: that Scripture was interpreted by Scripture, and events were shaped by God's presence in history. Therefore, they nurtured authentic spirituality and worship. The Spirit is not confined to accredited exegesis! For the allegorical was not just human poetic imagination but the sphere of God's mystery. It was not clarity that they desired, but moral effect. As Augustine put it: "For now treat the Scripture of God as the face of God. Melt in its presence."[18]

Fifth, the differing contexts of an oral culture, or of a scroll culture, or indeed of a print culture, provide distinctions of consciousness, which need to be recognized and taken into account.[19]

16. The anthology entitled *Theories of History,* ed. with introductions and commentaries by P. Gardiner (New York/London: The Free Press, 1959).

17. Henri de Lubac, *Medieval Exegesis,* trans. Mark Sebanc and E. M. Macierowski (Grand Rapids: Eerdmans, 1998-). This multivolume work is a basic text for appreciating the role of allegory in ancient and medieval commentaries.

18. Quoted by Robert Louis Wilken, *The Spirit of Early Christian Thought* (New Haven/London: Yale University Press, 2003), p. 50.

19. Anthony Grafton and Megan Williams, *Christianity and the Transformation of the Book* (Cambridge, MA, and London: The Belknap Press of Harvard University Press, 2006). This

Sixth, "reformation," as Ladner has argued,[20] is an ongoing process of church history, sometimes given other "names." During the Reformation the reformers aimed to recover the Spirit's intention in the original compositions, but their motto was *reformatio semper reformandum* ("reformed and always reforming"). Protestant thought tends to overlook the ongoing dynamism of faith, which requires two thousand years of reflection — not just that of "the Reformation" — to trace the renewal movements of God's people.

Finally, the selection of the psalms for this handbook made its own demands on how the contextual treatment of their history should be made.

IV. Commentary's Arrangement

The book is divided into two sections: an introduction, of which this prologue can be considered a part (chapters 1-3), and a commentary on the selected psalms (chapter 4-16). The introduction treats the history of the interpretation of the Psalter as a whole, and the commentary deals with the selected psalms. Among other functions, the Prologue introduces the reader to the history of this sort of commentary from the Church Fathers to the introduction of rationalism in the seventeenth and eighteenth centuries. As joint authors, we unite a Hebraic interpretation of the Old Testament text with the intertestamental linkage of the psalms into the New Testament (chapter 1), to then survey in chapter 2 the historical horizons of Christian orthodoxy from the early church to the Reformation. The third chapter traces the history of exegesis from the rise of historical Biblical criticism to the present.

In the first three chapters, we restrict ourselves to surveying the history of interpretation from the Second Temple period to the contemporary derivatives of historical Biblical criticism. In the second section, we selected the thirteen psalms for our in-depth study by way of several criteria.[21] First, we chose some psalms (i.e., Psalms 1, 23, and 51) that have played a basic and pivotal role in the life of the worshiping church. Second, we laid a solid foundation for Christian apologetics by studying psalms that Christ and his apostles used to validate the Christian faith (i.e., Psalms 2, 16, 22, and 110). Third, these and other psalms il-

is an example of the new interdisciplinary study of how scrolls and books became "read," over against the older oral tradition, where they were "heard." Walter Ong, S.J., has made a similar contribution to the study of the cultural impact of the "printed book" on the culture of the fifteenth and sixteenth centuries.

20. Gerhardt Ladner, *The Idea of Reform* (New York: Harper & Row, 1967).

21. Coincidentally, the Cappadocian Basil the Great (330-79) also wrote thirteen homilies on select psalms.

lustrate various genres and perspectives (i.e., Psalms 3, 4, 8, and 139). Fourth, we also chose psalms to highlight historical perspectives in the interpretation of the Psalter (i.e., Psalm 15). We leave it to other scholars to focus on the Jewish interpretations of the Psalms, other than brief references to the ongoing Christian-Jewish dialogue.

In the treatment of the selected psalms the history of interpretation is given first and then a commentary of the psalm. Following Luther, the exegesis begins with an original translation of the psalm before an exegesis of the psalm that includes an analysis of its literary aspects followed by a verse-by-verse commentary. The numbering of many psalms differs because the Greek translation unites or divides psalms somewhat differently from the Hebrew tradition, which the English versions follow, and versification in the Hebrew text differs from that of the English versions because the Hebrew tradition numbers a superscript with more than three words as a verse, whereas the tradition of English versions never numbers a superscript. We place the Hebrew numbering in brackets.

SECTION 1

SURVEY OF HISTORY OF INTERPRETATION OF THE BOOK OF PSALMS

CHAPTER 1

Survey of Second Temple Period Interpretation of the Psalms

I. Diversity in Judaism and the Psalter

The era commonly referred to as the "Second Temple" period dates from 516 BCE (the completion and dedication of the Second Temple) to 70 CE (the destruction of that temple by the Romans). The return to a demolished Judah after spending nearly seventy years in exile in Babylon, the reduction from an independent nation to a small province in the backwaters of the Persian empire, the building and dedication of the Second Temple, the continuing existence and growth of the Jewish Diaspora, the conquests of Alexander the Great and the encounter with Hellenism, the Maccabean revolt, the restored Jewish state, and the Roman conquest of Palestine all influenced the way in which the post-exilic community understood itself and how the various groups in that community interpreted and appropriated the Scriptures and the Psalms in particular.

In order to understand the various interpretive approaches to the Psalms, the diversity of this period must be appreciated in three main areas. First, according to some estimates, approximately 50,000 Jews[1] returned to Judah after Cyrus's decree in 538 BCE (Ezra 2:64-65), joining those who had been left behind after the Babylonian deportation in 586 BCE (2 Kings 25:1-12). Second, many exilic Jews had followed Jeremiah's instructions to "Build houses and settle down; plant gardens and eat what they produce. Marry and have sons and daughters. . . . Also, seek the peace and prosperity of the city to which I have carried you into exile" (Jer. 29:5-7, TNIV). For these folks and their children, Babylon had become "home," and so they remained in Babylon in spite of Isaiah's

1. For the nomenclature "Jew" see Bruce K. Waltke with Charles Yu, *An Old Testament Theology* (Grand Rapids: Zondervan, 2007), p. 17.

command: "Leave Babylon" (Isa. 48:20).[2] Third, a number of Jews responded to the Babylonian threat by settling in Egypt (2 Kings 25:26; Jer. 41:16–43:7). This recognition of geographical pockets of Judaism is to be distinguished from a simplistic designation of "Palestinian Judaism" and "Hellenistic Judaism."[3]

Despite the various geographic locations, the prevailing mood of the Jews during the Second Temple era can be distilled into a general set of tendencies. First, there was a crisis of faith. The Babylonian exile itself had led to an earlier crisis of faith regarding the trustworthiness and omnipotence of *I AM*. The promises of an eternal Davidic kingdom (2 Sam. 7:7-16; Ps. 89:3-4, 35-37; 132:11-12) and *I AM*'s vow to set up his abode forever in the temple at Jerusalem (Ps. 68:16; 132:13-14) seemed to fail. During the Babylonian crisis the Davidic promise was already under a cloud: Jehoiachin, the rightful heir of the line of David, had been taken into captivity to Babylon, and in his place Nebuchadnezzar set the puppet king Zedekiah. In addition, the land of Canaan had played a significant role in shaping the Israelites' understanding of themselves as *I AM*'s chosen people (Gen. 12:1-3; Deut. 4:37-38; 7:1-11). Because true worship of God was so closely aligned with the Israelites' inheritance of the land (Deuteronomy 12), to be outside of the land immediately raised grave concerns about their status before God (1 Sam. 26:19) and led to a questioning of whether or not true worship was even possible (Ps. 137:4). *I AM*'s power and/or character became suspect in the minds of many. To meet this crisis *I AM* made himself known by amazing prophecies (Isa. 41:22-29; and the recognition formula, "you will know that I am *I AM*" in Ezek. 5:13; 6:7, c. fifty times). The frustrated expectations of the restoration community — no restored monarchy, continuing threats from neighbors, economic hardships — led many in Palestine and the Diaspora to find ways to reconcile their present circumstances with the glorious future portrayed by various prophetic voices (Amos 9:11-15; Isa. 40–48; Obad. 17–21; Jer. 30–33; Ezek. 36:24-32; 37:15-28). Second Temple Judaism adopted an array of strategies to reconcile their present reality with Biblical expectation. One such strategy was renewed study of and reflection on the sacred texts. Hence, during this period there was considerable literary activity involving theological reflection on the Scriptures. Many remained faithful in the face of the nonfulfillment of the Messianic promises, rereading and adapting the Psalms to speak into their situation. This renewed interest in the Scriptures resulted, at

2. John Bright, *A History of Israel,* 3rd ed. (Philadelphia: Westminster Press, 1981), pp. 362-63.

3. See Charlesworth's plea to discard or at least refine such simplistic analysis in light of the significant number of newly discovered and/or translated into English pseudepigraphic documents. James H. Charlesworth, ed., *The Old Testament Pseudepigrapha: Apocalyptic Literature and Testaments,* vol. 1 (New York: Doubleday, 1983), pp. xxii-xxix.

least in part, in an eschatological reinterpretation of the Davidic promises and the prophetic passages found in the Psalter (see pp. 105-7). Second, persecution, resulting from Alexander the Great's policy of the rapid spread of Hellenistic culture and from the Roman occupation, caused many others to apostatize. Third, the Psalms were appropriated to address the theological concerns of the restoration community, in particular their relationship to God's covenant promises to their ancestors.

The complexity of the period was matched by the rich diversity of the Psalter itself. This diversity allowed for, even demanded, an equally diverse approach to its function in the community of believers. The Psalter was appropriated by the different communities as well as by individuals in the communities for various purposes, including liturgical, didactic, pietistic, and eschatological.[4]

II. The Composition and Shape of the Psalter

Before we seek to evaluate how the Second Temple community (re)interpreted and appropriated the Psalms, we first must ask, "What was the shape of the Psalter at this time?" Is there evidence that the Psalter underwent compositional changes and editorial adjustments during the Second Temple period?[5] The question as to when the Psalter, which is obviously made up of several smaller, earlier collections,[6] assumed its canonical form cannot be answered precisely, but certain parameters can be identified. The prologue to Ben Sirach (c. 180 BCE) refers to a tripartite canon.[7] Customarily, the Psalms were placed

4. See Harry P. Nasuti, *Defining the Sacred Songs: Genre, Tradition, and the Post-Critical Interpretation of the Psalms,* JSOT Suppl. 218, ed. David J. A. Clines and John Jarick (Sheffield: Sheffield Academic Press, 1999), p. 166.

5. J. Schaper notes the later tendency to treat the Psalter as a unified composition, not just a collection of individual compositions. To interpret a particular psalm text, language from any of the other psalms could be drawn upon, and not just for low-level questions such as the semantic range of a word or phrase, but also for thematic parallels or clues for a midrashic reinterpretation of a passage. Whether this later tendency is a distinct departure from or an extension of earlier interpretations that preceded the fixation of the Psalter's contents merits further research.

6. For example, Psalm 72 ends with the notation, "This concludes the prayers of David, son of Jesse" (v. 20), and Psalms 73–83 are all connected to Asaph. For more on the evidence of earlier collections, see Bruce K. Waltke, *An Old Testament Theology* (Grand Rapids: Zondervan, 2007), pp. 883-84; see also pp. 101-4 in this volume.

7. Roger Beckwith, *The Old Testament Canon of the New Testament Church* (Grand Rapids: Eerdmans, 1985), p. 111. In addition to Beckwith's thorough analysis of the historical development of the OT canon, see Charlesworth, ed., *The Old Testament Pseudepigrapha,* pp. xxiii-xxiv.

first in the third part of the canon, the Writings (Hebrew, *K^e^tûbîm*). Thus, the title "Psalter" as a metonymy for the third part of the Jewish canon, was an accepted conventional title (see also Luke 24:44). This conventional title appears in a Greek translation, allowing us to assume that the tripartite canon had existed in Hebrew for some time.[8] Additionally, the Septuagint translation (LXX) reflects a form of the Psalter virtually identical to ours. Although it is notoriously difficult to date this translation, recent attempts all place it mid-first century BCE or earlier.[9]

Most scholars believe that some of the smaller collections of psalms now included in the canonical Psalter were organized during the pre-exilic and exilic periods. During the earlier part of the Second Temple era more psalms were composed and organized into collections, and the pre-exilic and exilic psalms collections were brought together with them to form the bulk of the Psalter as we now have it.[10]

Many scholars have claimed to find evidence of editorial hands in the contents of individual psalms that have left us with clues about interpretation of the psalms in the Second Temple period. Unfortunately, nearly all of these claims are either no longer tenable or in dispute. Candidates for this alleged editorial activity include the addition and/or expansion of psalm superscriptions, the addition of concluding doxologies (Ps. 41:13; 72:19-20; 89:52; 106:48), and the addition of an initial and/or concluding "Praise the Lord" to some psalms (103–106, 111–113, 115–117, 135, 146–150). It is now widely believed that the "Praise the Lord" phrases and the doxologies were part of the original compositions to which they are now attached. While it is generally recognized that the Targums (Aramaic translations) and the LXX added historical and authorship notes to

8. Beckwith, *The Old Testament Canon,* p. 21.

9. See Schaper's discussion of recent attempts in *Eschatology in the Greek Psalter,* WUNT 76 (Tübingen: Mohr [Siebeck], 1995), pp. 39-45. He states at the outset that data for deciding the question is "unsatisfying." Munnich dates it to the early second century BCE based on comparative lexicography. Van der Kooij dates it to the mid-first century BCE based on similarities between LXX Psalms and the *kaige* recension of the Psalms found in the seventh column of Origen's *Hexapla.* Schaper rejects both in favor of a date in the late second century BCE, largely based on what he perceives to be references to the Maccabean dynasty in Psalms 59:8-10; 107:8-10 (MT: 60:8-10; 108:8-10). As he admits himself, he can only propose it as a tentative hypothesis.

10. The traditional fourth-century BCE date for the stabilization of the Psalter has come under review due in part to the study of the various psalm scrolls found at Qumran. Given the DSS evidence, Wilson argues for a middle first-century BCE date (Gerald Wilson, *The Editing of the Hebrew Psalter* [Chico, CA: Scholars Press, 1985], pp. 209-28). Tournay represents a dissenting view, contending that the bulk of the Psalter was a product of the Second Temple period. Raymond Jacques Tournay, *Seeing and Hearing God with the Psalms,* JSOT Suppl. 118, trans. J. Edward Crowley (Sheffield: Sheffield Academic Press, 1991), pp. 17-19.

psalms that lacked them in the Masoretic Text, evidence that similar superscriptions were added to the MT Psalter by later hands is questionable.[11] That some superscriptions were not part of the original composition of the psalms is suggested by cases such as that of Psalm 69. The authorship title attributes the psalm to David,[12] and yet verses 34-36 may suggest a post-exilic setting. According to Childs, the historical superscriptions found in Psalms 3, 7, 18, 34, 51–52, 54, 56–57, and 59–60 were added by editors to associate the contents of the psalm with an event in the story of David to serve as a model for individual response to the crises of life.[13] Jonker argues that the psalm superscriptions, especially those of Books II and III, were added as part of Levitical propaganda in the Second Temple period.[14] Wilson further suggests that the placement of Psalm 1 at the beginning of the Psalter is meant to provide hermeneutical reorientation for the rest of the Psalter. This Psalm leads the reader to treat the rest of the Psalter as material for individual study and edification. The historical superscriptions assist in this reorientation.[15]

Many scholars also believe that the editors of the Psalter succeeded in building out of pre-existing psalms and psalm collections a book with a distinct overall message. In addition, there exists a growing consensus among several leading scholars that there is a sequential "theological intentionality" in the Psalter's current shape, although they disagree about where the center of this intentional ordering lies (i.e., Brueggemann, Psalm 73; Wilson, Book 4 [Psalms 90–106]).[16] According to Gerald Wilson, there is a historical movement reflected in the arrangement of the Psalter: Books IV and V are a response to Psalm 89,[17] a psalm in which the issues of the failed Davidic monarchy and the crisis of the Babylonian exile are addressed.[18] Accordingly, the answer provided

11. See pp. 90-91.

12. For a discussion of various interpretive options for the prepositional phrase *l^e David*, see Uriel Simon, *Four Approaches to the Book of the Psalms: From Saadiah Gaon to Abraham Ibn Ezra*, trans. Lenn J. Schramm (New York: State University of New York Press, 1991), pp. 179-82; for a defense of the traditional interpretation, "by," see pp. 89-90 in this book.

13. Brevard S. Childs, "Psalm Titles and Midrashic Exegesis," *JSS* 16 (1971): 148-49.

14. Louis C. Jonker, "Revisiting the Psalm Headings: Second Temple Levitical Propoganda?" in Dirk J. Human and Cas J. A. Vos, eds., *Psalms and Liturgy* (New York: T. & T. Clark International, 2004), pp. 102-22.

15. Wilson, *The Editing of the Hebrew Psalter*, p. 143.

16. Nasuti, *Defining the Sacred Songs*, pp. 175-77; Claus Westermann, *Praise and Lament in the Psalms* (Atlanta: John Knox Press, 1981), p. 258; B. Childs, *Introduction to the Old Testament as Scripture* (Philadelphia: Fortress Press, 1979), pp. 515-17.

17. "The dark book of the Psalter." Waltke, *An Old Testament Theology*, p. 886. See p. 104 in this book.

18. Wilson, *The Editing of the Hebrew Psalter*, pp. 209-28.

to the exilic crisis by Books IV and V is a redirection from reliance on an earthly monarchy to an appreciation of God's eternal kingship.[19]

III. Common Features of Second Temple Interpretation of the Psalms

In the remainder of this chapter we will seek to identify common features of Second Temple Judaism's interpretive approaches to the Psalter, bearing in mind that what is described may not apply without exception to all the Jewish communities of this period. First, both the Biblical texts (Ezra, Nehemiah, Chronicles) and non-canonical materials from this period point to a renewed emphasis on the Torah among the Jewish people. One of the major religious concerns of the Second Temple period was seeking how the Torah applied to the contemporary situation.[20] As is noted elsewhere in this chapter,[21] there was a tendency to view the Psalter as a sourcebook for models of proper response to the Torah, for personal study and reflection — in short, as a supplement to Torah, another word from God.[22] Second, the faithful in this period of crisis used the psalms as resources for personal and corporate worship. Finally, there were gradual shifts in emphasis and understanding of the Davidic promises and prophetic counterparts as these Scriptures were now understood in Messianic terms to be speaking toward a future restoration of the Davidic monarchy (i.e., Psalms 2 and 72). In addition, without a monarchy, the royal psalms were democratized. For example, Psalm 101 was no longer interpreted as referring exclusively to royalty and could now be appropriated by any head of family.[23]

19. Nasuti, *Defining the Sacred Songs,* p. 177.

20. Waltke previously thought with Childs and others that *torah* ("catechetical teaching") in Psalm 1:2 referred to the book of Psalms: "Nevertheless, the book of Psalms was transformed from liturgy in the temple to reflective meditation in the postexilic synagogue." *An Old Testament Theology,* p. 885. But lexical data persuaded him that *torah* refers to the teachings of Moses (see p. 136). For more on the constitutive role Torah served in the post-exilic era, see Bright, *A History of Israel,* pp. 430-42. Bright notes that the post-exilic emphases on Sabbath, tithing, and the temple are not "external trivia, but distinguishing marks of a purified Israel" (p. 431).

21. See pp. 27, 29. Also, Tournay, *Seeing and Hearing God with the Psalms,* p. 25.

22. For more on the hermeneutical shift from the psalms as words of the faithful *to* God, to God's word to the faithful, see Childs, *Introduction,* pp. 513-15.

23. Sigmund Mowinckel, *The Psalms in Israel's Worship,* trans. D. R. Ap-Thomas, 2 vols. (Oxford: Blackwell; Nashville: Abingdon, 1962), vol. 1, p. 78; William L. Holladay, *The Psalms through Three Thousand Years: Prayerbook of a Cloud of Witnesses* (Minneapolis: Fortress Press,

A. Davidic Authorship of the Psalms

The traditional association between David and the Psalter was expanded during the Second Temple period. For example, the number of superscriptions that bear David's name increased from 73 in the Hebrew Psalter to 85 in the LXX.[24] Superscriptions describing the historical circumstances of a Psalm's composition were expanded or in some cases added where there was none in the MT.[25] According to the Qumran Psalms Scroll (11QPs), David wrote 3,600 psalms. From the Qumran remains also comes an indication that references to "David" could indicate an authoritative corpus of Scripture in similar fashion to the well-attested practice of citing "Moses" when referring to the Torah.[26]

B. Liturgical and Cultic

1. *Hymnbook of the Second Temple*

The Psalms have been referred to as the "hymnbook of the Second Temple." That is, the Psalter *functioned* as the cultic hymnbook of this period, not that it was compiled during this period for this reason.[27] According to Mowinckel, this does not necessarily mean that every psalm served a hymnic function in Second Temple Judaism. Rather, "there came a time when every psalm used in the temple service had to be from the Psalter. The Psalter attained such canonical authority and 'monopoly' that when a new festival was instituted and there was need of a special psalm for the festal offering, a new psalm would no longer be composed, but one of the psalms of the Psalter was chosen and interpreted in a way which would fit in with the festival."[28] For example, in 165 BCE, following the Jewish victory over Antiochus IV, when Judas Maccabeus and his brothers instituted the Hanukkah festival to celebrate the rededication of the temple, no new psalm was composed for the occasion. Rather, Psalm 30, a

1993), pp. 64-65. Sue Gillingham notes that the Psalms began to be explicitly cited as prophetic texts late in the Hellenistic period. "From Liturgy to Prophecy: The Use of Psalmody in Second Temple Judaism," *CBQ* 64 (2002): 488.

24. John J. Collins, *Introduction to the Hebrew Bible* (Minneapolis: Fortress Press, 2004), pp. 461-62.

25. For discussion regarding these additional superscriptions, see pp. 89-92.

26. Collins, *Introduction*, pp. 461-62.

27. Bernhard Duhm (see p. 93) is an example of a critical scholar who argued for the composition of the Psalter in this period.

28. Mowinckel, *The Psalms*, 2:202.

psalm originally concerned with an individual, was used and reinterpreted (1 Macc. 4:25).[29]

2. *Jewish Festivals and the Psalms*

The Psalms played a vital role in the religious life of the Second Temple Israelite community because the Psalter offered a rich liturgical deposit for Second Temple Judaism to speak to the contemporary crisis of faith and to depict a coming period of restoration. Various socio-liturgical settings for how the Psalms were used in this period can be identified. For example, there were various guilds of Levitical temple singers (i.e., Asaphites, Korahites) who used the Psalter in their liturgical practices in the temple service, for both festal days and daily sacrifices (1 Chron. 16; Sir. 50:16-17; 1 Macc. 4:54). These Levitical singers served, among other roles, a prophetic function.[30] Their sacred music functioned prophetically, either offering salvation or threatening punishment. In the temple they dialogued with *I AM* on behalf of the community. According to Tournay, in this period the psalms were sung, along with other sacred music, and they were given pride of place among liturgical celebrations, feasts, and pilgrimages in Jerusalem. He notes, "during the rule of the Persians, Greeks, and Romans, the singing of the psalms and sacred music had a privileged place among all the liturgical celebrations, sacrifices."[31] The Chronicler quotes three excerpts from the psalms (1 Chron. 16; Ps. 105:1-15; 96:1-13; 106:1, 47-49). Also, in 2 Chronicles 6:41-42, Psalm 132:8-10 is quoted.[32]

The liturgical appropriation of the psalms was not limited to the temple in Jerusalem. For example, the liturgical occasions listed in the 11QPsalms scroll poem found at Qumran match the occasions of all-Israel sacrifices in Numbers 28–29.[33]

29. Mowinckel, *The Psalms,* 2:199-202.

30. See 1 Chron. 15; 25; 2 Chron. 20.

31. Tournay, *Seeing and Hearing God with the Psalms,* p. 27.

32. Tournay, *Seeing and Hearing God with the Psalms,* p. 27.

33. Peter W. Flint, *The Dead Sea Psalms Scrolls and the Book of Psalms* (New York: Brill, 1997), p. 22; Michael Fishbane, "Use, Authority and Interpretation of Mikra at Qumran," in Martin Jan Mulder, ed., *Mikra: Text, Translation, Reading and Interpretation of the Hebrew Bible in Ancient Judaism and Early Christianity* (Minneapolis: Fortress Press, 1990), pp. 350-51.

C. The Psalms in Prayer

The psalms were also used to shape the private worship and prayer of pious Jews. A confessional prayer found in a fragmentary manuscript from Qumran Cave 4 expands on Moses' prayer recorded in Deuteronomy 9:26-29, incorporating language from Psalm 51 and Nehemiah 9. In acknowledging the community's guilt in light of God's righteous judgment, echoes of Psalm 51 may be heard: "and what is evil [in your eyes I have done], so that you are just in your sentence, you are pu[re . . . when] you [judge]. Behold, in our sins w[e] were founded [we] were [br]ought forth [ ] in imp[urity of . . .] and in [st]iffness of neck" (4Q393 1-2.ii.2-4).[34] The penitential prayer attributed to David in the superscription of Psalm 51 is here adapted for communal confession.

D. The Messianic and Eschatological Use of the Psalms

Alongside the liturgical use of the Psalter there was a gradual appropriation of the Psalms toward a future orientation.[35] The deaths of the post-exilic prophets (Haggai, Zechariah, and Malachi) signaled the end of the prophetic voice in Israel. The Levitical singers compensated for this prophetic silence in the Second Temple period by bringing an eschatologically oriented message of hope and consolation to the post-exilic community (1 Chron. 15:22ff.; 25:1ff.; 2 Chron. 20:19).[36] In particular, there was an increasingly eschatological appropriation of the explicitly royal psalms, interpreted as pointing to the judgment and vindication ushered in by the Day of *I AM*. Theological focus shifted from the historical Davidic monarchy to an indefinite future where the Davidic promises were expected to be fulfilled in the Messianic rulership.[37]

The Dead Sea Scrolls reflect the Qumran sectarians' belief in two Messiahs, one political and one priestly, the latter given more prominence in the literature.[38] The traditions of the past were pressed into service to console the new community gathered around the Second Temple. This Messianic interpretation

34. Daniel Falk, "Psalms and Prayers," in D. A. Carson, Peter T. O'Brien, and Mark A. Seifrid, eds., *Justification and Variegated Nomism*, vol. 1 (Grand Rapids: Baker Academic, 2001), p. 12.

35. For the development of the Messianic expectation see pp. 105-11.

36. D. L. Peterson observes that "liturgical singing became prophetic performance." Cited by Tournay, *Seeing and Hearing God with the Psalms*, p. 30.

37. Tournay seeks to demonstrate what he calls "'prophetic' stylistic features in the psalms of the Second Temple." *Seeing and Hearing God with the Psalms*, pp. 46, 67.

38. Philip R. Davies and John Rogerson, *The Old Testament World*, 2nd ed. (Louisville: Westminster/John Knox Press, 2005), p. 222.

of the Psalter appropriated a prophetic impulse already present in the original divine intention of the Psalter[39] and anticipated the NT treatment of the psalms as "prophecies" (i.e., John 19:23-24; Acts 2:25-36; 4:25-26; Heb. 1:1-14).[40] David was considered a prophet, and as such the Psalms were interpreted to be prophesying about the contemporary events and the Qumran community.[41]

This eschatological impulse is especially evident in how the psalms that were traditionally regarded as royal (see pp. 106-7) are appropriated in the Second Temple period. With the disappearance of the monarchy, there was "an increasingly eschatological awareness" of the importance of the royal psalms.[42] Evidence of this eschatological bias is seen in the LXX translations of both the superscriptions in the Psalter and the psalms themselves.[43] For example, in Psalm 1:5, "Therefore the wicked will not stand in the judgment," the LXX translates Hebrew *yqmw ("will stand") by* ἀναστήσονται (rise, i.e., from death), importing a more eschatological nuance in the Greek.[44]

IV. Distinctive Features of the Major Extant Witnesses to Second Temple Interpretation of the Psalms

A. Dead Sea Scrolls (DSS)

The earliest extant manuscripts of the book of Psalms come from the Qumran community. The Psalms played a central and significant role in the communal

39. Nasuti points out that, in Childs's discussion regarding the eschatological orientation of the Psalter, Childs does not deal with the question as to whether this orientation stems from a prophetic impulse already present in the original intent of the psalm (following Becker) or from a decisive reinterpretation during Second Temple Judaism (following Begrich). *Defining the Sacred Songs,* p. 164 n. 3.

40. According to Gillingham, "Of the 116 most obvious references to the psalms in the NT, at least 75 of these understood the psalms in a future-oriented way; when the psalms are quoted they are frequently referred to as "prophecies" ("From Liturgy to Prophecy," p. 471).

41. Qumran manuscript 11QPs[a], in referring to David's psalmic compositions, reads, "All these he uttered through prophecy which was given him from before the Most High." Gillingham, "From Liturgy to Prophecy," p. 483.

42. Gillingham, "From Liturgy to Prophecy," p. 477.

43. Schaper's assessment of the eschatological bias in the LXX translation of the Psalter is helpful. See Schaper, *Eschatology in the Greek Psalter.*

44. Gillingham, "From Liturgy to Prophecy," p. 480. Silva and Jobes note, "The semantic range of the Hebrew word *qum* includes both rising and standing. The Greek verb chosen by the translator, *anistēmi,* means specifically 'to rise up,' and the New Testament writers use it with reference to resurrection." Karen H. Jobes and Moises Silva, *Invitation to the Septuagint* (Grand Rapids: Baker Academic, 2000), p. 96.

life (worship in particular) of the Jewish sect at the Dead Sea, as is evidenced by the fact that more fragments of the Psalter have been found at Qumran than any other OT book, especially in caves 4 and 11. More than thirty copies contain fragments of 115 Biblical psalms.[45] The psalms were lovingly copied, commented on, and culled for inspiration as the sectarians produced their own psalms for worship.

The damaged Psalm scroll from Cave 11 contains all or portions of thirty-nine Biblical psalms. Of particular note is that it contains psalms from books IV and V of our canonical Psalter, though the order is markedly different from our canonical text. In another Psalm scroll found in Cave 4 that contains psalms from Books I and II the order is very close to our canonical order, suggesting that perhaps the order of the psalms in the earlier books had been set whereas that of the latter books was still in a state of flux. In a fragment from Cave 4 were found the words *sēper hattĕhillîm* ("the book of the psalms").[46] The Psalm scroll from Cave 11 has canonical psalms intermixed with non-canonical psalms (Psalms 151, 154, and 155), other portions of Scripture (i.e., 2 Sam. 12:1-7), part of an acrostic poem in Sirach (Ecclesiasticus) 51:13-30, three more poetic compositions of unknown origin, and a statement referring to David's compositions. Holladay suggests that such a compilation may point to a liturgical usage analogous to the breviaries of medieval Roman Catholicism, where poetic portions from other parts of the canon (Jer. 12:12-13) are interspersed with the canonical psalms.[47]

The Law of Moses played a prominent role in the community's life; as such it is not surprising that the sectarian writings contain references to both Psalms 1 and 119. Additionally, there are several references to both of these psalms in the sectarian document titled *Community Rule.*[48]

For the Qumran community, the Psalter provided proof-texts that supported their understanding that they were the righteous remnant living in the last days before the final judgment. "David's Compositions," found in column 27 of 11QPs[a] (11Q5), was the primary edition of the Psalter used at Qumran. What is of special note is that this document uses prophetic language with respect to David's composing the Psalms. For example, "And David, the son of Jesse, was wise . . . and the LORD gave him a discerning and enlightened spirit. And he wrote 3,600 psalms; and songs to sing before the altar. . . . All these he

45. Holladay, *The Psalms through Three Thousand Years,* pp. 95-112; Alan Hauser and Duane F. Watson, eds., *A History of Biblical Interpretation,* vol. 1: *The Ancient Period* (Grand Rapids: Eerdmans, 2003), pp. 144-46.

46. Tournay, *Seeing and Hearing God with the Psalms,* p. 13.

47. Holladay, *The Psalms through Three Thousand Years,* p. 102.

48. Holladay, *The Psalms through Three Thousand Years,* p. 109.

composed *through prophecy* which was given him from before the Most High" (italics mine).[49] In the *Florilegium* found in Cave 4 the community used the Psalms as part of their proof-texting. This sectarian document incorporates Psalm 1:1 and Psalm 2:1 into an anthology of canonical verses, which are then directly interpreted as referring to the community as the righteous remnant who have turned aside from sinful Israel.[50] Commenting on Psalm 2:1-2, the text reads, "the real interpretation of the matter (*pesher haddābār,* פשר הדבר) [is that "the nations" are the Kitt]im and those who take [refuge in Him are] the chosen ones of Israel in the latter days. . . ."[51] The central psalm in this text is Psalm 82:1-2, where Melchizedek is identified as a heavenly figure who executes divine judgment on Satan and all evil peoples.[52] Psalm 24, originally a hymnic celebration of *I AM*'s leadership in battle, is now recast as a celebration of God's victory in the eschatological battle.[53] The *Florilegium,* 1QFlor(4Q174), provides another example of eschatological interpretation of the Psalms (1 and 2), as does 4QCatena — a group of texts linked together by the phrase "at the end of days" — which refers to Psalms 6, 11–13, and 16 in an eschatological context.[54]

In addition to using the Psalter for proof-texting, the Qumran sectarians used the *pesher* method[55] of interpretation in their appropriation of the Psalter.

49. Peter W. Flint, "The Prophet David at Qumran," in Matthias Henze, ed., *Biblical Interpretation at Qumran* (Grand Rapids: Eerdmans, 2005), pp. 163-64.

50. Fishbane cites use of the common noun דרך to link citations from Psalm 1:1 and Isaiah 8:11 and *mô-šab* מושב in Psalm 1:1 and Ezekiel 37:23 in a discussion on sectarian separateness. Michael Fishbane, "Use, Authority and Interpretation of Mikra at Qumran," in *Mikra: Text, Translation, Reading and Interpretation,* p. 374.

51. Translated by G. J Brooke, *Exegesis at Qumran: 4QFlorilegium in Its Jewish Context,* JSOT Suppl. 29 (Sheffield: JSOT Press, 1985), pp. 88 and 93, as quoted in Gillingham, "From Liturgy to Prophecy," p. 486.

52. Holladay observes that the author of Hebrews may have drawn upon this interpretation in his portrayal of Melchizedek as a prefigurement of Christ, and also notes the seeming parallels between the chain of proof-texts in the Florilegium and Hebrews 1:5, where the latter quotes two of the verses (Ps. 2:7 and 2 Sam. 7:14) from this anthology. *The Psalms through Three Thousand Years,* pp. 103-4.

53. Holladay, *The Psalms through Three Thousand Years,* pp. 106-9.

54. Gillingham, "From Liturgy to Prophecy," pp. 484-85.

55. "The word *pesher* derives from an Aramaic root meaning 'solution.' The presupposition is that the text contains a mystery communicated by God that is not understood until the solution is made known by an inspired interpreter. . . . [T]he starting point for understanding is not the Old Testament text, but a historical event or person." Klyne Snodgrass, "The Use of the Old Testament in the New," in G. K. Beale, ed., *The Right Doctrine from the Wrong Texts? Essays on the Use of the Old Testament in the New* (Grand Rapids: Baker Books, 1994), pp. 41-42. Or, as is often more simply put, in *pesher* interpretation, "this [current event/institution/person] means that [Biblical reference]."

The pesharim (commentaries) from Qumran are limited to the prophetic books and Psalms (Psalms Pesher 1Q16; 4Q 171, 173).[56] Fragments from a commentary on Psalm 68 were found in Cave 1, and in Cave 4 a manuscript of a running commentary on Psalm 37 was discovered. Once again, Scripture was interpreted as finding fulfillment in the contemporary situation faced by the community. For example, referring to Psalm 137, the commentator notes: "This concerns the Wicked Priest, who tried to kill the Teacher of Righteousness." Psalm 37:7 is interpreted as referring to "the Liar who has led many astray by his lying words so that they chose frivolous things and heeded not the interpreter of knowledge, so that they perish by sword and famine and pestilence," and verses 18-19a are specifically interpreted as referring to "the penitents of the desert who, saved, shall live for a thousand generations and to whom all the inheritance of Adam shall belong, as also to their seed forever."[57] Further, Psalm 37:32-33 is interpreted as referring to the Wicked Priest's desire to kill the Teacher of Righteousness.[58] Another example is found in 4Q174. Once again, specific texts from the Psalms are explicitly interpreted as proof-texts announcing the dawn of the final eschatological age.[59]

Some of the Qumran community's constitutional documents contain allusions to the canonical psalms. For example, an echo of Psalm 1:2 can be heard in the following passage from the document entitled *Community Rule:* "And where ten [men of the community] are, there shall never lack a man among them who shall study the Law continually, day and night, concerning the right conduct of a man with his companion." Additionally, in the document known as the *War Rule,* which depicts the eschatological battle in which the "children of light" defeat the "children of darkness," echoes of psalmic phrases can be found. For example, on the trumpets will be inscribed these words: "The mighty Deeds of God shall crush the Enemy, putting to Flight all those who hate Righteousness and bringing Shame on those who hate Him." According to many scholars, this is derived from Numbers 10:35 or Psalm 68:2 (1).[60]

Finally, at Qumran, the Psalms served as models for the community's own original hymnic compositions. Holladay notes twenty-nine Scriptural echoes in "hymn 9" (Vermes's designation) from Qumran: fifteen from the canonical psalms and fourteen from other canonical sections. What is of particular in-

56. Hauser, *A History of Biblical Interpretation,* 1:158; Fishbane, "Use, Authority," p. 351.

57. Holladay, *The Psalms through Three Thousand Years,* p. 104.

58. Holladay, *The Psalms through Three Thousand Years,* pp. 104-5.

59. Holladay, *The Psalms through Three Thousand Years,* p. 104.

60. Holladay, *The Psalms through Three Thousand Years,* p. 105. Geza Vermes, *The Dead Sea Scrolls in English* (London: Penguin, 1987), p. 107.

terest is that, except for two echoes from thanksgiving psalms, all of these come from lament psalms. The community nuanced these allusions into words of thanksgiving for and rejoicing in God's triumph over evil.[61]

B. Septuagint (LXX)

By the middle of the second century BCE, the Psalms were being recited in Greek in the synagogues of Alexandria.[62] The LXX Psalter differs from the Masoretic Text in several respects. It contains an additional psalm (151) not found in the MT.[63] It also divides a few of the 150 psalms found in the MT differently.[64]

The LXX enhances the relationship between Psalms 1 and 2 already implicit in the canonical Psalter (see pp. 160-61) by translating 2:12b, "lest you perish from *the way of righteousness*" (cf. 1:6, "for the Lord watches over *the way of the righteous*") and by translating 2:10 and 2:12a to refer to being instructed or accepting instruction. The translator(s) appear to be promoting a view of the Psalter as an authoritative picture of the hopes, trials, and ultimate triumph of those who accept the wisdom of Torah, exemplified in the figure of David, the author of the Psalms.[65]

This view of the Psalter corresponds with the Torah-centric understand-

61. Holladay notes the curiosity that the community did not appropriate the "Messianic psalms" (i.e., Psalms 2, 72, 110) in their eschatological interpretations. See *The Psalms through Three Thousand Years,* p. 109.

62. Holladay, *The Psalms through Three Thousand Years,* p. 84.

63. Also, several LXX Psalter manuscripts have The Odes, a series of OT and NT prayers, appended to them. These Odes are incorporated into the liturgy of the Eastern Orthodox Church. See Jobes and Silva, *Invitation to the Septuagint,* p. 78 n. 22.

64. For example, Psalms 9 and 10 in the MT are a single psalm in the LXX, while Psalm 146 in the MT is divided into Psalms 146 and 147 in the LXX. See Jobes and Silva, *Invitation to the Septuagint,* p. 79.

65. Gerald Sheppard argues that, "By implication, the demand to read the Torah as a guide to wisdom is what the redactor [of Psalms 1 and 2 in the Hebrew Psalter] presupposes to be illustrated by the Psalter." The redactional placement of these psalms as the prologue to the Psalter emphasizes Torah as a source of and guide to wisdom and the way to right living. "The LXX seizes upon this functional resonance predisposed by the redactional association of the two psalms and heightens the effect." Sheppard identifies parallels (in structure, vocabulary, and imagery) between the Psalter and second-century BCE literature such as *Sirach* and *Baruch,* thus seeking to demonstrate that the redacted Psalter of early Second Temple Judaism shows a psalmic connection between the Torah and wisdom that anticipates a similar nexus demonstrated in later Second Temple writings. See Gerald Sheppard, *Wisdom as a Hermeneutical Construct* (New York: Walter de Gruyter, 1980), pp. 136-44.

ing of many strands of Second Temple interpretation of the TaNaK (Hebrew Bible composed of *T[ôrâ], N[ᵉbî'îm], K[ᵉtûbîm]*), and it would not be surprising to find in the rest of the LXX Psalter evidence of the translator(s)'s zeal to protect the Torah and the reputation of David as a Torah-observant prophet of God. The once fashionable idea that the LXX avoided the anthropomorphisms common in the MT has come under scrutiny as scholars have not been able to establish a consistently anthropomorphic bias in the LXX.[66] However, the evidence suggests that the LXX translators were consistent in their hesitancy to refer to God as a rock. The MT Psalter's use of rock or stone imagery likening I AM to a fortress (Ps. 18:31, 46) is translated in the LXX with words such as "helper, guardian, and protector, which preserve the sense but not the imagery of the metaphor."[67] One possible motivation is that it was "an apologetic endeavor to escape even the semblance of approval of the worshipping of stone images."[68]

C. Aramaic Targum on the Psalms

Fourteen manuscripts of the Psalms Targum (Tg. Ps.), dating from the seventh to the ninth centuries, have been preserved.[69] Sometimes several targumim[70] are noted for one verse, moving from a literal to a more aggadic interpretation of the text.[71] The Psalms Targum almost certainly contains interpretations of the Biblical psalms from the Second Temple period, although the text we have now reached its final form much later.[72]

Cook provides numerous examples of targumic expansions throughout

66. Jobes and Silva, *Invitation to the Septuagint*, pp. 94-95.

67. Jobes and Silva, *Invitation to the Septuagint*, p. 95. The authors note that this same tendency is evident also in the LXX of Deuteronomy, Isaiah, and Habakkuk. Quoted in Jobes and Silva, *Invitation to the Septuagint*, p. 96.

68. Isaac L. Seeligmann, quoted in Jobes and Silva, *Invitation to the Septuagint*, p. 96.

69. Hauser and Watson, eds., *A History of Biblical Interpretation*, 1:169. While the Pentateuch and Prophets sections of the Tanak have official Targums (Targum Onkelos and Targum Jonathan, respectively), according to the Talmud there is no official Targum to the Ketubim because this section of the Tanak foretold the date of the Messiah's coming. See Philip S. Alexander, "Jewish Aramaic Translations of Hebrew Scriptures," in Martin Jan Mulder, ed., *Mikra: Text, Translation, Reading and Interpretation*, p. 224.

70. "Targum" is the Aramaic word for "translation."

71. Alexander, "Jewish Aramaic Translations of Hebrew Scriptures," p. 225.

72. Edward M. Cook, "Covenantal Nomism in the Psalms Targum," in *The Concept of the Covenant in the Second Temple Period*, Supplements to the Journal for the Study of Judaism, vol. 71 (Leiden: E. J. Brill, 2003), p. 204.

the Psalter meant to highlight the centrality of study of and obedience to Torah for the life of the people of God. For example, in Psalm 114:4 the targum says that the mountains and hills skipped at the giving of Torah to Israel, not at the time of Israel's entrance into the promised land as in the Hebrew text.[73] Additionally, targumic additions suggest a cause-effect relationship between study of the Torah and blessing (and neglect of Torah and punishment). The enigmatic Hebrew of Psalm 68:30b [31b], "He who submits himself with pieces of silver," is translated in the Psalms Targum as "His favor is toward the people who are occupied willingly in the Torah, which is purer than silver."[74]

D. Other Second Temple Works on the Psalms

1. *The Psalms of Solomon*

Eighteen psalms attributed to Solomon are found in some editions of the LXX and also in Syriac. They were originally composed in Hebrew, though there are no extant Hebrew fragments. Perhaps the title is meant to suggest a contrast with the canonical psalms, presumed to be the work of David. These psalms reflect the crisis of faith felt by devout Jews due to the Roman invasion under Pompey in 63 BCE and express the desire for a Davidic Messiah to accomplish restoration.[75] They differ from the canonical psalms by making more frequent and explicit references to the immediate historical situation in which they were composed. Despite the troubles of the present time, the psalms repeatedly contrast the coming salvation of the righteous with the eventual destruction of the wicked. Psalms of Solomon 17 actualizes the coming salvation in the reign of the Messiah, using a catena of allusions to canonical psalms and the prophets to describe how, trusting in God rather than human power, he will make the land and people holy again, drive away evildoers, establish just rule over Israel and the nations, and bring glory to God and blessing to the righteous (Ps. Sol. 17:26-46). Gillingham notes, "In these so-called psalms of Solomon with their apocalyptic influence, the 'Messianic' figure from the Davidic line in the royal 'Psalms of David' is becoming a 'Messianic' figure for all time."[76] According to

73. Cook's translation of the Targum of Psalm 114:4 "When the Torah was given to his people, the mountains leapt like rams, the hills like offspring of the flock." "Covenantal Nomism in the Psalms Targum," p. 210.

74. Cook's translations, "Covenantal Nomism in the Psalms Targum," pp. 210-11.

75. Holladay, *The Psalms through Three Thousand Years*, p. 97; James Charlesworth and Paul Winter, "Psalms of Solomon," in *IDB* 3:959. Falk, "Psalms and Prayers," pp. 35-39.

76. Gillingham, "From Liturgy to Prophecy," pp. 487-88.

R. B. Wright, "There is more substance to the ideas concerning the Messiah in the Psalms of Solomon than in any other extant Jewish writing."[77] Wright also notes that the connection between the concepts of Messiah and lordship made in the Psalms of Solomon anticipates the identification of "Christ the Lord" *(Christos Kurios)* in NT Christology (i.e., Luke 2:11).[78]

In addition to the focus on Messianic redemption, the *Psalms of Solomon* are concerned with personal piety and the conflict between the sinners and the righteous in Israel. Falk notes, "Regardless of the specific format of their use, the frequently observed didactic and edifying character of these psalms, as well as their polemical content, leave little doubt that an intended function was to encourage and admonish a particular community that felt threatened within Israel."[79]

2. The Books of Maccabees

1 Maccabees 7:16-17 recounts an incident in 161 BCE when a delegation of Jewish scribes approached the Seleucid governor Bacchides to negotiate a peace settlement. Though the safety of the Jewish delegation was assured, the text notes, "So they trusted him; but he seized sixty of them and killed them in one day, in accordance with the word which was written, 'The flesh of thy saints and their blood they poured out round about Jerusalem, and there was none to bury them.'"[80] This paraphrase of Psalm 79:2-3 is used to honor and exalt the murdered Jewish scribes *(hasidim)*. The use of the phrase "the word which was written" indicates that the author of Maccabees understood Psalm 79 as a prophecy being fulfilled in the recorded events.[81]

Holladay also notes in passing the connection between 1 Maccabees 1:36-40; 2:7-13; 3:45 and Psalms 44, 74, and 79. We see the author of Maccabees min-

77. R. B. Wright, "Psalms of Solomon: A New Translation and Introduction," in James H. Charlesworth, ed., *The Old Testament Pseudepigrapha*, vol. 2, p. 643.

78. Wright, "Psalms of Solomon," p. 646.

79. Falk, "Psalms and Prayers," pp. 36-37.

80. Translation from G. Vermes, *The Complete Dead Sea Scrolls in English* (New York: Allen Lane/Penguin, 1997), p. 501, quoted by Gillingham, "From Liturgy to Prophecy," p. 487.

81. Or, with Devorah Dimant, "This verse offers another example of the exegetical procedure of actualization. . . . As a result, also the contemporary situation is read into the psalm, which is apparently considered as prophecy." "Use and Interpretation of Mikra in the Apocrypha and Pseudepigrapha," in *Mikra: Text, Translation, Reading, and Interpretation*, p. 391. Gillingham likens this appropriation of the Psalms to the pesher reading at Qumran. See "From Liturgy to Prophecy," p. 487.

ing the Psalms to articulate the laments of these Jews fighting what they considered to be the destructiveness of Hellenization.

3. *Non-Masoretic Psalms*

There is ample evidence of non-Masoretic psalms in use during this time period. For example, in the apotropaic prayer, *Plea for Deliverance* (11QPs[a] 19:1-18), the psalmist pleads for God's deliverance from some unknown danger.[82] Several non-Masoretic psalms associated with David are contained within the Qumran Psalter (11QPs[a]).[83] For example, *Psalm 155* (11QPs[a] 24:3-17 = Syriac Psalm III), in which the petitioner appeals to God for deliverance from wicked accusers who interpret his illness as divine judgment for his sins. In both these examples, the language and tone of the Biblical Psalter are reflected.[84]

V. Summary

During the Second Temple period the Psalter was still assuming its final shape. The various Jewish communities of this period appropriated the Psalter as a canonical interpretation of their current situation and future hope. Understanding how Second Temple Jewish interpreters appropriated the Psalter helps trace the Christological trajectory implicit in the Psalter to the New Testament.

82. Falk, "Psalms and Prayers," p. 22.

83. These psalms are 151A, 151B, 154, and 155. A different form of Psalm 151 is attested in LXX manuscripts with the superscription "outside the number." These psalms are part of a collection of five "apocryphal psalms" contained in the Peshitta Psalter (151-55). For more on the Non-Masoretic Psalms, see J. A. Sanders, "Non-Masoretic Psalms (4Q88=4QPs[f], 11Q5=11QPs[a], 11Q6=11QPs[b])," *The Dead Sea Scrolls: Hebrew, Aramaic, and Greek Texts with English Translations 4A: Pseudepigraphic and Non-Masoretic Psalms and Prayers* (The Princeton Theological Seminary Dead Sea Scrolls Project, ed. J. H. Charlesworth and H. W. L. Rietz, with P. W. Flint et al. (Tübingen: Mohr [Siebeck], 1997); J. H. Charlesworth with J. A. Sanders, "More Psalms of David (Third Century B.C.–First Century A.D.): A New Translation and Introduction," in Charlesworth, ed., *The Old Testament Pseudepigrapha*, vol. 2, pp. 610-24.

84. Falk, "Psalms and Prayers," pp. 22-23.

CHAPTER 2

Historical Introduction to the Interpretation of the Psalms in Church Orthodoxy

As angels live in heaven, so men live on earth who rejoice in the praises of God, in the pure heart of psalmody. No mortal man can fully declare the virtue of the psalms. In them are the confession of sins, the tears of the penitent, sorrow of heart. Here is foretold all the dispensations of our redemption, the wondrous delights of heaven's mirth. Here shall you find the Incarnation, Resurrection, and Ascension of the Word of God.[1]

For the past two millennia, the Psalms have been a vast spiritual hinterland of Christian devotion. It is shrinking fast today, not because of global warming, but nevertheless ultimately from the same causal source — the secularism of the human spirit, which seeks all satisfactions on this one planet, instead of seeking them from the Creator who "made heaven and earth." For over three thousand years, the Psalms have been Israel's prayer book, and the church's source of orthodoxy, as "truthful praise."

Various books of the Bible have served the church in the changing challenges to its faith. Ambrose advised the young convert Augustine to start with the book of Isaiah. The Song of Songs was hugely popular from the time of Origen to the legacy of Bernard of Clairvaux and his Cistercian followers a thousand years later. Certainly the epistle to the Romans was the text of the Reformers, Luther, Calvin, and their successors. Uniquely, however, the Psalms have been "the miniature Bible" of the Christian laity, always available — at least in theory — from the beginning of Christianity. Its recovery in the vernac-

1. Alcuin, Epistles IV, 391 PL C col. 497-98.

ular dates from the Council of Toulouse (c. 1225). Two-thirds of the Old Testament quotations in the New Testament are from the Psalms. Jesus lived by and recited from the Psalms. The apostles further interpreted the Psalms as prophetic of Christ, and of the distinctive teachings consequent upon the Incarnation, Resurrection, Ascension, and Pentecost. The early Christian Fathers based their commentaries on the Psalms upon the mystery of the Trinity, and their orthodoxy was tested accordingly. Meanwhile the poetic and lyrical qualities of the Psalms have been sung in numerous expressions of worship, since the beginnings of Christianity until the eighteenth century; since that time the singing of Psalms has become more rare. Only modern psychology has replaced its psalmo-therapy for cleansing, healing, and enriching the souls of the pious devotees of the Scriptures. With the contemporary "death of the Psalter," are we now seeing also "the death of the soul"? Our writing, then, is more than an expression of seminary scholarship; we write with deep concern for the future of the Psalms in our "postmodern" Christian lives and culture.

"No mortal man can fully declare the virtue of the psalms," confessed Alcuin, the brilliant educational advisor of the Emperor Charlemagne. We feel the same sentiment twelve hundred years later! Tracing their history is like cardiology, using complex instruments that record blood pressure, heartbeat, and other symptoms, except that we are trying to understand the heart of the soul, not the body. It requires sensitivity to changes of personal consciousness, the sense of the "self," of one's identity within the church, cultural contexts, new instruments of learning, and changing forms of heresy that threaten the orthodoxy or "true worship" of the communicants. Of all the books of the Bible, the Psalms have been the most sensitive to all these changes, penetrating "the heart" of the believer — in singing, chanting, memorizing, redeeming emotionally, rebuking, and confirming the life and faith of the church.

What we have observed in our reflections on the history of interpreting the Psalms is that each theologian is historically conditioned by his age. "A human being," the novelist Thomas Mann observed, "lives out not only his personal life as an individual, but also, consciously or subconsciously, the lives of his epoch and his contemporaries." The history of the Psalms' interpretation reflects the epochs of the interpreters. But beyond this there have also been significant "hinge periods of history" that have opened up new vistas. Four such pivotal moments in the history of psalm exegesis "hinge" this brief survey: the Augustinian allegorical debate at the end of the fourth century; Christian Hebraism and scholasticism in the High Middle Ages; the Reformation and John Calvin's "plain meaning"; and the effects of the Enlightenment on historical and form-criticism today. More detailed cultural changes occur within these major exegetical events, each in turn influencing the ongoing devotional usage of the

Psalms. These are reflected in our subheadings, as we begin with the early Church Fathers.

I. Interpretive Principles of Pre-Nicene and Post-Nicene Fathers

A. The Pre-Nicene Fathers

The composition of commentaries *(commentarii)* enjoyed a long and varied history in classical antiquity. Originally private documents, notebooks, and *aide-mémoire* for speeches by leading citizens, they became part of public life. Then in the great centers of learning established at Pergamum, Rome, Jerusalem, and later Alexandria, Antioch, and Constantinople, Hellenistic and Jewish scholars developed exegetical commentaries on their favorite authors. From this classical model of exposition, Christian commentaries then followed.[2]

The earliest fathers of the church were Greek in language skills, itself a critical departure from the Jewish/Hebraic interpretation of the Old Testament. Thus the Greek Septuagint, not the Hebrew, was their textual basis. Significantly, the Septuagint is both translation and exegesis, under the influence of Greek finesse and originality; for it is a rereading of the Old Testament that the apostles themselves used. Also, Christians considered the roles of prophecy and typology in their interpretations of the Messianic psalms, interpretations that were contested by the rabbis from the second century onwards.

Among the earliest Christian writers, **1 Clement** (c. 96 CE) interpreted the Old Testament perhaps too literally, whereas ***The Epistle of Barnabas***, originating in Syria-Palestine thirty to forty years later, was too Christological, and radically opposed to the literal. These two differing approaches remained unresolved until the Reformation.[3]

The Jews lived in active engagement with the Torah, reinforced by singing the Psalms in their synagogue worship. From antiquity, music was deeply associated with pagan worship, and music also remained expressive of Jewish and early Christian worship.[4] The very early hymnal expressions of confessional faith in

2. J. A. Cerrato, *Hippolytus between East and West* (Oxford: Oxford University Press, 2002), pp. 14-15.

3. Willy Rordorf, "The Bible in the Teaching and Liturgy of Early Christian Communities," in Paul M. Blowers, ed. and trans., *The Bible in Greek Christian Antiquity,* The Bible Through the Ages, vol. 1 (Notre Dame: University of Notre Dame Press, 1997), p. 73.

4. Johannes Quasten, *Music and Worship in Pagan and Christian Antiquity* (Washington, DC: National Association of Pastoral Musicians, 1973), pp. 59-95.

the deity of Christ, found in New Testament texts, may well echo this intrinsic feature of the earliest apostolic witness. Singing "a new song" may well have referred to the new interpretation of Christ having become the "new David," for the Psalms were now interpreted as having prophesied his advent. Thus the early church was born in psalmic song, and the joyful character of psalm singing was noted in the Pauline communities of Ephesus and Colossae (Eph. 5:18-20; Col. 3:16-17).[5] By the time of **Clement of Alexandria** (150-215), Clement was exhorting Christians not to use the pagan musical instruments, but instead, quoting from Psalm 150, "praise him in the psaltery," he proposed using musical instruments that are given allegorical meaning in the Psalms rather than instruments used in idolatry.[6] The *Didascalia,* by a Jewish-Christian bishop to a North Syrian congregation, instructed simply: "if you yearn for songs, you have the Psalms."[7]

Justin Martyr (c. 100-165) still belonged to a generation in touch with those who had known our Lord's apostles.[8] Born near Sychem in Samaria, he was a Greek in a Jewish environment, later trained by the Platonists, and probably familiar with rabbinical exegesis. He went to Rome, where he was martyred as a Christian apologist under Marcus Aurelius. He was familiar with several Old Testament books, especially the Psalms, and the main corpus of the New Testament.[9] He received his Old Testament exegetical tradition from the apostles.[10] It appears that Justin followed the style of Paul's missionary dialogues in the book of Acts, to prove from the Old Testament citations and from the resurrection of Jesus that truly Jesus is the Christ. This countered the military expectations of the Bar Kokhba rebellion of 131-35 CE, still fresh in the minds of Justin's Jewish contemporaries. Christ, as "the hidden Messiah," came to suffer and die, not to rule as an earthly king. He was raised again, but not to fulfill political expectations. It has been suggested that this political uprising gave new urgency to Jewish Christians to address their fellow Jews with greater missionary zeal, as apparently Justin demonstrated.[11]

5. Singing in the worship of the New Testament is mentioned in the following texts: Matt. 26:30; Mark 14:26; Luke 2:13-14; Acts 2:46-47; 16:25-26; Rom. 15:5-6; 1 Cor. 13:1; 14:7-8, 26-27; 15:51-52; 1 Tim. 3:16; Heb. 13:15; James 5:13; Rev. 4:8; 5:9-10.

6. Clement of Alexandria, *Paedagogus* ii, iv; PG viii, 441; James McKinnon, *Music in Early Christian Literature* (Cambridge: Cambridge University Press, 1987), pp. 32-33.

7. *Didascalia,* vi, 3-5; McKinnon, *Music in Early Christian Literature,* p. 41.

8. L. W. Barnard, *Justin Marytr, His Life and Thought* (Cambridge: Cambridge University Press, 1967), p. 5.

9. George T. Purves, *The Testimony of Justin Martyr to Early Christianity* (New York: Anson D. F. Randolph & Company, 1889), pp. 238-41.

10. Oskar Skarsaune, *The Proof from Prophecy, A Study in Justin Martyr's Proof-Text Tradition: Text-Type, Provenance, Theological Profile* (Leiden: E. J. Brill, 1987), p. 13.

11. Skarsaune, *The Proof from Prophecy,* p. 287.

The early Christians lay claim to their use and interpretation of the Scriptures. Justin Martyr argued with Rabbi Trypho: "Your Scriptures are rather not yours, but ours, for we are left persuaded by them, while you read them without comprehending the spirit that is in them."[12] Luke was the first to affirm Jesus' claim: "everything written about me in the Law of Moses, and in the prophets and the psalms must be fulfilled" (Luke 24:44). In the light of this claim Justin affirmed: "the Jews do not understand the Scriptures."[13]

Justin was one of the first Christian converts to leave us the story of his search for truth and how he was converted to Christianity.[14] Doing so in maturity, and finding it to be a new way of life, "sure and fulfilling," Justin had the confidence and ability to confront Jewish scholars directly. He did so by attesting that the Law is above all a *typos* of Christ and of the future of the church, for only the incarnation of Christ has unveiled the real meaning of the Old Testament. But Justin was not interested in hermeneutics, so he oscillated between being a "literalist" in his efforts to show that "prophecies" were fulfilled in Christ, and an "allegorist" in his typological interpretation of the Law in terms of Christ. Precise rules for the meaning and use of these terms came only later in Biblical studies. It appears that in his debates and dialogues with Jewish scholars, Justin engaged more directly with rabbinical sources for Jewish Messianic expectations than with the Old Testament texts themselves. Possibly this was in order to demonstrate the universal claims of the risen Savior of the world, as depicted by Luke. One theme in Justin was his anti-Hezekiah polemic, that Hezekiah (unlike Christ) was not a priest forever. "And who does not know that [Hezekiah] is not the redeemer of Jerusalem? And that he himself did not send a rod of power into Jerusalem, and rule in the midst of his enemies, but that it was God who turned his enemies away from him as he wept and wailed?"[15]

Irenaeus of Lyons (c. 130-200) subsumed all of the Old Testament under the category of "prophetic." **Tertullian of Carthage** (c. 160-220) used the Psalms to cite the heretics' misunderstanding of the Old Testament and to demonstrate the deity of Christ. **Hippolytus** (c. 170-235) gave us only fragments of psalm commentary to refute the Marcionites and Gnostics with their negative views of the Old Testament.

The **Alexandrians** engaged in more robust exegesis; indeed **Origen** (c.

12. *Dialogue with Trypho the Jew*, 29.2.

13. *Dialogue* 9.1.

14. Cited by Robert Louis Wilken, *The Spirit of Early Christian Thought* (New Haven and London: Yale University Press, 2003), p. 6.

15. Skarsaune, *The Proof from Prophecy*, p. 401.

185-254) was probably the first Christian Biblical textual critic.[16] In order to understand the literal sense of the Scriptures, he devised the *Hexapla* (c. 234), an elaborate tool for the textual criticism of the Hebrew Scriptures. The *Hexapla* consisted of a series of columns read vertically, in contrast to scrolls that traditionally had been read only horizontally. It was possibly the first book to display information in tabular form — a revolution as dramatic as the development of the printing press in the fifteenth century. In the six parallel columns of his *Hexapla,* Origen brought together respectively the Hebrew text, his transliteration of it, the traditional Septuagint, and three other Greek translations by Aquila, Symmachus, and Theodotion. In the fifth column he reconstructed his own Greek text based on the proto-Masoretic text. The differences between the various translations were now visually displayed by the parallel columns, which led to Christians accusing Jews of shortening the text, and Jews accusing Christians of adding to it.[17] Yet while devising this new reading technique, Origen clearly distinguished the apostolic authority of the New Testament writers and the continuity of their oral as well as written teachings, from the speculative scholarship he and others could now use in the extensive new and widening use of books, which could be accumulated conveniently in a library that he began to build up in Caesarea.[18]

Origen was able to blend the "literal" and the "typological" approaches more subtly perhaps than had been understood before him; yet he was criticized falsely as the allegorist *par excellence.* He saw the role of the Bible as being morally formative for both the unlettered and the educated. He thought he stood in the tradition of the apostle Paul, whom he frequently cited for his use of typology and allegory.[19] In his earliest writing on Psalm 1, he claimed he learned from a Jewish scholar to elicit the meaning of a text of Scripture from other Scriptures. But he added that this was now made possible by the Holy Spirit, who spoke in the texts to illuminate other passages also. This is "the spiritual meaning" of the text, deeper than what may appear literal. He also argued with his opponent Celsus that only the person "in Christ" can interpret obscure passages that the unbeliever may scornfully dismiss as meaningless. This required a broad understanding of all the Scriptures, becoming a person of

16. According to Henri Crouzel, *Origen* (San Francisco: Harper & Row, 1989), Origen settled in Caesarea from Alexandria in 234, and the Hexapla was composed soon after.

17. Marcel Simon, "The Bible in the Earliest Controversies between Jews and Christians," in Paul M. Blowers, ed. and trans., *The Bible in Greek Christian Antiquity,* p. 56.

18. See the pioneering study of this subject by Anthony Grafton and Megan Williams, *Christianity and the Transformation of the Book* (Cambridge, MA, and London: The Belknap Press of Harvard University Press, 2006).

19. Rom. 4:14; 1 Cor. 2:10-16; 9:9-10; 10:11; 2 Cor. 3:6, 15-16; Gal. 4:24.

prayer, living dialectically between the perceived sense of God's presence and the perceived sense of his absence as in the Song of Songs, and of seeking the imitation of Christ in his living under the Law. For, he said, "We can understand the Law correctly, if Jesus reads it to us, so that [as] he reads, we perceive his 'mind' and understanding."[20] The Biblical exegete thus requires "the mind of Christ."

The **Desert Fathers** who followed after Origen interpreted the Scriptures "literally" as they sang and memorized the Psalms daily. The Psalms were the most frequently cited book of the Bible in the *Sayings* of the Desert Fathers. A few, like Serapion, were said to have possessed "a Psalter," of which portable personal copies were known to have existed.[21] They lived in a "performative" listening of the Psalms, to embody what they had received. They insisted that interpretative skills must bear fruit in transformed lives. This removed any distance between the literate and the illiterate within an oral/aural culture, until later when "literal exegesis" was reversed to become the expertise of those with comparative language skills in Hebrew, Syriac, Arabic, and other Semitic languages. All this was happening from the third century onwards, in the eastern section of the Roman empire.

Eusebius (c. 260-339 CE) admired Origen deeply. He built a scriptorium in Caesarea and developed his *Chronicle* (c. 300 CE) and an annotated list of Biblical place names, *Onomasticon* (c. 330s), that surpassed any previous historical resources for the exegete.[22] He was bishop of Caesarea for the last two decades of his life. His collection of unique library resources was maintained by his successors, to be used by Jerome and later scholars.

B. Post-Nicene Fathers

While the pre-Nicene churches were semi-autonomous, and thus regional and ethnic differences produced diversity of commentary, the Christianization of the empire under Constantine sought for political unification that radically affected the rise of "Christendom." Thus the post-Nicene Fathers became much more "politicized" in their leadership and conflicts, and their commentaries became much more public and controversial.

Athanasius (296-373), the primary defender of Nicene orthodoxy (liter-

20. Quoted by Ronald Heine, "Reading the Bible with Origen," in Blowers, ed. and trans., *The Bible in Greek Christian Antiquity*, p. 142.

21. Douglas Burton-Christie, *The Word in the Desert* (New York and Oxford: Oxford University Press, 1995), pp. 96, 112.

22. Grafton and Williams, *Christianity and the Transformation of the Book*, pp. 133-77.

ally "right worship"), was appointed bishop of Alexandria three years after the Council of Nicea (325 CE). He was more a pastoral theologian than an exegete; thus we have no exegetical work from him. However, he describes uniquely what a marvelous garden of devotion is the Psalter, in his famous *Letter to Marcellinus.* It is a remarkable document in providing a précis of the diverse forms and pastoral applications of the Psalms.[23] Exiled five times, he first met with Anthony in the desert, where, during his many years of "desert life and experiences," it was the Psalms that brought him therapeutic healing and fortitude, thus enabling him to become the invincible defender of Nicene orthodoxy in the midst of intense personal hostility.

Hilary of Poitiers (c. 320-67/68) is the earliest recorded bishop of Poitiers in Gaul. It appears that it was Hilary's meditations on Exodus 3:14, where Moses experienced the revelation of God as the "I AM," in conjunction with Psalm 139, that brought him into the Christian life, in seeking to pursue a life that was "worthy of understanding that [his own mind] had been given by God." That one single statement, given to Moses, *I AM,* God the Creator "testifying about himself" as *I am who I am,* penetrated more deeply into Hilary's soul than anything he had ever heard or read before.

He suffered defamation of character in his struggles to uphold the Nicene Creed's doctrine of God against Liberius, the bishop of Rome, who failed to maintain the church's orthodoxy. As Robert L. Wilkens has recognized, "Hilary of Poitiers . . . discerned with uncommon perspicacity the inner logic of Christian thinking about God. If we wish to understand how Christians learned to think differently about God and broke with established patterns of Greek and Jewish thought, Hilary offers a unique vantage point."[24] Hilary united the depth of Eastern Trinitarian thought with Western Christianity, as the "western Athanasius." He summarized his thought in his lucid work on the Trinity, *De Trinitate* (356-60), and successfully eliminated Arianism from Gaul.

Hilary's fragmentary commentary on the psalms *(Tractatus super Psalmum)* was original, and important for later commentators.[25] Hilary was not polemical, but primarily grammatical and textual. Following Origen, he used classical prosopological criticism (see pp. 9, 147) to discern the speakers, identify diverse authors, and recognize different genres, for, as he explained in writ-

23. G. C. Stead, "Athanasius on the Psalms," *VC* 39 (1985): 65-78; Robert C. Gregg, trans. and introduction, *Athanasius, the Life of Anthony and the Letter to Marcellinus* (New York: Ramsay; Toronto: Paulist Press, 1980).

24. Robert Louis Wilken, *The Spirit of Early Christian Thought* (New Haven and London: Yale University Press, 2003), pp. 85-86.

25. Of Hilary's *Tractatus super Psalmum,* Psalms 1–2, 9, 15–16, 53–71, 93, and 120–150 remain.

ing on Psalm 1, "their composition is not uniform and they are distinct from one another." Careful exegesis makes Hilary a critical source who has been overlooked as a significant, reliable authority. Like Ambrose, however, he also used Origen's typological approach, not imitatively but with a sovereign purpose: so that "posterity . . . should contemplate the present also in the past and venerate the past in the present as well."[26] In the ecclesial controversies facing Hilary, he also recognized the need to seek for the "spiritual" meaning, when a literal meaning would be too shallow or inappropriate for the Christological defense of the church's orthodoxy.[27] The Arians quoted "literal" texts of Scripture, too, and Hilary was fully aware of their deceitful exegesis.

Ambrose of Milan (339-97) was also original, for while he followed Origen in typology and was textual like Hilary, he was also pastoral and liturgical in his intent.[28] Within the "Ambrosian chant" that he introduced into the liturgy, the psalms played a central role. They were sung antiphonally in the sacred calendar, but their verses also echoed in hymns he composed to defend the faith of the flock from Arianism.

Of the Cappadocians, **Basil the Great** (330-79) wrote thirteen homilies on select psalms, using a much more "literal" exegesis than his younger brother, **Gregory of Nyssa** (c. 335-94). Basil's appeal was for the spiritual and moral application of the psalms. Gregory of Nyssa wrote two essays on the *Inscriptions of the Psalms,* which he interpreted more allegorically. He saw that there is a "spiritually" progressive sequence *(akolouthia)* within the Psalter, reflecting man's ascent towards God. His focus was upon the goal *(skopos)* of the human soul, not on the prophetic role of Christology that preoccupied so many of his contemporaries.

Diodore of Tarsus (died c. 394) studied at Athens, and became founder of the Antiochene school of exegesis, when made bishop of Tarsus in 378. As such he was the great defender of orthodoxy against the pagan emperor Julian. His prologue to Psalm 119 spelled out his concern for the *sensus litteralis* of the text: "we much prefer the historical sense to the allegorical" (frag. 93). He assigned numerous psalms to the reign of Hezekiah, while suggesting that they were derived from David (Psalms 14, 15, 20, 21, 27–30, 32–34, 41, and 48). He identified Psalms 5, 31, 42, 43, and 51 as belonging to the Babylonian exile. He was fully

26. Quoted by Christoph Jacob, "The Reception of Origenist Tradition in Latin Exegesis," in Magne Saebø, ed., *Hebrew Bible/Old Testament,* vol. 1/1: *Antiquity* (Göttingen: Vandenhoeck & Ruprecht, 1996), p. 685; *Tractatus mysteriorum* 11.14 (SC 19bis; 160; Brisson).

27. Lionel R. Wickham, trans. with introduction, *Hilary of Poitiers: Conflicts of Conscience and Law in the Fourth-Century Church* (Liverpool: Liverpool University Press, 1997).

28. G. Nauroy, "L'Écriture dans la pastorale d'Ambroise de Milan," in J. Fontaine, ed., *Le Monde Latin antique et la Bible* (Paris: Ch. Pietri, 1985), pp. 371-408.

aware of the differing Greek and Hebrew traditions in numbering the psalms. He explained the absence of an ascription to a close relationship between such a psalm and the preceding one.[29] Later anathematized at a synod in Constantinople in 499, along with his disciple Theodore of Mopsuestia, his writings were destroyed, and so there is doubt about the authorship of these fragments.

Jerome (342-420) was born in the Balkans. He studied in Rome and later settled in Bethlehem, where he became a monk. There he revised the Old Latin version of some Old Testament books, including the Psalms *(Psalterium Vetus)* to reflect more closely the text of the Septuagint. His second revision, based on Greek texts, is the *Psalterium Romanum.* His revision of the liturgical text *(Psalterium Gallicanum),* based on Origen's *Hexapla,* was used later for the Vulgate version. In 391-93, he made a new Latin translation based on the Hebrew *(Psalterium Hebraicum).* In 402, with the aid of Origen's commentary, he wrote explanatory notes on the Psalms *(commentaiola).* Finally, a highly elaborate commentary, the *Tractatus in librum Psalmorum,* is also attributed to him.[30]

Unlike earlier exegetes who claimed the Septuagint to be inspired, Jerome rejected that view, becoming quite critical of its translators as men of erudition but not prophets. He also changed from the allegorical and spiritual levels, to make his focus "the literal text." He incorporated elements of Jewish scholarship into his Old Testament commentaries, including the Psalms, as no other exegete of late Antiquity ever did, as well as his own Hebrew scholarship in determing what the original Hebrew text might have been.

Despite all of this, Jerome was sometimes seen in a less favorable light because when Origen fell out of favor with the church leaders, Jerome joined in Origen's condemnation. Despite his indebtedness to Origen's scholarship, Jerome joined church leaders in their condemnation of Origen!

Also in the East, **John Chrysostom** (347-407) was taught by Diodore. Like his teacher, John gave a more literalist interpretation of the Psalms, but as a pastor bishop, his homilies on over fifty-eight psalms[31] are didactic and spiritual in focus. In contrast to his associates, nearly all his writings have been preserved. In his fifty-eight homilies on selected psalms, he searched for the *scopos* beyond the textual meaning by consulting other authors. He could offer three or four differing versions from his own *textus receptus.*[32] He also argued that

29. M.-J. Rondeau, "Le Commentaire des Psaumes de Diodore de Tarse," *RHR* 176 (1969): 5-33, 153-85; 177 (1970): 5-33.

30. René Kieffer, "Jerome: His Exegesis and Hermeneutics," in Saebø, ed., *Hebrew Bible/Old Testament,* 1/1, p. 669.

31. These are Psalms 4–13, 44–50, 109–18, 120–50.

32. Robert Charles Hill, trans., *St. John Chrysostom: Commentary on the Psalms* (Brookline, MA: Holy Cross Orthodox Press, 1998), vol. 1, p. 7.

human weakness is why God speaks with precision *(akribeia)* in the text. For John, even the most minute detail could have great significance in the text. He was reluctant to use allegory, in the belief that Scripture interprets Scripture. He accepted the use of Biblical typology, as the apostle Paul employed it, but not loose literary allegory. His Messianic interpretation was thus "Pauline," neither Jewish nor allegorical.[33]

Theodore of Mopsuestia (c. 350–c. 428), bishop of Cilicia, wrote on some eighty-one psalms; this was his first work, written as a youth.[34] He, too, read the psalms "historically" but dated them to the Babylonian exile and the Persian restoration. He rejected any value to the psalm headings and reworked the titles. His reworked headings were copied in early Irish Psalters, as well as in the ninth-century Paris Psalter. Eventually his Christology became suspect, and he was condemned later as a "Nestorian."

Theodoret of Cyrrhus (393-460), a bishop in Syria, commented on all the psalms still extant in the Syriac text or *Peshitta.* Last of the theologians of the Antiochene school, he was the most prolific writer of the Eastern church. He was restrained in his use of prophecy, preferring to place the psalms in their historical context. He was more concerned to nurture the Christian household than to use the psalms polemically against the Jews. He used typology only for a few psalms, where the speaker could not be a human ruler.[35]

As we are focused on the history of the Western church, we will not outline the Syriac tradition of interpretation, with which the Antiochenes had strong connections. Instead, we now consider the first significant "hinge" in the history of Biblical exegesis, at the beginning of the fifth century, when, under the influence of Augustine, the great diversity of Greek commentators with diverse interpretative approaches was succeeded by the Latin uniformity of Augustinian allegorical interpretation. Under Constantine, a political unity was imposed on a unified church with powers and property. "The Roman Augustine," defending the ecclesial doctrine of the *totius Christi* ("the whole body of professing Christians"), now used allegory with new persuasiveness.

33. Stan Hidal, "Exegesis in the Antiochene School," in Saebø, ed., *Hebrew Bible/Old Testament,* 1/1, pp. 561-62.

34. Robert C. Hill, trans., *Theodore of Mopsuestia, Commentary on Psalms 1–81* (Atlanta: Society of Biblical Literature, 2006).

35. The Antiochene school selects the following psalms as Messianic: Psalms 2, 8, 22, 45, 72, and 110. Theodoret adds also Psalms 67, 69, and 72.

II. Augustine and Medieval Monastic Exegesis

A. Augustine

Augustine (354-430) and Jerome (c. 347-420) were both in Rome in 383-84 — though they missed meeting each other. Augustine tried to open a correspondence with Jerome several times — in 395, again around 397, and then a decade later — but their relations were strained and complex.[36]

Unique among the preceding Fathers, Augustine covered the entire Psalter in his Homilies, composed over three decades. He often had two sermons on the same psalm — some dictated and the rest preached.

Unlike Jerome's remarkable linguistic skills in Hebrew, Syriac, Greek, and Latin, Augustine's were those of a Latin rhetorician. Augustine's Biblical initiation came through the Greek Septuagint, not through Jerome's Latin Vulgate. Augustine professed the spiritual inspiration of the Septuagint and criticized the audacity of Jerome in pointing out its textual errors. Augustine was prepared to accept variants as all being inspired by the Holy Spirit, but he was most convinced that the Septuagint writers had a special prophetic vision that he would follow.[37]

As a priest rapidly elected a bishop, Augustine was overly determined to establish his authority as a Christian teacher by writing his treatise *On Christian Doctrine.* Jerome had been dismissive of him as not being "a professional exegete." Augustine defended his abilities by redirecting the exegetical task into the literary-colloquial mode.[38] He said in a letter to Jerome in 404: "I neither have nor will possess a science of sacred Scriptures which is comparable to that which I recognize in you. If I have some small capacity in this field, I use it in the service of the people of God. Whenever I attempt to study scripture more diligently than the instruction of the people who listen to me demands, my ecclesial duties prevent me."[39]

During Augustine's doctrinal pilgrimage he was able to expose the Manichaean, Donatist, and then later Pelagian mishandlings of Scripture.

36. Allan D. Fitzgerald, ed., *Augustine through the Ages: An Encyclopedia* (Grand Rapids: Eerdmans, 1999), article on Jerome, pp. 460-62.

37. Anne-Marie La Bonnardière, "Does Augustine Use Jerome's Vulgate?" in Paula Bright, ed. and trans., *Augustine and the Bible* (Notre Dame: Notre Dame University Press, 1997), pp. 42-51.

38. Mark Vessey, "The Great Conference: Augustine and His Fellow Readers," in Bright, ed. and trans., *Augustine and the Bible,* p. 60.

39. Anne-Marie La Bonnardière, "Augustine, Minister of the Word of God," in Bright, ed. and trans., *Augustine and the Bible,* p. 245.

Jerome might have conversed with Moses in Hebrew if he wished, but Augustine's conferences were with Christ and his Body in rhetorical Latin.

Augustine inherited from Origen the allegorical and the historical senses, and indeed the four senses — literal, historical, moral, and spiritual — as well. But it was never a comfortable fit for Augustine, so he eventually amalgamated them into the comprehensive term *figura* or "figure."[40] This reflected his neo-Platonic culture, where the *anagogic* perspective of upward understanding was driven by likeness, usually discerned by rational observation, and the *dramatic* perspective involved horizontal, back-and-forth movement between a figure and a referent, that is, between a "thing" or *res* and a sign or *signum*. For Augustine, the anagogic was prophetic in Scripture, whereas the dramatic expressed the incarnational paradigm, where the humanity of Christ and his word provided a framework for living humanly by symbol and spirit.[41]

Augustine clearly set forth his exegetical principles in *On Christian Doctrine*. Having sat at Ambrose's feet as a young convert, he was forever haunted by the text: "the letter kills, the spirit gives life." With regard to the latter, he never resolved whether "spirit" referred to the "spirit of the orator" or to the Holy Spirit. From about 415 he took account of Jerome's Gallican Psalter, but for him the figural rather than textual accuracy ennobled Christian behavior. "Scripture teaches nothing but love, and condemns nothing but lust."[42]

In *On Christian Doctrine* Augustine generously acknowledged the guidance given him by the Donatist scholar, Tyconius (died c. 400).[43] Augustine's *Book of Rules* was the first Latin treatise we have on Biblical interpretation. As someone who was not a specialist in Hebrew, he walked historically, not "through the immense forest of prophecy."[44] He drew up seven rules, the first of which sought to distinguish between when Christ speaks in Scripture and when it is the voice of the church. The second rule concerned the admixture in the church of those who are true believers and those who are apostate. Augustine clashed with Tyconius's bi-partite ecclesiology. Rather, in accepting

40. Robert W. Bernard, "*In Figura:* Terminology Pertaining to Figurative Exegesis in the Works of Augustine of Hippo" (Ph.D. diss., Princeton University, 1984), pp. 105ff.

41. See Michael Cameron, "The Christological Substructure of Augustine's Figurative Exegesis," in Bright, ed. and trans., *Augustine and the Bible*, pp. 74-103; see also his thesis, "Augustine's Construction of Figurative Exegesis against the Donatists in the *Enarrationes in Psalmos*" (Ph.D. diss., University of Chicago, 1996).

42. Quoted by David F. Wright, "Augustine: His Exegesis and Hermeneutics," in Saebø, ed., *Hebrew Bible/Old Testament*, 1/1, p. 721.

43. Augustine shares with Tyconius the acceptance of the obscurity of Scripture as a good thing, to give room for the Spirit's guidance.

44. Quoted by Paula Fredriksen, "Tyconius," in Fitzgerald, ed., *Augustine through the Ages*, p. 855.

the *totius Christi,* he left "the separation of the sheep and the goats" to the end-time.

Augustine wanted to be grounded in a literal-grammatical-historical sense, but as an orator he wanted to take wing to flutter like a butterfly from one figural interpretation to another, where he was most at ease.[45] We might consider all this simply the musings of a Roman missionary bishop in proud Punic Carthage, were it not for the immense influence his homilies on the Psalms and other texts have had on western Europe ever since. Augustine asserted the uniqueness of the Psalms among the other books of the Bible, precisely because they provide us with words that we may recognize as describing ourselves within the body of Christ.[46] This prevents us from separating an abstract methodology from "a way of life." The medieval church that followed his "figural exegesis" profoundly shaped the Western church as being "Augustinian" and "Catholic."

B. Medieval Monastic Exegesis of the Psalms

1. *Its Exegetical Features*

"Knowing God as a way of life" has always been the *raison d'être* of the monk. Liturgy and life are interwoven with the Bible, especially with the Psalms. *Lectio divina* is expressive of this, in physically reading and chanting the Scriptures. Jean Leclercq in his significant study recognized this to be the distinctiveness of "monastic theology," and indeed "monastic exegesis."[47] First, their commentaries tend to be long[48] and personally distinctive, because they are based on verse-by-verse meditation. Second, they are also "anthological" until the twelfth century in that they incorporate extensive fragments of the patristic and "high" medieval texts of others. Third, they are oriented toward "tropology," the importance of moral interpretation and application. This could be true for

45. For contemporary scholarly debate on Augustine's misuse of Tyconius's Rules, see Bright, ed. and trans., *Augustine and the Bible,* pp. 109-281, and David F. Wright, "Augustine: His Exegesis and Hermeneutics," in Saebø, ed., *Hebrew Bible/Old Testament,* 1/1, pp. 701-30.

46. See Michael Cornelius McCarthy, S.J., "The Revelatory Psalm: A Fundamental Theology of Augustine's *Enarrationes in Psalmos*" (Ph.D. diss., Notre Dame University, 2003).

47. Jean Leclercq, *The Love of Learning and the Desire for God: A Study of Monastic Culture,* trans. Catherine Misrahi (New York: Fordham University Press, 1982), pp. 194-222.

48. Pascase Radbert's commentary on Psalm 45 (44) is 107 pages in the *Corpus Christianorum;* Rupert of Deutz is extensive; Bernard of Clairvaux has seventeen homilies on Psalm 24:3, "Who will ascend unto the hill of the Lord?"

Christians generally, but it is usually the case more specifically for the monastic community, which is thus also more introspective. Fourth, while allegory was exercised more generally in medieval consciousness than now, the monks took typology much more seriously, for to them "the literal text" was based on God's deeds in Israel's history. Grammar and rhetoric were the instruments used to understand God's intervention in human affairs. Thus the psalm commentary of Cassiodorus cites the numerous rhetorical expressions first used in classical grammar. Fifth, numerous commentators provide a preface to their commentary, which helps guide the reader to envisage how the commentary should be viewed by the meditative practitioner. This differs, then, from "the Rule of Faith," which several of the early Fathers wrote independently of their other works, as a polemic against pagan literary culture. In conclusion, it is worth repeating that "conversion" or monastic formation was the primary role of the psalm commentaries of the monks.

2. *Significant Monastic Authors*

While Jerome, John Chrysostom, writers in the Syriac tradition, and other authors of late Antiquity may be also cited, it is the Western Benedictine and later Cistercian orders that shaped institutionally this category of psalm commentary. Each generation of monks in these orders needed to understand the texts they were reciting and memorizing daily, as the entire Psalter was repeated weekly at least.

Cassiodorus (c. 485-580), a distinguished political leader in Lombardy, retired to his estate where he created his *Vivarium* as the first serious center for learned monks to use the liberal arts. He had already composed his commentary on the Psalms, following the example of Jerome, who advocated that the first book of the Bible Christians should read is the Psalms, before passing on to the New Testament. His passionate desire for the unity of the church (against the Donatist schism), his vehement condemnation of heresies (especially the Arians), his serious concern for the doctrine of the Trinity, and overall the orthodoxy of the Council of Chalcedon (in 451) are all his motives for his theological instruction in the psalm commentary. By adapting the instruction of the Psalms within the seven liberal arts (especially the *trivium*), these became the textbook for Christian literacy, even to a secular world.[49] About the same time or later, in Ireland, the Irish monks were using Theodore of Mopsuestia's psalm

49. P. G. Walsh, trans., *Cassiodorus: Explanation of the Psalms* (New York and Mahwah, NJ: Paulist Press, 1990), vol. 1, pp. 15-19.

commentary for children's education.[50] Cassiodorus also pioneered in using the Psalms to teach the *quadrivium,* especially the roles of music and astronomy. Latin was not the best language for this multiple use of the Psalms, so Cassiodorus had to explain or complain frequently in his text about this tension. As a comprehensive standard for subsequent monastic commentaries, Cassiodorus was uniquely important.

3. *The Northumbrian School and Later Carolingians*

As a territorial and cultural buffer between Scotland and England, the high monastic culture of monasteries at Jarrow and Lindisfarne, and the later cathedral school of York, educated several distinguished leaders. **The Venerable Bede** (673-735) at Jarrow was taught the daily psalmody by his abbot, Abbot Ceolfrith, who is reputed to have recited the Psalter twice daily.[51] Bede, in turn, composed his own précis of the Psalms in the old version of Jerome, the "Abbreviated Psalter," as his own *aide-memoire* to highlight the key themes of each psalm.[52] This became a primer for laymen and monks even centuries later. **Alcuin** (c. 735-804), a teacher at the cathedral school of York, was appointed by the Emperor Charlemagne as chancellor and head of his academy to direct the subsequent Carolingian reform; he adapts Bede's précis to teach the bishops.[53] The Second Council of Nicea (787) required all bishops to know the complete Psalter by heart in order to enable them to examine the daily exercise of each member of the clergy in their praying the Psalms. Later Carolingian monastic schools, notably Saint-Germain d'Auxerre, produced several distinguished commentators of the Psalms, such as **Haimo** (died c. 855) and **Remigius** (c. 841-908). They became more discursive and therefore more critical of their texts, blending tradition with new scholarship.[54]

The history of monasticism is marked by several phases. In the early period, around 400 to 700 CE, individuals sought perfection alone in hermit cells, cut off from the rest of the world. In the next phase, communities began to form, including communities such as the transplanted desert monks of Lérins, the transient camp of the Irish *peregrinus,* and the school of Benedict of Nursia.

50. M. McNamara, *The Psalms in the Early Irish Church,* JSOT Suppl. 165 (Sheffield: Sheffield Academic Press, 2000), pp. 239-301.

51. Benedicta Ward, *Bede and the Psalter* (Fairacres, Oxford: SLG Press, 2002), p. 5.

52. Ward, *Bede and the Psalter,* pp. 33-34.

53. Ward, *Bede and the Psalter,* p. 2.

54. Claudio Leonardi, "Old Testament Interpretation in the Church from the Seventh to the Tenth Century," in Saebø, ed., *Hebrew Bible/Old Testament,* 1/1, p. 194.

The Carolingian culture, a transitional culture, sought for a unification of Christian culture. After 1000 the bonds uniting monasteries were increasingly sufficient to fashion a common constitution, a standard regimen of activity, a uniform pattern of worship, a shared mode of interacting with ecclesiastical and political authorities, and a consistent message to the entire Christian community. This unification was achieved through several means, including a renaissance of learning, revival of psalm commentaries, and mastering a common language in order to teach and reach out to the secular world in a variety of ways.

In 811, Charlemagne issued a capitulary, asking his bishops, abbots, and counts: "Are we really Christians?" Great obstacles such as ignorance and pagan superstition prevented a clear response. The pursuit of learning was the answer to these problems. Neither asceticism nor mystical illumination was enough; books were fundamental. So Alcuin avowed that in the presence of books, "nothing was lacking that was needed for religious life and the pursuit of knowledge." He continued: "I wish to follow in the footsteps of the holy fathers, neither adding to nor subtracting from their most sacred writings."[55] The study and comprehension of Scripture were the ultimate goals of Carolingian education.

Charlemagne was known as "David" by his courtiers. The first major task of a student/scholar was mastery of the Psalter, combining, as Maurus sought, "growth in wisdom with growth in virtue."[56] The Psalms were embedded forever in the minds of Carolingian scholars and flowed from the tips of their pens into their writings more often than any other text. Contreni says: "The Psalms are songs, and while learning to read them, students learned to sing them and thus received their introduction to chant. The observation of the daily office made chant a lifelong practice."[57]

4. Commentators of the High Middle Ages

In addition to the "Great Schism" between the Western and Eastern branches of the church (1054), the crusades caused instability in the Eastern church. Meanwhile the Western church expanded its influence in western and northern Europe, with the impetus of the Gregorian reform. Among the later Benedictines

55. Richard E. Sullivan, "The Context of Cultural Activity in the Carolingian Age," in Richard E. Sullivan and John J. Contreni, eds., *The Gentle Voices of Teachers* (Columbus: Ohio State University Press, 1995), pp. 75-76.

56. John J. Contreni, "The Pursuit of Knowledge in Carolingian Europe," in *The Gentle Voices of Teachers*, p. 116.

57. Contreni, "The Pursuit of Knowledge in Carolingian Europe," p. 116.

were **Bruno of Asti/Segni** (died 1123), **Rupert of Deutz** (died 1129), and **Honorius Augustodunensis** (died 1156), who helped Gregory VII in his reform. **Lanfranc** and **Anselm** (c. 1033-1109) at Bec were remarkable for their more personalized approaches to prayer. **Geroch of Reichersberg** (c. 1093–c. 1169), as a reformer, used the Psalter to promote the laity's seriousness in living the *vita Christi,* and so to widen the understanding of "the religious" to extend beyond the clergy.[58] In composing his commentary (c. 1144-48), he relies quite heavily on the work of Gilbert of Poitiers and also on the work of Honorius of Autun. Gerhoh's commentary represented a transition from monastic to secular university scholarship, which would reshape psalm commentaries. Apart from his eighteen homilies on Psalm 91, **Bernard of Clairvaux** (1090-1153) was not a serious exegete, but he sustained the Augustinian allegorical/spiritual approach of a highly developed form of *lectio divina.*

III. Christian Hebraism and Scholasticism in the High to Late Middle Ages

With the twelfth century, we reach the second critical "hinge" in the history of Western Biblical interpretation. A fresh start in understanding the Hebrew text underlying the Septuagint and Vulgate was attempted by a few scholars, coupled with renewed interest in classical literature. This new impetus reflected the transition from "monastic theology," where *lectio divina* expressed the identity of the monk as *homo participans,* to the secular model of the scholar as more detachedly *homo spectans.* This change underlaid the debate between Bernard of Clairvaux and Peter Abelard at the Council of Sens in 1140. It also deepened the contrast between Cistercian scholarship, which remained "monastic," and the secular schools — certainly in France — which were offshoots of Benedictine roots.

A. Secular Schools of the Twelfth and Thirteenth Centuries

The beginning of urbanization in the twelfth century led to the spread of cathedral schools at Laon, Chartres, and Paris in France, as well as in other countries, each with their own style of commentators. The monastic "four senses" of Scriptural interpretation were gradually codified, particularly by **Stephen Langton** (died 1228). Another feature was the use of the *gloss* — notes in the

58. Contreni, "The Pursuit of Knowledge in Carolingian Europe," p. 28.

margins of the Biblical text — as a basic form of instruction to express at least the literal exegesis. They were first developed by **Gilbert of Poitiers** (died 1154). A third trait was the development of textual remarks on grammar, sources, and versions of a text, all giving a more scientific aspect to the exegesis. The Victorines, especially **Andrew of St. Victor** (died 1162), excelled in this. A fourth trait was the enlargement of sources, which the *Glossa*, later called *ordinaria*, contributed by adding many previous authors, especially the more recent ones. For now it was becoming appreciated that such commentary was progressive; accordingly, there was less emphasis on what previously had been esteemed as the authoritative tradition of the Fathers.

Alongside the cathedral schools were the growing universities, which began to distinguish between Biblical language as *non-scientific* (because of its use of metaphor and symbol) and theology as *scientific* (because of its univocal and rigorous use of language). Expressive of this change, the commentaries were much more *structured*, divided into three elements: the *divisio*, the section of the commented text; *expositio*, the verse-by-verse explanation; and the *dubia* or *questiones*, the doctrinal discussion. The commentary had a prologue providing an overview, which may conclude with the spiritual appreciation of the book or text. Authors like Bernard of Clairvaux, Andrew of St. Victor, Thomas Aquinas, and even Jewish scholars like Maimonides and Rashi were also more frequently cited. By now the "literal" exegesis of the text had become complicated; Hugh of St. Victor defined it as having three components: *littera*, textual and grammatical study; *sensus*, literary and historical study; and *sententia*, theological study. The ancient use of concordances by "rumination" of the text continued to help explain the Bible by the Bible.[59]

A new feature of these more "scholastic" scholars was that commentaries on the Psalms no longer remained their first priority. Indeed, many of the great scholars of this period did not write on the Psalms, choosing instead to comment on other Old Testament books, especially on Genesis, the Song of Songs, and Isaiah, or on the New Testament books, especially Matthew. At the same time, the Psalms continued to play a central role in lay devotions but in an increasing variety of ways, including illuminated Psalters, Books of Hours, Prymers (with over a third of the Psalter being represented in them), the seven "penitential psalms," lyrics, stained-glass windows in churches, and, by the Renaissance, the extraordinary expansion of sung psalmody.

59. Leclercq, *The Love of Learning and the Desire for God.*

B. Representative Commentators of the Twelfth Century

Due to the rapid changes in culture from monastery to cathedral school to university, representative commentators of the twelfth century reflected a significant amount of diversity. **Gilbert of Poitiers**, or Poretta (c. 1075-1154), the first bishop of Poitiers, better known as a philosopher than as an exegete, composed a commentary on the Psalms (c. 1117) that crossed from the monastic cell to the secular classroom. He devised a cross-index system that directed the reader to the various psalms that illuminate important doctrines.[60] He rejected Jerome's division of the Psalter into five books, arguing, like Hilary of Poitiers, for its unity. He glossed every verse of the Psalter, acknowledging his sources. Following Augustine, he saw the intersection between Christ and his Body in the Psalms as presenting *Christus integer.*

Gilbert's popular commentary was somewhat overshadowed by **Peter Lombard's** (1100-1160) commentary. Lombard defended the sole authorship of David, yet the Psalms' *materia* is Christ and his Body. He also grouped the psalms thematically. But as a theologian he excelled in giving theological insights into the exegetical text. His *Sentences* in conjunction with his *Magna Glosatura* of the Psalms set him apart in theological importance for centuries to come.

Student and successor of Albert of St. Victor, **Richard of St. Victor** (died 1175) linked exegesis and mystical life together, seeing Biblical truth as a gift from above. For him the *sensus literalis* led to the much fuller disclosure of the *mystica intelligentia,* when the reader could use Scripture as a mirror to see himself, ready to then receive the divine revelation of the Bible. In this way his exegesis was distinctive from his contemporaries.

Herbert of Bosham (c. 1120-94), close adviser of Archbishop Thomas à Becket, was the most accomplished "Christian Hebraist" after Jerome. Herbert's encounter with Rashi and his theological defense of his old teacher Peter Lombard stimulated his exegetical work. His exegetical method was independent of previous models, with an emphasis on the "literal," letting the Biblical text speak for itself.[61]

A century later, **Thomas Aquinas** (1225-74), as a Dominican, used the Psalms to inform the life of prayer in his *Postilla super Psalmos.* In Aristotelian fashion he set out four causes for the Psalms: their subject matter is Christ; their

60. Theresa Gross-Diaz, *The Psalms Commentary of Gilbert of Poitiers: From Lectio Divina to the Lecture Room* (Leiden, New York, Cologne: Brill, 1996), pp. 158-59.

61. Unfortunately his text is still not available in print; a copy exists only in St. Paul's Cathedral, London. See Deborah L. Goodwin, *"Take Hold of the Robe of a Jew": Herbert of Bosham's Christian Hebraism* (Leiden and Boston: Brill, 2006).

form is prayer; their origin is divinely inspired; and their goal is to be the gospel, where the apostles interpret their meaning. His psalm commentary on the first fifty-four psalms is commonly attributed to the end of his life (c. 1273), but the style has much in common with the topics of his earlier commentaries: defending the Davidic authorship; the nature of the Psalms as prophecy; and interpreting at two levels — the Davidic narrative and the prophetic role of Christ and his church.[62]

C. Christian-Jewish Exegesis in the High Middle Ages

Since Origen, Christian commentators, especially Jerome, had made use of Jewish scholars. Jerome's citations were continued into the later Middle Ages. But from the early tenth century renewed contacts with Jewish scholars occurred in Andalusia (Spain) and then in the next century in northern France, especially at Troyes, with **Solomon ben Isaac/Rashi** (1040-1105), who reverted to *peshat,* "the plain meaning" of the text. Following him, **Joseph Kara** (1050-1125) pursued further the *literal* text as a polemic against the Christians' use of the Psalms for supporting their Christology. The history of this "literal" textual development is complex, beginning with Arab-Jewish philology in Spain, followed by Rashi's own pursuits at Troyes in northern France, and then becoming more polemical from Kara onwards. Both Rashi and Kara[63] wrote psalm commentaries.

After Herbert of Bosham, the first significant Christian scholar to benefit most seriously from this Jewish contact was the French Franciscan **Nicholas of Lyra** (c. 1270-1349), who compiled a massive Biblical commentary, his *Postillae,* in two parts: on the literal sense of Scripture (1322-33) and on the moral senses of Scripture (1333-39). By *postilla* was meant a word-by-word or verse-by-verse account. It influenced Wyclif and later Luther in their exegesis as they sought "a plain text." For a monastic like Luther it was easily adapted to its use in preaching. The saying went: "If Lyra had not played his harp, Luther would never have gone dancing."[64] Indeed, we can appreciate Nicholas of Lyra as the first "modern" Christian commentator. Reading *with* the letter, with the help of Hebrew guides, Nicholas refused to read *through* the letter to some secret interpreta-

62. Karl Froehlich, "Christian Interpretation of the Old Testament in the High Middle Ages," in Saebø, ed., *Hebrew Bible/Old Testament,* 1/2, pp. 543-44.

63. Recently, fragments of his commentary have been found in Italian archives. See A. Grossman, "From the Italian *Geniza* — Fragments of R. Joseph Kara's Commentary on the Torah," *Pe'amim* 52 (1992): 16-32.

64. P. D. W. Wrey and L. Smith, *Nicholas of Lyra: The Senses of Scripture* (Leiden: Brill, 2000).

tion. But he was often misjudged as being too favorable to Jewish scholarship. He relied greatly on Rashi, with additional notes taken from the *Midrash*, suggesting he was more a copyist than a true Hebraic scholar. Hebrew was no longer a living vernacular language among the Jewish population, but a liturgical and cultural language.[65] But as the text of Lambeth Palace (folio 435; c. later thirteenth century) demonstrates, there were probably a significant number of Jewish scribes employed to copy the Hebrew text of the Old Testament, from which Christian scholars like Nicolas of Lyra would make their comments.[66] However, while Nicolas of Lyra preferred the literal meaning of the text from his Jewish contacts, he cited in his *Postillae* (c. 1330) the well-known adage on the epistle to the Galatians:

> The letter teaches events,
> Allegory what you should believe;
> Morality teaches what you should do,
> Anagogy what mark you should be aiming for.[67]

Nevertheless, the influence of Jewish-Christian textual studies was leading to a bias towards the more literal use of the text among the conciliar reformers.

D. Christian-Jewish Scholars of the Renaissance

Fostered by the Renaissance culture, eminent Jewish-Hebraic scholars throughout western Europe such as **Giannozzo Manetti** (1396-1459) in Italy, **Johannes Reuchlin** (1455-1522) in Germany, and **Benito Arias Montano** (1527-98) in Spain left their mark in Christian commentaries. The term "Christian-Hebraism" was coined to describe their scholarly pursuits. Significantly, the earliest printed Bible text is the book of Psalms (August 29, 1477), printed by Jewish printers. Pocket editions soon followed.

Nicholas of Cusa (1401-64) was the first of a new generation of Christian commentators who also benefited from Jewish scholarship. For this reason he was oriented to a more literal text, and therefore to a more historical context in identifying David. But he subsumed the intellect to the mystery of God, and therefore was more open to a "spiritual" interpretation. Like Lyra, Cusa saw Da-

65. Gilbert Dahan, *Les Intellectuals Chrétiens et les Juifs au Moyen Age* (Paris: Les Editions du Cerf, 2007), pp. 269, 303.

66. Dahan, *Les Intellectuals Chrétiens*, pp. 288-89.

67. Henri de Lubac, S.J., *Medieval Exegesis: The Four Senses of Scripture*, vol. 1, trans. Mark Sebanc (Grand Rapids: Eerdmans, 1998), p. 1.

vid's prophetic role to be more personal within those psalms ascribed to David, and both esteemed him as the greatest prophet of the Old Testament, greater even than Moses (in contrast to the estimate of Moses as supreme, made by scholars such as Thomas Aquinas). In his reforming zeal, Nicholas of Cusa interpreted David as the "Good Prelate." He illustrated from several of his psalm commentaries the ways in which David was both the good king and the good prelate.[68]

This was all in keeping with his predecessors **Pierre d'Ailly** (1350-1420) and **Jean Gerson** (1363-1429) in their church mission as conciliar reformers. But after 1437, when he saw the failure of the conciliar reform movement, Cusa reversed his position and returned to the advocacy of the papacy. Cusa still maintained the role of David as the exemplar of the Christian. David remained temptable, yet pursuant of the virtuous life. As David vowed to restore the religious community of Israel to its holy state, so Cusa sought to do the same in southern Germany. David was now seen to fulfill all the qualities of a good and holy churchman. Cusa advocated the *imitatio Davidis,* to be emulated now, not postponed as a fulfillment for a future time.

Denys the Carthusian (died 1471), also known as Dionysius the Carthusian, was linked with Cardinal Cusa in the cause of church reform in Germany, spending time with him there. Educated by the Brethren of the Common Life at Zwolle in the Netherlands, he compiled an extensive series of Bible commentaries while also editing works of Dionysius the Areopagite, John Climacus, and Peter Lombard. He was not original, like Nicholas of Cusa, yet he extended the personal/pastoral approach of his mentor. His psalm commentary included the first fifty psalms. He selected the psalms as a way of living what Christian teaching is, mindful of Thomas Aquinas's warning in book four of his *Sentences,* that whoever does not live practically according to what he teaches will indeed be judged. A Trinitarian theological focus is essential for this, as it is the Paraclete or Holy Spirit who teaches us appropriately. Denys reverted then to the fourfold interpretation of the Psalms: literally, allegorically, tropologically, and anagogically. He wrote: "history teaches what is done, allegory what ought to be believed, tropology what ought to be done, anagogy what ought to be hoped." This suggests that this medieval practice was slipping away and that he was desirous to revive it.[69]

Jacques Lefèvre D'Étaples (c. 1460-1536), engaged in the French reform,

68. Edward G. Gosselin, *The King's Progress to Jerusalem* (Malibu, CA: Undena Publications, 1976), pp. 25-48.

69. Denys the Carthusian, *D. Dionysii Cartusiani insigne commentariorum opus in psalmos omnes Davidicos,* in *Doctoris Ecstatici D. Dionysii Cartusiani Opera Omnia* (Monstolii: Typis Cartusiae S. M. De Pratis, 1898), vols. 5-6; 5.529-43. Article 7,405.

also attempted to liberate theology from the older scholasticism. Lefèvre explained that this degeneration of Christians' religious sensibility had been caused by their attempts to understand the psalms literally and historically, as Nicholas of Lyra had done (i.e., following Jewish scholarship too "literally"); these attempts caused their failure to taste the sweetness of the Psalter, along with their loss of heart and then their consequent disconsolation.[70]

Meanwhile in England, a new political purpose for the use of Hebrew developed in connection with "the king's great matter." Henry VIII had had a papal dispensation to marry his brother's widow, Catherine of Aragon. As part of Henry's attempt to seek a divorce, an obscure courtier of his, Robert Wakefield, cited Leviticus 18:16 and 20:21, forbidding such a union. Wakefield's knowledge of Hebrew became a great asset for his advancement. He then argued that the pope had no Scriptural authority for the papal dispensation. In turn, the queen's advisor, John Fisher, also a Hebraic scholar, used Deuteronomy 25:5, which enjoined such a union, when a deceased husband left behind a childless widow. Knowledge of Hebrew now became a career asset, not only in connection with Henry's divorce and the eventual independence of the English church from Rome, but also for the Reformers on the Continent. This issue of "the plain text" took on new significance with the exegesis of the Reformers in confronting the Catholic Church's Augustinian allegorization.

IV. "The Plain Text" of the Reformers

In several respects **Martin Luther** (1483-1546) is a transition from medieval to modern exegesis. Yet he also represented the new combination of providing translation as well as commentary, as the other leading Reformers would do after him. His first theology lectures at the University of Wittenberg were on Psalms 1–126, given in 1513-15. He made full use of the glosses of previous commentators, but especially Jerome, Augustine, and Cassiodorus (490-585). Following his master Augustine, he introduced the premise that all Biblical prophecy focuses upon Christ; accordingly, he would give a Christological commentary on the Psalms in connection with the fourfold method of interpretation. "In this way all four interpretations of Scripture come together to one magnificent stream."[71] He confessed frankly and modestly in his introduction,

70. We consider Jacques Lefèvre d'Étaples's contribution to Biblical studies in more detail in our survey of Psalm 23 (see pp. 422-24).

71. *Luther's Works,* ed. Hilton C. Oswald (St. Louis: Concordia, 1974), vol. 10, trans. Herbert J. A. Bouman, p. 52.

"even to this present day I do not understand many psalms, and unless the Lord enlightens me through your help, as I trust He will, I shall not be able to interpret them."[72] It was a traditional interpretation, except that possibly by the time he had reached the great penitential Psalm 51, he had become a "converted man," meeting Christ personally in the Psalms. But unlike Lefèvre, he interpreted Christ as speaking in the fourfold way of medieval hermeneutics, not to uphold the medieval system, but to overcome it, in a new, personally Christocentric wholeness, yet not in Christological restriction as Lefèvre had done.[73] But it was just a beginning, so in a letter of December 16, 1515, he referred to his first commentary as "trifles, quite worthy of being destroyed."[74]

He began a second commentary, *Operationes in Psalmos,* published in 1519-20. But this second attempt stopped with Psalm 22, as he was now caught up in the crisis of his excommunication. In 1519-21 Luther affirmed more clearly his Christological frame within the Psalms. He had discovered that "faith in Christ" is righteousness (Rom. 1:17). So even the fourfold sense is not "spirit" enough, for "the letter kills, but the Spirit gives life" (2 Cor. 3:6), that is, the Spirit of Christ. Knowing some Hebrew, he now used Jerome's *Psalterium Hebraicum* and Reuchlin's *De rudimentis hebraicis* in later studies.

In the period following, in the study of Paul's epistles, Luther identified the dialectic relationship between law and gospel to be the central issue of the Bible. Now he recognized clearly a single sense to Scripture, that is, "literal" and "spiritual" at the same time. In the Psalms, David as prophet speaks in "Spirit" and demands "faith." Grammatical detail becomes more important since it is the word of God, yet linguistic findings are made subordinate to the gospel of Christ, for it is proper that philology give way to theology. The Psalms remained the greatest influence on Luther's faith throughout his life. They were the sphere where the saints are always talking to God, himself included, as he describes in his Preface to the Psalter (1529). In 1531-33, he writes "summaries about the Psalms and reasons of translating." Luther now discerned five genres in the Psalms: prophecy, teaching, consolation, prayer, and thanksgiving.[75] In 1537 his translation of the Bible from Hebrew and Greek was published, a task he had started in 1522. But he saw translation as a form of interpretation, so once more he translated with a gospel sense of the text, and therefore continued to distrust more deeply rabbinical authority over the Hebrew text.[76]

72. *Luther's Works,* vol. 10, p. 8.

73. Siegfried Raeder, "The Exegetical and Hermeneutical Work of Martin Luther," in Saebø, ed., *Hebrew Bible/Old Testament,* 1/1, pp. 371-72.

74. Robert N. Fife, *Young Luther* (New York: AMS Press, 1970).

75. Luther, *WA* 38, 17, 24-28.

76. For more on Luther see Psalm 23 (pp. 425-27).

At first a humanist trained at Heidelberg and Tübingen, **Philipp Melanchthon** (1497-1560) joined Luther on the faculty at Wittenberg to focus on Hebrew teaching on Psalms and Proverbs, although he was also an accomplished Greek linguist. He wrote prefaces to the psalm commentaries of Luther. In his own commentaries Melanchthon studied Psalms 1–60 and 110–133. He sought simplicity of exposition, doing to prayerfully. Also, following Luther, he kept the distinction of law and grace central to his dialectic approach. He also used a prophetic and typological perspective on the layers of psalm interpretation. Above all, clarity of style and simplicity of method marked his commentaries.

An avid reader of Luther on the Psalms, **Martin Bucer** (1491-1551), a Dominican trained at Heidelberg, settled in Strasbourg and taught as a Hebraic scholar. In 1524 he started to set psalms in metrical hymnody for his congregation. Familiar with the Masoretic text, he consulted with Jewish scholars; and, believing Hebrew to be the basic language of the church, he looked forward to the day when it would be the language of all Christians! He composed a psalm commentary (in 1529, 1532, 1547, 1554) with a succinct introduction to each psalm, a new translation into Latin, and a verse-by-verse commentary. His purpose was to spread the Reformation pseudonymously through this new vernacular interpretation of the Psalms, using the French name "Aretius Felinus of Lyon" or "Felinus Lugdunensis." Within a few months an English translation was also in the underground market in a minuscule format.[77] He took issue with the strong distinction of law and gospel "promoted by certain modern theologians," an obvious reference to Luther and his disciples.

The accumulative scholarly benefits of these Reformers, spread widely by the printing press, broadened hermeneutical horizons during the sixteenth century. The greater understanding of the natural world, and the knowledge of its greater geographical dimensions through exploration, as well as the role of the telescope, were all contributing to a new awareness of divine creation. The medieval allegorical consciousness was being replaced by a more "literal" sense of things.

Trained as a humanist in law at Orléans (1528-31), **John Calvin** (1509-64) wrote his first commentary on Seneca's *De clementia* (1532). Erasmus had just completed his critical edition of this text in 1529, following all the rules of the arts of "philology" and "rhetoric." But Calvin showed his early independence by placing the text in the life and time of Seneca, in order to clarify allusions and to identify figures of speech. Later, as a second-generation reformer, Calvin realized he needed to take the human ability of reason very seriously, "as the instru-

77. R. Gerald Hobbs, *An Introduction to the Psalms Commentary of Martin Bucer: A Commentary in Its Historical and Exegetical Setting* (Strasbourg, 1971), vol. 1.

ment of determining the 'mens scriptoris' to know which God we worship, and what he calls us to," and "the means of the covenant he has concluded with us." It is God's word, accommodated for us in human transmission and speech. The multiplicity of extremists within the Protestant world, as well as confrontation with the Council of Trent in the Catholic world, challenged Calvin to focus upon Biblical interpretation. He spent time with "the Upper Rhine School" of exegetes at Strasbourg — Bucer, Bullinger, Melanchthon, Zwingli, and others. Learning from each, he exceeded them all in various ways.

Calvin saw Chrysostom as exemplary among the early Fathers because of his literal bias, by which Calvin meant that textual interpretation should be distinguished from argumentation, theological and otherwise. Calvin sought to recede behind the mind of the writer to let the Biblical author express himself. Thus exegesis remained subordinate to the self-explication of the truth of the Scriptural text *(mens scriptoris).* While he accepted with the early Fathers the need for the Rule of Faith, notably the Apostles' Creed, he saw that the ultimate authority was Scripture itself.[78] Likewise his writing rule was to seek brevity and perspicuity in his commentary, to allow the Bible to speak plainly for itself.[79]

Also vital for Calvin was the unity of the two Testaments, as proclaiming the same covenant between God and his people — a theme Martin Bucer and Bullinger had first developed in 1532/33. In his *Institutes* of 1559, Calvin put it plainly: "The Law was given, not to restrain the folk of the Old Covenant under itself, but to foster hope of salvation in Christ until his coming" (2.11.7). The Ten Commandments were not just for the people under Moses but were based on God's elective grace for all his people in Christ also. The unity of God's covenant throughout the ages, he reasoned, was based on three things: immortality as a common bond of all peoples at all times; divine promises under a covenant of grace, past and present; and fellowship with God as the divine intent for all ages.[80] The "old" was a shadow of things to come (Heb. 10:1), yet it remained a "spiritual covenant" in spite of its earthly promises of "the land" and "the ceremonial law." So the New Testament can, and does, reveal them all now more clearly "in Christ." Calvin thus removed the antithetical contrast between law and grace, which Luther and Melanchthon had presented so harshly. Instead, Calvin argues that grace is expressed in both Testaments and that the law remains. But now, with increasing light, the same immutable will of God is being progressively fulfilled from "the old" to "the new." For that reason Calvin was

78. Peter Opitz, "John Oecolampadius, Huldrych Zwingli and John Calvin," in Saebø, ed., *Hebrew Bible/Old Testament,* 1/1, p. 434.

79. R. C. Gamble, "Brevitas et Facilitas: Towards an Understanding of Calvin's Hermeneutic," *WTJ* 47 (1985): 1-17.

80. Calvin treats this unity in the *Institutes* 2.11.10.

restrained from bringing any forced Christology into the Psalms; there is no need, for it is all under one covenant. David points to Christ, serving as a "type" of the coming Christ. Yet David also represents our own humanity.

The first Bible commentary he intended for publication was the Psalms (1552). To aid his own Hebrew studies, he brought to his Academy (founded in 1559) the best Hebrew scholars he could recruit. He made his own Hebrew translations, displaying sensitivity to the variety of genres, the historical situation of the text, the circumstances around it, the author, and the addressees. He was critical of "baseless allegorization," seeking instead always "the plain sense" of the text. For it is through the Biblical text that "we learn to place our trust in God, and to go on our way in fear of him." Such "faith" is well illustrated in the praise of "the law" in Psalm 119. Compared with his contemporaries — even Bucer — Calvin was far more restrained in using "Christological interpretation." Under the one covenant, Calvin saw a sweep of divine sovereignty over both Testaments, enveloping them as united in an unfolding salvation history. Yet, as the Psalms are "the mirror of the soul," Calvin could live through and with all the psalms, too, in such a personal, rebuking, healing, and assuring way that he sees himself at all times wholly identified with them. In the foreword of his commentary he revealed so much about himself autobiographically, for indeed the Psalter is "An Anatomy of All Parts of the Soul"; Calvin shared so much together with David.[81] Surely, we can recognize Calvin's commentary to be "the most modern" of the Reformers' commentaries, for it is both remarkably "truthful" and intimately "personal" at the same time. Like no other commentator, Calvin finished what Augustine had begun by eliminating the perennial confusion about the merits and demerits of what is "literal" and what is "spiritual," or indeed what is "historical" also. The four levels of medieval interpretation are finally reduced to the "plain meaning" of the text.

However, as we can trace through church history, heresy is like a parasite, proliferating from one truth into an exaggerated distortion of it. Alas, such seems to have been the history of the "plain meaning" in the centuries that followed. So we enter into our fourth "hinge period" of Biblical exegesis,[82] a powerful indictment that was wholly ignored, even by other evangelical leaders.

81. J. A. De Jong, "'An Anatomy of All Parts of the Soul': Insights into Calvin's Spirituality from His Psalm Commentary," in W. H. Neuser, ed., *Calvinus Sacrae Scripturae Professor* (Grand Rapids: Eerdmans, 1994), pp. 1-14.

82. De Jong, "'An Anatomy of All Parts of the Soul,'" p. 990.

V. The Beginnings of Biblical Criticism During the Seventeenth and Eighteenth Centuries

A. Early Influences Toward the Triumph of Biblical Criticism

The "plain meaning" of the text that Calvin had advocated was strengthened in the seventeenth century by a culture that pursued "sincerity" through the writings of the great dramatists, Shakespeare and Calderón. A Puritan moral expression of this was "the examination of conscience." The rising influence of science to measure everything, observe everything, and classify everything was now aided by the roles of microscope and telescope, further energizing the desire for precision. Definition now required a new culture of dictionaries and encyclopedias. Thus as "precisians" of doctrine, the Puritans worshiped "a precise God."

The rapprochement between Christian and Jewish scholars in the preceding century bore further fruit in Biblical scholarship in the philological studies of Hebraists such as the two **Johannes Buxtorfs** at Basel, father (1564-1629) and son (1599-1664), whose influence extended long after their lives. No Christian before had been more concerned over the Masoretic text for non-Jewish audiences. After the elder Buxtorf's death, the son completed his father's works in his Bible concordance (1632) and his magnum opus, his *Lexicon chaldaicum talmudicum et rabbinicum.* He upheld his father's position that the Hebrew vowel points dated from the Biblical age, no later than the "great Synagogue" of Ezra and Nehemiah.[83]

Perhaps the most significant seventeenth-century insight was the recognition by Biblical scholars at the universities of Leiden, Paris, and Oxford that the Bible was subject to the same kinds of textual corruption as secular texts. The other feature of importance was the comparison of the Hebrew text with other Semitic languages such as Arabic, as exemplified by **Louis Cappel** (1585-1658), a French Huguenot scholar who knew Arabic as well as Hebrew. He tried to refute Buxtorf's position on the vowel points, and as a textual critic he introduced systematic textual comparisons. His work *Critica sacra* (1650) aroused suspicions among Protestant theologians, but comparative Semitic philology was launched further by **Albert Schultens** (1686-1750). The search was now on for "the true Hebrew Bible text," which scholarly entrepreneurs like the Oxford Kennicott (*Vetus Testamentum,* 1776-80) and the Italian De Rossi (*Variae lectiones Veteris Testamenti,* 1784-93) failed to find. They could go no further back

83. Stephen G. Burnett, "Later Christian Hebraists," in Saebø, ed., *Hebrew Bible/Old Testament,* 1/1, p. 788.

than medieval Hebrew manuscripts, all of which belonged to the Masoretic text type that was developing between 600 and 1000 CE. Prior to the work of the Masoretes — who vocalized the text and added marginal notes and other paratextual features to preserve it and assist in its reading — the proto-Masoretic text had become after 100 CE the *textus receptus* of the rabbis and of Christian scholars such as Origen and Jerome.[84]

While these textual scholars were predominantly conservative in faith, the Italian **Fausto Sozzini** (1539-1604) denied the doctrine of the Trinity. His book *De Sacrae Scripturae auctoritate* began to spread what later became known as "Socinian" teaching, with the assumption that natural human reason was in accord with divine revelation. With little Hebrew, he tried to promote a literal exegesis, denying both the Psalms' Christological sense and even the deity of Christ. While ostensibly conservative, the Dutch humanist **Hugo Grotius** (1583-1645) was latitudinarian in seeking a broad expression of Christianity, accepting the oral tradition of the early Fathers as well as the Biblical text as authoritative. Influenced by Sozzini, Maimonides, Cappel, and others, he argued for seeking textual explanations by clarifying the historical context. He did accept that Christ's activities had been predicted in the Old Testament, as he interpreted Psalms 2, 22, and 45 as Messianic .[85] As Laplanche notes, Grotius was loath to break irreversibly from orthodoxy, and yet his humanistic premise was the ultimate authority of the historical approach.[86] Like some contemporary "receptor commentators," he dismantled the unique authority of the New Testament over that of the Old Testament to appease the Jews. As the Dutch Calvinist A. Rivet attested, Grotius was indeed a "judaizing" teacher.[87]

While the French Catholic **René Descartes** (1596-1650) was well versed in the Bible, he preferred to leave exegesis in the hands of the experts and focus instead upon philosophy. In his thinking, the Bible was written for simple-minded believers, separating it from science and history. Science and faith were separate territories, not necessarily integrated. The Dutch Jewish philosopher **Baruch Spinoza** (1632-77) went much further in his *Tractatus Theologico-Politicus* (1670), horrifying Jews and Christians alike. His aim was political, namely, to undercut the state role of religious leaders by "naturalizing" the Old Testament and denying its status of being a "sacred book" and therefore of di-

84. Bruce K. Waltke, "The Reliability of the Old Testament Text," in *New International Dictionary of Theology and Exegesis* (Grand Rapids: Zondervan, 1997), pp. 51-67.

85. Grotius, *Opera omnia theologicae,* cited by H. J. M. Nellen, "Tension between Church Doctrines and Critical Exegesis," in Saebø, ed., *Hebrew Bible/Old Testament,* 2, p. 813.

86. François Laplanche, *L'Écriture, le sacre et l'histoire: Érudits et politiques protestants devant la Bible en France au XVIIe siècle* (Amsterdam: Maarssen, 1986), pp. 334-39.

87. Nellen, "Tension between Church Doctrines and Critical Exegesis," p. 816.

vine origin. Moses was denied authorship, as well as David, and the prophets were only using vivid imagination. For him the Jewish Bible was still a source of moral values, whose text should be studied carefully, but its divine revelation was wholly gone. He also reacted to Cartesian dualism in favor of a pantheistic god that was both matter and spirit. He was accused of atheism, even though he acted as if he was deeply religious.

Compounding such attacks on the Scriptures were the more insidious critics, like the French Catholic scholars **Richard Simon** (1638-1712), **Augustin Calmin** (1672-1757), **Jean Anstruc** (1684-1766), and **Charles François Houbigant** (1686-1784). In disagreement with Bishop Bossuet, Calmin was one of the first critics to discount the Psalm titles as inspired, and he stated the view that Ezra was the sole or principal author of the Psalms.[88]

B. The Rise of Deism

As E. Troeltsch put it, "Deism is the religious philosophy of the Enlightenment," but it goes back to Socinianism, and before that to an underground movement of free-thinkers in France and Italy in the sixteenth century; perhaps even to the Renaissance before that. Certainly **Thomas Hobbes** (1588-1679) was an early Biblical critic, while being a stout defender of a state church. **John Locke** (1632-1704), in his *Essay Concerning Human Understanding,* provided a methodological basis from which the Deists could advance. "Natural religion" gave rise to the later rivalry of "Nature" versus creation. **Edward Lord Herbert of Cherbury** (1582-1648) accepted "true believers" in all religions, but the Irish Catholic **John Toland** (1670-1722) and the Englishmen **Anthony Collins** (1676-1729) and **Matthew Tindal** (c. 1653-1733) were all clearly promoters of deism. As a deist **Thomas Morgan** (1680-1743) totally rejected the Old Testament as part of the Christian Bible. But as anti-deists, although rationalistic apologists, following upon John Newton, **Samuel Clarke** (1675-1729) and **William Warburton** (1698-79) both promoted a fatal dualism between the two Testaments.

What was now new in Biblical studies was the swelling growth and strength of cultural skepticism concerning Biblical authority, such as the church had never previously faced. This skepticism also stimulated Biblical scholarship, so that by the eighteenth century a substantial amount of Biblical erudition had been accumulated, especially on the Continent. It also provided

88. August Calmet, *Dictionnaire historique, critique, chronologique, géographique et littérale, 1719,* cited by John W. Rogerson, "Early Roman Catholic Critics," in Saebø, ed., *Hebrew Bible/Old Testament,* 2, p. 845.

ammunition for negative critics like the German **Hermann Samuel Reimarus** (1694-1768), who rejected the Bible as divine revelation, seeking instead a rationalistic, universal religion. He argued that the Old Testament had no historical credibility, while appreciating the poetic beauty of some of the psalms.[89] **Gotthold Ephraim Lessing** (1729-81) followed Reimarus's teaching, questioning the Exodus. In 1777-78 he challenged the Lutheran conservative, Goeze, to a public debate about Biblical hermeneutics. He attacked the use in Christian apologetics of arguments from history, distinguishing faith claims from claims of historical truth. He argued that Israel achieved monotheism *par excellence* through its late contact with the Persians, and not from the earlier religion of Moses; indeed, he argued that Moses did not convey the true notion of God to the Israelites.[90]

C. The Response of Pietism

Lutheran Pietism strongly set itself apart from the Enlightenment in giving priority to a godly life over nominal churchgoing, in emphasizing the central importance of Bible reading and serious study, and in encouraging believers to devote themselves to a life of prayer and communion rather than to rationalistic disputation. It was a latter-day reformation attempting to complete what the Reformation had not accomplished. *Tota Scriptura* now replaced *sola Scriptura,* to give awareness of one's sinfulness and to promote self-assessment and world-renunciation. **Johann Arndt** (1555-1621), a precursor rather than founder of Pietism, had published a massive collection of sermons on the Psalms as a form of mystical spirituality and internalized piety. More practically and articulately, **Philipp Jakob Spener** (1635-1705) did some of his exegetical studies with an Alsatian Jew, and then with Buxtorf. In spite of that, Spener virtually ignored the Old Testament in his teaching, admitting at the end of his life: "I have done nothing or only a little with the Old Testament, which I do not understand."[91] His doctrine of verbal inspiration made the use of historical Biblical criticism study impossible. He also denied the place of philosophy in Biblical studies, so philology tended to take its place. Spener's most important student was **August Hermann Francke** (1663-1726), who devoted some of his many skills to the Psalms, published posthumously as

89. R. A. Harrisville and W. Sundberg, *The Bible in Modern Culture* (Grand Rapids: Eerdmans, 2002), pp. 46-61.

90. Christoph Bultmann, "Early Rationalism and Biblical Criticism on the Continent," in Saebø, ed., *Hebrew Bible/Old Testament,* 2, p. 899.

91. Quoted by Johannes Wallman, in Saebø, ed., *Hebrew Bible/Old Testament,* 2, p. 907.

Introductio in Psalterium generalis et specialis (in 1734; 1229 pages). His approach was Christological. His successor, **Johann Heinrich Michaelis** (1668-1738), who taught Oriental Languages at Halle University, spent eighteen years working on a collaborative three-volume commentary of the Old Testament published in 1720 and containing over 4,000 pages! It still remains the most important contribution of Pietist scholarship. He published a commentary on the Psalms and Proverbs in 1745, with glosses that offered historical and linguistic notes on individual psalms. The honor of being the most important Pietist scholar as a Biblical critic goes to **Johann Albrecht Bengel** (1687-1752), but he remained almost exclusively a New Testament scholar.

D. The Expansion of Kantian Moralism

Immanuel Kant (1724-1804) came from a Pietist cultural background. But as a philosopher, he redefined religion as "perception of all duties as divine commandments." Christ then became "the moral example," the church was the necessary institution for morality, and the Scriptures were moral teaching.

He argued that the ways of God cannot be "explained," yet all rational thought must be explained. Since the positive must prevail, the empirical and the exact science have therefore no place for God. Accordingly, as a "science," history cannot include the ways of God; Biblical exegesis also cannot include God.

Johann Gottfried Herder (1744-1803) read the Bible as written by human beings for human beings, yet he attacked the rationalistic approach by a more mystical attitude. **Johannes Gottfried Eichhorn** (1752-1827), a protagonist of historical-critical exegesis, was a universalist who presented himself as a historian of literature, neglecting theological questions.

Johann Philipp Gabler (1753-1826) is considered the founding father of Biblical theology. Working within the climate of the Enlightenment, he defined history as a period of the past that can be characterized as a stage in the development of human knowledge and its opinions. He adhered to the idea of "progress." Historical questions about Jesus' relations to the Gospels led to similar questions about the historicity of David. At the same time, a growing interest in myth and ritual, rather than history, influenced the use of the psalms as prayers.

W. M. L. de Wette (1780-1849) then introduced "form-criticism" or *Gattungsgeschichte* by classifying four main types of psalms: individual laments, national laments, psalms reflecting on evil, and theodicy psalms. His commentary on the Psalms (1811) made use of Gesenius's Hebrew lexicon. In his second edition (1823), de Wette added two more categories. **Wilhelm Gesenius** (1786-

1842) lectured on the Psalms in 1826-27. His four categories of Psalms reflected de Wette's work.

VI. Separation of the "Literal" from the "Historical" in Biblical Studies During the Eighteenth Century

A number of factors led to the separation of the historical and spiritual dimensions of the text. First, later Calvinists perhaps exaggerated the continuity between the covenants of Israel and that of the church, and so neglected to note the differences in the administration of the Old Covenant, by which Israel was administered, and the New Covenant, by which the church is administered. Second, they so emphasized the woodenly literalistic interpretation of the text that this emphasis led to a later counter-reaction to recapture the text's spiritual dimension. Third, they subordinated hermeneutics to dogmatic theology so that texts were taken out of their historical contexts in order to prove a point of doctrine. In other words, they used the Bible text to prove doctrine *(dicta probantia),* not to arrive at doctrine. In place of this subjection of interpretation to dogmatic theology, many Pietist commentators accepted both a literal grammatical reading and a figural or "spiritual" reading, to which the technical term "emphasis" was now given, as a way of seeing beyond the grammatical text. A follower of August Hermann Francke, **Johann Jacob Rambach** (1693-1735) explored this approach, seeking to undo the unity of "literal" and "spiritual" that Luther had sought for the text. This passionate pursuit for the discovery of "saving truths" within the Scriptures contributed ironically to the opposing camp of radical historical criticism. The pursuit of "precision," which marked the culture generally, motivated great Biblical scholars like Johann Albrecht Bengel to seek the original or the more accurate Greek text of the New Testament, as part of that pursuit.[92]

In the light of these cultural dynamics, we can understand the beginnings of John Locke's empiricism. Luther had argued that the literal (i.e., the moral, figurative, and anagogical) sense and the historical sense of Scripture involved a cognate unity on the part of God, so that meaning and fact are one. But in the new culture, where these two aspects of Scripture were divided, the impact of John Locke's friend Anthony Collins (*A Discourse of the Grounds and Reasons of the Christian Religion,* 1724) was profound. Collins sought to fight faith issues (i.e., the spiritual) from proven "facts" (i.e., the historical).

92. Hans W. Frei, *The Eclipse of Biblical Narrative* (New Haven and London: Yale University Press, 1974), pp. 38-40.

According to this logic, if the texts in the Old Testament are not recited accurately (i.e., according to the historical meaning) in the New Testament, then the claims for Jesus' Messiahship are proven faulty. Hence the Psalms texts recited in the New Testament are now part of this "fight for accuracy." Collins disposed of the Biblical writers as "inspired," seeing them only as ordinary human beings just as prone to error as others. Like Rambach, he also separated completely literal (i.e., in Luther's sense) from historical statements — though for other reasons — to arbitrate on what is "meaningful" for the observer.[93] The end result a century later was "the hermeneutics of understanding," which Schleiermacher promoted. This suggests that the psychological/divinatory process of understanding had now become as indispensable as the grammatical aspect, for the psychological process was needed to make understanding "a fact within the thinker."[94] This resulted in marginalizing the historical dimension of understanding and exaggerating the subjective role of what seemed "acceptable to me" to think/believe. But it undercut all realistic narrative.[95] Thus Bultmann became Schleiermacher's heir when he released his project of de-mythologization. Alas, that the end result should be the exact opposite of what Luther had sought two centuries before!

Meanwhile, we may ask, what had become of Calvin's "plain sense"? By this he had meant in practice what could be as close as possible to consensus in Reformed thinking. Those who kept close to the theology of Calvin maintained "the plain sense." But there were others who followed Erasmus instead, including **Bishop George Horne** (1730-92). A pupil of the great Oxford Hebraic scholar **Robert Lowth** (1710-87), a pioneer in Hebrew poetry (*De sacra poesi Hebraeorum,* 1753), Horne published his *Commentary on the Psalms* in 1771. He refers to the patristic writers, then accepts the central importance of Erasmus, with no reference whatever to the Reformers. Luther and Calvin might never have existed! In his view, the continuity of covenant has ceased, so that "the spiritual ark/law/temple" are now not Christ, but the Christian community.[96] Now for our "modern age," Horne observes, "the repetition of the Psalms, as

93. Frei, *The Eclipse of Biblical Narrative,* pp. 66-86.

94. Frei, *The Eclipse of Biblical Narrative,* p. 292.

95. Frei, *The Eclipse of Biblical Narrative,* p. 322.

96. "In the titles, prefixed to some of the Psalms, there is so much obscurity, and in the conjectures which have been made concerning them, both in a literal and spiritual way, so great a variety and uncertainty, that the author, finding himself, after all his searches, unable to offer any thing which he thought could content the learned or edify the unlearned, at length determined to omit them; as the sight of them, explained, only distracts the eye and attention of the reader." Right Rev. George Horne, *A Commentary on the Book of Psalms* (London: Longman & Co., 1849), p. xiii.

performed by multitudes, is but one degree above mechanism."[97] "And is it not a melancholy reflection, to be made at the close of a long life, that, after reciting them, at proper seasons, through the greatest part of it, no more should be known of their true meaning and application, than when the Psalter was first taken in hand at school?" So the good bishop now desires to compose the first ever "spiritual Commentary" of the Psalms. He begins by dismissal of the Psalm titles and headings.[98]

What he calls "spiritual interpretation" occurred only in the sixteenth century. "When learning arose, as it were from the dead, . . . and the study of primitive theology by that means revived, the spiritual interpretation of the scriptures revived with it. It was adopted at that time by one admirably qualified to do it justice, and to recommend it to the world by every charm of genius, and every ornament of language. I mean the accomplished Erasmus."[99] In other words, a "spiritual interpretation" of the Psalms has become a Renaissance Humanist "spirit." He interprets very few Psalms prophetically, by which he means some type of "mystic allegory."[100] Contrary to Luther, he concludes: "I consider the literal and historical sense only as a kind of vehicle for it," that is, for the spiritual sense. He interprets Psalm 110 as a prophecy of David about the exaltation of Jesus, but he advises the Psalm to be read at Christmas, with no reference to the Ascension.[101]

Thus with the advance of eighteenth-century Rationalism, there took place what Hans Frei has called "the eclipse of Biblical narrative." What had seemed "the plain sense of the text" to Calvin no longer seemed so straightforward, even to Pietist scholars. German scholarship's proclivity to focus narrowly upon issues of the text, philology, language, and culture made exegesis vulnerable to hidden presuppositions in a theological vacuum. Luther's own influence, in his doctrine of the two kingdoms, intensified the open vulnerability of textual study to becoming non-confessional. John Locke's *On the Reasonableness of Christianity* near the beginning of the century and Immanuel Kant's *Religion within the Limits of Reason Alone* at the end of the century both reduced what had once appeared "reasonable" into a very circumscribed box, with no true sense of transcendence. Now Herder's *The Education of the Human Race* argued that the religious development of humankind was itself the revelation of God and not merely the instrument of that revelation.[102]

97. Horne, *A Commentary on the Book of Psalms*, p. xv.
98. Horne, *A Commentary on the Book of Psalms*, p. vii. See n. 96, above.
99. Horne, *A Commentary on the Book of Psalms*, p. xii.
100. Horne, *A Commentary on the Book of Psalms*, pp. xvi-xx.
101. Horne, *A Commentary on the Book of Psalms*, p. 481.
102. Horne, *A Commentary on the Book of Psalms*, p. 195.

VII. Conservative German and British Scholars of the Nineteenth Century

Early in the nineteenth century there were scholars such as **Augustus Tholuck** (1799-1877), who before he came to faith grew up as a student in the rationalistic environment of German universities, quite unaware of any Christian orthodox theology. All he knew was the psalm commentary of **Wilhelm M. L. de Wette** (1780-1849), who had first applied historical criticism to the Pentateuch. He found his materials on the Psalms dry and faithless — "particularly meager in religious knowledge" — and when he was asked by the government to take de Wette's university position at Heidelberg, in desperation he asked the Jewish scholar Neander to help him, for he at least shared a religious piety towards the Scriptures. Tholuck then found Calvin's commentary on the Psalms: "it disclosed to me a religious depth in that one book of the Old Testament, which opened my eyes for many other glories of the Old Testament scriptures. Progressing in this knowledge, I learned to understand that the Christian Revelation is indeed a tree without a root, so long as it is not understood in its intimate connection with God's revelation of salvation in the Old Testament."[103] Biblical scholars, too, can be "trees without roots," for what further impressed Tholuck was Calvin's faith.

He also discovered Pietist scholar A. H. Francke's *Devotional Exposition of the Psalms* (1731). In this work Francke stated clearly: "The man who has not the Spirit of Christ, nor denies himself, nor daily takes up his cross and follows Christ, has no relish for the Psalms."[104]

Tholuck's purpose became then "to interpret the Book of Psalms in the spirit of Calvin: and basing it on the helps of the newly-gained views of modern times, to adapt the volume to the wants of the people, and also to professional men, who, besides the strictly grammatical Commentaries, look for a guide to the spiritual-understanding of this portion of Holy Writ." We could not ask for a better description of what this new endeavor should be today! But in sharp contrast to Horne, Tholuck decries the abolition of the Psalm headings, as part of his *critical position* in scholarship:

103. Augustus Tholuck, *A Translation and Commentary of the Book of Psalms,* trans. Rev. J. Isidor Mombert (Philadelphia: William S. & Alfred Marten, 1858), pp. x-xi.

104. Tholuck continues: "They gladden not his heart, but appear to him as weathered straw — altogether stale. But let him be brought into similar courses of affliction and suffering, and experience the sneers and mockery of the world for righteousness' and Christ's sake . . . yet serve the Lord God in spirit and in truth . . . then he shall be like a tree planted by the rivers of water . . . and experience the intensity of the struggle which is required, and learn rightly to understand the Psalms" (*A Translation and Commentary of the Book of Psalms,* p. 10).

> Every candid theologian will admit that in the case of some of the titles there may be entertained by no means unfounded misgivings respecting their authenticity. But I feel constrained to confess that the manner in which the titles have in modern times been treated, appears to me nothing short of the highest degree of arbitrariness. Instead of winnowing where necessary the historical traditions, supported by weighty reasons, they are now from the outset set aside, for the purpose of substituting in their place the utterances of the most unbounded subjectivity. What confidence can be placed in a criticism, the judgments of which present among themselves such powerful contradictions?[105]

Tholuck was facing a losing battle. The German scholar Ewald rapidly dismissed any connection of Psalm 51 with David, dating it after the destruction of the temple! Further forms of subjectivism followed rapidly.

Like Tholuck, and in contrast to de Wette, **Hermann Hupfeld** (1796-1866) and **Ferdinand Hitzig** (1807-75) both favored a strong individual approach to the Psalms. As a Lutheran Pietist, Hitzig set each psalm within a strong historical context and gave a stronger personal concreteness to its characters. Hupfeld, while in agreement with Hitzig, admits he can give no evidence to his readers. **H. Olshausen** (1800-1882) combats Hitzig and Hupfeld, followed by **E. Reuss** (1804-91), **H. Gratz** (1817-91), and especially **R. Smend** (1851-1913), who all develop the "Collective I" of the Psalms, followed by **Thomas Kelly Cheyne** (1841-1915), with the loss of a historical context.

Franz Julius Delitzsch (1813-90) is one of the last great German scholars to take a conservative orthodox position, interpreting Psalm 110 as a prophetic and Messianic psalm, voiced personally by David to speak God's word. He concludes his commentary on Psalm 110: "The prophet who utters [this psalm] is David; He, whom he addresses as Lord, is the King, who is destined to become a king after the manner described in Ps. Lxxii, and therefore the one of whom God has spoken to him according to 2 Samuel xxiii, 3. David sees Him at a moment of His reign, which that moment of his own reign at which we find him in 2 Sam. xi 1 typically resembles."[106]

Meanwhile, in England, the Anglican scholar J. M. Neale was maintaining a strong patristic tradition in his psalm commentary, still sympathetic to the medieval exegesis of the *quadriga* and its liturgical music. Just as Luther had composed many hymns from the psalms he also commented upon, and just as Calvin was seeped in the hymns of the Huguenot Clement Marot, so we must appreciate that

105. Tholuck, *A Translation and Commentary of the Book of Psalms,* p. xiv.

106. *Delitzsch's Biblical Commentary on the Psalms,* trans. Rev. David Eaton (London: Hodder & Stoughton, 1889), vol. 3, p. 176.

such commentators had a lyricism behind their thoughts that academic scholarship on the Psalms has largely lost. But unlike Delitzsch, Neale sees no historical context to Psalm 110, other than Jesus' confrontation with the Pharisees over its interpretation. So he affirms that Psalm 110 "as a Messianic prophecy has no parallel throughout the Psalter."[107] Indeed, he further argues that it seems to stand unique in the Talmud and other Jewish sources. More familiar with historical sources than other commentators, Neale traces the interpretations of the Fathers and medieval commentators in careful scholarship. This enables him to ignore completely the rationalistic tendencies of his own day.

Bishop J. J. Stewart Perowne (1823-1904), a contemporary of Neale, does appropriate critically the German scholars, including Delitzsch, but he bases his work on his own Hebrew translation, with an appropoetic idiom. Like John Donne, he appreciates the Psalms as "the manna of the Church," quoting approvingly A. H. Francke's spiritual conditions of appropriating the psalms to one's personal life. His exegetical method is still typological, and therefore from a Biblically historical position. He devotes over a hundred pages to the outline of his background on the Psalms before he begins his commentary.[108] Both of these Anglican scholars, then, were aware of the rich context of faith that is required to appreciate the long historical process of Israelite devotion that provided us with the Psalms.

VIII. Contemporary Form-Criticism

The introduction of form-criticism in the early twentieth century added a new dimension to the historical aspect of Psalms research, further acerbating the loss of the spiritual dimension of the Psalms. Form-criticism has severely restricted the spiritual/doctrinal "hinterland" to "literary themes." As de Witte had pioneered form-criticism of the Pentateuch at the beginning of the nineteenth century, so a century later in 1926 **Hermann Gunkel** (1862-1932) did the same with the Psalms.[109] Within the "collective usage of the 'I'" in the Psalms, he set all of Israel's sacred songs within a cultic setting, the heritage of a worshiping community. Discernment of the types of poetry now requires an aesthetic sensitivity, rather than the traditional "spiritual" sensitivity. Classifica-

107. The Rev. J. M. Neale and the Rev. R. F. Littledale, *A Commentary on the Psalms: From Primitive and Medieval Writers* . . . , 4 vols. (London: Joseph Masters & Co., 1860-), vol. 3, p. 440.

108. J. J. Stewart Perowne, *The Book of Psalms,* vol. 1 (1864; repr. Grand Rapids: Zondervan, 1966), pp. 22-40.

109. For a sympathetic historical summary of "form criticism," see Harvey H. Guthrie, *Israel's Sacred Songs: A Study of Dominant Themes* (New York: Seabury Press, 1966).

tion of the types of Old Testament poetry then follows. He then draws parallels to the recovered literature of the neighboring peoples — Sumerians, Babylonians, Egyptians, Amorites, Assyrians. From this he identifies six major, six minor, and two special types of poetry. The most important types are individual and community laments, songs of trust, hymns of praise, and royal psalms. Influenced by Johannes Pedersen's anthropological studies of the ancient Near East, Gunkel identifies the ultimate source of these patterns in the cult.

This broad generalization of setting the Psalms in the cult and emphasizing their later use in the synagogue was objected to by his fellow Norwegian, **Sigmund Mowinckel** (1884-1965), who desired to investigate the pre-exilic *Sitz im Leben,* or the actual setting of worship, especially focusing upon the great New Year Festival near the autumn/fall equinox, when rains ended the prolonged summer drought and introduced a new agricultural year.[110] The importance that Mowinckel found in the institutions of worship seemed too close to foreign ritual and magic for some writers, although **A. R. Johnson** did suggest that rich insights could be gained by more critical investigation of the great religious rituals.[111]

Artur Weiser (1893-1978) reacted against too much reliance on form-criticism.[112] He was also critical of Mowinckel's acceptance of syncretistic elements in Israel's worship; instead, he traces the origins of Israel's unique tradition of covenant to the tribal league that preceded the monarchy. He regards developments after David as merely expansive of previous motifs. He identifies the anticipation of the coming Messiah expressed in Psalm 110 with the national religion of late Judaism.[113] **Hans-Joachim Kraus** collated the views of a number of Old Testament scholars, including Alt, Noth, and von Rad, to argue that these previous scholars had overlooked the complexity of Israel's tradition and cultic life, in an all-embracing "lump" theory.[114] Kraus contributes a new "theology of the Psalms" (1960, 1978), while retaining the idea that Israel's religion was syncretistic, incorporating elements of the religions of the surrounding nations. In spite of all these modifications, Gunkel's literary forms are still basic to contemporary studies. **Claus Westermann** also preferred the older view of the Psalms as evoking historical events and adjusted Gunkel's system of classification.[115]

110. Sigmund Mowinckel, *The Psalms in Israel's Worship,* trans. D. R. Ap-Thomas (Nashville: Abingdon, 1962).

111. A. R. Johnson, *Sacral Kingship in Ancient Israel,* 2nd ed. (Cardiff: University of Wales Press, 1967).

112. Artur Weiser, *The Psalms: A Commentary* (London: SCM Press, 1962).

113. Weiser, *The Psalms,* pp. 692-97.

114. H.-J. Kraus, *Psalms: A Commentary,* vol. 1 (Minneapolis: Augsburg, 1988), pp. 38-62.

115. Claus Westermann, *The Living Psalms* (Edinburgh: T. & T. Clark, 1990).

The climax of form-criticism is seen in the twenty-four volumes planned to present a form-critical analysis of the whole Old Testament, covering the last seven decades of research. In the two volumes by **Erhard Gerstenberger**, *Psalms and Lamentations,* fixed questions are asked of each psalm, such as its *genre,* its *setting,* and its *intention.* Only at the end is it acknowledged that Psalm 110 is the psalm most quoted in the New Testament, for it is quite irrelevant to the purpose of the research. So it is observed, "there is a cryptic air about Psalm 110. Very likely, songs like this had to use veiled language, in order not to arouse distrust and draw the attention of Persian officials."[116] Or is it now being viewed cryptically, not to upset the totalitarianism of contemporary secularism! Another subjective consequence of the exaggerated use of form-criticism is to open the way for sociological bias in the application of the Psalms today, just as a cult bias was opened originally by Gunkel. This is done persuasively by **W. Brueggemann** in his many works, who began with the perspectives of liberation theology and has since moved deeper into postmodern sociology.[117]

IX. Contemporary Trends

The publication of more recent psalm commentaries suggests that, as with all academic fashions, "form-criticism" may be running out of steam. Contextually, there has to be a theology of the Psalms. For **James L. Mays**, this lies first and foremost in the Psalms' use of the name YHWH, the God of Israel, and the recognition that the psalms are "the poetry of the reign of the Lord."[118] Mays would restore a more orthodox recovery of the Psalms, where the statement "'the Lord reigns,' is the basic truth about the world and life lived in it."[119] He therefore sees Psalm 110 as a commentary on the statement of the Apostles' Creed, "I believe in Jesus Christ . . . who sits at the right hand of God." It is a prophetic and Messianic psalm, both for a past event and for an eschatological anticipation.[120]

116. Erhard Gerstenberger, *Psalms and Lamentations* (Grand Rapids: Eerdmans, 1988, 2001), vol. 2, p. 267.

117. W. Brueggemann, *Israel's Praise: Doxology Against Idolatry and Ideology* (Philadelphia: Fortress, 1988); *Abiding Astonishment: Psalms, Modernity and the Making of History* (Louisville: Westminster/John Knox Press, 1991); *The Psalms and the Life of Faith* (Minneapolis: Augsburg, 1995).

118. James L. Mays, *Psalms,* Interpretation: A Bible Commentary for Teaching and Preaching (Louisville: John Knox Press, 1994), p. 30.

119. Mays, *Psalms,* p. 31.

120. Mays, *Psalms,* pp. 350-55.

Likewise, **Samuel Terrien** (1911-2001) in his final commentary, *The Psalms,* moves from a short appreciation of the literary genres of the individual psalms to the Psalter's theology, for indeed it can be described as "a little treatise of Biblical theology," which points to a grand design, whether God is sensed as present or absent, Creator of nature, sovereign of history, judge of the enemies, master of wisdom, or Lord of life.[121] However, in relating the Psalms only slightly with the New Testament, Terrien ties his commentary too much with Israel's neighbors.

The commentary of **John Eaton**, subtitled "A Historical and Spiritual Commentary," provides a comprehensive introduction to the Psalms. It even considers the musical use of Israel's hymnal, and it resists cultural syncretistic analogies. Eaton's focus is on the "holy God," the unique God of Israel, whose experience is celebrated in so many ways within the Psalter. His summary history of commentaries is also helpful.[122] The unique Kingship of *I Am* is his guiding significance. More clearly than many of his contemporary predecessors, he sees the theme for Psalm 110 as that of "the Son on the Throne of God." He blends ancient and modern discourse to view the Messiah and Savior as the King who should come.

EXCURSUS

Replacement of English Psalmody by Hymnody in the Eighteenth Century

Apparently, during the eighteenth century serious study of the Psalms by the opponents of historical criticism was diminished by a vaguely pious use of them in Sunday liturgy and/or an Evangelical reaction to them in favor of a more articulate gospel message in preaching and hymnody. In presenting in hymnody a more precise gospel rendering, Isaac Watts split the gospel truth of the new hymnody from the Old Testament Psalter.

It also divided Evangelical friends. **William Romaine** was familiar with the Hebrew text and sought to uphold the central use of the Psalms in the Anglican liturgy, so he condemned Isaac Watts for his substitution of new hymns for the Psalms. But his friends **John Newton** and **Lady Huntingdon**

121. Samuel Terrien, *The Psalms: Strophic Structure and Theological Commentary* (Grand Rapids: Eerdmans, 2003), pp. 44-59.

122. John Eaton, *The Psalms: A Historical and Spiritual Commentary with an Introduction and New Translation* (London and New York: Continuum, 2005), pp. 51-58.

wished he had never written his attack on Watts in 1775, entitled "An Essay on Psalmody."[123]

Romaine's text was "Give thanks unto the Lord, call upon his name, make known his deeds among the people: sing unto him, sing Psalms unto him" (1 Chron. 16:8-9). Romaine accepts the titles to the psalms for serious reflection, and he distinguishes their three names: "the Hymns contain the praises of Immanuel, our sun of righteousness; the Psalms treat of his taking our nature, and in it of being cut off for his people that through his death they might live — the Songs celebrate the glories of his kingdom, both in earth and heaven, time and eternity." Romaine argues that because of ignorance concerning the genres, meaning, and use of the Psalms in nominal church worship, "they are quite neglected in many congregations, as if there were no such hymns given by the inspiration of God, and as if they were not left for the use of the church and to be sung by the congregation. Human compositions are preferred to divine. Man's poetry is exalted above the poetry of the Holy Ghost. Is this right?" Again he explains, "I have no quarrel with Dr. Watts, or any living or dead versifier — my concern is to see Christian congregations shut out divinely inspired Psalms, and take Dr. Watts' flights of fancy; as if the words of a poet were better than the words of a prophet, or as if the wit of a man was preferred to the wisdom of God. . . . why should Dr. Watts, or any hymn-maker, not only take the precedence of the Holy Ghost, but also thrust him entirely out of the church?"[124]

123. Peter Toon, *William Romaine: The Life, Walk and Triumph of Faith, with an Account of His Life and Work* (Cambridge and London: James Clarke & Co. Ltd., 1970), p. xxi.

124. William Romaine, *Works* (1837), pp. 963, 968-70.

CHAPTER 3

History of Interpretation Since the Reformation: "Accredited Exegesis"

In this chapter we continue the survey of the history of Psalter interpretation from the post-Reformation (late sixteenth century) to the present. In that connection we evaluate the various movements in the development of interpreting the Psalter in order to hold on to that which is good — that is to say, to define what we mean by "an accredited exegesis."

In the post-Reformation history of the nominal church, the flow of the history of interpreting the Psalter became divided with the introduction of historical Biblical criticism (HBC) — and in the case of the Psalms, HBC depleted its spiritual power. After the Reformers, commentators who based their work on the Hebrew text increasingly replaced the *hermeneutica sacra* of orthodoxy with faith in reason. *Hermeneutica sacra* is based on faith in the triune God: God's Spirit reveals God's mind to the canonical writers, inspires them to produce an infallible text for faith and practice, and illumines his church to its meaning, thereby completing the cycle of revelation.[1] By contrast, HBC replaces faith in God with faith in man as the source of truth.

Since HBC is a briar patch of issues, our survey of the history of interpretation merely tries to separate the thorny branches enough to make our way through them. We begin by defining HBC (the reader should recall Jim's tracing its rise to ascendancy in chapter 2 [see pp. 65-68, 70-72]), then by critically appraising HBC, and finally by evaluating approaches that spring from HBC and that still dominate the field: form-criticism qualified by rhetorical criticism and liturgical criticism. We then consider the orthodox canonical-Messianic approach to interpreting the Psalms, which stands apart from HBC. As we shall

1. Bruce K. Waltke with Charles Yu, *An Old Testament Theology: An Exegetical, Thematic, and Canonical Approach* (Grand Rapids: Zondervan, 2007), pp. 29-48.

see, an accredited exegesis returns to Calvin's plain sense, but now enriched by the new tools of textual criticism, form-criticism, liturgical criticism, rhetorical criticism, and canonical criticism.

I. The Approach of Historical Biblical Criticism

The foundations of HBC were laid by philosophers and theologians during the sixteenth through the eighteenth centuries; by the nineteenth century it became for many the only way of interpreting the Bible. At first orthodoxy was questioned both in England and on the Continent, then marginalized in Germany during the nineteenth century and finally driven out of academic Biblical studies in many seminaries and churches.

HBC, Plantinga argues, takes three forms: Troeltschian, Duhemian, and Spinozistic.[2] All three forms, however, have as their common denominator faith in man, not in God.

Three fundamentals of Troeltschian HBC dominate Western scholarship: 1) skepticism (i.e., a hermeneutic of suspicion that doubts the Bible's truth, such as its divine inspiration and historical veracity and integrity); 2) coherence (i.e., every effect has a natural — this-worldly — not a supernatural, cause); and 3) analogy (i.e., the laws of nature in Biblical times are the same now as then; e.g., the dead are never resurrected).

Pierre Duhem, according to Plantinga, did not necessarily accept these assumptions, but his epistemology assumes commentators can work together in interpreting Scripture on the basis of reason alone. Apparently, exegesis stands apart from the *hermeneutica sacra* of orthodoxy and Troeltschian heterodoxy. As we shall see, there is some truth in Duhemian HBC.

Spinoza regarded reason alone as sole arbiter of truth and so of interpreting the Bible; for him faith has no role in Biblical interpretation. Troeltschian and Spinozistic HBC, for example, interpret prophecy as *vaticinium ex eventu* ("proclamation from the time of the event"). Though not usually expressing themselves in so many words, historical Biblical critics of these two stripes implicitly accuse the Bible of being morally tarnished by falsehood, whether deliberately fabricated and/or mistakenly believed.

As we have observed throughout our history, a commentator's social mi-

2. Alvin Plantinga, "Two (Or More) Kinds of Scripture Scholarship," in Craig Bartholomew, C. Stephen Evans, Mary Healy, Murray Rae, eds., *Behind the Text: History and Biblical Interpretation,* Scripture and Hermeneutic Series, vol. 4 (Grand Rapids: Zondervan, 2003), pp. 19-57.

lieu impacts his commentary. HBC has impacted all contemporary scholarly commentators on the Hebrew text. Our commentary is not an exception, for HBC has had the serendipitous effect, as we shall see, of spinning off form and liturgical criticism.

II. An Evaluation of HBC

A. Sacra Hermeneutica More Reasonable Than HBC

Although orthodox commentators presume a faith posture to do their work, they argue that the dependence on faith and the work of the Holy Spirit and on the testimony of Biblical writers and of the faithful church is more reasonable than a confession that human reason alone is sufficient for the task. In other words, they do not do their work apart from reason. Pascal (*Pensées*, 4.273) reasoned: "If we submit everything to reason, our religion will have no mystery and supernatural element. If we offend the principles of reason, our religion will be absurd and ridiculous." Let us consider, then, some reasons why orthodoxy's confession, a *hermeneutica sacra,* is more reasonable than that of HBC.[3]

1. *HBC Is a Confession of Faith*

Historical Biblical critics regard their enterprise as scientific because they restrict their inquiry to empirical data, ruling out Transcendence as a possibility of investigation apart from faith. Therefore, human reason alone is sufficient, and in fact the only appropriate tool for interpreting the empirical Biblical text. According to this approach to the Psalter, orthodox *hermeneutica sacra* is a hindrance to scientific Biblical scholarship.

In truth, however, their confession that reason restricted to empirical data is sufficient for understanding the Bible is based on faith in the human. Brevard Childs rightly argues:

> The role of the Bible is not being understood simply as a cultural expression of ancient peoples, but as a testimony pointing beyond itself to divine reality to which it bears witness. . . . Such an approach to the Bible is obviously confessional. Yet the Enlightenment's alternative proposal that was to

3. Waltke, *An Old Testament Theology,* pp. 78-92.

confine the Bible solely to the arena of human experience is just as much a philosophical commitment.[4]

Orthodox theologians defend the presuppositions of *hermeneutica sacra;* historical Biblical critics commonly offer no apology for their faith in Man.

2. *HBC Contradicts the Logic of the Bible's Nature*

T. F. Torrance rightly noted that any object to be studied has its own logic by which it must be researched.[5] Stars, separated as they are by numerous light years, by the logic of their nature must be investigated with a telescope, not a microscope; and micro-organisms by their infinitesimally small size must be studied with a microscope, not a telescope. By its own testimony, the Bible is Scripture inspired by God (2 Tim. 3:16). Accordingly, for the orthodox, the Bible's nature integrates into a holistic unity three essential components that in fact cannot be separated without destroying the whole: God, its divine author; the inspired human author; and the text.

As for God, the apostle Paul argued, since God is spirit, he must be known by possessing his Spirit (1 Cor. 2:6-15). Empirical data can be known objectively, but God must be known spiritually/personally. Personal transcendence cannot be known through the lens of science, so it cannot achieve the primary purpose of exegesis: to know God and be known by him in the sense of a spiritual participation of God and the mortal. Moreover, without God's Spirit, the depraved human spirit is insufficient to exegete the text (see below).

As for the human author, he is better understood, as Meir Sternberg recognized, by sympathy with his claim to be inspired, and we should add, with his covenant faith.[6] As for the text, which is experienced empirically, it must be studied scientifically. The latter reality makes it possible for the orthodox and historical Biblical critics to work together to some extent, but in truth the other two components of the Bible's nature, whether confessed or denied, influence the interpretation of the text and safeguard it against the tyranny of reason.[7]

4. Brevard S. Childs, *Biblical Theology: A Proposal* (Minneapolis: Fortress, 2002), p. 12.

5. In a personal communication of Houston to Waltke. See Waltke, *An Old Testament Theology,* p. 79.

6. Meir Sternberg, *The Poetics of Biblical Narrative: Ideological Literature and the Drama of Reading* (Bloomington: Indiana University Press, 1985).

7. Waltke, *An Old Testament Theology,* pp. 78-92.

3. *History Depends on Testimony and Tradition, Not Science*

All history, as I. Provan, V. P. Long, and T. Longman III argued so well, is based on testimony handed down by tradition. Without testimony and tradition no history is possible.[8]

4. *Credibility of Biblical Authors*

Historians who are credible to historical Biblical critics concede that the Biblical writers are not lunatics, and that they became martyrs for the sake of the truthfulness of what they testified to having heard and seen. A terrorist may be willing to commit suicide on behalf of a false testimony, but sane people do not suffer and/or die to give a false testimony about what they experienced.

5. *Testimony of Church*

Historical Biblical critics are deaf to and/or discount the testimony of millions of Christians over two millennia in regard to knowing God through the holy Bible and through his gift of faith to them. The Belgic Confession (Article 5) gave classic formulation to this orthodox conviction: "And we believe without a doubt all things contained in them [the canonical books that comprise the Bible] — not so much because the church receives them and approves them as such, but above all because the Holy Spirit testifies in our hearts that they are from God, and also because they prove themselves to be from God." The orthodox see light within the light of faith; they believe to understand.

6. *HBC Offers No Certainty*

Without faith, as the Biblical sages argued, the finite mind cannot be certain of any truth, including absolute values.[9] To come to absolute truth and sure values demands comprehensive knowledge. Unless reason can see data within a comprehensive whole, it cannot know anything absolutely or certainly. Unassisted

8. Iain Provan, V. Philips Long, Tremper Longman III, *A Biblical History* (Louisville: Westminster/John Knox, 2003).

9. Bruce K. Waltke, *Proverbs: Chapters 15–31* (Grand Rapids: Eerdmans, 2005), pp. 464-80.

human reason can attain only to relative evaluations, not absolute values. But the triune God of the Bible claims comprehensive knowledge of absolute truth and values, and the faithful can know them spiritually if they are willing to do God's revealed truth (John 8:31, 47). Moreover, the open mind, not committing itself to any cause, is more susceptible to evil. In other words, orthodoxy better meets the human need than HBC.

7. *Human Reason Is Depraved*

As Pascal (*Pensées,* 4.277) said so well: "The heart has its reasons, which reason does not know." Calvin (*Institutes,* 2.2.25), though recognizing the necessity of reason to be human, also recognized its limitations: "For we know all too well by experience how often we fall despite our good intention. Our reason is overwhelmed by so many forms of deception, is subject to so many errors, dashes against so many obstacles, is caught in so many difficulties, that it is far from directing us aright."[10] In other words, orthodoxy is more consistent than HBC with the reality of human nature.

8. *Salvation History Best Explained by a Transcendent Author*

From Genesis to Revelation the Bible presents a unified salvation history. Calvin's "plain text" interpretation interprets the earlier revelations of the Bible within the flow of the immutable will of God being progressively fulfilled from "the old" to "the new." **J. C. K. von Hofmann** (1810-77) coined the term *Heilsgeschichte* ("salvation history") to refer to this unified progressive flow of the sacred story.[11] This history occurs within God's covenant of grace with his people, a covenant that finds expression in, among others, the Abrahamic, Mosaic, Davidic, and New. God's fingerprint in this history is apparent to those that resonate with God's Spirit in the typology and prophecies that link the historical David with his greater Son, the supra-historical Jesus Christ.

10. Howard L. Rice, *Reformed Spirituality: An Introduction for Believers* (Louisville: Westminster/John Knox Press, 1991).

11. J. C. K. Hofmann, *Weissagung und Erfüllung im Alten und im Neuen Testament* (Nördlingen: C. H. Beck, 1841), was the first to use the term "salvation history." For Hofmann, world history can only be understood within the historical self-giving of the triune God who is love. Thus, for Hofmann all of history is salvation-history, a kind of history that embraces and fulfills God's purposes in the world. Cf. Waltke, *An Old Testament Theology,* p. 53.

B. The Abiding Value of HBC

In spite of its heterodoxy, HBC has serendipitously also contributed to a better understanding of the Bible. Skepticism regarding the Bible's claim of its human authorship led to a more sophisticated reading of its claims, such as the authorship of the book of Isaiah.[12] Also, the discrediting of the Psalter's superscripts to reconstruct the historical background of the Psalms gave birth to the new discipline of form-criticism in order to discover the origins of the Psalms and that in turn gave birth to the liturgical approach, commonly called "the cult-functional" approach. Moreover, naturalism led to the realization that "supernatural" would often be better defined as that which causes awe and wonder, rather than that which contravenes nature. And analogy led to a more sophisticated understanding of typology. Scientific precision in exegesis led to the development of sophisticated exegetical tools and an awareness of the Bible's rhetorical techniques.

III. Nineteenth-Century Division of Orthodox and Biblical Critics

HBC divided the flow of Psalter interpretation into two streams: expositors who accepted the veracity of the Psalter's superscripts to reconstruct the historical background for interpreting the Psalms and those who questioned that claim.[13] The traditionalists interpreted at least the seventy-three psalms labeled "by David," and especially the fourteen that are linked with specific incidents in his life, according to the biography of David in the books of Samuel and Chronicles. Over against the traditional approach there arose in the nineteenth century what we might call the "literary-analytical approach." Let us evaluate these two approaches.

A. The Traditional Approach

In spite of the increasing inroads of HBC, some commentators continued to give credence to the superscripts to establish a psalm's historical context. In

12. See Waltke, *An Old Testament Theology,* p. 67.

13. Some evangelicals find shelter in a halfway house. For them superscripts reflect an early interpretation of the psalm, but they are not inspired by the Holy Spirit. In fact, however, this resolution is a bromide, for it rejects the authority of the superscripts.

fact, some went beyond the fourteen superscripts that interfaced the Psalm with David's career to conjecture specific incidents in his career, such as Saul's hatred of David and Absalom's revolt against him. Notable among them are **E. W. Hengstenberg** (1802-69),[14] **Franz Delitzsch** (1813-90, Erlangen), **J. J. S. Perowne** (1823-1904, English bishop and general editor of the *Cambridge Bible for Schools and Colleges*),[15] **A. F. Kirkpatrick** (1849-1940),[16] and **D. Kidner** (formerly warden of Tyndale House, Cambridge).[17] However, under the impact of HBC, as Brevard Childs says in 1979, "a wide consensus has been reached among critical scholars for over a hundred years that the titles are secondary additions, which can afford no reliable information toward establishing the genuine historical setting of the Psalms."[18] As a result, psalm studies for over a century have been adrift in conflicting opinions about their dates and meaning, such as the identification of the "enemy."[19] Fortunately, the tide of academic opinion concerning the antiquity and reliability of the superscripts is slowly changing under the gravity of evidence.

First, however, we must define "superscript." We mean introductory historical notices that pertain to the psalm's composition: its genre (e.g., *mizmor* [see p. 195], song, prayer, and so forth), its author, and the historical occasion for its composition. References to a psalm's performance (e.g., "for the chief musician" plus instrument), which through a textual error introduce the superscripts of fifty-five psalms, are, we argue, subscripts to the preceding psalm.

Whether or not the superscripts should be taken at face value affects the interpretation and theology of the Psalter. If they are historical notices, the "I" of the psalms becomes a real character. In their petitions and praises the communion of saints hears theology being applied in the flesh and blood of a real person. The particular psalms give insight into his emotions, bring the numerous references to "the enemy" into focus, and give a theological depth in the interpretation of the psalms (see our commentaries on Psalms 3, 4, 51, and 110).

14. E. W. Hengstenberg, *Commentar über die Psalmen*, trans. P. Fairbairn and J. Thomson (Edinburgh: T. & T. Clark, 1846-1848).

15. J. J. Stewart Perowne, *Commentary on the Book of Psalms*, 2 vols., 1864-1868 (Grand Rapids: Zondervan, 1976).

16. A. F. Kirkpatrick, *The Book of Psalms: With Introduction and Notes* (Cambridge: Cambridge University Press, 1897).

17. D. Kidner, *Psalms 1–72: A Commentary on Books I-II of the Psalms* (London: InterVarsity, 1973); Kidner, *Psalms 73–150: A Commentary on Books III-V of the Psalms* (London: InterVarsity, 1975).

18. B. Childs, *Introduction to the Old Testament as Scripture* (Philadelphia: Fortress Press, 1979), p. 520.

19. Walter Wiens, "The Identification of the Enemy in the 'Lament' Psalms" (Th.M. thesis, Regent College, 1979).

The superscript of Psalm 63 says David composed the psalm in the wilderness of Judah while he was fleeing from Absalom. If so, David's choice to reflect upon God in the sanctuary (v. 2) and to remember him (v. 6), instead of opting to petition God to return the king to the sanctuary (cf. Pss. 42:4; 43:3-4), gives a sharp point to the role of reflection and remembering in the spiritual life of the pious.

Let it be noted that the traditional interpretation of the Psalter affects Biblical theology in several ways. 1) It allows the reader to hear the most intimate thoughts of Israel's greatest king. 2) It validates the New Testament attribution of select psalms to David as their author. 3) It provides the firm basis of the grammatico-historical method of interpretation for the canonical-Messianic approach and affirms that the New Testament's Messianic interpretation of the Psalter is not arbitrary but rooted in sound exegesis.

1. Superscripts and Subscripts

Before offering an apologia for the originality of the superscripts, we must first define our meanings. Waltke recovered Thirtle's theory that *lamĕnaṣṣēaḥ*, a prepositional phrase introducing fifty-five psalms, and probably meaning "for the director of music" (see p. 207-8 in Psalm 3), was originally a postscript to the preceding psalm, not an original part of the superscript. Among other things, Waltke argued for this theory on the basis of comparative ancient Near Eastern literature; of the paradigmatic example in Habakkuk 3 with its pattern of superscript, prayer, and postscript; of the theory's ability to explain several conundrums, including its resolution of the well-known *crux interpretum* in the superscript to Psalm 88, whose superscript illogically specifies two genres and two authors; and of parallels from the LXX and in 11QPs[a]. The lack of *lamĕnaṣṣēaḥ* in Psalm 3, after the introductory first two psalms, and its occurrence at the beginning of Psalm 4, further supports the theory that the prose superscript following the prose subscript caused the merging of the postscript of the preceding psalm with the superscript of the following psalm. If the theory is right, then the superscripts pertain to the psalm's composition and the postscripts to its liturgical performance.[20]

Moreover, **Diodore of Tarsus** (died c. 394) is probably right in thinking that the absence of an ascription means that such psalms are related closely to the preceding one (see p. 46 in chapter 2). This is obviously so in Psalms 1 and 2 (see pp. 160-61), Psalms 9 and 10, 42 and 43, and so forth.

20. Waltke, "Superscripts, Postscripts, or Both," *JBL* 110 (1991): 583-96.

2. *An Apologia for the Traditional Approach*

Our apologia for the traditional approach considers: 1) defense that *l^edāwīd* means "by David"; 2) the originality of the superscripts; 3) the evidence for an extensive royal interpretation of the psalms; 4) the credibility of the historical notices.

a. "Of David"

First, to defend the veracity of the superscripts it needs to be argued that in the Hebrew text the preposition *l^e* ("of/for/by"?) with a proper name, usually "David," means "by."[21] Though *l^e* can mean "belonging to a series,"[22] in the Semitic languages it commonly denotes authorship.[23] In hymns outside the Psalter, *l^e* in superscripts signifies "by" (cf. Isa. 38:9; Hab. 3:1). In the Old Testament as in other ancient Near Eastern literatures, poets, unlike narrators, are not anonymous (cf. Exod. 15:1; Judg. 5:1). The meaning "by" is certain in the synoptic superscripts of 2 Samuel 22:1 and Psalm 18:[1].

Other Scriptures abundantly testify that David was a musician and writer of sacred poetry. Saul discovered him in a talent hunt for a harpist (1 Sam. 16:14-23). Amos (6:5) associates his name with temple music. The Chronicler says that David and his officers assigned the inspired musical service to various guilds and that musicians were led under his hands (i.e., he led them by cheironomy [i.e., hand signals]) as pictured in Egyptian iconography already in the Old Kingdom; 1 Chron. 23:5; 2 Chron. 29:26; Neh. 12:36).[24] The Chronicler also represents King Hezekiah as renewing the Davidic appointments of psalmody; Hezekiah directed the sacrifices and accompanying praises, where the instruments of David and the compositions of David and his assistant Asaph are prominent (2 Chron. 29:25-30).[25] Sawyer says: "In the Chronicler's day . . . it can scarcely be doubted that the meaning was 'by David.'"[26] This was

21. Moses (Psalm 90), David (73 times), Solomon (72, 127), and the guilds and priests associated with David: the sons of Korah (42–49, 84–87), Asaph (50, 73–83), Heman (88), and Ethan (89).

22. BDB, p. 513, entry 5b.

23. GKC, 129c.

24. J. Wheeler, "Music of the Temple" in *Archaeology and Biblical Research* 2 (1989).

25. Although the genre identifications as "psalm" and "song" in the superscripts are well known, the musical notations in the postscripts are mostly not understood. The meaning of *selāh,* which occurs within the text of the psalm, is also not understood and so not translated in our translations.

26. J. F. A. Sawyer, "An Analysis of the Context and Meaning of the Psalm," *Transactions* 22 (1970): 6.

the interpretation of Ben Sirach (47:8-10); the Qumran scrolls (11QPs^a), Josephus,[27] and the rabbis.[28] The interpretation is foundational for the New Testament's interpretation of the Psalter as testimony to Jesus as the Messiah (Matt. 22:43, 45; Mark 12:36-37; Luke 20:42; Acts 1:16; 2:25; 4:25; Rom. 4:6; 11:9; Heb. 4:7).

b. Antiquity and Reliability of Superscripts in General

Seven arguments defend the originality of the superscripts: 1) No ancient version or Hebrew manuscript omits them, so denying their originality is conjecture. 2) Sumerian and Akkadian ritual texts dating from the third millennium contain rubrics corresponding to elements in the Psalter superscripts,[29] and so do Egyptian hymns from the Eighteenth Dynasty and later,[30] supporting the notion that they are original. 3) Some psalms ascribed to David are ancient, supporting the superscripts' originality; Psalm 29 depends on a Canaanite background. 4) Likewise, "Davidic" Psalms contain words, images, and parallelism attested in the Ugaritic texts (c. 1400 BCE),[31] so they are probably from his time. 5) No hymn in the Old Testament outside of the Psalter lacks a superscript (e.g., Exod. 15:1; Judg. 5:1; 1 Sam. 2:1; 2 Sam. 23:1 [see Psalm 18: superscript]; Isa. 38:9; Hab. 3:1), suggesting they are original with the composition. 6) Many technical terms in the superscripts were obscure to the Greek and Aramaic translators, pointing to an extended gap of time between their composition and the Tannaitic period,[32] agreeing with Davidic ascription. 7) By contrast, linguistic, stylistic, structural, thematic, and theological differences are so great between the Psalter and its imitative thanksgiving psalms at Qumran as to leave no doubt of the far greater antiquity of the Psalter — and if so, why not by David?

If it should be objected that Solomon's temple on Mount Zion is presupposed in Psalm 24:7, 9, note that the assumed "house of God" refers to any

27. *Antiquities,* viii. 305f.

28. Charles A. Briggs, *A Critical and Exegetical Commentary on the Book of Psalms* (New York: C. Scribner's Sons, 1906-1907), p. liv.

29. H. Wilson, *The Editing of the Hebrew Psalter* (Chico, CA: Scholars Press, 1985), pp. 13-24.

30. J. B. Pritchard, *Ancient Near Eastern Texts Relating to the Old Testament* (Princeton: Princeton University Press, 1969), pp. 365-81.

31. M. Dahood, *Psalms: Introduction, Translation, and Notes,* vol. 1 (Garden City, NY: Doubleday, 1966-1970), pp. xxix-xxx.

32. The Tannaim are rabbinic sages whose views are recorded in the Mishnah, from c. 70-200 CE.

dwelling where God resides, including the tent David pitched for the ark of the covenant, not exclusively to a building (cf. 1 Sam. 1:7). If it is objected that the Aramaisms in Psalm 139 point to a late date, note that it is now clear "that evidence of Aramaic influence alone cannot serve as decisive proof for arguing for a late date of a given text."[33] As Israel's poet laureate, there is good reason to suppose that David composed the dedicatory prayer for the temple (Psalm 30), just as he designed and prepared beforehand for its building (1 Chronicles 28).

c. An Extensive Royal Interpretation

Although the "I" in post-monarchic psalms refers to an anonymous leader or personifies Israel, the "I" of many pre-exilic psalms — all those that read "by David" — is the king; and if so, why not David? Eaton offers cogent arguments for an extensive royal interpretation, to which others can be added: 1) Even psalms by the sons of Korah (cf. Psalms 44, 84) and by Ethan (cf. 89) pertain to the king. 2) Temple music as a whole took its rise from the king (see 1 Chron. 15–16; 2 Chron. 29; Isa. 38:20). 3) Throughout the ancient Near East the king took responsibility for worship. In Mesopotamia the lament psalms were royal. 4) The enemies are frequently nations (e.g., Pss. 18:43 [44]; 20; 21; 28; 61; 63; 89; 144). 5) The royal interpretation gives integrity to psalms that otherwise lack unity (see Psalm 4). 6) "The only 'situation' that is certainly attested is that of the king; . . . he is the subject in a number of psalms, and the dispute is only about how many. This cannot be said of the other suggested usages."[34] 7) The representative character of the king explains the special problem presented by the psalms where "I" (i.e., the king) and "we" (i.e., the people/army) alternate (cf. 44; 60; 66; 75; 102). 8) Throughout the "psalms of the individual" there occur about twenty-four motifs or expressions that are specifically appropriate for a king. Gunkel[35] identified the following: all nations attend to his thanksgiving (18:49 [50]; 57:9 [10]; 119:46). His deliverance has vast repercussions (22:27-31 [28-32]); he invokes a world-judgment to rectify his cause (7:7-8); he depicts himself as victorious over the nations through God's intervention (118:10); he is like a bull raising horns in triumph (92:10).[36]

33. A. Hurvitz, "The Chronological Significance of 'Aramaisms' in Biblical Hebrew," in *Israel Exploration Journal* 18 (1968): 234.

34. J. H. Eaton, *Kingship and the Psalms* (Naperville, IL: Allenson, 1976), p. 22.

35. H. Gunkel, *Einleitung in die Psalmen: Die Gattungen der religiösen Lyrik Israels* (Göttingen: Vandenhoeck & Ruprecht, 1933), pp. 147f.

36. Eaton, *Kingship and the Psalms,* pp. 20-26.

d. Historical Notices

According to their superscripts, Psalms 34, 52, 54, 56, 57, 59, 142 date from the time of David's exile (1 Samuel 16–31); 18 and 60, from the time he is under blessing (2 Sam. 1–10); and 3, 51, 63, from when he is under wrath (2 Sam. 11–20). Psalms 7 and 30 are unclassified as to their precise dates (cf. 2 Sam. 21–24). In addition to the arguments given above for the credibility of the superscripts, we ask: Why, if they are secondary additions, are the remaining fifty-nine Davidic psalms left without historical notices, especially when many of them could have been easily ascribed to some event in David's life?[37] Also, why would later editors introduce materials in the superscripts of Psalms 7, 30, and 60, which are not found in historical books and not readily inferred from the psalms themselves? Finally, why should it be allowed that psalms in the historical books contain superscripts with historical notices (cf. Exod. 15:1; Deut. 31:30 [cf. 32:44]); Judg. 5:1; 2 Sam. 22:1; Jonah 2; Isa. 38:9), but not in the collection of psalms, even though the syntax is sometimes similar (b^e + infinitive cstr.)?

3. *Conclusion*

Against the prevalent skepticism of academics regarding the originality, and so the veracity, of the psalms' superscripts, both the universal tradition of Davidic authorship and empirical evidence support the notion that *l^{e}dāwīd* means "by David," that David authored the psalms attributed to him, and that the historical notices that associate fourteen psalms with his career are credible. Lacking superscripts, one can infer from the psalms' contents that Psalms 107, 126, 137 were composed after the Exile.

It is unwise, however, to reconstruct the historical background where none is given in a superscript or to overemphasize it and/or to pit it against other approaches, such as the form-critical approach. Most of the psalms, including those in which an author is identified, are written in abstract terms, not with reference to specific historical incidences, so that others could use them in their worship. In sum, an accredited exegesis includes in its toolbox the traditional approach to the superscripts' notice about their authors and historical circumstance.

37. Gleason L. Archer, *A Survey of Old Testament Introduction* (Chicago: Moody Press, 1964), p. 28.

B. 1875-1920: Literary-Analytical Approach

The literary-analytical approach of **J. Wellhausen** (1844-1918, Göttingen), **C. A. Briggs** (1841-1913, American Presbyterian scholar and later priest in the Protestant Episcopal Church),[38] **T. K. Cheyne** (1841-1915, an English divine),[39] and **B. Duhm** (1847-1928, Göttingen),[40] denies the superscripts are original and credible and instead reconstructs a psalm's historical horizon by philological and theological typologies. Other commentators, also between c. 1875 and 1920, thought they could precisely re-create the history of the Hebrew language and locate a psalm within its proper philological register, and assumed, on the basis of the evolution of religion, that the piety of the psalms belonged to a late period in that evolution. As a result of pegging the psalms within these typologies, they concluded that many psalms belong to the Second Temple period, after kings ceased in Israel. For example, Psalm 2 was interpreted against the historical background of the Maccabees.

Later evidence, however, especially from Ugarit, proved their linguistic typology wrong, and contemporary Old Testament scholars recognize that texts cannot be fitted into a Procrustean bed along the lines of the supposed evolution of religion.[41] So this approach cannot be regarded as an accredited exegesis.

IV. 1900: Form-Critical Approach

A. The Method

Throughout the church's history, some commentators recognized that psalms fell into various types, such as penitential psalms, and that they met differing emotional needs of the church. **Hermann Gunkel** (1862-1932, Halle), the great champion of form-criticism, scientifically refined form-criticism, first in an essay on selected psalms in 1904 and then in his commentary of 1926, which ignored psalm inscriptions and so evaded the question of their historicity.[42]

38. C. A. Briggs and Emilie Grace Briggs, *A Critical and Exegetical Commentary on the Book of Psalms,* ICC, 2 vols. (Edinburgh: T. & T. Clark, reprint 1986-87).

39. T. K. Cheyne, *The Book of Psalms,* translated from a revised text with notes and introduction (London: Kegan Paul, Trench, Trübner, 1904).

40. B. Duhm, *Die Psalmen übersetzt* (Freiburg im Breisgau: J. C. B. Mohr [Paul Siebeck], 1899).

41. M. Dahood, *Psalms.*

42. H. Gunkel, *Introduction to Psalms,* completed by Joachim Begrich (Macon, GA: Mercer University Press, 1998).

His widely accepted approach attempts to categorize the psalms into *Gattungen* by their common treasure of words, moods, ideas, motifs, and other literary criteria. This approach gains support from analogies with ancient Near Eastern hymns that belong to similar categories as those of the Psalter.

Using these commonalities to classify the psalms, Gunkel discerned five principal types of psalms: individual laments and communal laments (c. 50 psalms), thanksgiving (of individual or community), hymns of praise (Psalms 8; 19; 29; 33; 65; 67; 68; 96; 98; 100; 103; 104; 105; 111; 113; 114; 117; 135; 136; 139; 145–150), and royal psalms (see below), plus several minor types, such as songs of Zion (Psalms 46; 48; 76; 84; 87; 122), and songs of trust and wisdom (Psalms 1; 37; 49; 73; 91; 112; 127; 128; 133).

Form critics, having disregarded the superscripts, aim in part by their categorizations to determine the historical life-setting *(Sitz im Leben)* in which the genre circulated and developed. Gunkel assumed a long oral tradition in the history of a psalm and concluded that they reached their final form in the Second Temple period. C. Westermann made an important modification of the category labeled "thanksgiving" by demonstrating that public, not private, praise is meant.[43]

B. Critical Appraisal

There is much merit in categorizing the psalms into various types. The Chronicler identifies three primary types of psalms: petition, public thanksgiving, and praise (see 1 Chron. 16:4, NIV, NRSV), and comparative ancient Near Eastern literatures and the content of the psalms themselves support this analysis.

In contrast to the exegetical gain of understanding a psalm's motifs, the reconstructed life-settings for the genre are conjectural and rarely have a scholarly consensus. Moreover, form critics cannot reach a consensus about the identification of the "enemy" in petition psalms. Finally, an extended development in a flexible oral tradition lacks credible empirical support. In sum, no consensus can be reached about a psalm's history of tradition.

An accredited method of exegesis recognizes at least the three major types identified by the Chronicler, plus other minor forms. Among other merits, the recognition of a psalm's form is important for philology and literary analysis. For example, words mean different things in different genres (cf. the meaning of "ball" on the sports page versus the social page). Moreover, a recognition of forms guides one's reading strategy. The reader expects to read the

43. C. Westermann, *Praise and Lament in the Psalms,* trans. K. R. Crim and R. N. Soulen (Atlanta: John Knox Press, 1981).

Book of Revelation symbolically, but a Pauline letter more woodenly. Also significantly, as it helps to interpret a sonnet by recognizing its distinctive form, recognizing a poet's motifs assists an exegete in his or her interpretation of a poem. Variations from a typical form can also be significant.

Petition psalms typically contain four motifs: address to God; lament/complaint that the psalmist is close to death, his enemies are too strong, and God seems absent; confidence based on God's sublime attributes and/or Israel's experience; petition that God save the psalmist, to which is often added a petition that God punish the enemy; and praise of some sort. Psalm 3, the first of petition psalms, offers a textbook example of this kind of psalm.

Public thanksgiving for answered prayer typically contains a resolution to praise, the reason for praise, and the *tôdâ* (i.e., a thank offering of words and sacrifice). Praise psalms typically begin with a call for praise, followed by the cause of praise for God's mighty works in salvation history, which is often linked with his mighty works in creation.

In sum, an accredited method of exegesis takes into account form-critical analysis with respect to *Gattungen,* but rejects its conjectured history of tradition within a conjectured *Sitz im Leben.*

C. "Imprecatory" Psalms

The thirty-five psalms that add to the petition motif a plea that God punish the enemy are often incorrectly labeled "imprecatory psalms." The label is inappropriate, for they do not call curses down upon the enemy, but ask for justice that God avenge, not revenge, the wrong done to the psalmist.

The striking contrast, however, between David's petitions to punish his enemies and the absence of such petitions by Christ and his apostles who, though they predict judgment upon evildoers, instead instruct the church to love and forgive one's enemies is a gap within the canon, not a blank. By "gap" rhetorical critics mean that the omission is meaningful and so intended by the author (in this case, the Author of the canon). By a blank is meant that the omission is not intentional and so meaningless. A gap, especially one of this magnitude, calls for theological reflection. These thirty-five psalms — Psalm 137 is the usual textbook example, for it calls "blessed" those who dash against the rocks Babylonian babies — trouble many. C. S. Lewis speaks of them as "terrible or (dare we say?) contemptible Psalms."[44] In fact, however, upon re-

44. C. S. Lewis, *Reflections on the Psalms* (New York: Harcourt, Brace & World, 1958), p. 23.

flection they teach sound doctrine (2 Tim. 3:16) and are most holy for the following reasons:

1) These petitions are by saints (especially the innocently suffering king) who have suffered gross injustices. Few commentators have experienced the agony of utterly unprovoked, naked aggression and gross exploitation.

2) They are righteous and just: they ask for strict retribution (cf. Lev. 24:17-22). Here Lewis is helpful, for he notes that such expressions are lacking in pagan literature; Israel had a firmer grasp of right and wrong:[45]

> Thus the absence of anger, especially that sort of anger which we call *indignation,* can, in my opinion, be a most alarming symptom. . . . If the Jews [sic!] cursed more bitterly than the Pagans this was, I think, at least in part because they took right and wrong more seriously. For if we look at their railings we find they are usually angry not simply because these things have been done to them but because they are manifestly wrong, are hateful to God as well as to the victim. The thought of the "righteous Lord" — who surely must hate such doings as much as they do, who surely therefore must (but how terribly He delays!) "judge" or avenge, is always there, if only in the background.[46]

3) They express total trust in God. The New Testament upholds the justice of God and the legitimacy to pray for justice (Luke 18:6-8; cf. Matt. 7:23 with Ps. 6:8; Matt. 25:46; 2 Thess. 1:6-9). In that connection, the pious trust God, not themselves, to avenge the gross injustices against them. The wicked, by contrast, avenge themselves (cf. Ps. 8:2; Rom. 12:17-21).[47]

4) They are just. The psalmist is seeking to be avenged, not seeking for re-

45. Lewis, *Reflections,* p. 28.

46. Lewis, *Reflections,* p. 31.

47. The Biblical concept of "vengeance" (*NQM*) entails faith. B. W. Anderson oversimplifies the meaning of the word to mean "to save." Better, it means that the LORD secures his sovereignty and keeps his community whole by delivering his wronged subjects and punishing their guilty slayers. Viewed from the perspective of the sovereign acting on behalf of his besieged community, a translation such as "deliver" or "rescue" is called for, but where the perspective is between the ruler and the enemy, as in Micah 5:14, a translation such as "defeat" or "punishment" is appropriate. Only the sovereign himself has the legitimate right to use force to protect his imperium; the exercise of force by an individual is actually a hostile act. George E. Mendenhall notes: "With reference to the early usages of NQM, one must conclude that the normative value system of the early biblical society would never tolerate an individual's resorting to force in order to obtain redress for a wrong suffered. . . . Yahweh was the sovereign to whom alone belonged the monopoly of force. Self-help of individuals or even of society without authorization of Yahweh was an attack upon God himself" (*The Tenth Generation: The Origins of the Biblical Tradition* [Baltimore: Johns Hopkins University Press, 1974], p. 95).

venge. "There have been few men," says Kidner, "more capable of generosity under personal attack than David, as he proved by his attitudes toward Saul and Absalom, to say nothing of Shimei."[48]

5) These prayers are ethical, asking God to distinguish between right and wrong (cf. Ps. 7:8-9; cf. 2 Tim. 4:14-18).

6) They are theocratic, looking for the establishment of a kingdom of righteousness by the Moral Administrator of the Universe (cf. Psalms 72, 82). The earthly king asks no more of the Heavenly King than the latter asked of him (cf. Deut. 13:5; 17:7, 12; 19:13, 19; 21:9, 21; 22:22, 24).

7) They are theocentric, aiming to see God praised for manifesting his righteousness and justice in the eyes of all (cf. Ps. 35:27-28; 58:10-11).

8) They are evangelistic, aiming for conversion of the earth by letting all men see that the Lord is Most High over all the earth (83:17-18).

9) They are "covenantal"; a wrong against a saint is seen as a wrong against God (Ps. 69:7-9, 22-28; 139:19-22).[49]

10) The prayers are oriental, full of figures, especially hyperbole (cf. Jer. 20:14-18).[50]

11) They are political.[51] If we may presume the enemy heard the prayer, he would be publicly exposed as one who opposes the kingdom of God. Moreover, the righteous identify with the psalmist and rally around him (Ps. 142:7; cf. the complaint of Ps. 38:11). Indeed, the enemy and potential evildoer may be instructed and converted through prayer (cf. Ps. 51:13; 94:8-11).

Though theologically sound, however, these petitions for immediate retribution are inappropriate in the mouth of the church in the present dispensation. 1) Ultimate justice occurs in the eschaton (Rev. 20:11-15; cf. Isa. 61:1-2 with Matt. 13:30; 25:46; Luke 4:18-20; 2 Cor. 6:2; 2 Thess. 1:5-9), and it is appropriate to pray for the destruction of the wicked at that time of judgment and the avenging of the righteous (Luke 18:1-8; 2 Tim. 4:14; Rev. 6:9-10). 2) Sin and sinner are now more distinctly differentiated (cf. Eph. 6:11-18), allowing the saint both to hate sin and to love the sinner. 3) The saint's struggle is against spiritual powers of darkness, which he conquers by turning the other cheek and by pray-

48. D. Kidner, *Psalms 1–72* (TOTC; Leicester: InterVarsity Press, 1973), p. 26.

49. Chalmers Martin, "The Imprecations in the Psalms," *Princeton Theological Review* 1, no. 4 (1903): 537-53.

50. G. Fee and D. Stuart, *How to Read the Bible for All Its Worth* (Grand Rapids: Zondervan, 1981), p. 182. For hyperbole in Luke 17:2, see Kirkpatrick, *The Book of Psalms*, pp. xcii-xciii.

51. Gerald T. Sheppard, "'Enemies' and the Politics of Prayer in the Book of Psalms," in David Jobling, Peggy L. Day, Gerald T. Sheppard, eds., *The Bible and the Politics of Exegesis* (Cleveland: Pilgrim Press, 1991).

ing for the forgiveness of enemies through their repentance (Matt. 5:39-42, 43-48; 6:14; Luke 6:28, 35; Acts 7:60).

D. 1970: Rhetorical Criticism

A caveat regarding an accredited use of form-criticism is necessary. Form critics tended to stress the commonalities of forms and to neglect the rhetorical features that distinguish the psalms. In 1968, in his presidential address to the Society of Biblical Literature, **James Muilenberg** called for a correction of this imbalance and first used the term "rhetorical criticism."[52] Rhetorical criticism empowers the exegete to move beyond form-criticism to recognize the Biblical authors' known structural patterns, such as alternating structures (topics A, B, C, repeated in topic ABC), and chiastic or inverted structures (topics ABC repeated as CBA, sometimes around a pivot [topic X]). This new synchronic emphasis is primarily concerned with matters of texture. Wearing the lens of rhetorical criticism, the exegete discerns sounds, syllables, words, phrases, sentences, groups of sentences; the repetition of thoughts, key words, or motifs; word plays or paronomasia; repetition of sounds such as assonance or alliteration; or adumbration; inclusio; and a host of other literary devices. These considerations are important for theology, for the exegete does not know what a text means until he knows how it means. In addition to adorning the text, structure and texture direct the exegete to the poet's meaning. Theologians of all persuasions embrace rhetorical criticism, but some limit themselves to the synchronic phenomena of the text and disregard the history of tradition that led to the final composition.[53]

In sum, an accredited exegesis employs the form-critical analysis of literary genres qualified by rhetorical criticism to observe the text's distinctive texture.

V. 1920: Cult-Functional Approach

A. The Method

Sigmund Mowinckel (1884-1965, Oslo)[54] pioneered the cult-functional approach. His approach accepts the form-critical method, but unlike Gunkel he

52. James Muilenberg, "Form Criticism and Beyond," *JBL* 88 (1969): 1-18.
53. Waltke, *An Old Testament Theology,* pp. 113-28.
54. S. Mowinckel, *The Psalms in Israel's Worship,* 2 vols. (Oxford: Blackwell, 1967).

viewed the psalms as wholly cultic in origin and intent and so interprets the psalms against the historical background of Israel's first temple cultus, not upon their final function in the post-exilic synagogue. He aimed to reconstruct the precise cultic occasion that produced the psalm and so to mine its sociological function.

Gunkel recognized that ten royal psalms had their roots in the king's activity — his so-called "royal psalms" (Psalms 2; 18; 20; 21; 45; 72; 101; 110; 132; 144:1-11; cf. 89:47-52), but Mowinckel interpreted many more psalms in the light of the king's role in the temple. As there are royal psalms of enthronement (e.g., 2, 101, 110), of wedding (45), and of victory in battle (21), so also royal laments were uttered by the king on behalf of the nation in times of national crises. The king is understood to be the representative head of the nation: "all that concerned him and his house also concerned the people; nothing which happened to him was a purely private affair." However, Mowinckel thought these psalms were later democratized by the temple priests for the use of individual laymen.

Mowinckel also conjectured an Enthronement festival at the turning-of-fall new year, which he alleged is the historical background of forty-four psalms. At this festival, he conjectured, Yahweh was enthroned annually as king, guaranteeing the stability of the New Year in nature and in politics. Components of the festival, in his view, included: Yahweh's fight against cosmic chaos; victorious Yahweh ascends Zion; Yahweh is acclaimed king; Yahweh confirms the Davidic covenant and fixes the fate of the coming year.

B. Myth and Ritual

His conjectured reconstruction of an Enthronement festival deteriorates further in the myth-and-ritual approach of commentators like **I. Engnell, G. Widengren,** and **S. H. Hooke.** According to them, the Israelite king was regarded, like the kings of other ancient Near Eastern cultures, as the incarnation of the god: a "son of God" (Ps. 2:7; 2 Sam. 7:14), born from the goddess Dawn (Ps. 110:3), and addressed as "god" (Ps. 45:6). On the basis of the pagan Babylonian *Akitu* festival, it is claimed that at the fall festival the king played the ritualistic role of a dying and rising god in the cult, to represent the annual death and resurrection of the deity, corresponding to the cycle of nature. To effect the annual re-creation, the king, representing God, recites the myth of God's victory over the forces of chaos. This is followed by a ritual combat: cries of distress of the psalmist-king, along with tensions with enemies, are liturgical accompaniments of a dramatic sham fight in which the king emerges triumphant, followed by a sacred marriage with his consort — a representative of the deity —

to ensure the fertility of the land. The conjectured ritual ends with a triumphal procession: the king leading a triumphal procession to the temple to symbolize the annual enthronement of the deity in his proper home on Mount Zion. Thus many psalms that speak of humiliation or deliverance, of conflict, enemies, death and life, relate to this dramatic ritual.

C. Covenant Renewal Festival

A. Weiser[55] also interprets psalms against a fall festival, but regards it as a time of covenant renewal. He has not been followed.

D. Critical Appraisal

Recall that John Eaton argued cogently for an extensive royal interpretation of the psalms and in fact supports the conviction that the traditional interpretation belongs in the exegete's toolbox. By contrast, Mowinckel's fall Enthronement festival, and its myth-and-ritual bastardization, is based on pagan liturgy, not on the Mosaic covenant. The notion of a festival to reactivate creation finds its starting point in pagan magic, not in Israel's covenant faith with its essential doctrine that *I AM* rules history on the basis of ethics (see Psalm 1, pp. 142-44). Perhaps some psalms were composed for a fall new year festival, but the precise function of these psalms in such a festival is unknown, as the lack of academic consensus shows. The history of a tradition in any reconstruction is conjecture and not an accredited method.

In sum, an accredited exegesis accepts the notion that the psalms functioned as a libretto to the temple cultus in which the king played a prominent role, but rejects interpreting the psalms sociologically in the light of a conjectured fall festival.

VI. The Canonical-Messianic Approach

Although the conjectured history of a psalm's tradition cannot be incorporated into an accredited exegesis, obviously a psalm was given an expanding literary context within a developing canon. The whole is greater than its parts, and so an accredited exegesis should interpret a psalm within its canonical framework.

55. A. Weiser, *The Psalms* (London: SCM; Philadelphia: Westminster, 1962).

Brevard Childs (1923-2007, Yale)[56] pioneered this approach, but in fact it returns to Calvin's plain sense. Nevertheless, the canonical approach is often ignored, even by conservative exegetes, and so we develop and defend this approach more fully than the spin-offs from HBC. This study lays a firm historical foundation for the church's continuing interpretation of the psalms as referring to Jesus Christ, although they often did so apart from a historical consciousness.

A. Editing the Psalter[57]

1. Earlier Collections of the Psalms

The Psalter began with songs by individuals, often composed under unique historical circumstances, then used in the liturgical life of worshiping Israel and gathered into earlier collections. Psalm 72:20, "This concludes the prayers of David the son of Jesse" is "the eggshell" of an earlier collection. The notice in 2 Chronicles 29:30 suggests that two collections, "the words of David" (cf. Psalms 3–41) and "the words of Asaph" (50, 73–83), existed in Hezekiah's time. Psalms by the sons of Korah (42–49, 84–88 [not 86]) probably constituted another collection. Whether the "Elohistic Psalter" (Psalms 42–83), which bridges Books II and III, ever constituted a separate collection is unknown.[58]

2. Five Books

The 150 psalms we have in hand are now collected into five books. These books are marked off by original doxologies consisting of priestly benedictions, "Blessed be the Lord," and the congregation's responses, "Amen," at the end of

56. See n. 4.

57. For the history of commentators in their understanding the divisions of the Psalter, see chapter 1, pp. 22-24.

58. This grouping is marked by a striking statistical contrast between use of the divine names, *YHWH* and *Elohim*. Whereas in Psalm 1–41 and 84–150, *YHWH* occurs 584 times and *Elohim* 94 times, in 42–83 *YHWH* occurs 45 times and *Elohim* 210 times. Moreover *YHWH* usually occurs elsewhere in verset "a" and *Elohim* in verset "b," but in 42–83 the situation is reversed. Finally, in synoptic psalms the names are reversed (cf. 14:2, 4, 7 with 53:2, 4, 6; 40:13 [14], 17 with 70:1 [2], 5). The number 42 figures prominently in this collection: there are 42 psalms and it begins with Psalm 42. Elsewhere, in the Old Testament the numeral 42 is used in the contexts of judgment (Num. 35:6; Judg. 12:6; 2 Kings 2:24; 10:14; Rev. 13:5), but the significance of this number to shape the Elohistic Psalter is uncertain. See Joel S. Burnett, "Forty-Two Songs for Elohim: An Organizing Principle in the Shaping of the Elohistic Psalter," *Journal for the Study of the Old Testament* 36 (2006): 81-101.

Psalms 41, 72, 89, 106. Change of authors also occurs at these seams.[59] The division between Books III and IV probably occurred after the Exile (see below). The Dead Sea Scrolls (c. 150 BCE) also display this five-book arrangement.[60]

Jewish tradition explained this second "Pentateuch" as a conscious echo of the first. A midrash from the Talmudic period on Psalm 1 states: "as Moses gave five books of laws to Israel, so David gave five books of Psalms to Israel."[61] This analogy is appropriate. Moses instituted Israel's liturgical elements: its sacred objects, festivals, personnel, and activities, and David (Israel's "Mozart") transformed the Mosaic liturgy into opera by prescribing the staging of Solomon's temple, giving it musical accompaniment and the libretto of his psalms.

Within the five books, contemporary scholars are becoming more aware of a conscious arranging of the psalms, such as Psalms 1–8, 15–24, et cetera (see commentaries). An accredited exegesis will take into account assured results of this research.

3. *Exegetical and Theological Significance of Five Books*

Perhaps as early as 520 BCE the psalms were edited in such a way as to focus upon the king. This final editing significantly affects both the Psalter's interpretation and theology.

a. Introduction: Psalm 1

Most agree that Psalms 1–2 are the Psalter's introduction (see pp. 145-46) and that Psalms 146–150 are its climactic finale of praise. The first two psalms lack a superscription, unlike the rest of Book I (except Psalms 10, 33); share similar vocabulary (see pp. 160-61); and expound a uniform message: the pious and righteous are fully rewarded and in the time of judgment triumph over the wicked. This didactic generalization is stated in Psalm 1 and fleshed out in salvation history as happening through *I AM*'s anointed king in Psalm 2.[62]

Some suggest that the *torah* (catechistic teaching, traditionally "law") in

59. Wilson, *Editing of the Hebrew Psalter*, pp. 183-86.

60. See DJD I:133 and Anton Arens, *Die Psalmen im Gottesdienst des Alten Bundes. Eine Untersuchung zur Vorgeschichte des christlichen Psalmengesanges* (Trier: Paulinus-Verlag, 1961), p. 107. Rabbinic Judaism was also conscious of this division; see William G. Braude, trans., *The Midrash on the Psalms* (New Haven: Yale University Press, 1959).

61. William G. Braude, *The Midrash on the Psalms* (New Haven: Yale University Press, 1959), vol. 1, p. 5.

62. Cf. Proverbs 1–9, 10–16 (Waltke, *Proverbs: Chapters 15–31*, pp. 8-22).

Psalm 1:2 refers to the book of Psalms, transforming the book of Psalms from liturgical hymns of praise and petition into a book to be read, studied, and meditated upon.[63] Elsewhere in the Psalter, however, *torah* in similar contexts refers to the covenant God gave Israel at Sinai (Ps. 19:7; cf. Ps. 119:1). Nevertheless, the Book of Psalms was transformed from liturgy in the temple to reflective meditation in the synagogue. According to Jenni, "the people's 'Amen' no longer responds to the deeds of God but to the mighty words of God" (trans. mine).[64]

Psalm 1 functions as gate, protecting Israel's sacred hymns against the heresy of substituting liturgy for ethics (see pp. 118-19).

Psalm 2 escalates the wicked of Psalm 1 to whole nations and narrows the righteous individual to the Davidic king. The wicked in Psalm 2 form a cabal of nations at war against *I AM* and against his anointed king, who rules *I AM*'s righteous kingdom. Psalm 1 profiles the cause and consequence of the righteous individual against the wicked; Psalm 2 profiles the cause and consequence of the rebels. The way of the wicked is at war against *I AM*'s rule (Psalm 1) and against his ruler (Psalm 2).

The editor's two introductory psalms prepare those who meditate on his anthology of petitions and praises to interpret the psalms both with respect to the king and to themselves as individuals within his kingdom. The church by its baptism into Christ Jesus is "a royal priesthood, a holy nation" that prays with its king (1 Peter 2:9).

b. Books I and II (Psalms 1–72)

Psalm 2 introduces the Psalter's principal subject, the king in prayer. At the king's coronation he recites a poetic entailment of the Davidic covenant (cf. 2 Sam. 7:14): "You are my son; today I give you birth. Ask of me, my son, and I will give you the heathen for your inheritance and the ends of the earth for your possession" (Ps. 2:7-8). Beginning with Psalm 3 we hear the king's prayers. The king, "the anointed," plays a prominent role not only in this introduction but also at the Psalter's seams, between Books II and III and III and IV. Books I through III are clearly royal, as the colophon of Psalm 72:20 infers.[65] Psalm 72 contains multiple petitions for the king's son: "May he rule justly; may his domain be secure from his enemies; may he live long and be blessed." Wilson argues: "so the covenant which YHWH made with David (Psalm 2) and in whose

63. Childs, *Introduction to the Old Testament as Scripture,* p. 513; Wilson, *Editing of the Hebrew Psalter,* p. 207.

64. Ernst Jenni, "Zu den doxologischen Schlussformeln des Psalters," *Theologische Zeitschrift* 40 (1984): 117f.

65. Wilson, *Editing of the Hebrew Psalter,* p. 208.

promises David rested secure (Psalm 41) is now passed on to his descendants in this series of petitions in behalf of the king's son (Psalm 72)."[66]

c. Book III (Psalms 73–89)

With Book III and its concluding hymn, Psalm 89, a new but dark perspective is achieved. The Davidic covenant is viewed as established in the dim past, and more importantly, now considered as fractured. Wilson says: "The Davidic covenant introduced in Ps. 2 has come to nothing and the combination of three books concludes with the anguished cry of the Davidic descendants."[67] But there is hope!

d. Book IV (Psalms 90–106)

With Book IV yet another perspective is achieved. Without a king, Israel falls back upon its heritage. They look back to Moses, who is now mentioned seven times (90:1; 99:6; 103:7; 105:26; 106:16, 23, 32), whereas heretofore he was mentioned only once (77:20 [21]), and whose only song in the Psalter introduces Book IV. So Israel looks to their eternal king, *I AM:* "O God our help in ages past, our hope in years to come" (cf. 90:1-2). Psalms 93–99, the so-called enthronement psalms, celebrate "*I AM* is king!" He has been Israel's refuge in the past, long before monarchy existed; he will continue to be Israel's refuge now that monarchy is gone; and blessed are they that trust in him.

e. Book V (Psalms 107–150)

Psalm 106:47 concludes Book IV with the petition, "Save us, *I AM* our God, and gather us from the nations," and Book V begins with praise to *I AM* for answering their prayer: "he gathered us from the lands." The troubles of the Exile have been overcome. Two groups of Davidic collections are found in this book: 108–110, and 138–145, which probably serve as a model in response to the concerns of the psalms that precede them. Moreover, there is a prominent Messianic hope in some of these Davidic psalms.

66. Wilson, *Editing of the Hebrew Psalter,* p. 211.
67. Wilson, *Editing of the Hebrew Psalter,* p. 213.

B. Messianism

Within salvation history striking similarities between Israel's persons, events, and situations and Jesus Christ and his church confirm the New Testament's hermeneutic of seeing the Old Testament as a divinely intended type of Jesus Christ and his church, an Authorial intention unknown to the human authors of the Old Testament. So King David and Israel are earthly types of Christ and the church.

1. Term "Anoint"/"Anointed"

The term "Messiah" (Heb. *māšîaḥ*) derives from the root *māšaḥ*: "to paint, smear, sprinkle, daub, anoint" (Ps. 45:7; 89:20). God's Spirit comes upon the "anointed" (*māšîaḥ;* 1 Sam. 2:35; Ps. 84:10; 132:17; *passim*) to qualify and equip him for the task (1 Sam. 10:6; 16:13; Isa. 61:1-3). His anointing with sacred oil designates and appoints him publicly for divine status with divine authority (1 Sam. 10:1; 15:1, 17; 16:1-13; 2 Sam. 2:4, 7; 5:3, 17) and consecrates him as God's property (Exod. 29:7; 40:9-11; Lev. 8:10-11; Num. 7:10-11), entailing his invincibility and divine protection (see Ps. 2:2, pp. 164-65; 1 Sam. 24:6-11; 26:9-24; Ps. 2:10-12; Ps. 105:15; Lev. 10:1-2).

2. Development of Concept of "Messiah" in the Old Testament

a. In the Davidic Covenant

The concept of an ideal king who will rule Israel in the eschaton is rooted in the Davidic covenant, which promised David an eternal house, kingdom, and throne (2 Sam. 7:16, see ch. 23). By divine anointing and the gift of God's Spirit, the king becomes a superhuman divine being, "a son of God," filled with superhuman power and wisdom. Endowed with righteousness (i.e., with ability to rule justly), he defends the people and relieves the oppressed (Ps. 21:9ff.); he is the people's source of strength and life (Lam. 4:20; 2 Sam. 21:7; Hos. 3:4-5; Ps. 72:6, 16). As a priest he is in corporate solidarity with the people and represents them before Yahweh. The concerns of the king are the people's concern; his sin infects the whole nation; he bears Israel's religious and moral ideals and conveys *I AM*'s blessing on the people according to his obedience.

b. In the Prophets

Although the prophets did not use the term "the Messiah," they contributed significantly to the doctrine of a future king that would rule Israel and the world in the last days.[68] For example, Isaiah saw a glorious future son of David ruling over Israel in contrast to corrupt Ahaz (c. 735 BCE); he would be born of a virgin and called "Immanuel" ("God with us," Isa. 7:14). Micah 5:2-6 announces the birth of the humble Messiah at inauspicious Bethlehem and his glorious reign.

So-called Second Isaiah foresaw an anonymous suffering Servant who gives his life as an atonement for sin and after his resurrection assumes his glorious throne (42:1-7; 49:1-6; 50:4-11; 52:13–53:12). God says of him in 52:13, "Behold my servant will act wisely; he will be raised and [then] lifted up and [then] highly exalted." Since the rest of the oracle features his atoning death — *I AM* makes his life a guilt offering (53:10) — "he will be raised" must refer to his resurrection from the dead. His resurrection is then followed by his ascension ("lifted up") and glorification ("highly exalted").

c. In the Royal Psalms

The concept of Messiah was also augmented in the royal ideology of the Psalter. The Psalter's royal ideal was not due to the *Hofstil* of the ancient Near East, as Gunkel claimed, but Israel's genuine hope based on God's covenants. The psalms represent the king visually and *ideally* to the people and were always pregnant with Messianic expectations. Some royal psalms contain ideals that surpass historical reality and give birth to the Messianic expectation: the "anointed" rules to the ends of the earth (2:7-8) and as long as the sun and moon endure (Ps. 72:5). Israel salutes this king who is his sovereign and who sits at God's right hand (Ps. 110:1). On the other hand, some royal psalms — such as the penitential psalms — contain elements that are less than ideal. This is so because discontinuity is a necessary dimension of typology for history to progress. Sacred history progressively rises from the less than ideal toward the

68. Some have been troubled by God's judgment on Jehoiachin son of Jehoiakin. Regarding that king *YHWH* swears, "even if you . . . were a signet ring [i.e., a representation of the owner] on my right hand I would still pull you off [i.e., revoke the Davidic covenant in your case]" (Jer. 22:24). As for Jehoiakin's children *I AM* prophesies, not swears, "Record this man as if childless, . . . for none of his offspring will sit on the throne of David or rule anymore in Judah," yet Jeconiah (i.e., Jehoiakin) is in the lineage of Jesus Christ (Jer. 22:30). *I AM,* in keeping with his character to change his prophecies according to the righteousness or unrighteousness of a person (see Jer. 28), graciously reversed this judgment. He offered to make his servant Zerubbabel son of Shealtiel son of Jehoiakin his signet ring (Hag. 2:23), but this did not take place until Jesus (Matt. 1:12).

ideal. The outward carnal forms of the Abrahamic and Davidic covenants had to fail to make way for the fulfillment of their inward, spiritual perfections.

d. In the Editing of the Psalter

The concept of Messiah was also developed in the editing of the Psalter. In Israel's temple liturgy, the successive heirs of David's throne were draped with the magnificent robes of the psalms, but generation after generation, the shoulders of the reigning monarch proved too narrow and the robe slipped off to be draped on his successor. Finally, in the Exile, Israel was left without a king; and so a wardrobe of royal robes in their hymnody lay waiting, on the basis of God's covenants, for a king with shoulders broad enough to wear them. In other words, the editors of the Psalter re-signified the psalms from the historical king and made them Messianic — that is to say, the eschatological king. More specifically, in the petition psalms the Messiah, like David, suffers before he triumphs. Satan understood Psalm 91, a psalm of confidence, as referring to Messiah — and Jesus did not correct him. Moreover, the so-called enthronement psalms in Book IV must refer in the context of the Psalter's editing to Messiah. *I AM* reigns at the end of the ages in Messiah, not apart from a human agent. In Book V exemplary David finds his fulfillment in Messiah.

Samuel Terrien, commenting on Psalm 21, agrees: "The theology of kingship and divine power had to be re-examined in the light of the historical events. Psalm 21 needed to be interpreted eschatologically. The Anointed One began to be viewed as the Messiah at the end of time."[69] Similarly, the prophets Haggai and Zechariah, who prophesied c. 520, when the returnees had no king, fueled the prophetic expectation of the hoped-for king by applying it to Zerubbabel, son of David, and to Joshua, the high priest. When this hope fell through, Israel pinned its hope on a future Messiah.

An accredited exegesis recognizes this Messianic hue. For example, in the petition psalms the Messiah, like David, first suffers and then enters his glory.

e. Messiah in Later Judaism

The terms *hammāšîaḥ* "the anointed," *mᵉšîḥāʾ* in Aramaic, and *Christos* (Greek) for the eschatological king originate in later Jewish literature. The concept of the Messiah intensified in apocalyptic literature.[70] In this literature the righ-

69. Samuel Terrien, *The Psalms: Strophic Structure and Theological Commentary* (Grand Rapids and Cambridge: Eerdmans, 2003), p. 223.

70. Daniel the man (c. 550 BCE); 1 Enoch (just before 161 BCE); the Syriac Apocalypse of

teous future kingdom of heaven under Messiah is seen as imminently breaking into the evil kingdoms of earth. Here the Messiah becomes strikingly profiled as Israel's coming king who ushers in the righteous kingdom of God at the end of the ages.

The central figure of 1 Enoch is "the Son of man" (cf. Dan. 7:9-14), referred to in 1 Enoch 46:1-3; the chosen One (cf. Isa. 42:1) or the Righteous One (38:2); and the "Anointed One" (52:6). This heavenly figure, who is regarded as having been with God from the beginning (48:3, 6) and remains in God's presence, reveals all things to the elect, is the judge of the world, and the champion of righteousness who destroys the enemies of the righteous.

The Syriac Apocalypse of Baruch refers "my Anointed" (39:7; 40:1; 72:2), "my servant, the Anointed One" (70:9), and "the Anointed One" (29:3; 30:1) to a royal figure who introduces a limited period of complete bliss and incorruptibility. "That time marks the end of what is corruptible and beginning of what is incorruptible" (74:2). The Messiah will reign over the remnant of God's people in the place God has chosen (40:2): "His kingdom will stand forever, until this work of corruption comes to an end and the times appointed are fulfilled" (40:3). When the Messiah's presence on earth has come to an end, he will return in glory, and general resurrection will follow.

In 4 Ezra (= 2 Esdras) the divine agent who finally ushers in after his death the new aeon of incorruptibility, bringing with it resurrection and judgment (7:30-44), is called "my/the Anointed One." In another vision he is likened to a lion, "The Anointed One whom the Most High has kept back to the end of days, who will spring from the seed of David."

Other Second Temple Jewish literature (200 BCE-100 CE), although preoccupied with the priesthood, also makes its contribution to a royal Messiah.[71] Ben-Sirach is clearly interested in God's promises concerning the (high) priesthood in the line of Aaron. He does not neglect God's promises to David, but they do not seem to be relevant. The book of 1 Maccabees was written to legitimize the Hasmoneans' leadership in cultic and political matters as high priests and princes. The Jews and their priests make Simon their leader *(hēgoumenos)* and high priest forever (14:35, 41; vv. 42, 47), and "commander" *(stratēgos)* and "ethnarch" (v. 47). This arrangement will last "until a trustworthy prophet should arise" (v. 41). The book of 2 Maccabees features the intrigues to replace Onias, son of Simon, and his murder. He is clearly thought to be with God in heaven.

Baruch (after the destruction of Jerusalem in 70 CE); Apocalypse of Abraham (some time after 70 CE); 4 Ezra (= 2 Esdras) (c. 100 CE). See Marinus de Jonge, *Anchor Bible Dictionary,* 4, pp. 785-86.

71. De Jonge, *Anchor Bible Dictionary,* 4, pp. 781-83.

The Book of Jubilees features Jacob's blessing of Levi and Judah in 31:13-17 and 18-20 respectively. This passage emphasizes the functions to be exercised by the two patriarchs and their descendants on behalf of Israel. Of Judah it is said: "A prince shall you be, you and one of your sons." Not only the patriarch and tribe are in view but also David and/or a future ideal Davidic king.

The extant Testament of the Twelve Patriarchs achieved its final shape in the hands of Christians, and isolating the earlier traditions upon which it is based remains a hazardous undertaking. The Testaments in their present form are interested in the juxtaposition of Levi and Judah and of the priesthood and of kingship, but the former is superior to the latter. Levi's descendants are, however, singled out as sinners against Jesus Christ (T. Levi 4:4; ch. 10, 14-15, and 16). In 5:2 Levi's priesthood will be limited to the period before God's decisive intervention in the history of Israel. Whenever the Testaments mention an agent of the divine deliverance in connection with these two tribes or with one of them, they mean Jesus.

The Qumran community, which is represented in the writings discovered in the caves at Qumran, was a priestly sect led by Zadokite priests. Under the leadership of their "Teacher of Righteousness" they separated from the Jerusalem temple and the Hasmonean priesthood officiating there. The people at Qumran looked forward to the time when the meaning of the Law would be fully clear and when God would be obeyed completely. A duly appointed high priest and a Davidic prince would then discharge their respective functions properly. As may be expected from a priestly community, of these two the future high priest is the more important figure. When God brings about this decisive turn of events, the final battle against the demonic forces and human enemies would be won.

The authors of the *Psalms of Solomon*, which were written about 50-40 BCE, were clearly opposed to the Hasmoneans, who had not discharged their priestly duties properly and had usurped the high priesthood (8:11) as well as royal authority (17:5-6). They anticipate God's deliverance through a Davidic king (e.g., Ps. Sol. 17:21): "Behold, Lord, rule over Israel your servant." This king will rule as God's representative forever and ever and will free Israel from its enemies, the people in the dispersion will return, and the nations will serve God. The king will serve the Lord as the ideal pious, obedient, and wise man. In 17:32 and 18:5, 7 he is called "The Anointed" and in 18:5, 7 "the anointed of the LORD."

3. *Messiah and the New Testament*

a. Jesus of Nazareth Identified as Messiah

Jesus of Nazareth and his apostles identified the Lord Jesus of Nazareth as the Messiah, combining in his one person the future prophet, priest, and king. With his death, resurrection, and ascension, the temple and its priesthood cease. Jesus is a Priest-King after the order of Melchizedek and the prophet to come like Moses. In fact, he is greater than Moses because Jesus is identified with *I AM*.

The New Testament regards David and Israel, including the priesthood, the representatives of the kingdom of God under the Old Covenant, as types of Christ and his church, the quintessential representatives of the kingdom under the New Covenant arrangements. Of the 283 direct quotes from the Old Testament in the New Testament, 116 (41 percent) are from the Psalter. Jesus Christ alluded to the Psalms over fifty times (see Luke 24:44). In other words, when New Testament writers explicitly cite Psalms, which are written in small letters with reference to David, they write in capital letters with reference to Christ. For example, in Psalm 2:7 "son," with reference to first temple kings, should be glossed in lowercase, "son," but with reference to Christ by uppercase, "Son."[72] The anointed's *fervor* (Ps. 69:9) typifies the Anointed's (John 2:17). The *authoritative teaching* of the psalmist presages the authoritative teaching of Jesus Christ (cf. Ps. 37:11 with Matt. 5:5; Ps. 78:2 with Matt. 13:35; Ps. 78:24 with John 6:31; Ps. 82:6 with John 10:34). The *glory* of the anointed king in the Old Testament becomes the glory of the Anointed King in the New Testament (cf. Ps. 2:1-2 with Acts 4:25-28; 2:7 with Heb. 1:5; 5:5; Ps. 8 with Heb. 2:5-10 and 1 Cor. 15:27; Ps. 16:8-11 with Acts 2:25-31; Ps. 18:49 [50] with Rom. 15:9; Ps. 22:22 [23] with Heb. 2:10-12; Ps. 45:6 [7] with Heb. 1:8-9; 110:1 with Matt. 22:44; 118:22-23 with Matt. 21:42).

The New Testament introduces a realized eschatology, an already and a not yet, fulfillment of prophecy. The Messianic expectation is *fulfilled* in Jesus Christ and his church (cf. Matt. 28:18-20; John 17:2) and *will be consummated* at his Parousia (Second Coming) and the resurrection of his saints in the new

72. Cf. 2:1 with Acts 4:25-26; Ps. 6:3 [4] with John 12:27; Ps. 22:1 with Matt. 27:46; Ps. 22:18 with John 19:24; Ps. 31:5 [6] with Luke 23:46; Ps. 34:20 with John 19:36; Ps. 35:19 with John 15:25; Ps. 40:6 with Heb. 10:5-10; Ps. 41:9 [10] with John 13:18; Ps. 41:9 with John 13:18; 42:6 with Matt. 26:38; Ps. 69:21 with Matt. 27:34, 48; Ps. 109:25 with Matt. 27:39; Ps. 109:8 with Acts 1:20. See Frank Thielman, *Theology of the New Testament* (Grand Rapids: Zondervan, 2005), pp. 185-96. Thielman, however, fails to distinguish sharply enough between the Jewish leaders and the Jewish people. Many of the latter, especially in Galilee, believed in him.

heaven and the new earth (cf. 1 Cor. 15:23-28). The specific predictions of some Psalms that find their fulfillment in Jesus Christ combined with the use of the Psalter in the New Testament suggest that the entire Psalter pertains to Jesus Christ and his church.

But Christ and his apostles radically transform the notion of Messiah from a superhuman figure to revealing he is One who is united with God from eternity past to eternity future. He is the unique Son of God (John 3:16), fulfilling Israel's expectations and exceeding them by as much as the heavens are higher than the earth.[73] Moreover, he came not to satisfy Israel's cravings for a national, political, and even military Jewish restoration, but to transform radically the spiritual temper of the nation by repentance from confidence in both their corrupt priesthood and temple and also their self-righteousness to repentance of sin and trust in Jesus. This difference in understanding between the people's understanding of "Messiah" differed so radically from Jesus' understanding that Jesus used this title *least,* preferring instead the title "Son of Man," in order to avoid confusion.[74]

b. Kinds of Messianic Psalms

1) Indirect and Typical

Some of the psalms cited above are so indirectly typical that the New Testament use of them strongly suggests that all the psalms are a type of Christ. For example, psalms that indirectly speak of Christ include: "my soul is troubled" (Ps. 6:3 [4]), "into your hands I commit my spirit" (31:5 [6]), "they hated me without reason" (35:19), and "my soul is downcast" (42:6). Kidner says: "But a closer look at the way these psalms are handled will suggest that they are regarded as samples of a much larger corpus. It would scarcely seem too much to infer from this treatment that wherever David or the Davidic king appears in the Psalter . . . , he foreshadows to some degree the Messiah."[75] As noted, of course, the anti-type must be greater than the type in order for history to advance. Moreover, whereas the type is the son of God as the heir of the Davidic covenant (cf. John 1:49), Christ is additionally the Son of God by virgin birth (Luke 1:34f.) and by his pre-incarnate glory with the Father (John 17).

73. Thielman, *Theology of the New Testament,* pp. 150-62, 182.

74. Christopher J. H. Wright, *Knowing Jesus Through the Old Testament* (Downers Grove, IL: InterVarsity, 1992), p. 145.

75. Kidner, *Psalms 1–72,* pp. 23f.

2) Typico-Prophetic

David's sufferings and glory typify Jesus Christ, but sometimes his language transcends his own experience and finds its fulfillment in Jesus Christ (e.g., Psalms 2, 22). Psalms of this category include: "they divided my garments among them and cast lots for my clothing" (22:18); "he protects all of his bones, not one of them will be broken" (34:20). Unfortunately, under the impact of HBC, academics restrict the prophetic gift to the dictum of *vaticinium ex eventu* and so undermine the New Testament apologetic (see p. 81).

3) Prophetic?

Some think that Psalm 110 predicts exclusively David's greater Son, for he is greater than David (see Matt. 22:41-46), and envisions the king as seated at God's right hand. Ehrlich argues: "from the OT point of view it was wholly unthinkable, even in metaphor, to describe a mortal as seated on Yahweh's right hand" (trans. mine).[76] Our exegesis, however, leads to the conclusion that it too is typico-prophetic.

4) Enthronement (Psalms 93–99) and Other Psalms

As for the enthronement psalms (see above), they find their fulfillment in the church and their consummation in the coming reign of Jesus Christ in the new heaven and the new earth. As for other psalms, the New Testament identifies the everlasting Creator with Jesus Christ (cf. Ps. 102:25-27 [26-28] with Heb. 1:10-12). The apostles did not hesitate to use the Psalter with reference to their own time (cf. Ps. 34:12-16 with 1 Peter 3:10-12; 55:22 [23] with 1 Peter 5:7; 90:4 with 2 Peter 3:8; 4:4 [5] with Eph. 4:26; 112:9 with 2 Cor. 9:9; 116:10 with 2 Cor. 4:13; 24:1 with 1 Cor. 10:26; 146:6 with Acts 4:24).

VII. Conclusion: Accredited Exegesis

In sum, an accredited exegesis of the Psalter employs the grammatico-historical method as qualified by the traditional approach in contradistinction to the literary-analytical approach, by a judicious use of the form-critical, rhetorical-critical, and cult-functional approaches, and by the canonical-Messianic approach. In sum, we return to Calvin's plain sense of the text approach, appropriately enriched by these new disciplines.

76. A. B. Ehrlich, *Die Psalmen* (Berlin: M. Poppelauer, 1905).

SECTION II

COMMENTARY ON SELECTED PSALMS

CHAPTER 4

Psalm 1: The Rewarded Life

Part I. Voice of the Church

I. Seeking the Presence of *I AM*

As we shall trace, the Psalms invite participation between God and humankind. How some entered into that participation more clearly than others will remain a strong theme of this work. As the prayer book of Israel, the Psalms reflect that deep relationship in manifold ways. The early church experienced that relationship by being drawn into the triune community by the Spirit through the Son to the Father. Being "in the Psalter" now becomes expressive of being "in Christ." A personal encounter with God is the *sine qua non* for all faithful commentary on the meaning of the Psalms. In contrast with the Platonic role of human ascent to the divine, the Psalms celebrate the experiences of divine descent to the needs of the penitent and humble in spirit.[1]

Justin Martyr (see pp. 40-41) is probably the first apologist of the second century to apply the Middle-Platonic term "participation," but it is further developed by Irenaeus, Gregory of Nyssa, and later fathers as a renewed way of living.[2] However, since the available data is fragmentary, its integration with theology is sketchy. As a result, our choice of exemplars is restricted.

Hilary of Poitiers (c. 320-67/68; see chapter 2, pp. 44-45) illustrates vividly how the early fathers approached the Psalter, as indeed all Scripture, as par-

1. David L. Balas, "Christian Transformation of Greek Philosophy Illustrated by Gregory of Nyssa's Use of the Notion of Participation," in George McLean, ed., *Proceedings of the American Catholic Philosophical Association* (Washington, DC: Catholic University of America Press, 1966), vol. 40, pp. 152-57.

2. John Behr, "The Word of God in the Second Century," *Pro Ecclesia* 9 (2000): 85-107.

ticipants of the mysteries of God, and not as the pagan philosophers. "God can only be known by devotion"; He requires "warmth of faith." The knowledge of *I AM* begins with the receptivity of the eternally precedent Being, God. Thus, "only in receiving can we know."[3]

With these premises, Hilary then outlines his theology of the Trinity and enters appropriately into the psalms as a participant. Hilary illustrates well the quest of a wealthy, educated pagan in search of "happiness," or as Psalm 1 puts it, "of being blessed/fortunate." It is natural for human beings to seek leisure and riches, he begins, but these still leave us at the level of merely being animals. He admired the philosophers who had rejected this level in seeking to devote themselves, in an upward quest, to noble deeds and to the virtues of patience, temperance, and meekness. "Preserving one's conscience from every fault," as taught by those "who did not appear to me as fit teachers of a good and happy life," made Hilary skeptical about such a solution.[4] Instead, he confesses, "my soul was enkindled with the most ardent desire of comprehending and knowing God." Reading through the books of the Old Testament, he confesses, "in them I found the testimony of God the Creator about Himself, expressed in the following manner: 'I Am who I Am. . . .' I was filled with admiration at such a clear definition of God, which spoke of the incomprehensible nature in language most suitable to our human understanding."[5] This name of God expresses his eternal reality, without beginning or end. But it also defines the identity of the godly as *a personal participant,* not as *an individual spectator,* of truth.

Likewise, **Augustine of Hippo** (354-430; see pp. 48-50) began to seek after God, yet realizing he remained "far away in the region of unlikeness," he experienced that "from afar, You cried to me . . . 'I AM WHO I AM.' I heard it as one hears a word in my heart, and no possibility of doubt remained to it; I could more easily have doubted that I was alive than that truth exists, truth that is seen and understood through the things that are made."[6]

Yet while Hilary uses the incident of the burning bush to introduce both his teaching on the Trinity and his meditation on Psalm 1, Augustine uses Exodus 3:14 to conclude his short commentary on Psalm 1. Psalm 1:6, "for the Lord knows the way of the godly," is for Augustine a participatory and relational knowledge. Then quoting Matthew 7:23 in speaking of "sinners," "I never knew you," Augustine says: "[this] makes the point that to be unknown to the Lord is to perish, and to be known by him is to remain [alive]. For being corresponds

3. Hilary of Poitiers, *De Trinitate,* trans. Stephen McKenna, C.SS.R. (Washington, DC: The Catholic University of America Press, 1968), p. 4.

4. Hilary, *De Trinitate,* p. 4.

5. Hilary, *De Trinitate,* p. 6.

6. Augustine, *Confessions,* vii, 16, p. 173.

to God's knowledge, and non-existence is not being known of God, for the Lord said, I AM WHO I AM. Thus shall you say to the children of Israel, HE WHO IS has sent me to you (Ex. 3:14)."[7] For Augustine, our true identity, and indeed our life itself, are grounded in this divine assertion.

This distinction between *homo participans* and *homo spectans* was later to be interpreted by **William of St. Thierry** (c. 1085-c. 1147) in the twelfth century at a critical stage of the church.[8] It was cause for the ultimate confrontation and contest in 1141 between Peter Abelard's scholastic "love of learning" and Bernard of Clairvaux's monastic "learning for the love of God."[9] Beyond monasticism, it has remained ever since the contention between the humble devotion of "the godly" and the self-contained "humanist scholar."

II. Psalms as the Microcosm of the Bible

The early fathers thought the Psalms were uniquely the microcosm of the Bible. **Athanasius** (c. 296-373) likens them to the variety within a botanical garden, while **Basil the Great** (c. 329-79) describes them as a great storehouse. For most of the history of the church they were the layman's major Biblical source of faith and devotion. Since this requires critical personal identification, early Christians adopted a Greek form of literary interpretation: the prosopological approach of identifying the speaker and the subject of the literature.[10] With reference to Origen and Hilary of Poitiers, Augustine said: "The ability to discern who the speaker is and for what purpose the words ought to be understood" is the key to their interpretation.

III. Divisions of the Psalter

Christian antiquity knew many ways of organizing the Psalter, but the oldest was to divide it into three groups of fifty psalms each. Hilary of Poitiers favored

7. Saint Augustine, *Exposition of the Psalms*, trans. Maria Boulding, O.S.B. (Hyde Park, NY: New City Press, 2000), vol. 1, p. 70.

8. Thomas Michael Tomasic, "William of Saint Thierry against Peter Abelard: A Dispute on the Meaning of Being a Person," *Analecta Cisterciensia* 28 (1972): 3-76.

9. Jean Leclercq, O.S.B., *The Love of Learning and the Desire for God: A Study of Monastic Culture*, trans. Catharine Misrahi (New York: Fordham University Press, 1974).

10. Marie-Josèphe Rondeau, *Les Commentaires Patristiques du Psautier (III-Ve siècles)*, vol. 2, *Exégèse Prosopologique et Théologique* (Rome: Pontificium Institutum Studiorum Orientalium, 1985).

this as expressive of the economy of salvation: our life on earth "after the flesh"; our life within the kingdom of Christ after our death; and our life eternally within the kingdom of the Father.[11] Augustine of Hippo also favored a tripartite division, but he used the Vulgate notation that the 50th (Heb. 51st) expresses penitence;[12] in the 100th justice meets peace; while the 150th celebrates the glorified eternal life.[13] **Moses bar Kepha** (813-903) even saw the threefold homage as given to the Holy Trinity.[14] Such fanciful deductions are overruled by the Fathers' commoner division into five books, as evidenced by the doxologies at the end of Psalms 41 (LXX, 40), 72(71), 89(88), and 106(105). Psalm 150 then is interpreted as the conclusion of both the fifth book and the whole Psalter. It appears that the first evidence for this division is given in a text attributed to **Origen** (c. 245-49), who also affirmed that this division had a Jewish editorial origin. Jerome had strong reserve against it, as did Athanasius, but Eusebius accepted the division, and it was further endorsed by Gregory of Nyssa.[15] One of the fanciful medieval myths of numerology was cited uncritically by **Honorius Augustodunensis:** "the Psalter was edited by David in five days; and arranged in five books, through five thousand years, redeemed through the five wounds of Christ."[16]

IV. Psalm 1 as the Preface to the Psalter

Ever since Origen's first serious Biblical commentaries (beginning of the third century), Psalm 1 has been interpreted as the introduction to the whole Psalter. **Jerome** (342-420; see p. 46) describes Psalm 1 as *Praefatio Spiritus Sancti,* "the preface [to the psalms] as inspired by the Holy Spirit."[17] He likens the first psalm to the great door of a whole building, of which the Holy Spirit is the key to the great door, while other special keys are also needed for the different rooms of the other psalms.[18] When entering into the Psalms, he challenges the

11. Hilary of Poitiers, *Instructio psalmorum, 11* (pp. 10-11 Zingerle [CSEL xx:11] 1).

12. Jerome followed the LXX, which, unlike MT, treated Psalms 9 and 10 as one psalm, decreasing by one the enumeration of the psalms in the LXX (Vulgate).

13. Augustine, *Enarratio in Psalmos* 150, 3.

14. J.-M. Voste, "L'Introduction de Mose bar Kepa aux psaumes de David," *Revue Biblique* 38 (1929): 225.

15. J.-M. Auwers, "Organisation du psalmier chez les Pères grecs," *Cahiers de Biblia Patristica* 4 (Strasbourg, 1993): 37-54.

16. Honorius Augustodunensis, *Selectorum psalmorum expositio. In inedito ejusdem amplissimo Commentario in Psalmos excerpta* (PL 171:270).

17. Jerome, *Tractatus in librum Psalmos,* Ps. 1, CCL 78, 3.

18. Jerome, *Tractatus in librum Psalmos,* Ps. 1, CCL 78, 3.

reader to have the same spirit as expressed in Deuteronomy 30:15-20. One of his two favorite texts is, "But his delight is in the law of the Lord; and in His law will he exercise himself day and night."[19] This he found impossible to do in Rome, which he left in 385, to take refuge in a grotto in Bethlehem, where Christ was thought to have been born, in order to practice his daily meditation on the psalms.

Remigius of Auxerre (c. 841-c. 908) states: "The first psalm does not have a title, since it is as it were the title of the whole book; for it opens up the whole purpose of how the book ought to be understood."[20] Then he adds, "the object of the whole book is to exhort us to be conformed to Christ through imitation: so that through Him we might return to the highest glory, which having been lost through Adam, we have come into the lowest misery."[21]

The absence of both a title and authorship ascription was repeatedly argued as evidence of Psalm 1's introductory character. **Peter Lombard** (c. 1110-c. 1160), in his succinct way, would give the Psalter the overall title: "Here begins the Book of Hymns or Soliloquies of the Prophet about Christ." In contrast with earlier commentators, who often drew up fanciful reasons for the "five books of Psalms," he asserts that we are dealing with one book. Instead of following Jerome's authority for "five books," he prefers the apostle Peter's statement in the Acts of the Apostles: "Just as it is written in the Book of the Psalms" (Acts 1:20). He then continues: "Accordingly, let us see concerning the first psalm, where it ought to be considered, why a title is not placed above it like the others . . . a title is not given to the first psalm for this reason, that this psalm is the beginning, both the preface and the head of the book, just as it said in the following: 'It is written of me at the head of the book' (Hebrews 10:7). And it treats of that One who is the beginning of all, Christ, who does not have a beginning. For that reason therefore it lacks a title, lest a title written above would be seen as the head and the beginning of the book, or also for that reason, that this psalm was only the introduction of the following work. For it contains the sum and subject matter of the whole book. But the subject matter of this psalm is the same as that found within the whole book, namely the whole Christ."[22]

19. Psalm 1:2; M. J. Rondeau, "Le Commentaire sur les Psaumes d'Évagre le Pontique," *Orientalia Christiana Periodica* 26 (1960): 307-48.

20. Rowland E. Prothero, *The Psalms in Human Life* (New York: E. P. Dutton, 1905), p. 25.

21. Remigius of Auxerre, *Enarrationum in psalmos liber unus* (PL 131:148D).

22. Peter Lombard, *In totum Psalterium commentarii* (PL 191:57D, 58A, 60B), pp. 57-59.

V. A Wisdom Psalm

Justin Martyr (see pp. 40-41), the first of the early Fathers to refer to Psalm 1, interprets the Psalm as expressive of "the present reign of the Messiah."[23] Later, **Diodore of Tarsus** (died c. 394; see pp. 45-46) identifies its genre as *katholikos,* as distinct from other psalms that he regards as "ethical" or "dogmatic." Presumably by *katholikos* he means it has the character of a "wisdom" psalm. Rather than a prayer or a hymn, Psalm 1 is a beatitude, celebrating wisdom. In his opinion, whereas *bārûk* refers to the "blessed source or environment" of the godly, the use here of *'ašrê,* "how blessed that one," specifies the whole social and personal life of experience, given to the wise person, as seen in all aspects of being "alive" before God. This is echoed in Jesus' Beatitudes given in his Sermon on the Mount, where the Word of God Himself teaches us dynamically a whole new way of living. For it is Christ himself who is "the beatific life," and in rejecting him there is only death. Pagan and Christian interpretations of "blessing" or "happiness" are contrasted, though each may conceive of it as a superlative. **Theodoret of Cyrrhus** (393-460; see p. 47) comments: "The epithet 'blessed' therefore constitutes the fruit of perfection as far as virtue is concerned. You see, every practice in life looks towards its goal: athletics looks towards olive wreaths; martial arts towards victories and spoils; medicine certainly towards good health and cure of disease; commerce towards amassing wealth and abundance of goods. Likewise, the practice of [Christian] virtue has as its fruit and goal the beatitude from God."[24]

Jerome, however, unlike his predecessors does not accept the Christological interpretation of the first verse; rather, in his view, it is the portrait of a just man in general. Certainly in Adam's race the malediction continues, but "the just one," exemplified by Abraham, is one who may still sin but at least is willing to repent when he recognizes this. "God may help us to avoid three things and to do two things: we may be compared to the tree of life, and not be evil men who are compared with dust; we ought not to be sinners who will not rise up in the council, because the evil way must perish; we ought to bless God, to whom belongs the glory for ever, Amen."[25] Jerome is not only the learned exegete; he can also be more loosely a homiletic commentator.

Thomas Aquinas (see pp. 56-57) summarizes his commentary on Psalm 1 by stating: "This first psalm expresses the feeling of a man who is lifting his

23. Justin, *1. Apol.* 39-46.

24. Theodoret of Cyrrhus, *Commentary on the Psalms,* vol. 1, p. 47.

25. Jerome, *Tractatus in librum Psalmos,* 11f., trans. René Kieffer, "Jerome: His Exegesis and Hermeneutics," in Magne Saebø, ed., *Hebrew Bible/Old Testament: The History of Its Interpretation* (Göttingen: Vandenhoeck and Ruprecht, 2000) vol. 1/1, p. 677.

eyes to the entire state of the world and considering how some do well, while others fall."[26]

VI. Hilary of Poitiers' Commentary on Psalm 1

Of all the commentaries of the early fathers, that of Hilary of Poitiers (c. 320-367/68) must be considered one of the most exegetically significant. Hilary begins by asking who is "the blessed person" in Psalm 1. To attribute every psalm to Christ, as some did, Hilary argues, is not a judgment based on the truth of rational knowledge (*rationabilis scientiae veritate*). Taking the text itself, he states, it is "not at all appropriate to his [Christ's] persona and dignity." How can "he" have his pleasure in the law of the Lord, when he is himself the Lord of the law? As the "I AM," how can he be "blessed" when he is the source of all blessings? Hilary's conclusion then is that the prophet speaks the words as inspired by the Holy Spirit, "that he might encourage human frailty to a true zeal for worship; . . . to teach the mystery of God; . . . to promise a sharing of heavenly glory; . . . to declare the penalty of judgment; . . . to reveal the difference of the resurrection; . . . to demonstrate the providence of God in his retribution."[27]

Hilary carefully distinguishes the Psalmist's three categories: the ungodly, the sinners, and those who sit in the seat of "pestilence."[28] "Those persons who disdain to seek out knowledge of God are indeed 'ungodly.'" While we are all sinners, there are those who still "walk in the path of sinners," that is, still practice the vices of sin, even within the life of the church. Those "who sit in the seat of pestilence" are those like Pilate who judge politically to guard their own professional ambitions; indeed, those whose priorities are wrong. Yet there are virtuous pagans who might be cleared of all these indictments, and yet they are not "blessed." For it is "pleasure in the law of the Lord" that is the key to such a truly blessed life. It is the exercise of the will, to desire only the will of God, as "he wills to meditate on His law day and night."

In explaining the remainder of the psalm, Hilary reverts to allegory, as the psalmist himself likens "the blessed one" to being like a tree planted by rivers of water. It is an "Edenic" scene, where all life is fructified by the Word of God. As God's Word never fails (Matt. 24:35), the foliage of this tree (who is Christ) will not fall. This, then, is the source of such blessing.

26. Thomas Aquinas, *Commentaire sur les Psaumes,* trans. Jean-Eric Stroobant de Saint-Eloy, O.S.B. (Paris: Les Editions du Cerf, 1996), p. 40.

27. *Sancti Hilarii Pictaviensis Tractatus super Psalmos,* ed. J. Doignon, Corpus Christianorum Series Latina, vol. 61 (Turnhout: Brepols, 1977), 2, p. 20.

28. LXX renders Heb. *lēṣîm* "mockers" by *loimōn* (*loimos,* "pestilence").

In contrast, the punishment meted out to the ungodly is that they will be crushed down into dust. This solemn warning implies that no one can call oneself a "Christian" in levity, or in lacking seriousness of purpose to live by God's word, or indeed from worldly ambition. Abraham's willingness even to offer up his only son Isaac is the standard of Christian ethics that Hilary suggests is implicit in this first psalm. It is absolute and unconditional. "Beatitude . . . is a possession of all things held to be good, from which nothing is absent that a good desire may want."[29] But for Hilary and the other Church Fathers, Christ alone fulfilled that Ultimate Good. For the Christian, then, having a beatific identity is an ongoing living within the Word of God. This was the entry then; and for the rest of the journey of life it was enveloped within the spiritual consciousness of the Psalter.

But Hilary, who was in the process of his own changing identity, now began to see his separation, indeed his alienation from God, for as a sinner he desired and longed to participate in divine things. "My soul, however, was filled with anxiety partly for itself and partly for the body. While it remained unshaken in its devout belief in God, it was gripped at the same time with fear about itself and its dwelling, which it thought was destined for destruction." Then he read John 1:1-14, that through the Word all things were made, and yes, He has come into the world as Man. Now the knowledge of the Father and the Son, and of their divine participation each in the other, gave Hilary hope for his own entry into the Christian life. "By these words my fearful and anxious soul found greater hope than it had anticipated."[30] Then Colossians 2:8-15 assured him: "See to it that no one robs you by philosophy and vain deceit, according to human traditions. . . ." of the Word of God himself.[31] "For this reason my soul was at rest, conscious of its own security and full of joy in its aspirations; it feared the coming of death so little as to regard it as the life of eternity."[32]

VII. Later Latin Fathers

Like Hilary, **Augustine of Hippo's** (354-430) study of the Psalms was the fruit of a very rich pastoral ministry, with frequent sermons each week over a period of some twenty years of ministry during the latter period of his life. His commentary on Psalm 1 is not his best — it is a formal piece, which was written rather

29. Gregory of Nyssa, *The Lord's Prayer, the Beatitudes,* Ancient Christian Writers, trans. Hilda C. Graef (Ramsey, NY: Newman Press, 1953), p. 87.

30. Hilary, *De Trinitate,* 1:11, p. 11.

31. Hilary, *De Trinitate,* 1:13, p. 13.

32. Hilary, *De Trinitate,* 1:14, p. 15.

than preached. Immediately he reminds us that we see everything in the context of the fall of man. When we disregard God's commandments, then pride, wrong doctrine, worldly allurement, all act as a disease or "pestilence" from which the human race cannot cure nor free itself. So Augustine associates "the council of the ungodly" with our first parents; "the seat of pestilence" with the baneful effects of sin in all our lives; and "the way of sinners" with the way of pride. To these three conditions, Augustine distinguishes the order of the verbs: "gone astray" when Adam and Eve drew back from God; "stood" when Man was seduced into sin; and then "sat" when, once established in his pride, he could not return unless he was set free.[33]

He interprets "the blessed man" as "the Lord-Man" or *homine dominico,* referring to Christ's *human nature* only. Then later in other texts he regrets that he ever adopted this view from other commentators. He then fancifully interprets the fruit of the tree as Christ establishing churches. But more critically, he interprets the non-being of the "wicked" to not being known by the Lord who is "I Am Who I Am."[34]

Cassiodorus (c. 490-585) follows Augustine's Christological typology on the psalm, fancifully adding the explanation that Psalm 1 has no heading because Christ himself is the "Beginning," quoting John 8:25 as his support. But he misses the reference to "I Am Who I Am," which his master had observed, as the basis for the eternal quality of the "Blessed." He explicates "thought," "word," and "deed" as the threefold counsel of the ungodly, the way of sinners, and as sitting in the seat of pestilence. Likewise he misses Hilary's emphasis that "the law of the Lord" is not just obedience to the Law but more holistically to the Word of God. So his conclusion is that "the psalm as a whole is concerned with the moral teaching in which a good man is steeped, and by which the wicked minds of sinners are terrified."[35]

Honorius Augustodunensis (died c. 1151) affirms that "the purpose of the whole book [of the Psalms] is to exhort us to be conformed to Christ through imitation, so that through Him we might return to the highest glory, which, having lost through Adam, we have come into the lowest misery."[36] This theme recurs throughout the Middle Ages, reaching its climax in the fifteenth-century movement of *Devotio Moderna.*

33. Saint Augustine, *Expositions of the Psalms,* vol. 1, trans. Maria Boulding, O.S.B. (Hyde Park, NY: New City Press, 2000), p. 67.

34. Saint Augustine, *Expositions of the Psalms,* vol. 1, pp. 67-70.

35. Cassiodorus, *Explanation of the Psalms,* in P. G.Walsh, trans. and ed., *Ancient Christian Writers,* vol. 1 (New York and Mahwah, NJ: Paulist Press, 1990), pp. 45-57.

36. Honorius Augustodunensis, *Selectorum psalmnorum expositio. Ex inedito ejusdem amplissimo Commentario in Psalmos excerpta* (PL 172:269).

Roger Bacon (c. 1214-c. 1292) argues that the church's discernment regarding the virtues and vices, rewards and penalties implicit in Christian doctrine, "is written in the hearts through the church's liturgical practice."[37] The profound influence of monasticism has reshaped Christian morality. He deplores also the lack of liberal arts education that meant young mendicant preachers were ignorant of the rhetorical interpretation of the Scriptures. Yet this too, we should recognize, was not the highly overrated ideal of the *Hebraica veritas,* for scarcely more than a few dozen Christians had any command of Hebrew between 500 and 1500, and less than a quarter of them had any constructive use of Hebrew. Indeed, even the doyen Hebraist, **Nicholas of Lyra** (c. 1270-1349), the most "Jewish" of the medieval Christian exegetes, might not have passed an examination in elementary Hebrew![38] Rather "the literal sense" was itself typological, in referring all the psalms to the life and imitation of Christ. Indeed, it is difficult to overestimate the emotional and spiritual power that the book of Psalms exercised throughout the Middle Ages and far into modern times.[39]

VIII. Renaissance and Reformation Commentators

Desiderius Erasmus (c. 1466-1536) epitomizes all the achievements of the Renaissance movement of Biblical humanism: the revival of philology, with the quest for authentic texts; a renewed pastoral theology; a collapse of the fourfold senses of medieval exegesis into a comprehensive spiritual or mystical sense. His criticism of the church lies in its pastoral failure to support and nurture the spiritual growth of the ecclesial flock, where liturgy had replaced scholarship.[40] The thrust of the Renaissance is now to move "ad fontes!" towards linguistic sources, rather than to traditional devotion. Erasmus formulates two hermeneutical principles that govern his Biblical scholarship: an emphasis on the tropological sense to shape the Christian character, as he states in the *Handbook of the Christian Soldier,* and an appreciation of the role of philology. So in his exposition of Psalm 1 (1515) he notes "that man is blessed who is 'transfigured' and, so to speak, made one with Christ." Thus the tropological method is "more conducive to reforming a man's life."[41] His study of Psalm 1

37. Quoted in Saebø, ed., *Hebrew Bible/Old Testament,* vol. 2, p. 156.

38. Karlfried Froehlich, "Christian Interpretation of the Old Testament in the High Middle Ages," in Magne Saebø, ed., *Hebrew Bible/Old Testament,* vol. 1/2, p. 555.

39. R. S. Wieck, ed., *Time Sanctified: The Book of Hours in Medieval Life and Art* (New York: Braziller, 1988).

40. Wieck, ed., *Time Sanctified,* p. xxxi.

41. Desiderius Erasmus, ASD V-2, 31.20 and 36.87.

was a publishing success, translated into German and Spanish, and reprinted seven times over the next ten years. He recommends the psalms as food for the spiritual life, connecting such spiritual nourishment with meditation, which then leads to transformation. "What I have described as digestion," he says, "Psalm 1 calls meditation," noting that the Latin *meditari* means not to "meditate," but "to practice."[42] But his humanist bias is subtly Pelagian, with little awareness of the presence of the Holy Spirit acting in the process of human transformation.

It is not a coincidence that the first attempt to print a book of the Bible into Hebrew was that of the Psalms at Bologna in 1477.[43] Nevertheless, it is not **Lefèvre d'Étaples** (c. 1450-1536), nor his admirer **Martin Luther** (1483-1546), who can effectively use Hebrew for the "plain meaning of the text." Rather, it is **John Calvin** (1509-64) who becomes the exemplary Reformed exegete. For him, "Scripture cannot be understood theologically, unless it is first understood grammatically."[44]

IX. John Calvin's Commentary on Psalm 1

Unlike Erasmus, who does not see the psalms as exposing the sinfulness of his own heart, John Calvin makes much of his identification with David in all his troubles, temptations, and trials. Within the psalms Calvin sees God as the living God, dynamic in his actions, closely interacting within the affairs of humanity, and who is both within history and constantly making history. For possibly ten or eleven years Calvin preached on the psalms on Sunday afternoons,[45] as well as compiling his commentary on the Psalms in 1557 at the same time as he also was revising his *Institutes* (final edition, 1559). Unlike Augustine's Christological approach to the Psalms, Calvin's thought is fundamentally informed by the doctrine of God, *doctrina de Deo.*[46] For God as the "I AM" is always at the center, keeping a curb on all human speculations. The kindness of

42. Erasmus, ASD V-2, 51.542.

43. Arjo Vanderjagt, "Early Humanist Concern for the *Hebraica veritas*," in Magne Saebø, ed., *Hebrew Bible/Old Testament,* vol. 2, p. 158.

44. John Calvin, *Commentary on the Book of Psalms,* trans. Rev. James Anderson (Edinburgh: Calvin Translation Society, 1895), vol. 1, p. vii.

45. John Calvin, *A Commentary on the Psalms,* ed. T. H. L. Parker (Edinburgh: James Clarke & Co. Ltd., 1965), vol. 1, p. 6.

46. Herman J. Selderhuis, *Calvin's Theology of the Psalms* (Grand Rapids: Baker Academic, 2007), pp. 45-48.

God embraces us in the constant celebration of his mercy, even while uncovering sins we would otherwise hide.

To make progress in the Christian life, Calvin sees it is essential to live within the Psalter, since it combines personal biography with theology. As a singing advocate, Calvin also had immense pastoral influence in the proper liturgical use of the psalms. He sees informed worship as the primary means of Christian growth in sanctification, lifting us above the world into the heavenly realm, where adoration is eternal praise.[47] Thus, for Calvin, the Psalms are the greatest possible antithesis to the humanistic spirit of Stoicism, setting bounds to the exercise of human emotions, and putting God always at the center of our lives, our thoughts, and our desires. There is thus some ground for believing that Calvin's commentary on the Psalms is a pastoral variation of his theological *Institutes.*[48]

Calvin begins his Commentary on Psalm 1 by reminding us that "earnest prayer springs, first, from a sense of our need, and next, from faith in the promises of God."[49] So it is within the Psalms that the Christian is "taught . . . not only how familiar access to God may be opened up to us, but how we may lawfully and freely lay bare before Him the infirmities which a sense of shame prevents our confessing to men. Nay further, here also is prescribed most exactly how we may offer acceptably the sacrifices of praises, which God declares to be most precious in His sight, and of most sweet savor. Nowhere are there read more evident commendations both of God's singular bounty towards his church and of all his works; nowhere are recorded so many deliverances; nowhere are the instances of His fatherly providence and care for us set forth more gloriously; lastly, nowhere is the method of praising God delivered more fully; or are we stimulated more powerfully to render to Him this office of godliness."[50] Calvin thus begins with his awareness of the doctrinal uniqueness of the Psalter.

He then proceeds to disclose how intimately his own personal narrative has been related to the experience of the Psalms within all of his own afflictions and difficulties. For in so many ways he identifies with David.

The first message the psalmist advocates, he sees, is to shun the ungodly. Then in verse 2 he sees that it is from the love of God's word and delight in true doctrine that there will flow the constant study of it, not because of intellectual vanity but from its wholesome truth. The permanence and the fruitfulness of

47. Selderhuis, *Calvin's Theology of the Psalms,* pp. 202-4.

48. Selderhuis, *Calvin's Theology of the Psalms,* pp. 283-85.

49. John Calvin, *Commentary on the Book of the Psalms. Author's Preface,* trans. Rev. James Anderson (Edinburgh: Calvin Translation Society, 1895), vol. 1, p. xxxvii.

50. Calvin, *Commentary on the Book of the Psalms,* vol. 1, p. xxxviii.

such a life are then depicted.[51] But ultimately it is not just by human perception that the instability and fruitlessness of the wicked are discerned. It is God who is the judge of the world, so that seeing everything from his perspective is where we are not deceived. So Calvin concludes with the admonition: "let us in all troubles and turmoil, set before our eyes the providence of God, to whom it belongs to settle the state of the world according to his perfect rule."[52]

Yet, according to the Reformers, by assuming "the wicked" are those who are viciously evil we can also miss the nature of sin. For them "the wicked" included all who live independently of God's Word. Martin Luther in his commentary on Psalm 1 speaks then of "the double sin," of those who justify or minimize the nature of sin,[53] as well as of those living in sin. Likewise, with moral realism, John Calvin realizes how "intermixed" we all are with "the wicked" in our everyday life. So the psalmist employs three metaphors of being in their "counsel," of having their lifestyle or "way," and of hardening the heart in stubbornness in being "seated" with them as "scorners," all to reinforce what "sin" really is.[54]

Interpreting Psalm 1 as the preface to the Psalter, the Puritan **Thomas Watson** (c. 1620-86) describes it as "the Psalm of Psalms, because it contains the vigor and extract of Christianity. It carries blessedness in its architecture."[55] Another Puritan, **Matthew Poole** (1624-79) observes: "Psalm 1 is put first as a preface to all the rest [of the Psalter], as a powerful persuasive to the diligent reading and serious study of the whole book, and of the rest of the Holy Scripture, taken from that blessedness which attends to its study and practice."[56] The life of the faithful will always start with trust in the Creator, obedience to the Savior, and then conclude with praise through the Holy Spirit. The damaging effects of later historical criticism have regressed rather than advanced on such "plain meaning."

An essential abiding value from this historical survey of the exegesis of Psalm 1 is the conviction that the Psalms invite participation between *I AM*, the only eternal Reality, and the mortal.

51. Calvin, *Commentary on the Book of the Psalms*, vol. 1, p. 5.

52. Calvin, *Commentary on the Book of the Psalms*, vol. 1, p. 8.

53. Martin Luther, in Hilton C. Oswald, ed., *Luther's Works* (St. Louis: Concordia, 1978), vol. 1, pp. 11-12.

54. Calvin, *Commentary on the Book of Psalms*, vol. 1, pp. 7-8.

55. Thomas Watson, *Discourses*, vol. 1: *The Saint's Spiritual Delight* (Ligonier, PA: Soli Deo Gloria, 1990, reprint), p. 170.

56. Matthew Poole, *A Commentary on the Holy Bible* (London: The Banner of Truth Trust, 1962), vol. 2, p. 1.

Part II. Voice of the Psalmist: Translation

1 How fortunate[57] are those[58] who do not walk in the counsel of the wicked,
or stand in the way that sinners take
or sit in the seat of mockers;
2 but who delight in the law of *I AM*,
and meditate on his law day and night.
3 They are like a tree planted by streams of water
which yields its fruit in season and whose leaf does not wither.
Whatever they do succeeds.[59]
4 Not so the wicked!
They are like chaff that the wind blows away.
5 Therefore the wicked will not stand in the judgment,
nor sinners in the assembly of the righteous.
6 For the Lord knows the way of the righteous,
but the way of the wicked will end in destruction.

57. *'ašrê* is a nominal exclamation (*IBHS*, p. 674, P. 40.2a) and traditionally glossed as "blessed." Its full notion is "how rewarding is the life of."

58. Although *'îsh* probably refers to an individual male, the poet scarcely intended to exclude a woman. Rabbi David Stein posits that even when *'îsh* refers to a particular individual, it makes a two-pronged reference: one that is direct (to the individual), and one that is indirect (to the group or party with which that individual is affiliated). That is to say, the word *'îsh* serves to relate those two referents to each other. Compared to the conventional views that various senses of *'îsh* extend from a concrete meaning of "adult male" or "human being," his thesis accounts more readily for the many nuances of *'îsh,* and thus is to be preferred to the conventional views. Grammarians of the Hebrew language speak of the masculine gender as "*the prior* gender" because its form sometimes refers to females (*IBHS*, p. 108, P. 6.5.3a). The sages address their sons, yet their wives were involved in the teaching of Israel's youths (see Bruce Waltke, *The Book of Proverbs: Chapters 1-15* [NICOT; Grand Rapids, Zondervan, 2004], pp. 117-18). To that end the daughters also had to be instructed, though no mention is made of them. Since in much of the contemporary English-speaking world "man" no longer has its traditional generic sense, it is best to use inclusive language. Translators are further bedeviled by the lack of a third common singular pronoun to refer to a single antecedent. Consequently they shift to gender-neutral pronouns: "I," "we," "you," and "they," and transform the antecedent appropriately. Readers intuitively recognize themselves as individuals within the group.

59. Interpreted as an internal *Hiphil* (i.e., "causes itself to prosper," *IBHS,* p. 440, P. 27.2f). It could be a two-place *Hiphil:* "he causes all he does to succeed" (cf. Josh. 1:8).

Part III. Commentary

I. Introduction

A. Psalm 1 and Liturgy

As the early fathers saw, Psalm 1 prepares the worshiper of *I AM* to participate in God's eternal life, or better yet, for him to participate with the worshiper with his life (see v. 6). Moreover, it instructs his covenant people in the acceptable way to worship God in singing Israel's liturgy. Moses prescribed a liturgy without music and singing, but David, like a Mozart, transformed that liturgy into opera (see pp. 97-98). Israel's maestro staged that ritual at the temple (Psalm 132), gave it choreography (Ps. 68:24-27), as well as the music and the libretto of the Psalter (1 Chron. 16:4-6; Psalm 150). The Psalter refers to every aspect of Israel's liturgy: its sacred site (Mount Zion, Ps. 2:6), its sacred objects (e.g., the altar, Psalm 26), its sacred seasons (e.g., Ps. 81:3), and its sacred personnel (especially the anointed king [Ps. 2:2] and rarely priests [Ps. 132:16]). The dramatic liturgy represents heaven on earth, and worshipers sing these songs to God and to one another in their personal and passionate relationship with the triune God.

The Bible's understanding of liturgy differs radically from Hegel and postmodernism. Hegel defined liturgy as "the participation of finite existence in essential being (i.e., the realization and enjoyment of true reality)."[60] In his worldview "essential being" or "true reality" connotes a higher realm in which human beings are *natural* participants. So the function of liturgy becomes a process whereby humanity is brought into a fuller manifestation of its true nature. In this view, a person enters into the *true* realm mystically, finding one's true self. Hegel's definition and postmodernism's understanding of "spirituality," however, fail because they do not take into account that God is righteous and humankind is sinful. In the Old Testament, an individual does not enter into the sacred sphere lightly or as a matter of right. There are barriers inherent in the Israelite religion that takes sin into account. This tension between *I AM* and his worshipers is resolved through the covenant and the liturgy. Only cove-

60. Martin J. Buss, "The Meaning of 'Cult' and the Interpretation of the Old Testament," *Journal of Bible and Religion* 32 (1964): 321 [317-25]. Here is Hegel's definition: "This is the general definition of the cultus: it is the eternal relationship, the eternal process of knowing in which the subject posits itself as identical with its essence." Moreover, according to Hegel in that moment of human consciousness the eternal spirit is reunited with itself. W. F. G. Hegel, *Lectures on the Philosophy of Religion,* vol. 1, trans. R. F. Brown, P. C. Hodgson, J. M. Stewart, et al.; ed. Peter C. Hodgson (Berkeley, Los Angeles, London: University of California Press), pp. 188-94, esp. 193.

nant faithfulness and heartfelt participation in the liturgy allow participation in worship. Spiritual performance of the prescribed liturgy "de-sins" and sanctifies the worshiper. God gave Israel instructions for the liturgy (Exodus 25–Leviticus 9:24) only after she confirmed the Ten Commandments and the Book of the Covenant (Exod. 24:3-8). When she reneged on her covenant commitment, God ceased giving instructions for the liturgy and forced her representatives to abandon Mount Sinai (Exodus 32–34). When Israel repented and trusted God's grace (Exod. 34:6), however, liturgical instruction resumed. Similarly, *I AM*'s prophets liken rebellion against the covenant that is papered over with liturgy to the sin of divination (1 Sam. 15:22-23: cf. Isa. 1:11-15; Jer. 7:22-23; Hos. 6:6; Mic. 6:6-8; Matt. 12:7; Mark 12:33; Heb. 10:6-9).

Liturgy inherently tempts people into rigidity and manipulation. Given to magical rituals, some worshipers throughout history have turned religion into a way to get what they want from God. Others have assumed that God is interested only in the proper execution of religious procedures without a corresponding life that is attentive to him.

Psalm 1 anticipates these problems. Before entering the Psalter one must say a hearty "Amen" to Psalm 1; the fortunate person delights in God's catechetical instruction from a regenerate heart. Only the covenant keeper can enter and dwell in God's presence (Psalms 15 and 24), and only the regenerate who delight by faith in the Lawgiver who graciously gave them his Law can enter the congregation of the righteous, who sing the psalms, hymns, and spiritual songs of the Psalter. The fear of *I AM* is the key that opens the book of Proverbs (1:7), and a resonating "Amen" to Psalm 1 is the straight and narrow gate into the Psalter. In this sense, Psalm 1 is "the main entrance to the mansion of the Psalter,"[61] or to change the figure, the Wicket Gate that gave Pilgrim entrance to the Way that leads to the celestial city.

B. Author

The author of the preface to the Psalter is anonymous, but we can infer important truths about him. First, he is a true covenant partner with *I AM*. On the one hand, he confesses *I AM* as his God and proves himself regenerate because he delights in the Law; the unregenerate do not welcome God's Law. On the other hand, he trusts God to be faithful to his covenants. Perhaps he or an edi-

61. Jerome, *The Homilies of St. Jerome*, trans. Sister Marie Liguori Ewald, I.H.M., The Fathers of the Church, vol. 48 (Washington, DC: The Catholic University of America Press, 1964), vol. 1, p. 3.

tor other than himself — date of the psalm is unknown[62] — placed the psalm at the head of the Psalter to teach that, despite the oppression of the pious expressed in many psalms, in the end God will reward the just.

Second, he is inspired, for he speaks with the authority of God. He proclaims covenant keepers are blessed (Heb. *'ašrê*, Greek *makarios;* see n. 57) and speaks with the same authority as the Lord Jesus Christ who called people who belong to his kingdom *makarios* ("blessed are"). He speaks authoritatively of a future judgment of the wicked and salvation of the righteous, and he knows that those who are not "known" by God will perish.

A segue into the nature of the psalm's inspiration is appropriate here. In times past, *I AM* spoke in various ways to his people: to Moses, the founder of the holy nation, he spoke in theophanies (i.e., in face-to-face appearances); to prophets, in visions and auditions, and in the psalms through meditations and songs of charismatic saints in need and trusting God. By collecting these psalms and including them in the canon of Scripture, the elect's words to God were made God's word to the elect to be reflected upon.

Third, he is a sage, as Diodore of Tarsus (c. 330-c. 390) early recognized (see above). Inspired sages pronounce their son-students *'ašrê* ("fortunate," traditionally, "blessed," Ps. 1:1; cf. Prov. 3:13, 18). Also, they commonly argue from cause to consequence (see outline below), use the metaphor of "way" for that notion (vv. 1, 6),[63] use images from nature, such as tree and chaff, to instruct (vv. 3-4), and only sages speak of "mockers" (v. 1). It is a fair inference that our anonymous poet has the circle of charismatic wise ones as his peers.

Fourth, he is a literary artist. His teaching-poem is as full of designs as Belgian lace. He stitches back and forth from positive virtue (+) to negative vice (-): -(v. 1), +(v. 2), +(v. 3), -(v. 4), -(v. 5a), +(v. 5b), +(v. 6a), -(v. 6b). His first three verses profile the righteous against the wicked, and his last three, the wicked against the righteous. Striking contrasts abound between them from the first word, "rewarded" (of the righteous), to the last word, "perish" (of the wicked). James Waltner diagrams the contrasts:

Verses	*Subject*	*Characterization*	*Focus*	*Like*	*Fate*
1:1-3	righteous	Blessed!	Teaching	tree	prosper
1:4-6	wicked	Not so!	Counsel	chaff	perish

Others discern a chiastic pattern in the poet's images:

62. See J. H. Eaton, *Psalms of the Way and the Kingdom: A Conference with the Commentators* (JSOTSup 199; Sheffield: Sheffield Academic Press, 1995), p. 39.

63. N. C. Habel, "The Symbolism of Wisdom in Proverbs 1–9," *Int* 26 (1972): 137; Bruce Waltke, *Proverbs 1–15* (Grand Rapids: Eerdmans, 2004), p. 193.

A. Description (and fate) of the righteous: **way**		1-2
	B. Simile of the righteous: **tree**	3a-b
	C. Objectifying conclusion: **success**	3c
	C′ Objectifying introduction: **lack of success**	4a
	B′ Metaphor for the wicked: **chaff**	4b
A′ Description (and fate) of the wicked: **way**		5-6

Others discern couplets, which is the structure followed here.

C. Structure

I. Cause of the Blessed Life	1-2
A. Renouncing Sinners	1
B. Meditating in Law	2
II. Consequences of the Blessed and Non-Blessed Pictured	3-4
A. Verdant Tree	3
B. Windblown Chaff	4
III. Consequences Plainly Stated	5-6
A. Judgment of Wicked; Salvation of Righteous	5
B. *I AM* Watches over Righteous. Wicked Perish	6

The symmetry, the cadenced rhythm and beauty of the poem, delight the altogether Beautiful One and enthralls his audience. The poet does not specify his audience because he assumes that the five books that comprise the Psalter belong to the covenant community. What he did not know, however, is that Gentiles through the church would be grafted into Israel's covenants.[64] The psalms belong to each individual within the kingdom of God.

II. Exegesis

A. Cause of the Rewarded Life vv. 1-2

1. Renouncing Sinners v. 1

The poet's first three Hebrew words have a memorable assonance of initial *'aleph /'/: 'ašrê 'îsh 'ᵃsher.* Sages reserve the laudatory exclamation *fortunate*

64. Bruce K. Waltke with Charles Yu, *An Old Testament Theology* (Grand Rapids: Eerdmans, 2007), pp. 325-32.

(*'ašrê*, see n. 57) or "how rewarding"[65] for people who experience life optimally, as the Creator intended. W. Janzen notes that the largest number of these twenty-six pronouncements have the near or distant future in view, but that future depends on a present relationship with God by covenant fidelity.[66] Eliphaz calls those whom *I AM* disciplines *'ašrê* (traditionally, "blessed" [Job 5:17]), and the Lord Jesus calls "blessed" the poor in spirit, mourners, the meek, the hungry and thirsty for righteousness, the merciful, the pure in heart, peacemakers, and those who suffer for righteousness (Matt. 5:3-12). The pronouncement does not confer blessing — that notion belongs to Hebrew *bārûk* — but serves to hold up a human being as a model before the addressee to be envied. In this case the individual models the kind of person that enters into God's liturgy and who has the assurance of arriving safely at the celestial city. The rest of the psalm shows clearly that the righteous are called "fortunate" because of their future hope. The wicked will perish at the time of God's judgment like wind-driven chaff, but the righteous will endure like an ever-green fruit tree because God knows them. The popular, modern rendering of *'ašrê* as "happy" conceals both that suffering saints are fortunate and that the focus is on life that outlasts clinical death.

The "fortunate" do not walk in step with the "wicked," "sinners," "mockers." The *wicked* (*rᵉšāᶜîm*, vv. 1, 5, 6), according to K. H. Richards, are the guilty and always spoken of in terms of a community.[67] *Rašaᶜ* is the antonym of *ṣedeq* ("righteousness," faithfulness to the community [see vv. 5, 6]).

"In contrast to the positive root *ṣdq*, *ršᶜ* expresses negative behavior — evil thoughts words, and deeds — antisocial behavior that simultaneously betrays a person's inner disharmony and unrest (Isa. 57:20)."[68] If the righteous advantage the community, even at the expense of disadvantaging themselves, then the wicked advantage themselves by disadvantaging the community who live according to God's order.[69] In other words, the wicked push and shove to get their way. As for its synonym, *sinners*, despite Koch's objection, the meaning of *ḥṭ'* is "miss [a mark]," "fall short." This concrete meaning is attested alongside its familiar religious meaning of "sin" (Judg. 20:16; Job 5:24; Prov. 8:36; 19:2). *Ḥṭ'* is used in all sorts of circumstances for disqualifying error.[70]

Its synonyms etymologically also assume a violated standard: *pešaʿ* "re-

65. M. Brown (*NIDOTTE*, 1:571, *'ašrê*) defends the gloss "how truly happy."

66. W. Janzen, "'Ašrê in the Old Testament," *HTR* 58 (1965): 223.

67. K. Richards, "A Form and Traditio-Historical Study of *ršʿ*" (Ph.D. diss., Claremont, CA, 1970; cf. *ZAW*, 83:402).

68. C. van Leeuwen, *TLOT*, 3:1262, s.v. *rsᶜ*.

69. Waltke, *Proverbs*, pp. 109f.

70. M. Saebø, *TLOT*, 1:406-8, s.v. *ḥṭ'*.

bel," and *ʿāwōn,* "iniquity," "guilt." That standard is *I AM*'s teaching through conscience and special revelation. "Sin is usually described as being against God or disobeying God's word (cf. Ps. 51:4 [6])."[71] However, since one's relationship to God and the community are inseparable, this comprehensive theological term for "sin" also refers to a disqualifying offense "against someone with whom one stands in an institutionalized community relationship."[72] The nominal pattern of *ḥaṭṭāʾîm (sinners)* signifies an occupation or a repeated action.[73]

The most hardened apostates are the "mockers" *(lēṣîm),* a word that occurs fourteen times in Proverbs and twice outside of it (Ps. 1:1; Isa. 29:20, a wisdom pericope). The noun, "mocking" *(lāṣôn),* occurs three times in the Old Testament (Prov. 1:22; 29:8; Isa. 28:14). The mocker is the antithesis both of the wise (Prov. 9:12; 13:1; 20:1; 21:24), whom he hates (9:7-8; 15:12), and of the discerning (14:6; 19:25); he or she is lumped together with fools (1:22; 3:34-35; 14:7-8; 19:29), gullible (1:22); they are proud and haughty (21:24). Their spiritual problem is rooted in their overweening pride (21:24). Supercilious arrogance blocks them from wisdom (14:6). They have a genius for invective and denigration that impresses the gullible as long as they have their way (19:25; 21:11). They open their big mouths and, unleashing the tensions and strains in a community, set the whole community at loggerheads (22:10; 29:8) and destroy it (21:24; 22:10; 29:8). Their bad influence is plain to most (24:9). "No man earns more universal detestation or deserves it more than he who wears a perpetual sneer, who is himself incapable of deep loyalty and reverence and who supposes that it is his mission in life to promote the corrosion of the values by which individuals and society live."[74] To restore order they must be driven out of the community by force (22:10). God himself ultimately scoffs at them, and so they will disappear (Isa. 29:20).

The dominant metaphor in this psalm and in Proverbs is *derek* ("way").[75] Woodenly, *derek* denotes a traversable road and infers "walking" on a road that leads to a destination. In its figurative sense "way" evokes three notions: 1) "course of life" (i.e., the character and context of life); 2) "conduct of life" (i.e., specific choices and behavior); and 3) "consequences of that conduct" (i.e., the

71. A. Luc, *NIDOTTE,* 2:87-88, s.v. *ḥṭʾ.*

72. K. Koch, *TDOT,* 3:272-73.

73. *IBHS,* p. 89, P. 5.4a.

74. W. McKane, *Proverbs: A New Approach* (Philadelphia: Westminster, 1970), p. 399.

75. *Derek* ("way" or "highway") occurs about 710 times in the OT, 75 times in Proverbs, and 30 times in Proverbs 1–9 (see N. C. Habel, "The Symbolism of Wisdom in Proverbs 1–9," *Int* 26 [1972]: 137, n. 13; and D. Dorsey, *The Roads and Highways of Ancient Israel* [Baltimore: Johns Hopkins University Press, 1991]).

inevitable destiny of such a lifestyle).[76] In short, "way" is a metaphor for the deed-destiny nexus (see outline above). Koch says: "A man's deeds cling to him as it were, wrapping themselves around him in an invisible domain, which one day is transformed into a corresponding condition or state, and then recoils on the doer."[77] This is so, but Koch wrongly thinks that it is so apart from divine interference. Verses 5 and 6 make clear that *I AM* upholds this moral nexus.

Implicitly, the wise poet warns his audience against even setting foot on this way lest they become hardened in sin (cf. Prov. 1:15; 4:14-15). He accelerates patterns of sinful behavior from *ʿēṣâ* ("counsel"), a pattern of thinking, to *derek* ("way"), a pattern of behavior, to *môšāb* ("sitting"/"seat"), a pattern of identification. At the same time he slows the pace down with each stage of degeneration, beginning with *hālak* ("walking"), slowing down to *ʿāmād* ("standing"), and finally to *yāšāb* ("sitting").

Alexander Pope's couplet is apt: "Vice is a monster of so frightful mien, as to be hated needs but to be seen. Yet seen too oft, too familiar that face, we may first endure, then pity, then embrace." We are old enough to remember a Western world when homosexuality was a vice of so frightful mien as to be hated on sight. But then the West pitied that behavior; then treated it as a sickness, and finally the president led the United States to embrace it as a viable lifestyle. The Western nations are becoming hardened in sin and are being cut off from the olive tree of blessing. The Greek god, the Medusa, had a face so hideous that it turned hearts to stone. Many Christians have "Medusas" in their living rooms, hardening their hearts to sex and violence. Robert Louis Stevenson captured this truth in his well-known fiction, *Dr. Jekyll and Mr. Hyde.* Dr. Jekyll made a concoction that when he drank it turned the kindly doctor by day into the diabolic Mr. Hyde by night. Dr. Jekyll became more and more addicted to his potion until finally he turned into Mr. Hyde without even drinking his brew. Evil took over, triumphed, and destroyed him.

76. The three inseparable notions pertain as well to its synonyms: *ʾōraḥ* (1:19; 2:15, 19, 20; 3:6; 4:18; 5:6; 9:15); *maʿgāl* (Prov. 2:9, 15; 4:11), *nᵉtîbâ* (7:25; 8:2, 20). *ʾŌraḥ* ("path") is virtually poetic — possibly apart from its metaphorical use in Genesis 18:11, 56 or 57 times in poetry — synonymous with *derek,* signifying the route, not some secondary path in the woods, the traveler has selected. It was not used in everyday speech. *Maʿgâl* ("track") seems to derive from the route marked out by wagon wheels (see 2:9, 15). Tracks are when men travel in the course of their labors. *Nᵉtîbâ* ("byway") seems to allude to a byway rather than a highway (Jer. 18:15; Judg. 5:6), "a passage" rather than an open road (Hos. 2:8; Job 18:10). Though *ʾōraḥ* is a poetic synonym for *derek,* Koch notes several ways in which they differ. First, *ʾōraḥ* occurs predominantly in the plural, *derek* predominantly in the singular. Second, a *derek* can be composed of several *ʾorāḥôt* (cf. Isa. 3:12). Finally, *ʾōraḥ* emphasizes more the state or condition of the wayfarer than his actions (Koch, *TDOT,* 2:281, s.v. *derek*).

77. K. Koch, *TDOT,* 3:272-73, s.v. *derek.*

2. *Meditating in Law v. 2*

The long delay of three negatives — the anaphora having a peculiar emphasis — frustrates the audience's appetite for a positive definition of *'ašrê* and makes the fulfillment in verse 2 more intense and satisfying. Instead of following the counsel and behavior of guilty sinners and scoffers, the "rewarded" delight in the Law (Heb. *tôrâ,* literally "catechetical teaching"). *I AM* authors his teachings out of his sublime nature. Some suggest that the catechetical teaching in view is Israel's hymns transformed into texts for meditation. Elsewhere in the Psalter, however, *tôrâ* in similar contexts refers to the covenant God gave Israel at Sinai (Ps. 19:7; Ps. 119:1, *passim*). This normal meaning is most appropriate as a preface to the book of Psalms. The regenerate delight in the *Torah* because it is the God-given structure and order that speaks of Christ and frees from sin and death; for the unregenerate it is an oppressive burden of "Thou shalt nots." Whoever delights in the Word of Scripture will delight in the *Logos* ("Word") of God, Jesus Christ, who fulfills Scripture and to whom it points.

This teaching is from *I AM,* the name that thrilled the pious and profoundly thoughtful Hilary and Augustine. In Exodus 3:14 God gives the etymology of his name *yhwh* ("I AM") and its meaning by revealing his full sentence name: *'ehyeh ᵃšer 'ehyeh* (glossed in TNIV as "I AM WHO I AM").[78] God abbreviates his full sentence name to a single verb: "*'ehyeh*" ("I am/will be").[79] In verse 15 God changes his abbreviated name from the first person *'hyh* to the third person *yhwh* ("*HE IS* has sent me") because the first person is appropriate only in God's mouth and the third person is appropriate in Israel's mouth when

78. Typically in the ancient Near East names are full sentences reduced to one word and/or a play upon the birth situation. Scholars not necessarily basing themselves on the Biblical text have not reached a consensus. For a survey of interpretations since 1700 see *Lexicon in Veteris Testamenti libros,* ed. L. Köhler and W. Baumgartner (Leiden: Brill, 1951), pp. 368f. Until 1957 see Rudolf Mayer, "Der Gottesname Jahwe im Lichte der neuesten Forschuung," *BZ* 2 (1958): 26-53; F. M. Cross, "Yahweh and the God of the Patriarchs," *HTR* 55 (1962): 251, note 116. Further, E. C. B. MacLaurin, "YHWH, The Origin of the Tetragrammaton," *VT* 12 (1962): 439-63. O. Eissfeldt, "Jahwe, der Gott der Väter," *TLZ* 88 (1963): 481-90; J. Lindblom, "Noch einmal die Deutung des Jahweh-Namens in Exod 3:14," *ASTI* 3 (1964): 4-15; H. Cazelles, "La révélation du Nom divin," *Assemblées du Seigneur* 12 (1964): 44-59; O. Eissfeldt, "Ähᵉyäh 'ašär 'ähᵉyäh und 'El 'ôlām," *FuF* 39 (1965): 298-300; W. Weidmüller, *Der rätselhafte 'JHWH, Archiv für Geschichte Buchwesens* 6, 5s (Frankfurt am Main, 1966). F. M. Cross considers Yahweh as a splitting off from El in the radical differentiation of his cult.

79. W. von Soden came to a similar conclusion by relating *YHWH* to the group of *Danknamen* as, for example, old Canaanite *ahwi-ilu* ("That God is"). If so, this evidence shows philologically that the name had been in use before the time of Moses.

they invoke/mention God's name.[80] So the meaning of the two shortened forms, *'hyh* and *yhwh,* depend on the meaning of the sentence name, *'ehyeh 'ᵃšer 'ehyeh.*

The verb *'ehyeh* comes from the Hebrew hollow root *hyh* (or *hwh*), whose meaning roughly correlates with the English verb "to be." The root may have a stative sense ("I am") or an active sense ("I happen/become"). These two senses are frequently attenuated in usage. The active sense sometimes occurs in the suffix conjugation (normally past tense), as in Exodus 7:10 where "Aaron cast his staff before Pharaoh and his people and it *became* [*hyh*] a serpent." In our text, the verb is in the prefix conjugation (indicated by the first /'e/ of *'ehyeh*), which designates either future tense "will be" (i.e., "I will be what I will be") or a stative present, "I am who I am." *I AM*'s preceding response to Moses in 3:12, "I am/will be *('ehyeh)* with you," favors an attenuated sense, with no sharp distinction between the two tenses. In the prefix conjugation, the active and stative senses become attenuated in curse and blessing formulae or in a wish for actualization: The word of *I AM* will *be/become* effective in the way predicted or wished for. Thus God says to Abraham: "you *will be/become* a blessing" (Gen. 12:2). A similar sense occurs in prophetic oracles to describe events embodying *I AM*'s personal intervention (e.g., "For Gaza *will be/become* desolate" (Zeph. 2:4). The sense of something that happened or will happen due to God's miraculous and/or personal intervention fits the context. In legal prescription, *hyh* dictates the relationship of the covenant people to God, to others, or to the environment (e.g., "anything [in the seas or in the rivers] which does not have scales . . . *shall be* to you an abomination" Lev. 11:10), but Exodus 3 does not per-

80. Maimonides said: "His name is pronounced as it is written." His point: God's written name is all consonants — *yhwh* — and cannot be pronounced. Until about 500 CE the Hebrew written text was mostly consonantal and the Hebrew oral tradition preserved the text's vocalization. In the case of *yhwh,* however, during the Second Temple period, scribes and rabbis read *'ᵃdōnāy* ("Lord") or *haššēm* ("the Name") with the Tetragrammaton, probably to be wary of attaching God's name to something *šaw'* "false" (see Bruce Waltke with Charles Yu, *An Old Testament Theology* [Grand Rapids: Zondervan, 2007], ch. 15). The combination of two traditions led to the mistaken reading "Jehovah." In any case, as a result the oral reading of *yhwh* was lost. (Most of the Dead Sea Scrolls out of reverence write the *tetragrammaton* in the archaic Hebrew script, not the contemporary Aramaic script, just as some in the contemporary church retain "thee" and "thou" with reference to God.) Most scholars, but only a few contemporary English translations, depending upon the shortened form of *Yah* (as in Elijah, "my God is Yah"), reconstruct the first syllable as *yah* and the second syllable, on the basis of Exodus 3:14, as *yahweh.* This historical reconstruction, however, is speculative because *yah* can be the old Qal prefix of the root *hy/wh,* but the form attested in first person is *'eh,* whose equivalent in third person is *yih,* not *yah.* Moreover, the final *e* may be a late phonological addition. Since God in his providence did not preserve the pronunciation, I opt to translate the Tetragrammaton, *yhwh,* "He is," in its first person form, *"I AM,"* not by the invention "Yahweh."

tain to legal prescription. In covenant formulae, *hyh* describes the relationship of the covenant partners, obligating each to a particular behavior (e.g., "I will be your God and you will be my people," Jer. 7:23; cf. 2 Sam. 7:14).

The pronoun *ʾᵃšer* introduces a relative clause qualifying *ʾehyeh* (i.e., *I AM the one who I AM*) — that is to say, God's nature is both mystery and defined by Scripture as the Holy One without mixture: pure being without dependence; pure power without limitation; pure love without self-regard; et cetera.[81] God defines who he is when Moses asks him to show his glory: "I AM, I AM, the compassionate and gracious God, slow to anger, abounding in love and faithfulness, maintaining love to thousands, and forgiving wickedness, rebellion and sin. Yet he does not leave the guilty unpunished; he punishes the children and their children for the sin of the parents to the third and fourth generations" (Exod. 34:6-7). The forgiven are those that turn to him and by faith accept his grace; the guilty are those that spurn his grace. Had he intended to say "I will become what I will become," we might expect the sign of direct object *ʾet* as in Exodus 33:19, "*ḥannōtî ʾet ʾᵃšer ʾāḥōn wᵉriḥamtî ʾet ʾᵃšer ʾᵃraḥēm*" — "I will have mercy on whom I will have mercy and I will show compassion on whom I will show compassion."[82]

In its function God's name suggests his pragmatic presence. This sense of God's being can be captured in the English phrase, "I am who I am for you." His simplicity shows there is no shadow of variability in him. God is dependable; he can be counted upon.

81. Waltke, *An Old Testament Theology*, ch. 17, pp. 445-511.

82. Scholars and translators have offered various options for interpreting this name. Because of its ambiguity, some think the form is deliberately enigmatic to prevent magical manipulation. This explanation harkens back to the mythic notion that knowing the names of deities allows magicians to use incantation to control or manipulate them. But though the Name entails mystery, this interpretation is unlikely, for it would not reassure Moses and Israel to throw themselves into the teeth of the dragon. The same objection calls into question the interpretations of "I am who I am" with the connotation, "What does that matter to you?" (C. Houtman, *Exodus*, trans. J. Rebel and S. Woudstra [Kampen: Kok, 1993-1999], 1.367) and of P. Enns's, "They know very well who I am. What a question!" (*Exodus*, pp. 102-3). Bruce Boston ("How Are Revelation and Revolution Related?" *Theology Today* 26 [July 1969]: 143 [142-55]) emphasizes the fully active sense of *hāyâ* in his interpretation: "The God of Israel is the one who 'happens' with his people, the one who, when he presents himself, does so as an event and in events." The emphasis of this approach is that the name of God focuses on his actions. But the notion "he becomes what he becomes" could have a transmogrifying sense, not inspiring confidence in him. Also, the preceding statement, "I am with you" *(ʾehyeh ʿimmāk)* in the same historical and literary contexts validates the stative sense of *hyh* and calls into question introducing ambiguity by adding the active sense of *hyh*. The Septuagint glosses the sentence name in 3:14 simply by, "I am the Being" *(ho Ōn)*. Indeed, God is the uniquely true Being, but it is somewhat unclear how this philosophical statement about God's being provides Moses with the reassurance he is asking for. It seems too philosophical, too abstract, too Greek — not a Hebraic thought.

Delights in (*b*^{e} . . . *ḥepṣô,* "his delight is in") denotes a psychic feeling of pleasure and expresses a person's affection for another. When a person *meditates* (*hgh,* etymologically "to utter inarticulate sounds") on *I AM*'s torah *day and night,*[83] a figure for constancy, one is transplanted from one's ego-centered world into a God-centered world that serves others.[84] Paraphrasing Edmund P. Clowney, *C[hristian] M[editation],* in contrast to T[ranscendental] M[editation], is directed by the truth (i.e., word) of God, derived from delighting in God and directed to the praise of God.[85] Delighting and meditating[86] in *Torah* are metonymies of cause, assuming the effect of living according to *Torah* — that is to say, in the way of righteousness. The metaphor, "the way of the righteous," in verse 6a includes behavior (see "way" [*derek,* vv. 1, 6]).

Since, as Augustine emphasized, all are mired in sin and by nature cannot welcome the things of God (1 Cor. 2:14), the repentant who renounce their self-centered lives must be born of God. Sinners can no more change their reptilian nature than a leopard can change its spots. "Every good and perfect gift is from above, coming down from the Father of the heavenly lights," says James (1:17). Paul calls faith an abiding virtue (1 Cor. 13:13) and part and parcel of God's gift of salvation (Eph. 2:8). Whoever so love God's words that they keep returning to it as to the fragrance of sweet-pea have the new covenant written on their heart (Jer. 31:31-34). Such a person delights in an active obedience to the One who can fulfill this beatific vision. In short, the new covenant through faith in Christ is the basis of being called "blessed" and the *sine qua non* for entering the Psalter.

83. A merismus is a figure of speech that employs a topic's opposite extremes to denote its totality.

84. "Labour to remember what you read [cf. Matt. 13:4, 19]. . . . The memory should be like the chest in the ark, where the Law was put. . . . Some can better remember an item of news than a line of Scripture; their memories are like these ponds, where frogs live, but the fish die. . . . In meditation there must be a fixing of the thoughts upon the object. . . . Meditation is the concoction of Scripture: reading brings a truth into our head, meditation brings it into our heart: reading and meditation must, like Castor and Pollux, appear together. Meditation without reading is erroneous; reading without meditation is barren. The bee sucks the flower, then works it in the hive, and so turns it to honey: by reading we suck the flower of the Word, by meditation we work it in the hive of our mind, and so it turns to profit. Meditation is the bellows of the affection: *'while I was musing the fire burned'* (Ps. 39:3). The reason we come away so cold from reading the Word is because we do not warm ourselves at the fire of meditation." Thomas Watson, *Puritan Sermons,* vol. 2, pp. 61-62.

85. Edmund P. Clowney, *CM: Christian Meditation* (Vancouver: Regent College Publishing, 2002; first published by Craig Press, Nutley, NJ, 1979).

86. For a helpful discussion on meditation, see Edmund P. Clowney, *Christian Meditation* (Vancouver: Regent College Publishing, 1979).

B. Rewarded and Non-Rewarded Lives Pictured vv. 3-4

1. Verdant Tree v. 3

The poet now arouses his audience's envy to be among the blessed by an arboreal image. Those who turn aside from the wicked and are charmed by God's teaching and guidance are *transplanted (šātûl)* from the arid dust of the world into a garden by *streams* (*palgê,*[87] "channels") *of water,* an incomplete metaphor for the Law. KBL define *peleg* as an "artificial water channel, canal" (cf. Sirach 48:17).[88] Water is especially precious in the parched Near East. Aside from Lamentations 3:48 and Psalm 119:136, *peleg* always connotes positively the channeling of abundant, gladdening, life-giving water in an otherwise dry place. Whereas a river *(nāhār)* might run wild and a wadi *(naḥal)* run dry, the "streams" of water provide a steady, directed, full supply of life-giving water. The incomplete metaphor is expanded in v. 3b to include its fruit and leaf. *Yields* (*ntn,* literally, "gives") connotes the character-conduct-consequence connection implied by the metaphor "way" (see above). To judge from the rest of the psalm, *its fruit* probably refers to the rewards of righteous living vis-à-vis eternal life in a future that outlasts God's judgment on the wicked (vv. 5-6). When his truth is ingested with passion, it leads to true godliness. *In its season* refers to the appropriate time according to *I AM*'s calendar. The sustained arboreal metaphor, *its leaf (ʿālēhû) does not wither* (*loʾ-yibbôl,* literally, "fall"), connotes that before the time when virtue is rewarded and evil is punished, the righteous enjoy eternal life. That life survives in spite of the drought of deprivation and suffering. God's eternal life in those who sink their faith-roots deep into his spirit through his word can never perish.

The Law covers every aspect of human life: toward God, others (friend and foe), and self (health and wealth). *Whatever* (literally, "all that") *they do* includes all that. *Succeeds* (*yaṣlîaḥ,* often "prosper"; see n. 3) glosses a root whose concrete meaning is "to penetrate." Saebø says: "The same concept seems to shine through in uses of causative hi[phil]. To state that God causes someone's way on a journey to 'progress,' 'reach the goal' (i.e., succeed)."[89] The line, which has intertextual links with Joshua 1:8, puts into plain language the intention of the figure of an ever-green fruit tree. The truth and explanation that this kind of person reaches the goal reinforces our definition of *ʾašrê* ("rewarded," "fortunate") in v. 1.

87. *Palgê* may be a countable plural ("streams"), as probably in Prov. 5:16 (see 5:17), or a plural of extension to indicate that the channel is inherently large and/or complex, as probably in the case of the one tree in Psalm 1:3 (*IBHS,* p. 120; P. 7.4.1c).

88. *KBL,* 3. 929, s.v. *peleg.*

89. M. Saebø, *TLOT,* 3:1078, s.v. *ṣlḥ.*

The Lord Jesus did not seem to succeed in his passions on Good Friday, but viewed from the empty tomb on Easter Sunday, he reached the goal more than any could have imagined. He atoned for sin, was buried and swallowed up death, and ascended into the presence of *I AM*'s joy forever.

2. *Windblown Chaff v. 4*

With a pulpit-thumping bang, the inspired sage declares: *Not so the wicked* (see v. 1). The rhetorical triple "not" in verse one, re-emphasized by the exclamatory "Not so," demands a sharp rejection of the anti-Mosaic viewpoint. The self-ambitious, the self-serving, and the proudly self-reliant are *like chaff that the wind drives away.* Tree and chaff are as opposite as righteous and wicked. Chaff, in contrast to a fruitful tree, has no eternal life, no worth, no stability, no place, and no roots, and cannot endure God's sifting wind of judgment when it blows. The scattering of chaff by wind is a common Biblical figure for sudden destruction (Job 21:18; Ps. 35:5; Isa. 17:13; Hos. 13:3).

Where are Babylon, Assyria, Persia, Rome, the Holy Roman Empire? Where are the Dutch, Belgian, Portuguese, British colonial empires? Where are the Third Reich, the Soviets? Their judgments are but a type and pledge of the final judgment. Ultimately God will separate the wheat from the tares, the sheep from the goats.

C. Rewards Plainly Stated vv. 5-6

1. *Judgment of Wicked; Salvation of Righteous v. 5*

Therefore *(ʿal-kēn)* introduces a statement of later effects, not a proposed or anticipated response (= *lākēn*).[90] "Taking into account" that the *the wicked* (see vv. 1, 4) are like chaff, they *will not stand in the judgment (loʾ-yāqūmû bammišpāṭ).* The polysemic verb *qûm* here means "to resist attack and endure" — the litotes signifies "they will perish."[91] As for "judgment" *(mišpaṭ),* G. Liedke notes, "the *šp̣ṭ* act transpired in a 'three-cornered relationship': two people, or groups of people, whose relationship is not intact are restored to a state of *shalom* through a third party."[92] The wicked oppress and do not do right by their community in their greed to gratify their swollen appetites. The judge or a legal assembly has

90. *IBHS,* p. 666, P. 39.3.4e.

91. S. Amsler, *TLOT,* 3:1138-39, s.v. *qum,* "to stand up."

92. Liedke, *TLOT,* 3:1394, s.v. *spt.*

the obligation to right the wrong. A "legal decision, judgment" brings about "peace" by "cutting the wicked off from the earth" (Prov. 2:22).

The *waw* ("nor") that introduces verse 5b adds the additional notion that the righteous will be left to inherit the earth (cf. Matt. 5:5). *Sinners* — note the same sequence of "wicked" and "sinners" as in v. 1 — *will not stand in the congregation (baʿᵃdat) of the righteous (ṣaddîqîm)* — note the assonance with *baʿᵃṣat rᵉšāʿîm* in v. 1. To judge from the parallel, *ʿēdâ* probably refers to more than a circle of family and friends,[93] but to a legal assembly that executes the *mišpāṭ*. Since the wicked are like chaff and their way will perish, the assembly of the righteous, we may presume, hand down and exact a death sentence against the wrongdoers.[94] The *ṣaddîqîm* refers to those who bring about right and harmony for all by submitting themselves to the Law/Word *(Logos)* of God. That law instructs them to love God with all their hearts and to love their neighbors as themselves, and they delight in it (see v. 2). In other words, the righteous community abides forever.

2. *I AM Watches over Righteous. Wicked Perish v. 6*

These opposite destinies — of eternal life for the righteous and eternal death for the wicked — are not due to some impersonal, inexorable reality but *because I AM knows (yōdēaʿ) the way* (see v. 1) *of the righteous* (v. 1). *Yādaʿ* denotes personal knowledge, intimate experience with a person's reality, and the participle indicates active knowing, not merely a state of knowing. God's spirit actively "knows," "resonates with," and is intimately acquainted with the character and conduct of the righteous. Paul says: "The Spirit searches all things, even the deep things of God. For who among men knows the thoughts of a man except the man's spirit within him? In the same way no one knows the thoughts of God except the Spirit of God" (1 Cor. 2:10b-11). Since the mind of Christ dwells in the righteous, the Spirit of God knows the righteous. The participation of *I AM* in the life of mortals guarantees their eternal life, and without that participation there is no eternal life, as Augustine noted (see pp. 116-17). The "leaf of the righteous" never withers.

By contrast *the way of the wicked* (v. 1) *will end in destruction (tōʾbēd). The word ʾābad* originally meant "to run away." Its meaning expanded to "to perish," with the nuances of becoming lost (Lev. 26:38), going astray (Ps. 2:12), or dying (Esther 4:16). The parallelism suggests that this is so because the Eternal does not "know" their way and so his spirit is not present to invest them with his

93. *HALOT,* p. 790, entry 2.3, but to a legal assembly, entry 4 s.v. *ʿēdâ.*
94. *HALOT,* p. 790, *ʿēdâ.*

eternal life (cf. Rom. 8:10-11). For the righteous, clinical death is only a shadow along the trail of the eternal pilgrimage to the holy city. "So the two ways, and there is no third, part forever," says Kidner.[95]

Part IV. Conclusion

Hans-Joachim Kraus, as commented upon by Eaton, "noting that the good life is represented by a singular figure in vv. 1-3, against the plurality of the wicked, sees here an archetype of the Christ who will delight in the divine will." Eaton comments: "Perhaps it is the plurality of the righteous in vv. 5-6 which leads him to speak of this Christ as the one in and through whom the many find life-giving relation to Scripture and the Psalms."[96] This is a bit of a stretch, but a recognition of a singular righteous man as an archetype in conjunction with a congregation of the righteous suggests they are types of Christ and his church. Jesus Christ uniquely corresponds to the portrait of the righteous man, and the congregation shares his spirit of delight in *I AM* and his word.

Psalm 1 uses the arboreal image to describe the fortunate state of the righteous as they hope for the celestial city after God has cut off the wicked from the earth. Ezekiel 47:12 uses the same image to describe the blessed state of the righteous in the celestial city: "Fruit trees of all kinds will grow on both banks of the river. Their leaves will not wither, nor will their fruit fail. Every month they will bear fruit, because the water from the sanctuary flows to them."

Today the arboreal image finds its fulfillment in the Lord Jesus Christ. His gospel fulfills the righteousness of the law for the elect, and his Spirit writes the law upon their hearts. He is the supreme object of their desire and the focus of their diligent reflection. He is the water that sustains their eternal life. By their baptism into Christ they are already seated with him in heaven, and at his appearing he will welcome them into Paradise.

Jesus Christ's death on the cross at the hands of the wicked and the testimony of the psalms that follow show that the psalm must be nuanced. The psalm looks at the final verdict of history, the time of judgment; before then, however, the wicked often thrive and the righteous perish. In other words, the righteous who obey *Torah* live by faith.

As earlier commentators noted, the psalm's sharp contrast between the righteous and wicked seems to contradict human experience, where people seem to be a combination of good and bad. In truth, however, the contrast be-

95. D. Kidner, *Psalms 1–72* (TOTC), p. 49.
96. Eaton, *Psalms of the Way*, p. 39.

tween those who trust and love God, as shown by their commitment to the Word of God, and those who trust and love self, as shown by their commitment to their own insights, is an unbridgeable gap. The contrast between a regenerate heart and an unregenerate heart is as great as the contrast between life and death.

CHAPTER 5

Psalm 2: Ask of Me, My Son

Part I. Voice of the Church

I. Unity of Psalms 1 and 2

From the earliest times the unity of Psalms 1 and 2 has been accepted on the authority of the apostles themselves. **Clement of Alexandria** accepts this in several passages.[1] In a letter to the Emperor Antoninus Pius, the early apologist **Justin Martyr** refers to Psalms 1 and 2 as one psalm in his discussion of the incident in Acts 4:23-29 when the believers "came to their own company" and joined in singing Ps. 2:1-2.[2] Later, **Origen** reiterates their unity, although he had before him two Hebrew manuscripts, one in which the psalms are separated, and another in which they are written as a single song.[3] **Tertullian** (c. 200 C.E.) also affirmed their unity, seeing both the historicity and the humanity of Jesus Christ as being demonstrated by the testimony of the Psalms to him. In his debate with the Gnostics, he states: "We shall also have the support of the Psalms at this point — not the 'psalms' indeed of Valentinus the apostate, the heretic, and the Platonist, but the Psalms of David, the illustrious saint and well-known prophet. He sings to us of Christ, and through his voice, Christ indeed also sang concerning himself."[4]

In his exposition on Psalm 2, **Hilary of Poitiers** begins by admitting "the

1. Clement of Alexandria, *Paed.* 3.12.87; *Strom.* 2.15.68.

2. Leslie William Barnard, *Justin Martyr: The First and Second Apologetics,* Ancient Christian Writers (Mahwah, NJ: Paulist Press, 1997), pp. 50-51.

3. The Western recension of the Greek New Testament at Acts 13:33 reads "the first," not second psalm.

4. Tertullian, *De Carne Christi* 20,3.

majority of us" (scholars) are uncertain whether to consider this psalm attached to the first or as a separate psalm. He puts the onus on the Septuagint translators for separating them, while he alleges the apostle Peter unites them. The apostle is a Hebrew speaking to Hebrews who, according to Hilary, do not separate the two psalms. The Septuagint translators, he argues, were translating from Hebrew into a Greek culture. Hilary then uses the context of Peter's audience, "God-fearing men from every nation which is under the sun" (Acts 2:5), but who could also have "foolish thoughts."

Augustine of Hippo makes no reference to the issue of the unity of Psalms 1 and 2, but simply proceeds with his homily. **Cassiodorus** notes that just as four Gospels all harmonize into one Gospel, so too, both Psalms 1 and 2 are psalms of David. **Erasmus** neatly interprets Psalm 1 as the preface to the Psalter and the next one as "Psalm 1." He places it as the first in the collection.[5] Later exegetes, including Calvin, pass over the issue of one or two psalms in silence. We shall examine this question further in our commentary (see pp. 160-61).

II. Prosopopoeia of Psalm 2

As we saw in Psalm 1, Greek literary commentary seeks to identify the speaker/recipients in the text. So too, **Hippolytus** (170-236), a martyr like Justin, recognizes that the David of the Psalter no longer represents simply a historical king, but serves as a prototype of the "Anointed One" (see pp. 105-7). Critically, he observes that not all the psalms are attributed to David; indeed only seventy-two. Twelve are attributed to Asaph, twelve to the sons of Korah, as well as to others like Solomon, Haggai and Zechariah. So he comments: "We must now consider the mystery by what rationale the Psalter is attributed to David when there are different singers and when not all of the psalms are by David. The rationale of the attribution is that he was himself the cause of all that came about. He chose the singers himself, and since he was himself the cause, he should be considered worthy of the honor that all the singers uttered should be reckoned to David."[6]

Hippolytus adopts a Trinitarian theology to interpret the Psalter, as expressive of the Father, Son and Holy Spirit within the Psalms themselves. He now sees "the Psalter as a revision of the rest of Scripture." "These beliefs," he affirms, "have their theological basis in the conviction that the Psalter has a

5. Erasmus, *Collected Works*, vol. 1, pp. 74-75.
6. Hippolytus, *Hom. Ps.* 6-7.

spirit-given prophetic and messianic dimension." He affirms then, the typico-prophetic nature of the psalm. This conviction, combined with the faith in the unity of Scripture, allows for a Christian Christological and ecclesiological re-interpretation of the Psalms. This in turn refers to both the earlier and later history of salvation. He describes the Psalter, then, as the sacrament of the *one* reality of salvation, which encompasses the whole history of salvation and the road to salvation of the individual; in the Psalter, David sings about "the glorious school of grace."[7]

III. Origen on the Awesome Realism of God's Rule

Origen (c. 185-254), while linking Psalm 2 with Acts 4:25-29, speculates that it is the angels (or "spiritual beings") who use the prosopological language of the beginning of the Psalm: "It seems to me that the first four lines are spoken by the angels who had come down with the Savior; they are full of rage at the ambush laid against Christ by the invisible kings and princes. At the same time they remain uncertain what this commotion is all about. Since earthly kings and princes were the ones who bound captive human beings and subjected them to impose their yokes upon them, the Son of God responds to the angels, urging them to imitate him in breaking the bonds of sinners, and casting off their yokes."[8] Origen suggests that Christ himself has promised to relieve us from our yoke. For he has substituted for it his "easy yoke," so we will carry instead his "light burden," as he promises in Matthew 11:30.

Origen further notes that the *Christos* of the LXX (cf. "anointed" Ps. 2:2) is personalized in Acts 4:27 to refer to Jesus. He interprets this to mean that the psalm is describing the unique and universal Kingship of Christ. As Augustine was to comment later, Christ in Psalm 1 is the uniquely "Righteous Man." Christ as Lord is then both the test of "history" and the standard of Christian "morality." Origen answers the "why" of Psalm 2:2 by referring to 1 Corinthians 2:6-8: as sinners, they are in intrinsic revolt against God, exercising "the wisdom of this world, sinful and fallen as it is."[9] He also points out that the prophets' indictment of "princes" may not refer to specific historical rulers but to the powers of darkness, demonic and cosmic.

Origen associates "You are my son, today I have begotten you" (v. 7) with

7. Hippolytus, *Hom. Ps.* 12.

8. Translation of William L. Holladay, *The Psalms through Three Thousand Years* (Minneapolis: Fortress Press, 1996), p. 170.

9. Origen, *Commentary on the Psalter,* 11,315C, Patrologia cursus completus, Series Latina, ed. J.-P. Migne.

John's Gospel of the *Logos,* having neither beginning nor end. "Instead, the 'time' spoken of is coextensive with his uncreated and eternal life, as indeed 'to-day' is when his birth can be found."[10] For Origen, the "relationally eternal day" cannot be a temporal "day," because of his eternal "begotten-ness."[11]

Origen suggests that the admonition in Ps. 2:11, "serve the Lord with fear, and rejoice with trembling," is necessary because of "the possibility of falling away, should God's assistance abandon the one who is doing something that is not praiseworthy."[12] So he links Scriptures together as inspired of God, not just as a scholarly exercise, but primarily to nurture his flock in holiness before God.[13] Origen develops this "spiritual exegesis" to be comprehensive of all the Scriptures, as being revelatory of the deep mysteries of the divine *Logos.* For God's kingship is expressive of God being All in All.[14]

Origen's contribution, the need of a "spiritual exegesis," views the scholarly saint as seeking primarily to become holy, and not merely intelligent. As monastic theology later developed, the Christian identity is primarily *participatory* of the truth of God, and only then, in a secondary capacity, *speculative.* Origen would thus argue that we cannot comment appropriately on the kingship of God without first becoming obedient servants of the King. In this sense he is much more a "Christian realist" and should not be dismissed as being "too mystical," or indeed as a "Neo-Platonist"!

10. *Commentary on John's Gospel,* 1,30, Migne, 14,78CD.

11. Again in his commentary on Jeremiah 9:23-24, where the prophet admonishes the wise not to boast of his wisdom, nor the strong to boast of his strength, but to boast that he understands and knows the covenant life of God, Origen exclaims: *"Blessed is the one who is always being born of God . . . not just once, but continually so, according to each good deed in which God begets the just."* This is contrasted with the eternal Son of God, for our human, yet new birth in God, remains of "to-day" as a continual rebirthing, "day by day." So now Origen echoes the words of the apostle writing to the Corinthians: "Though our outer nature is wasting away, our inner nature is being renewed every day" (2 Cor. 4:16).

12. Origen, *Commentary on the Psalter,* 12,1116B.

13. The conflicting interrelationship between human and divine wisdom plays a great role in Origen's thought. For he sees human life as divided into two simple, yet profound realities: of living under the sovereignty of God or of living subject to the fear of death. In this world, all that is not of God will be destroyed: "Therefore, of these things which are seen, nothing at all is to be hoped for in the future. For 'no eye has seen . . . what God has prepared for those who love him' (1 Cor. 2:9)." God's reign reflects then on an invisible world, far more sublime than anything we can humanly understand.

14. So Origen takes the posture that *"I must decrease for Him to increase."* He embraces the folly of the cross, and recognizes that the "helplessness" and the "weakness" of the Christian must be central to the Christian life. So "the world is crucified to me, and I unto the world," if Biblical exegesis is to be truly "Christian."

IV. Augustine on God's Continual Wrath Against Evil

Augustine of Hippo moves straight into Psalm 2, as if it were the apostles themselves who are describing the insurrection against Christ's rule. He defends this Christological approach citing Psalm 102:18: "Let this be written for another generation." He assumes there is little profit to be had from examining the original context of the psalm, since it was written to foretell the New Testament.[15] The enemies of Christ have not destroyed the church of his day, and Christ's name has instead become known throughout the world to be acknowledged among the nations. This was the Constantinian political inheritance Augustine readily appreciated. But instead of moral complacency, he would alert his audience to continue to recognize that the justice and anger of God are realities to be feared by all, in all times.[16]

Augustine advocates that the faith of the New Testament, as the Church fathers unfolded it, has a heuristic and regulatory function with regards to the Old Testament Scriptures. There is an inner logic within the whole of Scripture that is discernible within "the rule of faith." This, in turn, is based upon the divine inspiration of the text, as far as Augustine was concerned. The figural interpretation provides "depth" for meaning beyond the literal words of the text to provide a "spiritual" meaning. He gives Psalm 2 only a brief Christocentric commentary. Indeed, since Augustine had a strong liturgical use of the Psalter, its recitation by the audience was the place for expounding the psalms, which he did for a quarter of a century!

V. Eastern Fathers' Use of Typology

While Greek prosopology can readily slip into allegory, the Semitic precision of Near Eastern scholars makes a clear distinction between Biblical typology as based on history, and allegory based on literary appeal.[17] **Eusebius** (c. 260-340), Bishop of Caesarea, regards himself as the intellectual heir of Origen, admiring and making much use of his master's works and codical methods. Yet where Origen engages allegorically within his philosophical culture, Eusebius is viewed as the first great Christian historian.[18]

15. Augustine, *Expositions of the Psalms,* ed. Boniface Ramsey, trans. Maria Boulding, O.S.B., The Works of Saint Augustine (Hyde Park, NY: New City Press, 2005), vol. 5, p. 61.

16. Augustine, *Expositions of the Psalms,* pp. 74-75.

17. See Bruce Waltke, *An Old Testament Theology* (Grand Rapids: Zondervan, 2006), pp. 136-42.

18. He provides the topographical and chronological framework for the history of God's

John Chrysostom (347-407), trained in the Antiochene/Caesarean school, follows Origen in emphasizing the need of Christians to follow "the angelic life," by which he means the importance of becoming a "spiritual person." In his baptismal instructions he uses the analogy taken from Psalm 2:9 to express how radical the act of baptism must be for the new life of the believer. "The Psalmist of old," he points out, "hinted at this destruction [of the old man] and this mystical cleansing when he said: 'Thou shalt break them in pieces like a potter's vessel.'"[19] In his description of the radical nature required of the true Christian, Chrysostom can draw out the spiritual implications of the text as well as any Origenist, while still treating the text with exegetical specificity.

As we have seen in chapter 2 (see p. 47), **Theodoret of Cyrrhus** favors the historical/literal approach to interpreting Scripture. However, the apostles' usage of Psalm 2 in Acts 4:24-30 gives him the freedom to treat Psalm 2 figuratively. Thus, he interprets the psalm as referring to the tawdry plot of the Jews to eliminate Jesus. Indeed, it is the humanity of Jesus that gives credence for a "literal" approach to Scripture, while the divinity of Christ allows also for a "spiritual" sense of the text. Theodoret lived between the Trinitarian debate of the Council of Constantinople of 381 and the Chalcedon council of 451. In this debate his guiding principle was a middle-ground Antiochene position on these issues, avoiding the extreme of Nestorianism. Rather, he is guided by "the completeness and the distinction of the two natures" of the God-Man.[20] So he follows the apostle's description of his unity as seen in Philippians 2:9. In that context he refers to Psalm 2:7: "You are my Son, today I have begotten you."

---

people, both in his *Onomasticon* and *Church History* (Anthony Grafton and Megan Williams, *Christianity and the Transformation of the Book* [Cambridge, MA: Harvard University Press, 2008], p. 221). He sees the prophet Isaiah and the Psalms as foretelling the significant events in history from the creation to the Incarnation. For him, each psalm was composed at a specific time, and in principle, at a discoverable date. He writes both before and after Constantine, with an optimistic spirit about the historical success of Christianity. Unfortunately, Eusebius' commentary on Psalm 2 is unavailable. Timothy D. Barnes has outlined the contrast and complementarity of both Origen and Eusebius in their treatments of Psalm 37[38]. Psalm 2 is treated by Origen wholly figuratively, as the spiritual medicine of Christ to provide for the healing for the church. Whereas Eusebius notes that it repeats the same verse: "Lord, do not rebuke me in thy anger," and attributes the context historically to the rebellion of Absalom, Eusebius also wants to explore a "spiritual" meaning, and so contrasts the Christian exegetes from their Jewish counterparts, who can only flatly see a humanly historical connotation, not as under the Lord of history.

19. Paul W. Harkins, trans., *St. John Chrysostom: Baptismal Instructions,* Ancient Christian Writers (Westminster, MD: The Newman Press; London: Longmans, Green and Co., 1963), pp. 139-40.

20. J. N. D. Kelly, *Early Christian Doctrines,* 5th ed. (New York: Harper & Row, 1978), p. 65.

Like Eusebius, Theodoret is also optimistic about the events of history within the Roman Empire, and yet he is guided to sustain a balance between the literal/historical interpretation and the more Origenist "spiritual" or theological interpretation of the psalm. It is what Wallace-Hadrill has called "a moderate historicism."[21] He lives in the tension of a double reality, of the earthly Lord within the Christianized Roman Empire, and of the heavenly Christ within the sovereignty of the God of history.

VI. Changing Contexts of Medieval Commentaries

Flavius Magnus Aurelius Cassiodorus (485-580) contributed to the founding of the later Carolingian renaissance with many of the benefits already provided by Origen, Eusebius, and Augustine, drawing also from Hilary of Poitiers, Jerome, and Ambrose. Holding high political office as Governor of Milan, he created a center of learning on his estate of Vivarium in south Italy, where he had already created two monasteries. His *Institutes* served as a syllabus of sacred reading, with a systematic survey of the books of the Bible, while his complete exposition on the Psalms was much inspired by Hilary of Poitiers' *Tractatus super psalmos.* Original to Cassiodorus is a fourfold treatment of each psalm: an explication of the psalm heading; an attempt to identify the speaker or speakers; a verse-by-verse explanation of the meaning of the text; and the conclusion that may be drawn from the psalm to provide its main significance.

He summarizes Psalm 2 as follows: "The beautiful texture of this psalm is fashioned in four sections. In the first, the prophet speaks of the Jews in relation to Christ's passion. In the second come the words of the deranged Jews; in the third, the Lord Savior's words concerning the all-powerful kingdom and His own indescribable begetting, in so far as our human insignificance can grasp it. In the fourth, the prophet speaks, warning the nations to recognize the Lord's majesty and to be reconciled to the Christian faith, for unless they grasp the most true teaching of the Catholic religion they know that they will perish, separated from the right path."[22] In his conclusion, Cassiodorus sees the psalm revealing "the two unmingled and perfect natures . . . most fittingly set in the single Person of the Lord Christ. By one He reigns, and by the other He serves . . . His divinity united with His humanity." Such is the norm of Christian orthodoxy, and the test of who is a Christian in proclaiming "the one Christ as being of and in two united and perfect natures. If with the Lord's favor we store these

21. D. S. Wallace-Hadrill, *Christian Antioch: A Study of Early Christian Thought in the East* (Cambridge: Cambridge University Press, 1982), p. 35.

22. Wallace-Hadrill, *Christian Antioch,* p. 58.

facts in our memory, we always abide by the norms of the Church."[23] As Alcuin and later medieval scholars affirm, Cassidorus continued to be a major influence in medieval Christendom.

Alcuin of York (c. 730-804) was the scholarly advisor to the Emperor Charlemagne as Eusebius had been to the Emperor Constantine, both in establishing the basis for the continuity of Christian "history," and in developing scholarly tools for Biblical commentaries. As head of the court school, the emperor assigned to Alcuin the task of the revision of the Vulgate. He also directed a new focus on the church liturgy, as inspired by the Psalter.[24] He saw with Augustine that the entry into the spirit of the Psalms is seeing them all through the lens of the Incarnation. So "the mind must cleanse itself from present things and cling to the divine and spiritual praises, so that heavenly things might be revealed to it. There is nothing more in this mortal life in which we might cling to God than in his praises. Accordingly, no one is able — neither by word nor by mind — to explain the power of the psalms, unless praise unto the almighty powers of God is sung not merely superficially with the lips but with an intent mind." This was an age that envisioned Christ exalted as the "King of Kings,"[25] "high and lifted up," as in Isaiah's vision in the temple. Hence, the victorious Christ of Psalm 2 was a strong motif in Carolingian worship.

As we have seen (see pp. 54-55), the twelfth century reflects a critical change in medieval thought and culture, in which the move from the monastic to scholastic learning develops. **Richard of Saint Victor** (c. 1123-1173), at the school of St. Victor in Paris, represents the "best" of this new Biblical scholarship. He benefits from a new view of history that his master Hugh of St. Victor had developed in his *Didascalion*. It was a happy conjunction of monastic theology and the fruits of the new secular scholarship of the schools. For Hugh desired that true learning should indeed be "Christian" in its control and expression. "Contemplation" was the ultimate direction, not "curiosity." That is to say, seeking to please God, not promoting carnal desires, was its primary motive.

There is only a fragment of a larger work on Psalm 2:1-4 by Richard, in which he applies its verses to the condemnation of scholasticism. "Why have the nations raged and the people meditated on inane things? What do we understand by the 'nations' who do not know God, who worship idols, except as depraved and perverse thoughts? And what do we understand by 'the people,' who meditate on inane things, except vain and inept thoughts?" Quoting from

23. Wallace-Hadrill, *Christian Antioch*, p. 68.

24. Marcia L. Colish, *Medieval Foundations of the Western Intellectual Tradition, 400-1400* (New Haven and London: Yale University Press, 1997), pp. 66-67.

25. Jaroslav Pelikan, *The Illustrated Jesus through the Centuries* (New Haven: Yale University Press, 1997), pp. 47-56..

the book of Wisdom 1:3, Richard answers his own question: "perverse thoughts separate from God, . . . for the Holy Spirit of discipline will flee from the deceitful and will withdraw himself from thoughts which are without understanding."[26] "Rage," he adds, "is for depraved desires to arise against reason," and "this raging (fremitus) is characteristic of beasts, not men." It may be forgivable to think foolishly, but to "meditate upon them is reprehensible." "For it is one thing which we endure from negligence or when it is against one's will; it is another when we are willingly occupied with useless study." Richard suggests "nations" are figurative of human "thoughts," and "peoples" are expressive of "affections."[27] Richard is using his annotation to critique theological education as it was developing in Paris in the twelfth century!

Richard sees the seriousness of being "against 'the Lord'" as being against the "I AM" and against "his Christ" "with reference to the Savior."[28] He links this with how some say boastfully in Psalm 12:4-5, "our lips are our own, who is Lord over us?" Worse still is the misuse of human abilities given us for the miscarriage of justice. To abuse natural abilities is one thing, but to abuse gifts of grace, which we could not accomplish without the Savior, is still more reprehensible. "Let us break their chains asunder and let us cast away their yoke from us" suggests to Richard that a "chain" implies involuntary restraint, while a "yoke" is unwilling bondage. The implication is that sensual knowledge is a form of captivity of the soul, which should freely desire to ascend the heavenly realm. Instead, it is being impeded by the body. Our negative emotions, such as fear and pride, then hinder our spiritual progress. "It often happens," adds Richard, that when the wicked do evil with impunity, "they believe that God has little concern for human affairs." He quotes the thoughts of the wicked in Psalm 10:11: "God will never take notice; he covers his face and never sees." He could have added the words of Psalm 3:2, "Many are saying of me, 'God will not deliver him.'"[29] Yes, literally that is what happened, notes Richard, for when "David was weary from his own temptations, [and his enemies] were hastening to subvert him with their own snares, David was confidently secure from the protection of the Lord, and singing: He who dwells in the heavens will laugh at them and the Lord will deride them. They are laughed at when they boast that they are able to do something against the elect, but they are derided when they are judged to do something about it."[30]

One of the "enemies" such commentators identify is *curiositas*. When cu-

26. Richard of St. Victor, *Mysticae adnotationes in psalmos*, PL 196:265-404.
27. Richard of St. Victor, *Mysticae adnotationes in psalmos*, PL 196:267(C).
28. Richard of St. Victor, *Mysticae adnotationes in psalmos*, PL 196:269(D).
29. Richard of St. Victor, *Mysticae adnotationes in psalmos*, PL 196:272(C).
30. Richard of St. Victor, *Mysticae adnotationes in psalmos*, PL 196:274(A).

riosity is exercised for its own sake, this is identified with pride (**Bernard of Clairvaux,** 1090-1153), or immoderate and empty knowledge (**Aelred of Rievaulx,** c. 1110-1167).[31] It is defined also as *desiderium oculorum,* "the lust of the eyes," such as the celluloid surrealism of the film industry generated today.

VII. Commentaries in the Political Turbulence of the Sixteenth Century

Desiderius Erasmus (1469-1536) is possibly quite unaware of the use Richard of St. Victor had made of Psalm 2. He interprets it politically, as he states in 1528: this is "the most turbulent century." He sees the psalm as a messianic prophecy to be treated allegorically. Yet he does so almost arrogantly, as he comments on Psalm 2:6: "On the literal level, this verse is appropriate enough to David, who defeated the Jebusites and built his palace on Zion (that is, the citadel of Jersualem), but let us dismiss such an insipid, watered-down interpretation, a product of 'the letter which kills'; we prefer to drink from the new wine of our king. What interest do we have in David, who rules a precarious kingdom soon to be destroyed in Palestine, a mere dot on the map?"[32]

As a prophecy of Christ, he cites Luke 24:44, where Jesus speaks of the various sources that must be fulfilled, including "in the law of Moses, in the prophets, and in the psalms."[33] He assumes it is the prophet David who raises the question at the beginning of the psalm, in astonishment at the violence of the nations' rejection of the "Anointed One," or Messiah.

Erasmus then highlights the continual rejection of Christ as recorded in the New Testament: by the Scribes and Pharisees, the Israelite people, the Romans, indeed by all those pursuing their own vested interests. The same elements of opposition will affect us also as Christ's disciples, suggesting that Erasmus identifies his own afflictions and misunderstandings with the lament of the psalm. He stood back from the tumult of the rulers during the Reformation and witnessed bad judgment, foolish actions, evil events. As he observes: "If a monarch can threaten mankind with total ruin in following his foolish, untamed passions . . . it is all the more essential that those who are custodians of God's mysteries should overflow in the understanding of the divine, and that

31. G. R. Evans, "What We Are Supposed Not to Know," in *The Joy of Learning and the Love of God: Studies in Honor of Jean Leclercq,* ed. E. Rozanne Elder (Kalamazoo, MI and Spencer, MA: Cistercian Publications, 1995), pp. 309-26.

32. Craig R. Thompson, ed., *Collected Works of Erasmus* (Toronto: University of Toronto Press, 1997), vol. 1, p. 119.

33. *Collected Works of Erasmus,* vol. 1, p. 79.

their minds should be purged of all dangerous passions."[34] Indeed, we can see in this longest of all his commentaries (some 77 pages), Erasmus is describing all his private feelings about the state of the rulers in his own day.[35] In a much humbler spirit than when he started the psalm, he concludes:

> He [God] warns us that our instincts must be made to obey his laws, that human reason must conform to his decree, and that we must so serve this single ruler of us all that we must both rejoice in his boundless goodness towards us, and yet be always fearful; that is, we must mistrust our own deeds and our own strength, since we are not our own judges, but must place all our hope and trust in his inestimable kindliness, through which eternal salvation is won by those who turn to him for help with all their heart; to him be praise and thanksgiving, with the Father and the Holy Spirit, for all eternity.[36]

Martin Luther (1483-1546) also sees himself mirrored in Psalm 2. "The second Psalm is one of the best psalms. I love that psalm with all my heart. It strikes and flashes valiantly among kings, princes, counselors, judges, etc. If what this psalm says be true, then are the allegations and aims of the papists stark lies and folly. If I were as our Lord God, and had committed the government to my son, as He to His Son, and these vile people were as disobedient as now they be, I would knock the world in pieces."[37]

By 1532, when he had written a more reasoned, reflective interpretation, his spirit had quieted down, to write one of the longest of his later lectures on a psalm (some 89 pages). Like Erasmus he interprets it as a prophetic psalm, but applies it more openly to the circumstances of his own day: the Peasants' War of 1525, his break with Ulrich Zwingli, the Turkish invasion of Eastern Europe, and all his conflict with Rome and the papacy. "These people, then, are the causes of the tumults and scandals, not we who are moderate, peaceful and quiet."[38] Others did the same thing, such as the Huguenots in France. Sir Walter Raleigh, who was scarcely a Biblical man, thought it appropriate to cite Psalm 2 with the impending threat of the Spanish Armada in 1588.

Even when delivered as a classroom lecture, Luther delivers it as a rousing sermon, which he encourages his students to sing in their churches.[39] "Let us,

34. *Collected Works of Erasmus,* vol. 1, p. 138.

35. J. D. Tracy, *The Politics of Erasmus* (Toronto: University of Toronto Press, 1978).

36. *Collected Works of Erasmus,* vol. 1, p. 146.

37. Quoted from Rowland E. Prothero, *The Psalms in Human Life* (New York: E. P. Dutton & Company, 1905), p. 123.

38. *Luther's Works,* vol. 12, ed. Jaroslav Pelikan (St. Louis: Concordia, 1955), p. 11.

39. *Luther's Works,* p. 8.

therefore, console ourselves with this psalm." For it is not just ourselves the world is so bitterly against, continues Luther, but God himself. Furthermore, he argues, instead of being afraid, we should be laughing at this crazy effort of the world to think it can fight against God. No one will deprive Christ of his throne, for God the Father has placed him there for ever; so the fight is really all about the First Commandment, of acknowledging God to be God. Thus it is the Holy Spirit who "laughs" over the folly of the world's revolt against God. So in our adversities, we can "laugh" too.[40]

Luther then goes on to read the psalm as proclaiming the Gospel, having "the chief articles of faith set forth in this psalm, who and what sort of king Christ is, namely, begotten of the Father from eternity and set upon Mount Zion; then, what His kingdom is like, namely, that He is a teacher beyond the Law and Moses. For He does not teach about our work, but about Himself, that He is the eternal Son of God, in order to arouse us to receive Him and to put faith in His merits and works."[41]

Luther links the conclusion of the psalm with Christ's saying in John 12:47-48: "I did not come to judge the world but to save the world. He who rejects Me and does not receive My sayings has a judge; the Word that I have spoken will be his judge on the Last Day."[42] Then Luther draws a number of pastoral conclusions from the exhortation at the end of the psalm. We serve God with filial, not servile, fear. We serve Him by obedience to His word in whatever occupation we are in, not just within a "religious" life and calling. "For to fear God and to trust God is alone true religion. When these two are in correct balance, there the whole life is righteous and holy."[43] Here, Luther is getting at the assumption of monks, that they need a change of clothing and a change of social rank in order to serve God, while Luther is advocating the radical character of the priesthood of all believers. "Consequently, the true worship of God is to kiss the Son, that is, to adore Him in such a way that you see nothing in heaven and earth aside from Him and believe in nothing else than Him." Indeed, "to 'kiss' the Son is to embrace Him with our whole heart, and see and hear nothing else than Christ, and Him crucified."[44] The Church lies hidden within this world, but "blessed are all those who take refuge in Him," even in the very great difficulties the church was facing in Luther's day.

A first reading of **John Calvin's** long commentary on Psalm 2 impresses the reader with its restraint and objective engagement with the text. Unlike

40. *Luther's Works,* pp. 20, 22, 27.
41. *Luther's Works,* p. 53.
42. *Luther's Works,* p. 63.
43. *Luther's Works,* p. 81.
44. *Luther's Works,* pp. 87, 88.

Erasmus and Luther, who take the opportunity to apply the psalm to the turbulence around them, Calvin is wholly silent about his own political troubles. But further study suggests that this is because Calvin has already so wholly identified himself with David. So while it is all about "David," this becomes a *nom-de-plume* for Calvin's own afflictions.

Nine years after Luther's commentary on Psalm 2, **Peter Martyr Vermigli** (1499-1562), who was one of the most important theologians to give shape to Reformed theology — some say in certain instances more influential than Calvin — fled from Naples to Geneva, and then resided in Strasbourg, where he composed the following prayer in 1547 as a paraphrase of Psalm 2, a fitting conclusion to this brief historical survey:

> Regardless of how much the devil rages, great and good God, or the worldly powers rise up daily, or the flesh conspires with its slaves against the Kingdom of your Begotten Son, our Lord Jesus Christ, still we know and hold firmly as part of our steadfast faith that you mock and scorn all such things — you who are mighty to crush them in your wrath and anger as soon as it pleases you. Since we are sometimes weak in our faith, so that driven by various fears we obey your commandments less than we ought, we beseech you that in your goodness you show us your favor so that we may be firmly convinced that your Son is our King and Redeemer and holds complete power at your side over all things. When you begot Him, you handed over all the nations for Him to rule rightfully, as His heritage. Grant us now finally to realize that — and learn it so well — by serving you with all fear and honor, we may not be smashed on the last day like a clay pot by the rod of your anger. Through Jesus Christ, our Lord. Amen.

Part II. Voice of the Psalmist: Translation

1 Why do nations conspire,[45]
  and the peoples plot[46] in vain?

45. The traditional rendering of *rāgaš* by "rage" is based on cognate studies, especially Syriac, but the use of *rāgaš* in Biblical Hebrew suggests the meaning "conspire." Its nominal derivatives *regeš* (masc.) and *rigšâ* (fem.) are parallel to the noun *sôd* ("counsel") in Psalms 55:14; 64:2(3); even as here the verb is apparently an equivalent to the denominative of *sôd* ("to band together") in Psalm 2:2 (see n. 48). In Daniel 6:6, 11, 15 (Aramaic) *rgš* denotes rulers coming together in a conspiracy. Assuming Psalm 2 is by David, all three uses of the root *rgš* are ascribed to David.

46. "Imagine" (AV) in Old English means "to plot." Dahood's suggestion "to number their troops" lacks support in Hebrew usage, and "plot" offers a better parallel to "conspire."

2 The kings of the earth take their stand
and the rulers[47] band together[48]
against *I AM* and against[49] his anointed one:[50]
3 "Let us break their[51] chains,
and throw off their shackles."
4 The One enthroned[52] in heaven[53] laughs;[54]
The Sovereign[55] scoffs[56] at them.
5 Then he speaks[57] to them in his anger
and in his wrath[58] terrifies[59] them:
6 "I[60] install[61] my king

47. *Rôzᵉnîm* is a "stock-in-trade synonymous parallel to *malᵉkê 'ereṣ*" (Stanley Gevirtz, *Patterns in the Early Poetry of Israel* [Chicago: University of Chicago Press, 1963], p. 3, n. 11).

48. G. B. Koenig, *HALOT* against BDB distinguishes two roots for *ysd:* 1) "to lay the foundations," 2) "to conspire together," probably a denominative of *sôd* counsel." The same construction (*Niphal* of *ysd* + *yaḥad* + *'al*, "band together against") occurs also in Psalm 31:14 [13].

49. The unusual repetition of the preposition serves to distinguish the human king from the divine king.

50. In this terse poetry, "saying" is elided.

51. For the form of third masc. pl. suffix *êmô* see GKC, 91l. The antecedent is *yhwh* and *mᵉšîḥô.*

52. The participle of *yšb* "to sit" may be used more specifically, especially of *I AM,* to mean "sitting enthroned" (BDB, s.v. *yšb,* p. 449, entry 1.a).

53. Possibly, the article designates a unique referent (*IBHS,* p. 242, P. 13.5.1b).

54. "At them" is gapped.

55. Probably, many Heb. Mss. and Tg. read *yhwh* due to the Jews pronouncing *yhwh* as *'ᵃdōnāy. 'ᵃdōnāy* makes an excellent parallel with *yôšēb.*

56. Construed as a progressive situation (*IBHS,* p. 504, P. 31.3.b).

57. Although *'az* with the short prefix conjugation denotes a preterite situation (see *IBHS,* pp. 498, 501, PP. 31.1.d, f), semantic pertinence demands that this sequel to the present tense be understood as realized at the time of speaking, as with the suffix conjugation (see *IBHS,* p. 488, P. 30,5.1.d).

58. *ḥārôn* mostly occurs as a construct before *'ap.* Here the stereotype phrase is reversed and, as commonly in poetry, split apart as parallels.

59. Under the government of *'az* (see n. 57).

60. *Wa'ᵃnî* (literally, "But I").

61. *Nāsaktî* is derived from either 1) *nāsak* "to pour out" with the specific sense "to pour out [a libation] = consecrate" [GB, p. 508. s.v. I. *nsk, Kal* entry 4], or from 2) *Nāsak* "to weave," which is used in Psalm 139:13 of gestation and in parallel with *qānâ* and here followed by *yᵉlidtîkā* (2:7), or from 3) *Nsk* "install" (cf. *nasîk* "prince"), a derivative of Akkadian *nasāku,* whence *nasîku* "prince" (BDB, p. 651, s.v. III. *nāsak*). Dahood pointed the verb as though from *sûk* "to anoint," but that verb is reserved for cosmetic anointings. The suffix conjugation is an instantaneous perfective — that is to say, accomplished at the time of speaking. This performative speech act functions like "I pronounce you: 'Man and Wife'"; "I baptize you . . . ."

on Zion, my holy hill."[62]
7 I will[63] proclaim the decree;[64]
I AM[65] said to me:
"You are my son;[66]
today I give you birth.
8 Ask me, and[67] I will make the[68] nations your inheritance,
the ends of the earth your possession.[69]
9 Break[70] them with a rod of iron;
Like a potter's vessel dash them to pieces."[71]
10 Therefore, kings, be wise;
be warned, rulers[72] of the earth.
11 Serve *I AM* with fear
and celebrate his rule with trembling.

62. LXX reads the verb as passive and the suffixes as third masculine singular, which *HALOT* (p. 703, s.v. I. *nsk*) retroverts as *nissaktî malkô* [. . . *qodšô*]: "I have been consecrated [with a libation] as his king upon his holy mountain." Probably, LXX is a facilitating reading to retain the king as the antecedent of "I" in verses 6 and 7. MT, involving a change of speakers, is the more difficult reading and better suits the structural symmetry of the psalm (see III.B. "Structure" below).

63. Hebrew cohortative is rendered *I will* in the sense of the old English distinction "I shall" (simple future tense) and "I will" (resolve regarding the situation) (*IBHS*, p. 573, 34.5.1a).

64. Hebrew *'el ḥōq* confused the ancient translations. Nevertheless MT represents good Biblical Hebrew. For a rebuttal of the many critical attempts to correct the text of Psalm 2 according to a priori theories see H. H. Rowley, "The Text and Structure of Psalm II," *JTS* 42 (1941): 143-54. 4QFlor I, 18-19 confirms the MT of vv. 1-2. See J. M. Allegro, "Further Messianic References in Qumran Literature," *JBL* 75 (1960): 176f.; and Y. Yadin, "A Midrash on 2 Sam 7 and Ps 1–2 (4Q Florilegium)," *IEJ* 9 (1959): 95-98.

65. The translation follows MT's sensible punctuation against many translations and conjectures.

66. Hebrew construction answers the question, "What is the king like?" not "Who is the king?" (*IBHS*, pp. 130-32, PP. 8.4.1,2).

67. *Waw* with the cohortative after an imperative often signifies a final clause, "so that . . ." (*IBHS*, p. 575, P. 34.5.2b).

68. Often omitted in terse Hebrew poetry, the article is frequently dispensed with before words that would naturally take it in prose (BDB, p. 208d, s.v. *h*, entry 1.i, N.B.).

69. *Naḥ^{a}lâ* . . . *'^{a}ḥuzzâ* is probably a splitting of the stereotype phrase *'^{a}ḥuzzat-naḥ^{a}lâ* or *naḥ^{a} lat '^{a}ḥuzzâ* (cf. Num. 27:7; 32:32; 35:2).

70. For the textual variations *tirʿēm* ("you will rule them") and *t^{e}rōʿēm* ("you will break them"), see commentary.

71. Construing the prefix conjugation of *trʿm* and *tnpṣm* as imperfectives of injunction or of legislation (*IBHS*, pp. 509-10, P. 31.5a-c).

72. For the gloss of *šōpēṭ* by "rulers," see W. Richter, "Zu den Richtern Israels," *ZAW* 77, no. 1 (1965): 40-71, esp. 57f.

12 Kiss [his] son,[73] lest he become angry,[74]
  and you be destroyed in [your] way,
  for his wrath will soon flare up.
How fortunate are all who seek refuge in him!

Part III. Commentary

I. Introduction

A. Editing of Psalm

We agree with the Fathers that Psalms 1 and 2 are a unit.[75] Though they were originally unique psalms, an inspired editor linked them to form an introduction to the Psalter. In addition to the arguments marshaled in chapter 3 to defend that thesis (see pp. 102-3), other arguments may be added. First, it lacks a superscription, suggesting a close connection with the preceding psalm (see p. 46). Second, many verbal correspondences also link these two psalms. The first verse of Psalm 1 (1:1a) and the last verse of Psalm 2 (2:12b) begin with *'ašrê* ("fortunate"), forming an inclusio framing the introduction. The introductory stanzas of both psalms use *hāgâ* ("to meditate," 1:2; "to plot," 2:1). The last verses

73. Aq., Syr., and Amelli's text of Old Latin take the first word as *nšq* ("to kiss"); Sym. and Jerome paraphrase this by "worship." Aq., Sym., Jerome all read *br* as an adverb from the root *brr,* "to purify," "to select," not as Aramaic *bar* "son." LXX and Tg. gloss *naššeqû-bar* by "receive correction." Their Hebrew text is uncertain, but probably they read the Hebrew text in a way similar to Aq. et al. and extended the meaning of "kiss purity/purely." This explanation is probable because the Arabic version, which often follows the LXX, does not have "correction," but "good moral, virtue," a possible extension of "pure." Their interpretation, however, makes no advance on v. 11; instead it returns in thought to verse 10. Haupt (*AJSL* 19 [1902-3]: 134) takes *br* to mean "the open field" as in Job 39:4, and renders "kiss the ground" (see commentary). Rowley, following Bertholet, proposes instead of MT's *wgylw brʿdh nšqw-br* to read *brʿdh nšqw brglyw* "in trembling kiss his feet" (see *BHS*). He defends his proposal, which demands combining verse 11b with 12a, by noting: "We have merely the transfer of *gylw* to follow *br*." His emendation is adopted in RSV and NRSV, but many are uncomfortable with such a massive emendation. W. J. Holladay (*VT* 28 [1978]: 110-12), building on Dahood, conjectures *nōšê qeber* "forgetters of the grave." Still, no ancient Heb. Mss. or versions have this reading, and the verb *nšh* is never used for *nšk* ("forget") in the Psalms.

74. Construing the prefix conjugation *ye'ĕnap* to signify an incipient situation (*IBHS,* p. 503, P. 31.2c; p. 505, 3d).

75. See John T. Willis, "Psalm 1 — An Entity," *ZAW* 91 (1979): 381-401, for an extensive discussion of the evidence concerning those who read Psalm 1 and Psalm 2 as one psalm, as well as the far greater evidence of those who have Psalm 1 and Psalm 2 to be two distinct psalms.

of both psalms use the metaphor of *derek* ("way") in connection with *'ābad* ("perish," 1:6; 2:12). Both Psalms also employ terms belonging to the semantic domain of "mock" (*lēṣîm*, "mockers" [against *I AM*'s law], 1:1, and *lā'ag*, "derision" of [*I AM* against rebels to his rule], 2:4). Third, the two psalms expound a uniform message: the pious and righteous are fully rewarded, and in the time of judgment they triumph over the wicked. The didactic generalization that the righteous prevail over the wicked (Psalm 1) is fleshed out in salvation history as happening through *I AM*'s anointed king in Psalm 2. In Psalm 1 the righteous trust *I AM* to uphold his Torah, and in Psalm 2 the faithful trust *I AM* to uphold his anointed king.

The editor's two introductory psalms prepare those who meditate on his anthology of petitions and praises to interpret the psalms both with respect to the king and to themselves as individuals within his kingdom (see pp. 105-6). The Church by its baptism into Christ Jesus is "a royal priesthood, a holy nation" who prays with their king (1 Peter 2:9).

In addition to functioning as an introduction, Psalm 2 also functions as a janus transition to the rest of the Psalter (see p. 103). As argued in chapter 3, most of the psalms refer to the king (see above), and as will be argued below, Psalm 2 functions in Israel's liturgy as coronation poem asserting Israel's king's right to rule all nations with the mandate to establish his dominion through prayer. Psalms 3–7 are David's prayers asking *I AM* to establish his kingdom in spite of severe opposition from his own people (Psalm 3), his own officials (Psalm 4) and evil-doers of all sorts (Psalm 5).

B. Structure of Psalm

Psalm 2 is a fine artistic piece of literary fiction in the form of a four-act play. The protagonists are *I AM* and his sacred king, and their antagonists are a worldwide confederation of foreign kings. The plot begins with the antagonists conspiring a *coup d'état;* develops with scenes of *I AM*'s resolve to install his king on Mount Zion and of the king's resolve to accept God's resolve by faith and prayer; reaches a climax with *I AM*'s command to his anointed king to shatter the conspirators; and ends with a denouement as the playwright steps on stage to warn the kings of their fate.

The four acts take place in distinct scenes, each with different speakers. The first takes place in a foreign court where the psalmist quotes the kings of the earth who convene to plot the assassinations of *I AM* and his king. In this scene the audience overhears their nefarious conspiracy encouraging one another to throw off the galling rule of their overlords, *I AM* and his king. The second act takes place in heaven, where the psalmist opens the ears of his audience to hear *I AM*'s proclamation in blazing anger that installs his king on Mount Zion (vv. 4-6). The third act occurs on Mount Zion. In this scene the psalmist causes his audience to hear the new king declaring his divine right to rule the earth by smashing his antagonists (vv. 7-9). In the final act the psalmist steps on stage to admonish the kings to submit to the rule of *I AM* and his king and to seek refuge in *I AM* before his wrath breaks forth in battle (vv. 10-12).

The acts are artistically composed in three-verse stanzas:[76]

I.	Hostile Kings Conspire to Throw Off Rule of *I AM* and His King	1-3
II.	*I AM* Resolves to Install His King on Mount Zion	4-6
III.	King Resolves to Recite Decree Granting Him Dominion	7-9
IV.	Psalmist Admonishes Hostile Kings to Submit to *I AM*'s King	10-12

Each of the first two stanzas ends climactically with addresses: by the pagan kings (v. 2) and by *I AM* (v. 6). In spite of the uncertainty that invariably occurs with the transition from an older and experienced warrior-king to a new king, the artistic symmetry evokes the feeling of order and serenity.

C. Liturgical Use of Psalm 2

As can be inferred from the plot and scenes, the psalm probably functioned in Israel's liturgy as part of a coronation ceremony.[77] The coronation celebration features the Davidic covenant. The king's three sacred sobriquets — "his anointed one" (v. 3), "my king" (v. 6), "my son" (vv. 7, 12) — entail that *I AM* and his king are inseparably united by the immutable Davidic covenant. According to stipulations in this covenant *I AM* adopts his chosen Davidic king as his son. As his son he inherits the earth, which *I AM* owns by creation. His kingdom is universal in space and eternal in time. Whether the psalm was used on other occasions during the first temple than at the time of the coronation of a new Davidic king — for example, on the anniversary of the king's birth as king — is less certain.

In Israel's hymnbook the psalm functions to encourage Israel with the assurance that their king will win the battle. As will be seen in "theology" (below), the psalm is a prophecy that now is being fulfilled by Jesus Christ, the son of

76. For the many artful poetic subtleties in the Hebrew text, see Pierre Auffret, *The Literary Structure of Psalm 2* (JSOTSup 3; Sheffield: Sheffield Academic Press, 1977).

77. See chapter 1: "cult-functional approach" (pp. 98-100).

David (Matt. 1:1), and in the future will be consummated at the Second Coming of this Son, who is far greater than David. After the first temple was destroyed and no king sat on David's throne, this psalm within the canon became a prophecy of Christ's rule and is so interpreted in the New Testament (Luke 24:44; see pp. 106, 112 and "theology" below).

II. Exegesis

A. Nations Rebel against I AM and His King vv. 1-3

The first stanza assumes the nations opposed to the rule of *I AM* rebel against Moses' Book of the Law (see Ps. 1:2), which the Davidic king copies by his own hand upon his inauguration. Instead of submitting to his righteous rule, wherein *I AM*'s subjects love him and their neighbor, the pagan kings in corporate solidarity with their peoples are intent on practicing their false worship that demands no moral rectitude and panders to their selfish interests. In an opening general statement, the psalmist's quasi-rhetorical question, "why," infers what his parallel declaration asserts: "the peoples plot in vain." The next two acts by *I AM* and by his king explain why this is so.

The first stanza moves from the general to the specific. Verse 1 represents the nations as hatching a futile plot. Verse 2 represents their kings as revolting against *I AM* and his king. Verse 3 condemns them by quoting them, as they encourage one another to throw off God's rule.

1. Futility of Revolt v. 1

Why (lammâ) is a quasi-rhetorical question, introducing an undesirable alternative.[78] The desirable action is stated in the final stanza: "Serve *I AM* . . . Kiss the son." In other words, "do something else; why pursue a way that cannot possibly succeed." The rhetorical question vents the poet's exasperation, amazement and indignation at the stupidity of the nations to conspire their own death.

In the ancient Near East, kings commonly revolted at the coronation of a new foreign overlord. As part of the coronation liturgy in Egypt, the young Pharaoh contested against rebellious states in a sham battle.[79] "The El Amarna

78. *IBHS,* p. 324, P. 18.3c.

79. Sigmund Mowinckel, *He That Cometh,* trans. G. W. Anderson (New York: Abingdon, 1954), p. 83; Ivan Engnell, *Studies in Divine Kingship in the Ancient Near East* (Uppsala: Almqvist & Wiksell, 1943), s.v. "sham fight" (index); A. Erman, *Die aegyptische Religion* (Berlin, 1909)^2, pp. 64f.

correspondence offers graphic descriptions of the plottings (sic) and intrigues of the petty kings of Syria-Palestine against the Egyptian Suzerain and against one another."[80] The northern kingdom seceded from Israel when Rehoboam succeeded Solomon, and so on.

Nations (gôyīm) occurs fifty-three times in the Psalms and always refers to foreign nations. Its parallel, *peoples (lᵉʾummîm),* also refers to foreign peoples. The generic nouns "nations/peoples" and "kings/rulers" could be applied specifically to different nations in the liturgical use of the psalm throughout Israel's history. Peter and John applied "kings" and "rulers" to Herod and Pontius Pilate, and they specified "the nations" as "the Gentiles" (e.g. Rome) and "the people" as the people of Israel. Christ's apostles accuse the leaders of Israel of having joined the foreign conspiracy against God's "holy servant Jesus, whom God had anointed," and describe the locus of the conspiracy as "in this city" (i.e., Jerusalem). In other words, the city where God formerly anointed and installed his holy king in dramatic irony had become the city where Israel's historic enemies and his own people *conspire* (see n. 45) and *plot* (*hgh* see Ps. 1:2) the epistemological death of God by killing his king (Acts 4:27). The apostles referred to Jesus as "servant" as a reminder of the suffering servant prophesied in Isaiah 42:1-4; 49:1-6; 50:4-9; 52:13–53:12. As the Reformers recognized, this is also true in church history.

They plot, however, "in vain" — that is to say, their scheme is "devoid of benefit" (Heb. *rîq,* cf. Isa. 30:7; Ps. 73:13; Isa. 49:4; Job 39:16).

2. *Universal Revolution v. 2*

Verse 2 articulates the plot of the foreigners' conspiracy. The "nations" and "peoples" are represented by *the kings of the earth (malᵉkê ʾereṣ)* and their *rulers (rôzᵉnîm,* see n. 47) with whom the peoples are in corporate solidarity. In other words, the whole world, without exception, opposes the rule of *I AM* and his king (Rom. 3:9-18). "Conspire" and "plot," which refer to the cognitive activity of the nations, now find concrete expression in *take their stand [in battle] (yityaṣṣᵉbû)* and *band together (nôsᵉdû yāḥad).*

The poet reserves the climactic surprise for the B verset. The rulers and people fight *against I AM and against his anointed (ʿal yhwh wᵉʿal mᵉšîḥô).*[81] (In ancient Near Eastern royal ideology the king represents the deity.)[82] Behind Is-

80. M. Dahood, *Psalms I: 1–50: Introduction, Translation, and Notes,* vol. 1 (Garden City, NY: Doubleday, 1965), p. 8.

81. For meaning and pragmatic function of the name *I AM,* see 1:2.

82. O. Keel, *The Symbolism of the Biblical World: Ancient Near Eastern Iconography and the Book of Psalms,* trans. Timothy J. Hallett (New York: Seabury Press, 1978, 1972), pp. 26-27.

rael's king stands the throne of heaven itself (vv. 4-6, 7-9). From that perspective their mischievous conspiracy does not have a ghost-of-a-chance to succeed. Also, from that perspective, the battle is a spiritual battle between the "gods," better "demons," who stand behind the pagan kings (Deut. 32:17; Ps. 106:37; Rom. 8:38; 1 Cor. 10:20f). In other words, God's people are engaged in a spiritual battle against spiritual forces in heavenly places (Eph. 6:12; Col. 1:16; 2:15). The armor and weapons required for this warfare are spiritual (Isa. 59:15-19; 2 Cor. 10:4; Eph. 6:10-20).

The verbal root behind *his anointed (m^{e}šîḥô)* is *māšaḥ,* which means "to smear," "to paint," "to anoint" (see p. 105). Sacral anointing with olive oil mixed with scented spices was widely practiced in the ancient Near East as well as in Israel, applying to both sacred objects and sacred personnel, usually with reference to the king. The king's anointing symbolized his consecration to and authorization for divine service, and a promise of divine empowerment for that service. The anointing ritual by *I AM*'s prophet was the king's cachet to be recognized as *I AM*'s property. An assault against God's anointed king or any of his anointed property is an assault against God himself and incurs his anger for defiling his holy property.

The prophet "Samuel took the horn of oil and anointed David . . . and from that day on the spirit of *I AM* came on David in power" (1 Sam. 16:13). Zadok the priest and Nathan the prophet anointed Solomon king at the spring Gihon (1 Kings 1:45). Later the coronation anointing ceremony took place at the Temple (2 Kings. 11:4-12). In the Psalms "anointed one" designates the heirs to David's throne (Ps. 18:50 [51]; passim).

3. *Motivation of Rebels v. 3*

Semantic pertinence demands understanding that the antecedent of the first person plural pronoun "us" is the world rulers and that the antecedent of the third masculine "their" is *I AM* and his anointed. The world rulers seek to instigate and encourage each other to throw off *I AM*'s rule through his king: *let us break (n^{e}natt^{e}qâ) their chains (môs^{e}rôtēmô) and* [then] *let us cast off from us (w^{e}našlîkâ mimmenû) their shackles (ʿ^{a}bôtēmô). Môs^{e}rôt,* from the root *ʾsr* "to bind," refers to something that confines and restrains from motion, action or progress. *ʿ^{a}bôtôt* refers to twisted cord (i.e., "rope") or cordage. The metaphor is a reference to either the leather thongs which lashed in place the yoke bar(s) placed on oxen (cf. Jer. 2:20; 5:5; Ps. 129:4; so LXX), or the ropes and shackles conquering kings placed on their captives.[83] In other words, the world rulers, in

83. Keel, *The Symbolism of the Biblical World,* p. 302, pl. 406.

solidarity with their subjects, regard *I AM*'s Book of the Law, which his anointed king upholds, as a galling bondage. To the regenerate, who gladly submit themselves to God's rule, it is a law that gives freedom from Satan's and sin's enslavement (James 1:25; Matt. 11:30; 1 John 5:3). To the regenerate the Book of the Law is pure delight (Ps. 1:2), sweeter than dripping honey from the comb (Ps. 19:10).

B. I AM Installs His King on Mount Zion vv. 4-6

The poet's eagle-eye of faith lifts his audience above the resolve of the rebels on earth to the resolve of *I AM.* Surprisingly, God is laughing in derision at the insurrectionists (v. 4). Their challenge to his authority is as ludicrous as that of Lilliputians to shipwrecked Gulliver. As Gulliver awakens from his sleep on the island's shore, to his amazement he espies the islanders laying scaling ladders against his prone body. The Lilliputians are the size of his little finger. Whereupon the king of the Lilliputians, who is a fingernail taller than the others, mounts a ladder and walks upon Gulliver's breast giving orders. The Lilliputians had earlier pegged Gulliver's long locks of hair into the grassy knoll. With a clap of his hands, Gulliver could have smashed them, but instead he plays their ludicrous game.

But God will not play games with the world rulers. He speaks in anger for their waging war against his righteous rule and his sacred king (v. 5). His roar is as awesome as that of Aslan. His awesome proclamation installs his king upon his holy mountain, which symbolizes his universal rule (v. 6).

The poet frames the second stanza by beginning with *I AM* sitting enthroned in the heavens (v. 4) and ending with his anointed king on "my holy hill" (v. 6). The upper frame speaks of his universal transcendence over all the earth and the lower frame of his immanent presence through his charismatic king who extends his kingdom over all the earth. The earthly temple is only an epiphany of his universal temple, even as each believer and each local assembly of Christians are temporal manifestations of the heavenly temple where Christ lives to make intercession for the saints.

1. God Regards Revolution as Pathetically Ludicrous v. 4

Borrowing mythological imagery, not mythological theology, the poet pictures God as *the One enthroned in heaven* (*yôšēb baššamayim,* note the assonance). In Psalm 29:10 David portrays *I AM* as one who "sits enthroned over the flood" *(lammabûl yāšāb).* The flood is a metonymy for the blue sky that looks like water.[84] F. M. Cross Jr. has shown that "to sit [enthroned] *(yšb)* with reference to *I AM* speaks of his transcendence."[85] This vivid imagery displays the folly of the "Lilliputians." The parallel *Sovereign (ʾᵃdōnāy)* — a divine title that occurs 400 times — relates *I AM*'s transcendence specifically to the social order wherein he is "supreme lord and master," "the Lord par excellence," "Lord of all."[86] The divine title is best understood in terms of its opposite: the rest of creation is his "slave."

Because of the certainty of *I AM*'s overwhelming destructive power through his king, the cabal's opposition is laughably pathetic. *Laughs (yiśḥāq)* and *derides (yilʿag) them (lāmô)* express the inward joy and disdain the Conqueror feels toward the defeat of his enemies (37:13; 59:8). His victory is so lopsided that there is a comic side to the reversal of fortunes. Before *I AM*'s anointed dashes them to pieces, however, his inspired poet first tries to instill sense in them: submit to God's righteous rule that gives true liberty (see vv. 10-12).

2. *God Blazes in Anger Against Rebels v. 5*

The poet-prophet now turns from depicting *I AM*'s inward disdain for the pagan confederacy to his outward intervention in history. *Then* marks a consecution in an uninterrupted narration. While the enemy is raging and *I AM* is laughing, then *I AM spoke* (see n. 57) *to them* (i.e., "the kings of the earth" [v. 2]. *In his anger (ʾap) . . . wrath (ḥārôn)* expresses the war-like mood of the coronation ceremony. *ʾap* (lit. "nose") points to the physically visible state of excitement of an individual breathing heavily as a consequence of anger. *Ḥārôn* derives from the verb *ḥrh* "to blaze," which with *ʾap* as subject means "anger was kindled" and even when used absolutely means "become angry." The compound *ḥārôn ʿap* means "blaze of the nose" = "burning anger." Here the compound is split apart so that the modifying *ḥārôn* "blazing [anger]" is put in the intensifying B verset. This expression of ferocious anger is used exclusively of *I AM*.

3. *I AM Himself Installs His King on Zion v. 6*

Even as the first stanza was brought to a dramatic conclusion with the defiant words of the rebels, the second stanza is brought to a climactic conclusion with God's dramatic proclamation expressing his scorn and anger toward them. He

84. See Bruce K. Waltke with Charles Yu, *An Old Testament Theology* (Grand Rapids: Zondervan, 2007), p. 189.

85. F. M. Cross, *BAR,* 225-27.

86. The *-āy* suffix is a substantival affirmative denoting emphasis by reinforcing the root *ʾᵃdōn* (*IBHS,* p. 124, P. 7.4.3e, f).

meets the world-wide opposition to his rule with the sovereign declaration that it is he himself who installs his king in the royal city that *I AM* set apart for himself. *I AM* begins his address in mid-sentence with a conjunctive "But" (*waw,* see n. 60). By suppressing the first part of his thoughts and then blurting out the rest, he expresses the passion with which he speaks.[87] The emphatic flash of self-assertion *I* (*'ᵃnî*) further intensifies his heated emotions.[88] In other words, whereas the kings of the earth and the king of *I AM* express their resolve by a cohortative verb form (vv. 3, 7), *I AM* expresses his resolve by an unusual syntax.

The installation of the king is accomplished by the divine proclamation, *I install* (*nāsaktî,* see n. 61).[89] His speech act performs the installation, even as a minister brings a marriage into existence by his proclamation: "I pronounce you man and wife." The minister effects the marriage by the authority of the state, which in turn derives its authority from God. *I AM* effects the Davidic kingship by his own ultimate authority. *My king* implies the sacred character of the House of David. From a survey of the monarchies in the ancient Near East, Ishida drew two conclusions about the essential elements of kingship: (1) dynastic succession; and (2) divine election.[90]

As the A verset focused on God's election of the Davidic king, the B verset focuses on God's election of Zion as his royal city. In the Psalms *I AM*'s city on earth, representing his heavenly city, is called *Zion* (twenty-six times), "Jerusalem" (ten times) and "mountain[s]"[91] (twelve times, including compounds with Zion). The name "Zion" is probably of pre-Israelite origin, but its etymology is uncertain.[92] It was the original name of the Jebusite hill or fortress on the southeast hill of Jerusalem (2 Sam. 5:6ff.). After David had conquered this site and had placed the ark on the northeast hill of the city, the southern hill came to be known as the City of David or the "Ophel," and Zion came to designate in the poets and prophets the northern hill where the ark and temple were located

87. GKC, 154b.

88. *IBHS,* p. 296, P. 16.3.2e.

89. A performative perfective accomplished at the time of speaking (*IBHS,* p. 489, P. 30.5.1d).

90. See Waltke, *An Old Testament Theology* (Grand Rapids: Zondervan, 2007), pp. 680-82.

91. The plural (Ps. 87:1; 133:3) is an honorific plural of majesty because though the referent is singular it is regarded as so thoroughly characterized by the qualities of the noun that a plural is used (*IBHS,* p. 122, P. 7.4.3a). From a topographical viewpoint Zion, with its rise of 743 meters, is a modest mountain, but because of its great sacred significance the higher mountains around it look up to it, glowering with envy (Ps. 68:15-16). Nevertheless, topographically one must go up to Jerusalem to worship (Ps. 122:4), and it is asked of the pilgrim going there, "Who may ascend the mountain of *I AM?*" (Ps. 24:3).

92. *TDNT,* 7:294.

(Ps. 132:13; Isa. 10:12; Mic. 4:2), or by synecdoche the whole city (Isa. 10:24; Jer. 3:14; Amos 6:1) or by metonymy its inhabitants (Isa. 1:27; 33:5; Ps. 97:8) and finally the community of the exiles (Isa. 40:9; Jer. 14:19; Lam. 2:13). *I AM*'s presence, symbolized by the Glory cloud and by his Name being located there, made Mount Zion *"holy."*

I AM chose a *mountain* as the site of his earthly residence in order to communicate truth about himself in the cultural language of ancient Israel. In that world temples were located on mountains to symbolize the victory of the local deity over the forces of chaos.[93] Thus the mountain represented the whole creation.[94] In Egypt the site itself was inherently holy as the primordial hillock emerging from the abysmal flood. By contrast *I AM* chose Mount Zion to symbolize his victory over all the forces of chaos both in the orders of creation and of redemption. *I AM*'s victory over the forces of nature served as a harbinger of his final victory over his political enemies.

My holy (qodšî) means that Mount Zion is set apart as God's possession for his use. He signals its sanctification by locating there the sacred chest that housed the covenant between *I AM* and Israel. Solomon located the sacred chest in the temple, which David had designed. The suppliant, though himself not necessarily present at Mount Zion, must direct his prayer only to this holy mountain (Ps. 121:1-2; Dan. 6:10). To look in the direction of another mountain would be tantamount to turning to a false god. In other words, the sacred ark served as a pledge and guarantee of the well-being of the monarchy.

The palace of *I AM*'s anointed king, with its judgment hall-porch where the thrones of justice stood, was located at *I AM*'s "right hand" (i.e., on the south side). *I AM*'s throne, the sacred chest housing the Ten Commandments with the Book of the Law beside it, found concrete applications in the righteous rulings of the House of David (see Ps. 15, pp. 298-99).

C. King Recites Decree Granting Him Dominion vv. 7-9

The king now resolves to recite the solemn and authoritative decree of the Davidic covenant granting him dominion over the foreign nations. By this recitation he gives tangible expression to his becoming king, not unlike modern swearing-in ceremonies. Although the antecedent of the first person singular pronouns *"I"* and *"me"* is not stated, semantic pertinence demands the interpretation that the king is speaking.

93. Keel, *The Symbolism of the Biblical World,* pp. 113-14.

94. R. E. Clements, *God and Temple* (Minneapolis: Fortress Press, 1965), p. 3.

The second stanza progresses through three expanding relationships: of the king to God as a son (v. 7), of *I AM* and his son to the nations as his son's inheritance (v. 8), and of the king to the nations as their sovereign (v. 9).

1. *King Proclaims His Relationship to God: A Son v. 7*

The king takes a half verse (7A) to solemnly declare that the recitation he is about to give is from *I AM* himself. The second half of the verse is the declaration (7B).

I will proclaim (ʾ^{a}sapp^{e}râ) expresses the Davidic king's resolve to accept his divine installation with its entailment to risk death to establish *I AM*'s universal kingship through holy war (see n. 63). *Proclaim* glosses *spr* (Piel), which means literally "to count," "to recount," "to document." Rost drew the conclusion that the most important ingredient in David's prayer in response to the covenant *I AM* handed him is its dependence on and almost direct quotation from the divine revelation.[95] The solemnity of the royal proclamation may be indicated by the unusual preposition *ʾel* (not translated). Commenting on the unusual construction, Delitzsch suggests: "Such a decree! Majestic as to its author and its matter." The etymological meaning of *ḥôq (decree)* means "what is cut in or scratched" and thus may contain the notion of what is abiding. Informing most of its uses is the idea "what is prescribed," and usually in connection with the fixed stipulations of a covenant. The content of the decree shows that the stipulation of the Davidic covenant that is in view is "I will be his [the Davidic king's] father and he will be my son" (2 Sam. 7:14).[96]

The importance that the king rules by divine authority can be measured by the pleonastic elaboration of the parallels: first person, "I will recite" and third person, "*I AM* says." The contrast between the poet's heretofore terseness

95. L. Rost, *Die Überlieferung von der Thronnachfolge Davids* (Stuttgart: BWANT, 1926), p. 51.

96. Von Rad argued that "the decree" corresponds to the Egyptian "protocol" *(nekhbet)* whereby the gods conferred on the Pharaoh his fivefold title and his sovereign right and duties: "It designates the king's authority to rule as the surrogate of the god." According to von Rad, the taking of the crown and this written document of legitimization (cf. 2 Kings 11:12) constituted the most important moments in the royal ritual and served as the official act attesting his elevation to kingship. But the Egyptologist K. A. Kitchen (*Ancient Orient and the Old Testament* [Chicago: InterVarsity Press, 1966], p. 106) objects that "Egyptian *nekhbet*" refers solely to the Pharaoh's fivefold titles and not to the decree of "protocol" in any wider sense. The titulary and the legitimization of the Pharaoh are two distinct things, evaporating Von Rad's theory. Kitchen, however, wrongly suggests that the decree here "refers to a single statute without reference to a covenant . . ." (p. 109). His conclusion is especially confusing because earlier he defined *ḥōq* as "the statutes which . . . constitute the covenant stipulations."

to surplus in v. 7Ab is striking. In verses 3 and 6 and 7Aa he elided the subject and the indirect object. In these three quotations the interpreter has to infer the change of speakers by semantic pertinence. In 7Ab, however, the poet allows no misunderstanding, clearly specifying the subject, *I AM (yhwh),* the verb *says ('āmar),* and object *to me ('ēlay).* For *you are a son of mine (bᵉnî 'attâ)* see n. 66.

In v. 7Bb *I AM* re-enforces that the Davidic king is a son by a birth announcement. The pronoun *'anî* "I," spoken by the king, is emphatic; his birthday, *today (hayyôm)* is his coronation day (see above); *give birth to you (yᵉlidtîkā)* is a poetic variant of "I will be his father" (2 Sam. 7:14). In Egyptian and Canaanite cultures the king was believed to be an offspring of the gods in a mythological sense and to have been suckled at divine breasts.[97] The theory of Gerald Cooke,[98] and the majority view, is that "you are my son" with its elaboration "I have given you birth," is an adoption formula like one alluded to the Code of Hammurabi. Arguments for taking the formula in this sense, and not in a mythological, literal sense, include: 1) "son of God" when used of Israel also expresses an endearing, not literal and so mythical, relationship between God and Israel (Exod. 4:22; Prov. 30:4B; Hos. 11:1). 2) David, whose lineage is well-known, calls *I AM* "Father" (Ps. 89:26), and *I AM,* having first qualified David's successor (i.e., Solomon) as "who will come from your own body" (2 Sam 7:12), then immediately says of him: "he is the one who will build a house for My Name" (7:13) and "I will be his father, and he will be my son" (7:14; cf. 1 Chron. 22:9-10; 28:6). 3) The reference to "today" precludes a mythical notion. 4) "Beget/bear" is also used figuratively in Deut. 32:18; Isa. 1:2 (LXX) and Jer. 2:27. The notion of adoption is well known in the history of Israel (Gen. 15:2-3; Exod. 2:10; 1 Kings 11:20; Esther 2:7). The notion of taking an offspring up into one's bosom to care for it in place of the natural parentage served the same purpose (cf. Ruth 4:16). This representation of the king's relationship to *I AM,* which is adopted and adapted from the mythical understanding of the ancient Orient, evokes the notions of his distinction from God and of *I AM*'s tender and emotional concern to care for him (Ps. 89:26-29), to discipline him (2 Sam. 7:14), and to make him the legal heir of the earth, which *I AM* owns by having created it. Indeed, the word "son" in other ancient Near Eastern languages means "heir."[99]

Though the inference of "discipline" is not in view in this psalm (contra 2 Sam. 7:14-15), the expositor should bear in mind that at the time of coronation the king also copied under the tutelage of the priest the Book of the Law with its

97. Keel, *The Symbolism of the Biblical World,* pp. 251-55.
98. Gerald Cooke, *ZAW* 73 (1961): 202-5.
99. *TDOT,* 2:145-49.

commands to uphold *I AM*'s covenant with Israel that she love *I AM* and her neighbors (Deut. 17:18; cf. 1 Sam. 10:25; 2 Kings 11:12).

In the unfolding drama of salvation history the earlier naming of the nation of Israel as *I AM*'s firstborn (Exod. 4:22) and his son (v. 23) is now applied to the king as their representative head. All doubt about the strength and about the validity or the justice of the decree is dispelled by the resurrection of Jesus from the dead to his throne in heaven, which cast its shadow on earth in the form of David's throne in Zion.

2. *King's Relation to the Nations: His Inheritance v. 8*

In consequence of this filial relationship of the king to God, the Creator subjects all peoples to the authority of his royal son. In the Old Testament (Pss. 2:7-11; 89:22-29 [23-30]), as in Egyptian literature,[100] lordship is very closely attached to sonship.

But God commands his king: *ask (š^{e}ʾal).* Even as he accepted the claim to be the son of God by faith, he must ask in faith for his inheritance. "Inheritance is the natural right of sons," says Kirkpatrick, "yet even the son must plead the promise and claim its fulfillment." This immense "ask me" should be compared with 1 Kings 3:5 (of Solomon) and with those many passages in the psalms in which the king claims and is accorded a special grace in prayer (see Ps. 4:3 [4]).

The promise, which is dependent upon the asking (see n. 67), *and I will give (w^{e}ʾett^{e}nâ),* underscores once again that the rule depends not on the will of the flesh but on the will of God.

Your inheritance (naḥ^{a}lāt͏ekâ) refers to the king's patrimony, a lasting possession obtained without payment of a purchase price (cf. Num. 27:7). But as Israel had to possess its inheritance by conquest, so also the king must possess his dominion by commanding submission to him (Pss. 2; 72; 110).[101]

The royal son's inheritance, *nations (gôyīm) . . . ends of the earth (ʾapsê-ʾāreṣ),* matches the rebellious "nations" (v. 1) in corporate solidarity with "the kings of the earth" (v. 2). The Davidic kingdom will not only endure uprisings but will even be extended to the ends of the earth, beyond the limits of the empire established by David, whose hegemony extended from the River of Egypt to the Euphrates. H. Gunkel supposed that "the ends of the earth" is part and parcel of the hyperbolic language common to the "court style" of the ancient word, and ought not to be taken literally. Rather, the term should be taken at

100. Keel, *The Symbolism of the Biblical World,* p. 253.

101. Julian Obermann, "Wind, Water, and Light in an Archaic Inscription from Shechem," *JBL* 57, no. 3 (1938): 239-53.

face value because: 1) the presence of rebellious nations would pose a constant threat to Israel's security (Mic. 5:3 [4]). 2) The Old Testament ideal would not tolerate a notion of co-existence with pagan gods (cf. Jer. 16:19). 3) Since *I AM* is the Creator and Lord of all his creation, his son's inheritance rightly consists of all lands (cf. Gen. 48:4; Deut. 20:16; Ps. 72:8).

Whereas the Law limited Israel's inheritance to Canaan (Gen. 17:8; Deut. 4:21; 32:49), the Davidic covenant expanded that inheritance to include all the earth (cf. Ps. 111:6). The Abrahamic covenant envisioned a universal salvation through his offspring, but that the whole earth should become Israel's inheritance through their king had to await the revelation to David.

3. King's Relation to the Nations: Their Sovereign v. 9

The king's recitation thus far has established his relationship to *I AM* as his son, and the entailment that as a son he receives the earth as his inheritance. He now brings the plot to a climax, reciting his mandate to crush the rebels

The difference between "break them" (see n. 70; NIV note, TNIV text) and "rule [shepherd] them" (NIV text, TNIV note) reflects two textual traditions. LXX, followed by Rev. 2:27; 12:5; 19:15; Syr., Jerome, read *tirʿēm* ("you will rule them," from the root *rʿh*), but MT, Targ. Sym. read *tᵉrōʿēm* ("you will break them," from the root *rʿʿ*). The difference pertains to the oral reading of the consonants *trʿm*. The textual evidence supports MT as the original reading, not LXX, in spite of its support from the New Testament, because: 1) the received oral tradition of MT is normally superior to the innovative interpretations of the LXX.[102] 2) The rare Aramaic root *rʿʿ* is more difficult to explain away than the very common Hebrew root *rʿh*. 3) "To break" is used again with iron in Jer. 15:12. 4) *rʿh* literally means "to shepherd" and connotes "tender care," an unexpected meaning in this psalm. 5) "To shepherd with a rod of iron" is an oxymoron. 6) "To break" forms a better parallel with "to dash to pieces."

Rod (šēbeṭ) denotes a part of a tree from which a staff or weapon is made. A person in authority, such as God (Job 21:9; 37:13), a father (Prov. 13:23-24; 22:15; 29:15) or the king (Ps. 2:9), used it to inflict remedial punishment on a slave (Exod 21:20), a fool (Prov. 26:3), a son (13:24; 22:15; 29:15; cf. 2 Sam. 7:14; Isa. 10:15), rebellious kings (Ps. 2:9). To insure the rod carries the day, this rod, a mace, is to be made *of iron (barzel)*. "Iron" probably designates the smelted and worked iron that was introduced into Palestine about 1400 B.C., not the meteoric iron that was used before that. It is notable for its hardness and strength and used in many types of instruments (cf. Deut. 27:5; Josh. 17:16; Judg. 1:19).

102. *IBHS*, pp. 26-28, P. 1.6.3g-m.

The command *like a potter's vessel dash them to pieces (kikᵉlî yôṣēr tᵉnappᵉṣēm)* finds graphic depiction in the Egyptian execration texts. These texts illustrate the Egyptian practice of formally cursing persons and cities. The ritual involved writing the names of the person or city on a pottery figure and/or ceramic bowl, after which the curse was spoken and the bowl smashed.[103]

D. World Rulers Warned to Submit to I AM's King vv. 10-12

Finally David himself, the psalm's author, steps on stage to address the nations. Since the speaker of this stanza refers to *I AM* and his son in third person, presumably the speaker once again is the composer of this fine artistic piece of literary fiction.

In spite of David's menacing tone, his warning contains a large measure of grace with truth. He extends God's salvation beyond the limits of the covenant people to the whole uncircumcised world (cf. Ps. 94:10). He concludes his poem with a universal embrace: "Fortunate is the life of *all* who seek refuge in *I AM*." Moreover, he extends the Word of God to all nations, not to just Israel.

1. Be Wise v. 10

Therefore (*wᵉʿattâ,* lit. "now then") has an emphatic logical sense and signals a macro-syntactic transition in the poem, introducing a shift in argumentative tack with a continuity in subject and reference.[104] The antagonists continue to be the *kings (mᵉlākîm)* of the earth (v. 2), and the protagonists continue to be *I AM* and his royal son. The reference continues to be the relationships of all three, but this stanza aims to resolve the tension between the protagonists and antagonists by warning the kings to be reconciled to *I AM*'s rule.

Be wise (haśkîlû) derives from the noun *śekel,* which designates "the ability to grasp the meanings or implications of a situation or message, the ability to understand practical matters and interpersonal relations and make beneficial decisions." For example, the prudent person *(maśkîl)* gives attention to a threatening situation, has insight into its solution, acts decisively, and thereby effects success and life and prevents failure and death. David's success against the Philistines is a textbook example of this virtue (see 1 Sam. 18:5, 14, 15).[105]

103. For a picture of an execration figurine see *ANEP,* p. 196, P.l. 593.

104. *IBHS,* p. 634, P. 38.1e; p. 667, P. 39.3.4f.

105. Bruce K. Waltke, *Proverbs 1–15: A Commentary* (Grand Rapids: Eerdmans, 2004), p. 94.

Yāsar, the root of the verb glossed *be warned (hiwwāsᵉrû),* literally means "to instruct" or "to educate." The relationship between the educator and educated may be that of a parent to a child (Prov. 19:18), a master to a slave (9:9) or of *I AM* to his people (Deut. 8:5). Ultimate authority resides in God, but the term's interest lies especially in the educated. W. E. Lane observes that the root *ysr* ("to instruct"/ "to discipline") always presupposes an educational purpose and is never used to refer to the correction of animals, but he errs when he says it is never used of the divine discipline of foreign nations.[106] Here the psalmist, perhaps the king himself, as God's surrogate instructs the foreign kings to submit to *I AM*'s rule. Since *ysr* pertains to the edification of the individual, it is co-relative to its parallel *haśkîlû* in v. 10A. In Proverbs the nominal form of *ysr* is *mûsār,* a synonym with "wisdom" (*ḥokmâ,* 1:2, 7), "knowledge" (*dāʿat,* knowledge, 8:10), "insight" (*bînâ,* 1:2; 4:1; 23:23), and "counsel" (*ʿēṣâ,* 19:20). Moreover, since the education in view here is within the framework of true Israel's worldview, it is used with the following commands, "to serve *I AM,*" and "to kiss the son," with the promise of a rewarding life for seeking their refuge in *I AM* (vv. 11-12). The manner and strength of the discipline depend on the relationship and the situation. The meaning of *ysr* ranges from "to teach" with a teachable person as its object to prevent wrongdoing (Job 4:3; Ps. 16:7; Prov. 31:1), to "chasten," "to discipline" a dullard (Deut. 4:36), to "reprimand" the intractable (Prov. 9:7). Sometimes verbal correction is insufficient (cf. Prov. 29:19); *ysr* may refer to corporal punishment. Here too the severity depends upon the situation (cf. Jer. 10:24; 30:11; Ps 6:1 [2]). God disciplined his people in the Wilderness (Deut. 8:5) and punished them for disobedience (Lev. 26:28). Solomon allegedly "scourged" them with whips (1 Kings 12:11). This last instance is exceptional; elsewhere the superior has the best interest of the inferior in view. Here the psalmist's instruction to the foreign rulers is verbal to prevent corporal punishment. Since the instruction is addressed to rebels, the gloss "be warned" seems best.

Rulers of the earth (*šōpᵉṭê ʾāreṣ,* see n. 72) is a synonym for *rôzᵉnîm* in verse 2. The link between verses 2 and 10 is secured by using *ʾāreṣ* with the synonym for "rulers," not with "kings" as in verse 2.

2. *Worship I AM and Submit to the Son v. 11*

Joshua challenged Israel to serve *I AM* (Josh. 24:14-28); the psalmist extends the challenge to all nations (cf. Matt. 28:18-20). The command to *serve (ʿibᵉdû),* often translated "worship," means to recognize God as lord with one's whole existence. "Since 'serving God' indicates one's relationship to God as a whole, it

106. W. E. Lane, "Discipline," in *ISBE* 1 (1979): 948-50.

cannot mean 'to do God a service.' Instead, it signifies acknowledgment of God as Lord, an acknowledgment that requires one's entire existence."[107] "To believe in God" designates only a spiritual fact, "to serve God" refers to the right and necessary acts that spring from a decision to own him as lord. Sometimes the liturgical (Exod. 3:12; Num. 8:11; Isa. 19:21) and/or specific ethical acts (Deut. 6:13; 13:4 [5]) are emphasized; in other cases the spiritual decision of a lasting commitment is in the forefront (Josh. 24:14-16, seven times). In Psalm 2:11 the latter notion prevails, but the former notion is always present.

I AM keeps God as the consistent protagonist in all four stanzas (v. 2, 4a ["the one who sits in the heavens"], 7, 11).

It is possible to substitute ritual service for relationship, and so the spiritual qualification *with fear (bᵉyir'â)* is added to prevent misunderstanding. The emotion, "with fear," and its outward expression, *with trembling (birᵉʿādâ)*, seem antithetical to a healthy, interpersonal relationship, because that affection of the mind separates, not unites, people. The antithesis between committing oneself to God and fearing him is understood in the light of Israel's covenant relationship with God. In the Old Testament "to fear *I AM*" is often used with other terms such as "serve" with the added notion to observe the law. The relationship of "to fear *I AM*" with keeping the law can be properly defined and understood on the basis of the so-called covenant formula.[108] The term *yr' 'et-yhwh* "to fear *I AM*" in that relationship expresses the basic declaration of Israel's relationship to *I AM*. "Thus *yr' 'et-yhwh* should be understood solely as the worship of Yahweh with particular attention to the concept of being faithful to him as the covenant God."[109]

Moreover, "to love God" and "to fear God" are not psychological contradictions for both are rooted in "to trust God." Love and fear of God spring from faith in God, the conviction that God says what he means and means what he says. Love denotes a spontaneous commitment out of appreciation for his grace; fear denotes a commitment out of dread, awe, and respect for God to avoid his just punishment (cf. Exod. 14:31; 19:9–20:21). God appeared to Israel at Sinai in a way that created numinous dread in order that they might surrender to him and be kept from judgment. The wicked, by contrast, have no fear of God (Ps. 36:2; Isa. 63:17; Jer 2:19; Hos 10:3). "Fear" is appropriate in the human relationship with God, whose names and deeds are "terrible" (Deut. 28:58), and who is "great" and "holy" (2 Sam. 7:22; Ps. 99:3; 145:6).[110]

107. C. Westermann, *TLOT,* 2:829, s.v. *'ebed "servant."*

108. K. Baltzer, *Covenant Formulary* (1971), esp. 12f., 37f.

109. J. Becker, *Gottesfurcht im Alten Testament* (*AB;* Rome: Pontifical Biblical Institute, 1965), p. 85; H.-P Stähli, *TLOT* 2:575, s.v. *yr' "to fear."*

110. Bruce K. Waltke, "The Fear of the Lord: The Foundation for a Relationship with

A literal rendering "rejoice in *I AM* with trembling" is an insufferable oxymoron and does not do justice to the psalmist's thought, but the gloss *celebrate his rule* (*gîlû with trembling;* see *bir*^{e}*ʿādâ*) is both sensible and the sense of the text. *Gîl* is frequently parallel and a synonym to *śāmaḥ* "to rejoice," *śûś* and *śîś* "to exult," *rûaʿ (Hiphil)* "to shout," *rānan* "to cry aloud," *ʿālaz* "to exult," *pāṣaḥ* "to break forth with joyous shouts," *ṣāhal* "to cry shrilly." These words are found almost exclusively in the Psalter and prophetic books, and in a great number of the latter in hymns. In the Old Testament rejoicing is not merely a psychological state of mind but an expression of joy in spontaneous, enthusiastic cries in the liturgy of praising God. The different kinds of joyful cries designated by these words cannot be known because the etymologies in some instances are uncertain, the texts are not specific, the LXX rendered most of them by the same words, and Israel's vocabulary for her liturgical celebration is far richer than ours.

3. *Submit to the Son to Escape God's Wrath v. 12*

The psalmist now gives reason why the kings should fear and celebrate God's rule with trembling. *Kiss the son (našš*^{e}*qû bar)* symbolizes their submission and reverence to the Suzerain's representative king (1 Sam. 10:1; cf. 1 Kings 19:18; Hos. 13:2). Actually, vassal kings in the ancient Near East kissed the ground immediately before the feet of the Overlord's representative.[111] The text and meaning of *našš*^{e}*qû bar,* however, is somewhat uncertain. No ancient version, apart from the Syriac, understood the Hebrew text in this way (see n. 73). The problem centers on the word *bar,* translated "son." This is an Aramaic word, not the usual Hebrew word, *ben* (see v. 7). *Bar,* however, is used in the Hebrew text of Proverbs 31:2. Its use in Psalm 2:12 can be explained in more than one way. The Aramaic term would be appropriate here because many of the restless tribes on Israel's threatened borders were Arameans. Also, the poet may have wished to avoid a discordant rhyming assonance of *ben* with the next word *pen (lest).* The poet also used the Aramaic word *r*ʿʿ ("to break") in v. 9 instead of the normal Hebrew verb *rṣṣ.* The Aramaic word in that verse also confused the ancient translators.

The particle *lest (pen)* negates the contingent purpose clause *he become angry* (*yeʾ*^{e}*nap,* the verbal root of *ʾap* [see v. 5]). The double reference to "anger" in this verse, both as a verb and in a chiastic parallel as a noun, *his anger (ʾappô),* at

God," in J. I. Packer & Loren Wilkinson, eds., *Alive to God: Studies in Spirituality Presented to James Houston* (Downers Grove, IL: InterVarsity Press, 1992).

111. Keel, *The Symbolism of the Biblical World,* p. 268; *ANEP,* Pl. 35a — note on the famous Black Obelisk showing the symbols of the Assyrian deities over the Assyrian king, and Jehu licking the dust at Shalmaneser's feet.

the end of 12A, suggests the subject of the verb is *I AM*, not "the son" even though it is the nearest antecedent. Verse 5 speaks of *I AM*'s anger. This interpretation that the antecedent of the third masculine singular pronouns, "he," "his," "him," is *I AM* finds confirmation in "seek refuge in him." The object of *ḥsh*, which occurs thirty-seven times, is always elsewhere *I AM* or its equivalents.[112]

Some scholars deny the attribute of anger to God,[113] but the inspired writers of the Old and New Testament attribute anger as a sacred emotion of his. Some restrict the notion to his judgment that demands retributive justice, not to his emotion: "The anger of God is not a disturbing emotion of his mind, but a judgment by which punishment is inflicted upon sin."[114] Of course, God is impassible — that is to say, he is always in control of his emotions, including his anger. His emotion of anger, however, is a necessary correlative of his holiness (Ezek. 28:22; cf. 20:40). His anger against those who touch his property, such as his son, and in this way insult him, indicates and proves his holiness.[115] *The way* (*derek*, see Ps. 1:1, 6) of the pagan kings has been to assail *I AM*'s holiness by rebelling against his righteous rule and his anointed property, which even David refused to touch in the case of King Saul, and by refusing, unlike Israel, to tremble before his holy mountain. Their refusal to take their shoes off their feet in his presence assailed his inviolable character and position and therefore incurs his wrath. In contrast to the gods the pagan worshiped, who broke out in anger out of caprice and or an inherent ill-well, *I AM*'s anger wells up from the demeaning of his person. The insult must be dealt with.

Furthermore, since God's holiness involves his moral perfection and his anger protects his purity, human recognition of his anger makes humankind conscious of their own sinfulness and their need of divine cleansing (cf. Exod. 14:31). Serving *I AM* with fear is related to a recognition of his anger that keeps humans in line with the divine standard. The godless and wicked have no fear of him because they disregard his anger against them (Hos. 10:3; Ps. 36:2; Jer. 2:19; Isa. 63:17).

When *I AM* vents his anger, the psalmist warns the nations, "*then you will be destroyed*" (*wᵉtōʾbᵉdû*, see Ps. 1:6). Before his fierce anger the earth trembles (Ps. 18:7 [8]). God adorns himself with glory and honor when he unleashes the

112. Waltke, *Proverbs*, p. 582, n. 52.

113. See Nicolas Berdyaev, *Freedom and Spirit* (New York: C. Scribner's Sons, 1935), p. 175; A. Ritschl, *The Christian Doctrine of Justification and Reconciliation*, vol. 3, ed. H. R. Mackintosh and A. B. Macaulay (Edinburgh: T. & T. Clark, 1900), p. 324; R. Otto, *The Idea of the Holy: An Inquiry into the Non-Rational Factor in the Idea of the Divine and Its Relation to the Rational*, trans. J. W. Harvey (London: Oxford University Press, 1936).

114. Augustine, *City of God*, XV:25.

115. A. P. Saphir (Dissertation, Princeton Theological Seminary, 1964).

fury of his wrath and human hubris is brought low (cf. Job 40:1-11). This is so *because (ki) he will flare up (yibʿar).* The combination of "he will become angry" and "he will flare up" is equivalent to his *blazing anger* in 2:5. The intensity of the destruction is often suggested by associating his wrath with fire (cf. Ps. 21:9 [10]; Isa. 30:27; Ezek. 22:21). The figure "flare up" suggests the elimination of all hubris from the earth. This will occur in the consummate Day of the Lord.

Soon is probably a better translation of *kimʿat* than the ambiguous "in a moment" (NIV, TNIV), for that expression may mean "suddenly" (JPS, NLT). *Kimʿat* with the imperfective, as is the case with *yibʿar,* elsewhere means "just" (only 2 Sam. 19:37) or "soon" (Ps. 81:14-15; Job 32:22), but never "easily" or "quickly" in the sense of unexpectedly, suddenly. If this is so, the imperfective is better construed as denoting the future ("will"), not potentiality ("can"). The Bible represents God's intervention in history as imminent, not remote (cf. 2 Pet. 3:8-9; Rev. 22:20), though some texts speak of his judgment coming unexpectedly (1 Thess. 5:2-3).

His destruction will take concrete form in the victories God assigns his sacred king and armies (Pss. 2:8-9; 18:32-45; 45:3).

David draws his address to conclusion by offering God's salvation to all who seek refuge in Israel's God. *Fortunate* or "rewarded" (*ʾašrê,* see Ps. 1:1) are those who trust *I AM,* who is known through his inspired revelations, such as this psalm. God is at once either a Destroyer or a Savior. Destruction comes from *I AM,* and so he is the only source of refuge from it. David opens a sanctuary of hope for *all (kol) who seek refuge in him (ḥôsê bô),* a metonomy for his devout worshiper.[116] The coronation liturgy closes with God's mercy trumping his anger.

Part IV. Theology

Marco Treves[117] as recently as 1960 revised and expanded the theory that Psalms 2 and 110 are acrostic poems composed for the Hasmonean rulers: Janneus and Simeon respectively. This interpretation has not gained acceptance because: 1) the psalms' contents cannot be tied to the Hasmonean dynasty. 2) The acrostic that names the Hasmonean kings is a product of ingenuity, not of discovery.[118] 3) The language of the psalm belongs to pre-exilic Hebrew, not late Hebrew.

116. Waltke, *Proverbs,* p. 582, n. 52.

117. Marco Treves, *VT* 15 (1960): 81-90.

118. B. Lindars and Von G. Sauer conclude after a survey of alleged acrostics in Psalms 2 and 110 that all examples are questionable.

Kimchi, Rashi, *et al.* think the king in view is David himself. This is possible because: 1) After being crowned at Hebron, David was crowned at Jerusalem (2 Sam. 2:1-4; 5:1-3), not at Zion (Ps. 2:6). 2) Upon hearing of David's crowning the Philistines fought against him (cf. 2 Sam. 5:17-25). 3) David was regarded as son of God (Ps. 89:26-27). More probably, however, David composed the psalm for Solomon and his successors. Solomon was crowned on Mount Zion (1 Kings 1:43-48) over potentially insubordinate kings (cf. 1 Kings 1:26; 9:15-19; 11:27), was called "the son of God" (1 Chron. 22:9-10) and is said to have "sat on the throne of *I AM*" (1 Chron. 29:23).

But David clothed Solomon in this psalm with a larger and more magnificent purple robe than David's young successor could wear (see p. 107). Solomon's kingdom, though it fulfilled the dimensions of the Abrahamic covenant, extending from the Wadi el Arish to the Euphrates, did not extend to the ends of the earth. The mantle of this psalm in Solomon's old age slipped off his stooped shoulders because of Solomon's apostasy, and the rebellion of the nations against this kingdom proved successful (1 Kings 11:1-13).

No Davidic king fulfilled this psalm's vision of a Davidic king extending *I AM*'s rule to the ends of the earth. In 586 B.C.E. *I AM*'s temple was destroyed, the House of David carried into exile and never again regained its throne, the symbol of its rule.

The psalm of the Davidic House ruling the ends of the earth is a prophecy looking to a future beyond David's and Solomon's reigns (p. 106). The surviving Greek translation of the Psalm of Solomon, written in the first century C.E., when Rome ruled the Jews, alludes to this psalm in its prayer for a Davidic king to restore the peace and independence of his people (Ps. Sol. 17:23-24). In short, after the exile "Messiah" (Hebrew) and "Christos" (Greek) and "son of God" became technical terms for this ideal king (cf. John 1:49; Matt. 26:63).

Jesus Christ of Nazareth fulfilled this hope, and he himself and his apostles identify him as the fulfillment of the psalms. Within the canon of Scripture Jesus Christ is the king whom Psalm 2 celebrates. Although Jesus Christ fulfills the psalm, he has not as yet exhausted its promises, for he must reign until he has put all his enemies under his feet (1 Cor. 15:20-28; Phil. 2:9-10; Rev. 2:27; *passim*).

In sum, the psalm is typico-prophetic (see p. 112). During the existence of the first temple (960 B.C.E.–586 B.C.E.) the psalm was used in the coronation of David's successors to his throne. In that context, the sobriquets "king," "anointed one," "son" are written in lower case. But in the second temple period they referred to the Messiah, who in the New Testament is identified as the Son of God both by virgin birth in Matthean theology (Matt. 1:18-25) and by his being the Second Person of the Trinity in Johannine theology (John 17), not just the adopted son of God as in the Old Testament. In the context of the New Testament the king's titles are written in upper case: "Anointed One," "King," and "Son." As Amyrault (1596-1664), a Protestant scholar at the Academy of Saumur, France, put it: we must keep our left eye on the temporal king and our right on the eternal Christ.

Christ's authority and right to rule the world through Christian faith, which expresses itself both by baptism and by obeying his teachings (Matt. 28:18-20), has been extended to every continent. Jesus of Nazareth has more followers than any other religious figure. On the other hand, his rule has been challenged throughout history. The Roman emperor Diocletian set up in Spain two large pillars. One reads: "Diocletian Jovian Maximum Hercules Caesares Augusti, for having extended the Roman Empire in the east and west, and having extinguished the name of Christian, who brought the Republic to ruin." The second reads: "Diocletian Jovian Maximum Hercules Caesares Augusti . . . for having everywhere abolished the superstition of Christ, for having extended the worship of the gods." That opposition expresses itself today in the "Humanist Manifesto," drawn by the world's intellectual elite during the 1930s. Today that manifesto that asserted human autonomy finds expression in postmodernism, cultural relativism, utopian pacifism, moral equivalence, and missionaries for atheism, such as Richard Dawkins. Those "religions" have now filtered down from our media, universities, and government to the general public. And we are seeing the pernicious wages of such theories. For the first time in Western civilization marriage is no longer defined as between a man and woman and fruitless cohabitation of any form is tolerated. Those wages are also paid in the Western nonchalance toward Islamofascism. The devil is always on the lookout for the moral relativism that signals a latter-day Faust, and it seems he is finding eager recruits amongst some prominent spokespeople in the West.

These reflections infer the psalm's universal aspect. It extends salvation to all who put their trust in the God who authored the Book of the Law and is the Father of Jesus Christ, who is now revealed to be the Son of God in the full sense of that pregnant term. As such, he inherits the world, and all who have been baptized into his sufferings are co-heirs with him (Rom. 8:17). In the eschaton they will sit on thrones judging the twelve tribes of Israel; they will even judge the angels in heaven (Matt. 19:27-28; 1 Cor. 5:12-13).

CHAPTER 6

Psalm 3: Living in the Borderland

Morning Prayer After a Dark Night

Part I. Voice of the Church

I. Messianic Character of the Psalm

Clement of Rome (c. 96), gives the first specific reference to Psalm 3 we can find. He writes that verse 6 (Heb.), "I lay down and slept, and I awoke for the Lord sustained me," alludes to Christ's death and resurrection. But this is exceptional for Clement, as he uses his homily to follow the synagogal parenetic approach, urging hearers to imitate "the noble things." Clement is a vast collection of "*exempla*" (not "typoi"), given as hortatory admonitions. He attempts to draw a moral continuity between the Old and New Testaments.[1] It is only the subsequent Christian apologists who then use the Psalms to develop a prophecy-fulfillment motif to emphasize Biblical unity.

Barnabas (c. 125) argues that the Old Testament ordinances were never intended to be taken literally, but metaphorically, as pointing to the coming of Christ. The Apologists who follow, beginning with **Justin** (c. 100-165), make three explicit statements: Jesus is the Messiah, the Son of God; the Law has a different interpretation and position after Christ; and the community of Jesus is now the true "Israel." An early tradition has it that the first three psalms reflect on the life, death, and resurrection of Jesus Christ.[2]

1. Oskar Skarsaune, "The Development of Scriptural Interpretations in the Second and Third Centuries," in Magne Saebø, ed., *Hebrew Bible/Old Testament: The History of Its Interpretation* (Göttingen: Vandenhoeck & Ruprecht, 1996), vol. 1/1, p. 376.

2. John Eaton, *The Psalms: A Historical and Spiritual Commentary* (London and New York: Continuum, 2005), p. 49.

Origen (c. 185-254), as we have seen, uses prosopopoeia to flow into typology, whenever the text no longer allows "the I" of the psalmist to continue. Psalm 3 is a case in point. From its title, it is clear that Origen does not question the historicity of Absalom's rebellion against David. But he finds it impossible to read verses 6-8 exclusively within a Davidic context. So now the "letter" leads into the "analogue" of Christ the Messiah and also of Judas, no longer only of David and Absalom.[3] Just as Christ "assumed the form of a slave" in Philippians 2:7, so Origen argues that Christ also "assumed the condition of the dead"; nevertheless, God did not leave him there in either condition.[4] At the same time, Origen never identifies the distinct "persons" of the Father and the Son, without also distinguishing the divine Christ and the human Jesus. For example, he associates Psalm 3:5 with Jesus' humanity in death and the risen Lord "out of sleep."[5] For Origen, it is the soul of Christ that descends into hell, not the body of Jesus, based on Psalm 30:3, 9. In this context Origen is refuting the heresy that argued for two separate "persons" engaged in the "kenotic" work of the Incarnation, Jesus and Christ. He links the reality of the One "who knew no sin," and yet "was made sin for us" (2 Cor. 5:21).

From this prosopological approach, Origen then prepares the way for later commentators to reaffirm the solidarity of Jesus Christ with humankind as the second Adam, as we shall see in his comments on Psalm 4:1 (see p. 212). Subsequent commentators sustain the theme of this solidarity. This notion also becomes a key theme of **Augustine of Hippo** (354-430), who interprets Psalm 3 as a prayer of "the whole Christ," namely of Christ and his Body the Church *(totus Christi)*. He associates the distressful "I" of the psalm with all Christians, both the wretched "I" of Romans 7:24-25, and the declaration of 1 Corinthians 12:27: "Now you are the body of Christ, and each one of you is part of it." In the light of Ephesians 4:15, "speaking the truth in love, we will in all things grow up into Him who is the head, that is, Christ,"[6] Augustine also identifies the distressed "I" with the individual Christian. Reflecting on Matthew 6:6, he states: "the Lord himself taught that it was behind the closed doors of one's bedroom, that is to say, in the

3. Origen, *Ps. 3* (PG 12, 1117B-1132D); Marie-Josèphe Rondeau, *Les Commentaires Patristiques du Psaltier (III-Ve siècles)*, vol. 2, *Exégèse Prosopologique et Théologique* (Rome: Pontificium Institutum Studiorum Orientalium, 1985), pp. 70, 100.

4. Origen, *In Rom. V,10* (PG 14, 1051); Marie-Josèphe Rondeau, *Les Commentaires Patristiques du Psaltier*, p. 120.

5. Origen, *Ps. 3* (PG 12, 1125C-1129A); Marie-Josèphe Rondeau, *Les Commentaires Patristiques du Psaltier*, p. 103.

6. Saint Augustine, *Expositions on the Psalms*, ed. John E. Rotelle, O.S.A., trans. Maria Boulding, O.S.B. (Hyde Park, NY: New City Press, 2000), vol. 1, pp. 81-83.

recesses of the heart."[7] Indeed, Augustine assures us it is in the silence of one's inner thoughts where one prays that one can intimately and profoundly communicate all the words of this psalm in silent prayer to God.

II. Monastic Liturgy of the Night

Theodoret of Cyrrhus (393-460) assumes that for the benefit of lazier people (i.e., those who do not know their Bible), he has to summarize the story of Absalom's betrayal of his father. But he says nothing more about this historical reference. He too spends more space focusing on the pastoral application of the psalm for his contemporary readers, but now he considers the Biblical significance of the "night" as the context for "sleeping" in Psalm 3:5. The Scriptures often relate "the night" with disasters; he notes: "On the other hand, sleep is associated with nights; so it suggests troubles and release from them at the same time. You see, the words, 'I awoke because the Lord will defend me,' mean this, 'I benefited from divine intervention and so proved superior to the evils that further befell me' that make the afflicted think they are living in a kind of darkness."[8] At the same time, "sleep" may be identified with deliverance and with rest of soul.

The flexibility with which the early fathers of late antiquity developed the threefold sense of literal/historical, figurative or Christological, and tropological and personal application was promoted in the distinctive usage of the psalms by the Desert Fathers. **Palladius** (c. 363-c. 431) reports that "[the fathers] applied all the Psalms to their own lives and works, and to their passions, and to their spiritual life and to the wars which the devils waged against them. Each man did thus according to his capacity, whether he was engaged in a rule of life for the training of the body, or of the soul, or of the spirit, . . . he acquires daily the faculty of singing a song mingled with meditation of God and gaze [which is fixed] upon Him . . . and which is like that of the angels."[9] He also quotes the confession of Abba Isidore, a priest in Scete, just south of Alexandria: "When I was a young man and stayed in my cell, I made no limit to the number of psalms which I used in the service of God. Night and day alike were spent in psalmody."[10] Sleep deprivation was characteristic of the monks of the

7. Augustine, *Expositions on the Psalms,* vol. 1, p. 79.

8. Theodoret of Cyrrhus, in Marie-Josèphe Rondeau, *Les Commentaires Patristiques du Psaltier,* p. 61.

9. Quoted by Violet MacDermot, *The Cult of the Seer in the Ancient Middle East* (Berkeley and Los Angeles: University of California Press, 1971), p. 61.

10. *The Desert Christian: The Sayings of the Desert Fathers,* trans. Benedicta Ward, S.L.G. (New York: Macmillan, 1975), no. 4, p. 97.

Egyptian desert. This was the way non-literate Christians combated ancient Egyptian religion, with its frequent association of sleep with the afterlife in a solar religion, with the activity of demons, with the interpretation of dreams, and with the ceaseless vigil and wakefulness of angels. Therefore, the holy man exercised himself in ceaseless prayer.

Palladius further records "about Abba Pachomias that he spent much time in striving with devils like a true athlete, and after the manner of Saint Anthony. And because many devils came against him in the night season, he asked God to keep him away from sleep both by day and night . . . and bring low the might of the Enemy."[11] Palladius, like others following him, would pray on the night of the Sabbath, as if to await the resurrection dawn of Sunday morning. At Easter the Desert Fathers most intently commemorated Psalm 3:5.

In the transition from an oral form of communication to a written text or codex, chanting the psalms was something to participate in "doing," rather than something to "discourse about." Daily recitation of the psalms, commonly twelve psalms in the morning prayer within one's own cell, and twelve psalms at night, became the daily practice, beginning the early morning with Psalm 3 (also more commonly later, Psalm 63 [LXX, 62], see pp. 215-16) and ending with Psalm 140, and other prayers at the third, sixth, and ninth hours.[12] Such became the origin and long tradition of the liturgical "hours," with its variants in the diverse monastic foundations, East and West.[13] During the manual labor of the day, the psalms were constantly chanted. Palladius reports that around 3 p.m., "one can stand and hear the divine psalmody issuing forth from each cell and imagine one is high above, in paradise,"[14] that is, with the angels. This was the time of day for the main meal, or in more ascetic forms, the single meal of the day. Palladius also reports that when visitors arrived at the community, they would be welcomed, taken into the church accompanied by psalmody, and would then have their feet washed. So the psalms were also linked with the daily need of inner cleansing.

Haunted by Paul's admonition, "Pray without ceasing" (1 Thess. 5:17), living in the practice of "unceasing prayer" became the identity of the desert monk. Yet it was not a form of repetitious prayer, but a way of life, identified with purity of heart, expulsion of evil thoughts, and protection against the demonic, and practiced along with other expressions of asceticism.

Palladius, like so many other Desert Fathers, attributes nearly all the ills

11. Quoted by Violet MacDermot, *The Cult of the Seer in the Ancient Middle East*, p. 47.

12. Tertullian, *On Prayer*, ch. 25.

13. Robert Taft, S.J., *The Liturgy Hours in the East and West: The Origins of the Divine Office and Its Meaning for Today* (St. John's Abbey, Collegeville, MN: The Liturgical Press, 1986).

14. Taft, *The Liturgy Hours*, p. 280.

that come to their communities to the agency of demons. Demons also figure strongly in the works of **Evagrius of Ponticus** (c. 345-99), a friend of the Cappadocian fathers, and of Jerome. He was astutely aware of the human propensity for evil, and discerning the *logismoi,* or inner thoughts, was his *forte.* At the beginning of his work entitled *Praktikos* he lists eight evil thoughts: gluttony, fornication, love of money, sadness, anger, listlessness or *acedia,* vainglory, and pride. He calls them "thoughts," for they invade our consciousness, and it is not in our power to prevent their invasion. But it is our responsibility to control them, interpreting their habitat as belonging to the "night" and to "darkness." Thus, celebrating the advent of "the morning," as in Psalm 3, is to celebrate victory over vices and the demonic realm. In his treatise *On Prayer,* Evagrius advises: "Pray suitably and without disturbance and chant psalms with understanding and rhythmically, and you will be like a young eagle soaring in the heights." Then he adds: "Psalmody calms the passions and silences the body's bad temperament."[15] Cassian describes the ideal monk in *Conference* 12: "He is found to be the same at night as in the day, the same in bed as at prayer, the same alone as when surrounded by a crowd of people; he sees nothing in himself in private that he would be embarrassed for others to see, nor wants anything detected by the omnipresent Eye [of God] to be concealed from human sight."[16] The night, traditionally so fearsome, has become as the day. In monastic life then, Psalm 3 could be celebrative of such personal integrity in a life given over to psalmody.

III. Expansion and Changes in Western Monasticism

Benedict of Nursia (480-543) gives the West what the Desert Fathers had given to the East, a monastic way of life. But it differs significantly in that it challenges nominal Christianity, not Egyptian pagan religion. Battling against sleep had been an important tactic for the Egyptian monks. Palladius had written about Dorotheus: "Never did I see him stretch out his feet, or rest on a mattress or bed."[17] Now Benedict allows six to eight hours of sleep a night and the use of a blanket, mattress, and pillow, with Vigils beginning with Psalm 3 and 95. Benedict is also moderate regarding the length and times of prayer (unlike the con-

15. Evagrius Ponticus, *On Prayer,* 82, 83, in A. M. Casiday, trans., *Evagrius Ponticus* (London and New York: Routledge, 2006), p. 185.

16. Quoted by Columba Stewart, *Cassian the Monk* (Oxford: Oxford University Press, 1998), p. 83.

17. Quoted by Herbert B. Workman, *The Evolution of the Monastic Ideal* (London: Charles H. Kelly, 1915), p. 151.

tinuous prayers of the Egyptian monks), and he pays close attention to the systematized practice of worship, installing the canonical hours: Nocturns, Matins, Prime, Terce, Sext, None, Vespers, and Compline. At all these periods of prayer, the psalms are appropriately recited. But most significant of all is his theological reorientation. Up to this time the monks had focused upon self-conquest, but now Benedict teaches self-surrender, for this is the truth underlying *obedentia.* The Rule systematizes manual life, giving it human dignity instead of slavish status, and decrees that six hours of manual work should be linked with two hours of reading. Monasteries become then cells of a civilized culture, much less subjective than the lives of Desert Fathers, and more given to thought, theology, and Biblical commentary. *Laborare et orare* engendered community, learning, enterprise, and education. Significantly, nearly all the medieval commentaries on the Psalms are now composed by monks. Cassiodorus gives new boost to educational standards, and learned monks like Bede, Benedict of Aniane, and Anselm follow.

IV. Medieval Monastic Commentaries

The great period of monastic commentaries develops between **Cassiodorus** (490-583) and **Geroch of Reichersberg** (1093-1169), with such names as **Haimo of Halberstadt** (died c. 855), **Remigius of Auxerre** (c. 841-c. 908), **Bruno of Würzburg** (died 1045), **Bruno the Carthusian** (1030-1101), **Bruno of Segni** (1049-1123), **Odo of Segni** (mid-twelfth century), and **Honorius of Autun** (died c. 1151). Most of these psalm commentators also cover other books of the Bible, spending all their productive lives in Biblical study.

Building upon the threefold exegesis of Origen, and the more elaborated fourfold exegesis of Cassian, Western monastic commentators now build upon the clear teaching of **Pope Gregory the Great** (590-604) in his greatly influential work, *Moralia in Job* (591). He subjects nearly every verse in the book of Job to a three-part analysis: historical or literal, allegorical, and moral.[18] Although Gregory left no commentary on the Psalter,[19] his *Job* becomes the influential text for all later medieval exegesis. We do not have a commentary on Psalm 3 by Cassiodorus, but Bede makes frequent use of Psalms 3:3 and 7.

The Carolingian commentator, **Haimo of Auxerre** (c. 790-c. 855), follows

18. Gregory the Great, *Moralia in Job. Libri I-X,* ed. Marcus Adriaen, trans. Barbara H. Rosenwein, Series Latina 143 (Turnhout, Belgium: Brepols, 1979).

19. Traditionally Gregory has been attributed an anonymous commentary on the penitential psalms, but his authorship is disputed.

the Origenian/Gregorian model and treats Psalm 3 at three levels: the story of David and Absalom; the passion of Christ in conflict with Judas; and personal reflections upon our own lives. But he ends rather suddenly with awareness that the Christian benefits from "a risen life in Christ, so that with the Apostle, we are assured: For the sufferings of this present time are not worthy to be compared to the future glory which will be revealed in us (Rom. 8:18)."[20] Also in the ninth century, **Remigius of Auxerre** (c. 850-908) treats both David and Christ, "the spiritual David," briefly. He interprets Christ in his humanity making this lament, which then permits a transition to a personal appropriation of the psalm. But noticeably absent is the discernment of one's enemies as one's own inner passions, which we saw in the Desert Fathers. Rather, the Carolingian "enemies" are external threats to a Christianized society, analogous to the Constantinian world of the fourth century.[21]

Bruno of Segni (c. 1032-1101), who helped Gregory VI with his papal reform in the eleventh century, writes briefly in his commentary about the lament of the humanity of Christ. Bruno interprets the psalmist's enemies to be the whole world as it rises up against the church. The imagery of "breaking the teeth of sinners," he interprets as "their power, knowledge, fortitude, arguments, and all the other things by which they are able to defend themselves and fight against others,"[22] being taken from them. Clearly he writes feelingly in an age of political opposition.

Pseudo-Bede (died c. 1103) divides his study of the Psalms into explanation, followed by commentary. The former appears to be genuinely Bede, but the rest of the commentary was written much later by another commentator. In the *explanatio* of Psalm 3, considered genuinely Bede, it is noted: "This psalm, and many others which pertain to the treacheries of Saul, was sung after Quinquagesima; but certainly placed before on account of the mystery, since both this one which commemorates the resurrection after the three days was placed third, and that psalm . . . which reveals the fruit of forgiveness and repentance. This whole psalm is fitted to the person of Christ."[23] He is stating that Psalm 3 is being sung after Lent, to celebrate the resurrection of Christ, in the church's liturgy. It also commemorates the suffering of Christ, and is thus also sung during Lent. For him, it is significantly "the third" psalm, to reflect "the third day" when Christ rose again, and it is also united with another psalm, unspecified, but possibly "the fourth psalm."

20. Haimo of Auxerre, *In omnes psalmos pia, brevis ac dilucia explanatio* (PL 115:191-695), pp. 204-6.

21. Remigius of Auxerre, *Enarrationem in psalmos liber unus* (PL 131:133-844), pp. 158-61.

22. Bruno of Segni, *Expositio in psalmos* (PL 164:695-1228), pp. 719-22.

23. Pseudo-Bede, *De psalmorum libro exegesis* (PL 93:477-1098), p. 494.

After the Bede insertion of his *explanation*, Pseudo-Bede — identified as Manegold von Lautenbach in the eleventh century — then adds his own commentary — rhetorical, fulsome, and scholarly. He argues that the psalm is linked with Psalm 2, having a similar exhortation for the persecuted. He makes much of the lament of the Son addressed to the Father, but also suggests, "This psalm can be read in the person of the Head [i.e., Christ], reading the whole in the voice of the Church," in an echo of Augustine. But he adds, "Thirdly, the same psalm can also be read in the person of any one member of the Church, that is, of any believer surrounded by unnumbered multitude of vices and earthly desires."[24] So he then writes much more like the Desert Fathers of how "the taunting devil and his angels heap up vices and noxious delights, by depraved suggestions, endeavoring to lead the believer's resistant mind into the law of sin and death. In desperation the believer speaks, praying and bewailing his misery to God his Creator, to arouse God to have pity on him and assist him."[25] He concludes by observing, "for 'the thousands of people' persecuting [me] are not in this understanding . . . external enemies, but internal ones, that is to say, vices and depraved desires, which are rightly called a people, since they produce tumult and strife in the soul."[26]

The commentary of Pseudo-Bede represents the transition from the more communal mindset of the earlier Carolingian period, to the new, more individual consciousness now being expressed by the Aristotelian influence of twelfth-century scholarship. The language of Pseudo-Bede is now more reminiscent of twelfth-century Jewish commentators, and of scholars like Albert and Richard of St. Victor. Pseudo-Bede suggests that Psalm 3 could be applied to Ezekiel in fear of his enemies, as well as to Christ in speaking to the Father. Then he focuses on the story of David's dysfunctional family, and on Christ's earthly life and sufferings, to a much greater extent than other commentators. He concludes with an echo of Richard of St. Victor's suggestion that inner enemies, i.e., evil thoughts, also threaten the godly.

Geroch of Reichersberg (1093-1169) argues that one needs both the literal/historical and the spiritual/mystical levels of interpretation, suggesting "the New Learning" focused more on glosses than on the text itself. He further suggests that the link between the first three psalms is the move from the Incarnation in Psalm 1, to the faith in the passion in Psalm 2, to the resurrection and ascension in Psalm 3.[27] He interprets the Son as speaking to the Father in Psalm 3.

24. Pseudo-Bede, *De psalmorum libro exegesis* (PL 93:499 D).
25. Pseudo-Bede, *De psalmorum libro exegesis* (PL 93:500 C).
26. Pseudo-Bede, *De psalmorum libro exegesis* (PL 93:500 D).
27. Remigius of Auxerre, *Enarrationum in psalmos liber unus*, (PL 131:133-844), pp. 158-61.

Remigius does the same, but with a stronger focus on the inside enemies, i.e., false brethren. Bruno of Segni's identification of the Jews as the enemy of Christ in his passion is indicative of a new hostility developing towards them.[28]

Thomas Aquinas (c. 1225-74) summarizes much of the previous commentaries but adds his own figural reflection of "sleep." Just as Adam entered "a deep sleep" to be presented with his spouse Eve, so too, Christ's "deep sleep" in his death was for the sake of his Bride, the Church. In turn then, the church need not fear being wholly overwhelmed by her adversaries, "for Christ rising from the dead, dies no more" (Romans 6).[29] He repeats the three levels of exegesis, but also adds reference to the persecution of the church, as well as to the Victorines' psychological interpretation of the inner attacks by evil thoughts.

Denys the Carthusian (1402-71) has a fulsome introduction explaining his Biblical principles, essentially following the traditional threefold levels. Originally, he thinks of "sleep" as the mitigation of bad things, or as the cleansing of thoughts, or even as providing comfort. He distinguishes the literal/historical sufferings of Christ from the spiritual sufferings of Christ. He then expands on a tropological interpretation of the psalm in a separate section: Absalom being a type of the world and David as the figure of Christ, as well as a member of the church. Then after much self-application, he closes with a prayer.[30]

V. Living Paraphrase of Erasmus

As for **Luther**, we have found no commentary of his on Psalm 3 in his original lectures or in a later exposition. **Calvin** includes Psalm 3 in his commentary, but it does not stand out as one of his best. In contrast, the extended "paraphrase" of Psalm 3 that **Erasmus** (1466/69-1536) wrote quickly and published in 1524, must be considered among his finest devotional writing. At the conclusion of his commentary on Psalm 2, Erasmus says: "It is now time to go on to the next psalm, and I intend to do so, with the inspiration of Jesus Christ." The *paraphrasis in tertium psalmum* is the shortest of his writings on the psalms, but it was well received, with further issues and editions. Unlike his other psalm commentaries, he does not discuss textual problems, nor does he make use of the patristic commentaries. Instead, after a brief summary of the historical background — so frequently discussed by previous commentators on David

28. Bruno of Segni, *Expositio in psalmos* (PL 164:695-1228), pp. 702-5.

29. Thomas Aquinas, *In psalmos Davidis expositio,* vol. 14, pp. 148-312.

30. Denis the Carthusian, *D. Dionysii Cartusiani insigne opus commentariorum, in psalmos omnes Davidicos,* in *Doctoris Ecstatici D. Dionysii Cartusi opera Omnia* (Monstrolii: Typis Cartusiae S. M. de Pratis, 1898), vols. 5-6; 5:422-27.

and Absalom versus Christ and Judas — Erasmus gives us a movingly and personal application of it. His subtitle is taken from the psalm: "O Lord, How Have My Tormentors Multiplied!" He uses the first person plural to incorporate the sufferings of others, and the role of the psalm in providing comfort and an exhortation to devotion and piety. He refrains from satire or anger against his political enemies, making his allusions wholly Biblical. The result is a powerful literary work. It had been requested by the theologian Melchior, for the benefit of Christendom, and Erasmus in turn requested that Melchior write an indictment against the status of academic theology, for "the age is wasted solely in quarrelsome disputations and in bitter polemical pamphlets. This is a great scandal." And so he concludes, "and now for this psalm!"[31]

Speaking on behalf of all Christians, he voices David's lament of affliction. The irony is that God is mighty, our Creator indeed, and our defense is solely in his hands. Why, then, does he permit us to endure such affliction? Yes, we know that all stood up against Jesus also, "a whole rout of priests, Pharisees, Scribes, elders, Herod, Pilate, and finally the whole mass of people . . . who finally crushed him."[32] Prior to Christ, God's beloved servant David also had been betrayed by Absalom and by Ahithophel, one of his closest advisors, as Judas did later to Christ. Just as David, who had built Jerusalem, was driven out into a wilderness, so also Christ, by whom "the world was made," was driven there. As Shimei taunted David, so the crowd at the foot of the cross mocked Jesus. But with an eternal perspective upon universal history, as under the sovereignty of God, Erasmus confesses, "nothing happens on this earth by accident or by chance, but that all things are governed by your eternal design."[33] Likewise the people of God will also suffer as Christ and his servant David have.

Erasmus now sees the whole sweep of his own life in terms of all the misunderstanding, slander, injustice, bitter opposition, and isolation he has suffered during the past tumultuous twenty years of his public life. He feels like the apostle, saying "We are troubled on every side, but we are not distressed. . . . We appear to be dying, but, see, we are alive, chastened but not done to death" (2 Cor. 4:8-9; 6:9). But in the triumph of Christ's sufferings, death, and resurrection, "broken are the teeth of the wicked." But "Christ is the strong rock, and anyone who is in Christ is a rock: broken teeth cannot grind it down."[34] "So, here it is," Erasmus writes to his friend Melchior. "You may not like it, but I shall not be disappointed!" How could Erasmus be disappointed with a negative re-

31. Erasmus, *Expositions of the Psalms*, ed. Dominic Baker-Smith, trans. Michael J. Heath, Collected Works of Erasmus, vol. 63 (Toronto: University of Toronto Press, 1997), pp. 152-53.

32. Erasmus, *Expositions of the Psalms*, p. 154.

33. Erasmus, *Expositions of the Psalms*, p. 157.

34. Erasmus, *Expositions of the Psalms*, pp. 166-67.

sponse, when Psalm 3 had provided for him such transcendence of "being in Christ's death and resurrection"? Following him, the Reformation abolished the liturgical emphasis of the monastic interpretive tradition on the Psalter.

Part II. Voice of the Psalmist: Translation

A psalm of David. When he fled from Absalom his son.

1 *I AM,* how many are my foes!
Many rise up against me![35]
2 Many are saying of me,
"God[36] will not deliver him."[37]
3 But you, *I AM,* are a shield[38] around me;
you are my glory, the one who lifts up my head.
4 I cry[39] aloud[40] to *I AM,*
and he answers me from his holy mountain.
5 I lay down[41] and slept;[42]
I awoke because *I AM* sustains me.[43]

35. *Me* glosses *nepeš.* Its traditional gloss, "soul," misleads an English-speaking audience into thinking of "soul" in the New Testament sense of Greek *psychē,* "the seat and center of life that transcends the earthly" (W. Bauer, *A Greek-English Lexicon of the New Testament and Other Early Christian Literature,* trans. and adapt. William F. Arndt and F. Wilbur Gingrich; 2nd ed. revised and augmented by F. Wilbur Gingrich and Frederick W. Danker [Chicago: University of Chicago Press, 1979], p. 893). Hebrew *nepeš,* however, refers to the passionate drives and appetites of *all* breathing creatures, both animal and human. In the NT a person has a "soul"; in the OT a person is a *nepeš* (B. Waltke, *TWOT* 2:587-91).

36. LXX adds: "His God."

37. Literally, "He has no deliverance in God."

38. M. Dahood, *Psalms,* vol. 1 (AB; Garden City, NY: Doubleday, 1968). LXX renders it by *antilēptōr* ("protector," "helper"). But why read Punic instead of sensible Hebrew?

39. Briggs et al. interpret the imperfective as denoting frequentative action in past time and the following *waw* consecutive with the short prefix conjugation as an "aorist single act." But the same construction elsewhere refers to a habitual, universal experience and is best rendered by the English present tense (*IBHS,* p. 669, P. 33.3.3c, ## 5-10; cf. also Job 7:18; 14:10; 34:24; Ps. 42:5 [6]; 55:17 [18]; 120:1; Hab. 1:9-10).

40. Literally, "my voice . . . I cry out" *(qôlî . . . 'eqrā'). Qôlî* is a non-cognate internal accusative (*IBHS,* p. 167, P. 10.2.1e, ## 42, 43).

41. The shift from the prefix conjugation to the suffix conjugation suggests a change from a habitual situation to a unique event. Conceptually, praying and receiving an answer in trouble belong to a universal experience, but lying down and sleeping in the midst of peril tend to be unique.

42. A pseudo-cohortative (*IBHS,* p. 576, P. 34.5.3).

43. The suggestion that, like an Assyro-Babylonian king, the psalmist is seeking a reassuring encounter with God in a dream or an oracle on the eve of battle through an incubation

6 I do not fear the[44] tens of thousands of troops
Who are drawn up against me on every side.
7 Arise, *I AM*! Deliver me, my God!
Strike[45] all my enemies on the cheek;[46]
break the teeth of the wicked.
8 Deliverance belongs to *I AM*.
Your blessing be[47] on your people.[48]
For the director of music. With stringed instruments.

Part III. Commentary

I. Introduction

A. Literary Context

Psalm 3 is the first of "a group of 12 psalms composed of ten prayers . . . , divided into two groups of five (Pss 3–7; 9–13), each of which has appended to it a sixth that characterizes the human condition (Pss 8; 14)."[49] J. Brennan sees a conceptual connection between Psalms 1 and 3. "By aligning ourselves with the 'just' in Psalm 1, and with those who 'trust in Yahweh' in Psalm 2 . . . we become part of that people upon whom he invokes Yahweh's blessing (3:9 [EV 8])."[50] Psalms 2 and 3 share a conceptual kingship connection: "The king who is introduced by

---

ritual conflicts with and deprives the passage of its obvious intention to teach the merits of faith: "because *I AM* sustains me." See Louis Jacquet, *Les Psaumes et le Coeur de l'Homme* (Gembloux, Belgium: Duculot, 1975), p. 247.

44. *Min* probably means "on account of."

45. Precative perfective (*IBHS*, p. 494, P. 30.5.4c).

46. *Leḥî*, probably an accusative of state (*IBHS*, p. 172, P. 10.2.2d), may mean "jaw" or "cheek."

47. Literally, "Your blessing upon your people." Although a nominal clause is normally indicative, at the end of the psalm it is probably a wish. Moreover, since David regarded himself as under a curse and since the nation is wicked, he would not assert that God's blessing is on the vile people (cf. 2 Sam. 16:5-11).

48. The meaning of *selâ* at the end of the Hebrew verses 3, 5, and 9 is obscure. Aquila and Jerome glossed it "always" (from *neṣaḥ*) and the LXX, by *diapsalma* (interlude of instrumental music). The learned rabbis disagree about its meaning, and modern scholarship has suggested sixty etymologies, none of which has gained a consensus. A suggested emendation is *sll*, raising the voice to a higher pitch.

49. *TNIV Study Bible*, p. 825.

50. Joseph P. Brennan, "Psalms 1–8: Some Hidden Harmonies," *BTB* 10 (January 1980): 25-30, esp. p. 26.

Yahweh in Ps. 2, and the enemies who plot against him, reappear in Ps. 3, which is the first of a series of laments in which the king himself cries out to Yahweh for deliverance from those who press in upon him from every side."[51] Psalm 3 shares an even closer relationship with Psalm 4: both pertain to the king who is opposed by enemies within his own ranks. Moreover, Psalm 3 is a morning prayer, Psalm 4, an evening prayer. Finally, both contain a number of catchwords that crochet them together: *ṣar* ("foes" [3:1]; "distress" [4:1]); *rabbîm 'ōmᵉrim* ("many are saying," 3:2 [3], "asking," 4:6 [7]); *kᵉbôdî* ("my glory," 3:3 [4]; 4:2 [3]).

The political order of heaven envisioned in Psalm 2 is overturned on earth in Psalm 3. In Psalm 2, *I AM* installs his anointed king on his throne; in Psalm 3 the king's non-anointed son, the heir apparent, dethrones his anointed father. In Psalm 2 the father's anointed son, by faith, recites both his right to the throne and his prayer to inherit the earth; in Psalm 3 he prays for deliverance from his own people, including his son, who like a mad animal seeks to devour him. Symbolically, the king is driven from social-political order (his palace) to social disorder (the wilderness). Nevertheless, though the anointed king's "landscape" is in disarray, his faith in God gives his spiritual "inscape" order. His faith expresses itself in Psalm 3 and serves as a model prayer that turns an upside-down world right-side up. The basis of this prayer is his covenant relationship with God, who orders the world through his immutable covenants.

B. Structure

Within the prose frame of the superscript and postscript, which respectively inform us of the psalm's original composition and of its later temple performance (see p. 88), the psalm, like most petition psalms (see pp. 95, 197), consists of five parts: 1) his address to God (first word); 2) a description of his lamentable state (vv. 1-2); and 3) his confidence: an affirmation of trust (vv. 3-4) and validation of that faith (vv. 5-6). Having turned the upside-down landscape into a righted inscape, he offers 4) his twofold petition for his deliverance and punishment of the enemy (v. 7) in connection with 5) a benediction upon the nation (v. 8). This analysis shows that, apart from the prose frame, the psalm consists of four equal couplets (1-2, 3-4, 5-6, 7-8); its stylistic symmetry matches the psalmist's spiritual composure.

The key words "deliverance" (*yᵉšû'â,* vv. 2, 7, 8) and "answers" (*'ānâ,* v. 4), and the sevenfold repetition of *I AM* (*yhwh,* vv. 1, 3, 4, 5, 7, 8) and its equivalent "God" (*'ᵉlōhîm,* v. 7) unite the development from address to the crescendo

51. Brennan, "Psalms 1–8: Some Hidden Harmonies."

benediction (v. 8 [9]). The outer couplets (lament and petition/benediction) are addressed directly to God; the inner couplets of confidence are an apostrophe, albeit his direct address to God in verse 3 links his lament and confidence. Anglican and Roman Catholic Christians reflect that *lex orandi, lex credendi:* "The rule of prayer is the rule of faith." One's true beliefs are best expressed in prayers. One's theology is best discovered through one's prayers.

II. Exegesis

A. Superscript

Superscripts of more than three words are numbered as separate verses in the Hebrew Bible; they are an integral part of the psalms (see pp. 88-92).

1. Genre and Author

A *psalm* (Heb. *mizmôr*) refers to a song that is sung to the pizzicato of a stringed instrument. The psalmist helps to put the cacophony of his situation into harmony with music and song. There is a melody in Scripture. This is the harp — sweeter than that of angels — that drives away sadness of spirit. Psalm 3 vibrates with fervency from the repeated exclamations of danger (vv. 1-2 [2-3], to the resolve "I will not fear," to imperative petitions for deliverance and to be avenged in verse 7 [8] to the crescendo shout: "Victory belongs to *I AM,*" before trailing off into the benediction (v. 8 [9]). Fervent prayer is effective (James 5:16); it is the fire and the incense; without fervency it is no prayer.

Of David (lᵉdāwīd) signifies that Israel's greatest king before the coming of Jesus Christ composed this saving song (see pp. 89-90).

2. Historical Notice

Fourteen of the seventy-two psalms attributed to David state the historical circumstances that prompted the song's composition (see p. 92).[52] The particular features of David's petition song in Psalm 3 correspond with the superscript. 1) The psalmist is an embattled monarch: his numerous foes attack

52. Psalms 34, 52, 54, 56, 57, 59, 142 are dated to the time of David's exile from Saul (1 Sam. 16–31); Psalms 18 and 60, to the time he is under blessings (2 Sam. 1–10); and Psalms 3, 51, 63 to the time he is under God's judgment (2 Sam. 11:20). Psalms 7 and 30 are unclassified as to precise dates (2 Sam. 21–24).

him (v. 1 [2]), are deployed to encircle him (v. 6 [7]), and speak disdainful words against him (v. 2 [3]; cf. 2 Kings 18:19-35; Pss. 42:3 [4]; 44:13-16; 74:18; 79:10; 89:41 [42]). But the king, in whose salvation is wrapped up the blessing of the people (v. 8 [9]), finds *I AM* his shield who lifts his head high above the surging foe (v. 3 [4]); prays that *I AM* "arise," "deliver" him, and "strike" the bestial enemy (v. 7 [8]); and proclaims "victory" (v. 8 [9]), all of which sound like battle cries. It is gratuitous to suppose that an ordinary, pious Israelite is employing martial language coined from royal battles to express his own situation, which is altogether different.

The "many" (vv. 1, 2, 3, 6 [2, 3, 4, 7]) tallies well with 2 Samuel 15:12-14; cf. 18:8); in both texts the enemy is referred to as those that "rise up against" the king (v. 1 [2]; 2 Sam. 18:3). The reference to Zion, his holy hill, does not indicate a date later than Absalom's revolt, as some allege, because the historian explicitly records that David took steps on his flight from Absalom to have the ark, which marked *I AM*'s presence, on the holy hill (2 Sam. 15:25). In short, on the story level the subject is David, and the enemy is Absalom and all Israel; on the liturgical level the fugitive king's petition takes on a prophetic hue, looking forward to Messiah (The Anointed); on the canonical level the subject is Jesus Christ and the enemy is his own people who rejected him, including the high priest and Judas (see pp. 105-11). On the moral level the subject is the faithful saint and the enemy are those within the nominal Christian church. Moreover, the abstract "enemy" allows the faithful to apply the enemy to political foes without and — with the commentators throughout the church's history — to spiritual struggles within, although the Hebrew word "save" normally entails both political and spiritual salvation (see below).

In addition to facilitating the contrast between Psalms 2 and 3 (see above), the historical notice, "when David fled from Absalom his son," gives the psalm greater theological depth. The king's morning prayer, after his flight from the palace, might suggest the erroneous conclusion that prayer to God stands opposed to human means. The full story, however, reveals that in his flight David set up an espionage network within the capital.[53] He sent his trusted advisor, Hushai, to frustrate the counsel of the traitor Ahithophel, whom David regarded as insightful as a prophet (2 Sam. 16:21). Moreover, David instructed Hushai to tell *I AM*'s faithful priests, Zadok and Abiathar, whom he had already sent back as spies, anything he heard in the king's palace and that they in turn were to communicate to David through their fleet-footed sons the vital information (2 Sam. 15:24-35).

53. Today, ignorance of the Bible is due to the world's suppression of its knowledge as well as laziness (see pp. 4-5).

Nevertheless, though David devised a strategy, he depended upon God. Upon David's hearing that Ahithophel was among the conspirators, he prayed, "*I AM,* turn Ahithophel's counsel into foolishness," whereupon Hushai providentially met him on the summit of the Mount of Olives. Hushai's advice to Absalom and his espionage for David played a crucial role in David's salvation, but ultimately salvation comes from *I AM* and praise belongs to him. The prophet-historian of the book of Samuel agrees: "*I AM* had determined to frustrate the good advice of Ahithophel in order to bring disaster on Absalom" (2 Sam. 17:14b).

Likewise, when David toppled Goliath, the experienced "animal trainer" did not exercise faith without arming himself with a sling and five stones, nor did he arm himself without faith. True faith risks the use of means. It takes more faith to risk the surgeon's scalpel than to lie in bed and pray: "God, heal me."

B. Address v. 1A

Petitions always begin with a direct address to God, and so the vocative *I AM (yhwh)* opens this psalm (see pp. 95, 197). As instinctively as salmon return to their spawning grounds at death and as birds fly toward the warmth and light of the sun with the onset of the cold and darkness of winter, saints instinctively turn to God in crisis. By turning to God in distress and addressing him, petitioners show their dependence on God — to be acceptable to God that dependence must be complete. David incurred God's wrath when he counted his fighting men, because, as he confesses, "When I felt secure, I said, 'I will never be shaken'" (30:6; cf. 2 Sam. 24). Directing one's petition to God conforms to other psalms that emphasize that one can never rely on human resources, albeit without denying their legitimate use (cf. Ps. 20:7-9; 118:6-7; 146:3). The saint depends upon God; without *I AM* everything and everyone else is a delusion (33:16-18). The fool says there is no God (10:4, 11; 14:1). To not turn to God in crisis is what the Babylonians call "living *ina ramanishu*" (i.e., living by oneself, on one's own resources). This is the essence of sin.[54] In sum: "Only God, the Guardian of Justice, can turn the tide, can restore health and good fortune, bring back former bliss and security."[55]

54. H. Ringgren, *The Faith of the Psalmists* (Philadelphia: Fortress Press, 1963), p. 35.

55. Erhard Gerstenberger, "Enemies and Evil Doers in the Psalms: A Challenge to Christian Preaching," *HBT* 5 (1983): 67.

C. Lament vv. 1-2 [2-3]

Laments typically include a complaint that the foe is too strong, the psalmist too weak, and God absent. All three are mentioned or inferred in the enemies' taunt, "God will not deliver him" (v. 2 [3]). This cry of distress belongs to the events of deliverance.[56] Jesus exemplifies it for his church: when he feels abandoned by God, helpless, and taunted by his enemies, he cries out to God in a lament psalm (Psalm 22; Matt. 27:46; cf. Rom. 8:20-23).

1. Foes Are Many v. 1B

Though perilously outnumbered by the surging foe, the anointed king refuses to come to terms with his godless enemies. He underscores his apparently inescapable distress by a staccato anaphora, a threefold repetition of *many (rabbîm),* after an exclamatory *How! (mâ).* The conspirators, whom the anointed later numbers in the tens of thousands, greatly out-man and out-arm the anointed king and those "in" him. Overwhelming superiority of the enemy is a frequent motif in royal petitions (25:19; 27:3; 31:13; 38:19; 55:18; 56:1-2; 59:4; *passim*). God blesses human beings with fertility (Gen. 1:22; 9:1) and the seed of Abraham in particular (16:10; 26:3) in order that they might participate in *I AM*'s salvation history, but the depraved human heart turns God's grace into a threat against its rule. But God's intention to bless in order to save humanity must prevail in spite of human waywardness, and it finds expression in the benediction (see v. 8 [9]; cf. Jer. 23:3; 30:9; Zech. 10:8; cf. Isa. 53:11).

The attribution of the *foes* (*ṣārî,* see "deliverance" below) as those that *rise up against me (qāmîm ʿālāy)* does not so much speak of them as insurgents — though the Hebrew expression is translated "revolt" in Judges 9:18 — as "attackers" (cf. Deut. 19:11; 22:26; Pss. 54:3; 86:14; *passim*). S. Amsler reached the same conclusion: "*qûm* with *ʿal* describes the attack (Angriff) against an enemy (Deut. 22:26; Isa. 14:22; Ps. 3:1)."[57] The participle graphically portrays the battle as in progress.

2. Foes Disparage King and God v. 2 [3]

It is the anointed king's opponents, not faint-hearted and defeatist friends who have already abandoned him, who *are saying of me, "God will not deliver him"*

56. Claus Westermann, *Praise and Lament in the Psalms* (Atlanta: John Knox, 1981), pp. 260f.

57. S. Amsler, *THAT,* 2:638.

(*'ôm/ᵉrîm lᵉnapšî 'ên yᵉšû'ātâ lô,* see nn. 36 and 37), and thus employing the customary military propaganda disparaging faith in God (cf. 2 Kings 18:17-37; Ps. 42:3 [4]; 71:11; cf. Ps. 4:2 [3]). The taunt "God will not deliver him" reaches into his *nepeš,* a term that adds an intensely personal element to the notion of self (see n. 35); the taunt is painful and personal. The enemy's taunt finds confirmation in the mind of the disaffected mob, because the king, upon whom Providence once smiled, now appears to be under God's curse as he flees from his bloody-minded son (cf. 2 Sam. 16:5-11). His greater Son also appeared under a curse when he hung upon a tree (Deut. 21:23; Gal. 3:13). But in both instances, *I AM* vindicated his S/son (cf. Ps. 2:7). Today the world without and Satan within disparage the true Christian's faith in the triune God.

The enemy's boast that "God will not deliver him" (see n. 37) strikes at the very basis of the king's hope. The root glossed *deliver (yāša')* plays a large role in the book of Psalms.[58] Although its etymology is uncertain,[59] it clearly denotes deliverance in both the military (cf. Judg. 12:2; 1 Sam. 11:3) and juridical spheres (2 Sam. 14:4). The two ideas coalesce, for the word denotes military or physical intervention because it is one's due or right (Deut. 28:29, 31). Sawyer notes that other words in the semantic domain of deliverance, such as *nṣl,* stress the idea of violent action, not invariably intervention on behalf of justice.[60]

The responsibility to deliver for the cause of justice falls particularly upon the king (1 Sam. 1:27; 2 Kings 6:26) and, above all, upon *I AM.* If God fails to help the innocent sufferer, the afflicted is put to shame (Ps. 44:9). The wronged party, however, has the responsibility to cry out, as in the case of rape (Deut. 22:23-27). This is why the psalmists frequently emphasize that they have raised

58. In Psalm 3 the root appears in three different forms: *yᵉšû'ātâ,* v. 3; *hôšîa',* v. 7; *yᵉšû'â,* v. 8.

59. The customary etymology, which sees the basic meaning in Arabic *wasi'a* "to be wide, spacious," is now called into question because it meets with difficulties in the discrepancies in expected consonantal correspondences in South Arabic. Nevertheless, the etymology is enticing because its antonym is *ṣrr* "to be narrow" (cf. Isa. 63:8f.; Jer. 14:8) (cf. F. Stolz, *TLOT,* 2:584). The nominal form *ṣar* is glossed "foe" in v. 1.

60. J. Sawyer, "What Was a Mōšia'?," *VT* 15 (1965): 479. He summarizes his argument that *mošia',* the nomen opificum of the root yš', has forensic sense: "Negatively, 1) there are no cases in the Old Testament where a forensic meaning is impossible, and 2) there is no other word used so consistently in similarly contexts; and positively, 1) three quarters of its occurrences suggest . . . the language of the law court, 2) the most probably [sic!] etymology . . . suggests a forensic origin for the root yš', 3) there are other examples of forensic words appearing in wider and more general contexts, but still retaining forensic overtones, 4) the mošia' was always on the side of justice, 5) his activity seems to have been verbal rather than physical in many contexts, unlike its synonyms, and 6) there was a place in ancient Israel for an 'advocate' or a 'witness for the defense,' as also for a 'witness for the prosecution.'"

their voices, presumably in public (see 3:4). They count upon *I AM* to uphold the course of justice. God's help belongs especially to the king (Ps. 20:6 [7], 9 [10]), who in turn delivers the poor and needy (Ps. 72:4; 109:31). This is so because in the legal process the king is the authority to whom one can address a legal claim (2 Sam. 14:12; 2 Kings 6:26). "This is why," says F. Stolz, "the lament of the psalm is structured basically like profane legal contests."[61] In the case of the king, however, only God can deliver the wrongly afflicted monarch.

Sawyer says that in the Old Testament salvation and deliverance seldom, if ever, express a spiritual state exclusively: their common theological sense is that of a material deliverance attended by spiritual blessings. Parallels show that God's righteousness (Ps. 71:15), strength (21:1 [2]; 28:8), blessing (3:8[9]) and unfailing love (119:41) are bound up with his salvation. Accordingly, the human role is to trust God *alone,* as well as to ask (Ps. 33:10; 60:11, 12 [12, 13]; 146:3). But, as noted above, the superscript safeguards against the error that trust in God, not in others and especially not in self, excludes the use of human means.

D. Confidence vv. 3-6 [4-7]

Oesterley commented: "For the expression of sublime trust in God this psalm is not surpassed."[62] Salvation, we noted, depends on calling upon God in faith. The psalmist affirms his trust in God (v. 3 [4]) and his conviction that God answers his prayer (v. 4 [5]). He demonstrated his faith the preceding night by going to sleep (v. 5 [6]), and in the morning he again demonstrates it by confronting the new day without fear (v. 6 [7]). Though verses 3 and 4 [4 and 5] are a couplet, verse 3 [4] is linked with verse 2 [3] by continuing in direct address, while verse 4 [5] is linked with verses 5-6 [6-7] by being an apostrophe within the prayer. Whenever he calls, *I AM* answers him (v. 4 [5]), while he, having relinquished his own watchfulness, sleeps and makes himself most vulnerable (v. 5 [6]). With the credibility of his faith now tried and proven he fearlessly confronts the innumerable, perfidious hordes posted about him (v. 6 [7]). The significance of the Hebrew tenses in these verses is open to different interpretations, but along with Delitzsch it seems best to understand verses 4, 5, 6 [5, 6, 7] as references to the present, past, and future respectively (see n. 39). These references to David's confidence are types of those of the Antitype, who in similar circumstances also entrusted himself to the One who judges justly (1 Peter 2:23).

61. F. Stolz, *TLOT,* 2:585.

62. William Oscar Emil Oesterley, *The Psalms,* vol. 2 (London: Society for Promoting Christian Knowledge, 1939), p. 8.

1. *King's Affirmation of Faith vv. 3-4 [4-5]*

a. Affirmation of Election and Divine Protection v. 3 [4]

"But you, I AM" *(w^e attâ yhwh)* is the unequivocal mark of the change from lament to confidence.[63] It signals the change from the exposed king's portrayal of the surging enemy to expression of buoyant confidence in the One who anointed him king and made a covenant with him that his house would rule forever. God with him is greater than the innumerable hordes attacking him (cf. 2 Kings 6:8-23). God is: 1) his shield *(māgēn,* i.e., his source of protection; Ps. 28:7); 2) his glory *(k^e bôdî,* i.e., his source of victory); 3) his victory ("you lift up my head"). "Deliverance is equated with the height of the delivered one's head . . . (Ps. 27:6)."[64] He is confident in God and also of his calling to be king (see Ps. 4:3 [4]).

The *māgēn,* a round, light shield that is made of wood or wicker and covered with thick leather rubbed with oil (cf. Isa. 21:5) to preserve it and to make it glisten, is carried by the light infantry to ward off the enemy's swords, spears, or arrows; it is frequently employed to describe God's presence in warding off a foe's attack (Ps. 18:2 [3], 30 [31], 35 [36]). The larger shield *(ṣinnâ,* cf. 2 Chron. 14:8), which was either oblong or rectangular in shape and carried by the heavy infantry or armor bearer (cf. 1 Sam. 17:7, 41), is used figuratively of God's good will (Ps. 5:12 [13]) and truth (Ps. 91:4). *About me* is nicely rendered in NEB "to cover me." The metaphor of God as a shield is ancient: "Perhaps David remembered a promise made a thousand years before . . . 'Fear not Abram,' the ancient words had run, 'I am thy shield [*māgēn*] and exceeding great reward' (Gen. 15:1)."[65] Moses restates that truth in a praise song: "Who is like you, a people saved by the Lord? He is your shield [*māgēn*] and helper and your glorious sword" (Deut. 33:29). Not surprisingly, the warrior king picks up on this ancient credo in his triumphant praise song after he has defeated all his enemies: "*I AM* is my . . . shield [*māgēn*] and the horn of my salvation" (2 Sam. 22:2-3). Today too, the Christian is "strong in the Lord and in his mighty power" (Eph. 6:10).

"Glory" *(kābôd),* which literally means "heaviness" and from which is derived the notions of "weight, dignity, importance, honor," refers to objective reality, such as property (Ps. 59:16-17 [17-18]), a noble wife (Prov. 12:4), or political position (Ps. 45:13), which in turn gives the subject the respect of society. The last honor for which a king hopes is a burial of such magnificence that he sleeps in honor (2 Chron. 32:33; Isa. 14:18).

63. Westermann, *Praise and Lament in the Palms.*

64. A. Bowling, *TWOT,* 2:838.

65. E. M. Blaiklock, *The Psalms of the Great Rebellion: An Imaginative Exposition of Psalms 3 to 6 and 23* (London: Lakeland, 1970), p. 22.

Though some English versions interpret the ambiguous *k^ebôdî* by "my Glorious One," taking the expression as a metonymy of adjunct with reference to God (i.e., the One whom the king glorifies), it is better taken as a metonymy of effect with reference to the king (i.e., the One who bestows glory on the king), because of its parallels: "the one who lifts up my head" and "when I cry aloud, he answers me." The Hebrew tense has a gnomic force: "[The imperfective can be used] in the sphere of present time . . . to express facts known by experience, which occur at all times, and consequently hold good at any moment."[66] If so, glory here is a metonymy for the king's luster in victory, not for God's greatness; nevertheless, God is the source of his glory. The divine aura conveys majesty, power, and salvation on his king (Ps. 21:5 [6]; 62:7 [8]; 84:11 [12]). Here the royal reputation, his glory, is his objective, wondrous victories over his many foes, which gain him the respect of his people and of the nations. By contrast, should the enemy triumph over him, his glory would be turned into shame (Ps. 4:2 [3]; 7:5 [6]; 89:44).

The reference to God as the one who *lifts up my head (mērîm rō'šî)* means that God singles him out for honor and lifts him clear of perils (cf. Gen. 40:13; 2 Kings 25:27; Pss. 27:6; 110:7). Bowed by humiliation, David flees Jerusalem with his head covered (2 Sam. 15:30), but vindicated in victory he returns as king with head held high.[67] Similarly, the Son's sacred head is bowed low on a cross outside of Jerusalem, but today his head is exalted in the heavenly Jerusalem (cf. Luke 21:28). Today, Christians fill up the sufferings of Christ — not his soteriological sufferings but his passionate sufferings — before their glorification with Christ (Col. 1:24; Rom. 8:18).

b. Faith Affirmed in Public Prayer v. 4 [5]

As stated, the victim desiring salvation has responsibility to cry out aloud for help, and with reference to God it must be a cry of faith, for David says "I cry aloud to *I AM*," and then confesses by faith: "He answers me." Petition is an integral part of shaping salvation history. Hannah's prayer for a son and her praise for a king (cf. 1 Sam. 1:11; 2:10) give birth to Israel's last judge and the prophet who anoints Israel's first two kings. *Cry (qārā')* has the basic meaning of drawing to oneself the attention of someone by the voice; *answer ('ānâ)* designates

66. GKC, 107f.

67. Shimon Bar-Efrat, *Narrative Art in the Bible,* Bible and Literature Series 17 (Sheffield: Almond Press, 1989), notes: "When David crosses the Jordan eastward in his flight he is referred to as 'David,' while when he crosses the river westward on his return is called 'the king.' During his flight he is mere David, barefoot, tired, destitute, and accompanied by only a handful of loyal subjects; on his return he is the king once more, and is recognized as such by Judah and Israel."

the reaction or response.[68] The son need only raise his voice and his Father sends him help (cf. Ps. 2:8; 57:2 [3]; 20:1-4 [2-5]; 21:2, 5 [3, 6]; 91:15; 140:6 [7]). But cry he must, for failure to turn to God, his only source of hope, would be tantamount to abdication of his throne and his becoming an accomplice with the evildoers (cf. Deut. 22:24). The specific content of his prayer in his flight from Absalom is given in 2 Samuel 15:31. As J. Eaton notes: "Against all worldly probabilities the king's prayer is singularly answered; at once Hushai presents himself and the counter-measures proceed successfully."[69]

Kidner comments: "Not Absalom's decrees, but *I AM*'s will, issue from Mount Zion."[70] Resolutely, resisting the superstitious impulse to have God in his hands as a talisman, David leaves the ark in Zion (2 Sam. 15:25; cf. 1 Sam. 4:5-6), confident that *I AM* hears his prayer though he is remote from him. For the lexical meaning, geographical situation, and theological significance of *from his holy mountain* (i.e., Zion), see Psalm 2:6. Salvation is mediated through the liturgy: God is frequently pictured as a stronghold (Ps. 18:2 [3]), brings salvation from his holy hill Zion (14:7), and "makes his face to shine" (31:16 [17]).

David prays from the Jordanian rift, the lowest point on earth (1,385 ft. below sea level), to God on Mount Zion (2,500 feet above sea level), conceptualized as the loftiest mountain (Pss. 48:2 [3]; 68:15-16 [16-17]). Although not the highest ridge even in its environment, in its significance as the mountain of God it is the "highest" mountain in the world (see Ps. 2:6; Isa. 2:2; Mic. 4:1). The scenic depiction symbolizes that in prayer space does not separate the earthling from God in heaven. In prayer, the saint and God are united in spirit.

2. *Demonstration and Validation of Trust vv. 5-6 [6-7]*

a. Slept in Crisis and *I AM* Sustained v. 5 [6]

The exemplary king's confidence in God is based on God's track record of answered prayer as well as on his glory that he conferred upon the king. The change from the imperfective tense ("I cry" *'eqrā'*) in verse 4 [5] to the perfect tense *(šākabtî)* strongly supports the majority view that verse 5 [6] should be rendered in past time: *I lay down* (see n. 41). The initial emphatic *I ('ᵃnî)* indicates the resoluteness of his faith. God guards his servants by day and by night (Ps. 91:15; 121:6), but especially when asleep, at their most vulnerable (cf. 4:8 [9];

68. C. J. Labuschagne, *THAT*, 2.668.

69. J. H. Eaton, *Kingship and the Psalms* (Naperville, IL: Allenson, 1976), p. 195.

70. D. Kidner, *Psalms 1–72* (Leicester: InterVarsity Press, 1973), p. 54.

57:4 [5]). A Pharaoh warns his son: "Even when you sleep, guard your heart, because no man has adherents on the day of distress."[71] Sisera vividly illustrates the vulnerability of sleep. Jael seized the opportunity of the sleeping general to peg his head to the floor of her tent. *And I slept (wāʾîšānâ)* gives observable evidence of David's inner faith. "It is not the sleep of exhaustion but of trust in God," says Scroggie.[72]

The Christian catechism, following S. Clement of Rome (*Epistle to the Corinthians,* 26:2; *Apology,* I.38.5) and S. Justin (*Apology,* I. 38.5) and others (see above), understands it as "the voluntary and harmless sleep of Christ in the tomb and of his resurrection."[73] Also, like David, Christ is rejected without reason by his own people, taunted in similar terms (see v. 2 [3]), and knows his own glory (John 5), but unlike David, who is suffering for his crimes against Uriah and Bathsheba, Christ suffers for the sins of others. Nevertheless, in spite of David's historical guilt that meant the sword will not depart from his house, he is forgiven juridically (2 Sam. 12:10, 13) and so has the right to pray for deliverance from the consequence of his sin (2 Sam. 15:31).

If the king's falling asleep in crisis demonstrates his faith, *I awoke* demonstrates *I AM*'s faithfulness during the perilous night. His explanation for his survival, *because I AM sustains me,* validates this interpretation (cf. Ps. 54:4 [6]; 145:14). As one commentator put it: "God's hand is his pillow" (cf. Song 2:6). Fénélon once said: "Peace does not dwell in outward things but in the soul. We may preserve it in bitterest pain if we will remain firm and submissive. Peace in this life springs from acquiescence, not in exemption from suffering." But true faith is more than acquiescence and submission; it struggles and prevails with God and human beings because it knows that God delivers the just. If Israel had said with a stoic grin, "I'll bear Egypt's oppression," or had said with a false optimism, "All will be well," she would still be in Egypt.

b. Fearlessly Faces the Foes in the Future v. 6 [7]

With the crisis of the night safely behind, the king heroically exclaims: *I do not fear (lôʾ-ʾîrāʾ).* He escalates the thrice-repeated "many" to an insuperable number: *tens of thousands (ribᵉbôt),* which designates an indeterminate, immense number (1 Sam. 18:7; Mic. 6:7). *Of troops (ʿām)* is a collective term for a numerous company. In contrast to *gôy, ʿam* refers to the subjective and personal in-

71. *ANET,* p. 418. Many languages have one verb for the two notions "to be awake" and "to protect" (cf. Lat. *vigilare*).

72. W. Graham Scroggie, *The Psalms: Psalm I to CL* (London: Pickering & Inglis Ltd., 1965), p. 57.

73. Jacquet, *Les Psaumes,* p. 247.

stead of the objective and impersonal,[74] and in certain contexts, like this one, becomes an army because the whole group fights.[75] *Drawn up (satû)* in the other intransitive use of *šît* (Isa. 22:7) also occurs in a military context. Possibly this use is a technical military term for "posting" an army. The lesson: "Let us therefore learn, when in dangers, not to measure the assistance of God after the manner of men" (Calvin).

E. Petition and Benediction vv. 7-8 [8-9]

1. Petitions

a. Deliver Me v. 7a [8a]

With victorious faith the old soldier raises Moses' ancient war-cry, "Arise, I AM!" when the founder of the nation leads Israel on their triumphant march to the Land of Promise (Num. 10:35). But now the cry is raised against a pretender to the throne. Not a stranger but the king's own flesh has taken over the throne of *I AM*'s anointed and has raped his wives and concubines.

Arise (qûm), like *deliver (hôšîʿēnî),* "is frequently used in martial contexts. It refers to preparation for (Judg. 7:15), engagement in (Exod. 2:17) and victory in war (or struggle). . . . Sometimes *qûm* connotes anticipated or realized victory. When God engages in combat victory is certain."[76] By referring to *I AM* in its parallel as *my God* (see above), the king appeals to his own privileged position as God's son (see Ps. 2:7; cf. Ps. 89:27 [28]).

b. Destroy the Enemy v. 7b [8b]

His petition is twofold: Deliver me (*hôšîʿēnî,* see v. 2) and destroy the enemy in a humiliating defeat. His petition assumes God's justice and omnipotence. He emphasizes the latter by an emphatic *surely (kî),* and instead of using an abstraction graphically portrays his double wish in petitions structured as a chiasm: *Strike all my enemies on the cheek (hikkîtā ʾet-kol-ʾōyᵉbay)* and *break the teeth of the wicked* (*šinnê rᵉšāʿîm šibbartā* — note assonance of /š/). The parallelism between "all my enemies" and "the wicked" shows his cause is just and deliverance is his due (see v. 2 [3]). The pretender has shown himself to be wicked

74. E. A. Speiser, "'People' and 'Nation' of Israel," *JBL* 79 (1960): 157-66.
75. A. R. Hulst, *THAT,* 2:301f.
76. L. J. Coppes, *TWOT,* 2:793, s.v. *qûm.*

by murdering his brother out of revenge, rather than trusting God; by dishonoring his father through stealing the people's loyalty; by usurping the throne without divine prophetic authorization or consecration by anointing, and by raping his father's wives and concubines on the roof of the palace in the sight of all Israel! First, the anointed asks that with respect to the defense of the wicked conspirators, they be rendered defenseless, and with respect to their offense that they be made harmless. "The buffet on the cheek was a climax of insult which shewed that all spirit and power of resistance were gone. (Cp. 1 Kings xxii.24; Job xvi.10; Lam. iii.30; Mic. v.1)."[77] "Breaking the teeth" signifies that the enemy, who like wild beasts had been eager to devour him, has been rendered harmless and helpless (cf. 58:6 [7]; Job 29:17). This is the certain fate of *all* his enemies. (For the value of these petitions for retribution to Christian faith and practice see pp. 95-98.)

Father and son strikingly differ in their stance toward their enemy. David turned the wrong done to him over to God, but Absalom took justice into his own hands when he avenged the wrong done to Tamar. David is attacked, but Absalom is the attacker. David is innocent and in need of God to avenge him, but Absalom seeks personal revenge.

2. *Benediction v. 8 [9]*

The representative head of God's people concludes by adding to his petition a benediction. First, however, he cites a proverbial saying of the faithful, especially of a warrior before engaging battle, that functions as a directive, an expression of faith and a doxology: "Salvation (*yᵉšûʿâ,* see v. 2 [3]) belongs to *I AM*" (cf. Prov. 20:28; 21:31; 24:6; John 2:9; cf. 2 Chron. 32:2-8). These parallel passages show that the expression does not deny the use of military arms but implicitly warns the king against trust in them (Ps. 20:7 [8]). The secular capability of the war-horse threatened Israel's faith in *I AM* and drew heavy theological criticism (cf. Deut. 17:16; Isa. 31:1; Hos. 1:7; Mic. 1:13; Zech. 9:10). Micah equates trust in military hardware with idolatry and witchcraft (Mic. 5:10-15 [9-14]).

Blessing refers to God's filling a person with the potency to reproduce life, to produce wealth, and to overcome enemies. God is always understood as the giver of blessing, even when he is not mentioned. The Creator's blessing may be mediated through a sacred person such as a patriarch (cf. Gen. 27:7), a priest (cf. Lev. 9:23), a king (2 Sam. 6:18; Ps. 3:8 [9]), a dying man (cf. Job 29:13), and/or the sacred congregation (cf. Prov. 10:6; 11:26). When blessings are mediated

77. A. F. Kirkpatrick, ed., *The Book of Psalms* (Cambridge: Cambridge University Press, 1916), p. 16.

through others, benedictory words and power become mingled notions. The mediator conveys the blessing through faith in a performative speech act, similar to "I pronounce you man and wife," or "I baptize you in the Name of. . ." The benediction infers that solidarity, fellowship, goodwill, and appreciation exist between the benefactor and the recipient. *Upon your people* (*ʿal-ʿammᵉkā,* see v. 7) on the lips of the king refers to Israel, which is *I AM*'s elect nation. "The whole nation is still Jehovah's people, though they have been misled into revolt against His king."[78] In spite of the supine hosts of evildoers who failed to rally to the anointed, the noble king inferentially prays that they will again become loyal subjects and bring to fruition their promised destiny (Gen. 12:1-3), as his greater Son of whom he is a type explicitly prayed for his people's forgiveness. "So the psalm ends by looking beyond the 'I' and 'me' of all the previous verses, to *thy people* (not even 'my people'), and to *thy blessing,* which goes as far beyond victory as health and fruitfulness go beyond survival."[79]

Psalm 1 began and Psalm 2 ended with the exclamation that God's saints will be rewarded with eternal felicities; Psalm 3 ends with a benediction for their success in the midst of grave peril.

F. Postscript

The meaning of *lamnaṣṣēaḥ* is uncertain.[80] The traditional meaning "for the director of music" is plausible because the *Piel* of *nṣḥ* with and without *ʿal/lᵉ* refers to work and activities in conjunction with the temple, sometimes in contexts of its music. The term means "to inspect," often with the connotation "to supervise" (cf. Ezra 3:8; 1 Chron. 15:21; 23:4; 2 Chron. 2:1-17; 34:12-13). The Chronicler

78. Kirkpatrick, ed., *The Book of Psalms,* p. 16.

79. D. Kidner, *Psalms 1–72,* p. 55.

80. For theories as of 1951 about the meaning of the technical term *lamnaṣṣēaḥ* see G. A. Danell, *Psalm 139* (Uppsala: A.-B. Lundequistska Bokhandeln, 1951) *ad locum.* In 1964 L. Delekat, basing himself on the LXX's rendering *eis to telos* "for the end," supposes that *lamnaṣṣēaḥ* is a *Responsion,* meaning something between "forever" and "amen," to mark the end of the psalm (L. Delekat, *"Probleme der Psalmenüberschriften, ZAW* 76 [1964]: 280-97). This is unlikely because it is sometimes followed by other musical terms, suggesting it is a musical term and so conforms to other ancient Near Eastern texts. According to Delekat, this term occurs only in pre-exilic psalms. At any rate, he agrees with Waltke that 4:1A is a subscript (see B. Waltke, "Superscripts, Subscripts or Both," *JBL* [1991]) and provides evidence somewhat supporting that *ldwd* means "by David." In Jerome's first Latin translation, *lamnaṣṣēaḥ* is rendered *ad finem,* "unto the end," but in his later Hebraica he translates it as *"victori"*; a "victor" he identifies as the choirmaster or precentor (Raphael Loewe, "Herbert of Bosham's Commentary on Jerome's Hebrew Psalter," *Biblica* 34 [1953]: 44-77, 159-92, 275-98).

says that David and his officers assigned the inspired musical service to various priestly guilds and that its musicians were led "under the hands of David and Asaph" (1 Chron. 25:2, 3, 6; 2 Chron. 23:18; 29:27); i.e., they led the musicians by cheironomy, as pictured in Egyptian iconography already in the Old Kingdom.[81] J. Sawyer defines *m^{e}naṣṣēaḥ* as "to be recited by the official in charge" and its prepositional phrase as referring "to elements in or areas of cultic participation under the direction of *m^{e}naṣṣēaḥ*. Thus the *mnṣṣḥ ʿl-hššmynyt* means "to be recited by the official who is charge of the ritual *hašš^{e}mînît*."[82]

The Levites accompanied the singing *with stringed instruments* (see 1 Chron. 23:5; 25:1; Ps. 33:2).

These postscripts (see p. 88) show that the psalms were used in Israel's temple liturgy and included a much wider audience than that of its historical setting. The psalms' inclusion in the canon democratizes them for all the people of God, who in Christ are a royal priesthood (1 Peter 2:9).

Part IV. Conclusion

The psalm is indirectly Messianic — that is to say, within the canon of Scripture every motif of David's petition typifies the life and words of the Lord Jesus Christ (see pp. 105-11). According to the *superscript*, David was rejected without a cause and hounded to death by the heir apparent to his throne who said "No" to the chosen king. So also the Jewish authorities and Judas murdered David's son and God's elect Son (John 15:25). Moreover, as Erasmus recognized: "Just as David, who had built Jerusalem, was driven out into a wilderness, so also Christ, by whom 'the world was made,' was driven out into the wilderness. As Shimei taunted David, so the crowd at the foot of the cross mocked Jesus." In the wilderness, a symbol of chaos, type and Antitype by faith turned an upside-down world right-side up (Mark 1:12; Matt. 24:1-3),[83] even though both appeared to be under God's curse (see above).

Surrounded by enemies, both *address* God, crying out for deliverance (cf. Matt. 27:46).

David *laments* that his political and spiritual enemies are many and regard him as forsaken by God, and so does the Lord (Matt. 27:27-46). Nevertheless, David is *confident* that God has bestowed glory upon him and will answer

81. J. Wheeler, "Music of the Temple," *Archaeology and Biblical Research* 2 (1989): 12-20.

82. John F. A. Sawyer, "An Analysis of the Context and Meaning of the Psalms Headings," *Glasgow Oriental Society Transactions* 22 (1970): 26-38.

83. Bruce K. Waltke with Charles Yu, *An Old Testament Theology* (Grand Rapids: Zondervan, 2007), p. 567.

his prayer; and so is Christ Jesus (John 5:19-28; 17:1-26). Both demonstrate their confidence by, in the face of death, laying down their lives in peace (John 12:20-36; 1 Peter 2:23). Both lower their heads in humiliation before their glorification (Luke 21:28). Both by faith *petition* God to save them because it is their due (John 12:27; Heb. 2:12-13). And in his *benediction* David seeks the salvation of the elect nation, and so does Christ (Luke 23:34; cf. Acts 7:59). Unlike David, however, his greater Son does not pray that God punish his malefactors, but nevertheless prophesies their eternal punishment (Matt. 23:33-36; 25:46; Mark 12:9).

The postscript hands David's prayer over to the faithful for their use, and the Spirit hands the prayers of Christ over to the church by inspiring his apostles to give his words to the church for their worship of the triune God (cf. John 17). The five motifs of the K/king's prayer teach the church how to pray and so turn a dark night into morning light.

CHAPTER 7

Psalm 4: An Evening Prayer in Crisis

Part I. Voice of the Church

I. Indirect Messianic Psalm

A positive aspect of historical criticism is its attempt to set a psalm in its original context. Psalm 4 illustrates this, for in it, King David's immediate distress is caused by the drought in the land, which calls both his and his God's leadership into question (2 Sam. 21). In his last novel, *Till We Have Faces,* C. S. Lewis describes the critical situation within the ancient kingdom of Gnome when the rains fail and starvation threatens the kingdom. The king's rule is in jeopardy, so it is the time for a supreme sacrifice; his favorite and youngest daughter, Psyche, is called upon by the high priest to be offered as a sacrifice to appease the anger of the gods. This pagan response is the antithesis of that of the psalmist, who is being tested to put his trust intimately in the Creator, the "I AM," in spite of the disastrous drought.

II. Antiochene Commentators

Only **John Chrysostom** (347-407) in his homily on this psalm gave it a providential, precise context. He understood the geographical context of this psalm very well; his birthplace of Antioch was within a semi-arid environment, where the Greek god Zeus had replaced the original Canaanite god Baal as the rain-god. In the context of verse 7, where the psalmist is given "the gift of joy of heart" as expressive of God's gracious providence, Chrysostom challenges idolaters: How can they worship Zeus as the god of fertility when he is also such an immoral scoundrel?[1] Moreover, is God's providence adequately understood when it is related merely to material things, and not to the intimacy of joy within the heart, which God's covenant care alone can provide? Is this still not the issue today? We become post-secular precisely when we become disenchanted with both rationalism and materialism, with their failure to give us "joy of heart."[2] We have both intimacy and confidence in God because of his righteousness. "Let us therefore study how to converse with God." No intermediary, no oratorical skills are needed, reasons Chrysostom, only a humble, meek, and trusting heart. For it is only the ways and things of the world that will keep us separated from his providential care. Make this then an evening prayer, and before going to sleep confess everything before God, he urges, "giving thought to the day's transgressions."[3] Then one will find within the core of one's being, not in external things, "joy of heart," as "the effect of God's providence."[4] "Hope-filled," "secure," "recollected," Chrysostom describes the *hesychia,* or inner stillness of contemplative benefits, when one can enjoy "rest" in the Lord.[5] As a monk, he had experienced this himself. He is so taken up with the intimacy of the psalmist's trust in God, that he devotes almost double the space to this psalm that he normally allots in his commentary. Likewise it is with precision, *akribeia,* dependent on detail, that he gives his hearers a rich Scriptural diet, even if it is still commentary rather than textual exegesis.

Theodore of Mopsuestia (c. 350-c. 428), a colleague of Chrysostom, has left us with a collection of commentaries, from Psalm 1 to 81. He too has no command of Hebrew and Syriac by which to critique the local Septuagint version. But neither does he take a liturgical interest in the psalm titles, so his task is to be a psalm interpreter, giving the central message, as he understands it, with "narrative coherence."[6] As such he is restrained in the use of typology, and, as far as Psalm 4 is concerned, he focuses on the providence of God and the foolishness of those "who presume to say that no control is exercised over human affairs by providence."[7] Since the psalmist calls upon "God of my righ-

1. St. John Chrysostom, *Commentary on the Psalms,* vol. 1, trans. Robert Charles Hill (Brookline, MA: Holy Cross Orthodox Press, 1998), pp. 64-65.

2. See Msgr. Joseph Murphy, *Christ Our Joy: The Theological Vision of Pope Benedict XVI* (San Francisco: Ignatius Press, 2008).

3. Chrysostom, *Commentary on the Psalms,* pp. 51-52, 60.

4. Chrysostom, *Commentary on the Psalms,* p. 65.

5. Chrysostom, *Commentary on the Psalms,* p. 70.

6. Francis M. Young, *Biblical Exegesis and the Formation of Christian Culture* (Cambridge: Cambridge University Press, 1997), p. 182.

7. Theodore of Mopsuestia, *Commentary on Psalms 1–81,* trans. Robert C. Hill (Atlanta: Society of Biblical Literature, 2006), p. 41.

teousness," he feels justified in trusting that God will be provident in all his ways. The psalmist is not self-motivated in calling God "the Holy One," since all his purpose is to oppose those who deny divine providence. The evidence is personally experienced as "the light of God's countenance," and "the gladness you have put into my heart." "In peace I shall go to sleep and in the same instant find rest." It is all intimately personal, not just in material blessings. This is no idle boasting on the part of the psalmist, for only God could so convince the mind of the psalmist, itself a mark of his divine blessing.

III. Augustine's "Liturgical Eschatology"

As we have seen in Psalm 3, Origen and Augustine are preoccupied with the prosopological issue: Is the speaker David, or Christ, or both?[8] Now added to this is the musical direction at the heading of Psalm 4, "For the Director of music," which becomes wrongly translated: "Of the End." We segue here to **Theodoret of Cyrrhus** (393-460), who quotes Aquila and Theodotion as the authority for "unto the end," as tribute to "the author of victory." Theodoret himself more modestly suggests, "'Unto the end means that the foretold events will take place a long time afterwards," interpreting that the end of the psalm, in verse 8, foretells the resurrection from the dead. Others, he reports, interpret the present psalm as "offered to God, the author of victory, as a triumphal hymn by the blessed David after his victory over Absalom." Favorable to this suggestion, Theodoret applies the psalm to the importance of recognizing God's governance over all human affairs. He testifies for himself: "Since I have dismissed all panic and disturbance of mind and have gained relief from them, and have instructed others in reading your wonderful providence in these things, I await death in the hope of resurrection; he [i.e., David] called death 'sleep' in this verse."[9] As a rare exception in his critical commentary, Theodoret concedes that David might have an eschatological perspective in this psalm, all because of his probable textual mistranslation of "For the director of music"! We now return to Augustine.

Augustine of Hippo (354-430) elaborates this much further, "for now Christ is the end of the law, bringing justification to all who believe" (Rom. 10:4). The speaker is thus "the Lord-Man," but included is the voice of the

8. Marie-Josèphe Rondeau, *Les Commentaires Patristiques du Psaltier (III–Ve siècles),* vol. 2, *Exégèse Prosopologique et Théologique* (Rome: Pontificium Institutum Studiorum Orientalium, 1985), pp. 70, 101, 102, 104, 105, 137, 276, 367.

9. Theodoret of Cyrrhus, *Commentary on the Psalms, 1-72,* trans. Robert C. Hill (Washington, DC: Catholic University of America Press, 2000), p. 63.

church, the *totus Christi*. The "rest" of verse 5, is about the afterlife, in the light of resurrection. It is possible the Donatist, Tyconius, was Augustine's source for using "seven mystic rules" for his normative psalm interpretations in what he calls "the immense forest of prophecy." Rule 3 refers to "divine authority" as the basis of both law and promise, so that Scripture has both meanings, actual and anticipated.[10]

Psalm 4 had a special place in Augustine's life. He describes in the *Confessions* how he lived liturgically with the psalms, beginning with their appeal before his conversion. "How loudly I cried out to you, my God, as I read the psalms of David, songs full of faith, outbursts of devotion with no room in them for the breath of pride! . . . How loudly I began to cry out to you in these psalms; how I was inflamed by them with love for you and fired to recite them to the whole world, were I able, as a remedy against human pride!" (*Confessions* 9.4.8). In particular, he quotes Psalm 4 as expressive of the stages of his life experienced so far. "It all found an outlet through my eyes and voice when your good Spirit turned to us, saying, 'How long will you be heavy-hearted, human creatures? Why love emptiness and chase falsehood?' [Ps. 4:2] I, certainly, had loved emptiness and chased falsehood, and you, Lord, had already glorified your Holy One [Ps. 4:3], raising Him from the dead and setting Him at your right hand . . . ."[11] Augustine identifies the Manichees with the enemies of God (v. 2), who had led him astray for so long (in never teaching him about the Psalms, among other "errors"), saying: "I could wish that they had been somewhere nearby, without my knowing it, and had gazed upon my face and listened to my voice as I read the fourth psalm in that place of peace. 'When I called on Him he heard me, the God of my vindication; when I was hard beset, you led me into spacious freedom. Have mercy on me, Lord, and hearken to my prayer'" (Ps. 4:1).[12]

In addition to the personal appreciation Augustine now has for this psalm, his whole exposition is based on his adoption of the LXX's probable mistranslation of the psalm heading as "unto the end." This enables us to trace his influence in later medieval commentators, as we shall see.

We can illustrate from his homily on Psalm 4 both his dependence upon the LXX and his Christian, pastoral interpretation. Since the "End" (so LXX for *lamᵉnaṣṣēaḥ*, see p. 88) is Christ, the psalmist can call confidently upon God as

10. Robert A. Kugler, "Tyconius's Rules and the Rules of Augustine," in Pamela Bright, trans. and ed., *Augustine and the Bible* (Notre Dame: University of Notre Dame Press, 1986), p. 159.

11. *The Confessions of St. Augustine*, trans. Maria Boulding O.S.B. (London: Hodder & Stoughton, 1997), pp. 214-15.

12. *The Confessions of St. Augustine*, IX,8,9.

"the God of vindication." Augustine builds on *oikteirēson me,* "you made room for me," and affirms for believers: "When I was hard beset, you led me into spacious freedom [see below, n. 45]" (v. 1b). For the believer "does not have his heart live in a poky little room, even though his persecutors pile in against him from without, trying their best to drive him into a corner."[13] Augustine describes the way God enlarges our hearts, by his entering into our lives to converse with us. He suggests that "how long will you be slow of heart, human creatures [see below, n. 51]?" (v. 2) refers to those who have been deluded throughout Old Testament times until the advent of Christ. Augustine translates the "selah" at the end of verse 2: "Be sure of this: the Lord has glorified his Holy One." He is unsure if *selah* is a Hebrew word meaning "so be it" or a Greek word (*diapsalma,* "pause"), implying a break of silence in the singing. He notes, "this mode of expression is common to the language in which the prophets spoke. You often find an opening phrase like this: 'And the Lord said to him,' or 'And the word of the Lord came to him.' 'Take note then of its authority,'" is his argument (but see n. 25 in chapter 3). In verse 3b, "The Lord will hear me when I cry to him," he sees "the great earnestness of heart" with which we are "being warned to invoke God's assistance." He gives two positive interpretations to the command, "Be angry and sin not" (v. 4): if you are angry with a strong emotional reaction, which we cannot help, because our flesh is still fallen, at least make sure you do not sin. Or it might mean, "Go on! Repent!" "That is, be angry with yourselves about past sins and do not sin anymore in future."[14] The modern translation, "When you are on your beds, search your heart and be silent," is translated "Be pierced in your own rooms." This may be "the piercing of repentance," or a wake-up call, prompting us to rise from our sleep.

Augustine suggests that the "selah" that follows verse 4 implies the break between the old and the new way of life, brought about by repentance. "Offer a sacrifice of justice, and hope in the Lord," is his rendering of verse 5. He asks: Is this sacrifice of the just, of their repentance? Or is it that only with the death of the old man can it become a just sacrifice? "The mind now washed clean, offers itself and places itself on the altar of faith, to be consumed by the divine fire, that is, the Holy Spirit," he concludes. He interprets "Who has anything good to show us?" (v. 6a) to mean "the chatter, the daily questioning of all foolish and unjust people. . . . Or again, there are those who entertain doubts or despair of the future life which is promised to us. They often say, 'Who knows if it's true? Who has ever come back from the dead to tell us about these things?'"[15] Ac-

13. *The Confessions of St. Augustine,* p. 85.
14. *The Confessions of St. Augustine,* p. 88.
15. *The Confessions of St. Augustine,* p. 89.

cording to Augustine, the psalmist's joyous response to the question is, "The light of your countenance is stamped upon us, O Lord" (v. 6b) (but see commentary, pp. 224, 238-39, below). To this he adds: "The psalmist's phrase, 'stamped upon us' [*esēmeiōthē*], suggests a coin stamped with the king's picture. Likewise the human individual has been made in God's image and likeness, something that each has corrupted by sinning. Therefore true and eternal goodness is ours if we are minted afresh by being born again. And I believe that our Lord's exhortation when he saw Caesar's coin, 'Render to Caesar what is Caesar's and to God what is God's' (Matt. 22:21), refers to this, as some have aptly understood it. It is as if Christ said: 'Just as Caesar demands from you the mark of his likeness, so too does God: and just as money is rendered to Caesar, by the same principle the soul is rendered to God, illuminated and marked by the light of his face.'"[16] Here Augustine follows the distinction made by the early Fathers, that the *imago dei* has two elements: "the image" which we still bear, and the "likeness" we have lost by the Fall. Luther later on interpreted Genesis 1:26 as expressing synonyms, not distinctive terms.

In verses 7 and 8, Augustine sees the importance of seeking spiritual rather than material gains. For "when the mind is given over to temporal pleasure, it is always burning with desire and cannot be satisfied; when it is stretched this way and that by all sorts of conflicting and miserable thoughts, it does not allow itself to see the good which is uncompounded." In other words, such cannot find "rest" in God alone. "But," he adds, "this is not within our grasp at present, in this life. Instead it is something to be hoped for after this life. This is something which the verbs themselves, which are in the future tense, show; for what is said is neither, 'I rested and fell asleep,' but 'I will rest and fall asleep.' Then this corruptible nature will be clothed in incorruption and this mortal nature will be clothed in immortality; then will death be swallowed up in victory (1 Cor. 15:54)." Once more, Augustine interprets the psalm as eschatological.

IV. Liturgical Role of Psalm 4 in the Middle Ages

The liturgical use of Psalm 4 was adopted by the early church as a congregational evening psalm, following reflection, upon the close of the day. Just as Psalm 3 had been included in the earliest service of the day at 2 a.m., so later in Benedictine monasteries, Psalm 4 was sung every evening at Compline, as the monks gathered for the Canonical Hour. In the old Roman Breviary, this psalm

16. *The Confessions of St. Augustine*, p. 90.

was also part of each Sunday Completorium.[17] "An Order for Night Prayer (Compline)" (Anglican *Common Worship*), and "Prayer for the Evening" *(The Methodist Worship Book)*, echo the psalm's conclusion in their final prayers.[18] Traditionally, it is described as an individual lament, but it is more a prayer than a lament, and it is congregational rather than individual in its usage. But unfamiliar with the musical directions, from this liturgical use, medieval commentators persisted with the translation "Unto the End."

As we may expect, **Cassiodorus** (485-580) continues this liturgical-eschatological interpretation of "Mother Church." But he interprets verse 4 as referring to secret things, which we may hide in bed, but which God sees and knows,[19] speaking with the figure of speech of *mythopoeia*. At the same time Cassiodorus is anxious not to depict the church abstractly, "without living personality," for the church is "the aggregate of all the holy faithful, one soul and one heart, the bride of Christ."[20] He identifies two parts to the psalm with two musical instruments. In the first, "the Church asks that her prayer be heard, rebuking the faithless for worshipping false gods and neglecting the worship of true gods." In the second part, the church "warns the world at large that it must abandon deceitful superstition, and offer the sacrifice of justice. Then in her attempt to win over the minds of the pagans by the promise she has made, she relates that the Lord has bestowed great gifts on Christians."[21]

Following Augustine, Cassiodorus uses the analogy of the emperor's image stamped on his coinage: "so the signs of the heavenly Emperor are imprinted on the faithful."[22] As a church statesman, Cassiodorus offers a political manifesto for what he calls "our mother's preaching," which has an audience "throughout the world." It is a uniform morality for all Christendom, ruled by the four Stoic "virtues of prudence, justice, fortitude, and temperance," with a common psalmic liturgy.[23]

Quite different from the court life of Ravenna is the monastic cell of the Benedictine monk **Haimo of St.-Germain d'Auxerre** (died c. 875) in France. Yet he maintains the Augustinian interpretation of the title as "Unto the end a psalm song for David" *(psalmus cantici)*. He too hears the voice of the church in the psalm as "binding diabolical temptations" in rebuke and strong admoni-

17. Stanley L. Jaki, *Praying the Psalms* (Grand Rapids: Eerdmans, 2001), p. 39.

18. Adrian Curtis, *Psalms* (Peterborough, UK: Epworth Press, 2004), p. 8.

19. Cassiodorus, *Explanation of the Psalms,* in P. G.Walsh, trans. and ed., *Ancient Christian Writers,* vol. 1 (New York and Mahwah, NJ: Paulist Press, 1990), p. 76.

20. Cassiodorus, *Explanation of the Psalms,* vol. 1, pp. 73, 74.

21. Cassiodorus, *Explanation of the Psalms,* vol. 1, p. 74.

22. Cassiodorus, *Explanation of the Psalms,* vol. 1, p. 77.

23. Cassiodorus, *Explanation of the Psalms,* vol. 1, p. 80.

tion, commingled with promises of divine favor. But "the light of your countenance" is now interpreted to be the divine wisdom, the living image of Christ, imparted to us by him.[24]

A generation later, **Remigius of Auxerre** (c. 841-908) adds an original interpretation on the distinction between a "psalm" and a "song," still based on Augustine's distinction. "In a psalm in which 'psalm' precedes in the title, and 'song' follows, its early part exhorts us to labor, the later parts summon us to glory." Likewise, it is the "fleshly David" who is exemplified in the former, and "the spiritual David," "great David's greater son," who exemplifies the latter.[25]

Although **Bede** (673-735), called the Venerable, devoted his life to Biblical commentaries, we have only short fragments of his works on the psalms. These are mostly collations of previous commentators, notably Augustine, but also of Theodore of Mopsuestia, who had significant influence in the early Irish monasteries. **Manegold von Lautenbach** (died c. 1103), also known as **Pseudo-Bede** (see pp. 188-89 on Psalm 3), notes, "a psalm is a musical instrument . . . by which divine praises were sung," whereas a "song is that which sounds the heavenly praises by means of human voices." The words of the whole of Psalm 4 are interpreted as those of the church. "Unto the end" he interprets as expressive of Christ, "because he is the true end and perfection of the shadow of the old law" (citing again from Augustine, Rom. 10:4). As a "psalm-song," he interprets it as symbolic of the unity between Christ and the church, for "by 'psalm' proceeds . . . the invocation of Christ to God the Father before glorification; and from that very glorification follows that which is much more joyful than invocation, and on that account it is understood by 'song,' since it is a more joyful voice than psalm, as has been said above." Almost half of his text is devoted to this imaginative explanation of the psalm's musical directions, before he begins to apply the psalm pastorally.

Bruno of Segni (died 1123) is a much better commentator, who helped Gregory VII in his reform of the church. He too follows Augustine in relating Psalm 4 to Christ as "the end of the Law," so its "songs" are those of the church. Like Cassiodorus, he interprets this psalm as the prayer of the church, which he notes is "enlarged more in tribulation and adversity than in prosperity." But he notes that "just now it seems to have failed both in Africa and in many other parts of the earth, in which at one time it was glorious."[26] Commenting on verse 4 he notes that "the beds are the thoughts of our hearts; there they arise, there

24. Haimo of Auxerre, *In omnes psalmos pia, brevis ac dilucida explanatio* (PL 207B, 209B).

25. Remigius of Auxerre, *Enarrationum in psalmos liber unus* (PL 131:162A).

26. Bruno of Segni, *Expositio in psalmos* (PL 164:706A, B, and C).

they rest, there they bring forth fruit if they are good, and evil if they are evil," linking this with Matthew 15:17-19, of the evil things that stem from the heart. This and other suggestions indicate that he is an independent thinker, expressing his own reflections.

Herbert of Bosham (c. 1120-c. 1194) is a remarkable commentator. He was born in England, educated in Paris, a pupil of Peter Lombard, then attached to the household of Thomas à Becket. He is probably associated with Richard of St. Victor, and one of the most brilliant scholars of his time. He is a respecter of no man, and his commentary on the Psalms shows all the marks of independent thought.[27] Perhaps Herbert had more responsibility for Thomas à Becket's intransigence with Henry II than chronicles may have realized! A secular cleric, diplomat, and Hebraic scholar, he even knows how to assess the merits of various Jewish scholars' handling of Scripture. He rejects the prevailing allegorical interpretation of the psalms' titles and focuses instead on the Hebrew meaning of the words. With immense integrity he explores the literal Hebrew meaning of obscure psalm titles, even if it means rejecting such unquestioned authorities as Jerome himself. He does not abandon the traditional Christian interpretation that the psalms are "about Christ," but if a Hebrew/Jewish context and meaning can be accepted textually, he does so. Herbert's introduction to the Fourth Psalm is critically important in its challenge to traditional Augustinian interpretation.

Herbert's groundbreaking exegetical emphasis sets the stage for **Thomas Aquinas's** (1225-74) homilies on the Psalter. Aquinas's title to Psalm 4 ignores Hubert's work, continuing to use the traditional title, "Unto the end, in Song, a Psalm of David." But Aquinas now shares with the scholastics a desire for accuracy and a more critical use of sources, whether pagan, Jewish, or Christian (see pp. 54-55 in "Christian Hebraism and Scholasticism in the High to Late Middle Ages"). He cautiously appropriates the writings of Rashi and other Jewish scholars.[28] His style is sober and restrained, as he forsakes the liturgical/eschatological approach of his predecessors in order to give a clear pastoral exposition.

He quotes Jerome extensively, "according to the Hebrew," and interprets individual verses within the context of the entire psalm. He sees the psalm "divided into two parts: for the first it begins with giving of thanks for benefits received . . . second, it ends in the exhorting of others that they may be turned to

27. Beryl Smalley was the first scholar to discover Herbert of Bosham's work. See Beryl Smalley, "A Commentary on the *Hebraica* by Herbert of Bosham," *RTAM* 18 (1951): 29-65.

28. Marcia L. Colish, *Medieval Foundations of the Western Intellectual Tradition, 400-1400* (New Haven and London: Yale University Press, 1998), pp. 295-301.

29. Thomas Aquinas, *In Psalmos Davidis expositio,* in Sancti Thomae Aquinatis Opera Omnia, vol. 14 (Parma: Typis Petri Fiaccadori, 1863), pp. 148-312.

God."[29] In gratitude, "the psalmist gives thanks about the past," and then "he shows in what way he has been heard." Then "he prays for the future." He quotes Jerome about the meaning of "selah," as a pause in the division of the psalm. But he gives alternative renderings that do not distort his textual criticism.

V. Erasmus, a Renaissance Sermon

The fourth and last psalm commentary Erasmus undertook to publish on the Psalms is *In psalmum quartum concio,* published in 1525 as "a written sermon." Having used four differing experimental genres in treating the first four psalms (see pp. 124-25, 154-55, 190-92), Erasmus questions if the Psalter can ever be treated systematically. Instead, he envisages its multiform character. For him, conservative "Augustinian commentary," aligned with medieval chronicle (i.e., the uncritical acceptance of past records and statements, being passed on conservatively to the next generation), belongs to medieval historiography, which is now rapidly passing away. In revolt, Erasmus is protesting: "Where there is such a host of commentaries, if I am to hold the reader's attention, there must be some novelty in the treatment." This is no longer the mindset of the Middle Ages!

Already in his commentary on Psalm 2, he faces the difficult issue of the psalm headings (see p. 146). Hilary's ruling had been, observed Erasmus, that "whenever we meet a psalm which does not bear the author's name in the heading, we may ascribe it to the author whose name appears on the preceding heading, and continue until we reach a later psalm bearing the name of a different author."[30] Erasmus then continues: "I am not sure that this is a true or comprehensive rule." But as the First Psalm has no heading, how can it apply to the Second Psalm? Nicholas of Lyra, who Erasmus suggests should have known better, avoids this whole issue, as indeed others did later. He then turns to the musical ascriptions in psalm headings. He asks: What point is there in learning what particular musical instrument was used? "Christians do God more honor by leading godly lives than by singing hymns and praises."[31] But what follows is a depiction of moralistic humanism, which shows that Erasmus does not understand the Reformers' doctrine of justification *sola gratia.*[32]

30. Erasmus, *Expositions of the Psalms,* ed. Dominic Baker-Smith, trans. Michael J. Heath, Collected Works of Erasmus, vol. 63 (Toronto: University of Toronto Press, 1997), pp. 75-76.

31. Erasmus, *Expositions of the Psalms,* p. 176.

32. Erasmus, "A Sermon on Psalm 4," LB V 292A/ASD V-2, pp. 274-75.

VI. Reformation Commentaries

Near the end of his life **Martin Luther** (1483-1546) asks Ludwig Seuffel to compose a requiem for him. Luther reveals that Psalm 4:8 has been deeply formative for him. (Unfortunately, aside from his earlier lectures on the Psalter, we do not have a later commentary on the Psalms.) Verse 8 becomes ever more dear to him as he prepares himself hourly for death, constantly singing the soothing words, "Ich lieg und schlafe ganz mit Frieden." A genre of late medieval religious literature, *ars moriendi,* "the art of dying," focused on the theme of "how to die well" or of "being able to die" with a positive spirit. Books of exercises were available, to be memorized while in good health for this eventuality. Luther himself composes his *ars moriendi,* having been asked in early May 1519 to write such a work for his friend Markus Schart.

Since the time of Anselm (1033-1109), when the *ars moriendi* literature seeks reconciliation with God through Christ, emphasis was placed on the redeeming work of Christ. The genre was intended not just for the dying person, but also the relatives and friends in attendance. Luther uniquely and exclusively pays attention to the dying person in the presence of God, excluding advice to third parties, such as given in the conciliar materials of Jean Gerson. Luther emphasizes the need to have a comprehensive view of the images of death, sin, and hell, but from the perspective of eternal life, grace, and heaven. For, says Luther, "[Christ] on the cross presents himself to us in a threefold image. . . . He is the living and undying image against death. . . . He is the image of God's grace against death. . . . He is the image of heaven."[33] Thus Luther can comfort us in that the terrible image and fear of death is removed by its opposite, eternal life in Christ. Luther also moves away from the "imitation of Christ" tradition of the *devotio moderna* movement (i.e., imitating Jesus in his calm composure upon the cross), towards a recognition of the benefits we receive in Christ's victory over death. The great medieval fear had been to die suddenly without time to administer the last rites of confession, absolution, and receiving communion; Luther now sees these rites as unnecessary. Without faith they are nothing, so one must be more concerned about the forgiveness of one's sins than about the sacraments and their power.[34] It is unfortunate we do not have a full text of Luther's thoughts on Psalm 4, but verses 4-5, 8, are for him truly expressive of *ars moriendi: "lying on one's bed; searching one's heart in silence before God; trusting in the grace of God; and thus in peace, lying down to sleep,"* all in the

33. Quoted by Dick Akerboom, ". . . Only the Image of Christ in Us," p. 249.
34. Akerboom, ". . . Only the Image of Christ in Us," p. 238.

light of the Resurrection of Christ. The anticipation of this had been with him for most of his life.

Unlike Erasmus's dialectical engagement with Augustine's commentary of the Fourth Psalm, **John Calvin** deliberately chooses Chrysostom's commentary because of its more literal approach. He recognizes Augustine is too allegorical for his own adoption and recommends David Qimhi as the most reliable rabbinical scholar.[35] Nor does Calvin interpret Psalm 4 as *ars moriendi,* as Luther did. Rather we commune with our heart in our daily intimacy of reflection — not just at our death "bed" (v. 4): "here to learn, that in solitude we can give to any subject a closer attention. David therefore exhorts his enemies to withdraw and to be alone, that they may examine themselves more truthfully and honestly. There is nothing to which men are more prone than to deceive one another with empty applause, until each man enters into himself, and communes alone with his own heart."[36] The justification of the righteous leads them to have a low estimate of material prosperity in comparison with resting alone in God. So they are content to remain as pilgrims and strangers in this life in the light of having a better life in the world to come. They too may desire worldly comforts, but they do so with moderation.

Calvin is uncertain of the historical context of the psalm, possibly when "David was a fugitive and an exile . . . persecuted by Saul."[37] He expresses David's intimate trust in God to be such that he concludes: "David boasts that the protection of God was alone sufficient, and that under it he sleeps securely, although destitute of all human guardianship. . . . Let us, therefore, learn from his example . . . that though there appear no help for us from men, yet under His hand alone we are kept in peace and safety, as if we were surrounded by a great host."[38]

Robert Leighton (1611-84), Archbishop of Glasgow, gives us a series of "meditations" on a few selected psalms, which include Psalm 4. He uses his sources critically, and with him we conclude our historical survey. He notes that while the psalm heading of the Fourth Psalm should be translated "to the chief musician," the Latin fathers had translated it as "to the end." "Whence the Greek and Latin fathers imagined, that all the psalms which bear this inscription refer to the Messiah, the great end and the accomplishment of all things; a sentiment

35. Peter Opitz, "Calvin's Exegesis of the Old Testament," in Magne Saebø, ed., *Hebrew Bible/Old Testament: The History of Its Interpretation,* vol. 2 (Göttingen: Vandenhoeck & Ruprecht, 2008), pp. 439-40, 448-51.

36. John Calvin, *Commentary on the Book of Psalms* (Edinburgh: Calvin Translation Society, 1895), p. 44.

37. Calvin, *Commentary on the Book of Psalms,* pp. 36-37.

38. Calvin, *Commentary on the Book of Psalms,* p. 50.

which was rather pious than judicious, and led them often to wrest several passages in the psalms by violence and unnatural glosses. Yet I would not morosely reject all interpretations of that kind, seeing the apostles themselves apply to Christ many passages out of the psalms and other works of the Old Testament, which, if we had not been assured of it by their authority, we should hardly have imagined to have had a reference to him. . . . And it is certain the passage out of this psalm, which Austin [Augustine], and some others, suppose to refer to Christ, may be applied to him without any force of the expression: Ye sons of men, how long will ye turn my glory into shame?"[39]

As a former Principal of Edinburgh University, he writes with a student audience in mind, commenting on verse 4, "communing on your beds," as the need to become self-reflective: "Dear youths, if amid all your other studies, you do not learn to converse with your own selves, whatever you know, or else, whatever you imagine you know, I would not purchase it at the expense of a straw."[40] He renders "lie upon your bed" as the need to remove oneself from the noise of the world and all its activity, to exercise self-reflection, especially when "the reflections of the night are the deepest." Quoting Pythagoras, he states: "We should not allow ourselves to go to sleep, till we have seriously revolved the actions of the day, and ask ourselves: 'What have I done amiss? What good have I done, or neglected to do? That so we may reprove ourselves for what has been wrong, and take the comfort of what has been as it ought." To "be still" is not so much the silence of the tongue, as the tranquility of the mind, reposing in a deep trust of God. He quotes Bernard of Clairvaux concerning verse 5, on "the sacrifice of righteousness": "Nothing, Lord, that is Thine can suffice me without thyself, nor can anything that is mine, without myself, be pleasing to thee."[41] Selflessness in adoration of Him is the true holocaust, to present ourselves a living sacrifice. Leighton concludes his meditation: "God fixes his gracious dwelling in the pure and holy soul which has learned to despise the vanity of riches, and makes it calm in the midst of hurries and scurries in the deepest solicitudes."[42]

39. *The Whole Works of Robert Leighton,* arranged by John Norman Pearson (New York: J. C. Riker, 1852), p. 357.

40. *The Whole Works of Robert Leighton,* p. 362.

41. *The Whole Works of Robert Leighton,* p. 363.

42. *The Whole Works of Robert Leighton,* p. 364.

Part II. Voice of the Psalmist: Translation

A Psalm of David

1 Answer[43] me when I call to you, my righteous God.[44]
Give me relief[45] from distress;[46]
be merciful to me and hear my[47] prayer.
2 How long, highborn men,[48]
while[49] my glory is turned to[50] shame,[51]
will you love delusions and seek false gods?
3 Now know that *I AM* has set apart the godly for himself;
I AM will hear when I call to him.
4 Tremble and do not sin;
search your hearts while you are in bed,
and be silent.[52]

43. LXX, followed by Vulgate, read all the verbs in v. 1 [2] as perfects, not as imperatives, a vocalization adopted by Lagarde, Kessler, Gunkel, et al. This "revocalization" of the text is due to the failure to recognize the parallel *hirḥabtâ* as a precative perfective.

44. On the one hand, the pronominal suffix may modify the construct chain. In that case *ṣedeq* may be an attributive genitive, "my righteous God" (*IBHS*, p. 149, P. 9.5.3a.), and the sense is, "the God who does right by me." Or *ṣedeq* may be a genitive of effect (*IBHS*, p. 146, 9.5.2c), in which case *ṣedeq* has the sense of "success, well-being" and the pronominal suffix is possessive (i.e., "God who grants me success"). On the other hand, "my" may modify "righteous" (i.e., "my righteousness"), as understood by Theodore of Mopsuestia (see above).

45. A precative perfective, not a preterite perfective (as in LXX and most EVV), because of its imperative parallels (see 3:7, note 45). There is no need to emend the text to an imperative (contra Budde, Graetz, Staerk, et al.). Literally, "make room," which does not mean to make converts (against Cassiodorus) or "to enlarge the heart" (i.e., "to have God . . . shed abroad in the heart," against Augustine), but a metaphor "to save" (Ps. 18:19 [20]; 31:8 [9]).

46. Heb. *ṣār* (root I. *ṣrr* "to bind, be restricted"), a homonym of *ṣār* "adversary" (root *ṣrr* "to show hostility toward").

47. Genitive of authorship (*IBHS*, p. 143, P. 9.5.1c).

48. Not *huioi anthrōpōn*, "human beings," but highborn officials (see commentary).

49. Construed as a nominal circumstantial clause.

50. Initial *lamedh* of *lklmh* implies a verb of motion (*IBHS*, p. 224, P. 11.4.3d).

51. LXX, Vulgate, and Ethiopic read less happily: "How long will you be slow of heart? Wherefore . . . ?" Their "Vorlage" confounded *kbdy klmh* with *kbdy lb lmh*.

52. Lexicographers differ whether *dmm* is a homonym, and if so, of how many roots. *HALOT* proposes three: 1) = "be motionless, still," a root no one questions; 2) = "to wail, lament," a root attested in Ugaritic and possibly in Akkadian; and 3) = "to be destroyed, perish." BDB finds the first two, citing only Isaiah 23:2 for root 2, whereas *HALOT* lists Psalm 4:4 [5] and Lamentations 2:10 as also belonging to this root. The meaning "to be still, silent, motionless," however, satisfies all Biblical texts; so, it is best to acknowledge with GB and KBL only one root.

5 Offer the sacrifices[53] of the righteous
and trust in the *I AM*.
6 Many are saying, "O that one would show us good!
Lift up[54] the light of your face upon us, *I AM*."
7 Fill[55] my heart with great joy
when[56] their grain, and new wine and oil[57] abound.
8 In peace I will lie down and fall asleep at once,
for you, *I AM*, make me dwell apart, in safety.

For the director of music. For flutes.

53. An effected cognate accusative (literally, "sacrifice sacrifices," *IBHS*, p. 166, P. 10.2.1f).

54. Literally, "Lift up upon us the light of your face." "Lift up" renders the anomalous form *n^{e}sâ*. This *hapax legomenon* is rendered in the LXX by *esēmeiōthē* ("has been manifested," rendered in Vulgate by *signatum est*), perhaps questionably reading *niśśâ* and interpreting it as a *Niphal* perfective of *nss*, a denominative of *nēs* ("standard"). Dahood and Anderson emend the text to *nāsâ*, understanding the form to be a *Qal* perfect with an archaic third masculine singular ending (so Dahood) or a third feminine singular (so Anderson) of *nûs* (= has fled, so NEB). This conjectural emendation stumbles on the -*â* suffix and the preposition *'al* ("upon"). Bardtke *(BHS)* escapes these philological objections by reading *nās^{e}'â*, from the root *nāsa'*, "to start out on a journey," a curious figure for light departing. The Masoretes probably understood the form as a *Qal* imperative, masculine singular of *nāśa'*. This is the preferred understanding because: 1) although the form is normally *śā'* (cf. Ps. 25:18), the *nun* recurs in Psalm 10:12. 2) The interchange of /*ś*/ and /*s*/ and of /*'*/ and /*h*/ is not uncommon. GKC (762[a]) regards the form as merely an orthographic variant of *n^{e}śā'*, the reading in one ms. 3) It was so construed by Aquila, Theodotion, Targum, and most older commentators. 4) This interpretation suits well the apparent intertextuality of the petition with the Aaronic benediction (Num. 6:26).

55. Dahood thinks that "the *scriptio plena* of the final syllable /āh/ may correspond to the energic ending of the imperative [see *n^{e}sâ* in v. 6 (7)], especially since an impressive number of precative perfects are written fully in the final syllable: Pss. 10:14; 31:6; 35:22; 44:27; 56:9; 60:6; 140:8; Lam 3:59, 60."

56. Literally, "from the time." The LXX, followed by Vulgate, reads "from the fruit of," which is due to confounding within the Greek tradition *kairou* ("time") with *karpou* ("fruit"). Many ancient psalteries read *a tempore* (Moll).

57. The LXX, Syriac, and Qumran texts read "their new wine and their oil." The intertextuality with Deuteronomy 33:23, which omits *w^{e}yiṣhār* (see commentary), may suggest that *w^{e}yiṣhārām* is a gloss because of the frequent pairing of *tîrôš w^{e}yiṣhārām*. More probably *w^{e}yiṣhārām* dropped out of the MT by haplography due to three words ending with /*ām*/.

Part III. Commentary

I. Introduction

A. Historical Context

The importance of rain and dew for life in Israel cannot be overemphasized; the chosen nation's existence depended on them. Rain is God's good gift to his people in the Land he swore to give them (Deut. 11:11-12), and the dew of heaven is the first blessing promised to Jacob (Gen. 27:28). In *I AM*'s covenant with Israel, that promise is conditioned upon their obedience to the Law of love for *I AM* and service to him (Deut. 11:13-14; 28:12). At the dedication of the temple, Solomon prayed that *I AM* would grant the petitions of *I AM*'s people for rain when they pray toward the temple (1 Kings 8:35-36), and as the anointed leader of the people, the king is expected to lead them in prayer for rain in drought.

Psalm 4 is such a prayer, as seen as early as Chrysostom and more recently defended by Oesterley and Dahood in their commentaries and by John Eaton in his *Kingship and the Psalms*. In verse 6 [7] the people pray for "good," a metonymy elsewhere for rain (see commentary), and in verse 7 [8] the king backs up their prayer: "Fill my heart with joy when their grain and new wine abound."

Drought, however, plunges the king into an even greater crisis: loss of confidence in his leadership. Because of the drought and a bad harvest, such as the three-year drought described in 2 Samuel 21, the nation's rich and powerful were turning to pagan fertility deities. Baal ("Lord"), an epithet for Hadad, the storm god, was the principal fertility god in the Canaanite pantheon. His escutcheon was a fertility bull, so very much unlike *I AM*'s escutcheon, the ark of the covenant symbolizing his justice with mercy. A statue of Baal pictures the rain god brandishing in his left hand a twisted spear, representing the lightning, and holding in his right hand a club, representing the thunderclap.[58] The rites associated with his worship include kissing his image (1 Kings 19:18), lascivious fertility practices,[59] and child sacrifice (Jer. 19:5).

The defection of the highborn from the cultus of *I AM*, whose patron head is the House of David, becomes more understandable in their historical context. In the ancient Near East abundant rain, crops, and life were thought to be intertwined with the divine election and favor upon the king. The king was

58. For texts from ancient Ugarit attributing rain to Baal, see Leila Leah Bronner, *The Stories of Elijah and Elisha as Polemics Against Baal Worship* (Leiden: E. J. Brill, 1968).

59. W. F. Albright, *Yahweh and the Gods of Canaan: A Historical Analysis of Two Contrasting Faiths* (Garden City, NY: Doubleday, 1968).

like a shaman figure, who mediated between the forces of heaven and earth. Assurbanipal claims in an inscription: "Since the time that I sat on the throne of my father, my progenitor, Adad [the storm god] has loosed his downpours, Ea [the fountain god] has opened his fountains, the forests have grown abundantly."[60] In Egypt, the pharaoh attributes the bountiful harvests reaped during his reign to his good and magical relations to the grain god: "It is I," he boasts, "who produced the grain because I was beloved by the grain god. No one was hungry in my years."[61] Had not *I AM* promised his people food when he chose the House of David and Mount Zion as the site for his temple that guaranteed provision and protection (Ps. 132:11-15)? In their crisis of doubts about *I AM*'s fidelity to his promise to David and about his anointed scion's favor with him, the rich and powerful turn to the sensual fertility rituals of the Baal cultus that demands no moral rectitude of them.

Moreover, to make matters worse, the king was supposed to be potent in prayer.[62] Of the pharaoh it was said: "Everything proceeding from the lips of his majesty, his father [the god] Amon causes to be realized there and then." And of the Assyrian king it was said: "his prayer will be well received by the god." But *I AM*'s king thus far has found no answer to his prayer. His question to the feckless rich: "How long?" assumes an extended period of their defection. Pagan religions believe in instantaneous answer to prayers — a sort of "name it, claim it" religion.

But the saints of the triune God often feel abandoned by him with no answer to their prayer (cf. Ps. 13:1-2). In *A Grief Observed,* C. S. Lewis likens his prayer for his wife's healing from cancer to knocking on the door, as the Lord Jesus instructed. Lewis says he knocked until his knuckles were bloody raw, and when he examined the door it was double-bolted. And sometimes, when we step back and look upstairs, the lights are out and no one seems at home. Perplexity is normal Christian experience, but saints do not despair because the verities of the metanarrative transcend the immediate narrative (2 Cor. 4:7).

In the crisis David's petitions establish the intimate relation he has with *I AM,* who does what is right by his covenant partner (v. 1a [2a]). The petition is summarized in the words "extricate me from distress" (v. 1b [2b]). David then rebukes his feckless subordinates for their apostasy (v. 2 [3]) and aims to restore

60. B. Meissner, *Assyrische Jagden: Auf Grund alter Berichte und Darstellungen/ geschildert* (Leipzig: J. C. Hinrichs, 1911), p. 23.

61. O. Keel, *The Symbolism of the Biblical World: Ancient Near Eastern Iconography and the Book of Psalms,* trans. Timothy J. Hallett (New York: Seabury Press, 1978, 1972), p. 286.

62. J. Eaton, *Kingship and the Psalms* (Naperville, IL: Allenson, 1976), p. 195, brings together the studies of Posener, Labat, and Dussaud to show the king's claim to power in prayer in Egypt, Assyria, and Hatti respectively.

faith in the cultus of *I AM* by giving seven imperatives to the backsliders. These seven admonitions also serve to express his own confidence in his election, and give reasons for Israel to trust *I AM*. The first calls upon them to know his unique intimacy with *I AM* and so power in prayer. The last six fall into three pairs: dread the consequences of apostasy (4a [5a]), let your conscience confirm your faith (4b [5b]), and trust *I AM* (v. 5 [6]). In other words, David by faith lays hold of verities that bring his house through the crisis. Buoyed by these verities he petitions God to end the drought for the sake of the people (vv. 6-7 [7-8]), and shows his confidence by going to sleep while the drought still afflicts the land (v. 8 [9]). He sets his prayer to music to teach the people how to pray according to sound doctrine (subscript).

B. Form and Rhetorical Criticism

From a form-critical viewpoint David composes his prayer using the typical motifs of a lament psalm (see Psalm 3, pp. 194-95): Address (v. 1 [2]), Lament (v. 2 [3]), Confidence (vv. 3-5 [4-6]), Petition (vv. 6-7 [7-8]), and Praise, implied in his going to sleep (v. 8 [9]). From a rhetorical viewpoint it may be analyzed as having a one-line introduction and a conclusion around three quatrains. These occur in connection with his changing of addressees, first to *I AM* (v. 1 [2]), then to the highborn (vv. 2-5 [3-6]), and finally to *I AM* (vv. 6-8 [7-9]). In sum, its rhetoric suggests the following outline:

Superscript: genre and author	
I. Address to God: Introductory petitions for God's favor	1 [2]
II. Address to highborn	2-5 [3-6]
A. Accusation and admonition	2-3 [3-4]
1. Accusation: apostasy	2 [3]
2. First admonition: know the king's power in prayer	3 [4]
B. Further admonitions:	4-5 [5-6]
1. Dread the consequences of apostasy	4a [5a]
2. Let your conscience confirm your faith	4b [5b]
3. Trust *I AM*	5 [6]
III. Address to *I AM*	6-8 [7-9]
A. Petition for rain	6-7 [7-8]
1. By the people	6 [7]
2. By the king	7 [8]
B. Resolve to sleep in peace	8 [9]
Subscript: liturgical performance	

II. Exegesis

A. Superscript

The following internal evidence of the psalm supports the superscript's claim that David composed the psalm (*mizmôr,* see chapter 3, pp. 87-88): 1) He is opposed by highborn men (v. 2). 2) He claims a special grace and glory in prayer, a royal prerogative throughout the ancient Near East.[63] This trait is generally ascribed to the king, particularly in psalms conceded by form-critics to be of royal origin (2:8; 20:1-5 [2-6]; 21:2, 4 [3, 5]; 89:26 [27]). 3) He is in corporate solidarity with prayers of the people (3:6-7 [7-8]) and speaks of himself as having glory (v. 2 [3], cf. 3:3 [4]). 4) There is no reason to question the superscript's claim.

B. Address to I AM: Invocation for Favor and Relief v. 1 [2]

The introductory petitions invoke God's favor and salvation. Each verset ends with the first person singular suffix /*î*/ (= "I, me, my"), and of the nine accented words this suffix occurs six times. And so, the introductory petitions establish an intimate "I — Thou" relationship between God and his king. As in Psalm 3, the king must assert his intimacy with God in a context of adversaries who deny this relationship. His petitions for God's favor are threefold:

1. "Answer me." The compound "to call" and "to answer" means respectively "to draw attention to oneself" and "respond" (see 3:4 [5]). His only hope is in God.

2. "Be merciful to me" derives from a verb "to show *ḥēn* ['favor,' 'grace'] to someone." It entails three notions at one and the same time: a) "Condescend to take note of someone" (cf. Ruth 2:10). If human beings take note on the needy (Ruth 2:10; cf. 2 Sam. 20:3), how much more will God note the needs of his anointed king! b) "To feel goodwill," which precedes the actual doing of a generous deed (cf. Gen. 19:19; 32:5–33:10). c) "To have mercy," because the person taking note with an attitude of goodwill has the capacity as a benefactor to meet the need of the favored beneficiary.[64] Mercy entails no obligation to meet the need: "It is entirely free and wholly undeserved."[65] Nevertheless, God's favor and generosity must be held in dialectical tension with his justice. Noah found

63. Eaton, *Kingship and the Psalms,* p. 195.
64. L. Reed, *JBL* 73 (1954): 58f.
65. Snaith, *TWBOB,* p. 101.

favor in the eyes of *I AM* and he was a righteous man (Gen. 6:7-8). This benevolent attribute of God's unmerited favor is consistently connected with his other sublime virtues: gracious, longsuffering, abounding in love, and faithful (Exod. 34:6; Ps. 86:15; 103:8; 145:8; Jonah 4:2). His mercy is not an arbitrary, capricious condescension of a monarch's will, but the characteristic outreach of a loving God (cf. Jer. 31:2-3; Neh. 9:17, 31) toward a repentant individual who does not spurn his grace. God's attitude of condescending to human needs constitutes the basis for his performing deed of *ḥesed* ("unfailing love"). When a gift of love is received, it is proof that the benefactor has an attitude of goodwill toward the recipient (2 Sam. 14:22; 16:4; Ruth 2:13).[66]

3. *Hear (š^{e}maʿ) my prayer (t^{e}pillātî).* "Hear" may have the same broad range of meanings as covered by the English word "to hear." In prayer it signifies both outwardly that God gives his ear to the speaker's words and inwardly consents to them. The force of the command is weakened to a request by the object of "to hear": "prayer" *(t^{e}pillâ). T^{e}pillâ* means "a request for an assessment, a consideration," either for others (= "intercession," Ps. 35:13; 84:8 [9]; 109:4) or for self ("prayer," "petition"). Almost half of the usages of *t^{e}pillâ* occur in petition psalms, either in introductory petitions, imploring God to be favorable (17:1; *passim*), or in the praise section, rejoicing that God heard his prayer (65:2 [3]; *passim*). In a superscript it functions as a technical term to designate the genre of petition/lament/complaint psalms (17:1; 86:1; 102:1; 142:1). Its parallels are "cry for mercy" (*t^{e}ḥinnâ, taḥ^{a}nûn, taḥ^{a}nûnôt,* Ps. 6:9 [10]; 86:6; 143:1) and "cry for help" (*rinnâ,* 17:1; 61:1 [2]; 88:2 [3]); *šawʿâ,* 39:12 [13]; 102:1 [2]), *dimʿâ* (39:12 [13]).[67]

The king addresses *I AM* by his title *God (ʾ^{e}lōhê),* because that title, which refers to God's transcendence as Creator, is appropriate in a prayer for rain. The form is plural (a *pluralis majestatis*) to signify that God is thoroughly characterized by his transcendence: no aspect of creation or history lies beyond his purview.

The root translated *righteous (ṣedeq)* occurs 534 times in the Old Testament, and of these, 139 times in the Psalms. Olley defines *ṣedeq* ("righteousness") as that which brings about "right and harmony for all, for individuals, related in the community and the physical and spiritual realms. It finds its basis in God's rule of the world."[68] In other words, *ṣedeq* signifies serving one's neigh-

66. J. Stoebe, *THAT,* 1:589.

67. Mentioned postures in prayer are: "stand" (1 Kings 8:22), "kneel" (1 Kings 8:54), "touch forehead to ground" (Isa. 44:17), "throw oneself down" (Ezra 10:1), "bow" (Isa. 44:17), "spread palms wide apart" (1 Kings 8:38, 54), "raise hands" (Ps. 141:2). Weeping or fasting in sackcloth and ashes is also mentioned.

68. J. W. Olley, "'Righteous' and Wealth? The Description of the *Ṣaddîq* in Wisdom Literature," *Colloquium* 22 (1990): 38-45.

bor, not self (see Ps. 4:1 [2]), as defined by God's *torah.* The precise sense of the term here, however, depends in part on the syntax (see n. 44). If the psalmist intends "my righteous God," his thought is that God does right by his covenant partner. The frequent references to the righteousness of *I AM* in the Old Testament and in the Psalms entail that *I AM* is faithful in keeping his covenant promises to his servant nation and to his king. If God called David through the universally recognized prophet, Samuel, who poured fine oils upon him as his cachet to be God's king, and if God credentialed him by performing glorious feats over the uncircumcised, it would be diabolical to turn a deaf ear to him and not to rescue him in the drought.

On the other hand, if the construction signifies "God grants me success," "righteousness" becomes a synonym for justice, salvation, and unfailing love (Ps. 7:17 [18]; 22:31 [32]; 35:28; 40:9 [10]; 48:10 [11]; 51:14 [16]). When the king extols *I AM* as the shepherd who leads him in paths of righteousness, he means that *I AM* protects him from his enemies (Ps. 23:3-4; 5:8 [9]). *I AM*'s forgiveness and restoration of his elect slave is spoken of as an act of his righteousness (Ps. 51:14 [16]; Mic. 7:9). This circumstance of a "sound, unassailed and favorable success,"[69] assumes the innocence of the beneficiary. The Judge of the earth (Ps. 94:2) fulfills his commitment to Israel and David by punishing their oppressors and delivering them, two sides of one coin. The obverse side of his judgment pictures the preservation of the elect, and its reverse side pictures the punishment of their enemies. In Psalm 69:27 [28] the psalmist prays that his foes not enter into *I AM*'s righteousness (= salvation).

Both grammatical possibilities fit the context well, suggesting both metonymies of cause, in connection with the former notion, and effect in connection with the latter. The former interpretation puts the accent on God's doing what is right by his covenant partner; the second accents the benefits flowing from that action. In sum, God's righteous acts based on the ethics of his elect are indissolubly coupled with beneficial results.

His second petition asks God to extricate him from his distress. His petition for salvation pictures his *distress* (*ṣār,* "strait") as a situation from which he cannot extricate himself and his salvation as *make room, enlarge the space* (to escape the strait). *Me* (literally, "for me," see n. 45) denotes "for my advantage," not merely an indirect object, "to me." Verse 2 [3] clarifies his distress and verse 7 [8] clarifies how God will deliver him from his distress. That abstract petition becomes specific in verses 6-7 [7-8]).

69. K. Koch, *TLOT,* 2:1052, s.v. *ṣedeq.*

C. Address to the Apostates vv. 2-5 [3-6]

In an apostrophe within his petition, the king imaginatively turns to the faithless rich and influential and reproaches them for their defection from him, and correlatively, from *I AM* who anointed him. The warm intimacy in the I-Thou encounter between God and his king is replaced by hostility in the I-Thou relationship between the king and the apostate leaders. He displays the same spirit of faith that led Moses to destroy the apostates (Exod. 32:20), Elijah to defeat them (1 Kings 18:19-40), and the prophets to denounce them (Jer. 14:22).

1. Worthless Fertility Deities Versus Potent King vv. 2-3 [3-4]

Though the king's admonition to the pusillanimous highborn to "know" his power in prayer is the first of his seven commands to them, it is uniquely bound to his accusation against them in verse 3 [4] by the conjunction *waw* ("and/but") and by the semantic pertinence of contrasting the futility of false gods with his unique power. In other words, verse 4 [5] is a janus between verses 3 [4] and 5-6 [6-7].

a. Accusation Against the Highborn of Turning to Fertility Deities v. 2 [3]

The vocative, *highborn men (bᵉne ʾîš),* albeit not recognized by most English versions, refers to men of rank and of social eminence and wealth (see Ps. 49:2 [3]; 62:9 [10], NIV, TNIV). Weiser calls attention to analogous Egyptian and Babylonian linguistic usage of the term to signify "wealthy and influential people."

The rhetorical question *how long* posits an extended historical past and vents exasperation at the apparently hopeless, yet urgent, situation that cannot continue. In other words, the question condemns the feckless apostates for their perverse obstinacy against *I AM*'s established rule.

The Hebrew syntax and Masoretic accents link the king's glory being turned to shame with "you love a delusion." How the king's glory is degraded depends on the interpretation of "you love a delusion."

In Psalm 3:3 [4] the metonymy, *my glory (kᵉbôdî),* referred to the king's luster in victory that gave him social weight; here it attends his power in prayer. The anointed frequently refers to his grace and power in his petitions and praises (cf. 5:3 [4]). The apostates, however, turn his former luster in *tᵉpillâ* into *shame (kᵉlimmâ),* a disintegration and degradation of a person both subjectively ("disgrace") and objectively ("insult"). The degraded person "is isolated within his previous world, and his own sense of worth is impugned. He becomes subject to scorn, insult and mockery, and is cut off from communication."[70]

But Israel's pusillanimous wealthy *love (te'ᵉhābûn)* to worship at the cult of the pagan gods for answers to their prayers. *'āhab* designates the emotional feeling of strongly desiring something that flows out of one's perceptions and as a result causes one to go after (Jer. 2:25b), seek (Prov. 8:17 [Q]), run after (Isa. 1:23), cleave (Deut. 11:22; 30:20; Prov. 18:24), and continue faithful to the loved person or thing. Instead of a disposition to retain *I AM* and his king, the wealthy yearn with passionate desire to seek fertility gods that demand no moral rectitude or justice. They love to attain their wealth by injustice, not by keeping *Torah. "Delusions"* glosses *rîq* (LXX *mataiotēta,* see 2:1) and may have the sense of "empty" and be a metonymy for their baseless rumors and accusations against the king (so NRSV, NLT, et al.). More probably, however, in light of the overall context and the historical background that gives the psalm integrity (see introduction), it signifies "useless," "worthless," and is a metonymy for false fertility deities as elsewhere in Scripture (1 Sam. 12:21; Acts 14:15 [*mataiōn*]; so NIV, TNIV, Beck). Note that the king and people pray for "good" — that is to say, for "grain and new wine" (vv. 6-7), not for salvation from apostates who slander him. The singular is probably a collective for all the fertility deities in the Canaanite pantheon of gods.

The parallel "will you seek false gods" escalates their apostasy. *Seek (tᵉbaqᵉšû)* means "to strive to fulfill a wish," not to locate a goal. In the sphere of worship it means "to ask, pray, implore" — with fear, reverence and trust — in order to realize the goal (Pss. 24:6; 27:8; Exod. 33:7). "Those who seek *I AM*" (i.e., the faithful covenant people, Pss. 40:16 [17]; 69:6 [7]; 105:3-4), stand opposed to "those who do not seek him," who are apostates (Zeph. 1:6; cf. Prov. 28:5). Significantly, in the famine David "sought the face of *I AM*" (2 Sam. 21:1).

Rîq (literally, "empty") is escalated to *false gods* (*kāzāb* "lie," a collective singular). Truth, whether according to correspondence, coherence, or relational theory of truth, is founded in the character of God. The triune God is truth and all else is surreal. If *rîq* is a metonymy for empty accusation — the interpretation of most English versions — then *lies* also refers to unfounded accusation. As argued, however, a holistic exegesis of the psalms suggests it is a metonymy for idols. David petitions God to give the nation rain, not to silence or punish the apostates for calumnies against him. *Kāzāb* is probably used of false gods in Psalm 40:4 [5]; Amos 2:4; cf. Jonah 2:9; *passim.*[71]

70. S. Wagner, *TDOT,* 7:186, s.v. *klm.*

71. V. Maag, *Text, Wortschatz und Begriffswelt des Buches Amos* (Leiden: Brill, 1951), pp. 11, 81; M. A. Klopfenstein, *THAT,* 1.821, s.v. *kzb.*

b. Admonition: Know the King's Potency in Prayer v. 3 [4]

Implicitly, the king commands the apostates to repent of their apostasy. First, he admonishes them to acknowledge that *I AM* distinguished him from the masses of men by responding to his petitions.

The conjunction *waw (ûdᵉʿû kî, and/but know that)* links verses 2 [3] and 3 [4]. As in Psalm 2:6 the conjunction entails an ellipsis, suggesting emotional indignation. The full thought is: "How long will you turn my glory to shame as you love delusions and seek false gods? Stop seeking gods who cannot hear and answer prayer, *but know* that . . ." In other words, *waw* is a disjunctive that contrasts two spiritual realities: "seeking false gods to achieve your goal" versus "know that . . . *I AM* hears me when I call to him." For the meaning and pragmatic function of God's name, "I AM," see Psalm 1:2.

Whereas "to know" by itself refers to the subject's internalization of external knowledge, allowing no dichotomy between the knower and the object known (Ps. 1:6), *know that* objectifies the object to be known from the knower. For example, *I AM* says of Cyrus *tēdaʿ kî ʾᵃnî yhwh* ("you know that *I AM* [is the God of Israel], Isa. 45:3) . . . *wᵉlōʾ yᵉdaʿtānî* ("but you do not know me," 45:5). In other words, the king admonishes the apostates to become conscious of, become aware of, observe, perceive, and realize *that* he is extraordinary.

I AM has set apart (hiplâ) means "to distinguish one in a remarkable way from others in order that people might recognize the dignity of the elected." In Exodus 8:22 [18]; 9:4; 11:7 the word used of God's action is distinguishing Israel from Egypt. *Plʾ* does not refer to his consecration for service (contra Alexander) — that notion belongs to *qdš*, "to be holy."

The distinguished object is the *godly (ḥāsîd)*, a metonymy for the king. *Ḥāsîd,* which is also glossed "holy one" (Ps. 16:10) and "saints" (Pss. 30:4 [5]; 31:23 [24]; 52:9 [11]; 79:2; 85:8-9 [9-10]), means more precisely one who is "faithful" to God (2 Sam. 22:26; Ps. 89:20; 97:10), one "devoted" to him (86:2), "those who made a covenant" (Ps. 50:5). Loving loyalty to one's covenant commitment involves loving God's person and obeying his commands. Its root, *ḥsd,* has two concomitant ideas: loyalty to a person or a group with whom one has relationship and love for the party or parties. K. D. Sakenfeld[72] contends that the infix pattern /ā~î/ must have a passive sense, and therefore *ḥāsîd* must denote one who is the recipient of the covenant, but H. J. Stoebe[73] has demonstrated that this pattern may have an active sense in passages, as, for example, where God is

72. K. D. Sakenfeld, *The Meaning of Ḥesed in the Hebrew Bible: A New Inquiry* (Missoula, MT: Scholars Press, 1978).

73. *THAT,* 1:619, s.v. *ḥesed.*

called *ḥāsîd.* Other nouns with this pattern also may have an active sense.[74] The active sense is corroborated by its parallels: "blameless" (2 Sam. 22:26); "faithful" (Pss. 12:1 [2]; 31:23 [24]); "those who love *I AM*" (97:10); "servant" (79:2); "those who fear him" (85:8-9 [9-10]); "those who trust in you" (86:2). By contrast the "ungodly" *(lōʾ ḥāsîd)* are parallel to "deceitful and vile" (43:1), and the opposite of *ḥāsîd* are "those who return to folly" (85:8-9 [9-10]) and the "proud" (31:23 [24]). This adjectival substantive may be used of the priests (Deut. 33:8; 2 Chron. 6:41), the nation Israel (Pss. 50:5; 85:8-9 [9-10]; 149:5), and the king (Pss. 4:3 [4]; 16:10; *passim*). The king sometimes speaks of himself, as here, in the third person.

I AM has set apart his godly king *for himself.* What is in the king's interest is also in God's interest, for God and king love and serve each other.

The king's unfeigned commitment to *I AM* guarantees to all the "godly" that *I AM hears* (*yišmaʿ*, see v. 1 [2]). In particular he hears with favor the king's prayer *when I* [the king] *call* (*bᵉqorʾî*, see 1:1 [2]) *to him* (*ʾēlāyw*). The king's potency in prayer is his royal escutcheon.

2. *Further Admonitions to Apostates*

a. Dread the Consequences of Apostasy v. 4A [5A]

The king's second admonition to the apostate highborn consists of four imperatives in two pairs: "Tremble in fear and do not sin"; "search your hearts . . . and be silent in dread." The second pair clarifies the first. They are to tremble in fear because their conscience will condemn them, and they will not sin because they dread the outcome of their apostasy.

Tremble (*rigzû*, pl.) means "to shake," "to quake" physically in trauma. The verb is used of the whole creation shaking before God when, in his anger, he brings victory for his elect and judgment upon his enemies. Specific aspects of the creation that shake include the ground (1 Sam. 14:15); the mountains (2 Sam. 22:8 [= Ps. 18:7 [8]; Isa. 5:25); the earth/land (Joel 2:10; Amos 8:8; Ps. 77:18 [19]); the tents of Cushan (Hab. 3:7); and the depths of the sea (Ps. 77:16 [17]). The whole earth trembles when the social order is turned on its head (Prov. 30:21). An emotional disturbance connected with *rāgaz,* though uncertain, may also be detected in Genesis 45:24; 2 Samuel 7:10; 18:33 [19:1]; and Isaiah 14:9.

Only three times out of thirty in *Qal, rgz* refers to shaking in the passion of anger, "to be enraged" (Isa. 28:21 [with reference to *I AM* rousing himself

74. *IBHS,* p. 88, P5.3c.

from sleep]; Ezek. 16:43 [with the preposition *lamed*], and Prov. 29:9). The LXX (*orgizesthe* "be angry," quoted by Paul in Eph. 4:26[75]) opted for this meaning in Psalm 4:4 [5]. But this meaning is both unlikely and unclear. Kirkpatrick, followed by Delitzsch, argues that "in your anger sin not" means: "If you must needs be angry and discontented with my government, do not be carried away by passion into rebellion." It is unlikely, however, the king would exhort apostates to "rage" and "rail" silently against God's rule (so also Calvin, see p. 221). Alexander, following Hengstenberg, interpreted it to mean: "do not sin by raging"; but Hebrew syntax disallows that interpretation. Augustine offers the option that it means "be ye angry with yourselves for your past sin," but the *rgz* is never used with reference to anger against oneself. Others (Moll et al.) suppose that David is no longer addressing his foes but his overzealous friends, but the interpretation is arbitrary, for no other vocative than "highborn men" has been mentioned. Possibly — and this is probably the way Paul uses "be angry" — the king means: "be angry with righteous indignation against apostasy." But that sense has to be read into the text, for the object of anger, "apostasy," is not stated.

A command to quiver in fear before impending doom better suits the two other imperatives in the verse. Although grammatically the two commands, tremble *and do not sin* (*wᵉ'al teḥᵉṭā'û,* see 1:1), could be simply a compound expression like "eat" and "drink," the commands probably have a sequential connection like "divide and [so] conquer."[76] By trembling in fear of the impending doom, they will cease running headlong in their rebellion against God's rule.

b. Third Admonition: Let Your Conscience Confirm Your Faith v. 4B [5B]

But what shall bring the pusillanimous highborn to tremble and not sin, and so save themselves from doom? David gives the answer in two more imperatives: "Search your hearts *('imrû bilᵉbabkem)* . . . and be silent." Normally *'mr blbb* means "to say to oneself" (literally, "say in one's heart"),[77] but no citation follows. Psalm 4:4 [5] is the only case where *'mr,* which is one of the most common words in the Old Testament, occurs absolutely — that is to say, without an indication of the content of what is said or without one that cannot be instantly supplied (cf. Gen. 4:8;[78] Exod. 19:25). In that light, Dahood's proposal that *'mr*

75. Paul may have used the LXX as a handy way of expressing his point "to display righteous indignation," an exhortation appropriate to the church, but appropriate for apostates.

76. GKC 110g.

77. N. Bartsiotis, "Der Monolog im AT," *ZAW* 73 (1961): 30-70, esp. 46f.

78. The Samaritan Pentateuch and the ancient versions retain the original reading, which supplies the indication of the content of what Cain said: "Let us go into the field."

means "to see," "to look into," which is the root's meaning in Akkadian, Ugaritic, and Ethiopic, should be adopted here and the verb glossed by "search."[79]

Your hearts (bilᵉbabkem) denotes the inner forum where a person decides his or her religious and moral conduct on the interplay of thoughts, feelings, desires, and religious affections.[80] Delitzsch comments: "The heart is the seat of the conscience, and the Spirit of God . . . disguises itself as our own voice that we may see His exhortation, His counsel, and His wisdom well up out of our own stony heart."[81] Instead of hardening their hearts in self-confidence and hubris, the highborn should allow their conscience to be God's vicegerent to rule them. Whereas the conscience of the faithful to *I AM*'s cultus fortifies and encourages them, the conscience of the unfaithful condemns them and brings them to the realization of their inevitable doom.

This searching should take place *upon your bed (ʿal-miškabkem).* In a group one is inclined to think and act rashly and hypocritically; whereas, when offstage and in the privacy of one's own bedroom, one is more authentic. In that spiritual state God has the best opportunity to speak clearly to a person through the conscience and to convince one of moral truth.[82] In other words, "upon your bed" need not be taken literally, but figuratively to represent a condition and/or situation of quiet contemplation.

The conjunction in the complementary imperative, *and be silent (wᵉdommû),* also probably expresses a logical consequence: "and so be silent." "Be still" (see n. 52) is used literally of the sun (Josh. 10:12, 13), of men (1 Sam. 14:9), of the sword (Jer. 47:6), of churning bowels (Job 30:27), and of speech and other noises (Ezek. 24:17; Pss. 30:12 [13]; 35:15; Job 29:21). Sometimes silence expresses faith, as in "Be still before *I AM*" (Ps. 37:7; 62:5 [6]). Other times it is a metonymy of effect: one is silent as a result of destruction and death (Jer. 8:14; 48:2; Ps. 31:17 [18]) or in grief — as in English "numb with grief" — (Lev. 10:3; Isa. 23:2; Amos 5:13; Lam. 2:10; 3:28), or in fear and terror — cf. English "nailed to the spot" — (Exod. 15:16; Job 31:34). The parallel "tremble" suggests such a metonymy of effect: "be silent (out of dread)."

In sum, the conscience of the apostates will make them tremble, filling them with dread, so that they will not sin by seeking false gods, instead of seeking *I AM* who stands behind his king.

79. M. Dahood, "Hebrew-Ugaritic Lexicography I," *Biblica* 44 (1963): 289-303, esp. 295f.

80. B. Waltke, *Proverbs 1–15* (Grand Rapids: Eerdmans, 2005), pp. 90-92.

81. F. Delitzsch, *Psalms,* vol. 5 in C. F. Keil and F. Delitzsch, *Commentary on the Old Testament,* trans. Francis Bolton (Peabody, MA: Hendrickson, 1996), p. 68.

82. Recall that Calvin (see p. 221) and Bishop Leighton (see pp. 221-22) had earlier made the same point.

c. Trust *I AM* v. 5 [6]

Now that the king, the patron-head of *I AM*'s cultus, has admonished the apostates to acknowledge his potency in prayer within the cultus of *I AM*, to tremble at the consequences of turning aside from that cultus, he admonishes them to repent and return to the cultus of *I AM*. The cultus has two aspects: an outward, external aspect of offering sacrifices (5a [6a]) and an inward, spiritual aspect of trust in *I AM* (5b [6b]).

Offer . . . sacrifices (*zibḥû zibḥê,* see n. 53) means to slaughter animals (sheep, goats, or cattle) and to eat their flesh in a communal meal with God and the other worshipers.

The sacrifice is qualified by *of the righteous* (*ṣedeq*). Woodenly the Hebrew reads "sacrifices of righteousness." The sense, however, is probably not that the sacrifices conform to the Law (contra Buttenwieser and Briggs) — although this idea cannot be excluded — but is a metonymy for the one offering the sacrifice — that is to say, he is righteous (see v. 1 [2]). Just as the one qualified to enter the sacred temple site is said to enter the "gates of righteousness" (Ps. 118:19) — surely not a reference to the standards for the gate itself — so the sacrifices offered by the one admitted through the gates into the temple's precincts are said to be righteousness. For the apostates to be reckoned as righteous entails that they repent and accept by faith God's grace of forgiveness through Israel's sacrificial system, a system that points ultimately to the sacrifice of Jesus Christ. God shows his glory in his being compassionate and gracious, slow to anger, abounding in love and faithfulness (Exod. 34:6; see above). But those who do not live by faith in him and accept his forgiveness are left in their guilt, and he "does not leave the guilty unpunished" (Exod. 34:6-7). *I AM* loathes sacrifices offered by those who are unrepentant, not righteous by faith and so disobedient to his teachings that his people love him and their neighbors (1 Sam. 15:22-23; Isa. 1:11-17; Hos. 6:6; Amos 5:21-24; Mic. 6:6-8). In other words, the external aspect of the cult points to social, ethical behavior.

The parallel, "and trust in *I AM*," makes explicit the worshiper's spiritual state, which empowers him to offer sacrifices pleasing to God in connection with serving others. The conjunctive "and" binds together into a unity the outward sacrifices and the inward spiritual state. *Trust in I AM* (*biṭḥû 'el yhwh,* literally "rely unto *I AM*") means "to rely on *I AM* out of a sense of security in the face of danger." Normally the Scripture uses *bṭḥ* negatively, of trusting a human being and human devices (wealth, fortifications, idols, ritual); they are deceptive objects of trust. Only *I AM* is worthy of their confidence, and he validates his sublimities in crises. The confession that *I AM* alone is worthy of faith gives these confessional statements in the psalms their peculiar strength and inner dynamic.

D. Address to I AM: Petition to End Drought vv. 6-7 [7-8]

After the king has turned the dark accusations into bright admonitions that inspire faith, the king returns to make his petition: to send the rain that will produce the spring grain harvest and the fall grape harvest. He models his command, "trust in *I AM*," by resolving to go to sleep.

In his petition for rain the king anticipates Elijah's prayer for rain (1 Kings 18:41-46), a model used by James (5:17-18). The king first joins his people in corporate solidarity in their petition for rain (v. 7b [8b]) and then exercises his glory by himself, petitioning *I AM* for bountiful harvests. The petitions of the people and of the king are bound together by the inclusio *rabbîm,* the first word of verse 6 [7], *rabbû,* the last word of verse 7 [8], and by splitting apart the pronoun "us" in versets 7 [8]A and B into "my [heart]" and "their [grain]."

1. People's Petition for Rain v. 6 [7]

Commentators differ in identifying the speakers in verse 6 because the adjectival substantive *many (rabbîm)* has no clear antecedent. Nevertheless, the content of their petition removes the ambiguity. If the interpretation that follows is valid, the "many" are not the opponents of the psalmist (cf. Anderson), or the adherents of Absalom (cf. Cohen), or the disheartened followers of David (cf. Delitzsch), or depraved humanity (cf. Calvin), but the great number within Israel that remain loyal to David and of the repentant apostates who join the faithful in prayer.

The durative participle *are saying (ʾōmᵉrîm)* signifies that the petition is their constant prayer. Their petition *mî yarʾḥēnû* may signify a real question: "Who will show us?" or a rhetorical exclamation, "O that one would show us." According to the former interpretation the people, like the apostates, are hanging a question mark over the cultus of *I AM,* for they are uncertain who will answer their petition. If the latter, their use of *mî* expresses their extreme desire that *I AM* answer their prayer. The following matching parallels of verse 6a/b [7a/b] favor the latter interpretation: the same volitional mood (i.e., a request), the same request ("good" and *I AM*'s favor, which entails his granting what is good [i.e., beneficial and desirable]), and the same object "us" (i.e., "the many"). These parallels suggest that in both halves the petition is directed to *I AM,* first by the people and then by the king who leads them. BDB cites many instances of this rhetorical use of *mî,* including this verse as one of them.[83]

Good (ṭôb) is a substantival adjective for something or someone that is

83. BDB, p. 566 entry f.

beneficial and so desirable. Often it refers to happiness, prosperity, and success in general (Pss. 23:6; 34:12 [13]; 122:9). Dahood produces a number of examples where it refers to rain (Deut. 28:12; Jer. 5:24-25; 17:6; Ps. 85:12 [13]). The king's petition that follows certifies this meaning.

In texts from Babylon, El Amarna, and Ugarit *lift up* (*nᵉsâ*, see n. 54) *upon us the light of your face (ʿalênû ʾôr pāneykâ)* is a frequent metaphor to signify a ruler lifting up his countenance to look with favor toward someone. The figure probably has a solar background, because the king is called "sun" in connection with the shining of his face.[84] A Ugaritic text reads: "and the face of the sun (i.e., Pharaoh) shone bright on me" (UT 1126.6). In the Old Testament "light," "sun," "lamps," and a verb meaning "to shine" with God as its subject, serve as frequent metaphors of prosperity and salvation (Judg. 5:31; Job 17:12; 18:5f.; 22:28; 29:3; 33:30; Ps. 18:28 [29]; 36:9 [10]; 43:3 [4]; 67:1 [2]; 118:27; 139:11f.; Prov. 13:9; 24:20; Isa. 9:2 [1]; 58:8; Jer. 15:9; Amos 5:18, 20; Mal. 4:2 [3:20]). The metaphors "the light of God's countenance" or "God makes his face to shine" are used in parallel with victory in battle (Ps. 44:3); with salvation (31:16 [17]; 80:3, 7, 19 [4, 8, 20]; 119:135); with favor and blessing (67:1 [2], 6 [7]; esp. the Aaronic benediction, Num. 6:25). In the petition of Psalm 4:6 [7] the king and people fuse into one petition the two parts of the Aaronic benediction: "*I AM* make his face to shine *(ʾwr)* upon you," "*I AM* lift up his face toward you" (Num. 6:25, 26). The king and people appropriate by faith the Aaronic benediction to petition God for his favor, blessing, security, and peace. In other words, they pray according to God's will.

2. *King's Petition for Harvests v. 7 [8]*

The king's petition manifests his servant heart. He prays for joy that will be his when his nation prospers. His joy is intertwined with their prosperity, not with his own. *Fill my heart* (literally, "give" *nātatâ,* see n. 55) interprets the suffix form as a precative perfective (see 3:7 [8]; 4:1 [2], note 45), not as a perfect (= "you have given," so LXX [cf. Chrysostom] and most English Versions). Independently from Buttenwieser and Dahood (so also NIV, TNIV), Waltke drew this conclusion because it best suits the imperative in verse 6 [7] — recall the tight pairing of verses 6-7 [7-8] — and it matches the introductory petition, *hirḥabtā* ("make room") in verse 1 [2].

The goal of his prayer, *joy (śimḥâ) in my heart* (*bᵉlibbî,* see v. 4 [5]). *śimḥâ* signifies being glad or joyful with the whole disposition, as indicated by its association with heart.

84. Gustav Aalen, *TDOT,* 1:165 s.v. *ʾôr.*

The people pray for rain; the king anticipates the spring grain harvests and the fall grape harvest. With Aben Ezra, Kimchi, et al., the *min* of *mēʿēt* should be interpreted as temporal (*when,* literally "from the time of"), not as a comparative (= "more than [the time of]," so most English versions) because: 1) Elsewhere *mēʿēt* is always temporal, never comparative (1 Chron. 9:25; 2 Chron. 25:27; Isa. 48:16; Ezek. 4:10, 11; Dan. 12:11). 2) *Min* by itself after *simḥâ* has a temporal meaning in Deuteronomy 28:47. 3) If the *min* is comparative, the psalmist gives no reason for any joy apart from God answering his request. In contrast, by taking it temporally, his joy, or festive mirth, is connected with the increase of crops, a common motif in the Old Testament (Deut. 28:47; 29:22; Neh. 8:12; Esther 9:17-18; Prov. 14:10; Eccl. 9:7; Isa. 9:3 [2]; 16:10; 22:13; 24:11; Jer. 25:10; 33:11-12) The common English rendering demands supplying to the text *ṭôb miśśimḥâ hāʿēt* (Briggs). The addition of an adjective *ṭôb* ("greater" or "better") and of the thing compared, "joy," seems highly dubious when the text makes better sense without the additions. 5) The antecedent of "their" (with "grain" and "new wine") is now clearly the "many" who prayed for God's favor. Otherwise, its antecedent is ambiguous: common men (Calvin), impersonal or indefinite (Briggs), Absalom (Delitzsch), his enemies (Perowne), the defeatists (Kidner).

Their grain (dᵉgānām) is the general term for ripe grain. With a variance of as much as two weeks, depending on the location in Israel, harvesting started in the spring, first with the barley in early April, then wheat in late May. *Their new wine and their oil* (*tîrôšām wᵉyiṣhārām,* see n. 57) pertain to the fruit harvests at the end of September. The pairing of the spring and fall harvests is a merism for all the produce of the earth that sustains Israel's life. New wine, according to F. S. Fitzsimmons, "represents wine made from the first drippings of the juice before the winepress was trodden. As such it would be particularly potent."[85]

Abound (rabbû) emphasizes the great quantity of the harvests, guaranteeing that "the many" *(rabbîm)* will be well fed.

E. King Sleeps in Peace v. 8 [9]

The king draws his prayer to conclusion with a resolve to lie down, confident he will fall asleep because he at peace. Whereas the king counseled the unfaithful and faithless rich to search their hearts upon their bed, he himself cheerfully lies down in the crisis and immediately falls asleep (v. 8a [9a]). In so doing, he also models for his nation trust in *I AM.* His sleep is assured because he lies

85. F. S. Fitzsimmons, "Wine and Strong Drink," in *NBD,* p. 1254.

down *in peace (bᵉšālōm).* The first word of the concluding verse emphasizes his spiritual state. *šālōm* may mean "to be free of conflict and hostility," or "to enjoy prosperity and good fortune," or "to possess an inner contentment, delight, and joy." The latter is its normal sense, with the preposition *bᵉ* ("in") in connection with verbs of motion.[86] The basis for his peace is the security *I AM* grants him.

NIV/TNIV fail to render *yaḥdaw* (literally, "together"). "I will lie down and fall asleep at once" captures the literal wording: "together I will lie down and sleep." The cohortative form *'eškᵉbâ* ("will lie down," see 3:5 [6]) signifies resolve, not a simple future (= "I shall lie down"). *And I will sleep (wᵉ'îšān)* demonstrates the reality of his inner peace.

This is so *because (kî)* of his faith in God, as expressed in the intimacy of his *I-Thou* relationship with *I AM:* "*You,* I AM *('attâ yhwh).* Syntactically, *lᵉbādād* modifies *tôšîbēni* ("cause me to dwell"), but its meaning is disputed. LXX (*kata monas,* "only") and most English versions (e.g., ASV, KJV, NLT, NRSV, JPS, TNIV) interpret it as a reference to the exclusive action by God. *Bādād,* an accusative of state, has this sense in Deuteronomy 32:12: *Yhwh bādād yanḥennû wᵉ'ên 'immô 'ēl nēkār* ("*I AM* alone led him; no foreign god was with him"). This interpretation, however, faces three objections: 1) For this sense, the form should be, as in several manuscripts,[87] *lᵉbaddekâ* (cf. Ps. 83:18 [19]; 86:10; *passim*). 2) It lacks a parallel, although it could be inferred as a polemic against the pusillanimous highborn who turn to false gods (4:2 [3]). 3) Elsewhere, apart from Deuteronomy 32:12, it is always used in connection with verbs of "dwelling" (*škn* or *yšb*) in the sense of living alone, apart, often with the sense of security (cf. Deut. 33:28; Jer. 49:31; Num. 23:9; Mic. 7:14). This otherwise exclusive sense of *bādād* faces no objections and the interpretation agrees with its parallel, *lᵉbeṭaḥ, securely* (i.e., the psychological state of feeling secure, "trust," 4:5 [6]). JPS rightly renders the sense: "for Thou, Lord, makest me dwell alone in safety." As there is an intertextuality between the king's and people's prayer in 4:7 [8] with the Aaronic benediction, so also 4:7-8 [8-9] has an intertextuality with Moses' blessing: "So Israel will live in safety *(beṭaḥ);* Jacob will dwell secure *(bādād)* in a land of grain and new wine (*dāgān wᵉtîrôš,* Deut. 33:28). In sum, as a result of their abundant crop harvests, the king and his nation dwell apart in secure seclusion, like the Sidonians and the people of Laish (cf. Judg. 18:7).

The root of *tôšîbēnî, yāšab,* can mean to "to sit enthroned" as in Psalm 2:4,

86. G. Gerleman, *THAT,* 2:928, s.v. *šlm.*

87. The reading *lᵉbaddekâ* may be due to a scribal error of confounding final *daleth* with similarly formed final *kaph* in the Aramaic script, not vice versa, because it is the facilitating reading.

but more probably it has its general sense of "to dwell" (cf. Lev. 13:46; Jer. 15:17; 49:31; Lam. 1:1; 3:26). The tense could be present ("you cause"), but after "I will lie down and sleep," probably the future is intended ("you will cause me"). His audience can infer that in the state of salvation, he will praise *I AM* for answering the petitions for rain and abundant harvests. When God's promises and life's realities seem far apart, saints live by faith; when they meet and touch each other they celebrate their God in praise.

F. Subscript

For the director of music see p. 88; *'el-hann^{e}ḥîlôt* is an unexplained technical term in music or hymnody; possibly "played on the flutes" from *(ḥālîl)*. As part of the temple performance the psalm found an extended use beyond David.

By laying himself down in peaceful sleep when earth's troubles seemed utterly detached from heaven's promises, the king evinced the same spirit of faith that has sustained God's people throughout their history. The godly Abel, the righteous prophets, the called apostles, and saintly martyrs all laid themselves down in death at the hand of the wicked while committing themselves into the hand of God who authors life. Above all, the Lord Jesus Christ displayed this faith by accepting a criminal's death while commending his spirit into his Father's hand and was vindicated by rising from the grave.

A Vietnam veteran wrote Waltke the following letter: "In one of the battles I fought in Vietnam there were dead and wounded all around me. Having gone for three days without sleep my ability to make wise decisions was at a dangerously low level. At 3:00 A.M. I found a hole in a jungle base, virtually under a battery of cannons. The heat of the jungle night combined with that of the cannons, which fired volleys about every twenty seconds, was insufferable. Even in the stench of the gunpowder, the mosquitoes relentlessly pursued their bloodthirsty duty. As I lay there, this verse of Scripture came to me as audibly as any human voice: 'I will lie down in peace and I will sleep; for you alone, O Lord, make me dwell in safety.' I think I had the best two hours' sleep in my entire life."

Part IV. Conclusion

The psalm is indirectly Messianic, for in every motif of the psalm David typifies the Lord Jesus Christ. None enjoyed more intimacy with his father than he, and none is more potent in prayer than he. Nevertheless, he too experienced the unbelief of the nation's leadership when he was nailed to the cross and his prayers were considered worthless. He too interceded for his nation (cf. 1 Peter 2:9) for his and his Father's glory (see John 17). He laid himself down in the sleep of death, and his Father answered his prayer by raising him from the dead.

CHAPTER 8

Psalm 8: I AM Rules Through "Infants"

Part I: Voice of the Church

I. Introduction

Psalm 8 well exemplifies how culture affects interpretation. Jewish interpreters favored reading it as a hymn of creation, whereas in medieval Christian liturgy it was celebrated on Ascension Day. This usage, which assumes a Messianic interpretation, can be traced to the book of Hebrews. Christian interpreters, however, favored a Messianic interpretation in differing ways. At various periods it was used to express the theme of *imago dei* in the sense that the dignity of humankind has been given and then restored by salvation/redemption. The psalm also featured prominently in the commentators' reflections on the "two natures" of Jesus Christ, a keenly controversial theme in church history.

Other considerations also complicated its history of interpretation. When one additionally examines allegorical interpretations against cultural values, as well as the efforts to explain the superscript to the musical direction at the heading of Psalm 8, meaning "Gittith" or "winepress," or "stringed instrument" (as also in Ps. 81, 84) — which in Bruce's theory is a postscript to Psalm 7 (see p. 88), not part of the heading of Psalm 8! — one can appreciate the psalm's complex history of interpretation.

II. Francis of Assisi on Creation

Psalm 8 echoes Genesis 1, and yet it has its own distinct voice in doing so, enriching the psalmist's praise all the more. **Francis of Assisi** (c. 1181-1226) embodied such praise of creation, while his companion **Clare** whispered its echoes just before she died, praying: "I thank you God for having created me."[1] Francis too intoned Psalm 141, "Bring my soul out of prison, that I may praise Thy name!" as he died.[2] His unforgettable *Canticle to the Sun* echoes the sufferings Francis experienced as the movement he had founded passed into other, sometimes cruel hands, and as he was losing his eyesight as well.

III. Interpretations of Eastern Greek Fathers

For some fathers in both the Eastern Greek Church and the Western Church "the eighth psalm" was interpreted in the light of the resurrection; it celebrated "the first day of the week," not the Sabbath or seventh day — that is to say, it celebrated *I AM* as Lord of the new covenant for the "New Israel." It was later appropriately sung on the Feast of the Ascension. Once composed to reflect on the creation narrative of Genesis 1, it now becomes for the Church Fathers a hymn recomposed and seasonally reused to reflect upon redemption.[3]

Athanasius (296-373) suggests using Psalm 8 as a song of thanksgiving. "When you behold the Savior's grace, which has been extended everywhere, and the human race, which has been rescued, if you wish to address the Lord, sing the eighth."[4] He is following Origen in interpreting the psalm as a hymn of redemption.

Theodore of Mopsuestia (350-429) is typical of many commentators when he writes concerning this psalm: "In this psalm blessed David, filled with a prophetic spirit, predicts the Lord's incarnation, and speaks of events concerning Christ later fulfilled, thus soundly refuting the dishonesty of all the Jewish opposition." He interprets "Gittith" in the heading "as on the winepresses," deriving it from the Hebrew term "gat": "Some commentators claim that this psalm was composed by blessed David even for people in general on the Feast of Tabernacles, when the feast of crops happens, and hence it is given the title 'on the winepresses'" (see Jerome below). He sweeps aside such a dis-

1. Quoted by Stanley Jaki, *Praying the Psalms: A Commentary* (Grand Rapids: Eerdmans, 2001), p. 49.

2. Jean Leclercq, François Vandenbroucke, Louis Bouyer, *The Spirituality of the Middle Ages,* A History of Christian Spirituality, vol. 2 (New York: Seabury Press, 1968), pp. 294-95.

3. Susan E. Gillingham, *One Bible, Many Voices: Different Approaches to Biblical Studies* (Grand Rapids and London: SPCK, 1998), p. 244.

4. Athanasius, in Robert C. Gregg, trans. and introduction, *Athanasius: The Life of Anthony and the Letter to Marcellinus* (New York, Ramsay, Toronto: Paulist Press, 1980), pp. 113, 115.

traction to study the actual text. Theodore is following his master Diodore in this regard, who had also ignored "Gittith."

In his commentary on Psalm 8, Theodore of Mopsuestia stresses the independence of the two natures of Christ, human and divine, two persons loosely united by a moral union. He writes, "How great is the diversity of natures in him emerges here in that so lowly and insignificant is the condition of him whom God deigned to call to mind that blessed David was struck with astonishment and wonder at their combination . . . what is the human being for whom you are mindful?" He explains that the one who is "mindful" is God the Word (Logos), who paid the visit, who made the human being a little less than the angels, and who crowned him with glory and honor. He then cites Hebrews 2:6-9, seeing "'Jesus as the one who was made a little lower than the angels, now crowned with glory and honor on account of the suffering of death.' Hence, therefore, it is the psalm that brings out for us such a great distinction between God the Word and the man, [which in the psalm is] assumed they are found distinguished in the New Testament. The Lord takes upon himself the beginning of the psalm, where he is the maker of created things and his magnificence is exalted above all the heavens and marveled at in all the earth, whereas the apostle applies the second part to the human being Jesus, who was the object of such favor. How could it fail to be obvious that the divine Scripture clearly teaches us that God the Word is one thing and the human being another, and shows the great difference between them?" This last critical statement was repeated verbatim in the condemnation of the Nestorians by Pope Virgilius in 553. It suggested the heresy that there was a split between the Logos and the manhood of Jesus, rather than Jesus' being the incarnate Logos. Theodore of Mopsuestia implies that the question "What is man that you are mindful of him?" refers to the human Jesus, and that this psalm is a specific prophecy of the incident when the children shouted "Hosannas" at the beginning of his Passion (Matt. 21:16). He was condemned by the Council of Ephesus in 431 for these Nestorian leanings.

John Chrysostom (347-407) uses this psalm also as a polemic against the followers of Paul of Samosata, who denied the deity of Christ. In their view, "Christ belongs to the time when he came from Mary." But Chrysostom asks: How then did Christ create the heavens, if he was limited only in space and time to his birth from Mary?[5] He can so argue because he had already alluded to the hymn-singing by the children in the Temple as an echo of verse 2. Then he concludes with a Trinitarian affirmation that this psalm implies that whoever does not honor the Son, cannot give glory to the Father, and if the Father and the Son "were not the same substance, how would equal honor be re-

5. *Athanasius,* p. 171.

quired?"[6] Finally, he finds that more of God's character is revealed in his delegating to humanity authority over his creation than in merely describing God in terms such as the divine attributes of his creative power, his absolute authority, or his infinitude.

John Chrysostom does not even mention the musical title. Instead, assuming the psalm is a hymn of praise, he enters immediately into the psalm as if joining the celestial music of the angels, whose heavenly choirs are contrasted with the lurid and pernicious song of the pagan theatre, celebrating evil things. For it is an angelic privilege to sing the praise, "Lord, our Lord, how wonderful your name is in all the earth!" "It is really wonderful. To what degree wonderful, however, he did not say; measuring it, you see, was beyond him — instead, he had recourse to exaggeration and hyperbole. Where are those who busy themselves with prying into the being of God?" Then already having condemned Nestorius or Arius, he adds: "You excuse those people who claim to know his being while the inspired author does not succeed in discovering to what degree his name is wonderful." The wonder of the incarnation, argues John, is sufficiently mysterious, so why speak of angels when their focus is upon "God who became man, and man became God"? Again in indictment of the theological speculators, John notes that just as "little children" hailed the coming Messiah on Palm Sunday (Matt. 21: 15-16), so too the psalmist notes it is "little ones" who inherit the kingdom of Heaven (Matt. 18:3).

In the second half of the psalm, John reflects on the blessedness of the new status redeemed humanity now has in Christ. "You see the glory and the honor that occur in the New Covenant are greater, when they have Christ as their head, when they come to fulfillment in his body, when they become brother and co-heir with him." The earthly dominion given humankind at their original creation was glorious, but how much more glorious, in spite of the Fall, will our redeemed destiny become! But all this John relates to a glorified Christ who is not subservient in being to the Father, but co-equal, "of the same substance."[7] Yet in his ministry, why does Christ make mention of many humble matters? Is it not to teach us humility, especially in speculating about the nature of the Trinity, and of the twofold nature of Christ. So in a polemic against both Jews and Christian heretics, he concludes: "let us shun their gatherings; and when we come to learn his origin before all ages, his creative power, his absolute authority, his unchanging relation to the Father, the considerateness of his dealings with us, the varied nature of his providential care of us . . . let us hold fast the precision [*akribeia*] of the teachings and give evidence of a worthy way

6. *Athanasius,* p. 172.
7. *Athanasius,* p. 172.

of living. . . ."[8] Perhaps not until Calvin do we have such an attempt at a careful commentary on Psalm 8.

Meanwhile, preoccupation with the psalm title "Gittith," translated as "winepress," waylaid other commentators. **Gregory of Nyssa** (330-95) notes that good wine requires the selection of good grapes, not those already putrid, otherwise the wine too will become sour and undrinkable. So it can only be out of the storehouse of our mind, expressive of good works, that we can anticipate eternal blessings.[9] Unfortunately we do not have a commentary on the whole psalm by him. **Theodoret** (393-460), bishop in Syria, suggests that Jesus claimed to be the true Vine, from whom "believers make the mystical vine," to expose the infidelity of the Jews, who still "refused to admit" that "the ancient ways had come to an end." Whereas "now, the eighth psalm, entitled 'On the Winepresses,' foretells salvation of the world and teaches God's care for people, and predicts the Incarnation of the Only-begotten."[10]

IV. Augustine's Allegorical Heritage

Taking the title of the Eighth Psalm, "to the end" (see pp. 212-13), as a hermeneutical "threshold," **Augustine of Hippo** (354-430) uses it to control the allegorical orientation and meaning that follow. "To the end" (Psalm 3) is a key orientation for Augustine, which qualifies its allegorical character, in requiring a "spiritual" reading. So he expounds the psalm as "For her [i.e., the church] who receives the inheritance."[11] The *totus Christus* is his hermeneutical center, reading "Christ in all the scriptures," as well as his body the church, and also every individual Christian benefiting from his grace. Following Jerome's translation of *Gittith* as "winepress," Augustine speculates even more on the term and elaborates how it refers to the churches. In Augustine's open-endedness, he interprets the term in three differing ways. Just as the grain is separated from the husk, or the juice is extracted from the grape, so he argues, Christians are separated from the ways of the world, "so that the good may be separated from the evil."[12] Second, it can refer to the fermentation of the word of God, which can

8. *Athanasius,* p. 173.

9. Gregory of Nyssa, *Commentary on the Inscriptions of the Psalms,* trans. Casimir McCambley (Brookline, MA: Hellenic College Press, 1990), pp. 73-74.

10. Robert C. Hill, *Theodoret of Cyrus: Commentary on the Psalms, 1–72* (Washington, DC: Catholic University of America Press, 2000), pp. 82, 83.

11. *Expositions of the Psalms,* ed. John E. Rotelle, O.S.A., trans. Maria Boulding, O.S.B. (Hyde Park, NY: New City Press, 2001), vol. 1, p. 93.

12. Augustine, *Expositions of the Psalms,* vol. 1, p. 129.

become vinegar when the Jews mistreat it, and offer it to the dying Christ, a religion gone sour indeed! Third, it can refer to the persecution of the churches, stripped like grapes and crushed, and yet in the resurrection and ascension of Christ, now emboldened by the indwelling Holy Spirit. "Once filled by the Spirit, the disciples preached with boldness to gather the churches together."[13]

Augustine's Christological interpretation of the psalm contrasts sharply with Theodore of Mopsuestia's Nestorian understanding. It is the humbled Jesus, who is now exalted above the heavens. It is the magnificence of his incarnate life which "has been raised above the heavens." Augustine links the "infants and nurslings" (verse 2) with the Jews on Palm Sunday, still spiritually immature, and also the Corinthians whom Paul rebukes (1 Cor. 3:1-2). Such people need to be nurtured in the history of God's purposes, climaxed in the Incarnation. Only then is divine praise "perfected." This however requires "faith," faith that precedes understanding, for God's enemies are the "faithless," who can give no recognition to the Incarnation. Faith begins then in reading the Scriptures, even though "the magnificence" that is "above the heavens" is the incarnate Lord, who transcends the Scriptures in his glory. Later, Bernard of Clairvaux uses Augustine to suggest that while Christ transcends Scripture, the reading of Scriptures is where Christ appears again to us. The incarnate Christ has "visited" those who have faith in Him, to be called "sons," while for those in unbelief, God is still "mindful of" them, yet they do not recognize the God-Man. Like the heretics of Augustine's day, they cannot recognize the humility of the One "made a little lower than the angels for the suffering of death," now also "crowned with glory and honor."

The poetic repetition of "son" and "son of man" in verse 4 is interpreted by Augustine as the distinction between "the old man" and the "new": the former is Adam and his fallen race, the latter is Christ and those in him. So he translates the verse "What is a mere man that you remember him, a son of man that you visit him?" to mean that sin has "separated [the earthly man] from God at a great distance, and that is why God remembers the one, as far away from him, but the other [i.e., 'the spiritual man'] he comes to visit."[14] In the concluding verses, Augustine's allegorical imagination goes even further as he tries to categorize all those with no recognition of the glory of Christ. For Augustine, the Eighth Psalm is a hymn of thanksgiving — not for God's purpose in creation — but in redemption.

While close to Augustine, **Cassiodorus's** (485-580) format of the fourfold presentation of each commentary controls his otherwise strongly allegorical

13. Augustine, *Expositions of the Psalms,* vol. 1, p. 130.
14. Augustine, *Expositions of the Psalms,* vol. 1, p. 134.

approach. He states simply that it is the church who is praising God in Psalm 8.[15] This theme is traceable all through the Carolingian commentators into the High Middle Ages. By the time **Geroch of Reichersberg** (1093-1169) writes on Psalm 8, the church has become a winepress in a threefold way: where the "good" and "bad" need to be sorted out; where the sweetness of God's name has been separated from the dregs; where the martyrs of the church are indeed afflicted and crushed. They all contribute to this wonderful hymn of praise to the Lord.[16] These are then finally reinforced by **Peter Lombard** (c. 1100-1160), who reiterates Augustine's various interpretations of the church as the winepress. But now, with a clearer understanding of Christian historiography, he argues: "Here the intention of the prophet [David] is to confute the errors of the Jews, who say that God is only known in Judea, and of the Donatists, who say that God is only known in Africa, and of those like them."[17] The cosmic scope of divine Lordship is obvious to Peter Lombard. As **Rupert of Deutz** (c. 1075/80-1129) averred, "We are not reckless worshipers of the blessed Augustine."[18] Far more important now is the importance of a strong Chalcedonian Christology as reflected in the works of commentators such as Cassiodorus, **Gilbert of Poitiers** (1079-1154), **Thomas Aquinas** (1224/25-1274), and later commentators.

V. Christian Hebraism in the High Middle Ages

Meanwhile the Midrash Tehillim 8.1 had commented on the "winepress," to see it as a symbol of judgment upon their enemies, namely, the Edomites, quoting Joel 3:13 and Jeremiah 51:33.[19] Now in the twelfth century, scholarly dialogue between Jews and Christians enabled a few Christian scholars to interpret the Hebrew titles of the psalms very differently.

Herbert of Bosham (c. 1120-c. 1194) (see p. 56) refers to Jewish exegetes, notably rabbi Solomon ben Isaac of Troyes (known by his acronym, Rashi [died 1105]) in several psalms, including Psalm 8. Unlike all other Christian commen-

15. Cassiodorus, *Explanation of the Psalms,* in P. G.Walsh, trans. and ed., *Ancient Christian Writers,* vol. 1 (New York and Mahwah, NJ: Paulist Press, 1990), p. 109.

16. Geroch of Reichersberg, *Commentarius aureus in psalmos et cantica ferialia* (PL 193-94), pp. 738-42.

17. Peter Lombard, *In totium psalterium commentarii* (PL 191:123B).

18. Quoted by Theresa Gross-Diaz, *The Psalms Commentary of Gilbert of Poitiers* (Leiden and London: E. J. Brill, 1996), p. 98.

19. Cited by Susan Gillingham, *Psalms through the Centuries* (Oxford: Blackwell, 2008), p. 119, although she uses the texts as if the Christians were being condemned, instead of Israel's traditional enemy, the Edomites.

tators, Herbert resolves the tension between Jewish and Christian scholars by using the plain sense of the Hebrew text as being often more accurate than the textual sources used from the Vulgate.[20] Thus we recognize in his commentary on the psalms a hermeneutical change: "Our ecclesiastics, having abandoned the literal sense, flee to a spiritual understanding of the psalms and in various places in the Scriptures according to the[ir] interpretations of Hebrew words. Whence it often happens in countless places in Scripture, but especially in the titles of the psalms, that the interpretation of the word is found in place of the [Hebrew] word."[21] Herbert follows Rashi to assert *"gittith"* is a musical term denoting an instrument manufactured in *geth ad quem fugit david,* as the Targum title had rendered it: "To be sung to the harp which David brought from Gath."[22]

VI. Reformers: Luther and Calvin

Martin Luther (1483-1546) provides us with two commentaries on the Eighth Psalm, which can be studied comparatively. The first dates probably from the end of 1513, when he was giving his first lectures on the Psalms at the University of Wittenberg, while the second was preached on All Saints' Day, November 1, 1537. It was later elaborated, on the basis of Luther's notes, by **Andreas Poach** (1516-1585) into a lengthy commentary (1572).[23] The contrast between them is a fascinating indicator of how far Luther had advanced theologically in just over twenty years, the formative years of the Lutheran Reformation. In the former his Christology is scarcely visible, while his robust Chalcedonian understanding is fully mature by 1537.[24] In the former he follows the fourfold interpretation of a passage and repeats Augustine on several verses of the psalm — not cited above: "the heavens" as referring to the apostles and/or their books; and the various creatures at the end having reference to the various wayward sinners, who are still all subject to Christ. The second treatment is light years away in theological commentary. It is as if he now summarizes all the controversies of

20. See Eva DeVisscher's study, "The Jewish-Christian Dialogue in Twelfth-Century Western Europe: Herbert of Bosham's *Commentary on the Psalms*" (Ph.D. diss., University of Leeds, 2003, chapter 2 *passim*).

21. Raphael Loewe, "Herbert of Bosham's Commentary on Jerome's Hebrew Psalter," *Biblica* 34 (1953): 71.

22. J. M. Neale and R. F. Littledale, *A Commentary on the Psalms, from Primitive and Medieval Writers,* vol. 1 (London: Joseph Masters & Co., 1884), p. 141.

23. Jaroslav Pelikan, ed., *Luther's Works,* vol. 12 (St. Louis: Concordia, 1955), p. ix.

24. Vidar L. Haanes, "Christological Themes in Luther's Theology," *ST* 61 (2007): 21-46.

Chalcedon and settles the issues of the two natures of Christ as fully God, yet fully man. Earlier he had scarcely any theological awareness of the Trinity; now he is quite clear. "Christ is the true and eternal God with the Father and Holy Spirit in an undivided divine being and true natural man."[25] Again, "David keeps the unity of the person firm and sure. He gives Christ the King two names — a great divine name, Lord; and a small human name, ruler. Thus he indicates the two natures in Christ, the divine and human nature; yet he speaks not of two, but of one single Lord and Ruler, to show the unity of the person."[26] So three doctrines are spelled out: this King has two natures, true God and true man; He is an undivided Person; and this Lord, that is, God, became man and received dominion, power, and glory from the Father. Luther sees the whole psalm as a glorious prophecy of the future kingdom of God, using babes and sucklings to describe the kingdom's unique character of humility. He contrasts its nature with that of the Turks and the Papacy, and, feeling his own weakness, he sees the power of the Word as being expressed through children, the unlearned, the weak, and the despised. For Luther the whole psalm is all about Christ and his kingdom, described and celebrated in short simple statements over thirty-eight pages of commentary.

John Calvin's (1509-64) *Commentary on the Psalms,* which was published late in his life (in 1557), is a summary of many previous lectures and sermons and differs greatly from that of Luther's. Exegetically, Calvin is much more cautious than Luther about looking prematurely for Christological meaning in all the psalms. Calvin was not converted through the psalms as Luther apparently was; he does not discard the fourfold interpretations of Scripture, for he had no monastic background; and Calvin contrasts the Old and New Covenants by means of "anagogue," not in the medieval sense of having a future meaning, but as a comparative application of the text.[27] Even when verse 5 ("You have made him a little lower than the angels") is applied by the writer to the Hebrews (2:7) to Christ, Calvin is prepared to admit it can be certainly applied to Christ, but the original psalm may have had another context. Unlike the early Fathers, who claim that the soul of Christ entered hell, Calvin rejects such speculation.[28]

For Calvin, the witness of "babes and sucklings" (v. 2) only underscores God's sovereignty: God needs no human abilities to demonstrate his authority and power. If he creates the whole universe with his "finger," he needs nothing of humankind. Yet he is "mindful" of humans, as much to embrace them in his

25. Haanes, "Christological Themes in Luther's Theology," p. 100.

26. Haanes, "Christological Themes in Luther's Theology," p. 102.

27. Herman J. Selderhuis, *Calvin's Theology of the Psalms: Texts and Studies in Reformation and Post-Reformation Thought* (Grand Rapids: Baker Academic, 2007), pp. 129-30.

28. Selderhuis, *Calvin's Theology of the Psalms,* pp. 56-57.

Fatherly love, for he has created us "in his image and likeness." Calvin then enumerates some of the qualities he associates with the *imago dei:* as "endued with reason whereby they may discern good and evil; in that the seed of religion is sown in them; in that there is a mutual communion knit together with certain holy bonds; in that there grows among them a regard of honesty, and shamefulness, and governance of laws."[29] Unlike Luther, Calvin sees these gifts of God's "mindfulness" as expressive of the original creation of human beings, although subsequently corrupted by sin.[30] Nevertheless Calvin also recognizes that God's creation purpose for man will only occur with the final defeat of sin and death.[31] The gist of it all is that this psalm celebrates God's "immeasurable grace": while man's divine dignity is not clearly seen because of sin, yet with "Christ as their Head," it will be restored finally, giving us the incentive "to follow after godliness," and "not be slothful in celebrating His praises."[32]

VII. Post-Reformation Commentators

Bishop George Horne (1730-92), with a more "churchly" approach to Psalm 8, as the first of the psalms appointed for Ascension Day, interprets it as showing the grace of God in being so "mindful of man," to reveal greater glory than merely in his physical powers of creation. It is a twofold glory he expresses, as Creator and Redeemer. "Messiah's praises have in them a strength and a power which nothing can withstand," not even the powers of Hell. He then conjoins the New Testament passages of Hebrews 2:6, 1 Corinthians 15:27, Philippians 2:8, and Matthew 28:18, to anticipate "the universal chorus of people and angels joined in their voices together, and making their sound to be heard as one, in honor of the Redeemer, evermore praising Him."[33]

Only later, with the rise of the Newtonian universe, did the grandeur and vastness of the scale of creation begin to be appreciated. Indeed, it is a much later Puritan, **Charles H. Spurgeon**, who can state: "Astronomy shows us what an insignificant being a human being appears amidst the immensity of creation. Though he is an object of the paternal care [echoing Calvin], and the mercy of the Most High, yet he is but a grain of sand to the whole earth, when compared with the myriads of beings that people the amplitudes of creation.

29. *A Commentary on the Psalms,* vol. 1 (Edinburgh: James Clarke & Co., 1965), p. 92.

30. Calvin, *A Commentary on the Psalms,* p. 93.

31. Calvin, *A Commentary on the Psalms,* p. 95.

32. Calvin, *A Commentary on the Psalms,* p. 96.

33. George Horne, *A Commentary on the Book of Psalms* (London: Thomas Tegg, 1824), vol. 1, p. 41.

What is the whole of this globe in comparison of the hundred millions of suns and worlds which by the telescope have been descried? What are they in comparison with the glories of the sky?" We wonder what Spurgeon would say today, if he could see through the Hubble Space Telescope, now observing billions of stars — indeed billions of galaxies — to see so enlarged the scope of God's mercy to humankind.

Yet neither poetic diction nor even hymnody can fully express the gracious purposes of man's creation. So perhaps it is more fitting to conclude with another prayer of **Peter Martyr** (1499-1562) as he meditates on Psalm 8:

> From the things which have come to be both in heaven and on earth through your power and providence, O almighty God, your magnificence and glory manifest themselves not just well but excellently. Your power reveals itself even better and stirs the souls (which are heavier than lead) in children and babies. We are wretched and cast off, not because of the effort and care with which you fashioned us, but because of our own sins and infinite guilt which we ourselves have accumulated. We pray nonetheless that you be not angry with us over them but rather you come to us frequently, as you used to do, and make those whom you wanted to be a little less than the angels in your own divine nature. And since you have set us up as rightful lords over all your creatures, grant that we may use them to the praise and glory of your name so that your word and Gospel may be spread to all mortals. Through Jesus Christ, our Lord. Amen.[34]

Part II. Voice of the Psalmist: Translation

A psalm of David.[35]

1 *I AM,* our Lord, how majestic is your name in all the earth!
  You who have set[36] your glory upon the heavens.

34. Peter Martyr Vermigli, *Sacred Prayers Drawn from the Psalms,* trans. and ed. John Patrick Donnelly, SJ (Kirksville, MO: Sixteenth Century Essays and Studies, 1996), p. 12.

35. For the division of superscripts and postscripts, see pp. 88, 207 n. 80.

36. There is no need to emend *tᵉnâ* with Bradtke *(BHS).* Dwight W. Young, "Notes on the Root ntn in Biblical Hebrew," *VT* 10, no. 4 (1960): 457-59, confirmed Delitzsch et al., that the form is infinitive construct of the root *tn,* which expanded in Northwest Semitic as I-*nun* or I-*waw/yodh* verbs (cf. inf. constr. *rᵉdâ* of *yrd* in Gen. 46:3; cf. Hos. 9:11; Exod. 2:4). Herbert Donner, "Ugaritischen in der Psalmenforschung," *ZAW* 79, no. 3 (1967): 322-50, esp. 322f., refuted the proposal of Dahood and Weiser to read the form as *Qal* perfective (3rd masc. sing.) of a root *ṯnh,* "to repeat in antiphonal song." Ugaritic *ṯny* comes over into Hebrew as *šnh* and

2 From the mouth of children and infants you have laid the foundation of a strong bulwark
in order to [eliminate] your foes, to eliminate the enemy and the avenger.
3 When I[37] consider your heavens, the works of your fingers,[38]
the moon and the stars, which you have set in place,
4 what is a mere mortal that you are mindful of him,
a common human being that you care for him?
5 And so you made him lack a trifle from the heavenly beings
and you crown him with glory and honor.
6 You cause him to rule over the[39] works of your hands;
you put everything under his feet:
7 all flocks and herds,
and even the wild animals;
8 the birds of the air, and the fish of the sea,
the one that swims the paths of the seas.
9 *I AM*, our Lord,
how majestic is your name in all the earth!

Part III. Commentary

I. Introduction

A. Form: Praise Hymn

Psalm 8 is what Westerman calls "a descriptive praise psalm." Praise psalms celebrate *I AM*'s greatness and goodness, his lordship over the cosmos as its Creator, his commitment to Israel as its covenant-keeping God who saves them to fulfill their mission to rule the earth. Moreover, praise psalms develop their theme analytically, not synthetically: "that is, we do not have sentences heaped on one another, but one sentence is developed."[40] Psalm 8 does not disappoint

---

means nothing other than "to repeat" and is always in parallel with *rgm*. The rendering "place" has the support of the ancient versions.

37. No need to follow the Syriac "they" for consistency with "our" in verse 1. David embodies the nation.

38. Genitive of cause ("fingers effected the work").

39. LXX probably invested the article with the force of a pronoun to avoid redundancy.

40. Claus Westermann, *Praise of God in the Psalms*, trans. Keith R. Crim (Richmond, VA: John Knox Press, 1965), p. 123.

these expectations, wielding the two notions of God's great deeds in creation and history into a unique unity of profound reflection and of incomparable beauty. As for celebrating *I AM*'s mighty deeds in creation, the occasion is the writer's looking up into the night sky and observing "the moon and the stars." The spectacle calls forth reflection on God's mighty deeds in history. "When I consider," the poet-king says, whereupon he reflects on the mortal's cultural mandate to rule the earth in history. The two notions come together in the psalm's theme: "*I AM*, our Lord, how majestic is your name in all the earth" (vv. 1, 9 [2, 10]). That theme frames the psalm (vv. 1a, 9 [2a, 10]) and, as will be seen (see "Rhetoric" below), is developed analytically through two stanzas: a summarizing stanza of his rule over the heavens and his vicegerent's rule over the earth (1b-2 [2b, 3]), which is developed in the second stanza with reference to the heavens (v. 3 [4]) and to the mortal's rule over all the earth (4b-8 [5b-9]).

Although there are no references to liturgical rites, processions, or festivals, its being a psalm handed over to the choir director, its individual and corporate character, and its repetition of the same refrain at the beginning and the end, all suggest it was originally composed as a hymn to be used in Israel's liturgy.

B. Inter-Literary Context

As its framing refrain shows, the psalm celebrates the name of *I AM*: "*I AM*, how majestic is your name." As an opening refrain, it connects with Psalm 7, whose closing verse gives the promise: "I will praise *I AM* (*ʿôdeh yhwh*) because of his righteousness; / I will sing to the plucking of stringed instruments[41] the praises of **the name of *I AM***, the Most High" (*ʾazammᵉrâ šēm-yhwh ʿelyôn*). Then Psalm 8, a *mizmōr* (a song sung to the pizzicato of a stringed instrument), takes up the pledge, "***I AM***, our Lord, how majestic and great is **your name** in all the earth." Now as a concluding refrain it segues into Psalm 9, which begins: "I will praise ***I AM*** (*ʿôdeh yhwh*) with my whole heart; . . . I will sing praises **to your name**, Most High (*ʾazammᵉrâ šimᵉkâ ʿelyôn*)."

C. Message

This magnificent hymn of praise to *I AM* as Creator of the cosmos and as Ruler of history paradoxically celebrates *I AM*'s greatness by celebrating the grandeur of the *humble*, not the proud, human being to whom he gave the cultural man-

41. "Sing" glosses *zāmar* ("to sing to the pizzicato of a stringed instrument"); the root of *mizmōr* glosses "psalm" (8: superscript).

date to rule the earth. Irenaeus put it succinctly: "The glory of God is man fully alive." Amandus Polanus, sixteenth-century Basel professor and Reformer, stated the complementary truth: "the glory of man is the living God."[42] The mortal fully alive is childlike, not a tyrant.

D. Outline

	Superscript	[v. 1]
I.	Theme Stated: *I AM*'s Name Majestic in All the Earth	v. 1a [v. 2a]
II.	Theme Developed:	vv. 1b-7 [2-8]
	A. Splendor in Heavens, and "Infants" Defeat God's Foes	vv. 1b-2 [vv. 2b-3]
	1. Displays Glory in Heavens	v. 1b [v. 2b]
	2. Uses "Lips of Infants" to Annihilate the Wicked	v. 2 [v. 3]
	B. Glory in Heavens and Splendor in Mortals' Rule of All the Earth	vv. 3-8 [vv. 4-9]
	1. Glory in Heavens at Night and Stoops to Help Mortals	vv. 3-4 [vv. 4-5]
	a. Glory in Heavens at Night	v. 3 [v. 4]
	b. Stoops to Help Mere Mortals	v. 4 [v. 5]
	2. Crowned Mortals to Rule All the Earth:	vv. 5-6 [vv. 6-7]
	a. Mortals Crowned with Splendor	v. 5 [v. 6]
	b. Mortals Commissioned to Rule All the Earth	v. 6 [v. 7]
	3. Ruled Creatures	vv. 7-8 [vv. 8-9]
	a. Land Creatures	v. 7 [v. 8]
	b. Air and Water Creatures	v. 8 [v. 9]
III.	Theme Restated: *I AM*'s Name Majestic in All the Earth	v. 9 [v. 10]

I AM's name is majestic in both the spheres of creation (v. 1b, 3 [2b, 4]) and in salvation history (vv. 2, 4-8 [3, 5-9]). With regard to the order of creation, he set his glory upon the heavens — more particularly, according to the second stanza, in the moon and bright stars that rule over the night sky (see Gen. 1:16). The scenic depiction of the bright luminaries against the black sky aptly profiles the triumph of the saints over *I AM's* enemies in the order of redemption. In that order his name becomes majestic on earth through using "infants and children" — a hyperbolic metaphor for people who depend totally upon him — to

42. Donald G. Bloesch, *The Future of Evangelical Christianity: A Call for Unity Amid Diversity* (Garden City, NY: Doubleday, 1983), pp. 19-20.

eliminate his foes from the earth, the bulk of humankind, which rebels against him (v. 2 [3]). That notion is then developed in verses 3-8 [4-9]. In the first stanza, the meek saint petitions and praises *I AM*. In the second stanza, *I AM* stoops to care for them.

He crowns and commissions the humble mortal to rule all creatures — none excepted — and empowers the meek to achieve the cultural mandate. In sum, the psalmist makes God's majesty in all the earth even more awesome by contrasting *I AM*'s obvious splendor bestowed upon the stars (vv. 1b-4 [2b-5]) with the frailty of the mortal who must look to him to fulfill the commission to rule. The heavens are the work of the Creator's fingers, but his rule on earth in salvation history is his work through the mouth of "children," "infants."

E. Rhetoric

The theme, which is stated in a single-line inclusio, is developed in two alternating stanzas:

A. Creator of heavens, Ruler of earth through praise and petition of "infants"
   1. Order of Creation: Creator of Heavens
   2. Order of Redemption: Conquest of Enemies

B. Creator of stars, Ruler through the mere mortal
   1. Order of Creation: Creator of stars in night sky
   2. Order of Redemption: Crowns and Commissions the mortal to rule earth

Moreover, the theme is developed in quatrains: verses 1b-2 [2b-3], 3-4 [4-5], 5-6 [6-7], 7-8 [8-9]. Verse 1b [2b] is a janus. It is linked to the superscript 1a [2a] by an exceptional relative "who," by the Masoretic accents that retain the earliest known interpretation of the psalm, and by this parallelism:

I AM	*how majestic is your name*	*in all the earth*
You who	place *your splendor*	*upon the heavens.*

This janus is linked to verse 2 [3] by the psalm's thematic structure in two alternating parallel stanzas of quatrains.

Some scholars, probably not understanding verse 1b [2b] as a janus, dispute the Masoretic accents of verse 1 [2] and instead couple verse 1b [2b] with verse 2a [2b], yielding the translation:

Thou whose glory above the heavens is chanted
by the mouth of babes and infants, thou hast founded a bulwark
because of thy foes, to still the enemy and the avenger (RSV).[43]

The insertion of "chanted," however, is made of whole cloth; the NRSV returned to the traditional versification.

Perhaps the embroidered psalm also is crocheted as a chiasm:

A. Inclusio: How majestic your name in all the earth
  B. First Quatrain: Splendor upon the heavens
    C. Second Quatrain: Work of your fingers . . . you have set in place
      D. Pivot Quatrain:
        1. What is the mortal you care for?
        2. You made him a little lower than heavenly beings to rule
    C′. Third quatrain: Work of your hands . . . you put
  B′. Fourth quatrain: birds of the heavens
A′. Inclusio: How majestic your name in all the earth

II. Exegesis

A. Superscript [1]

While it is true that the poet as "a creature" could be anyone — king, priest, or ordinary worshiper — who, having poetic gifts, views the whole creation as God's temple (see Psalm 104), it is also true the theme of human dominion is most appropriate on the lips of a king, as the superscript asserts. For the integrity of superscript with the psalm and for the meaning of its genre, "a psalm," and of its author, "David," see pp. 87, 89-90.

B. Theme Stated v. 1a [2a]

God's name, "I AM" [*yhwh*], signifies his eternal reality both as an aseity and as an ever-present help with Israel (see 1:2); both concepts comport well with the

43. "Whoever keeps singing of your majesty higher than the heavens, even through the mouths of children, or of babes in arms, you make him a fortress, firm against your foes, to subdue the enemy and the rebel" (NJB).

theme of Psalm 8. God's name gives concrete form on earth to all his sublime perfection "in so far as He makes Himself known to His people" (Calvin).

The ascription of the psalm to David shows that *our* refers to the king and the nation embodied in him. The royal poet is zealous for the establishment of God's universal rule through his elect people who own *I AM* as their supreme *lord* (*'ᵃdōnay,* see 2:5), not to foster jingoistic nationalism. Under this Sovereign they establish a universal, just, and merciful kingdom, not a reign of tyranny.

The question *what (mâ)* functions as a rhetorical exclamation, *how*! Rendering of *'addîr* by *majestic* is superior to the familiar KJV rendering "excellent." The adjective denotes someone or something that commands respect through the excellence of power. It is used of the "mighty" Reed Sea when it engulfed the Egyptian army (Exod. 15:10), of *I AM*'s dominion over the stormy seas (Ps. 93:3-4), and of his right hand when he shattered Pharaoh's picked troops (Exod. 15:6).

In all the earth (bᵉkol — ha'āreṣ) designates the humanly inhabited earth; it never designates the entire universe and is contrasted with "the heavens": "The highest heavens belong to *I AM,* but the earth he has given to humankind" (Ps. 115:16). Psalm 8 contrasts *I AM's* unmediated splendor in the heavens with his splendor on earth, which is mediated by humankind.

The psalm has an already-not-yet character. His majesty on earth through faithful saints is being fulfilled but is not yet consummated (see below, "Conclusion"). The name of *I AM* is not majestic where his enemies revile his name, ignore it (Ps. 79:6), or misuse it (Ps. 139:20). The psalm will be consummated when God answers our Lord's prayer: "Our Father in heaven, hallowed be your name, your kingdom come, your will be done on earth as it is in heaven" (Matt. 6:9-10).

C. Theme Developed vv. 1b-7 [2b-8]

The psalm develops the theme by explaining that the name *I AM* becomes majestic by his use of the mere mortal to vanquish his adversaries and by his empowering his deputies to establish dominion over the earth.

1. I AM's Splendor in Heavens and in "Infants" Who Defeat Foes vv. 1b-2 [2b-3]

The first stanza combines his glory that he places upon the heavens with his mediated splendor upon earth through people who trust him.

a. Places His Splendor upon the Heavens v. 1b [2b]

Many translations fail to render the relative pronoun *who* (*'ᵃšer*), linking the theme with its development (see above). *You* is added for smooth English. For the form *tᵉnâ* (see note 36). The infinitive is best rendered as a present tense *places*. Delitzsch rightly notes: "the setting out of the heavens with divine splendor is being constantly repeated and not done once and for all." *Hôd* means "splendor," a different word from *kābôd* ("glory") in verse 5 [6]. *'addîr,* like its parallel *hôd,* commonly refers to a leader, but unlike that adjective is never used of an unrighteous ruler (cf. Ps. 21:6; 45:3; Zech. 6:13; Jer. 22:18; Dan. 11:21). Although *'al* with "heavens" elsewhere means "above" or "over," in the four other passages where it occurs with *ntn* and *hôd* it means "upon" (Num. 27:23; 1 Chron. 29:5; Ps. 21:6; Dan. 11:21), and this sense fits better with its parallel in the second stanza (v. 3 [4]). The *heavens (šāmāyim)* designates the space above the earth, specifically what the ancients thought of as a visual dome, *raqîa'* (see Gen. 1:6; Ps. 19:1). In their phenomenal world they conceptualized the blue sky as water being held up by the *raqîa'*. In their cosmology *I AM* sat upon his throne above the Flood (*mabbûl,* Ps. 29:10).

The parallel in verse 3 [4] suggests "heavens" functions in this stanza as a metonymy for the heavenly host in the night sky (v. 3). The bright stars, free from all impurity (cf. Job 37:21), encompassing the broad expanse of the night sky, serve to reveal to all people the Creator's splendor. Their majesty and beauty (Song 6:10), their endurance and longevity (Ps. 72:5, 7, 17), and their great number (Nah. 3:16) derive from the Creator and so reflect his splendor (cf. Job 11:8; 22:12; 38:31-33; Isa. 40:25-26).

b. Uses Prayers of the Meek to Destroy Enemies v. 2 [3]

The psalmist now develops his theme of *I AM*'s name becoming majestic in all the earth. *From the mouth of (mippî),* a collective noun, is a common metonymy for speech, and since this speech defeats *I AM*'s enemies, it is presumably the speech of prayers, including both petition and praise to God. The LXX, followed by Darby, NLT, NIV, partially captures the meaning through paraphrasing *'ôz* by "praise" *(ainon).* The prayers are by *children ('ôlᵉlîm) and infants (wᵉyônᵉqîm).* The former *('ôlᵉlîm)* may refer to an unborn child (Job 3:16) or a child yet unable to supply bread for itself. In other words, "children" refers to the tender age where the child depends upon an adult for support. *Yônᵉqîm* (literally, "sucklings") denotes a child not yet weaned, an act accomplished by the child's third year. The compound, "children and infants," in its seven occurrences refers to the helpless offspring of a people threatened with annihilation by a ruthless foe (1 Sam. 15:3; 22:19; Jer. 44:7; Lam. 1:16; 4:4; Joel 2:16).[44] It is an apt metaphor for ancient Israel who, trapped as a small and insignificant state between the giant superpowers of Egypt and Mesopotamia, found strength in their dependence upon their God. It is also apt for the church which, in a world armed with military and political power, also conquers by faith. Luther (see above) rightly interpreted babes and sucklings as a figure to describe the kingdom of God's unique character of humility. The psalm found a literal and symbolic fulfillment when children praised the lowly Jesus as he rode on the colt of a donkey and then later "cleansed" the temple precincts — perhaps as a sign of judgment to come — where arrogant priests and scribes usurped the place of God's king, King Jesus (Matt. 21:16).

The NIV gloss of *yissadtā* by "you have ordained" (cf. LXX *katērtisō,* "to arrange harmoniously") could be supported were this a post-exilic text (cf. 1 Chron. 9:22; Esther 1:8). Also, in those texts, unlike this one, *ysd* has no object. But *Piel ysd* in its seven other occurrences in pre-exilic Hebrew, where it always occurs with an object, means "to lay the foundation": of a city (Josh. 6:26; cf. 1 Kings 16:34); of Zion (Isa. 14:32); of a tested stone (Isa. 28:16); of the temple (1 Kings 5:17 [31]; Ezra 3:10; Zech. 4:9). The last text shows the focus is on the commencement of the work. So petition and praise, the gratitude of the poor in spirit for answered prayer, begin the process of banishing from the earth those who make humankind, not *I AM,* their lord.

The object *strength (ʿôz)* entails two figures of speech. First, the inapposite juxtaposition of an abstract noun as the object of a concrete verb (i.e., "lay the foundation of strength") shows that it functions as a metonymy for a structure such as a "bulwark," "rampart," "citadel."[45] What matters is not the specific kind of structure, but that the defensive structure protects those walled up behind it to withstand attack. Second, the inapposite juxtaposition of petition and praise of children laying the foundation of such a structure shows that the poet is using an incomplete metaphor, implying that the petition and praise of the meek withstand the assault of *I AM*'s enemies against them. In sum, through the grateful praise of *I AM*'s dependent people — not the rhetoric of eloquent orators — *I AM* commences his work of defending them and of slaying their attackers. The thought is expressed more fully in Psalm 149:6-7:

44. It is methodologically unsound to appeal, as some do, to Ugaritic texts and to advance the meaning "heavenly beings," "sons of god," against the unambiguous Hebrew evidence.

45. Dahood's proposal to interpret *ʿôz* as a poetic name for heaven is unconvincing because it is based on the gratuitous assumption that *ʿôz* must be a precise parallel for "heaven" in Psalm 78:26 and that Psalm 150:1 is an exact equivalent to Genesis 1:14, 15, 17.

6 May the praise of God be in their mouths and a double-edged sword in their hands,
7 to inflict vengeance on the nations and punishment on the peoples.

Calvin comments: "The faithful prayer and praise of God's people — not necessarily their eloquence — commences the work of slaying the foe. What majesty accrues to God when he brings onto the field of battle the poor in spirit against the arrogant hordes of wickedness in order to slay their intolerable pride in the dust."

Calvin rightly understood *lᵉmaʿan* to mean *in order to,*[46] but since this construction demands a verb we should probably assume that *lᵉhašbît (to eliminate)* has been gapped. The object *your foes (ṣôrᵉreykā)* is a substantival participle of the root *ṣrr,* "to be hostile," and, according to the figure of a "strong structure" providing defense, more specifically refers to "attackers" (cf. *ṣar* in Ps. 3:1 [2]). The plural number emphasizes that their enemy is not an individual but many, for even in the singular the noun is used of a collection. Probably we should think of many nations, because this praise psalm is sung by the nation under David (see "our lord," v. 1 [2]).

Hašbît, the *Hiphil* of *šābat,* means *to cause to cease.* In the majority of cases *I AM* is its subject. That he is the subject here can be inferred because the petition and praise are the mediated means of silencing the enemy, who are designated as "your foes." *I AM* prepares to do battle against those who attack his people by laying the foundation of a strong defense through their petition and praise (cf. Ps. 89:45). In Psalm 46:9 [10] he victoriously ends the battle against the hostile nations.

Having made clear that the adversaries are many, the poet uses collective singulars in the two synonyms. *The enemy (ʾôyēb)* can be defined by its descriptive predicates: "oppress" (Deut. 28:53), "persecute" (1 Kings 8:37), "smite" (Lev. 26:16; Jer. 30:14), "pursue" or "persecute" (Hos. 8:3), "deal treacherously with, deceive" (Lam. 1:2). "Furthermore," says the editor of *TDOT,* "the proud behavior of the enemies is often mentioned: they exalt themselves (Ps. 13:4 [5]), make themselves great (Lam. 1:9), scoff and revile (Ps. 74:10, 18; Lam 1:21; Ezek. 26:2), rejoice (Lam. 2:17), open wide their mouths, i.e., rail (2:16), gnash with their teeth (2:16), etc."[47]

The notion of proud behavior is made explicit by the last synonym: *and the avenger (ûmitnaqqēm).* Vengeance *(nqm),* according to F. Horst, refers to

46. H. A. Brongers, "Die Partikel *lᵉmaʿan* in der biblisch-hebräischen Sprache," *Oudetestamentische Studiën* 18 (1973): 84-96, esp. 87.

47. H. Ringgren, *TDOT,* 1:215, s.v. *ʾāyabh.*

the "typical private penalty that properly pertains to persons located outside one's own jurisdiction and authority."[48] The infliction of a penalty for a perceived wrong belongs solely to *I AM* because he alone is qualified to judge the guilt and to assess the appropriate compensation. Normally, as probably here, the avenger is communities or nations, not individuals. The action normally foregrounds strong emotions, as can be seen with special clarity in Proverbs 6:34, which speaks of the merciless vengeance of a jealous husband. The *Hithpael* form of the root *nqm* indicates that God's enemies act for themselves. In contrast to this private assessment of guilt and punishment to be exacted, *pqd* "to visit" (see 8:4 [5]) refers to "the official investigation executed in one's own jurisdiction that holds those concerned responsible for failures and offenses and takes action against them." Only the "omnicompetent" God has the authority to legitimate the penalty as righteous. So the concluding compound, "the enemy and the avenger," which connotes the self-confident and arrogant without regard to God, stands antithetically opposed to the initial compound "children and infants," which connotes the helpless and poor in spirit. The faith of the latter must prevail over the foolish pretensions of the former (cf. 1 Cor. 1:27-29).

2. *I AM's Glory in Heavens and Splendor in Mortals' Rule of the Earth vv. 3-8 [4-9]*

The second stanza (vv. 3-8 [4-9]), an alternating parallel, reinforces and expands the first (vv. 1b-2 [2b-3]). The celebration of the nation pertaining to *I AM* as Creator and Ruler is now narrowed down to the confession of their king, who represents them: "when I consider." The general "heavens" of verse 1 [2] is now specified as "the heavens" housing the moon and the stars. The elimination of *I AM*'s enemies through mediation of the meek is now expanded to the mortals' rule over all the earth, and their prayers are matched with *I AM*'s stooping down to care for the mortals.

a. Splendor in Night Heavens and Stoops to Help Mortals vv. 3-4 [4-5]

Verses 3 and 4 [4 and 5] are linked grammatically by linking the protasis, "when I consider," with the apodosis "[I exclaim] what is a mere mortal." In this way the celebration of *I AM* as Creator is inseparably linked to his celebration as Ruler of history.

48. F. Horst, "Recht und Religion im Bereich des AT," *EvT* 16 (1956): 49-75 = *Gottes Recht* (1961): 260-91 [esp. 73, 289].

(1) Splendor in Heavens at Night v. 3 [4]

The particle *when (kî)* introduces a conditional clause, having the sense "supposing that," and more specifically a temporal clause, which with the imperfect means "as often as."[49] The gloss, *I consider ('er'eh),* invests the superordinate verb "to see" with its particular notions of to "look at, see, by direct volition" with mental observation.[50] "When man gazes up at the illimitable expanse of the heavens studded with stars, the difference between God and man is revealed in all its magnitude, and the whole contradictory quality of that difference is made manifest" (Weiser).

The "heavens" now becomes *your heavens (šāmeykā).* They belong to *I AM* because he created them. The apposition, *the works of your fingers (maʿᵃśê ʿeṣbᵉʿōteykā),* explicates the "your" as signifying possession. Ownership by creation probably functions as a subtle polemic against the universal pagan worship of these brilliant bodies. The plural intensifies the immensity of God's handiwork, and the anthropomorphism, *of your fingers,* implies the ease with which the Creator established the myriad of stars. The majority of manuscripts and ancient versions read plural, "works," against the collective, singular "work."

In the chiastic parallelism, *moon and stars* (see v. 3 [4]), specifies *works of your fingers* in the core of the verse, and *which you have established (kônāntâ, Polel of kûn)* matches "your heavens," again explicating ownership by creative work in its outer boundaries. *Kûn* connotes permanence, firmness. Like the strong bulwark that withstands attack, the moon and stars stand firm at their stations in the night sky. As for verbs in the semantic domain of "work," the emphasis of the verb *kōnēn* "set in place," as E. Gerstenberger notes, "lies on the stability and dependability of the work."[51] The night cannot overcome them; nothing can dislodge them.

(2) *I AM* Cares for the Mortal v. 4 [5]

The rhetorical question *what (mâ)* connects the apodosis to the temporal protasis in verse 3, while heightening the qualitative difference between *I AM* as Creator and Ruler of the sidereal spheres and the mortal who has dominion on earth.[52] His smallness under a Ruler who with deft ease creates an infinite number of stars and maintains them in their appointed courses over countless generations is brought home forcibly by the poet's choice of terms for the human

49. GKC, 159bb, 164d.
50. BDB, p. 907, entry 6 and 7 s.v. *r'h.*
51. E. Gerstenberger, *TLOT,* 2:605, s.v. *kwn.*
52. GKC, 150h.

being.[53] His first term, *a mere mortal,* glosses *ʾ*ᵉ*nôš,* which refers to the male in his weakness, in contrast to *geber,* which refers to the male in his strength. Job says: "If even the moon is not bright and the stars are not pure in his eyes, how much less man *(ʾᵉnôš)* who is but a maggot — a son of man (*ben ʾādām* [see below]), who is only a worm" (Job 25:6; Isa. 51:12). The addition of *the* with "the mortal" is used as an article of class to leave open the ambiguity that it may refer either to an individual and/or to the generic collectivity. With reference to the individual it could refer to David and/or Israel's coming hoped-for universal ruler (see Psalms 2 and 110). With reference to the collectivity, which seems to be in mind according to the plural "children" and "infants," "the mortal" refers to the nation the king represents and is embodied in him. The divine Author had in mind the resurrected mortal, Jesus Christ and his church, as the writer of Hebrews argues (Heb. 2:5-13).

That (kî) introduces a final clause ("so that") and "expresses consecution, specially, after a question implying a question implying surprise or deprecation,"[54] and in the present time may denote a factual result (cf. Job 7:17; Isa. 7:13). From his study of *zkr,* the root of the verb glossed *to be mindful of (tizkᵉrennû),* B. Childs draws the conclusion: "The essence of God's remembering lies in his acting toward someone because of a previous commitment." Here he acts on behalf of his vicegerent whom he commissioned to rule all the earth (see Gen. 1:26).

The synonymous parallel (v. 4b [5b]) gaps *what is* but repeats *that (kî). Ben-ʾādam,* woodenly, "the son of a human being," is best interpreted as "son" with the qualifying genitive, "human being," to represent the nature, quality, character, or condition of the son as human.[55] As in Job 25:6, the same parallel with *ʾᵉnôš,* the term also points to the weakness and frailty of the mortal.[56] Whereas *ben-ʾîš* in Psalm 4:2 [3] refers to the "highborn," *ben-ʾādam* refers to *a common human being.* In pre-exilic Hebrew the term is never a technical term for the Messiah as it became in later Jewish literature and as reinterpreted by the writer of Hebrews.

You care for him glosses *tipqᵉdennû. Pāqad* means "to visit" in the sense to take careful notice of one's situation and to act appropriately, not to come into someone's presence. NIV sometimes renders the verb "to come to the aid of" (Gen. 50:24, 25; Ruth 1:6; cf. Gen. 21:1; 1 Sam. 2:21; Exod. 3:16). When God committed to his human image the rule of the earth, he did not abandon him. Implicitly, by his taking careful note of his vicegerent's situation and acting appro-

53. J. Barr (*SBL,* pp. 144ff.) holds that the terms of "man" are mere synonyms without any specific emphasis, but most commentators rightly disagree.

54. BDB, p. 472d s.v. *kî.*

55. *IBHS,* pp. 149f., P. 9.5.3b.

56. Haag, *TDOT,* 2:162, s.v. *ʾādām.*

priately "he visits" with salvation those who in childlike meekness depend on him. In contrast, he "visits" his enemies, who usurp his prerogative to right wrongs (see v. 2 [3]), with judgment (Lev. 18:25). The significance and success of the human being in fulfilling the cultural mandate is based on relationship, through faith, with the omnicompetent Creator and Sovereign, who rules creation and history, not on human greatness. The constellations lose their austerity and the stars their cold stare in the knowledge that the Creator stoops to raise up his frail image to whom he entrusted the rule of the earth.

b. Crowned the Mortal to Rule All the Earth vv. 5-6 [6-7]

(1) Crowned with Splendor v. 5 [6]

The psalmist celebrates the mortal's elevated status among the Creator's creatures: *And so you made him (watt^{e}ḥass^{e}rēhû) a trifle lower (m^{eʿ}aṭ) than heavenly beings (mēʾ^{e}lōhîm).* This is a paraphrase of the Genesis creation account: "Let us make human beings in our image." Most scholars recognize in the Genesis statement that the first person plural pronouns, "us" and "our," refer to the heavenly court.[57] The *waw-consecutive* construction with *watt^{e}ḥass^{e}rēhû* points to the human being's elevated status as a logical consequence *(and so)*. Because God remembers his commitment to his image to rule and so stoops to care for him, the human lacks only a little from the exalted status of the beings in the heavenly court. The verb *ḥāsar* signifies to "diminish," "decrease," "lack," and implies comparison to a state where all necessary components to function are present. The components of that ideal state, which is only realized in the heavenly court, include transcendence in space (universal) and time (eternal), comprehensive knowledge, immortality, and so on. The *Piel* stem signifies that God appointed the mortal to rule in a diminished state. Nevertheless, that reduced status is only a trifle less than the ideal. The noun *m^{eʿ}aṭ* signifies a small quantity and/or quality, "little," "trifle," and functions as a double accusative: person appointed + rank: "you diminished *him* (i.e., the mortal) a little."[58] In light of Jesus' resurrection and exaltation to the heavenly spheres, the writer of Hebrews, in connection with his interpreting "son of man" as the eschatological Messiah Jesus, interprets the noun (Greek *braxu ti*) to mean "for a little while" (Heb. 2:9).[59] The

57. Bruce K. Waltke with Charles Yu, *An Old Testament Theology* (Grand Rapids: Zondervan, 2007), pp. 212-15.

58. *IBHS*, p. 175, 10.2.3c.

59. According to Christopher Stanley, *Paul and the Language of Scripture: Citation Technique in the Pauline Epistles and Contemporary Literature*, Society for New Testament Studies Monograph Series 74 (Cambridge: Cambridge University Press, 1992), pp. 342-47, ancient writ-

preposition *min* in *mē'ᵉlōhîm* designates the movement away from a specified beginning point.[60]

'ᵉlōhîm has been interpreted as a reference to God (Aq., Sum. Theod., PIH, NAB, NJB, NRSV), or to "angels" (LXX, Syr. Targ., Heb. 2:7, KJV, JPS) and to "heavenly beings" (NIV, cf. TNK). The literary form, a paean of praise to God, argues against its normal meaning, "God." Had the poet intended God, he might be expected to use "yourself," because in the rest of the psalm he addresses God as second person, not as third. Although Hebrew poets frequently shift their perspective from direct address to God to indirect statements about God, they do not normally alter their stance in the same clause. Though it is true that elsewhere in the Hebrew Bible unqualified *'ᵉlōhîm* never means "angels," *'ᵉlōhîm* may refer to supernatural beings, as for example in 1 Samuel 28:13, where the medium at Endor calls Samuel's ascended spirit an *'ᵉlōhîm* (cf. Isa. 8:19). Commenting on Psalm 8:5 [6], Ringgren drew the conclusion: "The most natural meaning of *'ᵉlōhîm* is divine nature (cf. the LXX *par' angelous,* 'than angels'): the crucial thing here is the similarity with the divine in general."[61] Gesenius-Buhl defines it: "divine, supernatural being . . . in Ps 8:6 of mankind, who in comparison with the rest of nature approximates an *'ᵉlōhîm*."[62] The LXX is probably best construed as a dynamic equivalent. B. Childs says: "The Greek translation has offered an interpretation, but one which does not in itself do an injustice to the Hebrew."[63] In his mortality and weakness the human being stands in antithesis to God (cf. Num. 23:19f.; Isa. 31:3), but in his role of ruler he approximates a heavenly being.

The mortal has such an exalted state because, as the parallelism says, "and with glory and honor crowned him." The "and" is conjunctive, not consequential, unlike "and you made him lack." In the outer frame, "you made him lack" is parallel with "you crown him," and in the inner core "glory and honor" is parallel with "a trifle from divine beings." *Glory (kābôd)* means literally "weight," a metonymy for the social esteem that his status as king over the creation gives. The term is often used of a leader, but never of an unrighteous ruler (cf. Ps. 21:6; 45:4[5]; Zech. 6:13; Jer. 22:18; Dan. 11:21). *Honor (hādār)* signifies splendor, majesty, glory, and grandeur, a visual display of majesty and splendor. Its parallels are "glory" (Ps. 21:5 [6]), "wondrous works" (*niplᵉ'ôt,* Ps. 145:5), "mighty deeds" (*gᵉbûrôt,* Ps. 145:12), "beauty" (*tip'eret,* Ps. 96:6; Prov. 20:29), "majesty" and "dig-

---

ers adapted quotations according to "how well the original wording coincided with the point the later author wanted to make in adducing the passage."

60. The LXX, followed by most English versions, interprets *mᵉʿaṭ* as an adjective and *min* as a comparative (= "a little lower than"), but in its 100 uses *mᵉʿaṭ* is a noun, not an adjective.

61. H. Ringgren, *TDOT,* 1:282, s.v. *'ᵉlōhîm.* So also BDB, p. 43, s.v. *'ᵉlōhîm* entry 1b.

62. Gesenius-Buhl, p. 40, *'ᵉlōhîm,* entry 3.

63. B. Childs, *Int* 23 (1969): 25.

nity" (*gāʾôn* and *gōbah,* Job 40:10). The compound "glory and splendor" is issued elsewhere primarily of royalty (Ps. 21:5 [6]; 45:3 [4]; 96:6; 145:5). Its association with kingship is supported by the verb *you crown him* (*t*^{e}*ʿaṭ*^{e}*ṭrēhû; ʿṭr* in *Qal* means "to surround, encircle," but in *Piel* "to crown with a wreath" [Ps. 65:11 [12]; 103:4][64]; or "to entwine a wreath" [Song 3:11]). The thought is not that God surrounded the mortal with the glory and honor of heavenly beings — a possible sense had the parallel, "you made him lack significantly from a heavenly being." The following verb "to rule" certifies the notion of "to crown." The incomplete metaphor for kingship is drawn from the creation narrative (Gen. 1:26-28). Elmer Martens says: "If one were to imagine a scale of 1 to 10 with living creatures such as beasts as 1 and God as 10, then, so high is the writer's estimation of humanity, he should have to put him at 8 or 9. It is God, and not animals, who is man's closest relative." He then adds C. S. Lewis's remark at the coronation of Queen Elizabeth II: "the pressing of that huge, heavy crown on that small, young head is a symbol of the situation of all men. God has called humanity to be his vice-gerent . . . on earth."[65]

(2) **Commissioned to Rule All the Earth v. 6 [7]**
Whereas *ʿṭr Piel* represents the human being as the passive recipient of God's crowning, *you cause him to rule over (tamšîlēhû b*^{e}*, Hiphil)* represents God as empowering the mortal as the agent to rule. With both verbs, the prefix conjugation signifies iterative present action, in contrast to the narrative form "you made him lack." As "you have made him lack a trifle from the heavenly beings" (v. 5 [6]) paraphrases "let us make man in our image," so verses 5-7 [6-8] and verses 6-8 [7-9] paraphrase "and let them rule over the fish of the sea . . ." (Gen. 1:26). *Māšal* designates governing the conduct of a subordinate, as Eliezer ruled over Abraham's household (Gen. 24:2) and Joseph ruled over Pharaoh's Egypt (45:8, 26). Whereas the apposition of moon and stars narrows the anthropomorphic metonymy of "the works of your fingers," the apposition of the fish, birds, and land animals in verses 7-8 [8-9] narrows *the works of your hands (ma*^{ʿa}*śê yādeykā)* to earth-creatures. Psalm 8 does not rule out human exploration of space, but it does rule out a divine intention for human beings to rule and subdue it.

Once again verset B underscores and expands the A verset in an A B B′ A′ structure. In B and B′ "works of your hands" is explicated as "everything" *(kôl),* which comprehends all that the context suggests. In this case the apposition mentions only animal life, fish and birds, but this is so because the poem sets

64. *HALOT,* 3:815, s.v. *ʿṭr.*

65. Elmer Martens, *God's Design: A Focus on Old Testament Theology,* 3rd ed. (North Richland Hills, TX: BIPAL Press, 1998), pp. 202-3.

the first creation account to music. Genesis 1:26-28 limits human dominion to this sphere, but in the second creation account (Genesis 2) *I AM* places humankind over the garden. The poet does not intend to exclude the flora from human dominion. *You have put under his feet (šattâ taḥat-raglāyw)* is a figurative way of representing "subdue" *(kābaš)* in the Genesis account. "To subdue" and its poetic equivalent, "to put under feet," imply that mortals must struggle to win dominion over the creatures. There is within the creation, even before the Fall, a nature that resists domination. Humans must subdue the horse to harness it to their chariots; the oxen, to plow their fields; and flocks to give them milk and fleece. Whereas *I AM* has inscribed his own splendor on the celestial bodies (v. 1), he gives his image honor in its own right by empowering him to rule over all things (1 Chron. 29:12). Mortals have not gained power over the creation by a chance mechanistic process but by a mandate from the Creator to establish a culture that expresses God's character. This mandate suggests that history will end in humankind's triumph, not in tragedy.

c. Ruled Creatures vv. 7-8 [8-9]

The roll call of the ruled creatures includes both the domestic and the wild animals, represented as created on the sixth day, and the birds and fish on the fifth day. Only animate creatures are cited because "only they can be considered a possible rival to the mortal."[66]

(1) Land Animals v. 7 [8]

The A verset mentions the domestic flock and herds. "Flocks" (*ṣōneh,* collective singular) include the small, domesticated animals — sheep and goats; and "herds" *(wa'ᵃlāpîm)* denotes the large, domesticated cattle such as oxen. *Kullām* refers to all within those species of fauna, including both clean and unclean.

Gam that introduces v. 7b [8b] can mean simply "also" (i.e., adding something) but commonly denotes an intensifying and/or emphatic force, *even.* This notion is appropriate with *wild animals* (*bahᵃmôt śādāy,* literally "beasts of the field"), the non-domesticated cattle (cf. 1 Sam. 17:44; Joel 1:20).[67]

(2) Air and Water Creatures v. 8 [9]

The Genesis creation account also lists the human being's dominion extending to the birds and fish (Gen. 1:28). *Birds (ṣippôr)* refers to "chirpers," and is the

66. H. Wolff, *Anthropology of the Old Testament,* trans. Margaret Kohl (Philadelphia: Fortress Press, 1974), p. 163.

67. Gesenius-Buhl, p. 86, s.v. *bᵉhēmâ.*

general word for commensal birds. *Of the heavens (šāmayim)* is commonly added to *ṣippôr*, so that "birds of the heavens/sky" is a Hebraism for "birds," but here the poet is emphasizing the three spheres that house life: "fields," "heavens," and "sea." *Fish (d^{e}gê)* is plural, not a collective singular (cf. Neh. 13:16) to designate the variety of fish *of the sea (hayyām)*. In sum, the poet envisions a tripartite universe with human beings having dominion over the creatures in all three spheres.

The B verset again sets up something of a contrast with the A verset. *The one swimming* is singular. By changing from the plural "fish" to the substantival participle singular the poet suggests either a collective that includes the great sea creatures, including Leviathan, or only Leviathan (cf. Ps. 104:26), the dreaded dragon who in pagan thought of the ancient Near East rivaled the gods. As the "wild animals" in verse 7b [8b] contrasts with the domesticated animals, so also "the one that passes through the paths of the sea" probably stands in opposition to non-threatening fish. *The paths ('orḥôt)* is virtually a poetic synonym for *derek* "way," signifying the route, not some secondary path in the wood, that the traveler has selected. In contrast to *derek*, *'ōrēaḥ* usually occurs in the plural (see also p. 135, n. 76). With *of the waters (yammîm)* "paths" refers to the recognized traveling patterns of the sea creature.

In sum, the last quatrain emphasizes the universal rule of humankind over the earth. It stands in apposition to *kōl* in verse 6 [7], repeats *kōl* in verse 7 [8], names the animates in earth's three spheres, and uses a series of merisms: the land animals created on the sixth day (v. 7 [8]) and the birds and fish created on the fifth day (v. 8 [9]); the non-threatening creatures in the A verset and the threatening creatures in the B verset, and the domesticated animals (flocks and herds in 7A [8A]) and wild animals ("beasts of the field") to represent the fauna.

D. Theme Restated v. 9 [10]

The emphasis on the mortal's rule over all the earth through God's appointment and empowerment prepares the way for the restatement of the psalm's theme: the glory of God over all the earth (see v. 1 [2]).

In contrast to Darwin's thought that humans gained mastery over their environment by their own strength, the psalm teaches that this dominion is a gift of God, not involving itself in the question of whether this came about by creation from without or from within. Darwin's view opens up the possibility that human beings may behave as arrogant tyrants over the earth, but the psalm teaches that in praise to the Creator and by dependence upon him the mortal rules in meekness under the Creator. The Creator's law for humankind protected the animals (Exod. 23:12) and the birds (Deut. 22:6f) against abuse, and distinguishing between clean and unclean animals in the tripartite spheres of the earth restricted humankind's greed. The greedy appetite of fallen humanity extinguishes species, and the gift has "withered in his selfish hand."[68]

Part IV. Conclusion

The poet's vision encompasses the whole drama of human history from the creation to the eschaton, from God's original commission to human beings — to rule the earth (Gen. 1:26-28) — to the consummation of that mandate, when human beings will have put all things under their feet (v. 6). Its intertextuality with Genesis 1:26-28; Job 7:17-18; 15:14-15; and Hebrews 2:8-9 clarifies that encompassing vision.[69]

I. Genesis 1:26-28

Psalm 8 is Genesis 1:26-28 set to music. The roll call of creatures in Psalm 8:6-8 [7-9] strikingly parallels the Genesis cosmogony: "let them rule over the fish of the sea and the birds of air, over the livestock, over all the earth" (Gen. 1:26). The parallel puts beyond reasonable doubt the poet's transformation of the creation narrative in Genesis 1 into a hymn.

In Darwin's theory of evolution (i.e., evolution without divine direction) *homo sapiens* is only on a continuum with animals; the only issue is what kind of animal. The concept of human beings as animals is reflected in the writings of earlier non-Christian intellectuals as well. Aristotle defined humanity as a political animal; Edmund Burke, a religious animal; Benjamin Franklin, a tool-producing animal; and Thomas Carlyle refined that to a tool-using animal. For others, we are less than animals. Robert Louis Stevenson considered humanity as but "a devil weakly fettered by some generous beliefs." For Gilbert, doubtless with Sullivan's approval, we are nature's sole mistake. B. F. Skinner said that because humans are entirely shaped by forces outside their will, they have no will, no freedom, and so no dignity.[70] In this view evolutionism is too optimistic.

68. E. M. Blaiklock, *The Psalms of the Great Rebellion: An Imaginative Exposition of Psalms 3 to 6 and 23* (London: Lakeland, 1970), p. 22.

69. Richard Pratt, *He Gave Us Stories: The Bible Student's Guide to Interpreting Old Testament Narratives* (Brentwood, TN: Wolgemuth & Hyatt, 1990), p. 246, defines "allusion" in this way.

70. B. F. Skinner, *Beyond Freedom and Dignity* (New York: Knopf, 1971), pp. 42-43, 58-59.

Humankind is a thing made of chemicals, no different from plants and rocks and so nothing more than an object subject to the same physical laws as other objects and without moral accountability. Tillich said: "God died in the nineteenth century and man died in the twentieth century."

On the other hand, some philosophers proclaim the "imperial self." This view is based on natural theology, not on science, and constitutes the foundational notion of postmodernism. The sovereign self decides truth by itself for itself, not by a source of authority outside of itself. Its credo is "believe in yourself." Both the "diminished self" and the "imperial self" reject external authority, be it the Bible and/or the institutional church. Postmodernism loves self as god, not a God external to self. This is the essence of sin. Without revelation, *homo sapiens* knows neither its identity nor its rightful place in the scheme of things. That revelation crowns humankind as God's delegated authority over all the earth and instructs the deputy to rule in meekness and dependence upon God.

II. Job 7:17-18; 15:14-15

Job inverts David's rhetorical question of praise, "What is man?" into a satirical sneer vis-à-vis his personal misfortunes: "What [*mh*] are mere mortals [*'enôš* — same vocabulary as Ps. 8:4 [5]], that [*kî*] you raise him up, and that you put [*tašît*] your mind on him? You take account of him [*tpqdnnu* — same vocabulary as Ps. 8:5] every morning, and test him continually" (Job 7:17-18). For Job, God's exaltation of humankind results in a scrupulous divine presence holding him accountable for every offense and so liable to guilt and punishment.

Eliphaz, Job's "friend," transforms David's question to rebut Job's complaint against God: "What is man that he could be pure?" Eliphaz also plays with David's testimony, "You have made him a little lower than the angels": "If God places no trust in his holy ones [i.e., angels] . . . how much less man, who is vile and corrupt?" (Job 15:14-15). According to Eliphaz, what Job is saying of himself is the just fate of all mortals. Although intending to debunk Job's self-pity, Eliphaz actually compounds the discrepancy between the divine intention for humanity and the historical reality of its fate because of sin. In Eliphaz's theology mortals do not fulfill their destiny but suffer instead because they are guilty before God and deserve his judgment.

Though the theologies of Job and his "friend" are seriously flawed, by noting the harsh reality that humankind's destiny and standing before God have been reversed by the Fall, they strip human beings of an unthinking piety that believes God is majestic through humanity's grandeur and of a human self-pretension to an exalted status.

When the creation is empowered by hostile spiritual powers, such as Satan, human beings prove no match. The Serpent — with a capital "S" to represent its uniqueness[71] — brings unaided humanity under its rule. As a result of the Fall, humanity's mastery of the earth, its technical, scientific, and artistic achievements, prove a mixed blessing. Nuclear power lights up our cities but threatens the extinction of all life; flight conquers space but opens new frontiers to terror; beauty in art ennobles humanity and pornography degrades it.

Job and Eliphaz, along with many modern commentators, miss David's resolution to the tension between the Creator's intention for humanity's glorious status as the pinnacle of all creation and the obvious reality that human beings, after their Fall, are defeated by sin and do not fulfill their cultural mandate according to the divine intention. For David, fallen humanity fulfills the cultural mandate through childlike faith. God's intention for mortals is realized in a fallen world from the petitions and praises of dependent saints, who lay the foundations of a strong bulwark in their struggle to silence the enemy and the one who avenges himself rather than trusting God (v. 2).[72] For this reason the psalmist praises *I AM*, not humanity. David's allusion to Genesis 1:26-28 develops the theme of humankind's mandated dominion over creation to its fulfillment after the Fall by asserting that mortals triumph in achieving their destiny through childlike trust in God.

III. Hebrew 2:8-9

The writer of Hebrews comments on Psalm 8:6 [7]: "Yet at present we do not see everything subject to them" (Heb. 2:8), and the faithful do not see *I AM*'s enemies eliminated from the earth (Ps. 8:2 [3]). What we see is the continuing struggle between the wicked and the righteous, between the rebel and the saint. Both the kingdom of God and the kingdom of Satan are expanding as wheat and tares, as good fish and bad fish.

The writer of Hebrews further notes: "But we do see Jesus, who was made lower than the angels for a little while, now crowned with glory and honor because he suffered death, so that by the grace of God he might taste death for everyone" (Heb. 2:9). The Pioneer of our faith, as Son of God and as son of man, has extended humankind's dominion over sin and death. Jesus Christ began the

71. Hebrew *hannāḥāš*. The article cannot be anaphoric but refers to an intrinsically definite noun so that it functions as a proper name. Bruce K. Waltke and M. O'Connor, *An Introduction to Biblical Hebrew Syntax* (Winona Lake, IN: Eisenbrauns, 1990), p. 249, P.13.6a.

72. The NIV, along with other translations, substitutes "ordain praise" to clarify the metaphor of "lay the foundation of strength" in v. 2.

dominion over all things, including sin and death, and his followers are bringing that dominion to its full realization. The full realization of humankind's manifest destiny is still a thing in the future, but details of its further course and its completion are already beginning to stand out clearly even in the present age as the faithful conquer under their resurrected, ascended, and exalted Head, who pioneered their faith.

As Christians step onto the stage of life they wear the victor's crown over all things through their faith in Jesus Christ who conquered even death. To the triune God belongs all the glory. He works in his vicegerents both to will and to do his good pleasure in establishing his rule over all things, including sin and death.

CHAPTER 9

Psalm 15: A Liturgical Decalogue

Part I: Voice of the Church

Psalm 15 was recognized early as a catechetical psalm of the Decalogue. Only recently, however, has the possibility been suggested that it introduces a collection, Psalms 15 to 24 (see commentary). Early commentators, however, linked Psalms 14 and 15 together. As a liturgical psalm, Psalm 15 was frequently repeated throughout the week by the monks.

Psalm 15 has been interpreted differently as a source of moral renewal within various historical contexts. One of the earliest interpretations of Psalm 15, traceable to Syriac sources, is as a mandate for conversion. Chrysostom (c. 400) interprets this psalm as expressive of the beginning of the Christian life. He links it with the previous psalm where the pronouncement, "There is no one who does good" (Ps. 14:1), raises the question, "Who then does good?" Despairingly the questioner turns to God to witness him (i.e., Christ) as the High Priest before the Holy of Holies. **Jerome** (c. 400) interprets the psalm to be preparatory for those seeking baptism, challenging them to make radical changes in their life. **Basil** (329-79) sees the psalm directed towards the Christian with particular focus upon the use of usury. **Benedict** (480-550) introduces his monastic Rule with citations from Psalms 15, 34, and 95. In the late Middle Ages, Psalm 15 was used prominently in calls for church reform.

I. In the Early Fathers

Before the unification of Christendom (late in the fifth century), commentaries reflected the regional differences and the independent voices of the various Fathers. **Hilary of Poitiers** (315-67) posited that the Psalter should be considered in groups of three, dedicated to judgment and mercy, to penitence, and then to praise. In the first category he highlights Psalm 15, because of its moral importance. He concludes that Psalm 15 should be "preserved in the inner parts . . . inscribed on the heart . . . stamped on the memory, and the treasure of this copious brevity ought to be bought by us day and night." Indeed, Hilary concludes his commentary by assuming this psalm is our guide on the journey to eternity, which we have undertaken as the body of Christ "at length to rest in the glory of the body of Christ."[1] He accepts the heading given as "a psalm of David," "since the Holy Spirit has spoken these things through him. And David is so rightly suited for this psalm," giving us an exhortation for "the present time," in simple, straightforward language that is neither designed for another time, nor mystical in its character. Rather, its brevity "summarizes all the instructions and commandments of the Old and New Testaments."[2]

As for the question, "Who may live on your holy mountain?," in a fresh way Hilary, who distinguishes the "tabernacle" or *paroikia,* from "the mountain" or God's eternal abode, does not take the tabernacle/temple too literally. Whether it was the desire of Moses to make a copy of what he had seen on the mount (Exod. 25:40), or what David longed for in the courts of the Lord (Ps. 84:2), or what Solomon built more ornately (1 Kings 6–8), or indeed whatever house or building every Christian community in the various Roman cities now worship in, all are pointing beyond themselves to the future eternal reality of being part of the Body of Christ, "the One in the Many." What counts is the daily communion we can all cultivate, of dwelling constantly in the presence of the Lord. This applies to all, whether as young Joshua, who "did not depart from the tabernacle" (Exod. 33:11), or as the prophetess Anna, who "did not leave the temple, serving day and night with fastings and prayers" (Luke 2:37). But since there is no "mountain of the Lord" on earth, Hilary argues that Isaiah rightly pointed to a future/eternal state, when we shall finally enter "the hill of the Lord, and into his holy place" (Isa. 2:2-3). It is this promise that the author of Hebrews refers to when he says, "you have come to mount Zion, and to Jerusalem, the city of the living God" (Heb. 12:22).

Hilary goes on to argue that just as Christ took on flesh, living in a human body, so we too within our human existence should live out morally the reality of our faith as Christians. "Doing justice, and speaking truth in the heart," may

1. Hilary of Poitiers, *In Psalmos I-XCI, Sancti Hilarii Pictaviensis Tractatus super Psalmos,* in J. Doignon, ed., Corpus Christianorum Series Latina, vol. 61 (Turnhout: Brepols, 1977), p. 91.

2. Hilary of Poitiers, *In Psalmos,* p. 81.

not appear norms any higher than what good pagans also practice. So the motive for "our bodies not being contaminated with debauchery, eyes not sordid with theatrical spectacles, a mind not drunk with wine, nor our life in service to money" — all of which Tertullian and Cyprian had already spoken against[3] — was because our bodies, while living within Roman pagan society, were the temple of the Holy Spirit.

With this distinctive reason, the moral behavior of Christians remains always motivated to ascend towards the eternal state, where Christ dwells in ascended glory. "So that there may be a worthy ascent unto the rest of God, one ought to live in the truth of one's words and tongue, so that through the faith of works the meaning of our words may not be false."[4] For Hilary the moral key is the exercise of constant humility, for it is pride that is the source of all vices. It is with the prayer of the Publican, "Lord, be merciful to me a sinner," rather than with the pride of the Pharisee, "I thank you, Lord, I am not like other sinners" (Luke 18:11-14), that one makes ascent to Mount Zion.

In his conclusion, Hilary highlights the issue of usury, which he connects with the practice of bribing judges, in verse 5. The seriousness of extorting from a poor brother in this abusive way is that "Christ died for him," so as a Christian the abusive lender is behaving in a manner that contradicts the whole event of the Incarnation, when "He who was rich, yet for our sakes became poor" (2 Cor. 8:9). Actually good pagans like Cicero, whom Hilary also quotes in his indictment of usury, saw this as a social ill within Roman society.[5]

Basil of Caesarea, also referred to as **Basil the Great** (329-79), was a Cappadocian bishop who wrote some fifteen homilies on the psalms, including two on Psalm 15.[6] His interest is more in Christian behavior rather than in the doctrinal polemics of other contemporaries. He sees the psalm as exercising "great power in the affairs of life," brief though the text may be. His homily is directed to verse 5: "he has not put out his money to usury." Basil sees this sin censored in several Scriptures: Ezekiel 22:12; Jeremiah 9:6. He cites Jesus' command in Matthew 5:42, "from him who would borrow from you, do not turn away." Basil is speaking of "robbing the poor," of making profits from those deprived, vulnerable, and defenseless. But he also condemns the borrower, who is thoughtless in his actions, so he addresses both: "Are you rich? Do not borrow; Are you poor? Do not borrow." All are equally condemned, although the last

3. Tertullian, *De baptismo* 4.5 (CCSL 1:280); Cyprian, *Ad Donatum* 8 (CSEL 3/1:9).

4. Hilary of Poitiers, *In Psalmos,* section 9.

5. Cicero, *De officiis,* 2.15, 53-54.

6. "With his friend Gregory of Nazianzus and his brother Gregory of Nyssa, he makes up the trio known as 'The Three Cappadocians,' far outclassing the other two in practical genius and actual achievement" *(New Advent Catholic Encyclopedia).*

word of judgment he heaps upon the heartlessness of the rich who exploit the poor.[7]

Basil expounds on Psalm 15 in two homilies, but unfortunately we do not have the first general overview of the psalm, where Basil might have described the Christian's aspirations for the eternal state of his moral life. In the second homily he focuses attention on verse 5, on the issue of usury. He shows how seriously it was censored by the prophets, especially Ezekiel, who condemns it as among the greatest of social evils: "you take usury and excessive interest and make unjust gain from your neighbors by extortion" (Ezek. 22:12). While the law had expressly forbidden this in Deuteronomy 23:19: "Thou shalt not lend to thy brother money to usury, nor corn, nor any other thing." "Truly," notes Basil, "usury involves the act of the greatest inhumanity, that the one in need of necessities seeks a loan for the relief of his life, and the other, not satisfied with the capital, contrives revenues for himself from the misfortunes of the poor man and gathers wealth."[8] Basil proceeds in the remainder of his homily to describe all the moral consequences of the evil of usury, which Basil had seen firsthand, as evidenced by his vivid understanding of its evil social consequences.

Jerome (342-420), in his *Tractatus in psalmos,* notes the significance of this being the fourteenth psalm (in the Vulgate). For it was on the fourteenth day of the month, that is, at full moon, that the lamb was sacrificed (Exod. 12:6). Implied is that the psalm describes a sacrificial life, lived transparently "beneath the light of the moon." He then distinguishes the tabernacle and the holy mountain (or hill) of the Lord. "A tabernacle is not an established house . . . but travels with the one traveling." Thereby Jerome distinguishes our mortal life on a journey towards our eternal destination. He contrasts the Stoic virtues that give us self-satisfaction, with "doing justice," which imitates God, and is therefore God-directed. What follows is "to speak truth in one's heart," such as expressed by the Good Samaritan, who again reflects the character of God's mercy. So "he does not accept slander against his neighbors." Rather he "glories in those fearing the Lord." As for "he has not lent his money for usury," Jerome suggests much could be said about this, as possibly he himself had devoted a previous treatise to this matter, described by him as a *katēchēsis.* Jerome does not exegete the psalm but instead gives a pastoral homily, which clearly distinguishes Christian from Stoic virtues.

Jerome also preaches on Psalm 15, repeating some of his *Tractatus,* but it is within the more restrictive context of teaching baptismal candidates. Like

7. Saint Basil, *Homilies,* The Fathers of the Church (Washington, DC: Catholic University of America Press, 1951), Homily 12, pp. 181-91.

8. Basil, *Homily 12,* p. 182.

Hilary, he distinguishes the "tabernacle" or *paroikia* from "the mountain" or God's eternal abode. He, too, adopts the metaphor of travel or pilgrimage of those who in passing through the world meet, like the Good Samaritan, those who are "neighbor to us" in their relations and needs. So our mortal life should be directed by how we love our neighbor as ourselves, in doing justice, speaking truth, and not doing evil to others. But the abrupt termination suggests we do not have the whole text of his homily.[9]

Theodore of Mopsuestia (350-428), a bishop of Mopsuestia, suggests that the sequencing of Psalms 14 and 15 is intentional, for the former is concerned about the moral complacency of the Israelites who assume they live in safety, and the latter is urging them to make every effort to strive towards a blameless life. It is about "what we should do: walk blameless, live righteously, speak truthfully; and what we should avoid: commit no guile, nor harm our neighbor by usury." Again, he too elaborates on the sin of usury. All these things are appropriate to those seeking to become citizens of heaven.[10]

Theodoret of Cyrrhus (c. 393-c. 460), following Hilary, suggests that Psalm 15 is post-exilic, composed to train the returning exiles how to relive as inhabitants of Jerusalem. He translates "tabernacle" as the Temple, and the "holy hill/mountain" as Jerusalem. He also interprets "performs righteously" (v. 2) as the ultimate virtue, from which all others derive. Likewise, he sees the logical flow that proceeds from "speaking truth in the heart" to "not deceiving with the tongue," and then to not "doing evil to his neighbor," as first the inner heart, then the tongue, and then the outward deed.[11]

In contrast to these earlier commentators, **Augustine of Hippo** (354-430) gives a very slim exposition on Psalm 15. To him the word "tabernacle" here applies to the military use of soldiers' tents, and metaphorically to the behavior appropriate to soldiers of Christ engaged in fighting the Devil. So the great Augustine leaves us with a hasty summary of 2 Corinthians 5:1-2 and of 1 Peter 1:13-14, to apply doubtfully to the psalmist's exhortation, and then also to the Christians in their earthly campaign.[12]

Cassiodorus, Roman statesman, writer, and monk (born c. 490, died c.

9. Jerome, *Tractatus in psalmos,* in S. Hieronymi Presbyteri Opera, Pars II: *Homiletica,* D. Germanus Morin, ed., Corpus Christianorum Series Latina, vol. 78 (Turnhout: Brepols, 1958), pp. 30-34.

10. Robert C. Hill, trans., *Theodore of Mopsuestia, Commentary on Psalms 1–81* (Atlanta: Society of Biblical Literature, 2006), pp. 173-81.

11. Theodoret of Cyrrhus, *Commentary on the Psalms,* trans. Robert C. Hill (Washington, DC: Catholic University of America Press, 2000), vol. 1, p. 111.

12. Saint Augustine, *Expositions of the Psalms,* ed. John E. Rotelle, O.S.A., trans. Maria Boulding, O.S.B. (Hyde Park, NY: New City Press, 2001), vol. 1, pp. 179-81.

583), interprets Psalm 15 as a simple summary of the Ten Commandments. Rhetorically, he suggests the figure of speech *erōtēma* is being illustrated, where an apt reply is given to a questioner. Who is worthy of the church? Clearly only Christ is without blemish, who alone has fulfilled the Law. Christ uniquely lives the truth, and without guile he can affirm: "Whatsoever I have heard from my Father I have made known to you." As for his neighbors, he prays for them on the cross, "Father forgive them, for they know not what they do." He even delegates to Judas the money to be given to the poor, the opposite of usury. And so through ten virtues Cassiodorus illustrates how each in turn demonstrates the uniqueness of Christ's earthly, moral life. No doubt thinking of his singing audience, who could so easily sing the psalms unreflectively, Cassiodorus emphasizes that only Christ could, by doing all these things, fully embody the Decalogue.[13]

The Carolingian reformer **Remigius of Auxerre** (c. 841-908), with a renewed appreciation of the Biblical text, also unites this psalm with the previous one. He makes the link with the last verse of Psalm 14:7, asking who is the true Israel, as his covenant people. He suggests that Psalm 15 defines who they are.[14]

II. In the Moral Reform of the Later Middle Ages

In defining the senses of Scripture, Origen had called its moral application or moral exposition "the third sense,"[15] following upon the narrative of the facts and the allegorical exploration of its depths as a "spiritual application." From then on, every other level or expository aspect became "spiritual." But within the vocabulary of exegesis, "tropology" took on new significance during the twelfth century. Literally, *tropologia* was "speech turned around," or speech that "converted," now implying a new way of living as a consequence of the knowledge being disclosed. Both Origen and Gregory the Great had been the great masters of tropology in applying the mystery of Christ to the Christian way of life. But in the twelfth century **Bernard of Clairvaux** (c. 1091-1153) took tropology to a new level, or indeed a new "depth," because he associated it with "conversion." By this term *conversion* he meant the change of life from feudal knighthood to the simple and obedient life of a monk. Literally, it was a new form of "monastification," the spiritual formation of monks or the *conversi*. The

13. Cassiodorus, *Explanation of the Psalms*, in P. G.Walsh, trans. and ed., *Ancient Christian Writers*, vol. 1 (New York and Mahwah, NJ: Paulist Press, 1990), pp. 155-60.

14. J. M. Neale and R. F. Littledale, *A Commentary on the Psalms from Primitive and Medieval Writers* (London: Joseph Masters & Co., 1884), p. 197.

15. Origen, *In Cant.*, Bk. 1,90; Bk. 11,133.

traditional Benedictine model of accepting children to grow up unreflectively within the monastic community was now being replaced by the Cistercian reform of recruiting youths, voluntarily. These postulants needed "conversion" — consciously and radically — from their worldly ways, to become true monks. So a Cistercian commentary on Psalm 15 would be very illuminating. But since early Cistercian theology "ruminated" rather than gave an "exposition," we find literally hundreds of echoes to the Psalter within their homilies, but not a straightforward textual exposition. Significantly, the only commentary on a selected psalm that Bernard composed was contained within his seventeen sermons on Psalm 91. But everywhere, Bernard is quoting and using the psalms tropologically for this intent of "conversion."[16] In his seventh sermon, on Psalm 91, he does quote Psalm 15:4; the converted monk will despise the reprobate and honor those who fear the Lord.[17] As Bernard puts it, everything that the gospel history contains can therefore be interpreted "according to tropology, so that what has proceeded from Christ as 'the head,' may consequently also be acted out morally within 'the body.'"[18]

At the same time, there were robust Benedictine commentators like **Rupert of Deutz**, who were quite affirmed in the existing order of monasticism, as he saw "splendid things . . . in the deeds of David and Solomon, seeking everywhere the glory of Christ the king." "Foremost was David," the "greatest of the prophets," "a great . . . mighty . . . and victorious king."[19] He links Psalms 15–16 together as reflective of the earthly and risen life of Christ.[20]

III. In the Reform Movements, Twelfth to Fifteenth Centuries

As we have seen (chapter 2, pp. 54-55), the twelfth century is a turning point or "hinge period" of history. It is so regarded because this turning point involves several factors: Bernard's Cistercian reform movement of adult recruits in monasticism; secular schools of theology; dialogue with Jewish exegetes; and the social unrest associated with Jewish usury. Regarding the latter, Christian

16. Bernard of Clairvaux, *Sermons on Conversion,* trans. Marie-Bernard Said, O.S.B. (Kalamazoo, MI and Spencer, MA: Cistercian Publications, 1981), pp. 11-25.

17. Bernard of Clairvaux, *Sermons on Conversion,* p. 159.

18. Quoted by Henri de Lubac, S.J., *Medieval Exegesis: The Four Senses of Scripture,* vol. 2, trans. Mark Sebanc (Grand Rapids: Eerdmans, 1998), p. 135.

19. Rupert of Deutz, *De sancta Trinitate et operibus eius,* in Hrabanus Haack, ed., *Corpus Christianorum Continuo Christianorum Continuo Mediaevalis* (Turnhout: Brepols, 1972), vol. 22, pp. 1338-40.

20. Rupert of Deutz, *De sancta Trinitate et operibus eius,* p. 1346.

scholars like **Robert Grosseteste** (1175-1253), bishop of Lincoln, are favorable to the Jews, reasoning on their behalf that the church has grown out of the synagogue, as indeed Sarah shares Abram with Hagar. Later, William Langland reasons that since the Hebrews "know the first clause of our creed, Credo in unum Deum, [teach them] little by little [to believe also] in Jesum Christum filium and in Spiritum Sanctum."[21] By 1187, the Jews are reckoned to have one-fourth of the moveable wealth of the kingdom, and one Jew alone, Aaron of Lincoln, keeps Henry XI solvent. Edward I tries to carry out the ideals of Grosseteste, and yet also to ban all usury in 1275, but the economic change is imposed too suddenly and the legislation fails; instead, Edward expels all Jews from England (in 1290).[22] We have no psalm commentary by Grosseteste, although we have already referred to the Christian Hebraic scholarship of Herbert of Bosham.

In the political climate of the twelfth century (see pp. 250, 385-88), a new use of the Psalter by the laity arises, in which Psalm 15 plays a uniquely prominent role in the moral reform movements of the following centuries. Meanwhile in 1246, the Council of Toulouse reiterated that the Psalter could be translated into vernacular languages.[23] Following upon this renewed freedom, **Richard Rolle** (c. 1300-1349), educated at Oxford, writes in Middle English the first lay commentary on the whole Psalter. He spends over thirty years as a hermit, remaining independent of the church hierarchy and even local priests. He becomes the most influential and popular English commentator of the Psalter, and widely read by the educated laity.[24] Indeed, for the following two centuries his Psalter commentary is the only authorized translation of part of the Bible into English that did not need diocesan permission for its use. He may be described as "the Franciscan reformer of England," whose mystical writings influenced the rise of the Lollards and of Wyclif's teaching, as well as giving stimulus to later English mystics.[25] He breaks the Psalter loose both from its long monastic way of life, and from the much shorter period of scholasticism, to put it into the hands of "the ploughman," as William Langland describes a generation later.[26]

21. Ruth M. Ames, *The Fulfillment of the Scriptures: Abraham, Moses and Piers* (Evanston, IL: Northwestern University Press, 1970), p. 35.

22. Ames, *The Fulfillment of the Scriptures,* p. 36.

23. This was the lay movement the Desert Fathers had practiced in their daily use, at least since the fourth century.

24. There are at least thirty-eight extant copies of his vernacular commentary, mainly in private homes and university colleges.

25. Margaret Deanesly, *The Lollard Bible and Other Medieval Biblical Versions* (Cambridge: Cambridge University Press, 1966), p. 120.

26. Ames, *The Fulfillment of the Scriptures,* p. 73.

There are two strands of devotion in Richard Rolle, one indebted to Anselm's personalized prayers and the other to Bernard of Clairvaux's sweet love of Jesus. He wrote two independent commentaries, first a Latin version, then later a more mature, richer, vernacular commentary on the Psalter. He is also indebted to Augustine, Cassiodorus, Peter Lombard, and Gilbert of Poitiers. From the latter he adopts the analogy of the psalms being "verbal medicine," for the cure of the sick soul. He sees the unique role of the Psalms as the Bible in miniature, as Athanasius had first recognized. Now the Psalter becomes increasingly significant for the laity. Rolle's intent is to recover David as God's prophet for the common people, whose lyre was a ten-stringed instrument, as the Law had ten commandments.[27] Yet the psalms are "ful derke," with many obscure passages which his text is intended both to clarify for the reader, and to stir up deeper devotion, in teaching God's ways to sinners.

Richard Rolle begins his Prologue of his psalm commentary: "A great fullness of spiritual comfort and joy in God comes into the hearts of those who recite or devoutly intone the psalms as an act of praise to Jesus Christ. They drop sweetness in men's souls and pour delight into their thoughts and kindle their wills with the fire of love, making them hot and burning within, and beautiful and lovely in Christ's eyes. And those who persevere in their devotion he raises up to the life of meditation and on many occasions; he exalts them to the melody and celebrations of heaven. The song of the psalms chases away devils, stirs up the angels to help us; it drives out and destroys discontent and resentment in the soul and makes a peace between body and soul; it brings desire of heaven and contempt of earthly things. Indeed, this radiant book is a choice song in God's presence."[28]

In Psalm 15, he comments on each verse in turn, giving a balanced devotional précis, with a brief statement on usury in verse 5. This summary of the ideal Christian life expresses what we have received from God's grace: "When we were baptized we proclaimed to Jesus Christ to keep his commandments and to forsake the Devil and all his works." Covetousness, of which usury is one expression, is seeking our rewards from this world and denying our spiritual nature, which seeks only heavenly things. So then, "do not take gifts from the innocent . . . gifts that might destroy the judgment of a righteous man, who

27. Peter Lombard had possibly first made this analogy of the Ten Commandments and the ten-stringed lyre of David. Later, Joachim of Fiore, an apocalyptic mystic, used symbolism extensively, and one of his favorites in his *Liber Figurae* was the harp. This he identified with the Psalter, its meaning being "that of the disciplined soul which has curbed its passions and achieved harmony by being attuned to God and transformed by love."

28. Richard Rolle, *The English Writings*, trans. and ed. Rosamund S. Allen (New York and Mahwah, NJ: Paulist Press, 1988), pp. 66-67.

loves righteousness above all things." Then he dwells here in the tabernacle of the church, but rests in his final destiny of "God's holy hill, in eternal bliss."[29]

William Langland (c. 1330-c. 1400), in his radical reform poem, *Piers Plowman,* uses Rolle's commentary, referring five times to the central question of Psalm 15:1, "Lord, who may dwell in your sanctuary? Who may live on your holy hill?" The psalms command a preeminent place in his moral and literary imagination. Indeed he may have been an official "psalmist" in the local church, whose task was to read the psalms in the church services.[30] At least 107 times over, he quotes the psalms in his poem. Covetousness and the abuse of usury are key indictments of the need of social reform, as voiced by Langland's biographical *persona,* Will the Dreamer. The triumphal moment of the poem is in Passus XVIII, when the reconciliation of Mercy and Peace with Justice and Truth occurs. In the universe of *Piers Plowman,* psalms and psalm verses do not merely have the force of ideas, but the palpability of directives; words become commands, for psalm phrases are not only to be sung, but to be acted upon with moral intent. "Charity" becomes a Davidic figure, whose honest labor is the antitype of the negligence of priests, in the same way that Will's incessant questioning is the converse of their blithe disregard for the faithful. Langland's most radical use of the Psalms occurs when he makes his key psalmic figure not a priest, but a humble plowman, Piers himself, who lives out Psalm 15.[31]

Geoffrey Chaucer (c. 1342-1400), whose poem *Canterbury Tales* ranks him as one of England's greatest poets, also uses the Plowman as the idealized Christian. It has become an occupation of critical importance after the Black Death (1349) for the revival of the agricultural economy, previously so socially despised.[32] As the antitype of pride, the plowman now becomes the true inheritor of the legacy of Christ and his apostles, and the last best hope of the church. Chaucer's "Poure Persoun" (1386) fits idealistically the portraiture of "the righteous one" of Psalm 15. Just as Jerome had seen the psalmist on pilgrimage between an earthly abode and a heavenly Zion, Chaucer too sets out on pilgrimage, even though it is only to Canterbury. The intent is the reform of God's house. Like Langland's Plowman, Chaucer's Poor Parson illustrates well many of the traits depicted in Psalm 15. As a flyleaf of a fifteenth-century copy of Rolle's

29. Rolle, *The English Writings,* pp. 66, 67.

30. E. T. Donaldson, *Piers Plowman: The C Text and Its Poet,* Yale Studies in English (New Haven: Yale University Press, 1949), pp. 205-6.

31. Michael P. Kuczynski, *Prophetic Discourse: The Psalms as Moral Discourse in Late Medieval England* (Philadelphia: University of Pennsylvania Press, 1995), p. 209.

32. Joseph Horrell, "Chaucer's Symbolic Plowman," in Richard Schoeck and Jerome Taylor, eds., *Chaucer Criticism: The Canterbury Tales,* vol. 1 (Notre Dame: University of Notre Dame Press, 1960), pp. 84-97.

English *Psalter* quotes: *Inter sapientes sapientior est qui humilior est.* ("Among the wise the more wise is he who is more humble.") For it is in the meekness of David and of Christ that wisdom is truly gained through humility.[33]

As a concluding comment on reform movements in the twelfth to fifteenth centuries, we note that Langland and the Lollard writers attempt to break the hold which the concept of "Meed" or "Reward" has had over the individual, and over society at large in the fourteenth century. Those who are "Covetous," and exhibit a life of moral "Sloth" are severely condemned. In the anticlericalism of the times, the priests too are being exposed and judged. Bluntly, they are told that they need to withdraw from misdirected worldly activity, to rededicate themselves to learning the Psalter both intelligently and devotionally, and to communicate its moral precepts to the faithful. For there are two kinds of rewards, observes the poet: that truly given by God, and that selfishly and carnally sought by the ungodly — an echo of Rolle's earlier reflections on Psalm 15.[34]

IV. In the Ongoing Reform of "Devotio Moderna"

Denys the Carthusian (1402-71) is probably also inspired by Rolle, for his Psalms commentary has the same simplicity of expression in a plain Latin style, accessible to the educated families of Rhineland burghers. Their movement, "Devotio Moderna," is "modern" in the sense of becoming "renewed devotion." Their reading of the psalms is motivated to live in "imitation of Christ," as expressed in Thomas à Kempis's great classic. Seeing Christ in the Psalter feeds this devotional outpouring, of which Denys is a prominent example. It is an ideal of treating Christ as a historical figure, whose own earthly existence is grounded in his devotional use of the Psalter within his daily life.[35]

Denys notes Psalm 15 is not just "a psalm of David," but of "Saint David speaking here. For the Prophet wishing to form us morally, that we might truly be able to belong to the number of the elect, in the present through grace, and the future through glory, asks God: 'Lord, who shall dwell in your tabernacle?' . . . For many dwell in the Church in name only, such as immoral Christians and heretics."[36] He takes up the military analogy of Augustine (see p. 280), interpreting

33. Horrell, "Chaucer's Symbolic Plowman," p. 215.

34. See Nicolette Zeeman, *Piers Plowman and the Medieval Discourse of Desire* (Cambridge: Cambridge University Press, 2006).

35. Gordon Leff, *The Dissolution of the Medieval Outlook* (New York: New York University Press, 1976), p. 132.

36. Denys the Carthusian, *D. Dionysii Carthusiani insigne opus commentariorum, in*

Psalm 15 as expressive of the "Church Militant." But he understands the psalm to speak most clearly about Christ in all his perfections. He quotes Zechariah 6:12-13 to identify the coming Messiah: "Here is the man whose name is the Branch, and he will branch out from his place and build the temple of the Lord. It is he who will build the temple of the Lord, and he will be clothed with majesty and will sit and rule on his throne. And he will be a priest on his throne." Is he then anticipating the rising militancy of the next century that will bring conciliar reform to its end, with the cataclysmic break of the Reformation? Significantly, when Denys comes to verse 5 on the issue of usury, he reveals he is now living in a much more developed economic way of life than William Langland ever knew. So he appeals to the teaching of Jesus in the parable of the talents, when he translates the message to the wicked servant: "'You ought to have given my money to the bankers; and at my coming I would have received it with interest' (Matt. 25:27). But there money is taken for the commissioned talent, that is, for grace given, and especially for the knowledge of the Holy Scripture: he who would receive ought to instruct others. And so usury is the fruit of knowledge given, or of grace, or of benefit. For from it, he who receives more, more will be demanded."[37]

Denys comments on the virtuous conditions of righteousness by his interpretation of the ten acts of virtue he finds in Psalm 15. Unlike social reformers such as William Langland, who focus upon specific social ills, Denys is more concerned about the qualities of those who consider themselves to be "a member of Christ, and an inhabitant of the church, and in a state of salvation."[38]

There were various reactions to the use of the Psalter with the breakdown of a purely institutional church. The rise of the Hussites, Waldensians, and Lollards as such popular lay approaches are strongly reacted against by such conciliar reformers as Pierre d'Ailly and Jean Gerson. We know they write their own commentaries on the Psalter, but unfortunately we do not have access to them because they write topical pamphlets, a new genre, quickly printed. The closest we have to a commentary is that of **Nicholas of Cusa** (1401-64). He is their most outstanding intellectual contemporary.[39] His language is the opposite of Rolle's and Denys's, leading his readers to the edge of incomprehensibility in imaginative and profound insights. Truth may be precise, but it must be held in "learned ignorance," he tells us. So, like the conciliar reformers, he puts a brake upon the popular use of the psalms and even inhibits any devotional use of Scripture.

---

psalmos omnes Davidicos, in *Doctoris Ecstatici D. Dionysii Carthusiani Opera Omnia* (Monstrolii: Typis Cartusiae S. M. de Pratis, 1898), vol. 5, p. 482.

37. *D. Dionysii Carthusiani insigne opus commentariorum,* vol. 5, pp. 483-84.

38. *D. Dionysii Carthusiani insigne opus commentariorum,* vol. 5, p. 484.

39. Nicholas of Cusa, *Selected Spiritual Writings,* trans. H. Lawrence Bond (New York and Mahwah, NJ: Paulist Press, 1997).

V. In John Calvin's "Reformed" Summary

Erasmus and Luther do not leave any commentaries on Psalm 15, so we now come to **John Calvin** (1509-64) as an example of a "modern interpreter." He begins: "This psalm teaches upon what condition God chose the Jews to be his people, and placed his sanctuary in the midst of them; namely, that they should show themselves to be His peculiar and holy people by living justly and uprightly."[40] Nothing is more common, he observes, than the infringement of the third commandment, in taking God's name in vain. For this is what the unrighteous do by their evil way of life. So the initial questioning of the psalmist, Calvin interprets, is at the wonderment of the crowds entering the sanctuary, full of "god-talk," and yet so wholly unaware of their own unrighteousness. Thus the third commandment serves three purposes: to desire to be counted among the righteous we must show this by the integrity of our own life; to dwell permanently within God's house, we must act accordingly, as distinct from the many who come and go; and we must actively seek to reform the church of God, even though in this life it will always remain tarnished.

Calvin suggests that the conditions of being worthy residents of God's house may not be what we expect. Should emphasis not be given to such marks of godliness as the exercise of faith and prayer? No, he argues; hypocrites too can show these exercises! It is not so much then in outward behavior, as in such inner dispositions such as singleness of heart, righteousness towards others, and sincerity of speech, in concord of attitudes, motives, and social relations. David has listed some of the vices particularly to avoid: slander and false censure of others; all forms of unrighteousness that would destroy community; and insensitive cruelty to others. Flattery indulges in the same vice(s). Instead, honoring the godly is necessary, as well as keeping one's word, even when it hurts to do so. Again, the faithful do not oppress their poor neighbor with usury or unfair business practices, but act with fairness and consideration of others at all times. Succinctly, Calvin is describing behavior he expects of the citizens of Geneva, as also of "the citizens of Zion." Had we the data, no doubt the idealistic Puritan colonists would exemplify the same way of life. For usury is now all but forgotten, and mercantilism now revolves around it! But the prayer of Denys the Carthusian, reflecting on Psalm 15, would still be appropriate today:

> Visit us, we ask, Lord, sojourning in the body far from you, and in your holy service, grant to strengthen us so that, assiduously intent on the working

40. John Calvin, *A Commentary on the Psalms,* ed. T. H. L. Parker (Edinburgh: James Clarke & Co. Ltd., 1965), vol. 1, p. 203.

of justice, we might without spot deserve to be inhabitants of the eternal tabernacle.[41]

Part II. Voice of the Psalmist: Translation

1A A psalm by David
1Ba *I AM,* who may sojourn[42] in your tent?[43]
1Bb Who may dwell[44] on your holy mountain?
2Aa Whoever[45] lives[46] as a person of integrity:[47]
  2Ab who does[48] what is right;
  2B and speaks truth from[49] his heart.
3Aa He does not slander[50] with his tongue,[51]
  3Ab does not harm his neighbor;[52]
  3B and does not vilify his close neighbor.[53]

41. *D. Dionysii Carthusiani insigne opus commentariorum,* vol. 5, p. 484.

42. Interpreting *yāgûr* and *yiškōn* as imperfects of permission (*IBHS,* p. 507l, P. 31.4d).

43. Fragments of Hebrew codices in the Cairo Geniza and more than twenty mss. in the Kennicott–de Rossi collection read *bᵉʾohᵒleykā* (pl.) against the majority of Hebrew manuscripts and the ancient versions. Perhaps the pl. is an auricular error and was understood as a plural of extension to indicate the tent is inherently large and/or complex (*IBHS,* p. 120, P. 7.4.1c); there is no significant difference in meaning.

44. See note 42.

45. An independent relative pronoun as subject (*IBHS,* p. 621, P. 37.5a) with the implied predicates "may sojourn . . ." (see v. 1).

46. Literally, "walks" (see commentary).

47. Accusative of state specifying a feature of the subject in relation to the verbal action (*IBHS,* p. 171, P. 10.2.2d).

48. Interpreting *waw* as epexegetical to clarify or specify the sense of the preceding clause, and signified as such by the colon with "integrity:".

49. Literally, "in" or "with."

50. Interpreting the suffix conjugation as denoting a gnomic perfective situation (*IBHS,* p. 488, P. 30.5.1c).

51. Instead of the tri-colon of the MT, BHS scans 2A as a bi-colon and instead of scanning verse 3 as a tri-colon combines 3Aa with 2B: "speaks truth from his heart/does not slander with the tongue," forming the typical parallels of "heart" and "tongue." MT, however, has the advantage of linking the three participles of verse 2 and the three occurrences of *lōʾ* with three gnomic perfectives in verse 3 and of making performing the virtues of verse 2 parallel to abstaining from the vices of verse 3 (see commentary).

52. One of a small group of nouns that takes *-ēhû, not ô,* as their third person singular masculine pronominal suffix (GKC 91k).

53. Literally, "to reproach he does not lift up [the name] of his close friend" (so most versions). If so, *ḥerpâ* is an adverbial accusative of place with a verb of motion (*IBHS,* pp. 8-10,

4Aa Whoever is vile,[54] in his eyes[55] is one to be rejected,[56]
    4Ab but he honors[57] those who fear *I AM;*
4B He promises on oath[58] to his own hurt,[59]
    and he does not change.[60]
5Aa He charges no interest when he gives[61] his silver to the poor,
    5Ab nor takes a bribe against the innocent.
5Ba Whoever does these things,
    5Bb will never be toppled.[62]

Part III: Commentary

I. Introduction

A. Literary Context

The TNIV Study Bible notes that Psalms 15 and 24 frame a cluster of psalms that have been arranged in a chiastic pattern, with Psalm 19 as the hinge. Thus:

15Who has access to the temple?	24Who may ascend the holy hill?
16Confession of trust in *I AM*	23Confession of trust in *I AM*
17Plea for deliverance from foes	22Plea for deliverance from foes
18Royal praise for deliverance	20-21Prayer and praise for king's victory

19*I AM*'s glory in Creation and Torah[63]

P. 10.2.2c). TNK, however, glosses v. 3B by "or borne reproach for *his acts toward* his neighbor" (see commentary).

54. *Niphal* participle functions as a gerundive (*IBHS,* p. 387, P. 23.3d).

55. *Paseq* syntactically links *b^{e}ʿênāyw* with *nimʾās.*

56. Here the gerundive *Niphal* participle signifies what is proper (*IBHS,* p. 387, P. 23.3d).

57. Construed as a habitual imperfective (*IBHS,* p. 506, P. 31.3e).

58. *Niphal* is unclassified (*IBHS,* p. 391, P. 23.5b), but it may be a productive denominative of *šebaʿ.* The perfective is gnomic (see n. 50), an elegant variation of the habitual imperfective.

59. A one-place internal *Hiphil* (literally, "to hurt himself," *IBHS,* pp. 39-40, P. 27.2f). The LXX (Syr.) reversed the consonants from *hrʿ* to *lrʿhw* (*l^{e}rēʿêhû,* "to his neighbor"). The unique *plene* spelling speaks against this facilitating reading for difficult Hebrew syntax.

60. Literally, "He promises on oath . . . and does not change."

61. Gnomic perfective (see n. 50).

62. The prefix conjugation, when used with reference to future time, represents a real situation that arises as a consequence of some other situation (*IBHS,* p. 511, P. 31.6.1c).

63. TNIV Study Bible, p. 819.

The framing psalms share the same form of question followed by answer (15:1-5; 24:3-4) and the same theme of their insistence on the inextricable connection between worship and ethics. Moreover, these two framing psalms move from general, abstract positive statements to a more specific negative statement.

At the pivot, Psalm 19 celebrates *I AM* as the transcendent Creator and immanent Redeemer, who provides his worshipers with moral purity through his Torah, forgiveness, and shepherding care. "Together, these three psalms (15, 19, 24) provide instructive words concerning the petitioners heard in the enclosed psalm, offer a counterpoint to Psalm 14, and reinforce the instruction of Psalm 1," which introduces the whole collection.[64]

B. Literary Form and Structure

Psalm 15, as early commentators recognized, is a *torah* (catechetical teaching) psalm to teach piety and ethics, using a liturgical temple entrance formula of question-and-answer (cf. Ps. 24:3-5; Mic. 6:1-8; Isa. 33:14-16). The connection of liturgy with piety and ethics suggests that liturgy depends on pure ethics and religion, and that liturgy reinforces Israel's covenant values (see Psalm 1, pp. 129-30). But "purity" is a matter of the heart, as the psalm makes clear. Though commentators commonly assume that the psalm was used by a temple warden to evaluate the aspiring worshiper, in truth the psalm looks to one's conscience to be the temple warden. It calls for self-examination, not judgment by others (cf. 1 Cor. 11:28, 30), for who but the worshiper knows what is in his own heart (see vv. 2, 4)? In this psalm spirituality, morality, and liturgy unite as a holy trinity. However, external evaluation also has a proper place. In Psalm 101 David sets forth the qualifications of those who function in his administration.

Its structure, like other features of the psalm, is complex.[65] On the one hand, the psalm's introduction raises the question about who is worthy to sojourn in *I AM*'s protective sanctuary (v. 1); its body answers the question (vv. 2-5A), and its conclusion promises the worthy eternal security (v. 5C). This structure is similar to Psalm 24:3-6 and Isaiah 33:14B-16. The body consists of a Decalogue of stipulations (to be counted on the fingers): 1-3 [v. 2]; 4-6 [v. 3], 7-8 [vv. 4A, B]; and 9-10 [vv. 5Aa, b]. The seventh, usually the favored slot in a series, pertains to the crucial requirement to fear *I AM*. On the other hand, this

64. TNIV Study Bible, p. 837.

65. Many scholars see three parts: a question in verse 1, its answer in verses 2-5A, and a promise of blessing (inviolability) in 5B.

structure of introduction, body, and conclusion is presented rhetorically in a chiasm housing other chiasms:

A. Question: Who may dwell in *I AM*'s sanctuary?	v. 1Ba, b
B. Summary and particulars of required action and speech	vv. 2-4
1. Summary of prescribed virtues (participles):	
a. Summary: Walks *(hōlēk)* with integrity	v. 2Aa
b. Action: Does *(pōʿēl)* righteousness	v. 2Ab
c. Speech: Speaks *(dōbēr)* truth	v. 2B
2. Particular proscribed vices (*lōʾ* plus perfectives)	v. 3
a.′ Speech: No going about as slander (*lōʾ rāgal,* "foot")	v. 3Aa
b.′ Action: No evil to neighbor *(lōʾ ʿāśâ)*	v. 3Ab
a.′ Speech: No reproach against neighbor *(lōʾ nāśāʾ)*	v. 3B
X. Fears *I AM*	v. 4
1. Socially: Positively, rejects non-God-fearers but honors them	v. 4A
2. Personally: Negatively, no changing of vows (i.e., fears *I AM*)	v. 4B
B′ Particulars and summary of righteous action and speech	v. 5
1. Particular proscribed vices (*lōʾ* plus perfectives)	v. 5A
a. Action: No interest from poor *(lōʾ nātan)*	v. 5Aa
b. Speech and Action: No bribes against innocent *(lōʾ lāqaḥ)*	v. 5Ab
2. Summary: Does (participle, *ʿōśeh*) these things	v. 5Ba
A′ Benediction: Assurance of eternal security	v. 5Bb[66]

The above analysis reveals the psalm's obvious theme: What does God, a consuming fire against the wicked, require of his worshipers? Not surprisingly, in true covenant theology, so unlike pagan religion, the answer pertains to spirituality and ethics, not ritual. The psalm's chiastic structure pivots on the requirement to fear *I AM,* which entails faith in him. Biblical ethics and faith are two sides of the same coin, which has eternal currency.

Let us consider this chiastic structure more closely.

A/A′ (vv. 1, 5Bb): The question of who may sojourn in *I AM*'s sanctuary is raised in A, and the reason one wants to dwell there is stated in A′: it provides eternal security.[67] Guests of God were protected against pursuers (Ps. 23:5-6;

66. Cf. P. Auffret, "Essai sur la structure littéraire du Psaume XV," *VT* 31 (1981): 383-99; L. M. Barre, "Recovering the Literary Structure of Psalm XV," *VT* 34 (1984): 207-10.

67. That climactic consequence is signaled by the shift from participles and perfectives to the future imperfective ("will not be toppled").

27:4-5f.; 61:4-5 [5-6]), granting them deliverance and peace. With regard to parallelism the psalm moves from a bi-colon (v. 1), to two tri-cola (vv. 2 [Aa, b, B]-3 [Aa, b, B]), to two quatrains (4 [Aa, b, Ba, b]-5[Aa, b, Ba, b]).

B/B′ (vv. 2-4, 5A-Ba): An accepted worshiper's social obligations are stated in B, moving from a summary statement to particulars and reversing that sequence in B′. Moreover, in B the requirements become more and more focused, moving from the generalization "walks" (i.e., lives, v. 2Aa) with integrity, to summary statements of action (does right, v. 2Ab, and speaks truth, v. 2B). Conjunctive *waw* links the three clauses. The three positive, generalizing virtues of verse 2 are followed by three particular prohibited vices in verse 3, which has yet another chiastic pattern of a/a′ (speech: not slander, not malign) around the pivot b′ (action: do not do evil to neighbor). Also, the tri-colon of virtues in verse 2 are held together grammatically by the use of three *Qal* participles having the assonance of its infix pattern of ōē. Likewise, the tri-colon of vices in verse 3 are linked grammatically by *lō'* plus a *Qal* perfective, having the assonance of its infix pattern /ā and a/.[68] Turning now to B′ (v. 5A) on the other side of the pivot, it states specific prohibited vices with regard to action (v. 5Aa) and speech (v. 5Ab), using the same grammar in sense and sound of verse 3. In yet another chiasm verse 5B summarizes the requirements in a positive statement, using the participle infix pattern, matching the form and assonance of the *Qal* participle in verse 2.

X (v. 4): Whereas the teachings pertain to social obligations, the two teachings of the pivot pertain to God. The pivot can be analyzed as a quatrain, which consists of antithetical clauses (v. 4A), linked by disjunctive *waw* (4Aa, b), and a semantically conditional clause ("[when] he promises on oath") and its apodosis ("then, he does not change"). Both bi-cola of the quatrain are linked by *waw* and divided by the conjunctive accent *r^{e}bî^{a}'*. The king hinges the two semantic halves of his Decalogue on the "fear of *I AM*" (v. 4), which has the social dimension of honoring God-fearers and rejecting the despicable, and of keeping one's vow even to one's own hurt (cf. Eccl. 5:4-6).

An escalating length of verses matches the escalating particularization, moving from six stressed syllables (v. 1), to seven (v. 2), to eight (v. 3), to ten (v. 4), to eleven (v. 5).

Throughout the Old Testament the key to social ethics is true piety, whose non-negotiable virtue is faith. Though ethics and piety are commonly treated separately by theologians, in reality ethics on the horizontal axis is in-

68. Note too the alliteration of the gutturals [18x]: /ʾ [4x]/, /h~ḥ [4x]/, /ʿ [5x]/ and /r [5x]/. Note too the assonance of *ʿal-l^{e}šōnô* and *ʿal-q^{e}rōbô* at the end of vv. 3Aa, 3B, of *rēʿē-hû* and *rāʿâ*, and of *ʿāśâ* ("does," 3Ab) and *nāśāʾ* ("lifts up" 3B).

separable from piety (faith) on the vertical axis and vice-versa. Since the focus of the psalm is on ethics, the pivot gives pride of place to the accepted worshiper's posture toward the impious and pious (i.e., the impious versus the faithful) before insisting that he himself fears *I AM* as shown by the litmus test that he keeps his oaths. Note the chiasms of the negative frame: rejects (4Aa) and does not change (4B), around a positive pivot, honors God-fearers (4Ab).

Psalm 15 is filled with intentional ambiguities.[69] "Speaks truth from the heart" (v. 2B) forms an excellent antithetical parallel with "does not slander with the tongue" (v. 3Aa), matching the inner organ that contrives speech with the outer organ that performs it. This parallelism is so good, some rearrange verses 2 and 3 into three bi-cola:

2 Who lives as a person of integrity
  Who does what is right
Who speaks truth from the heart
3 Who does not slander with the tongue
Who does not harm his neighbor
  And does not vilify his close neighbor (so BHS)

This structure of three bi-cola, however, should not override the parallelism of the tri-cola of verses 2 and 3 (see n. 51). Both structures are intentional. Moreover, "[speaking truth] in his heart [*blbbw*]" may mean either that his inmost thought treasures honesty or that he speaks accurately and sincerely. Also, in verse 3 *ḥerpâ lo'-nāśā' ʿal-q^{e}rōbô* means either "he does not vilify his neighbor" or "he does not bear reproach on account of his neighbor"; and in verse 4 *b^{e}ʿênāyw* ("in his eyes") can modify either "the vile" or "the one to be rejected" (but see n. 55). The negative prohibition ("not change [oath]") of verse 4B joins the next two ("not take interest and/or bribes"), forming a trilogy of prohibitions matching the trilogy of verse 3. *Lāqaḥ* ("take") in verse 5 can refer to taking a bribe out of one's pocket or to taking a bribe and putting it in one's pocket. This piling up of ambiguities suggests that all are intentional; in other words, they are double entendres.

69. See also P. D. Miller, Jr., "Poetic Ambiguity and Balance in Psalm XV," *VT* 29 (1979): 416-24.

II. Exegesis

A. Superscript: see pp. 88-89.

The author of our psalm is none other than the inspired David, Israel's greatest, covenant-keeping king. As his time of death drew near, David instructed Solomon to keep *I AM*'s *torah* in order to secure his throne forever (1 Kings 2:1-4). As soon as David transferred the ark to Zion, that mountain became holy by *I AM*'s presence. The reference to the tent uniquely applies to David's tent for housing the ark. Although the psalm pertains to Israel's liturgy, it does not follow that, as Weiser insists, it "obviously originated in the cultus."[70] David drew

70. A. Weiser, *The Psalms* (OTL; Philadelphia: Westminster Press, 1959), p. 167. Form-critics who reject Davidic authorship commonly interpret Psalm 15 as part of an entrance liturgy. Most think that pilgrims or worshipers ask a priest at the gate of the temple area the requirements of entrance (v. 1) to which gives the priest answers (vv. 2-5A). J. T. Willis, "Ethics in a Cultic Setting," in James L. Crenshaw and John T. Willis, eds., *Essays in Old Testament Ethics* (New York: Ktav, 1974), pp. 145-70, finds this point of view reasonable: 1) Many religions in the ancient world required worshipers to meet certain conditions before allowing them to enter the sanctuary, but the entrance requirements were usually ritualistic, though sometimes they include high ethical standards. 2) There is evidence of worshipers being asked entrance questions (Deut. 26:1-15; Ps. 118:19ff.). 3) Several texts indicate that a gatekeeper refused worshipers entrance (2 Chron. 23:19; cf. Deut. 23:1-4 [2-5]). 4) The psalm contains cultic language, such as "tent of *I AM*" and "holy hill" (v. 1). But Willis does not think this liturgical setting is beyond reasonable doubt, for one can speculate on other possibilities. Perhaps the priest asks the question, the worshipers provide the answer, and the priest pronounces a benediction (v. 5B). Or maybe a righteous priest raises the question for wicked priests; after all, corrupt priests allowed all sorts of wicked people to enter the sanctuary (Amos 5:21-24; Hos. 6:4-6; Isa. 1:10-17; Mic. 6:6-8; Jer. 7:1-11; Isa. 58:1-8). Or perhaps the questions and answers were sung antiphonally as part of the worship. Or maybe a prophet raised the question and/or answered it (cf. Isa. 33:14-16; Mic. 6:6-8; cf. Jer. 7:1-11; Hag. 2:11-13). The psalm, Willis notes (p. 156), has strong affinities with prophetic literature and with wisdom literature, but he fails to note that the wisdom literature was composed by kings and/or their courtiers (see Bruce K. Waltke, *Proverbs: Chapters 15-31* [Grand Rapids: Eerdmans, 2005], p. 58f.). Obviously, the form-critical method of establishing the psalm's origins by its *Sitz im Leben* is based on conjecture. Even apart from the question of who is asking the question of whom, the notion that it was used as an entrance liturgy is problematic. Can a gatekeeper determine a person's character — his or her integrity, justice, truthfulness, or heartfelt fear of *I AM* (vv. 2B, 4)? C. C. Broyles (*Psalms* [NIBC; Peabody, MA: Hendrickson, 1999], p. 92) rightly comments with reference to "walk with integrity" and "speak truth in one's heart": "one's judgment could not be conceded to another; self-examination under the scrutiny of conscience was required (cf. . . . 1 Cor. 11:28, 31)." M. Buttenwieser (*The Psalms Chronologically Treated* [Chicago: University of Chicago Press, 1938], p. 203) issued this warning: "The treatment Psalm 15 has received at the hands of present-day interpreters is anything but adequate. Preoccupied with its literary type more than with its spiritual content, they have missed the spirit and purpose of the psalm and have underrated its ethical standard."

up the plans for the temple and composed the music and libretto for its liturgy, so a question of a person's worthiness to worship there was apt as soon as that mountain was sanctified by the divine presence. Perhaps David originally intended the psalm for an individual, such as a priest or king, to secure inviolability by an affirming conscience, but more probably he intended it for all who ventured on that sacred mountain. As the psalm functions in the Psalter, it teaches all the people of God to keep covenant, especially brotherly love, with all their heart in order to secure eternal life. But that love is rooted in faith (see v. 5, below). As Chrysostom (see above) recognized, David implicitly points to his greater Son, for only the Son of God perfectly satisfies these covenant requirements. Nothing less than his perfect obedience and sacrifice for his people can secure eternal inviolability in God's presence. The triune God grants that perfection and salvation to all who fear (i.e., believe in) him.

B. Question: Who May Dwell in I AM's Tent v. 1

The wise king introduces his catechetical teaching by asking, probably his students (i.e., his people), what are *I AM*'s conditions for the individual and nation to enjoy his security in his sanctuary. As Cassiodorus (see "survey") recognized, the interrogative pronoun *mî* ("who") asks a real, not a rhetorical, question (contra Ps. 2:1). In the Old Testament an individual does not enter into the sacred sphere lightly or as a matter of right. There are barriers inherent in the Israelite religion that take ethics into account (see pp. 129-30). The king likens the worshiper at the sanctuary to a resident alien. *Gûr* ("sojourn") signifies to leave one's homeland for political, economic, religious, or other circumstances and to dwell as a newcomer and resident alien without the original rights of the host community for a (definite or indefinite, Ps. 61:4 [5]) time in order to find protection, a resting place and home in another community, as Abraham sojourned in Egypt and Gerar (Gen. 12:10; 20:1), Lot in Sodom (19:9), the Bethlehemite Elimelech and his family in Moab (Ruth 1:2), the Ephraimite in Benjamin territory (Judg. 19:16), and especially Israel in Babylon (Jer. 42–50, 12 times). Its semantically equivalent substantival participle *gēr* ("sojourner") is used of Abraham in Hebron, Moses in Midian, Israel in Egypt (Exod. 22:21), and so forth. The *gēr* possesses no land and so is usually poor and depends on the good will of the host. The relationship between the landless Levite and the *gēr* bears comparison (Judg. 17:7-9; 19:1; Deut. 14:29; 26:11-13). In Israel's daily life, apart from ownership of land, no distinction between a *gēr* and an Israelite existed: the *gēr* stands under *I AM*'s divine protection (Deut. 10:18; Ps. 146:9; Mal. 3:5), is to be loved as one loves himself (Lev. 19:34; Deut. 10:19), and is not to be oppressed (Exod. 22:20-23); they participate in the tithe (Deut. 14:29), Sabbath year (Lev. 25:6), and cities of refuge (Num. 35:15), and they are subject to the same law (Lev. 20:2; 24:16, 22; Deut. 1:16).[71] The word is used here poetically and figuratively of the worshiper's relationship to *I AM* in God's tent. "The Arabs give the title of *jār allāh* to one who resides in Mecca beside the Caaba."[72] A sojourner has no natural right but depends upon God's favor to give him the *protection, provision, and rest* that his tent affords. The Decalogue of requirements specifies that the *gēr* must have a heartfelt commitment to *I AM,* a requirement that demands a new heart (i.e., regeneration; Jer. 31:31-33). Nothing short of being a new species of humanity will do. The rest of Scripture makes clear that this new creation occurs by being spiritually baptized into Christ Jesus. Today, David's language of dwelling in God's tent is a type of the Christian's belonging to God's household (Eph. 2:19).

'ōhel ("tent") refers to a collapsible tent made of cloth and/or skins stretched over a wooden frame, fastened down to pegs with cords, in contrast to a more permanent *bayit* ("house") or any other kind of dwelling.[73] Of the 435 occurrences of *'ōhel,* 60 percent of the texts occur in the cultic sense of the "tent of *I AM,*" "tent of meeting," etc. *I AM*'s tent, the Tabernacle, during Israel's sojourn in the wilderness was an elaborate royal tent in contrast to a booth *(sukkâ),* which was a temporary shelter composed from whatever materials were at hand. Here *in your tent* *(bᵉ'ohᵒlekā)* refers to the sacred tent David pitched on Mount Zion to house the ark of the covenant, pending its installation in a permanent structure (2 Sam. 6:17; 7:2, 6; 1 Kings 1:39; 2:28-30; Ps. 132:1-9; 1 Chron. 15:1; 16:1; 2 Chron. 1:4). References to the sacred "tent" in the Psalter are all in psalms attributed to David (Ps. 27:5, 6; 61:4 [5]).[74] These texts suggest that though a tent is the essence of the nomadic way of life (Jer. 35:7-10; Hos. 12:10), the tent David pitched was more complex, permanent, and beautiful than a nomad's tent.

In verset B *who* is emphatically repeated; its predicate escalates God's resi-

71. In this paragraph I leaned heavily on R. Martin-Achard, *TLOT,* 1:308, s.v. *gûr* to sojourn.

72. Robertson Smith, *Lectures on the Religion of the Semites: The Fundamental Institutions* (London: Adam and Charles Black, 1894), p. 77.

73. From the Old Testament little can be gleaned concerning the form or construction of tents; they may have been matted or pointed. A nomad lived in a bell tent, supported in the middle by a wooden pole and composed of several dark goatskin curtains.

74. Critics who deny David authorship avoid the obvious inference that the mention of a tent sanctuary points to David's authorship and dubiously argue that the Psalter's reference to the tent preserves the memory of that tent. In Solomon's day the Tent of Meeting was at Gibeon (2 Chron. 1:3; cf. 1 Kings 8:4), and in Chronicles "tent" is used of the Second Temple as a memory of the Tent of Meeting (cf. 1 Chron. 9:23; 17:5).

dence from a transient tent to the security and permanence of a mountain. *šākan* ("dwell") means "to stay, spend time, dwell." The verb indicates nothing concerning the nature and/or duration of the stay. The rest of the psalm specifies those details. However, its substantival participle, *šākēn,* denotes "one who resides in some geographically proximate relationship to another and thus may designate a next-door . . . neighbor (the neighbor close[st] 'to his house[hold]')."[75] The rest of the psalm shows that God's closest neighbors dwell on his holy mountain as his welcome guests (Ps. 23:6; 27:4-6; 61:4 [5]; 84:10; 2 Sam. 12:20).

On your holy mountain (bᵉhar qodšekā); see Psalm 2:6. *I AM* chose Zion for his dwelling, saying:

> "This is my resting-place for ever and ever;
> Here I will sit enthroned, for I have desired it.
> I will bless her with abundant provisions;
> Her poor I will satisfy with food.
> I will clothe her priests with salvation,
> And her faithful people will ever sing for joy. (Ps. 132:13-16)

C. Summary and Particular Requirements vv. 2-4

The royal Decalogue demands duty to neighbor, moving, as Theodoret of Cyrrhus recognized, from broadly axiomatic abstract virtues to more specific virtues and prohibited vices, moving back and forth between speech to action. More specifically David's Decalogue, using independent relative participles, which tend to characterize a person, first demands the individual be a person of integrity in his behavior and speech (v. 2). Then it requires specific acts, using perfectives for complete, specific situations with regard to speech (not slander . . . not bring reproach upon a neighbor) and action, "does not harm his neighbor" (v. 3). The seventh requirement demands a right response to neighbor based on fear of *I AM,* and the eighth cites oath-keeping as the test of one's fear of *I AM.* Finally, the ninth and tenth require not to use money to disadvantage the poor. The Biblical teaching on money is that it should be used to help the poor, not to hurt them. Surprisingly, from a pagan perspective, David, the elaborator of Israel's liturgy, makes no mention of cultic matters such as sacrifices, ritual purity, and so forth (cf. Hos. 6:6; Amos 5:21ff.; Isa. 1:11ff.). This is so because ritual without spiritual and moral virtue is an abomination to God (1 Sam. 15:22-23). Broyles comments on the requirements: "They do not allow

75. R. H. O'Connell, *NIDOTTE,* 4:112, s.v. *šākēn.*

one to hide behind a cloak of religiosity."[76] The Lord's famous Sermon on the Mount shares the same spiritual impetus as the Decalogues of Moses and of David. It is surprising, however, that no mention is made of heinous crimes, such as murder, adultery, and theft, as in the Mosaic Decalogue. The prescribed virtues of David's Decalogue are more spiritually subtle (e.g., walking with integrity) and its proscriptions are commonly violated: taking advantage of others, gossiping about them, and breaking vows. More fundamentally, the issue is one of the heart, demanding of the worshiper self-examination.

1. *Summary of Virtues v. 2*

a. Summary: Lives as a Person of Integrity v. 2Aa

In verse 2Aa, *hôlēk* ("lives," see n. 46) is a verbal complement of *derek* ("way"), a common metaphor signifying broadly to live according to one's world and life views and, more specifically, to 1) course of life (i.e., the character and context of life); 2) conduct of life (i.e., specific choices and behavior); and 3) consequence of that lifestyle (i.e., the inevitable destiny of one's lifestyle).[77] *Tammîm (a person of integrity),* from the root *tmm* (*tām* [adj.]/*tōm* [noun]/*tammîm* [adjectival substantive]), denotes completeness and integrity with reference to a process that has already been accomplished in a person and "that through imminent necessity will produce either good or bad result."[78] (The traditional gloss "blameless" [Greek *amōmos*] may be misleading, for "blameless" may denote legal perfection.) With "walk" *tmm* denotes consistent behavior "to do something with the completeness of one's heart." When ascending a sheer rockface, a climber wants a *tammîm* holding the rope, keeping him on belay. *Tmm* is a comprehensive term for a total commitment to the way of *I AM.* The next two clauses clarify what is meant by "walk as a person of integrity" with regard to action and speech.

b. Action: Does What Is Right v. 2Ab

The summary, "lives with integrity," is now broken down by two more broad abstractions pertaining to action and speech. *Pōʿēl (who does)* means "to execute" — that is to say, the worker puts into action the necessary means to secure the success of his enterprise, namely *ṣedeq,* glossed "what is right" (see Ps. 4:1 [2]).

76. Broyles, *Psalms,* p. 92.

77. Waltke, *Proverbs,* p. 194.

78. K. Koch, *TLOT,* 3:1, 425, s.v. *tmm.*

c. Speech: Speaks the Truth v. 2B

And joins righteous action (2Ab) with truthful speaking (2B). In Biblical ethics righteous speech and actions are inseparable; one cannot do righteousness and speak vilely, and vice versa. *Dōbēr (who speaks)* indicates primarily "the activity of speaking," whereas its synonym, *'mr* ("say"), directs attention to the contents of the speech (see Ps. 4:4 [5]).[79] *'emeth (truth)* denotes words upon which one can rely. Although righteous behavior and righteous speech are inseparable, speech may be hypocritical, not righteous. Consequently, an accepted worshiper speaks truth *from the heart* (literally, "in the heart"), aiming to conform his speech to reality and to speak it sincerely, not with hypocritical flattery (see Ps. 4:4 [5], 7 [8]; cf. 12:2 [3]). He intends to speak truth, not to mislead by lies and/or flattery. The old joke has it that a captain wrote in his ship's log: "The first mate was drunk today." The first mate complained, "Aye, captain, you didn't have to write that into the log." The captain replied: "The truth is the truth." On the next day the first mate wrote in the log: "The captain was sober today."

2. *Particular Prohibited Vices v. 3*

The three prescribed virtues of verse 2 are now paired with three prohibited vices, which give the abstractions of verse 2 more specificity: *lō' rāgal* ("to not slander" [with the tongue], a derivative of *regel* "foot") specifies *hālak* ("walk"); *lō' 'āśa* ("to not do" [evil against a neighbor]) specifies by *pā'al* ("to execute [what is right]"); *ḥerpâ lō' nāśā'* ("to not vilify" [one close by]) matches *dābar* ("to speak truth [from the heart]"). The use of *lō'* ("not") resembles the form of Moses' Decalogue. The trilogy of proscriptions will receive finer specification in verse 5.

a. Speech: No Slander v. 3Aa

Slander glosses Heb. *rāgal,* a denominative of *regel* "foot." The verb occurs uniquely here in *Qal.* BDB connects the denominative to the etymological root by the gloss: "foot it," "go about" (maliciously, *as slanderer*). *With his tongue* (*'al lᵉšōnô,* literally, "upon his tongue"), the body part that performs the speech act, balances the "heart" in verse 2B, where the speech act is conceived (see above).

79. G. Gerleman, *TLOT,* 1:327, s.v. *dābar.*

b. Action: No Evil to Neighbor v. 3Ab

The second prohibition disallows "to do evil/harm" to the worshiper's innocent neighbor. The semantic range of *'āśâ (do)* is very large, like its English equivalent "to make," "do." Its manifold uses depend on its subjects and objects, ranging from production ("to make") to action ("to do"), which is the sense here and so in parallel with *p'l* (v. 2). It is commonly used with *rā'a* to signify the action of inflicting harm, not a consequence. Lexicographers gloss the feminine *rā'â* ("evil") and its gender masculine doublet *ra'*, with no difference in meaning, by "evil" (ill-disposed and sinful), "wickedness," "injustice," "wrong," "calamity," "distress," "disaster," "deprivation," or "misfortune," recognizing that the differences between these synonyms is often attenuated. Stoebe suggests that the basic meaning of *rā'â* is what harms life, not what benefits it.[80] More fundamentally its root, *r''*, conveys the factual judgment that something is bad, whether it be a concrete physical state (e.g., "ugly" cows, Gen. 41:3; "poor/bad" figs, Jer. 24:2), an abstraction ("calamity/disaster"), or moral behavior that injures others (Ps. 15:3). The value judgment that something is bad depends on the taste of the one making the evaluation, so "in one's eyes" is often added to the word (see 15:4). In the phrase *to his neighbor (lᵉrē 'ēhû)* is a broad term for "those persons with whom one is brought into contact and with whom one must live on account of the circumstances of life."[81] Its range extends from a close friend (see Prov. 17:17) to a person with whom one "keeps table company and exchanges peaceful greetings,"[82] to another in any relationship (see Prov. 3:28). Jesus defined, not redefined, neighbor as anyone encountered (Luke 10:29-36).

c. Speech: No Maligning of Neighbor v. 3B

Also, the worshiper must not defame an innocent community member. *He does not vilify* glosses *ḥerpâ lo'-nāśā'* (literally, "he does not lift up reproach"). *ḥerpâ (reproach)* refers to the indelible disgrace that society heaps on an individual who seeks to break up its foundation and its social coherence; they punish him by maligning him in order to denigrate his significance, worth, and potential influence. "Lift up" (*nāśā'*) is probably elliptical for "you shall not lift up the name of," i.e., lift up his hand and speak (that which causes society to heap insults against someone); cf. Exod. 20:7: "you shall not lift up the name of [i.e., lift up your hand and speak the name of] the LORD your God falsely or frivolously." In the phrase *against his close neighbor ('al-qᵉrōbô)*, the preposition *'al*

80. Stoebe, *TLOT*, 2:491, s.v. *ṭôb*.

81. *HALOT*, 3:1254, s.v. *rē'a*.

82. Gemser, *Sprüche*, p. 23.

("against" [LXX *epi*]) has its hostile sense and *qārōb* denotes a neighbor who is "close" both literally in space and metaphorically in sympathy and spirit (cf. Lev. 21:3; Ruth 2:20; cf. Ps. 148:14; Prov. 27:10). Reproaches and insults are rightly heaped upon sinners (cf. Jer. 29:18; 42:18; 44:8 *passim*), but not upon an innocent neighbor who dwells trustingly in the neighborhood and who has not done wrong (Prov. 3:29-30). *ḥerpâ lō'-nāśā' 'al-qᵉrōbô* can also mean "or borne reproach for *his acts toward* his neighbor" (see n. 53), investing *nāśâ'* with its usual meaning and *'al* with the sense of "on account of." However, though the ambiguity may be intentional (see above), in a Decalogue of prescribed virtues and proscribed vices that pertain to others, the clause more likely means to inflict scorn, not to suffer it. This inference is further supported by the parallelism between verses 2 and 3 (see above), suggesting that 3B is parallel to *dōbēr 'emet* that entails affecting others, not self.

3. *Fears I AM v. 4*

Teachings about having a right relationship with God stand at the pivot of teachings regarding maintaining a right relationship with neighbors. Foundational to acceptable ethics is the fear of *I AM,* which entails faith in him. The true worshiper shows his or her fear of *I AM* both socially by rejecting the vile, who do not fear *I AM,* and honoring those that fear him (v. 4Aa, b) and personally by keeping his oath whatever the cost.

a. Socially: Rejects Despicable (Non-God-Fearers) but Honors God-Fearers v. 4A

Although true worshipers never slander a neighbor or alienate from society an innocent neighbor by heaping scorn upon them, they draw a line with regard to piety: they reject the impious but aim to give the pious social weight. *Nibzeh* (*one who is vile/despicable,* see n. 54) signifies that the adjectival state is a necessary condition of the person in view. The root *bzh* means to regard as worthless and vile (see Prov. 1:7). Its bi-form, *bûz* ("to despise"), stands in antithetical parallelism to "fear of *I AM*" in Proverbs 1:7, the key verse of that book. So too here, the vile stand in opposition to God-fearers, suggesting that by "vile" David means those that are irreverent. *In his eyes (bᵉ'ênāyw)* may be literal, because in the ancient Near East one's attitude is shown on the face, "by the look in someone's eyes."[83] The MT accents favor the interpretation of connecting "in his eyes" with "is one who should be rejected" (i.e., he views the reprobate as one to be ostra-

83. Cf. J. Fabry, *TDOT,* 5:24, s.v. *ḥānan.*

cized, not honored; cf. Isa. 32:5; Prov. 26:8). One cannot understand anyone or anything without explanation and that explanation depends upon a prior understanding of reality. James M. Houston observes: "We are always experiencing two landscapes at the same time: the landscape before our eyes — the phenomenal world — and the landscape in our minds, what Gerard Manley Hopkins [one of the Victorian era's greatest poets] has called 'inscape.' The one is constantly interacting with the other. If, therefore, we conceive the world to be a desert, we also make it such."[84] William Blake, I am told, makes the point tellingly: "We do not see with the eye, but through the eye." By "inscape" is meant the presuppositions one brings to the task. In this case the accepted worshiper brings to a situation the "fear of *I AM*," and interprets people and/or situations with that preunderstanding of reality. In the God-fearer's evaluation it is proper (see n. 56) to regard the vile non-God-fearer as *one to be rejected (nimʾās).* The root *mʾs* means: "to want nothing to do with someone or something."[85]

In this single requirement of properly relating to people with regard to their piety, the *waw (but)* is disjunctive, pitting *those who fear God* against "the vile," "the despicable." One can neither honor God-fearers and the despicable nor reject both. A person loves either the pious or impious, never both. One who fears *I AM* loves *I AM* with all his being and so trusts him and obeys his catechetical teaching. He does so because he holds *I AM* in awe, knowing that God holds in his hands life for the pious and covenant-keepers, and death for the impious and disobedient to his teachings.[86] Whereas the accepted worshiper rejects the contemptible, he always *honors (yᵉkabbēd)* those who fear *I AM.* The root *kbd* means "to be heavy"; in *Piel* it means to esteem a person as having value and to declare him such to give him social weight or prominence.[87] In other words, the acceptable worshiper aims to divest the vile from social significance and to invest the ethical God-fearer with social weight.

b. Personally: Keeps Oath at Any Cost v. 4B

The true worshiper also demonstrates his fear of *I AM* by his keeping oaths made before *I AM,* whatever the cost. *He promises on oath (nišbaʿ)* means "to bind oneself to a future obligation," never to confirm an existing circumstance with an oath. To swear an oath to do something assumes God's awareness of the oath. Sometimes *šbʿ, niphal,* involves a solemn obligation accompanied by a conditional curse (e.g., "thus may *I AM* do to me and even more if I do not . . .")

84. James Houston, *I Believe in the Creator* (Grand Rapids: Eerdmans, 1980), p. 15.

85. H. Wildberger, *TLOT,* 2:653, s.v. *mʾs.*

86. See Waltke, *Proverbs,* pp. 100-101.

87. *IBHS,* pp. 402-4, P. 24.2f, g.

or strengthened by a reference to God. David swears that Solomon will become king (1 Kings 1:13, 17, 29f.), that he will not eat for a day in sorrow over Abner (2 Sam. 3:35), and that he will "find a place for *I AM*" (Ps. 132:2-5). The root of the phrase *to his own hurt* (*lᵉhāraʿ*, see n. 59) is *raʿ* (see v. 3). The oath includes an imprecation against the one making it. Even though his oath damages his well-being *he does not exchange* (*yāmīr*, see n. 60) [it] by a different oath or by negating his original oath. The object "oath" is elided. Even a lightly spoken promise must be honored (Lev. 5:4). A promise made dishonestly or with false intentions, or one that simply cannot be fulfilled, is called "fraudulent" or "deceitful" and will be harshly condemned by *I AM* (Lev. 19:12; Jer. 5:2; 7:9). For this reason the wise caution their students against taking oaths. *Qoheleth* (traditionally, "the preacher" or "the teacher") ends his sayings on the danger of not keeping vows with the exhortation: "Therefore fear God" (Eccl. 5:1-7). And so to keep an oath at any cost infers that the oath-keeper fears *I AM*, for he believes God will hold him accountable to keep it. Saul, in contrast to David, failed this litmus test of piety (cf. 1 Sam. 19:6).

D. Particulars and Summary of Social Action and Speech v. 5ABa

Whereas the teachings in verses 2 and 3 moved from admonishing positive virtues to prohibited vices, now in the chiastic complement of verse 5A to verse 3 they move from prohibited vices to a positive summarizing statement in verse 5Ba. The accepted worshiper, who inferentially has economic power, refuses to use it to take advantage of the misery of the poor: he rejects taking interest from them and using bribes to steal from them.

1. Particular Prohibited Vices of Action and Speech v. 5A

As the bi-colon of verse 2, so too its chiastic parallel bi-colon in verse 5A moves from action to speech, but uses the negative *lōʾ* plus the perfective form, as a matching chiasm to verse 3.

a. No Interest from Poor v. 5Aa

His silver (kaspô) refers to silver as mined and smelted, not as a precious metal in its native state. The reference to silver instead of gold may indicate an early time when silver was priced higher than gold.[88] *Nātan* "basically indicates the process

88. C. A. Robinson, "God the Refiner of Silver," *CBQ* 11 (1949): 188-90.

through which an object or matter is set in motion," more specifically either to cause something to come to some ("to give") or in the sense of to cause, to effect, to occasion ("to do") as in Proverbs 10:10.[89] Since the one giving the silver does not exact interest, one may assume that the true worshiper either gives his silver outright to the destitute or, more probably, with the expectation the borrower will repay the loan when they are no longer destitute. *The poor* is added to *with interest (b^e^nešek),* because, as most early Christian commentators recognized, the destitute, not the investor, is in view. Of the ten Biblical occurrences of *nešek* half (three in the Pentateuch, Exod. 22:25 [24]; Lev. 25:36, 37; and two in Ezekiel based on the Pentateuch, Ezek. 18:8, 13) explicitly refer to a charge to the poor for borrowed money. In Psalm 15:5 and Ezekiel 22:12 that precise reference is not as clear, but the latter is in the context of keeping the Mosaic covenant. According to Deuteronomy 23:20 [21], where *nešek* occurs twice, an Israelite could charge interest from foreigners — the Gentiles charged interest from their own poor — but not from fellow Israelites. The parallel, "poor," in Proverbs 28:8 and the context (see vv. 3, 6, 11) strongly favors restricting its meaning to charging interest from the needy. In Biblical times the charge on borrowed money was about 30 percent of the amount borrowed. In any case, most scholars agree that all ten passages refer to loans made as "acts of charity for the relief of destitution as opposed to loans of a commercial nature for expanding business."[90] To make profit on another person's misery is unconscionable.

b. No Bribes Taken Against Innocent v. 5Ab

Bribe (šōḥad) refers to a gift, usually monetary, given to or taken by a judge or a witness to convict an innocent person (Exod. 23:8; Deut. 10:17; 16:19; 27:25). So bribes pertain to both action and speech and appropriately draw this Decalogue of "dos and don'ts" to its conclusion. According to J. Finkelstein, although there is sufficient evidence that bribery of judges was regarded at least as a moral offense in other ancient Near Eastern cultures, "there is no known cuneiform law outlawing bribery specifically." He draws his essay on bribery to this conclusion: "It was not only a common practice, but was recognized as a legal transaction."[91] *Accepts* glosses *lqḥ* ("to take"), which can mean "to take (i.e., to draw out of the pocket)" with reference to the one who proffers the bribe (cf. Prov. 7:20; 20:16; 22:27), or "to accept" with reference to the one who takes it (cf. Prov. 1:3; 2:1). The latter interpretation accords better with Proverbs 15:27 and

89. C. J. Labuschagne, *TLOT,* 2:776, s.v. *ntn.*

90. Robin Wakely, *NIDOTTE,* 3:186, s.v. *nšk.*

91. J. Finkelstein, "The Middle Assyrian *Shulmanu*-Texts," *JAOS* 72 (1952): 77-80.

fits the parallel of taking interest in Psalm 15:5Aa, but the ambiguity is probably intentional. *The innocent (nāqî)* means "free from guilt." Both the briber and bribed aim to pervert justice *against (ʿal)* the guiltless.

2. *Summary v. 5Ba*

The relative participle, *one who does* (*ʿôśēh,* see v. 5Ba), complements as an inclusio the initial summarizing relative participle *(hōlēk),* one who walks (i.e., "lives"). The deictic relative pronoun, *these things (ʾēleh),* refers back to the Decalogue of prescribed virtues and prohibited vices. As a consequence of meeting these requirements, the true worshiper, who has already begun in the eternal way that God watches over (Ps. 1:6), dwells forever on *I AM*'s holy hill. *Never* glosses *lōʾ* ("not") and *lᵉʿōlām*[92] ("forever," "for eternity"). *ʿôlām,* according to E. Jenni,[93] means "the most distant time," "of unlimited and unforeseeable duration." *Môṭ,* the root of *will not be toppled (yimmôṭ),* means concretely "to rock or shake and to fall off a base," and in Proverbs 10:30 "to never be toppled" stands in antithesis to "not dwell" (*škn,* see v. 1). The metaphor of never toppled connotes durability, stability, unalterability, finality, and permanence. This is so because the accepted worshiper dwells on the Eternal's holy mountain, a type of heaven. The world may collapse but God never will (cf. Isa. 24:19; 54:10; Ps. 46:5 [6]). In short, David draws his Decalogue to conclusion with a benediction of eternal life upon the worshiper who by faith keeps these requirements.

Left unstated is the divine curse upon those who do not do these things, especially upon those who would venture to enter the holy hill of the Consuming Fire. If one does not examine his heart and conduct, the divine Judge will. God's salvation from human failure to keep these virtues and to abstain from these vices comes about through the obedience of faith in reliance upon God's grace for forgiveness of sins for spiritual enablement.

Part IV. Conclusion

We draw our commentary to conclusion by recalling **Denys the Carthusian's** comment that the psalm speaks most clearly about Christ in all his moral perfections. He alone can satisfy these righteous requirements, the proofs of true faith, for those who are empowered by his Holy Spirit in them so that they may live eternally with *I AM* both now and forever in heavenly Zion.

92. Temporal and terminative *lᵉ* (*IBHS,* p. 206, P. 11.2.10c).

93. E. Jenni, *THAT,* 2:230, s.v. *ʿôlām* means "the most distant time," "of unlimited and unforeseeable duration."

CHAPTER 10

Psalm 16: My Body Will Not Decay

Part I: Voice of the Church

As we saw in the previous psalm, the apostle Peter preached his Pentecost sermon reciting various psalms, of which Psalm 16:8-11 is quoted in the context of the resurrection. The apostle Paul also cites verse 10 in his sermon at Pisidian Antioch (Acts 13:35) to verify from Scripture the apostolic witness to and tradition of Christ's resurrection. If the original author of the psalm merely intended, as some argue, to relate the recovery from a near-death experience that the apostles used as a prophecy of Christ's resurrection by investing it with a second, not authorial intended meaning, their apologia for the gospel of Jesus Christ is seriously weakened, for Peter argued, as reported by Luke:

> Brothers and sisters, we all know that the patriarch David died and was buried, and his tomb is here to this day. But he was a prophet and knew that God had promised him on oath that he would place one of his descendants on his throne. Seeing what was ahead, he spoke of the resurrection of the Christ, that he was not abandoned to the grave, nor did his body see decay. God has raised this Jesus to life, and we are all witnesses of the fact. (Acts 2:29-32)

Since the so-called scientific studies of HBC, the orthodox interpretation that invested Peter's words with their plain sense has been almost shouted down. The contemporary church needs to hear loud and clear the voice of orthodoxy: the voice of Scripture and of the church's response.

I. Pre-Reformation Commentaries

Of the known commentaries on the Psalms, there are eight early fathers who all affirm that in Psalm 16 it is Christ who is spoken of, not David: Hippolytus, Clement of Alexandria, Origen, Cyprian, Commodianus, Lactantius, Eusebius of Caesarea, and Asterios Sophistes. Commodianus states in *Carmen de duobus populis,* "that [Christ once] placed in the grave would rise, was preached before in Psalm 30:3; 3:5; and 16:10. In these texts David does not refer to himself, rather to the death of the Lord."[1] **Eusebius** (260-340), using Origen's prosopological approach, links Psalm 16:10, "For you do not give me up to Sheol," with Psalm 30:3, "O Lord, you brought up my soul from Sheol," stating that these statements could not have been applied to David, only to Christ.[2]

Differently, **Diodore of Tarsus** (died c. 390), founder of the Antiochene school, left a critical commentary on some fifty-one psalms, including Psalm 16. These psalms he sees as a poetic gloss on the history of Israel from the time of David to the reign of Hezekiah, serving as a commentary on Isaiah, Jeremiah, and Samuel/Kings. David is the author, but he is speaking prophetically about Hezekiah, and not about Christ. Diodore ignores the apostles' use of these psalms, and only cites Psalms 2, 8, 45, and 110 as being applied to Christ.[3] He attributes authorship of Psalm 16 to David speaking as a prophet in the name of the Jewish people liberated by God from their enemies. In regard to the apostles' use of the psalm, he makes only brief mention, as if the verses quoted were cut off from the rest of the psalm. Vaguely he applies the term "similarity" to messianic themes between the words of David and allusions to Christ, as if the Christian interpretation is a rereading of the original text.[4]

As a pupil of Diodore, **Theodore of Mopsuestia** (c. 350–c. 428) follows closely the same interpretation. He interprets the psalm as a Jew might do, to describe the faith of Israel, and refers only briefly to the apostles' use of the psalms. Like Diodore, he thinks David is speaking on behalf of the people, "David giving thanks for the destruction of the neighboring peoples," done "with God's assistance."[5] He is silent on the theme of the resurrection, with no expla-

1. Quoted by Hansjörg auf der Maur, "Zur Deutung con Ps. 15(16)," *Bijdragen* 41 (1980): 404.

2. Eusebius, *Demonstratio evangelica,* 11, 16, 1-8; 111 2, 71.

3. Susan Gillingham, *Psalms through the Centuries,* vol. 1 (Oxford: Blackwell, 2008), pp. 31-32.

4. Marie-Josèphe Rondeau, *Les Commentaires Patristiques du Psaltier (III-Ve siècles),* vol. 2, *Exégèse Prosopologique et Théologique* (Rome: Pontificium Institutum Studiorum Orientalium, 1985), pp. 275-312.

5. Theodore of Mopsuestia, *Commentary on Psalms 1–81,* trans. Robert C. Hill (Atlanta: Society of Biblical Literature, 2006), pp. 181-99.

nation of the phrase "you will not abandon my soul in Hades." Only in his last statements does he admit the apostle Peter cites verse 10.[6]

Unfortunately, we have no commentary on Psalm 16 from John Chrysostom, whose approach would no doubt have been very different. **Augustine of Hippo** (354-430) has only a very short interpretation, ascribing it to "Christ the King."[7] Surprisingly, he makes no reference to the New Testament citations of the psalm, nor to verse 10, concerning the Christian hope based on the resurrection of Christ. Instead, he assumes that friendship with God, which has become real in this life, cannot be extinguished by death, as hinted also in Psalm 49:15 [16].

The first serious commentary on Psalm 16, a full treatise of nineteen pages, is given by **Jerome** (342-420). He carefully consults the texts of Aquila, Symmachus, Theodotion, as alternative Greek versions more closely aligned with the Hebrew text than the LXX, and he refers to them frequently in his commentary. He notes that five other psalms share the title "David's *Miktam*": 16, 56, 57, 58, 59, 60. All these share in the suffering of our Lord, as expressing Messianic action, to "make us mindful of our Lord's death," and "so engrave in our hearts the inscription and memory of our Lord's passion." He relates the term *Miktam* to "humility," "purity," "perfection," all expressive of the character of our Savior, whom he identifies as the subject of the whole psalm. He bases this upon the apostolic statement of Acts 2:29-33.

Jerome interprets "guard me" or "keep me safe" as referring to Christ's body, the church, which needs protection against the evil powers that beset his people. But when the psalmist states, "'you are my Lord,' as the universal 'I AM,' who created all-things," he also sees him become "the Lord of his holy people, saying 'I AM the God of Abraham, Isaac, and Jacob,' so you are especially mine." Jerome conjoins the uniquely universal Lordship of *I AM* with being also his personal lord. All good stems from this relationship, for "my good does not exist without you," and, reciting Psalm 127:1, "Unless the Lord has built the house, those who build it labor in vain. Unless the Lord guards the city, those who guard it keep watch in vain." "The saints or holy ones, who are in the land," he identifies as the church. The church, however, is in the course of transformation, for once they were those foolish ones "who ran after other gods," but now "they have been converted to the faith of Christ." But we need to know our weaknesses apart from God in order to seek his help all the more. "No longer then will we continue in the old covenant of bloody sacrifices but seek after the new covenant." The response of God is not to recall their old names, given be-

6. Theodore of Mopsuestia, *Commentary on Psalms 1–81*, p. 181.

7. Saint Augustine, *Expositions of the Psalms*, vol. 1, trans. Maria Boulding, O.S.B. (Hyde Park, NY: New City Press, 2000), p. 182.

fore baptism, but "the new names, as Simon I shall make Peter, and as the sons of Zebedee will become the sons of thunder to entrust the sublime mysteries of my gospel."

Jerome sees Christ depicted from verse 5 onwards, as both Priest and King. As the sons of Levi were told, "'You will not have an inheritance among the sons of Israel, since I am your share,' says the Lord" (Num. 18:20), "So Lord, you have assigned me my portion." The Son has his inheritance in his relationship with the Father. Yet "he emptied himself" in his humanity, and the Father has now restored "his inheritance" in his deity. "Just as our food and drink is our Savior — since we eat His flesh and drink his cup — so the Father is the food and drink of that human who was assumed by the Savior, i.e. one common divinity with God the Father, while the Savior has received a beautiful inheritance in the saints."

To avoid "the madness of the Arian heresy," Jerome carefully does not state that Jesus received wisdom from God which he had not possessed before. Rather he quotes Proverbs 8:12ff. to indicate Wisdom was God's companion even at the creation. The assertion of Psalm 16:7, "deep into the night my heart has rebuked me," Jerome finds as a unique statement, never made "by any one of the philosophers, nor rhetoricians, nor poets, nor physicians themselves, as referring to the seat of understanding."[8] Jerome applies this intimacy of divine wisdom which Christ always possessed as never leaving him when he took on human flesh, even in the dark night of his Passion. Likewise Christ remained sinless throughout his human condition, "not because the one is God and the other is Man; but because the Son of Man and the Son of God are one and the same." The psalmist states: "because God is at my right hand I will not be moved/shaken" (v. 8). When the believer "sets God always before him," the "right hand" of dignity and authority is where God always is present, for "the length of eternity and the years of life [are] in her right hand" (Prov. 3:16). "This then is the reason for joy and exultation . . . for the Lord who endured the death of the cross . . . stands at my right hand," and what is expressive of "glory" is what has been fully accomplished. Just as the glory of the athlete is courage, or the glory of a physician is his healing care, so the glory of the rhetorician lies in the disciplined use of the tongue: "my tongue exulted." "Furthermore, my flesh also will rest in hope. Because you will not abandon my soul in the underworld, nor will you allow your holy one

8. The Latin *renes* actually refers to the kidneys and is sometimes translated as "reins" (see Ps. 139:13). It is used as a superlative as it states in Psalm 7:9, "O God, who searches the heart and soul" *(corda et renes)*, to suggest the heart is mysterious enough, but the most secret part of the heart is the *renes*.

to see decay" (vv. 9-10). Jerome notes "the Lord had both flesh and soul: flesh that was placed in the tomb and soul that descended to the dead. . . . Certainly, with the Savior dead and past suffering, that flesh was placed in the tomb which had also been living; therefore, that very flesh rose again, which had lain lifeless and dead in the tomb. If, however, the same flesh rose again, how do certain people argue that a spiritual, so to speak, and a great and non-human human arose in the Lord?" Now transformed and glorified, the corruptible has put on incorruption, and the mortal has taken on immortality. So like the apostle Paul, Jerome finds himself forced to exclaim, "O the depths of the riches, wisdom, and knowledge of God: how inscrutable his judgments and unsearchable his paths!"

Jerome identifies the statement of verse 11, "'you have made known to me the paths of life,' as the manifestation of Christ's resurrection, which has dramatically changed our outlook on life. As a result, we do not know anyone after the flesh" (Rom. 11:33), for we now have a new state of being. "Joy" is the outcome of such a new life: "You fill me with joy with your presence; delights at your right hand which will never end."

Cassiodorus (485-580) expands on the twofold ways Christ speaks to the Father throughout the psalm. The first expresses his human form, as putting all his trust in him. "By this he does not in any sense lessen his divinity, but reflects on the nature of his humanity." The second expresses his divine form, as giving thanks to the Father that he now sits at God's right hand, having overcome the evil in the world, including his conquest of death, by his resurrection. The two natures of Christ are thus finely balanced, in his human weakness dependent upon the Father, and in his exaltation beyond the tyranny of hell. As a polemic against the Pelagians, he sees the emphasis is placed upon divine grace, causing the Son to rejoice. As Jerome opposed the Apollinarians, so too Cassiodorus reflects on them in verse 10: "Where are the misguided Apollinarians who say that the Lord Christ had not a rational soul? See how he himself cries out and gives thanks to the Father because his soul was not in the usual way abandoned in hell, but is glorified by swift resurrection and has passed to the kingdom of heaven."[9] Cassiodorus concludes joyously, with the immensity of the gift of salvation this psalm offers for our instruction. "It gives us confidence in sufferings and promises eternal glory in hope, so that through this teaching of our future happiness we do not fear the hardships of the present."[10]

9. Cassiodorus, *Explanation of the Psalms,* in P. G. Walsh, trans. and ed., *Ancient Christian Writers,* vol. 1 (New York and Mahwah, NJ: Paulist Press, 1990), p. 165.

10. Cassiodorus, *Explanation of the Psalms,* vol. 1, p. 167.

The *Utrecht Psalter* (c. 820-35), commissioned by Ebbo, the archbishop of Rheims, has 166 ink and pen drawings to illustrate each psalm. The text is Jerome's Gallican Psalter, and the drawing to illustrate Psalm 16:10 depicts the resurrection with three women approaching Christ's tomb, and with Christ drawing Adam and Eve out of hell. It expresses the central character of the resurrection in popular devotion.

Rupert of Deutz (c. 1075-1130) reflects the same interpretation three centuries later. For him Psalm 16 is "a recapitulation of what is foundational to the Christian faith." The "inheritance" of verse 6 implies the first state of Adam before the Fall, which by redemption has now been restored to those made righteous. With reference to verse 10a, he adds "plainly by these words in the passion he treats of the resurrection and the eternal reward — so that he may deserve to obtain all of which he in the form of a servant prays to God the Father."[11]

Geroch of Reichersberg (1093-1169), as we have already seen, gives fresh, original insights in his commentaries. Here he melds Psalm 8 with Psalm 16, and both with Johannine Christology.[12] He has Christ praying to the Father, "preserve me," not for his own sake but for the sake of his disciples, "those whom you have given me, and also for those who are going to believe in me through their word" (John 17:6, 20). In his warmly devotional meditation, Geroch marvels with the psalmist, "He [Christ] has made all my desires wonderful in these my saints who have denied their own desires" (v. 3). With the Lord as one's inheritance, with the Son exalted on the cross, this has become a great redemptive inheritance indeed (v. 5). But the Lord's own inheritance is hereditary, as the divine Son of the Father, though Arius tried to obscure it. But through the death-resurrection, "this has been restored [to the Son] through the Passion."[13] Like other commentators before him, Geroch believes the soul of Christ entered *Hades/Sheol,* while his body lay in the grave, as the counter of verse 10, "you will not leave my soul in hell." But he then links this with the theme of *totus Christi,* to affirm, neither was the thief on the cross left in *Hades,* but rescued into paradise. "Because of this the holy Evangelist calls the following day of the Sabbath the great day of the Sabbath; for the faithful souls freed from hell were celebrating a great Sabbath rest with the soul of Christ — the soul of the robber associated with theirs through the power of the Lord's Pas-

11. Rupert of Deutz, *De sancta Trinitate et operibus eius,* in Hrabanus Haack, ed., *Corpus Christianorum Continuo Christianorum Continuo Mediaevalis* (Turnhout: Brepols, 1972), vol. 22, p. 1347.

12. Geroch of Reichersberg, *Commentarius aureus in psalmos et cantica ferialia* (PL 193-94).

13. Geroch of Reichersberg, *Commentarius,* p. 838A.

sion."[14] To Geroch, "the paths of life" were made known to the psalmist and indeed to Christ "through the Resurrection and the Ascension, and through the Ascension to your [Christ's] co-sitting at your [the Father's] right hand."[15] Geroch must be rated as one of the finest commentators within the tradition of "monastic theology." He concludes with a prayer that summarizes his commentary: "Glory to the eternal Father, who restores the eminent inheritance to his Son, and fills him with joy. Glory to the Son, who is filled with joy not only in himself but also in his members. Glory to the Holy Spirit, who is this very everlasting joy by which Christ is filled, the Head without measure, and the members with measure, namely, 'according to the measure of the giving of Christ'" (Eph. 4:7).

In sharp contrast, **Peter Lombard** (1100-1160) writes tersely in a series of glossia as lecture notes, within the new model of the secular schools. Hence he quotes his authorities frequently, giving the double meaning of the psalm, as expressed by the psalmist, and as expressed by Christ. His desires are made wonderful by his dying and rising again, even though his adversities have been manifold in the process. The "inheritance" has also a double meaning. The Fall occasioned the loss of our inheritance, but the redemptive work of Christ redeemed it for us. The inheritance is also realized in the glorification of Christ after his earthly life. But the bias is towards interpreting the text as the experiences of the Christian, rather than of the psalmist or of Christ.

Thomas Aquinas (1225-74) delivered his pastoral meditations on Psalms 1–54, at the end of his life (1272-73).[16] They reflect a new spiritual depth to his previous writings. Familiar with all three versions of Jerome's texts, they are based on the Vulgate (i.e., the LXX Iuxta LXX or Gallican Psalter), because it was long used liturgically, even though Thomas is aware the Hebrew version is more accurate. Since the age of five, when he first learnt the psalms by heart in the Benedictine monastery at Monte Cassino,[17] his prayerful and meditative reflections are framed within the fourfold use of *lectio divina* — perhaps at its climax in his usage of this genre — which he then teaches the reader/audience to use with him.[18]

14. Geroch of Reichersberg, *Commentarius,* p. 839D.

15. Geroch of Reichersberg, *Commentarius,* p. 840C.

16. The oldest manuscript of Aquinas's commentary on Psalms 1–51, dating from the thirteenth century, was destroyed by fire in Naples in 1943, leaving only four others of later date. The text we have used is a modern French edition, by Jean-Eric Stroobant de Saint-Eloy and Mark D. Jordan, *Commentaire sur les Psaumes* (Paris: Les Editions du Cerf, 1996), pp. 167-74.

17. *Commentaire sur les Psaumes,* p. 15.

18. Suggestively, he calls his collection "*Super Psalmos,*" signifying he can only be humbly apprehensive, with no claim to being comprehensive of their depths.

As a literal approach, he begins with a précis/translation of the text. He suggests the title *"miktam"* acknowledges it is "from David himself." "But because David represents also the person of Christ, born as a human in his descent, these human features of David, are also said of Christ"; this is claimed by the authority of the apostle Peter in Acts 2:25. He notes that Jerome had titled the psalm, "A psalm of David for the humble and the poor in heart," which David was, and which also prefigured our Lord. The psalm is divided into two parts, observes Thomas. The first part, verses 1-4, speaks of David (or of Christ), as David (or Christ) relates first to God, then to the saints, and finally to their enemies. As for his relationship to God, like Geroch he renders the psalmist's trust in God with the Johannine representation of the intimacy between the Father and Son (John 17:11). As for his relationship to the saints (v. 3), Aquinas relates it to Christ's entering this world, not to do his own will but the will of him who sent him (John 6:38). The psalmist then, in verse 4, describes his negative relations with his enemies, in spite of whom, "where sin abounded grace did much more abound" (Rom. 5:20).

In the second half of the psalm, from verse 5 onwards, Thomas suggests the psalmist explains why he trusts only in God: for God is both his heritage and his full satisfaction. "Here in this world humans seek possessions that will make them happy, but for him [the psalmist] his possession is God . . . so all passions are directed towards God." Thus he is given a double benefit: first, he is endowed with blessings (vv. 5-6), and second, his passions are guarded from the evil powers (vv. 7-8). Having then received these double blessings, the psalmist enumerates the benefits he can also hope to receive beyond death (vv. 9-10). For in the light of the resurrection, he has hope for a bodily renewal of immortal life, and his soul can anticipate fullness of wisdom in seeing the full plenitude of God, whereas now in the flesh we have only partial vision. In that eternal future there will be fullness of joy.

Thomas's sparing use of allegory is distinctive, for his mind is saturated instead with the Scriptures.[19]

Denys the Carthusian (died 1471), while greatly influenced by the mystical writings of Pseudo-Dionysius, also writes some lovely devotional Biblical commentaries, including one on the Psalms. He contributes as a leader of the *Devotio Moderna,* which had produced such classics as Thomas à Kempis's *Imitation of Christ* and Ludolph of Saxony's *Life of Christ.* Pivotal for him is to interpret the Scriptures prophetically, reflecting on four kinds of prophecy: predestination, the threat of judgment, promise, and foreknow-

19. Identifiable in this short meditative commentary, there are at least thirty-five direct Scriptural quotations: eighteen from the New Testament, eleven from the Psalms.

ledge of events.[20] In this regard David is esteemed as the most excellent prophet, for he anticipates the mysteries of Christ most clearly and fully, including his prophecies in Psalm 16. Following Augustine, Denys interprets all the Psalter as being authored by David, while he acknowledges that Jerome, Hilary, Chrysostom, and Nicholas of Lyra all accept multiple authorship.[21]

II. Commentaries of the Reformers

We refer to Martin Luther in other contexts,[22] so we pass over him to focus on his colleague at Wittenberg, **Philipp Melanchthon** (1497-1560), a humanist educator, with inconsistent, irenic traits. He is a "modern commentator" in the sense that he appreciates the need to have critical exegesis, so he admits that his Hebrew is defective and his interpretation is not definitive. He begins by stating "this psalm is didaskalikos, a prophecy . . . a narration concerning the resurrection of the Messiah, and Christ principally should be understood to speak, even if for this reason it behooves the Church both to suffer for Christ's sake and be raised again through Christ." Then he divides the psalm into four parts: "the Petition of Christ to be preserved; the Application of the passion; the Narration of the Resurrection; and the End of the narration, that the eternal Church gathered would celebrate God." Pastorally, he asks in reference to verse 3, "'Do you suffer for a purpose?' If it is for the saints, then there are meaning and comfort. But the defenders of idols, even when they are called bishops and priests, as well as Jews and pagans, will accumulate sorrows unto themselves. Christ our Priest does not pray for them, but in John 17 he prays "for those who believe in me through their word" (John 17:20). This is an echo of what we first heard in Geroch of Reichersberg. His commentary is short and succinct in its clarity.

John Calvin (1509-64) believes profoundly in congregational participation, so his first use of the Psalms is to nurture lay piety in *sola scriptura* by singing the psalms. In 1539, he publishes his first collection of twenty-two metrical psalms, assisted by a French poet, Clément Marot. Then later, as we have seen, he preaches regularly on the Psalms and from this ministry composed his commentary; it is first translated into English in 1571. He proceeds on the prin-

20. Denys the Carthusian, *D. Dionysii insigne opus commentariorum, in psalmos omnes Davidicos*, in *Doctoris Ecstatici D. Dionysii Cartusiani Opera* (Monstrolii: Typis Cartusiae S. de Pratis, 1898), vol. 5, pp. 389-90.

21. Denys the Carthusian, *D. Dionysii insigne opus commentariorum*, p. 483.

22. See pp. 60-61.

ciple laid down by Melanchthon: "Scripture cannot be understood theologically, unless it is first understood grammatically."[23]

Calvin's great aversion to allegorical interpretation leads him to be perhaps too sparing in his use of Christology in the psalms. In Psalm 16, he refers wholly within the context of David, as if he was following Jewish commentators. He is inclined to translate "*miktam* of David" as "some kind of musical tune," rejecting the long allegorical tradition on this title. He names none of the commentaries of the Fathers, but interprets the Hebrew text with critical comments, as if he is doing his study completely afresh.

Calvin sees the psalm as a prayer of the psalmist's trust in God. This is what makes the psalmist firm and unmovable, for he can bestow nothing upon God, and can only use soliloquy with his own soul to encourage himself more effectually in his absolute trust in God. By calling him uniquely "Lord," the psalmist acknowledges he is wholly bound to him. All-sufficiency lies in God, nowhere else. It is impossible for humans to claim any merit of their own, so we must lay aside all presumption when we come to him. Any good deeds we are enabled to do only magnify and praise God. Being "on the earth" implies that here in this world, wicked though it is, God is being praised and acknowledged. But such concord with the saints needs us to have nothing to do with the erring and impure; such deserve only God's judgment.

In verse 5, the psalmist shows further why he separates himself from idolaters. They cannot trust God for they do not know him, whereas David by calling God "the portion of his lot" is fully satisfied with God alone. This conviction shared with David frees us from the world, to provide us with complete rest of soul. Such trust dwells most intimately within the believer, growing the more we experience God in our lives, as "under his tuition." In verse 9 the psalmist commends the inestimable fruit of faith, as joyful indeed, most intimately within the heart, but publicly expressed also by the lips. In verse 10, Calvin notes that God in delivering his people has often prolonged their life, yet eventually the sentence of Adam is upon all humanity: "Dust thou art, and unto dust shalt thou return" (Gen. 3:19). This did not prevent David from seeing prophetically that Christ would be exempted, and by rising again would provide immortality to all his people. So Peter and Paul contend that this is what has happened; Christ was wholly exempted from the grave and its corruption. "To know the path of life" (v. 11) is the prospect of those who put their trust in Christ; "fullness of joy" lies both in the face of God and in those who behold him, infinitely blessed and satisfied. "David therefore testifies that true and

23. John Calvin, *Commentary on the Book of Psalms,* trans. Rev. James Anderson (Edinburgh: Calvin Translation Society, 1895), vol. 1, p. vii.

solid joy in which the minds of men may rest will never be found anywhere else but in God; and that therefore, none but the faithful, who are contented with his grace alone, can be truly and perfectly happy."[24]

III. Effects of Historical Critical Commentary

"The plain meaning," for which Calvin has probably set the highest standard of commentary, could only be sustained by the deep sense Calvin had of the Holy Spirit's illuminating and guiding the commentator. But when the "plain meaning" became the humanistic rendering of a rationalistic culture as the seventeenth century moved towards the Age of Enlightenment, then "plain" degenerated to become disbelieving, skeptical, and destructive of the authority of Scripture, as we traced in chapter 3. We select a few examples.

George Horne (1730-92), bishop of Norwich and previous President of Magdalen College, Oxford, is an early mild example of the cultural change. His commentary is titled: "A Commentary of the Psalms; in which their literal or historical sense, as they relate to King David and the people of Israel, is illustrated; and their application to Messiah, to the Church, and to individuals thereof, is pointed out; with a view to render the use of the Psalter pleasing and profitable to all orders and degrees of Christians."[25] He argues that, unique to the Holy Scriptures as expressive of the Sovereign Lord of History, they have a double sense, with a "spiritual sense" that differs from the historical data. The Hebrew scholar Bishop Lowth had called this "Mystical allegory," in which "the literal and historical sense is only a kind of vehicle for the spiritual sense."[26] Horne gives one of the earliest classifications of the Psalms.[27] He sees that what is styled "as the Prophetical, Evangelical, Mystical, or Spiritual sense" is what separates a Jewish from a Christian interpretation, yet "the spiritual interpretation of Scripture like all good things is liable to abuse." The first test he uses is to list all the psalms cited and interpreted by the New Testament apostles, as united in their prophetic intent. Some fifty psalms can thus be understood from within their New Testament reinterpretation. The problem begins when the remainder are given a second or "spiri-

24. Calvin, *Commentary on the Book of Psalms,* p. 234.

25. George Horne, *A Commentary on the Book of Psalms* (London: Thomas Tegg, 1824).

26. Horne, *A Commentary on the Book of Psalms,* p. xli.

27. His six categories are: Prayers (of which there are eight types); Thanksgiving (two types); Praise and Adoration (two types); Instructive psalms (five types); Psalms distinctly prophetic; and Historical psalms. He places Psalm 16, with 2, 22, 40, 45, 72, 87, 110, and 118, as "prophetic" psalms.

tual sense," and where Horne speaks of them as being "allegorical" and never understands the role of Biblical "typology." Then "spiritual allegory" becomes confused with "literary allegory," and the subjective imagination plays its tricks. His bias is towards the humanist Erasmus as the authority of the Reformation, not Calvin. Also significant, he accepts the term "Nature," and makes no reference to "Creation."

Following his own principles, Horne acknowledges in his introduction that the speaker of Psalm 16 is identified by the apostles in Acts 2:25 and 13:35 to be Christ himself. "First there is a prayer for support (v. 1); then a declaration of love to the saints (vv. 2, 3); followed by a protestation against idolaters (v. 4); acts of love, joy and confidence in Jehovah are expressed (vv. 5-8); and verses 9-11 close with hope in an approaching resurrection and glorification."[28] What is missing is the specificity of the resurrection as a historic event of divine intervention. Instead "it was part of the covenant of grace, and promised by the mouth of God's prophets, that after the death of the Messiah, his animal frame should not continue like other men, in the grave, nor should corruption be permitted to seize on the body, by which all others were to be raised to incorruption and immortality."[29] For the true David is both Christ and the contemporary idealized Christian. In consequence the historicity of Jesus Christ is becoming lost. He accepts the Platonic notion of the immortality of the soul in a curious statement: "Although our mortal part must see corruption, yet it shall not finally be left under the power of the enemy, but shall be raised again, and reunited to its old companion the soul, which exists meanwhile in secret and undiscerned regions there waiting for the day when its Redeemer shall triumph over corruption, in his mystical, as he hath already done in his natural body. As members of Christ, this same promise and assurance is so for us."[30] David's confidence that God would not leave his soul in Hades has now become Horne's assurance that because our immortal soul will be reunited with our bodies, death will not have the final action with us. The uniqueness of the Messianic "Holy One" has also been lost, as reference to Christ himself, and is now merged with his "mystical body," the church. The door is now open to the effects of subsequent historical criticism, to deny the historical reality of Christ's own resurrection.

One way in which this occurred is by assuming there is a single *persona* in verse 10, who uses poetic repetition to express the same thing: "being held in Sheol," and "to see corruption." **Ernst Wilhelm Hengstenberg** (1802-69), who

28. Horne, *A Commentary on the Book of Psalms,* p. 77.
29. Horne, *A Commentary on the Book of Psalms,* p. 81.
30. Horne, *A Commentary on the Book of Psalms,* p. 81.

defended Lutheran orthodoxy, upheld the Messianic nature of the psalm, and thought he was supporting Peter's use of the psalm. Yet he denies that for verse 9, "dwelling secure or in hope" has any reference to the period after death. "You will not see the grave," he interprets as saying that beyond death the Christian has hope in Christ. David then, as a believer, experiences victory over death, as a member of Christ. But "the victory" is vaguely defined.

Another German conservative scholar, **Franz Julius Delitzsch** (1813-90), takes a more open position on the Hebrew text, translating *Sheol* and "the pit" as ambiguous terms. For him, David was hoping not to come under the ultimate power of death in verse 9, but he accepts the interpretation of the apostles that the twofold aspect of verse 10 applies only to Christ, as in Acts 2:31. The "Holy One" he interprets as "the mystic relation" that the *ḥsyd* "the devoted one") had with Yahweh. It is comparable to the seed promised in the covenant to David, as that which "Christ gives back to his Church." Here at the end of his commentary, Delitzsch is tacitly admitting this rendering does not come from the grammatical sense of the text.

Another "conservative," **J. J. S. Perowne** (1823-1904), suggests the psalm was composed by David while in the wilderness of Ziph (1 Sam. 26:19), inspired in the latter part of the psalm to be prophetic of Christ, as Peter attests.[31] But Perowne interprets *Sheol* in verse 10 as "the unseen world," not hell, as Luther had interpreted, but simply David's confidence that he would not be left destitute by God, and so "given over" to whatever threat he faced, even the physical threats of his enemies. As for the "Holy One," Perowne likewise dilutes its Messianic distinctive to "Thy pious" or "godly one," a human category.[32] But when applied to Christ, these verses are deepened by the resurrection of Christ to have another meaning. Implicit for Perowne is that the primary referent is David, with a secondary Messianic meaning in the background. So he sees a single persona in verse 10, with a shadowy double meaning in the text. His ambiguity leaves the reader to decide whether the psalm has primarily reference to the hope of the church or else directly to the resurrection of Christ.

S. R. Driver (1846-1914) now denies any Messianic prophecy in Psalm 16. "The Psalmist does not speak explicitly of a future life, for verse 11 does not refer to it at all," he affirms, "but he expresses the hope of superiority over death grounded on the close personal relation in which he himself stands towards God, and which he cannot believe will be interrupted by death. . . . The Psalm is

31. J. J. Stewart Perowne, *The Book of Psalms* (Grand Rapids: Zondervan, reprint 1966), vol. 1, p. 190.

32. Perowne, *The Book of Psalms*, p. 195.

thus 'Messianic,' not in being a prediction of Christ's resurrection . . . but in expressing an ideal . . . a hope of superiority to death . . . which transcended experience, and was fully realized by Christ. Even by him, however, it was not realized literally, but only in substance; for Christ did in the literal sense of the words, 'see the pit.'" Were the apostles wrong then in their interpretation of the Psalm? Yes, argues Driver, because of their use of the mistranslations of the Septuagint ("shall dwell in hope," "wilt not leave my soul in Hades," and "to see corruption"). The apostles were using arguments cogent to their contemporaries, which no longer are so for modern commentators. He concludes: "The Psalm cannot be appealed to, in the way in which they [i.e., the apostles] appealed to it, as a proof of the resurrection of Christ."[33]

Following Driver, many modern commentators have either argued the apostles were wrong in their interpretation of verses 9-11 or else have ignored the apostolic use of the Psalm and instead have interpreted it as a message of comfort to be unafraid of death, with no clear doctrine of Christian resurrection. Artur Weiser actually commends the inner polemic of the psalmist for keeping the idea of resurrection muted because of the pagan mythologies of (a) dying and rising god(s).[34] **John Goldingay** (born 1928) illustrates the increasing loss of transcendence in contemporary "western" Christianity, by suggesting that among the psalm's numerous "readings," we should opt for its original meaning, which, according to his interpretation, would cut us off from all history of its usage by the early church and later in order to settle upon its original immanent meaning.[35] Yet even the original was facing the transcendence of death. Others, like Craig Broyles,[36] wholly ignore the apostolic references to the psalm. While Samuel Terrien (born 1911) assures us that the hope of the psalmist was that "As the beloved of Yahweh, he will never see the lower depths of the underworld . . . [o]n account of the Presence."[37] But he gives no reference to the New Testament doctrine of the Resurrection of Christ.

33. S. R. Driver, "The Method of Studying the Psalter," *Expositor* 10 (1910, 7th series): 35-37.

34. A. Weiser, *The Psalms: A Commentary,* trans. Herbert Hartwell (Philadelphia: Westminster Press, 1962), p. 177.

35. John Goldingay, *Psalms,* vol. 1 (Grand Rapids: Baker Academic, 2006), p. 234.

36. Craig C. Broyles, *Psalms,* in New International Biblical Commentary (Peabody, MA: Hendrickson, 1999), p. 97.

37. Samuel Terrien, *The Psalms: Strophic Structure and Theological Commentary* (Grand Rapids and Cambridge: Eerdmans, 2003), p. 178.

Part II. Voice of the Psalmist: Translation

A *miktam* of David.[38]

1 Keep me safe,[39] El,
because I take[40] refuge in you.
2 I say[41] to *I AM,* "You are the Lord;[42]
I have no good thing[43] apart from you."[44]
3 As for[45] the holy ones in the Land,[46] they,

38. Commentators complain that the text is often uncertain. In truth, the MT makes good sense, assuming David is adopting a Canaanite psalm.

39. In spite of the *methegh* the vowel is /o/ ("keep me safe"), not /ā/ ("you have kept me safe"), because it is followed by *shewa* (see GKC, 9v, 48i, n).

40. Construing the suffix conjugation as a persistent (present) perfective (*IBHS,* pp. 487f., P. 30.5.1c).

41. Reading with many mss. and with the ancient versions 1st com. sing. — perhaps written defectively as in Phoenician (see also *nḥlt* [v. 6] and cf. *mnt* [v. 5]) — and construing the suffix conjugation as an instantaneous perfective (*IBHS,* p. 488, P. 30.5.1d). Possibly, the apparently 2nd fem. sing. implies an ellipsis of *nep̱eš,* so that David is dialoguing with himself ("you, my soul, say[s]"; so Targ., KJV, ASV; cf. Ps. 42:5 and Lam. 3:24 without ellipsis). The ellipsis, however, is unlikely, and if he is dialoguing with somebody else, addressing them as "you," the text has to be reinterpreted differently from its normal meaning in Hebrew.

42. LXX's error in reading *Kurios mou* ("my Lord") may be due to reading *ʾᵃdōnay* instead of MT's *ʾᵃdōnāy,* an epithet meaning "the Lord of all" (*IBHS,* pp. 123f., P. 7.4.3e,f). Apparently Jerome *(Dominus meus)* and the many English versions that read "my lord" make no distinction in the forms. Or do they repoint the text? The long form */āy/* with the *munaḥ* cannot be pausal.

43. A gloss of *ṭôbî* construes the pronominal suffix as a genitive of advantage (*IBHS,* p. 147, P. 9.5.2e): "good thing to/for me."

44. Perhaps polysemic *ʿal* signifies here "over against [you]," as in Exodus 20:3 (*IBHS,* p. 218, P. 11.2.13e): "would the pious think of something as 'good' that stood opposed to God?" LXX reads *hoti tōn agathōn ou chreian exeis* ("you have no need of my goodness"), either interpreting *ʿal* in the sense of "for the sake" as in Psalm 105:14 (cf. 45:4[5]; 79:9; literally, "my good is not for your sake") or having read [*kî*?] *ṭôbatî bᵉlîyal lᵉkā* ("my goodness is worthless to you," see S. Mowinckel, "Zu Ps 16, 2-4," *TLZ* 82 [1957]: 649-54). Some (cf. *BHS*) emend the text to read: *ṭôbî: bᵉlîyal kol qᵉdôšîm . . . hēmâ:* "I say to *I AM:* 'Lord, you are my good. As for the gods (literally, "holy things") in the land, they are worthless.'" Such a radical emendation, also entailing other emendations in verse 3b, is unwarranted. MT, though difficult, is sensible, and the emendation invests *qᵉdôšîm* with an otherwise unattested use in the Biblical Hebrew. Jerome reads *bene mihi non est sine te,* perhaps having read *ṭôbî bal bilᵉyadᵉkā* ("my well-being is not without you"). This seems to be the best interpretation.

45. Construing the substantive introduced by *lamedh* to function as a casus pendens (GKC, 143e, p. 458).

46. Interpreting *ʾereṣ* as the land of Israel. Or, "on earth."

— indeed the noble people[47] — are those in whom is all my delight.[48]

4 Their pains[49] will increase[50] who[51] have acquired[52] another god.[53]
I will not pour out[54] to them[55] libations of blood,
or take up their names on my lips.

5 *I AM*, my allotted portion[56] and my cup,[57]
you hold[58] my lot.

6 The boundary lines have fallen for me in pleasant places;
indeed, the inheritance[59] is beautiful[60] to[61] me.

47. Construing *waw* as epexegetical and translated as an emphatic.

48. Literally, "noble ones of my delight is in them." The construct governs the independent nominal clause (GKC, 130d, p. 422). LXX, probably not understanding the exceptional Hebrew, renders as *tois hagiois tois en tę̄ gę̄ autou ethaumastōse panta ta thelēmata autou en autois* ("on behalf of the saints in his lands, he magnifies his pleasure in them"), reading and/or interpreting *'arṣô*, not *'areṣ; hû'*, not *hēmâ; yadîr*, not *'addîrê;* and *ḥepṣô*, not *ḥepṣî.*

49. For masculine predicate with feminine subject see GKC, 145p, p. 465. Syr. Targ. read *yarbîm* (Hiphil, "they multiply"), not *yirbû* (Qal), and so avoided the grammatical disagreement in gender.

50. Construed as a simple future non-perfective (*IBHS*, p. 512, P. 31.6.2b).

51. Literally, "Their pains . . . who have acquired. . . . The retrospective pronoun is the subject of the asyndetic relative clause and is contained in the verb *mhrw* (GKC, 155f, p. 486).

52. Construed as a present perfect perfective (*IBHS*, p. 490, P. 30/5/2b) of II *mhr* (*HALOT*, 2.554; cf. Ps. 106:20; Jer. 2:11).

53. *'aḥēr* ("another") functions as an adjectival substantive for "another god" (see BDB, p. 29, s.v. I. *'aḥēr*).

54. Construed as a non-perfective of obligation (*IBHS*, p. 508, P. 31.4g).

55. The pronominal suffix probably refers to the nearest antecedent in v. 4A, "other gods"; "their names" probably refers to the same antecedent. If so, the pronominal suffix of *niskêhem* is a genitive of the mediated object, not a genitive of agency or subject genitive (*IBHS*, pp. 146f., P. 5.2.b; pp. 143f., PP. 9.5.1b, e).

56. Literally, "the portion of my tract of territory," a genitive of species (*IBHS*, p. 152, P. 9.5.3g). Dahood emends *m^enot* to *mānîtâ* "you apportioned," explaining *mnt* as another example of defective Phoenician spelling, not understood by the Masoretes.

57. Most EVV construe it as a nominal clause: "*I AM* is . . . my cup." The change to second person in the middle of a verse, however, is improbable. More probably, the whole verse is addressed to *I AM* so that grammatically "my allotted portion and my cup" is in apposition to *I AM* (so also NAB).

58. *Tômîk,* an anomaly, is a bi-form of *tômēk* (GKC, 50e, p. 136). Though the form could be the *Hiphil* prefix conjugation of *ymk,* that lexeme is unattested in Biblical Hebrew. Dahood (*Psalms 1–50* [AB; New York: Doubleday, 1965]) suggests plausibly *ymk* is a bi-form of *mmk* ("to sink," "to fall") and so — less plausibly — means "to cast [the lot]."

59. Anomalous *naḥ^alāt* may be a feminine bi-form of *naḥ^alâ,* or to be read with the LXX as *naḥ^alātî* ("my inheritance"; cf. GKC, 50g, p. 223), or a defectively written Phoenician form.

60. Construing the *hapax šāpar* as stative (*IBHS*, P. 22.2.2, pp. 364f.).

61. *'al* expresses the subject's psychological state of feeling (*IBHS*, P. 11.2.13c, p. 217).

7 I will bless[62] *I AM,* who counsels[63] me;
indeed, at[64] night[65] my conscience[66] instructs[67] me.
8 I place *I AM* always before me.
Because he is[68] at[69] my right hand, I will[70] not be toppled.
9 Therefore my heart is glad and my liver[71] rejoices;[72]
indeed, my body rests[73] secure,
10 because you will not abandon me to the grave,
nor will you allow[74] your devoted one[75] to see corruption.[76]

62. Construed as a non-perfective of obligation (*IBHS,* p. 506, P. 31.4g).

63. See n. 101.

64. Adverbial accusative of time (*IBHS,* p. 171, P. 10.2.2c).

65. Form is plural (cf. "night seasons," AV, ASV, ESV).

66. Literally, "kidneys."

67. See n. 40.

68. The personal pronoun may be omitted in Biblical Hebrew (GKC, 116s, p. 360).

69. Spatial *min* to designate the direction where someone/thing is located (*IBHS,* p. 212, P. 11.2.11b).

70. Construing the non-perfective as representing a real future situation that arises as a consequence of some other situation (*IBHS,* p. 511, P. 31.6.2a). It could be a non-perfective of capability ("I cannot be moved," *IBHS,* p. 507, P. 31.4c).

71. LXX *(hē glōssa mou),* followed by Vulgate *(lingua mea),* NLT ("mouth") and TNIV, apparently understood *kāḇôḏ* (trad. "glory") as a metonymy of effect for David's "tongue" that glorifies God. This is possible (cf. Ps. 30:12; Acts 2:26; James 3:5-9) but questionable in Psalm 57:8, where TNIV glosses it "soul." The NJB consistently translates it as "soul" both in Psalm 16:9 and 57:8. *TaNaK,* followed by ESV, renders "my whole being," perhaps over-stretching the sense of *kāḇôḏ* from "wealth and respect" to "whole being," or, more probably, thinking "my glory" is a metonymy for the king's whole impressive being. But this is too questionable a jump, especially with "to exult." The best solution is to emend the text to *kᵉbēdî* ("my liver"), supposing that when the early use of liver to designate emotions in Canaanite literature was lost, its textual tradition came to be vocalized as *kāḇôḏ.*

72. *Waw*-consecutive in present time (*IBHS,* p. 559, P. 33.3.3c).

73. More literally, "settles down," "dwells."

74. "The technical expression [found here] *ntn* + accusative + *lᵉ* means 'to allow (something) to be done'" (C. J. Labuschagne, *TLOT,* 2:785, s.v. *ntn*).

75. Heb. *ḥāsiḏ* is glossed in the LXX (cf. TNIV) as *hosios* ("holy one," so also Acts 2:27; 13:35).

76. According to G. E. Whitney ("Survey of the History of the Interpretation of Prophecy: How Interpreters Deal with Peter's Use of Psalm 16 in Acts 2," *Evangelical Theological Society* [Eastern Regional Conference, April 3, 1987, Myerstown, PA]: 15), Reinke's defense of *šḥt* meaning "decay" (against historical critics) is even more thorough than that given by P. A. Vaccari ("Salmo 16"; and "Il Salmo della Risurrezione," *La Redenzione* [Rome, 1934]: 165-90). Building on their studies, I argued in 1993 (*NIDOTTE,* 4:1113):

The nom. *šaḥat* occurs twenty-five times in the OT, always in poetry. It can be derived from the verb *šḥt,* "sink down," or from the verb *šāḥaṯ,* "to go to ruin." Noms. of the pattern

11 You will[77] make known to me the path of life;[78]
you will fill me with joy[79] in your presence,
with eternal pleasures at your right hand.[80]

Part III. Commentary

The author of this psalm of confidence, unlike the mortal's natural fear over the mystery of death, confronts that unexplored realm with hope: "Therefore my

---

šaḥaṯ derived from hollow *wāw* roots (e.g., *šwḥ*) are fem. (i.e, final *ṯ* is the fem. suff.); noms. of the latter verb are masc. (i.e., the *ṯ* is part of the root). As a result homonyms, a masc. and a fem. form, are possible. For example, *naḥat* (fem.; BDB, 629), a derivative from *nwḥ*, means "quietness/rest," but *naḥat* (masc.; BDB, 639) from *nāḥat* means "descent/descending." All the ancient versions understood *šaḥaṯ* as a homonym. No scholar denies it sometimes means "pit," but the LXX and Vulgate understood it to mean "corruption" or "decay" in Ps. 9:16; 29[30]:10; 34[35]:7; 48[49]:9[10]; 54[55]:23[24]; 102[103]:4. Sym. so understood it in Ps. 35:7; 55:23[24]; Aq. in Ps. 7:15[16]; 30:9[10]; Theod. in Job 33:22, 30. In addition to the LXX, Jerome and Syr. understood it this way in Ps. 16:10. Pope (*Job*, 1965, AB, 75), seemingly unaware of *šaḥaṯ* (masc.), recognizes that it must mean "filth" in Job 9:31 and tries to explain it as due to the netherworld's putrescent nature. A clear example, however, of masc. *šaḥaṯ* is found in Job 17:14: "If I say to . . . *(šaḥaṯ)* 'You are my father,' and to the worm (*rimmâ*, worms; fem. coll.), 'My mother,' or 'my sister'" (NRSV). K. Brugmann showed at the end of the last century that grammatical gender guided the poetic imagination in personification (cited by *IBHS*, p. 100, P. 6.3.1e). "Worm" *(rimmâ)* is fem., hence its personification by "mother" and "sister." We may confidently infer, therefore, that *šaḥaṯ*, personified as "father," is the masc. form, "decay/corruption."

Moreover, it can be established that the masc. form, "corruption," not the fem. form, "pit," is in view in Ps. 16:10 by the verb "to see" *(lir'ôṯ)*. "To see" expresses the ideas of "experiencing," "enduring," "proving," and the like, and takes for its object a nom. of *state* of the soul or of the body; e.g., to see death (Ps. 89:48 [49]), to see trouble/evil (90:15; Jer. 44:17), to see sorrow (Jer. 20:18), to see famine (5:12), to see affliction (Lam. 3:1). On the contrary, when indicating the idea of *place* (e.g., pit, grave, Sheol, gates of death, etc.), the Hebrew authors use a verb of motion; e.g., to descend (Job 21:13), to fall (Ps. 7:15 [16]; 57:6). The expression "to go down to the pit" occurs four times in the Psalter; nine times in Ezek.; cf. Prov. 1:12; Isa. 38:18. Having demonstrated that the masc. *šaḥaṯ* "decay" exists and that the verb [dictates this meaning] in Ps. 16:10, I conclude the ancient versions, not modern lexicographers, have the better of the argument, and so does the NT [see below IV. Conclusion].

77. Theologically *tôdîʿēnî* could be construed as a present progressive non-perfective (*IBHS*, pp. 504f., P. 31.3b, "you make known to me"), but exegetically the term more probably signifies a specific future (*IBHS*, P. 31.6.2b, p. 512), because verse 10, using the prefix conjugation, 1) clearly refers to the future; 2) the context suggests a future beyond the grave; 3) "forever" in 11Bb clearly looks to the future; 4) verses 5-8, using the suffix conjugation, refer to the same blessings of instruction and of an abundant life in the present.

78. Genitive of species, like "tree of life" (*IBHS*, p. 152, P. 9.5.3g).

79. Contruing *śᵉmāḥôt* as abstract plural (*IBHS*, pp. 120f., P. 7.4.2).

80. *Nᵉʿīmôt* is the feminine equivalent of *nᵉʿimîm* (v. 6).

heart is glad and my tongue rejoices; my body also will rest secure" (16:9). He lies himself down in death confident that God will raise him from the dead, not even allowing his body to decay.

Three approaches to the psalm's prophecy of his body's resurrection without decay have been suggested. First, for those skeptics described in the modern movement of HBC (see chapter 3) the issue is clear: interpret the psalm in such a way that it speaks of salvation from a premature death and ignore or reject the apostolic testimony of the psalm as a messianic prophecy. The second approach interprets the psalm as Bishop Horne does, as having both a historical sense that finds its fulfillment in the career of David and as having a spiritual or allegorical sense that finds its fulfillment in Jesus Christ. Two centuries later, Raymond Brown argued similarly in his highly influential 1955 doctoral dissertation. He labeled his hermeneutical principle *sensus plenior* ("fuller sense"). By this Brown meant that the words of the Old Testament, not just its types (i.e., of words representing events), contained a fuller sense that added to and deepened the original author's intention. Later, Brown wisely rejected his own thesis as unworkable. Others, especially those scholars in the Roman Catholic tradition, strive to defend the *sensus plenior* interpretative principle, for it offers them a way to explain those discrepancies between the results of the so-called scientific studies and the authority of the church's traditional hermeneutic.[81] As noted in the historical survey, that approach finds increasing sympathy among those in the evangelical tradition who are opting for a polyvalence of meanings in the Biblical text.

Calvin's plain sense, which includes spiritual illumination such as the gift of faith to believe the whole counsel of God, interprets the psalm as typico-prophetic (see pp. 316-17).[82] The psalm presents a textbook example of HBC

81. See Matthew W. I. Dunn, "Raymond Brown and the *sensus plenior* Interpretation of the Bible," *Studies in Religion/Sciences Religieuses* 36, no. 3-4 (2007): 531-51.

82. The TNIV Study Bible offers — following Weiser's interpretation without noting it — only a typological interpretation of verses 9-11: "David speaks of himself and of the life he enjoys by the gracious provision and care of God. The Lord, in whom the psalmist takes refuge, wills life for him. . . . But implicit in these words of assurance . . . is the confidence that with the Lord as his refuge, even the grave cannot rob him of life. . . . If this could be said of David — and of all those godly Israelites who made David's prayer their own — how much more of David's promised Son! So Peter quotes vv. 8-11 and declares that with these words David prophesied of Christ and his resurrection." All this is good and true but what is missing is troubling: no mention of the corpse's preservation from decay — the chief point of Peter's apologia; no mention that Peter says David is speaking of Messiah, not of himself; and no mention that according to Peter, David saw this preservation of Messiah's body from decay beforehand. I say "troubling," because, like HBC, the note — though sounding as if in agreement with Peter's interpretation — in fact ignores or rejects it.

versus orthodoxy, or of a compromise between them. Let us now exegete the psalm, employing Calvin's plain sense. We already took a major step forward exegetically in note 76.

I. Introduction: Form, Structure, and Message

Here is one conceptual and structural outline of Psalm 16:[83]

I. Superscription	
II. Introduction: Petition in Peril	1
III. Body: Confidence with Praise	2-8
A. Confession of trust	2-4
1. Sole loyalty to *I AM*	2
2. Sole loyalty to people of *I AM*	3-4
a. Delight in people of *I AM*	3
b. Refusal to join apostates	4
B. Cause for trust	5-8
1. Inheritance from *I AM*	5-6
a. Inheritance of *I AM*	5
b. Inheritance of possessions	6
2. Instruction from *I AM*	7-8
a. Praise for *I AM*'s instruction	7
b. *I AM*'s presence and protection	8
IV. Conclusion: Commitment of Corpse to God	9-11
A. Confidence of God's presence in death	9-10
1. Emotions joyful for body secure	9
2. Body secure with reference to grave	10
B. Confidence of presence with God after death forevermore	11

The introduction, verse 1, contains three of the four typical motifs of a petition psalm: direct address, "El/God"; petition, "keep me safe"; and confidence, "for I trust in you." The remainder of the psalm (vv. 2-11) is a paean of trust and praise, so much so that it could be classified as a song of trust. Recall from Psalm 15 ("Literary Context") that Psalms 16 and 23 are paired: "Together these two psalms underscore faith/trust as the second essential characteristic (alongside conformity to God's law of those who bring their prayers to God)."[84]

83. Aquinas plausibly fused the last two stanzas into one, analyzing the psalm as Confession of Trust (vv. 1-4) and Reasons for Trust (vv. 5-11, see p. 314).

84. *Zondervan TNIV Study Bible* (Grand Rapids: Zondervan, 2006).

After the introduction, which serves like an introit to a Mass or to a piece of music, the psalm conceptually and structurally consists of three stanzas: Confession of trust (vv. 2-4), Cause for trust (vv. 5-8), and Commitment of dead body to God (vv. 9-11). The first and last stanzas consist of three verses each, arranged chiastically in two strophes of 1 + 2 verses and 2 + 1 verses. The second stanza consists of two quatrains of two verses each. Counting the central stanza with both the first and last stanzas, each grouping consists of seven verses, the number of perfection.[85]

The first stanza, confessing trust in *I AM*, lays the foundation for the next two. The logical particle "therefore," introducing the last stanza, signals that the poet is now ready to draw his climactic conclusion. In other words, the second stanza presents the cause to be at ease even in death. The history of interpretation has so focused on verse 10 that one might think the antithesis of the psalm is this world and the next. Rather, the antithesis is a life with God versus a life without God. Indeed, the psalm teaches that a life lived by faith in communion with God, with all its attendant benefits, will continue in the next world forever: "The Psalm is a joyous profession of faith and hope, springing from the sense of a living fellowship with Jehovah."[86] That faith and hope, according to the New Testament, is validated within history by the fulfillment of this psalm in the death, burial for three days, and resurrection of Jesus Christ.

II. Exegesis

A. Superscript

The psalm's genre is a *miktam,* whose meaning is uncertain.[87] The term occurs six times in the superscripts of petition psalms *by David* (see pp. 88-89) that celebrate the salvation of the righteous in contrast to the damnation of apostates (Psalms 56–60), as Jerome observed (see pp. 309-11). But that data is not helpful here, because other psalms by David not labeled *miktam* have these same features.[88]

85. This analysis, arrived at independently, essentially conforms to the paragraph breaks of Psalm 16 in TNIV.

86. A. F. Kirkpatrick, *The Book of Psalms,* Cambridge Bible for Schools and Colleges (Cambridge: Cambridge University Press, 1916), p. 72.

87. For a comprehensive bibliography of scholarly opinions see P. Craigie, *Psalms 1–50* (WBC; Nelson Reference & Electronics, 2004), p. 154. n. 1. Of these Craigie rightly thinks the meaning of "inscription" is best, based on the LXX (*stēlographia*), Theod. Targ.

88. John F. A. Sawyer, "An Analysis of the Context and Meaning of the Psalm-Headings," *Glasgow University Oriental Society Transactions* 22 (1970): 26-38, esp. 33.

B. Introduction v. 1

The petition is one word: *šāmᵉrēnî,* "preserve me," an ambiguous notion in English, and so glossed *keep me safe. šāmar* means "to exercise great care over something." When its object is "teaching," or "wisdom," and the like it takes on the nuance "to observe it carefully so as to do it," but when the subject is "God" — as here — it means "to observe the object carefully so as to protect it." What the danger may be lies in the background, though it may be inferred from verse 10 that it involves death.

The vocative, *'ēl (God),* which is the ancient Canaanite designation of the chief of the ancient Canaanite religion and of the only God in the patriarchal religion,[89] presumably has the same meaning as *'ᵉlôah* (singular) and its intensive plural *'ᵉlôhîm,* both of which are also translated "God," and signifies the quintessence of divine transcendence.[90] *'ᵉlôah* is what humanity is not. *'El* emphasizes God's inhabitance of the heavenly sphere, focusing on his transcendence over human qualities: immortality and power. *Because (kî)* introduces the reason God should protect him and keep him safe: *I take refuge in you (ḥāsîṯî ḇāḵ). Ḥsh* occurs thirty-seven times and always with the meaning "to seek refuge," never to "have found refuge."[91] Danger impels the faithful to seek refuge in the arms of God and to enter into dialogue with him. "A constant life of prayer is the natural way in which faith manifests itself in life."[92] Moreover, the psalmist publicly stakes his fate on God, implicitly entailing that the reputation of God himself is at stake in this temple dialogue with God and the congregation.

C. Confession of Trust vv. 2-4

The psalmist implicitly confesses his trust in *I AM* by asserting his sole loyalty to *I AM* (v. 2). The flip side is his identification with *I AM*'s saints (v. 3), not with apostates, who look to other gods for their salvation (v. 4).

89. Cf. the names for Israel's God involving combinations of *'ēl* with a qualifier: *'ēl 'ᵉlôhê yiśrā'ēl* ("*El,* the God of Israel" [Gen. 33:20]), *'ēl-'elyôn* ("El Most High" [Gen. 14:18-22]), *'ēl-rᵒ'î* ("El Who Sees Me" [Gen. 16:13]), *'ēl-'ôlām* ("El Eternal" [Gen. 21:33]), and *'ēl-šadday* ("El, Ruler of All" [Gen. 17:1; 28:3; 35:11; 43:14; 48:3]).

90. It is not clear how the meaning of *'ᵉlôah* is distinct from *'ēl.* The significance of the *h* ending is unknown. Furthermore, *'ᵉlôah/'ᵉlôhîm* can both be either indefinite or definite nouns. When it refers to the only God, *I AM,* who is Israel's patron deity, it is capitalized ("God"). However, if it is referring to the essence of divinity, it is not capitalized ("god").

91. See B. K. Waltke, *The Book of Proverbs: Chapters 1–15* (Grand Rapids: Eerdmans, 2004), p. 582, n. 52.

92. A. Weiser, *The Psalms* (OTL; Philadelphia: Westminster Press, 1962), p. 173.

1. Loyalty to I AM Alone v. 2

I say to I AM signals that David's pledge of allegiance to *I AM* is made in the congregation, not privately. "The glory of God may be revealed to the world both by God's dealing with his people and through their witness."[93] "You are the Lord [of all]," not "my lord" (see n. 42). His confession entails his acknowledgment of God's claim on him, and "I have no good thing (*ṭôbātî*, 'what is beneficial and desirable,' see notes 43, 44) apart from you" (cf. James 1:17). The rest of the psalm rests on this foundation.

2. Loyalty to the People of God vv. 3-4

a. Saints Are His Sole Pleasure v. 3

Saints (qᵉdôšîm) signifies those separate from human infirmity, impurity, and sin; those who by faith accept God's forgiveness and spiritual enablement to be holy as God is holy. *Qᵉdôšîm* often refers to angels or to God, but *who are in the land* (or "on earth") shows earthly, not heavenly, beings are in view. Human referents elsewhere in the OT include priests, Aaron, Levites, prophets, Nazirites, the remnant in Jerusalem, and as here, Israel (cf. Exod. 19:6; Num. 16:3).[94] Emphatically *they (hēmmâ)* are the ones in whom the king delights; he regards them as the true *nobles* (*'addîrê;* "respected for excellence in power"; cf. Ps. 8:1). Those who trust *I AM* have true, not false, strength (see 1 Sam. 2:1-10). *In them is all my delight (kol-hepṣî ḇām,)* — "all" (*kol,* "the whole of") is limited by the context to those on earth, not in heaven. Any happiness apart from the Lord, the Author of all good, and from his saints is sin against God, for it defiles that relationship.

b. Refusal to Worship with Apostates v. 4

His confession of *I AM* as his sole good and of saints as his sole pleasure excludes the worship of other gods in the congregation of apostates. *Their pains will increase* (notes 49, 50) implies that the king will not join the apostates to avoid the trajectory of their lives ending in death. *Who have acquired another god* (notes 51-53) implies the apostates looked to someone/thing to give them life apart from *I AM,* the Lord of all and of all good. Apostates, however, have no faith in *I AM*'s covenant promises. In addition to his confession in verse 3,

93. Weiser, *Psalms,* p. 174.
94. BDB, p. 872, s.v. *qādôš.*

the king proves his faith by asserting *I will not pour out to them libations of blood* (notes 54, 55). Elsewhere in the Old Testament *nēsek* (pl. *niskêhem,* "their libations") refers to drink offerings of wine in combination with other offerings.[95] Libations of blood probably were not drunk but were acts of pouring a liquid — in this case *of blood (middām).* Libations may be offered in a correct ritual (Exod. 29:40; 30:9; *passim*) or in forbidden rituals that prompt *I AM*'s anger (cf. Isa. 57:5f.; 65:11; 66:3; Jer. 7:18; 19:13; *passim*). Apostates slaughter animals to gain the favor of gods and to appease them, gods who never saved Israel and demand no moral rectitude. The king will not even "take up their names on my lips," a Hebraism for "I will not speak their names."

D. Cause for Trust vv. 5-8

The poet is at ease in crisis because the sublime God is his possession and this God bestows on him all the good he possesses. This is so for all who see by faith God's providence: "If man turns his thoughts to the providential rule of God and envisages that providential rule with gratitude and joy, he is thus taught to discern in material benefits the visible proof of the benevolence of his God."[96]

1. Inheritance from I AM vv. 5-6

Distributed over the four versets of the first of two quatrains in this stanza are four hyponyms for a land grant: "portion of land," "lot," "lines," "inheritance" (vv. 5a, b; 6a, b respectively). His allotted inheritance is twofold: *I AM* himself (v. 5) and his beneficence (v. 6). The land grant imagery derives from Joshua's tribal allotment of the land by casting lots (Joshua 15–19; especially 18:10).

a. Inheritance of *I AM* v. 5

NIV/TNIV uniquely interprets verse 5, "LORD, you have assigned me my portion and my cup," giving it a similar sense to verse 6, not that *I AM* himself is his portion, as was the inheritance of the Levites. Presumably it either emends the text (see n. 56) or thinks *tômîk* in the B verset is gapped in the A verset. The former is unnecessary and the latter is unlikely. *Portion* (*m*^{e}*nāṯ* or *m*^{e}*noṯ*) signifies "choice portion,"[97] and "allotted" (see n. 56) metaphorically depicts the rela-

95. *Nāsak* is used of pouring out water in 2 Samuel 23:16 (1 Chron. 11:18), but in this use David interprets the water as blood of those who risked their lives to get it (2 Sam. 23:17).

96. Weiser, *Psalms,* p. 175.

97. BDB, p. 584, s.v., *mānâ.*

tionship between God and his people. *I AM* determines the boundaries of all nations, but uniquely possesses Israel (Deut. 32:8f.) and the Levites (Num. 18:20; Deut. 10:9; 18:1); the psalmist possesses *I AM* (cf. 73:26; 119:57; 142:5 [6]; Lam. 3:24). The imagery may derive more specifically from the Levites, who had no portion or inheritance of land; *I AM* was their portion. Moreover, Israel was a kingdom of priests (Exod. 19:6), and as such *I AM* was spiritually the portion of Israel (Jer. 10:16).

My cup also signifies good fortune. The imagery depicts God's handing a cup of wine to someone to drink its portion and signifies that he determines their destiny (cf. Jer. 25:15). David drinks from a metaphorical cup that contains the provision of *I AM* himself and all the benefits entailed in God. The additional metaphor, "my cup," shows that "the allotted portion" does not refer to the Levite's portion at *I AM*'s altar. Augustine captures the thought: "Let others choose for themselves portions, earthly and temporal, to enjoy; the portion of saints in the Lord is eternal. Let others drink of deadly pleasures, the portion of my cup is the Lord."[98]

NJB captures emphatic *you ('attâ)* by "you, you alone." *Hold (tômîḵ*, see n. 58) is ambiguous, for *tmk* may mean "to take hold of" or "to hold fast." If the former, *my lot (gôrālî)* refers to "a lot" held in the hand and cast for the decision of questions, and the suffix is a genitive of mediated object ("for me") = "you decide my destiny." If the latter, then "lot" by metonymy refers to "the thing assigned, apportioned, allotted esp. of land,"[99] and the genitive is a possessive genitive: "You hold my lot [of blessings] secure" (TNIV). This referent functions well as a janus to his possessions other than *I AM* himself in verse 6, but is not as apt as the former in parallel with *I AM* as his portion — that is to say, *I AM* predestined his relationship to himself (cf. Ps. 139:16B). The proposed translation preserves this ambiguity.

b. Inheritance of Possessions v. 6

"The boundary lines" glosses *ḥᵃḇālîm* (pl. of *ḥeḇel*). *Ḥebel* refers to a cord or line and more strictly to a measuring line. By metonymy the sense is extended to a *measured portion, lot, part, region* (cf. Ps. 78:55; Mic. 2:5; Amos 7:17). The plural suggests it is a metaphor of his favored life (cf. the summary of his gifts in 1 Sam. 16:18), including *I AM*'s counsel that guides him (v. 11), not of his being granted the land of Israel in the sense that he is king over the entire land. *Have*

98. Cited by Charles Augustus Briggs, *A Critical and Exegetical Commentary on the Book of Psalms* (ICC; Edinburgh: T. & T. Clark, 1906), p. 120.

99. BDB, p. 174, s.v. *gôrāl*.

fallen (*nāpᵉlû)* assumes the image of casting lots for the allotment of territory. *In pleasant places (bannᵉʿīmîm)* with "boundary lines" refers to good soil, a figure for a rich, full, and abundant life.[100]

Indeed (ʾap) intensifies verse 6A. *My inheritance* (*naḥᵃlōṯ*, see n. 59; Ps. 2:8) is a synonymous parallel to the metaphor "boundary lines have fallen to me." *Is beautiful* (see n. 60) intensifies "pleasant places." Since beauty is relative to the beholder, "to me" (see n. 61) is added. What the pious regard as pleasant, the impious may regard as distasteful.

2. *Instruction from I AM vv. 7-8*

The second strophe, praising *I AM* for his instruction, supports this understanding of "to me." His pleasant inheritance includes ethical behavior. The first strophe, a quatrain, first mentions his inheritance of *I AM* himself and then *I AM*'s blessings; this strophe, also a quatrain, chiastically mentions first *I AM*'s instruction (v. 7) and then his commitment to *I AM*'s person (v. 8).

a. Praise for *I AM*'s Instruction v. 7

I will bless I AM *(ʾᵃbārēḵ)* is a shortened way of saying "to pronounce *I AM* as blessed *(bārûk)*. It describes *I AM* as possessing beneficial power that he benevolently bestows on the one praising him as such. Thus here it signifies the poet's admiration of God and his joyous praise of him and his exclamation of thanksgiving to him. Grounds for this laudatory thanksgiving in the psalms are for anything. The reason is usually, as here, introduced by "who": *who (ʾᵃšer)* and the personal experience that David lauds is that *I AM counsels me (yᵉʿāṣānî)*.[101] *Yāʿaṣ* signifies that one with authority to advise lays a plan of action for success. No wonder David's inheritance is pleasant and agreeable to him. *Indeed (ʾaṗ)* again intensifies the A verset, rhetorically linking the two strophes. *At night* (see n. 65) escalates David's praising by implying he extols *I AM* constantly. *Instructs me (yissᵉrûnî)* intensifies the parallel "to counsel, to advise." Although *yāsar* "to instruct" often connotes "to rebuke" or "to chasten" either by words or the rod (cf. Prov. 9:7),[102] here it probably has simply its essential meaning, "to communicate knowledge in order to shape specific conduct"[103] (cf. Prov. 31:1), without connoting rebuke for wrongdoing (cf. Isa.

100. *HALOT*, 2:705, s.v. *nᵉʿîm*.
101. C. A. Keller, G. Wehmeier, *TLOT*, 2:269, s.v. *brk*.
102. Waltke, *Proverbs 1–15*, pp. 175-76.
103. R. D. Branson, *TDOT*, 6:129, s.v. *yāsar*.

28:26). Though without sin the Son of God, Christ "learned obedience from what he suffered, and, once made perfect, he became the source of eternal salvation for all who obey him" (Heb. 4:15; 5:8-9). God is the ultimate mentor who instructs David, but his immediate tutor is *my conscience* (*kilyôtāy*, literally "my kidneys"). "Of all human organs," says Kellermann, "the OT associates the kidneys in particular with a variety of emotions," from joy (Prov. 23:15f.) to deepest agony (Ps. 73:21). In a Ugaritic text it is said of Aqahat: "his inward parts instruct him."[104] These nocturnal instructors probably function by inflicting pangs of conscience. Psalm 139:13f. mentions these organs in the context of God's testing. In 1 Enoch 68:3 the word of judgment disquiets the kidneys. According to Babylonian *Ber.* 61a, "the right kidney counsels what is good, the left kidney what is evil."[105] In the quietness of the night, without the distractions of the world, the voice of conscience speaks louder and clearer (see Ps. 4:4 [5]).

I place I AM *(šiwwîtî)* glosses the relatively rare lexeme II *šwh.* In Psalm 119:30 the psalmist locates on the way that lies before him *I AM*'s judgments. David keeps his eyes on *I AM,* whether he reveals himself by his written *Torah* or by conscience, because he has chosen him as his admired instructor to lead him in the right way (cf. v. 7). As "at night" implies constantly, *continually (tāmîd)* explicitly states his constant looking to *I AM* to instruct him in the right way, both through *I AM*'s *tôrâ* and his conscience.

b. *I AM*'s Presence and Protection v. 8

The thought of *I AM* as lying on the path before him to give him direction segues into the thought that *I AM* is at his right hand to preserve and protect him, bringing us full circle to his opening petition: "keep me safe." *Because* (*kî*, see 22:9, 16, 24 [10, 17, 25]) introduces the situation that constitutes the basis for the apodosis: *I will not be toppled ('emmôṭ). The right hand* is the favored and stronger hand (cf. Gen. 48:14, 18; 1 Kings 2:19), and "since time immemorial, the 'right hand' has been used figuratively in the sense of 'power' or 'might'" (cf. Isa. 63:12).[106] At God's powerful right hand, no powers in heaven or on earth can shake the king's favored position. *Mûṭ* signifies "to rock or shake and to fall off base." Death, according to verse 10, is like being hit by a shadow of a truck, not the truck.

104. C. Gordon, *Ugaritic Textbook* (Rome: Pontifical Biblical Institute, 1965), p. 19, Text 127 (26).

105. D. Kellermann, *TDOT,* 7:179f.

106. Soggin, *TDOT,* 6:101, s.v. *yāmîn.*

E. Commitment of Body to God vv. 9-11

Therefore (lākēn) "introduces an anticipated response after a statement of certain conditions ('the foregoing being the case, therefore')",[107] namely his having *I AM* as his possession and protector. He commits himself to God with joy, not just serenely (v. 9a), and his body rests in faith's security (v. 9b). His ease is based on faith's certainty that God will not hand his body over to the grave to have the last word (v. 10a). Indeed, to show that *I AM* is present with him in death, he predicts God will raise "his holy one" before his body has time to decay (v. 10b). Beyond the shadow of the grave, his path leads on to an abundant life in God's presence (v. 11a) that protects him forever (v. 11b).

1. Confidence of God's Presence in Death vv. 9-10

a. Emotions Joyful for Body Is Secure v. 9

My heart (*libbî*, see Ps. 4:4 [5]) is *glad* (*śāmaḥ*, cf. Ps. 4:7; Luke 10:21-22), *and my liver* (*wayyāgel kāḇôḏî* [see Ps. 3:3 [4]] *kᵉḇēḏî* see n. 71) *exults* finds a close parallel in a Ugaritic text. Of the goddess Anath it says: "Her liver swells with laughter, / Her heart fills up with joy, Anath's liver exults."[108] In this text "liver" also stands in parallel with "heart" in connection with a verb meaning "to exult."

The third *indeed ('ap̱)* combines more strongly a conjunctive nuance with its enhancing sense. In addition to his inward joy, even his physical body confronting death rests in security. *Body (bāśār)* signifies "flesh" and is used to refer to the "whole body." As "kidneys" in verse 7B is the most comprehensive, important, and frequently used term for emotions, and heart is the same for spiritual state (v. 9A), *bāśār* is for the external, material aspect of a human being. It denotes the body's fleshy consistency and the whole exterior form of a living being. *Rests secure (yiškōn lābeṭaḥ)* also signifies to be at ease. *škn* means "to stay, spend time, dwell" and says nothing of the time, place, or extent of the staying (see Ps. 15:1). Those notions are developed in verse 11 and by *secure* (*lābeṭaḥ*, literally "with reference to security"). *Beṭaḥ* normally has a negative notion when security is sought in humanity because the human being(s) on whom one relies turn(s) out to be deceptive. It has positive connotations when the object is God.

107. *IBHS*, p. 666, P. 39.3.4e.
108. *ANET*, p. 136. Cf. *UT*, p. 417, entry 1187.

b. Body Secure with Reference to the Grave v. 10

Like the syntax of "therefore" and "because" in Psalm 1:5 and 6, in Psalm 16:9 "therefore" introduces the anticipated response of being at ease after a statement of the cause for trust in verses 4-8. In verse 10, logical *because* looks ahead to a further reason why his body rests secure. The verse qualifies the time and place of his body's secure rest: in the grave: *you will not abandon (lōʾ ṯaʿ^{a}zōb) me* (*nap̱šî*, see Ps. 3:3). *ʿzb* means "to hand over and leave" (Exod. 23:5 with *l*^{e}; Job 39:11 with *ʾel;* cf. Gen. 39:6 with *b*^{e}*yad*). As for *the grave* (*liš*^{e}*ʾôl*):

> Traditionally *š*^{e}*ʾôl* has been transliterated by "Sheol," but the NIV rightly glosses it by "grave." The noun occurs sixty-six times in the Old Testament, fifty-eight times in poetry. The frequent prepositions with it show that it is the grave below the earth. The biblical poets use rich and varied figures to depict it. Sheol has a "mouth" (Ps. 141:7), which it "enlarges" (Isa. 5:14), and it is "never satisfied" (Prov. 27:20; 30:16). It is so powerful that none escapes its "grip" (Ps. 89:48 [49]; Song 8:6), but some are redeemed from it (Ps. 49:15 [16]; Prov. 15:24; Hos. 13:14). It is like a prison with "cords" (2 Sam. 22:6) and land that has "gates" (Isa. 38:10) with "bars" (Job 17:16). Here corruption is "the father," and the worm "the mother and sister" (Job 17:16). It is "a land" of no return to this life (Job 7:9); an abode where socioeconomic distinctions cease. Rich and poor (Job 3:18-19), righteous and wicked (3:17) lie together. It is a land of silence (Ps. 94:17), darkness (13:3 [4]), weakness, and oblivion (88:11-18 [12-19]). The destructive nature of this realm is intensified by the addition "Abaddon" (Prov. 15:11; 27:20).
>
> One errs in using this figurative language to build a doctrine of the intermediate state. On the other hand, these vivid and powerful figures transform the grave from a six-foot pit into a metaphorical and transcendent realm distinct from life on the top of the earth inhabited by living mortals and from heaven inhabited by the immortal God and his court. Those who descend there will never again participate in salvation history or join the holy throng at the earthly temple (Ps. 6:5 [6]; Isa. 38:18). Like the Jordan River and Mount Zion, the grave symbolizes eternal realities that transcend their physical space.[109]

Driver rightly says: "He expects to die and to go to Sheol, but he prays [sic! asserts] that God will not abandon him there; will not leave him in the power of Sheol; but will go with him and remain with him there" (Ps. 139:8).[110] If *I AM*

109. Waltke, *Proverbs 1–15*, p. 116.

110. S. R. Driver, *Studies in the Psalms* (New York: Hodder and Stoughton, 1915), p. 121.

deserted him in death, then Death trumps *I AM*. But David's God will have the final word in his chosen king's destiny, and that is life in his presence, not the grave.

Verset B clarifies the full force of verset A: *you will not allow* (see n. 74) *your devoted one* (see Ps. 4:3 [4]) *to see corruption* (*lōʾ ṯittēn ḥ^{a}sîd^{e}kā šaḥat,* see n. 76). Since the body's decomposition becomes apparent between the third and fourth days (cf. John 11:38f.), he must be raised from the dead within three days. But who is this devoted one that is raised from the dead presumably on the third day? A few scholars maintain that "me" (v. 10a) and "devoted one" have different referents because David has himself as the referent, whereas the apostles regard Jesus Christ as the referent. To harmonize the discrepancy they argue that "me" (v. 10a) refers to David and that "devoted one" (*ḥāsîḏ*) refers to Jesus Christ. Hebrew parallelism allows this possibility, but the parallels otherwise so closely match one another that their distinction is tortuous.[111] In fact, Peter refers "me" in 10a to Jesus. According to the superscript, parallelism, and use of *ḥāsîḏ* in Psalm 4:3 [4], the reference is to David. Possibly David is using hyperbole with reference to his own body in order to imply several truths. First, that he will not see decay entails he envisions himself in the grave, not merely as being delivered from a premature death. (If the Old Testament has no hope beyond the grave, as is often alleged, the Old Testament is an anomaly in ancient Near Eastern religions.)[112] Second, it implies that God raises his body from the grave. If his body goes to the grave and does not decay, then beyond any cavil God must have raised it. Third and correlatively, it implies God's presence with his saint even in the grave.

But this is not the plain meaning of the text. Though David, the human author, may be using hyperbole, God, the divine Author, speaks prophetically of David's greater Son, his heir, to validate his claim to be the promised Christ. Moreover, by his death and resurrection he proved the truths that the putative hyperbole infers.

111. G. E. Whitney, "Survey of the History of the Interpretation of Prophecy: How Interpreters Deal with Peter's Use of Psalm 16 in Acts 2," Evangelical Theological Society (Eastern Regional Conference, April 3, 1987, Myerstown, PA): 13-16.

112. For example, a Ugaritic text, where the goddess Anat addresses the hero Aqhat, says: "Ask for life and I'll give it thee, for deathlessness, and I'll bestow't on thee. I'll make thee count years with Balal, with the sons of El shalt thou count months." H. L. Ginsburg notes: "i.e. shalt be immortal like them" (*ANET,* p. 151, vi: 26-29). Expositors who deny that some Old Testament texts teach life after death typically argue in a circle. First, they tortuously divest texts of that notion, and then appeal to this global evidence to call into question the notion in any text. See Waltke, *Proverbs 1–15,* pp. 104-9.

2. *Confidence of Presence with God After Death v. 11*

If God will not hand over the psalmist's body to the grave as its final resting place, what then is his final destiny? Verse 11 answers that question: it will be the same for the resurrected body as his present good fortune but forever; namely, God will instruct him in the right way (cf. vv. 7-8) and bestow on him an abundant life (cf. vv. 5-6). Like all of God's rewards, they are not separate from the virtue. A parent may reward a child for practicing scales on a piano with an ice-cream, but the reward is unrelated to the investment. God's reward consummates the investment. The child who practices today can anticipate playing beautiful music in years to come. So the joy of fellowship with God in this world will be rewarded with the reward of overflowing joy when we see him face to face. Tears of joy will flow like a river. How that reward will happen is mostly a mystery (cf. 1 Cor. 15:35-58).

You will make known to (tôdîʿēnî) entails both that *I AM* will continue to point out to him the path of life (see v. 7) and that he will internalize and experience it (Ps. 1:6; 4:3 [4]). The metaphor *path (ʾōraḥ)* combines the ideas of action and outcome (see p. 135 n. 76).[113] It is a poetic hyponym for the semantic domain of "way" (see Ps. 1:1).[114]

Verse 11B clarifies that *life (ḥayyîm)* signifies both qualitatively an abundant life in fellowship with *I AM* (v. 11bA) and quantitatively eternal life under his protection (v. 11Bb). First, a qualitatively abundant life: *You will fill me with joy*[115] *in your presence (śōḇaʿ śᵉmāḥôṯ ʾeṯ pāneyḵā,* literally, "fullness of joy with your face," 11:bA). *Śōḇaʿ* ("you will fill") signifies satiety. His joy in God's presence will be gratified to or beyond his emotional capacity to contain. *Śᵉmāḥôṯ* (see n. 79) denotes being glad or joyful with the whole disposition and is a metonymy for all the future blessings the psalmist will receive beyond death. As the "tree of life" in the Garden of Eden symbolizes an abundant life that qualitatively and quantitatively transcends clinical life represented by Adam's "breath," so the path of life refers to a spiritual state that transcends clinical life. *ʾet* ("with," of accompaniment) with *pāneyḵā* (literally, "your face") is a Hebraism for "before you, in your presence."[116] Abundant life depends upon a relationship with *I AM*. D. Kidner comments, "In several places it is not too much to

113. For a distinction of the hyponyms in the semantic range of "way," see D. Dorsey, *The Roads and Highways of Ancient Israel* (Baltimore: Johns Hopkins University Press, 1991).

114. Waltke, *Proverbs 1–15*, p. 194.

115. Construing *śᵉmāḥôt* as abstract plural (*IBHS*, pp. 120f., P. 7.4.2).

116. *HALOT*, 3:941, s.v. *pāneh* (D. 2). To be sure Exodus 21:6, where the slave is described as serving his master forever (i.e., for life), is a relative "forever," but that context is unlike this Psalm 16:11, which, according to our exegesis, speaks of life after death.

say that 'life' means fellowship with God. . . . Some of the major Old Testament expressions for godliness are interchangeable with 'life' or to 'live.'"[117] By contrast, the clinically alive wicked are in the realm of darkness and death, a state of being already dead because they are separated from the Source of Life.

Second, "path of life" infers a quantitative eternal life: "with eternal pleasures at your right hand" (*nᵉʿīmôṯ bîmînᵉḵa neṣaḥ;* literally, "pleasant [things]" [see v. 6] "are at your right hand" [see v. 8] "forever" [11Bb]). Protected by being at the Eternal's powerful right hand, his abundant life is guaranteed to be forever in duration.[118] Driver comments well: "Such a hope he could not express for this life; he is thinking of everlasting life in the presence of Yahweh."[119]

Part IV. Conclusion

In their apologias to the Jews that the crucified Jesus of Nazareth is the Messiah, Peter and Paul appeal to Psalm 16:8-11 (Acts 2:25-32; 13:35). They argue that David is talking about Jesus Christ, not himself, because, among other things, the after-death experience of David's body, which decayed, contrasts with that of Christ's body, which did not decay. Since the experience of Christ's body after death uniquely matches Psalm 16:10, "your holy one will not see decay," David, they argue, is speaking of Christ's death and resurrection, not of his own death. Moreover, Peter says of all of Psalm 16:8-11: "David said of him [Jesus of Nazareth]," implicitly putting the first person statements in these verses, such as "you will not abandon me to the grave," in the mouth of Jesus. Indeed, Psalm 16:10 is probably one of the texts the original church had in mind in their basic kerygma "that Christ was raised on the third day according to the Scriptures" (see v. 10b; 1 Cor. 15:4).[120] This early interpretation of Psalm 16 probably derives from Jesus himself (Luke 24:44-45). It is the traditional interpretation of the church until the ascendancy of HBC.

Yet the exegesis given above argues these are the words of David and that they refer to him. The contrast between a normal interpretation of the psalm by a hermeneutical method credible to most modern interpreters and the apostles' use of the Psalm is a critical issue in the history of interpretation. According to Weiser, "[The great majority of more recent expositors] hold the view that what the author has in mind is that God will protect him from a sudden, untimely, or

117. Derek Kidner, *The Proverbs* (TOTC; Downers Grove, IL: InterVarsity, 1964), p. 53.

118. The normal form for this notion, *lāneṣaḥ,* is here abbreviated to *neṣaḥ* (cf. Ps. 13:1).

119. Driver, *Psalms,* p. 122.

120. I reached the conclusion independently from L. Reinke, *Die Messianischen Psalmen,* 2 vols. (Geisen: Roth, 1857), vol. 1, p. 179. d by.

evil death." But Weiser rightly objects: "Neither the wording of the verse nor the general circumstances and attitude of the poet suggest such an interpretation; moreover, it is precisely the decisive feature of that interpretation — the specific kind of death — which is read into the text." Rather, in Weiser's opinion, the psalmist is speaking of his overcoming his fear of death. "There is no reason to doubt that the poet, speaking of death in quite general terms, has in mind death as such, that is, death in general, and that by virtue of his faith in God he is progressing towards the conquest of the fear of death in his heart."[121]

According to the majority of contemporary commentators, the apostles erred. These commentators validate their position by wrongly insisting with Driver that *šaḥaṯ* derives from *šûaḥ* "to descend" and so must mean "pit," not corruption.[122] Curiously, the classic lexicon by Brown, Driver, and Briggs does not have an entry for *šaḥaṯ* as a derivative of *šaḥaṯ*, "to go to ruin," "decay," though they recognize the existence of that root.[123] If they are right, the psalm in David's mouth cannot apply to Jesus, for Christ died a premature, evil death, contrary to a normal interpretation of the psalm. We are not aware, however, of any rebuttal to the arguments that *šaḥaṯ* must be II. *šaḥaṯ*, meaning "corruption" (see n. 76).

The resolution of the tension between the historical horizon where Psalm 16 refers to David and the apostles' horizon where it refers to Christ is best resolved by interpreting Psalm 16 as a typico-prophetic psalm. As heir of the Davidic covenant David is a type of the quintessential Fulfillment of that covenant. But beyond that typology David, while possibly using hyperbole with reference to himself, prophesies that the body presumably of his final Heir — God's fully devoted one, though experiencing death, will not experience decay. Was David reflecting, as Calvin suggests (see p. 316), that this Heir will be so perfect in his faith toward *I AM* that he will not fall under Adam's curse that "dust you are and to dust you must return" (Gen. 3:19)? David's statement "your devoted one will not see corruption" also clarifies that his previous statement, "you will not abandon me to Sheol," means deliverance from the grave, not deliverance from a premature death.

This prophecy of David's son is so unexpected that it makes one marvel and admire. Today, the church has no excuse not to be orthodox. In the light of its fulfillment and its blessings, including light of the everlasting fellowship with God, for the orthodox death fades away.

121. Weiser, *Psalms*, pp. 176f.

122. S. R. Driver, "The Method of Studying the Psalter," *Expositor* 10 (1910; 7th Series): 35-37. Cf. Kirkpatrick, Gunkel, Chr. Barth, Kraus, Mowinckel, et al.

123. BDB, pp. 1001, 1007-8. *HALOT* think the noun *šaḥat* is a primary, not a derivative, noun, meaning "pit," "grave," citing Psalm 16:10 as one of its occurrences.

CHAPTER 11

Psalm 19: A Royal Sage Praises and Petitions I AM

Part I: Voice of the Church

Probably no psalm has generated more diversity of modern interpretation than Psalm 19. For that reason we now focus our survey on interpreters since the introduction of historical Biblical criticism (see pp. 80-82). Early in the history of HBC, Delitzsch represents an orthodox commentator at the hinge period of the new approach. We then go back to the pastoral Luther and Calvin to show the shift from the allegorical (as impacted by social contextualization) to the plain sense, and draw our survey to conclusion with Aquinas, a monk writing in his cell just prior to the Reformation.

In his *Reflections on the Psalms,* C. S. Lewis wrote of Psalm 19, "I take this to be the greatest poem in the Psalter and one of the greatest lyrics in the world." Christian poets from Thomas Campion (1567-1620) to Gerard Manley Hopkins and Charles Péguy have given us diverse renderings of this psalm. Haydn's *Creation* suggests the power this psalm can still express in a work of music. But poetry tends to be suggestive rather than explicit. We feel that understanding Psalm 19 only as a poem fails to grasp its theological unity — its unique character as a psalm of wisdom, thanksgiving, and petition.

By Biblical wisdom we mean that it is God who is the source and giver of knowledge, as applied to life and all its relationships. It is what Augustine calls *intellectus Christi,* an understanding that only Christ can give us. God then is both the source and premise for the study, and the benefit we may receive in reflecting upon this psalm and discerning its unity. Both creation and *torah* are expressive of God. But we believe the integration of creation and *torah* is more profound than previously recognized, even in commentaries that accept the psalm's unity. Orthodox theologians have long recognized the diverse forms of

God's general revelation in creation and of his special revelation in Scripture, but they have failed to recognize that without comprehensive knowledge — which only the Creator of all things possesses — absolute or certain knowledge of right and wrong is not possible. Unless one knows ontologically, as only the Creator of all things knows, a mortal's epistemology is at best relative and uncertain. Hence, though unquestionably the psalm has a major break in substance and style at verse 7, shifting from celebrating God as Creator to God as Lawgiver to make mortals wise to salvation, from the psalmist's perspective God's redemptive knowledge revealed in Scripture is absolute and certain because, as the Creator, he is omnicompetent in wisdom/knowledge and power (see commentary). By contrast, introducing alien aspects such as the concept of "nature," and Pharisaic practices of "the Law," causes tensions in the exegesis of Psalm 19. When the Biblical focus of "I AM" is set before us, both creation and divine revelation together express the same integrated reality in diverse ways. But when unbiblical notions of "nature" and "history" exclude "I AM" as creator and redeemer, then Scripture loses all sense of divine inspiration. By this criterion we assess modern commentaries, testing their theological acumen in their understanding and acceptance of the nature of Biblical wisdom, or their lack thereof.

The psalmist's praise of God, the *I AM,* is based on the acceptance of both general revelation given in creation and of the special revelation of Scripture, and of their integration as understood by Israel's sages. If we fail to see this, the divine revelation in the text is not celebrated, and it becomes handled, at best, as a non-revelatory unity for its rhetorical features (see commentary), or, at worst, as a non-revelatory scrapbook of ancient texts. We can then tacitly ignore any theological claims for the Christian doctrine of Creation and of Scriptural revelation that makes the mortal wise to salvation.

In science, the Heisenberg principle states that the outcome of a given experiment is very heavily influenced by the point of view of the observer. Likewise, the exegetical observer needs to consider the weight of his own interpretation. For the word "interpretation" implies a reciprocal entry, both into the mind of the interpreter and into the text being penetrated. This we are attempting to demonstrate in these historical outlines.

I. Modern Interpreters

John Eaton (2005) accepts a Biblical premise for the doctrine of creation, since it is set in the Biblical canon. He reflects on the psalm as "one of the greatest treasures of religious devotion, which echoes ancient hymnody in vv. 1-6, with later theological teaching in vv. 7-10, that anticipates the more elaborate and developed teaching on the *torah* of Psalm 119."[1] A late, post-exilic date seems unjustified, so he sees it reasonable to date the psalm to a middle or late monarchy period. But like Delitzsch in the mid-nineteenth century, he is a minority voice among the pundits today.

Rabbi Martin Samuel Cohen, at the opposite pole, sees the psalm simply as a poem, whose poet goes off in two entirely different directions, one in viewing the physical universe, the other in praising the laws of God. "The stars and the planets are no less splendid today than they were in the psalmist's time, but can moderns still look towards heaven and hear them speak of God?" he asks. Since the answer for a secular society is obviously negative, what then can a secular rabbi get out of the psalm? The secular rabbi argues that human beings, in having intelligence to know how to obey laws morally, are more ennobled than mindless planets that have no choice but to obey the laws of science![2]

The crux is whether creation is personified, or nature is deified in either open or concealed ways. If it is the former, then Psalm 19 is a wisdom psalm to the Creator-Redeemer. If it is deified, then all the praise is made on behalf of "Nature," as our secular society manifests today. Linguistically, meter, style, and topic change abruptly at verse 7 [8], but its unity has been maintained theologically since the early Church Fathers. Its disunity has been the result of modern criticism. For this reason, in this historical commentary we will reverse the chronological approach taken so far, and instead trace back from contemporary studies some of the changes of theological perspective, as reflected mostly in modern German scholarship.

John Goldingay (2006) is one of the most recent commentators to "plausibly maintain that these [two parts] were originally separate psalms or parts of psalms that have been combined."[3] This may be so, but for sound theology what needs to be emphasized is their unification.

William P. Brown (2002) puts on a *son et lumière* show, to collate archaeological, iconographical, and later syngagogal data, into a novel unity of Sun and *torah* cosmology that syncretizes ancient and modern perspectives. Wholly absent is the apostolic interpretation of the psalm, or that of the Church Fathers.[4]

1. John Eaton, *The Psalms: Historical and Spiritual Commentary with an Introduction and New Translation* (London and New York: Continuum, 2005), p. 109.

2. Martin Samuel Cohen, *Our Haven and Our Strength: The Book of Psalms* (New York: Aviv Press, 2004), p. 57.

3. John Goldingay, *The Psalms,* vol. 1 (Grand Rapids: Baker Academic, 2006), pp. 284, 285, 290, 297-99.

4. William P. Brown, *Seeing the Psalms: A Theology of Metaphor* (Louisville and London: Westminster/John Knox Press, 2002).

Georg Fohrer (1993) makes no pretense of having any orthodox premise for the doctrine of creation. He treats a selection of thirty-five psalms in his *Psalmen.* He accepts that Psalm 19 is divided in two parts (vv. 2-7, 8-14 [3-8, 9-15]), the first as a remnant of a creation psalm incorporated by a later author as an introduction to his *torah*-psalm. Fohrer drops verse 4 into a footnote, thus editorially removing the psalm's expression of wonderful mystery.[5] Rather than a call to praise, it is praise that personifies the heaven itself and its alternating rulers Day and Night.

H. Spieckermann (1989) in similar critical fashion disparages even the twofold approach, and divides the psalm into four parts (1-4a, 4b-6, 7-10, 11-14 [2-5a, 5b-7, 8-11, 12-15]), with differing sources: Canaanite meditation; temple theology; later expansion; and anxious rigidity. He interprets anxiety rather than praise and trust as the tone of the psalm.[6]

E. Gerstenberger also interprets the two parts as having unrelated sources, one a "Hymn to Creation," the other a "Hymn to the Torah," stitched together as a personal prayer, in "synagogal" settings.[7]

C. Westermann (1984) likewise treats only verses 2-7 [3-8] of the psalm, as "a fragment," "a psalm in praise of the Creator," to which praise of the Law came later. So his too is a retrograde and subjective critique, in refusing any unity to the whole psalm.[8]

Mitchell Dahood (1966, 1968, 1970) with a predominant interest in language, and pioneering in spirit, is inspired by Ugaritic studies to give a fresh textual suggestion, but sides with those who find "two distinct but related parts." The first is an adaptation of an ancient Canaanite hymn, while the second praises the Law in terms appropriate to the praise of the sun.[9]

Hans-Joachim Kraus (1960, 1978) attempts a new grouping of the Psalter, in which Psalm 19 is in the category of "Instructional Compositions." He too sees two psalms, with 19A belonging to a much older praise song *(Loblieder),* while 19B he sets as a "Torah psalm." He suggests they both came from materials of the autumn festival. In his theology of the psalm he acknowledges no double witness to God, but a contrast between Nature and revelation. Consequently other elements of the psalm are ignored, especially its meditative spirit.

5. Georg Fohrer, *Psalmen* (Berlin and New York: De Gruyter, 1993).

6. H. Spieckermann, *Heilsgegenwart: Eine Theologie der Psalmen* (Göttingen: Vandenhoeck & Ruprecht, 1989).

7. E. Gerstenberger, *Psalms Part 1* (FOTL 14; Grand Rapids: Eerdmans, 1988).

8. C. Westermann, *Ausgewählte Psalmen,* translated as *The Living Psalms* (Edinburgh: T. & T. Clark, 1989), pp. 252-55.

9. Mitchell Dahood, *Psalms* (AB; New York: Doubleday, 1966-70).

Sigmund Mowinckel (1955), drawing on over forty years of research,[10] gives full emphasis to the distinction of the two parts, but respects the final unity. The first he sees as a mythologically tainted view of Nature, while the second part's praise of the Law he considers abstract and monotonous. The Near East's association of the sun with righteousness is the unity that binds the two parts, as we have seen likewise in the interpretation of William P. Brown. So the *Torah* author has adopted an ancient text for the first part, in order to praise the Lord.[11]

Hermann Gunkel (1929) sought with Lutheran piety to enter "the soul" of each psalm, appreciating it from within, by classifying it by type or genre *(Gattung).*[12] In Gunkel's estimation Psalm 19 was originally two wholly independent pieces, "falsely" joined together by a later editor. He hears the echo of the Greek theory of "the music of the spheres" in the heavenly song.[13] He rejects the idea of prophetic meditation and of a hearing with the inner ear. Rather it is expressive of the fantasy of the poet himself. Do we hear here an echo of the subjective theology of Schleiermacher in Gunkel? Reviving the spirit of J. G. Herder, he is determined to see each piece in its own context. He traces the original context of the second half of the psalm back to an age when the Law's requirements were not so rigid as they were in Pharisaic times (as Duhm dates it). Gunkel's interpretation is not directed to God himself, nor does he comment on the circumstances surrounding the uniting of these two distinct compositions.

Rudolph Kittel (1914) also sees two disparate compositions joined by a redactor, on the common theme of divine revelation.[14] In 19A (vv. 1-6 [2-7]) he sees poetic imagination treating the great elements of Nature as living beings. His is a rational explanation that obscures all sense of divine mystery. In 19B (vv. 7-12 [8-13]), a "hymn on the Law," he sees a later addition, before the law had become heavily elaborated by the scribes. Once more, he does not comment on the unity of the psalm, and he betrays no awareness of the psalm's preoccupation with spiritual concerns.

Charles Briggs's (1906-7) two-volume work, *A Critical and Exegetical Commentary on the Book of Psalms,* is an example of a radical textual-critical

10. S. Mowinckel, *The Psalms in Israel's Worship,* trans. D. R. Ap-Thomas (Oxford: Oxford University Press, 1962).

11. J. H. Eaton, *Psalms of the Way and the Kingdom: A Conference with the Commentators* (Sheffield: Sheffield Academic Press, 1995), p. 36.

12. Hermann Gunkel, *Die Psalmen* (Göttingen: Vandenhoeck & Ruprecht, 1929, reprinted 1968).

13. Eaton, *Psalms of the Way and the Kingdom of God,* p. 30.

14. R. Kittel, *Die Psalmen übersetzt und erklärt* (Leipzig: Deichertsche, 1914, 1929).

handling of Psalm 19.[15] He seeks for an original text, so he is prepared to discard all later glosses; he refuses to date any of the psalms as pre-exilic. Psalm 19 is seen as two separate poems, 19A being adapted from a sun-hymn of the Babylonian period, while 19B is a didactic poem in praise of the Law, no earlier than the Greek period. No theological assessment is given of the psalm, since he focuses on textual criticism.

Bernhard Duhm (1899) interprets the psalms as popular and conventional materials, even platitudinous, befitting the attitude of the crowd.[16] Dogmatically, he sees them all as late, Psalm 137 being the oldest, because of its reference to the Exile! Between 19A and 19B he makes no connection. He appreciates the poetic flair concerning God's glory in Nature in 19A, while 19B is at least better than its dreadful successor, Psalm 119! How narrow-minded one must be to interpret all one's life within the compass of the Law. So the best one can say is that this is a good text for psychologists and historians of religion to examine, to see how narrow-minded primitive religious people have been.[17] For Duhm, Psalm 19 betrays the mindset of the Scribes and Pharisees that Jesus condemned. In other words, not even secular scholars today might go so far negatively as Duhm would lead us to go!

Franz Delitzsch (1859-60), a conservative scholar who faced up to the radical challenges of Wellhausen's interpretation of Old Testament history, updates the various editions of his commentary on the Psalms to incorporate subsequent scholars, such as Hupfeld, Hitzig, Baer, Bickell, and Jewish scholars. He explains his inclusion of the latter as "owing to my desire to see the partition wall between Synagogue and Church broken down," although he does not mention them by name.[18] He also incorporates language discoveries, including Syriac, Assyrian, and Hebrew manuscripts. The introduction of his commentary includes the following quote from Johannes Arndt, the father of Lutheran Pietism: "What the heart is in man, that the Psalter is in the Bible." He rejects the twofold composition of Psalm 19, aware that this was already being asserted by Hupfeld.

Delitzsch observes that David is named "Servant of the Lord" in the superscription of Psalm 18 and again in Psalm 19:13 [14] and that in both psalms, David calls the Lord "my Rock" (18:2 [3]; 19:14 [15]). Delitzsch titles his commentary: "Prayer to God, the God who is revealed in a twofold manner." As

15. C. A. Briggs and E. G. Briggs, *A Critical and Exegetical Commentary on the Book of Psalms* (ICC; Edinburgh: T. & T. Clark, 1906-7).

16. Bernhard Duhm, *Die Psalmen* (Tübingen: Mohr, 1899, 1922).

17. J. H. Eaton, *Psalms of the Way and the Kingdom*, pp. 21-25.

18. Franz Delitzsch, *Biblical Commentary on the Psalms*, trans. David Eaton, 4th ed. (London: Hodder & Stoughton, 1887), p. xvi.

Psalm 18 is an evening psalm, so this is a morning psalm, he argues, witnessing the new day with the rising of the sun, and then of the need to live out the day's practicalities by the further illumination of the law of God. He counts fourteen lines in both parts, dividing naturally into a six- and an eight-line strophe. "If we take Ps. 32 along with it, we have the whole of the way of salvation in almost Pauline clearness and definiteness." He adds, "Paul often quotes these psalms; they were certainly his favorites."[19]

Instead of associating "Torah" with the encomium of legalism, Delitzsch sees it as "a mirror of the God who is gracious in holiness, a mirror into which he can look without slavish fear, and a norm of hearty and willing obedience. And how totally different is the love of the psalmists and the prophets for the law, a love that had regard to that which was essential and of universal ethical significance in the commandments, which aimed at spiritualizing the letter and enjoying the consolation that was involved in the promises, from the pharisaical and rabbinical worship of the letter and of ceremonies that was characteristic of the post-exile period!"[20]

In our brief survey of modern interpretive approaches to Psalm 19, we have omitted, due to space constraints, New Testament scholars, such as Martin Dibelius and Rudolf Bultmann. In place of engaging in debate about what they thought was the arbitrariness of deciding what is "historical" or not, they seek to impose strictly only literary criteria on the text. They assume discontinuity, between Old and New Testament, and between the historical Jesus and the post-resurrection Christ, as well as between the apostolic teaching and the later Church Fathers. Discontinuity between later phases of psalm commentary would also be their premise, not the continuity we are seeking here. The Bultmannian demand that all must be "de-mythologized" means to analyze everything in evolutionary categories, to arrive finally at an unquestioned contemporary "science of exegesis."

II. Study in Contrast: The Reformers, Calvin and Luther

As we have noted, **John Calvin** develops a strong doctrine of God as Creator (see pp. 252-53). He rejects the idea of a fixed or static God, for he is the living God. So he comments: "of a truth it is a great matter, that there is offered to our eyes a lively image of God, in the brightness of the heavens. But because the utterance of a sounding voice does better stir up our senses, or at least teaches

19. Delitzsch, *Biblical Commentary on the Psalms*, pp. 346-47.
20. Delitzsch, *Biblical Commentary on the Psalms*, pp. 352-53.

more certainly, and with much more profit, than simple beholding . . . the expressive force of this figure is to be noted, in that he says the heavens tell forth the glory of God by their own preaching."[21]

The universal power of God was unquestioned by Calvin, so he adds that while his glory may be visible in the heavens, "there is nothing so obscure or despised, even in the most confined corners of the earth, wherein there is not some mark of God's might and wisdom to be seen."[22] Calvin is outraged at the Greek notion of nature as "physis," an organic coming-to-be, that is eternal, emanating from particles, as Epicurus, Lucretius, and other philosophers had postulated. So in Psalm 148:7, he affirms, "neither has the world emerged from itself, but it has been created through the Word, the only-Begotten Son."[23] On Psalm 19:1 [2], he comments, "For David shows in what way the heavens declare God's glory to us; namely, because they openly give us to understand, that they are not huddled together by chance, but created wonderfully by some most excellent workmaster."[24]

Moving then from the doctrine of *Creatio per Verbum* ("Creation by Word"), he extols the doctrine of *Creatio Continuans,* the evident record of his providence, for "day after day they pour forth speech." One day would be enough to convince us perhaps, but "when we see the sun and moon compass the work daily with their going about; the sun by day appearing over our heads, the moon succeeding by turns; the sun to mount up by degrees, and at the same time to approach nearer unto us, and afterwards to take his journey back again, and to depart from us little by little; and that thereby the length of the days or nights is determined; and that this variation is so ordered according to a uniform law, that it recurs annually; this is a far more evident record."[25] Thus long before Isaac Newton was to describe the planetary movements, Calvin had appreciated the planetary ordered movements in the light of God's providence.

The third statement of the doctrine of creation is *Creatio ex Nihilo,* that God has created all things without recourse to any pre-existing substance or reality. All is expressive of God's grace, so any approach we may make to God is the consequence of divine initiative. It is indeed *sola gratia.* One of Calvin's basic principles is that God has created everything in order that man would glorify his name; we are born into the world to praise him.

All this is plain enough, so Calvin states simply: "Hitherto I have set forth

21. John Calvin, *A Commentary on the Psalms,* vol. 1, rev. and ed. T. H. L. Parker (London: James Clarke & Co. Ltd., 1965), p. 216.

22. Calvin, *A Commentary on the Psalms,* p. 216.

23. Calvin, *A Commentary on the Psalms,* vol. 4, p. 435, on Psalm 148:7.

24. Calvin, *A Commentary on the Psalms,* vol. 1, p. 217.

25. Calvin, *A Commentary on the Psalms,* pp. 217-18.

the native meaning of the prophet; for whereas this part of the Psalm has been wrested to allegories, the readers will easily perceive that there is no reason why it should be so."[26] Here Calvin is taking a dig at Augustine who had overdone his allegory of Psalm 19, equating the sun with Christ as the Bridegroom, the stars with the apostles, and their speech with the Gospel. Augustine had even distinguished how with his word God expressed his wisdom, but with his hands he did so with power. Then Cassiodorus (485-580) and later medieval commentators repeat the same allegorization.

In response, Calvin admits, it is true the apostle Paul uses allegory in Galatians 4, concerning Rachel and Hagar. But he limits it in a way Augustine and his successors did not. "Only, because these allegorical interpreters have taken occasion from the words of Paul, this knot must be untwisted." So the general revelation given to all humanity in the first part of the psalm is now shown to be a specific revelation also by the giving of the *Torah,* as specifically — not allegorically — as it was first revealed to the children of Abraham. This, explains Calvin, is more than about the Ten Commandments, or even the statutes of the covenant. It is "the whole body of doctrine whereof consists true religion and godliness."[27]

In describing the nuances of the synonyms of the *Torah,* Calvin, trained as a lawyer, is in his element. But he repeats the importance of realizing that "David treats not the bare commandments, but comprehends the whole covenant," as later they reflect on the whole gospel as preached by the apostles. "Therefore, under the rule of living well, he joins the promises of salvation, or rather Christ Himself, in whom the adoption was grounded." Then he warns all scholars that just as the law was deadly without the Spirit of God affecting Moses, so too without the Spirit of Christ, the text can be unprofitable, indeed "deadly to the use scholars may make of it."[28] Calvin was persuaded that the grammatical sense of the text was the genuine sense, so his rejection of the allegorical reading was more pronounced than Luther's. He also had a stronger conviction of the Spirit's internal testimony inspiring the reader to accept the word of God. Unlike Luther, he saw the pervasiveness of the law of God in all of Scripture, without the conflict Luther brought in of always interpreting the tension and split between law and grace.[29] All these nuances can be sensed in the comparison of their two commentaries on Psalm 19.

Martin Luther's commentary on Psalm 19 underwent several changes be-

26. Calvin, *A Commentary on the Psalms,* p. 219.

27. Calvin, *A Commentary on the Psalms,* p. 222.

28. Calvin, *A Commentary on the Psalms,* p. 224.

29. Hans W. Frei, *The Eclipse of Biblical Narrative: A Study in Eighteenth and Nineteenth Century Hermeneutics* (New Haven and London: Yale University Press, 1977), pp. 21-25.

fore it was published. Unfortunately we have no version of his original lectures in 1513-14. Some think that it was in residence in Coburg in 1530 that he expounded on this psalm. A. F. Hoppe suggests it was first made in 1524. Both are agreed it was neither a pulpit nor a lecture address, but a private exposition delivered personally to Melanchthon, who transcribed it into Latin. It was published in 1531. Certainly, it appears out of the ferment of the early days of the Reformation. Its first statement is like a manifesto: "This is a prophetic and didactic psalm. It prophesies that the Gospel will be preached in the whole world. Secondly, it talks about the manifold and great value of the Gospel, how it acquired this, and what it works and accomplishes."[30]

It is therefore a clarion call for the Reformation, teaching how God's word will be active, and will accomplish great things. No more than the sun can be hindered in its course, can the gospel be held back from being preached, as a new Word from God. Moreover the psalm teaches that the kingdom of Christ will be a spiritual kingdom, unlike the German politics that Luther found himself embroiled in. In addition, at the end of the psalm, there is given a very helpful lesson on repentance, showing that while we are all sinners, by God's grace we can be redeemed.

In other words, Luther is still echoing his Augustinian heritage, applying the allegorical approach of his master, and adapting it to the new situation of the Reformation. Verse by verse, he places his own allegorical substitutes: "The heavens are telling" — the gospel is being preached everywhere; "The glory of God" — the gospel; "The handiwork" of God — all the works wrought by justification, sanctification, deliverance from the devil, etc.; "There is no speech or language" — no part of the world will not hear the gospel; "Their rule has gone into all the world" — in the future God's grace will be preached everywhere; "He has set a tent for the sun" — Christ, who will rule the church in all lands; "As a Bridegroom" — Christ is loving and friendly, giving great comfort to the conscience "for there is nothing hid from its heat." Then comes the break from the allegorical, for in verse 7 [8] Luther sees God's Law speak directly in plain words. It would be intriguing to know what Melanchthon's response would have been to this allegorical commentary, for this was not his style!

From verse 11 [12], Luther sees a third section, a prayer, which begins with confession and repentance. Yes, acknowledges Luther, I am a sinner as David was, but I stay with the Word of God and do not give approval to the proud persecutors of the church: whether the pope, Campegius as cardinal legate in Germany, or Matthew Lang, cardinal archbishop of Salzburg, or Johann Eck, Luther's opponent in Leipzig in 1519. For Luther, "innocent of the great

30. *Luther's Works,* vol. 12, ed. Jaroslav Pelikan (St. Louis: Concordia, 1955), p. 139.

transgression" was to be innocent of blasphemy and ungodliness, as he had been accused. Indeed, Luther felt the same need as David, to cry unto the Lord, "my Rock and my Redeemer." Rarely then has a psalm become so intimately appropriated to the commentator's personal circumstances as it was with Martin Luther. Yet we sense the subtle reaction of Calvin, that perhaps Luther had taken allegory too far!

III. Aquinas

Thomas Aquinas neatly suggests that the psalm "according to the letter refers to David, but according to the mystery it refers to Christ." He sees it divided into two parts: God reveals generally to all humanity, and he reveals specifically to the faithful by his law. Like Augustine he sees the physical realm being expressed figuratively, so that "by the skies the apostles are understood, in whom God resides as in the skies. And they are called skies on account of the sublimity of their behavior." "Again they are covered in stars because of the abundances of many virtues . . . they are shining by teaching." Here he quotes Jesus in Matthew 5:16: "Let your light shine before me, that they may see your good works and glorify your Father who is in the heavens." The Apostles are also called "the firmament, because they have been made firm by virtue of the Holy Spirit."

It all suggests the night sky is not appreciated by this scholar monk in his cell, and indeed he states: "the night-time is the time of meditation because of the quiet," finding it is the time of inward discoveries, the time of knowledge, indeed knowledge of God. But "the night" is also the time of ignorance, the life of the carnal who do not know God nor can discern spiritual truths. Whereas "the day" is that of clear revelation to the faithful, suggesting that is the spiritual condition we need to have to participate in the second part of the psalm, when we delight in the law of the Lord. Yet such is the authority of apostolic teaching that it is universal, having "gone to the ends of the earth."

So what then of "the sun"? Like Augustine, Aquinas states "by the sun we understand Christ . . . and some prophecies say this of Christ under the figure of the sun." With the appearance of Christ, the night has dissipated, and in the clear day of revelation, we have joy in place of sadness, magnitude in place of "small things," regularity that gives us certainty as to the way, and height by which to measure all things. Aquinas then uses further figural images by which to unfold the mysteries of Christ's incarnation.

Next, Aquinas describes the law of God, as he reflects on the second part of the psalm. He contrasts human law and "the Old law," perhaps unconvincingly so for us, since his comments upon the synonyms used by the psalmist are given somewhat too legalistic treatment by Aquinas. His conclusion on "the fear of the Lord" is suggestive. "Now, all fear is caused by love, since a man fears to lose that which he loves." So an unholy love fears God negatively, while a "holy fear" loves God righteously. An unholy fear originates from the world and from the servility of self-love. Whereas a "holy fear" has three traits: "it fears to offend God; it is unwilling to be separated from Him; and it submits itself to God through reverence." With this holy fear as the basis for the exegete to comment upon Scripture, we complete the trail from modern skepticism regarding the divine authority of the I AM, to the godly reverence with which God's revelation was once treasured.

Part II: Voice of the Psalmist: Translation

A psalm by David

1 The heavens are telling the glory of God,
And the firmament is declaring his handiwork.
2 Day by day it pours forth words,
And night by night it proclaims knowledge.
3 There is no speech, and there are no words;
Their[31] voice is inaudible.
4 The measuring cord[32] [of their voice] stretches out to all the earth,
Even at the remotest point of the world are their words.
And God[33] has pitched[34] a tent in the heavens[35] for the sun.
5 It is like a bridegroom who emerges from his chamber;
It rejoices like a strong man to run a course.
6 It emerges from the edge of the earth,
And its orbit extends from one edge to another;
And nothing can be hidden from its glowing heat.

31. The addition of "where," "in which" in some EVV is grammatically unwarranted. The ancient versions read: "It is not a speech or words whose voice is unintelligible," but this is unnatural and does not satisfy the parallelism.

32. There is no need to seek new meanings for *qav* (e.g., from II *qvh*, "to assemble") or to alter the text (e.g., to *qôlām*, "their voice") on the basis of LXX's *hai phōnai autōn* ("their voice"), for it may be a dynamic equivalent. I added ["of their voice"] to clarify the metaphor.

33. Literally, "he."

34. *Śām* is better construed as a perfect than a participle, for the poet more probably intends a tent God pitched at the creation of the world than a tent he is in process of setting up.

35. Literally, "for them."

7 The law of *I AM* is perfect, renewing vitality;
The stipulations of *I AM* are reliable, making wise the simple.
8 The regulations of *I AM* are right, rejoicing the heart;
The commands[36] of *I AM* are clean, causing the eyes to sparkle.
9 The fear of *I AM* is pure, enduring forever;
The judgments of *I AM* are true; they are altogether righteous.
10 They are[37] more desirable than gold, even much fine gold;
And they are sweeter than honey, than virgin honey flowing from the comb.
11 Also, by them your slave is warned;[38]
And in keeping them is great reward.
12 As for errors, who can discern them?[39]
For hidden faults,[40] declare me free from punishment.[41]
13 Moreover, hold back your slave from insolent men,
let them not rule over me.
Then I will retain integrity,
and be free from the punishment for a great transgression.
14 Let the words of my mouth and the meditation of my heart find favor[42] before you,[43]
I AM, my Rock and my Redeemer.

36. Construing the singular as a collective to designate the group (*IBHS*, p. 113; P. 7.2.1b).

37. Literally, "the ones [which are] more desirable." *Hanneḥ^{e}mādîm* consists of a cataphoric article (literally, the judgments . . . the ones, *IBHS*, p. 247, P. 13.5.2c) with a dependent relative participle modifying "judgments" (i.e., "judgments, which are," *IBHS*, p. 621, P. 37.5.b.).

38. A tolerative *Niphal* (= allow oneself to be warned; to take heed; *IBHS*, p. 389, P. 23.4f).

39. *š^{e}nî'ôt* may be the object of "who can understand," but more probably, to judge from the normal pattern of the rhetorical use of *mî*, it is an absolute nominative. If so, the typical object of the verb is elided: "who can perceive [that he does them]?"

40. *Nistārôt* is an independent relative participle (*IBHS*, p. 621, P. 37.5), functioning as a substantival adjective (*IBHS*, pp. 261-63, P. 14.3.3).

41. Declarative/delocative *Piel* (*IBHS*, p. 402).

42. Literally, "let be with reference to favor."

43. The Hebrew text breaks up the stereotype phrase, "favor before you," over parallel members.

Part III. Commentary

I. Introduction

A. Author and Date

No empirical reason calls into question the superscription's claim that David authored Psalm 19. Most scholars, however, think the firmament's hymn of praise (vv. 1-6 [2-7]) is older than the rest of the psalm. There may be some truth here (see below). David may have adopted and *adapted* an old hymn to the Canaanite god, 'El (proper name), to the praise of the God of the patriarchs, using *'ēl* as a generic term for God (see superscript below). The connections of Psalms 18 and 19, as observed by Delitzsch (see pp. 345-46), may point to Davidic authorship, because David is almost certainly the author of Psalm 18 (see Ps. 18:50; 2 Sam. 22:1). That David is the one praising *I AM*'s Torah (vv. 7-10 [8-11]) finds confirmation in his closing charges to Solomon, where he uses essentially the same vocabulary (apart from *huqqâ* instead of poetic *piqqûdîm*) as hyponyms[44] for the Law (see vv. 7-10 [8-11]): "Keep *I AM*'s decrees *(huqqâ)* and commands *(miṣwâ)*, his judgments *(mišpāṭ)*, regulations *(ʿēdâ)*, as written in the Law *(tôrâ)* of Moses" (1 Kings 2:3).

B. Rhetoric and Content

Form and rhetorical critical analyses show the psalm consists of a superscript, two stanzas of praise (1-6, 7-10 [2-7, 8-11]), one stanza of petition (11-13 [12-14]), a dedicatory prayer (14 [15]), and a subscript (see p. 88).

Superscript	Superscript [1]B
I. Firmament's Praise of God's Glory and Knowledge	vv. 1-6 [2-7]
A. Temporal and Spatial Universality of Its Inaudible Praise	vv. 1-4 [2-5]
1. Temporal Universality of Firmament's Praise	vv. 1-2 [2-3]
2. Spatial Universality of the Heavens' Inaudible Praise	vv. 3-4 [4-5]
B. Sun's Universal Testimony	vv. 5-6 [6-7]
II. Psalmist's Praise of *I AM*'s Torah	vv. 7-10 [8-11]
A. Strophe 1: ab//a′b′ structure	vv. 7-8 [8-9]

44. Hyponym is a word or phrase whose semantic range is included within that of another word; e.g., scarlet, vermilion, carmine.

B. Strophe 2: ab structure	vv. 9-10 [10-11]
III. Psalmist's Petitions for Salvation	vv. 11-13 [12-14]
A. Pardon for Hidden Guilt	vv. 11-12 [12-13]
B. Preserve from Guilt of Apostasy	v. 13 [14]
Epilogue: Dedicatory Prayer	v. 14 [15]
Subscript: to the chief musician	Psalm 20:superscript A [1A]

The three stanzas consist of seven quatrains (i.e., two bi-cola): 1-2, 3-4, 5-6, 7-8, 9-10, 11-12, 13-14. The number seven signifies perfection, completeness, and so suggests that whatever the origin of the stanzas, an author composed a unified poem.[45] The psalm is a conceptual unity, focusing on God's two books of revelation: the general revelation of creation and the special revelation of Scripture (see Survey of History; cf. Romans 2): "Both books magnify the Author's excellence."[46] Some find a unity in the movement of the stanzas: for M. Fishbane, from the heavens speak (vv. 1-6), to *I AM* speaks (vv. 7-10) to the psalmist speaks (vv. 11-14);[47] for A. Meinhold, from words about God, to words from God, to words to God;[48] for C. Broyles a contracting movement, from the vastness of God's skies, to *I AM*'s law, to the worshiper himself. "This threefold movement is also reflected in the divine names: 'God' (or 'El'), the LORD (Yahweh) and my rock and my Redeemer."[49] Are these movements the intended creations of the artist or the creations of ingenious interpreters? Are the stanzas related by the psychology of awe? "The starry sky above me," said Kant, "and the moral law in me . . . are the two things which fill the soul with ever new and increasing admiration and reverence."[50] R. Clifford sees a logical unity (see below).

The striking formal differences (i.e., subject matter, mood, language, and meter[51]) between the first two stanzas of hymns to God and to *I AM* and the abrupt way they are joined together, lacking any transition, suggest the author pieced together two originally independent poems. Ancient Near Eastern poets

45. He uses the name *I AM* seven times in the second half, reaching a crescendo of three names in a climactic conclusion: "I AM, my Rock, my Redeemer."

46. C. Spurgeon, *Treasury of David,* updated by Roy H. Clarke (Nashville: Thomas Nelson, 1997), p. 125.

47. M. A. Fishbane, *Text and Texture* (New York: Schocken, 1979), p. 86.

48. A. Meinhold, "Überlegungen zur Theologie des 19. Psalms," *ZTK* 80 (1983): 119-36.

49. C. Broyles, *Psalms* (NIBC; Grand Rapids: Zondervan, 1999), p. 109.

50. Wallace, *Kant,* p. 53, cited by A. F. Kirkpatrick, *The Book of Psalms* (CBSC; Cambridge: Cambridge University Press, 1916), p. 101.

51. The more extended verses — especially the two tri-cola in verses 5-6 — match the theme of the heavens' expansive praise.

had no scruples about joining together pieces of literature (cf. Psalm 108).[52] Ancient Near Eastern evidence put forward by Schröder[53] and Dürr[54] also favors seeing the psalm as a unity. Whatever the stanzas' origins, the poet who composed the whole, as in so much of Biblical literature, allows his audience to tease out the connection.

To understand the poet's images in his personifying the firmament's praise of God, one needs to understand his ancient Near Eastern cosmology. In brief, the firmament is the phenomenal dome or vault that was thought to separate the supernal ocean above from the earth and water below.[55] Moreover, knowledge that Near Eastern religions associated the sun with righteousness and law,[56] reflected in many Old Testament passages (e.g., Job 38:12-15), provides an understanding of the immediate link between the celebration of the sun in the conclusion of the first stanza and of the law in the second, as Delitzsch recognized (see pp. 345-46). The physical light of the sun that exposes the hideaways of the wicked corresponds to the spiritual light of the law that exposes hidden sins.

C. Form and Theology

Psalm 19 is obviously a poem, characterized as it is by parallelism, terseness, and heightened style, including manifold figures of speech (metaphors, metonymies, personification, etc.). Recall that C. S. Lewis regarded Psalm 19 as the greatest poem in the Psalter and one of the greatest lyrics in the world (see p. 340). It is not scientific literature.

More specifically it is a song, a hymn. The superscript labels its genre **a psalm** (*mizmôr,* a song sung to the pizzicato of a stringed instrument) and an inspired editor included it in Israel's hymnbook. The Psalter's songs are mostly hymns of praise and petition. Psalm 19 is both. The first two stanzas resemble

52. It can be said that Israel's authors are redactors. Put that way, it becomes apparent that a distinction between author and redactor is a false dichotomy.

53. O. Schröder, "Zu Psalm 19," *ZAW* 34 (1914): 69-70.

54. L. Dürr, "Zur Frage nach der Einheit von Ps. 19," in *Festschrift für E. Sellin* (BWANT 13; Stuttgart, 1927), pp. 37-48.

55. For a fuller discussion see Bruce K. Waltke with Charles Yu, *An Old Testament Theology: An Exegetical, Canonical, and Thematic Approach* (Grand Rapids: Zondervan, 2007), pp. 194-96.

56. The diorite stele on which is written the famous law-code of Hammurabi is topped "by a bas-relief showing Hammurabi in the act of receiving the commission to write the law-book from the god of justice, the sun-god Shamash" (*ANET,* p. 163; see *ANEP,* p. 77, fig. 246).

hymns of praise: praise to God the Creator (vv. 1-6; cf. Psalms 104, 148) and praise of *I AM* as author of *Torah* (vv. 7-10; cf. Psalms 1 and 119).[57] As for the first hymn, I say "resemble" because there is no call to the congregation to praise and no address to God, unlike typical praise hymns. The praise of Torah is a janus. In the light of God's law, his slave is warned and offers his penitential petition in a third stanza. Like petition psalms, Psalm 19 typically includes the motifs of petition and praise, but atypically it reverses the movement; instead of moving from petition to praise, it escalates from praise to petition. In other words, praise is the basis, not the result, of petition. This unique sequence leads to our classifying the psalm as both praise and penitence. The third stanza is a penitential petition for salvation, pardon, and preservation (vv. 11-13).

Even more specifically, Psalm 19 is a wisdom psalm — that is to say, it belongs to the genres of both hymnic and wisdom literatures. David expresses himself in the form of a praise psalm and a petition psalm, but he thinks as a sage.[58] First, he uses the vocabulary of wisdom literature: "knowledge," "simple," "wise," "fear of *I AM*," "warned." Second, in typical wisdom fashion he connects God's revelation in creation with his special revelation in *Torah* by using the former to buttress and/or illustrate the latter.[59] R. Clifford, as mentioned above, sees a logical unity holding the psalm together. "The poetic logic is clear: The divine wisdom (meaning ability to govern) discernible in the daily movements of the heavens (vv. 1-4b), especially in the sun's course (vv. 4c-6), is also visible in the teaching (vv. 7-9) to which human beings have access through humble prayer (vv. 10-14)." But his attempt to show analogies between the creation and the Law are not all equally convincing.[60] Third, more specifically, the first hymn (vv. 1-6) celebrates the creation that displays God's knowledge (see v. 2), and the second stanza celebrates the *Torah* that gives humankind wisdom (v. 7). Fourth, and most importantly, because the Creator of all things knows comprehensively, he knows absolutely and certainly. The heavens declare that God's knowledge is vast. Therefore, it may be inferred that his special revelation is based on his com-

57. The two names of God, El (God as Creator) and *I AM* (God as Israel's Covenant Keeper), used in its two halves respectively, superficially seem to point to two unrelated psalms. But when it is recalled that descriptive praise psalms normally praise God as both Creator and as Israel's Covenant Keeper, the twofold names point to the psalm's unity.

58. Most recently M. Futato, *Interpreting the Psalms: An Exegetical Handbook,* Handbooks for Old Testament Exegesis (Kregel, 2007), p. 179, classified Psalm 19 as a wisdom psalm.

59. For the wisdom-like ethos of verses 1-4a see O. H. Steck, "Bemerkungen zur thematischen Einheit von Psalm 19:2-7," in *Werden und Wirken des Alten Testament: Festschrift für Claus Westermann,* ed. Rainer Albertz et al. (Göttingen: Vandenhoeck & Ruprecht, 1980), pp. 318-24.

60. R. Clifford, *Psalms 1–72* (AOTC; Nashville: Abingdon Press, 2002), pp. 111-12.

prehensive knowledge as Creator; God alone sees "ontologically" (i.e., the whole of what actually is). To be wise, a person must transcend the relativity and depravity of human epistemology. Earthbound mortals cannot find transcendent wisdom apart from the transcendent *I AM.* Real wisdom must find its starting point in the order of creation: in his light, we see light (Ps. 36:9 [10]).[61] Only the Creator knows what is true and false, what is right and wrong. And only the humble, who are willing to live by faith, are wise; the unbeliever is a fool.

The subscript shows that all Israel should join the king's praises and petitions. Without using direct address, the king implicitly addresses the nation in the first two stanzas, and though he explicitly addresses *I AM* by referring to himself as "your slave"[62] in the third stanza, he implicitly exemplifies for the nation a godly response to *Torah* and wisdom (see below on the psalm as mystery, pp. 366-73).[63] In sum, the psalm is a unified mixture of hymns praising the Creator and *Torah,* a penitential psalm, both of which function to instruct the nation, and, as will be seen in the conclusion, a mystery that veils the Christian faith.

II. Exegesis

A. Superscript s/s [v. 1]

For **a psalm by David** see pp. 89-90.

B. Firmament and Heavens Declare God's Glory vv. 1-4 [2-5]

The first stanza consists of two strophes: the heavens' universal proclamation of God's glory and knowledge (1-4), and the sun's proclamation in particular (5-6). The first strophe consists of two quatrains that have an alternating pattern: a/a′: the firmament and heavens are declaring God's glory (a, v. 1) in inaudible words (a′, v. 3); b/b′: the universality of their proclamation in time (b, v. 2) and in space (b′, v. 4). The distinction between singular and plural heavens shows that the firmament is the subject of verse 2 and the heavens, of verses 3-4. The heavens' vastness, splendor, order, and mystery should prompt rational creatures to celebrate the Creator's glory. Aristotle speculated: "Should a man live under-

61. B. K. Waltke, *The Book of Proverbs Chapters 15–31* (Grand Rapids: Eerdmans, 2006), p. 471.

62. Cf. Psalm 18: superscript, where the epithet clearly refers to David.

63. Cf. L. C. Allen, "David as an Exemplar of Spirituality," *Biblica* 67 (1986): 544-46.

ground, and converse with the works of art and mechanism, and afterwards be brought up into the day to see the several glories of the heaven and earth, he would immediately pronounce them the work of such a Being as we define God to be."[64] Compare Addison's paraphrase:

What though in solemn silence all
    Move round the dark terrestrial ball?
What though nor real voice nor sound
    Amid their radiant orbs be found?
In reason's ear they all rejoice,
    And utter forth a glorious voice,
For ever singing, as they shine,
    "The hand that made us is divine."[65]

1. *Temporal Universality of the Firmament's Praise vv. 1-2 [2-3]*

Verse 2 is linked to verse 1 by the subject of the firmament, by verbs of speaking, and by a chiasm of the verbs' stems: *Piel* and *Hiphil* // *Hiphil* and *Piel.*

a. The Firmament Praises God's Glory v. 1 [2]

In the introductory summary statement of this stanza the synonyms "heavens" and "firmament" constitute its outer frame (a/a′), "announcing" and "declaring" occupy the b/b′ slot, and its inner core matches "glory of God," a metonymy of effect, with "work of his hands," a metonymy of cause (c/c′).[66]

The firmament and heavens, personified as hymnists, proclaim that God's government over them shows his glory and knowledge. His skill and knowledge should encourage covenant people to submit to *I AM*'s government of society through *Torah* (see Psalm 1; above, "Form and Theology"). Moreover, God's order of creation lays the firm foundation for his order of redemption through *Torah.* Pope John Paul II noted in his remarks to Roman Catholic bishops, "Grace never casts nature aside or cancels it out, but rather perfects it and ennobles it."[67]

64. Aristotle (384 BCE), cited by Spurgeon, *Treasury of David,* p. 125.

65. J. Barr, *The Concept of Biblical Theology: An Old Testament Perspective* (Minneapolis: Fortress Press, 1999), rightly restores the role of natural theology and of science and reason to overcome dialectical theology.

66. E. W. Bullinger, *Figures of Speech Used in the Bible* (Grand Rapids: Baker Book House, reprinted 1968), pp. 539, 560.k.

67. Richard John Neuhaus, "True Christian Feminism," *National Review,* November 25, 1988, p. 24.

The heavens *(haššāmāyim)* may refer to everything above the earth, the firmament (cf. Gen. 1:8) and/or the supernal waters held up by **the firmament** (*hārāqîa*ʿ). The firmament is metonymy associated with the sun, moon, and stars, which make their orbits within it (cf. Ps. 8:3 [4]). The Bible images the expansive firmament and the high heavens as inhabited by God and his angelic court to represent among other sublimities God's omniscience. In this metaphor, God sees the world holistically and clearly and so can "speak" absolutely and with certainty, unlike earthbound mortals, who apart from revelation must speak tentatively because of their limited vision (see Job 28:12-24).

Mᵉsappᵉrîm ***(are telling)*** means "to count again," and/or "to enumerate (that is, to relate or narrate in detail)."[68] Both senses are intended; the former, because of the synonyms of speaking in this strophe, and the latter, because it repeats its proclamation day and night, "to count again" also may be intended. The grammatical form is a participle, signifying a durative (i.e., a continuous) situation.[69] This is also true of *maggîd* (**are declaring**), which signifies the process whereby a speaker communicates to the addressee a *vitally important* message, namely, the Creator's *handiwork* (*maʿᵉśēh yādāyw,* literally "the work of his hands"), a metonymy of source for the effect *glory (kābôd).* Israel tells *I AM*'s glory — his weight, dignity, importance, honor — among the nations (Ps. 96:3); the heavens tell God's glory to the whole earth. David speaks of *God ('ēl),* because *'ēl* represents his transcendence over the creation, whereas *I AM,* which he uses in his Torah praise, connotes his immanence with his covenant people. Recall Calvin's comment that "the heavens declaring" stirs up our senses and teaches more clearly and more profitably than simply "our beholding" (see pp. 346-47).

b. Temporal Universality of Their Praise v. 2 [3]

The chiastic pattern of verse 1 is replaced with an alternating pattern: slot a ("day by day"), slot b ("pours forth") and slot c ("words") //a′ ("night by night") b′ ("declares") c′ ("knowledge"). The note of the constancy of heaven's praise sounds quietly in the durative participles (v. 1), then intensifies in the merism of "day and night" (= "all the time," see Ps. 1:2), and comes to a resounding climax in the distributives "day by day" and "night by night" (i.e., every day and every night).[70] *Day (yôm)* refers to the cycle of daylight (cf. Prov. 4:18), not of twenty-

68. The *Piel* is used with verbs of speaking to express a "frequentative" situation (cf. *IBHS,* 414-15, P. 24.5).

69. *IBHS,* p. 626, P. 37.6e.

70. *IBHS,* pp. 115-16, P. 7.2.3.

four hours. The firmament proclaims God's glory from the rising of the sun in the east to the fading sun in the west, whereupon it replaces that witness to God's glory with the heliacal orbit of the moon and stars at *night (layᵉlâ).*

The personified firmament is the subject of *pours forth (yabbîaʿ),* because the predicate continues to be verbs of speaking. *Yabbîaʿ* denotes an uncontrollable or uncontrolled gushing forth of words, like that of the swollen waters of a gushing wadi. The metaphor derives from conceiving the mouth as a fountain (cf. Prov. 18:4; Matt. 12:34).[71] The firmament's uninterrupted proclamation of God's glory is copious, extravagant, powerful, and inescapable. If the naked eye can "hear" the sight-language of the heavens' proclamation, how much more when its sight-hearing is amplified a billion-fold by the Hubble telescope. Stars, many times much larger than our modest sun, thousands of light years apart, are more numerous than the grains of sand on earth's beaches. The synonym **declare** (*ḥawwâ,* "to make known," "to inform someone") is used only in poetry (Job 13:17; 15:17; 32:6, 10, 17; 36:2; Ps. 52:11; Hab. 3:2 *(Qere).* Both verbs occur in the iterative imperfective conjugation in conformity with the distributive singulars of "day by day" and "night by night." *'ōmer* ("words," "sayings," "news") also occurs only in poetry (Job 22:28; Pss. 19:2 [3], 3 [4]; 68:11 [12]; 77:8 [9]; Hab. 3:9). "Word" refers to the expression; its parallel *knowledge (daʿat)* refers to the substance communicated. According to C. Kayatz, in the theological system of the Egyptian city of Heliopolis, the creator god, Re, is characterized by *sja,* "knowledge," and *hû,* "expression."[72] Knowledge signifies the fact or condition of knowing something, of understanding, of having information. God's apparent vast knowledge as seen in his masterpiece garners him glory. Unlike human knowledge that must be learned or acquired (Isa. 40:12-14), God's knowledge is inherent in his being.

2. *Spatial Universality of the Heavens' Inaudible Praise vv. 3-4 [4-5]*

The second strophe is linked to the first by the rare catchword *'ōmer,* "words"; by shifting from the masculine singular pronoun ("it"), having "firmament" of verse 1b as its antecedent, to the third masculine plural pronoun ("their, them"), having "heavens" of verse 1a as its antecedent; by using other synonyms of speaking; and by the alternating pattern of representing the notion of the heavens' witness followed by the universality of that witness.

71. See Bruce K. Waltke, *The Book of Proverbs: Chapters 1–15* (Grand Rapids: Eerdmans, 2004), p. 71.

72. C. Kayatz, *Studien zu Proverbien 1–9; Eine form- und motivgeschichtliche Untersuchung unter Einbeziehung ägyptischen Vergleichsmaterials* (WMANT 22; Neukirchen-Vluyn: Neukirchener, 1966), p. 11.

a. Unspoken Eloquence v. 3 [4]

Three negations emphasize that their "voice" is inaudible. Twice repeating *there is no* (Heb. *'ên,* a predicator of non-existence) in construct with *'ōmer* ("words," see v. 2) and its synonym "speech" *(dᵉbārîm).* Whereas the root *'mr* directs attention to the contents of the speech, *dbr* points to the activity of speaking.[73] The third negation is *bᵉlî* ("without"), which is replaced in late Hebrew by *'ên lᵉ*.[74] The oxymoron of a silent declaration can be felt more fully when it is understood that *qôl voice* describes everything that can be perceived acoustically. But their voice *is inaudible* (*bᵉlî nišmā',* literally, "without being able to hear"). *šm',* like English "to hear," refers minimally to acoustic perception. The point of the oxymoron: though the heavens are seen with the eye, like a portrait, they "speak" the language of sight to the ear of reason and of the heart to generate the worship of God (cf. Rom. 10:17). As my wife Elaine and I (Bruce) were traveling through the Alaskan Inland Passage, a geologist lectured on the rocks, and a naturalist discoursed on the flora and fauna, but neither one mentioned the Creator. I expressed my appreciation for their knowledge, likening the geologist's work to that of an art critic's comments on the pigment of the paint Michelangelo used in the Sistine Chapel, and I compared the naturalist's explanation to the art critic's exposition of his brushstrokes. But I noted that it was the landscape itself that attracts and delights the tourists, and that the Artist of such a masterpiece must be what we call God. They now include the analogy in their lectures.

b. Spatial Universality of the Heavens' Witness v. 4 [5]

The second quatrain highlights the heavens' spatial universality. Its structure alternates ab/a′b′: "In all the earth" (slot a) emphatically introduces the theme of this quatrain. By its contrast to the heavens, *earth (hā'āreṣ)* has its cosmological nuance, not its normal geographical sense of "land." *All (kôl)* is quantitative (= totality), not qualitative ("all sorts of"). "Even in the extremities of the world" (slot a′) intensifies the spatial universality. Since the slot a′ heightens slot a and does not add a new thought, *waw* is ascensive *even,* not conjunctive ("and").[75] *Extremities (qāṣēh,* from the root *qṣh,* "to cut off") refers to earth's "farthest, most remote" places. *World (tēbēl)* is a stock-in-trade parallel of "earth," but in contrast to the earth it refers to the inhabited and cultivated areas of the mainland, what we would call continents.

73. Cf. G. Gerleman, *TLOT,* 1:327, s.v. *dābār.*

74. *IBHS,* p. 603, P. 36.2.1g.

75. See *IBHS,* pp. 652-53, P. 39.2.4b.

In slot b *their measuring cord (qaw)* denotes the ancients' tape-measure. Israel's prophets use it as a metaphor for the extent of *I AM*'s judgment or salvation of a land. As a person's allotment of land is measured or marked off (2 Sam. 8:2), so land is marked off by God or some other agent for ruin or restoration (Isa. 34:11, 17). Here the metaphor refers to the extent of land reached by the heavens' message. *Their voice* is added to clarify the metaphor (see n. 32). *Qaw* commonly occurs with *nṭh* "to stretch out," but here, as in Jeremiah 31:39 *(Qere), qaw* occurs with *yṣ'* "to go out," probably because no agent stretches it out. Nevertheless, for the sake of the English idiom, *yṣ'* is glossed *stretches out.* The parallel in slot b′, *their words (millêhem),* validates this interpretation of the metaphor. *Millim,* another synonym for "words," is borrowed from Aramaic and occurs exclusively in poetry.

3. *Sun's Universal Testimony vv. 4c-6 [5c-7]*

Verse 4c is a janus linking the universality of heaven's witness (vv. 4a, b) to the particular universal witness of the sun (vv. 5-6). The Masoretic text combines "And God has pitched . . ." with verse 4. But it is better to combine it with verses 5 and 6, for their topic is the sun, which is introduced in 4c. Moreover, by emending the versification, 5a and b give two similes in two balanced tri-cola. Syntactically the two strophes are linked by *in them* (i.e., "the heavens"). Rhetorically the strophes are linked by three catchwords: *yṣ'*, "goes forth" (vv. 4a and 5a, 6a); *qṣh:* "edge" (vv. 4a, 6a); *'ên,* "there is no"/"nothing" (vv. 3a, 6b); and by the inclusio *haššāmayim,* "the heavens" (vv. 1a, 6a). The sun implicitly testifies to God's knowledge and glory all the time (v. 5, cf. v. 2) and everywhere (v. 6, cf. v. 4 [5]). The strophe traces the course of the sun at night and in the morning, and its orbit from sunrise to sunset.

a. Sun's Tent at Night v. 4 [5]c

Though unseen at night, the sun is still present in the heavens, implying its universal presence in space as well as in time. At the earth's most remote horizon God (literally, "he") pitched **a** metaphorical tent (*'ōhel,* see Ps. 15:1) *for the sun (laššemeš)* to spend the night. The antecedent of "he" is ambiguous, but conceptually Israel's monotheism demands the clarifying gloss **God** (see v. 1). The sun becomes theologically significant in the Old Testament because of the importance it plays in the pantheon of ancient Near Eastern gods. *Pitched* glosses *śām* (literally, "set," "set up"). In verse 5a the poet transforms the image of the tent into a marriage chamber from which the sun emerges in the morning.

b. Sun's Morning Radiance v. 5 [6]

Semantic pertinence demands interpreting *haššemeš (the sun)* as the antecedent of *hû'* (it). The comparative *kᵉ (like)* has its qualitative sense, expressing resemblance in respect of some attribute, action, character, to the appearance of a *bridegroom (ḥātān).* Elsewhere, in its seven uses in simile the newly married husband of the bride is used with reference to his adorning (Isa. 61:10) and his rejoicing with exuberance over his bride (Isa. 62:5; Jer. 7:34; 16:9; 25:10; 33:11; cf. Joel 2:16). So the personification and simile connote the morning sun's glorious radiance, *who emerges* (literally, *going forth* [*yōṣē'*], see vv. 4, 6) *like a bridegroom (kᵉḥātān) from his chamber (mēḥuppātô).*[76] The simile connotes youthful freshness, beauty, vigor, and joy. *Ḥuppâ* occurs only three times in the Hebrew Bible and refers broadly to "shelter" (Isa. 4:5), a hyponym of "tent" in verse 4c. In Joel 2:16 the bride's chamber is distinguished from the bridegroom's room (Joel 2:16), and in Psalm 19:5 the "shelter" refers to the bridegroom's chamber where presumably he takes his bride to consummate their marriage.

The parallel simile in the B verset, *it rejoices (yāśîś),* supports the interpretation that the bridegroom simile images the rising sun as radiantly exulting. The simile marked by *like (kᵉ)* supplements the joy of a bridegroom with the strength of a *strong man (gibbôr).* The strong man rejoices about *to run (lārûṣ)* a [race] course (*'ōraḥ*, a poetic word for "track") because none can compete with him for either speed or distance. The metaphorical track — he is no cross-country runner — refers to the sun's orbit in the firmament. The sun has the speed of a sprinter and the endurance and strength of a marathon runner.

c. Sun's Universal Heat Throughout the Day v. 6 [7]

It emerges glosses "its going forth" *(môṣā'ô),* the nominal form of *yṣ'* (see vv. 4a, 5a, and 6). This is the third occurrence of this catchword and shows that the verset opens with reference to the morning sun of verse 5. Conjunctive *and (û)* links the rising sun to *its orbit (tᵉqûpātô),* a gloss for this rare word that in its three other occurrences means cycle (Exod. 34:22; 1 Sam. 1:20; 2 Chron. 24:23). That orbit extends from one edge of the earth to the other (*'al-qᵉṣôtām,* literally, "upon[77] their edges"). Conjunctive *and* adds the further thought that the sun's heat is felt universally. *Nothing* (*'ên,* see its construct use in v. 3 [4]) *can be hidden* (*nistār*), which here, like English "to hide" (with reference to sight), has

76. Note the alliteration of *ḥtn* and *ḥpt.*

77. Some mss. read *'ad,* not *'al,* but the correction is unnecessary; the preposition implies a verb of motion such as "extend" (*IBHS,* p. 224, P. 11.4.3d).

both negative and positive nuances. It can mean to prevent a person or thing from being perceived by another or to protect them. *From its glowing heat (mēḥammātô)* is appropriate with both notions: none can be prevented from feeling the sun's heat or be protected from it. *Ḥammâ* refers to glowing heat and so is used by poets as a metonymy for the sun in its five other occurrences: Job 30:28; Song 6:10; Isa. 24:23; 30:26 (twice).

C. Psalmist's Praise of I AM's Torah vv. 7-10 [8-11]

David now shifts his praise of God's knowledge and glory through the mediated proclamation of the firmament to his own praise of the *Torah* of Israel's covenant-keeping God, *I AM.* His praise of the *Torah* is unified by a steady beat of three words in the A versets and two words in their B versets of the first two quatrains (vv. 7-8), which is slowed down to two beats in each verset in verses 9-10, though in verse 9A there are still three words. Matching this cadence is a similar structure, using qualifying adjectives/nouns to praise the *Torah* and assertions of its beneficences to the covenant community. However, whereas in the A versets of verses 7-8 adjectives celebrate the Law's moral beauty and in their B versets celebrate its social benefits, in verse 9 the whole quatrain uses only adjectives for its moral perfection, and verse 10 speaks of its beneficences. So there are two strophes of contrasting rhythms and structures: verses 7-8 and 9-10.

The A versets of verses 7-10 have an abc pattern. The /a/ slot features a hyponym for *Torah*: Law, statutes, precepts, commands, fear of *I AM,* and court verdicts, or judgments.[78] The /b/ slot cites the author: *I AM (yhwh).* The /c/ slot features the predicate adjectives: perfect, reliable, right, clean, pure, firm. The B versets of verses 7-8 praise the beneficences of the hyponyms for the Law using participles with the initial letter /m/ and denoting a durative situation and a causing of the verbal notion: "renewing, making wise, rejoicing, enlightening," with objects appropriate to them. The sustained cadence and the anaphora of structure have a rhetorical effect similar to that of Lincoln's Gettysburg Address: "we cannot dedicate — we cannot consecrate — we cannot hallow." The manifold anaphora of verses 7-10 elevates step by step the moral sublimity of *I AM*'s Torah. Verse 10 crowns the whole: its judgments are more valuable than much pure gold and more delightful than virgin honey from the comb.

78. *Huqqîm* ("apodictic laws") is not used in Psalm 19.

1. Strophe 1: Pattern ab//a'/b' vv. 7-8 [8-9]

Verse 7 is the basic step in the elevation of *torah.* Its A verset uses the most comprehensive term for the Law, *torah,* and its B verset states its most basic benefit, renewing vitality.[79] *Law* (*tôrâ,* catechetical teaching) refers to the Law of Moses (see Ps. 1:2). Though mediated through Moses, its author is I AM *(yhwh).* Its most comprehensive sublimity *is* its being *perfect* (*t*ᵉ*mîmâ,*[80] "complete," and "having integrity," see Ps. 15:2; 19:13). Spurgeon reflects: "It is a crime to add to it, treason to alter it, and felony to take from it."[81] The first-cited and most essential benefit of the *Torah* is that of *renewing (m*ᵉ*šîḇaṯ) vitality* (*nep̱eš,* passionate vitality; traditionally, "soul," see Ps. 3 n. 35). *šûb* ("renew") has the central meaning of having moved in a particular direction to move thereupon in the opposite direction. In a context pertaining to evil, it means "to convert [from evil]" (so some EVV), but the beneficiaries of *Torah*'s blessings are implicitly true covenant people. Better, then, to invest *šûb* with the nuance of "to restore," "to put back into order" as in the case of Jerusalem (Dan. 9:25), a territory (2 Kings 14:25), people (Ps. 80:3, 7, 19 [4, 8, 20]). In connection with the human psyche and spirit it is best glossed to restore/renew/revive liveliness, vitality *(joie de vivre)* to the sad and discouraged (Ruth 4:15; Ps. 19:8; Lam. 1:11).

The second step escalates reviving life to making wise the simple. The hyponym *stipulations* (*ʿēdût,* "written expressions *of* I AM's solemn will") were first written by God's own fingers and then mediated through Moses. As such they are totally *reliable (ne*ʾᵉ*mānâ).* Its root *ʾmn* (cf. "amen") means "to be firm, secure, dependable." Inferentially, it is reliable because it is based on God's comprehensive knowledge (v. 2) and derives from his sublime character. Such a firm spiritual foundation has the benefit of *making wise (maḥkîmat).* The root *ḥkm* means generally "to have masterful understanding," "to be skillful," "become an expert"[82] (see "Form and Theology" above). That function is beneficial to *the simple* (*p*ᵉ*tî,* from the verb *pth*). *Pth* means "to be open." Its nominal derivative denotes a person who is open to teaching. This can be bad, as in the book of Proverbs, where "the simple" love to be open to everything, and so gullible, having never made a commitment to God and his wisdom (cf. Prov. 1:32).[83] In the Psalter, however, the simple are open to God's teaching, having made a faith commitment to God and his word.

79. Verse 7 is united phonetically by a memorable sevenfold alliteration of /t/ in its ten words: twice in the first and in the last constructions: *trt yhwh* and *mḥkymt pty.*

80. Note also initial /t/.

81. Spurgeon, *Treasury of David,* p. 129.

82. See Waltke, *Proverbs 1–15,* pp. 76-77.

83. Waltke, *Proverbs 1–15,* p. 111.

Consequently, in the book of Proverbs the simple are categorized with fools; in the book of Psalms, with the wise.

The third step celebrates the Law's capacity to cause rejoicing by its artistic form. The gloss *regulations (piqqûdîm)* is uncertain because *piqqûdîm* occurs only as a parallel hyponym to *torah,* with no definitive benchmarks except that it occurs in contexts of divine commands (Ps. 103:18; 111:7; 119 [21 times]). Their sublimity is that they are *right (y*ᵉ*šārîm). Yāšār* has the geometric notion of being straight, either horizontally or vertically, or, when a surface is involved, flat. This geometric use assumes a fixed order to which something can be compared. God's teachings/commands conform to a fixed order by which they can be judged. But that raises the question of truth: Who decides something is right? Plato in his Dialogue *Euthyphro* posed the moral problem in its classic form by placing his audience on the horns of a dilemma: 1) "Is something good/right because God wills it?" or 2) "Does God will it because it is good/upright?" If the former, God could be a diabolical tyrant and we would be forced to turn the moral order upside down. If the latter, God is not sovereign and bows to a higher order. The Bible cuts through the nonsense: *I AM* is inherently good/upright and from his character issue his teachings that by nature are right.

Their straight form is the cause of *rejoicing (m*ᵉ*śamm*ᵉ*ḥê).* "*Śāmaḥ* denotes being glad or joyful with the whole disposition as indicated by its association with the heart (cf. Ex 4:14; Ps 19:8 [9]; 104:15; 105:3), the soul (Ps 86:4) and with the lighting up of the eyes (Prov 15:30)."[84] The precepts are like a piece of art that includes both a formal and informal aspect. The external form in art refers to the visible elements of a piece, independent of their meaning. For example, in Leonardo's *Mona Lisa,* the formal elements are color, dimension, lines, mass, shape, etc. But art also consists of the informal products of the viewer's imagination; in the case of the *Mona Lisa,* the feelings of mystery and intrigue. If the form of being upright rejoices the heart, then the heart brings to it an imagination of the righteous that delights in an upright moral order, unlike the wicked who prefer no boundaries. *The heart (lēb)* combines the complex interplay of intellect, sensibility, and will.[85]

The fourth step, making the eyes to sparkle without, builds on the third step of rejoicing the heart within. The *Torah*'s moral rightness carries a moral imperative that must be obeyed — that is to say, they are *commands*[86] *of* I AM. They *are radiant* (*bārâ,* literally, "clean") for they have been scoured from all

84. Waltke, *TWOT,* 2:879, s.v. *śāmaḥ.*

85. Waltke, *Proverbs 1–15,* pp. 90-92.

86. See C. H. Dodd, *The Bible and the Greeks* (London: Hodder & Stoughton, 1954), pp. 25ff. for crucial terms.

moral impurity. No stain of sin defiles them. A derivative of *brr* is *bôr*, "lye" (a cleaning agent made from ashes). Daniel 11:35 combines "to cleanse" *(lᵉbārēr)* with "to make white" *(lalbēn)*, and Song of Solomon 6:10 speaks of the bright sun as clean. In Akkadian and Ugaritic, *brr* means to be metallically "pure" and to glitter. This shining cleanness may account for *enlightening* (*mᵉʾîrat*, literally, causing to light up, illuminate) and explains the gloss "radiant." The clean and radiant commands within a person's heart light up the *eyes* (*ʿênāyim*, see Ps. 15:4) without, visible for all to see. The light of the eyes in Proverbs 15:30 connotes the manifestation of the inward vitality and joy of a person. Scripture associates sparkling eyes with righteousness (Prov. 13:9; Matt. 6:22-23), life, and good fortune (Job 3:16; 33:23; Prov. 4:18; 6:23; 13:9; 16:15).

2. *Strophe 2: Pattern of ab vv. 9-10 [10-11]*

The second flight of the praise of *I AM*'s torah does so by adjectives (v. 9 [10]) and then by its benefits (v. 10 [11]). Though the second flight, it is the first in the fifth step and builds on the fourth, for the Law's purity assumes it has been purged of any impurity. Moreover, it points to its eternal nature: it will never pass away (Matt. 5:17-18). The *fear of I AM (yirʾat yhwh)* refers to *I AM*'s special revelation in the Bible, in contrast to the "fear of God," which according to the late R. N. Whybray refers "to a standard of moral conduct known and accepted by men in general."[87] The collocation, "fear of *I AM*," refers to both the rational aspect of understanding the revelation and the non-rational, emotional aspect of responding to the revelation in fear, love, and trust.[88] The "fear of I AM" opens the door to wisdom (Prov. 1:7; Job 28:28; Eccl. 12:13)[89] and so probably associates this opening verse of the second strophe with that of the first, which speaks of "making wise" (v. 7B). It is *pure (ṭāhôr)*, the opposite of being mixed. Pure incense has no wood mixed in; pure gold is without alloys; and pure animals are like our notions of a purebred dog or pedigreed horse.[90] So the "fear of I AM" is free of any mixture with moral impurity. Like being free of a disease, *they endure* (*ʿômedet*, literally "stand," see Ps. 1:5) *forever (lāʿad)*. *ʿd* was probably

87. R. N. Whybray, *Wisdom in Proverbs: The Concept of Wisdom in Proverbs 1–9* (London: SCM Press, 1955), p. 96.

88. B. Waltke, "The Fear of the Lord," in J. I. Packer and L. Wilkinson, eds., *Alive to God* (Downers Grove, IL: InterVarsity, 1992), pp. 17-33.

89. In Ecclesiastes 12:13 "fear of God" is a synonym for "fear of I AM" in other Scriptures.

90. Mary Douglas, in *Purity and Danger: An Analysis of the Concepts of Pollution and Taboo* (London: Routledge & Kegan Paul, 1966), argues that the purity laws had the sociological purpose of helping Israel grasp the unity and perfection of God's creation, a worldview that set them apart from their neighbors.

chosen instead of the more frequent *l*^{e}*ʿôlām* for its alliteration with *ʿmd.* Perpetuity normally denotes the unforeseeable future, but when applied to God and his word, it takes on the philosophical nuance of being eternal.

The sixth step assures us that the stairway is firm because the whole has been built according to righteousness. *The judgments of I AM (mišp*^{e}*ṭê yhwh)* refer to the judicial verdicts such as those found in Exodus 21–23. *I AM*'s case laws are *firm* (*ʾemet,* "true," "steady," "reliable," see v. 7) — that is to say, they cannot be overturned, unlike human judgments. This is so because *they are righteous* (*ṣād*^{e}*qû,* see Ps. 1:5; 4:1 [2]) — that is to say, in conformity with God's rule they serve the interest of the entire community, not the self in preference to others.[91] *Altogether* (*yaḥdaw,* Ps. 4:8 [9]) adds that the verdicts in unison, without an exception, are righteous.

We have finally arrived at the top: the value and delight of God's judgments are breathtaking. Old people desire money; young people crave pleasure. The word of God meets both needs. *They are . . . desirable* (*hanneḥ*^{e}*mādîm,* see n. 37) syntactically refers to "judgments," for both words are masculine plurals. The root *ḥāmad* designates the disposition of the self in the direction of appealing property, usually for its beauty and/or its power.[92] When the desired object belongs to a neighbor (i.e., "coveted," Exod. 20:17), it is a vice that must be renounced and not entertained out of love for God and neighbor (James 1:13-15), but when the desire is for the beauty and the power for life found in the morally perfect Law, it is a virtue. The comparative "more . . . than" (Heb. *min*) indicates a positive comparison; both *I AM*'s judgments and gold are desirable for their value. *Gold (zāhāb)* may refer to "to gold-ore, gold in a raw state; or gold dust," or wealth in general.[93] Since it is further qualified as *than pure gold (mippaz),* which designates gold separated from its ore and from alloys, the first sense is intended. Money puts food on the table, but not love around it; builds a house,

91. Waltke, *Proverbs 1–15,* p. 97.

92. Marvin L. Chaney ("'Coveting Your Neighbor's House' in Social Context," *The Ten Commandments: The Reciprocity of Faithfulness* [Louisville: Westminster/John Knox Press, 2004], pp. 302-17) hopes to overthrow the ancient versions, Paul (Rom. 7:7; 13:9), Luther (Larger Catechism), Calvin (*Institutes* 2.8.49), and many moderns. He argues with Hermann and Alt that the verb entails the taking of property in addition to coveting it. His argument fails because he ignores that in the instances he cites, a second verb of taking is added (e.g., Mic. 2:2), an addition lacking in the tenth commandment. The eighth commandment pertains to the taking of property and entails "to covet it." If "to covet" entails "to take," then there is little difference between the two commandments, unless one restricts the eighth commandment to kidnapping. Most scholars, however, refer the eighth commandment to ordinary theft (B. S. Jackson, "Liability for Mere Intention in Early Jewish Law," in *Essays in Jewish and Comparative Legal History* [Leiden: Brill, 1975], p. 206, n. 12).

93. BDB, p. 262, s.v. *zāhāb.*

but not a home; bestows luxuries, but not love. When the religio-ethical virtues of God's verdicts are delighted in, they give both material and spiritual benefits. As pure gold shows that the quality of gold makes no difference in this comparison, so *much (rab)* shows that the quantity of gold also does not matter.

Conjunctive *and* adds a second benefit: God's judgments are *sweeter (mᵉtûqîm) than honey (middᵉbaš)*. The positive comparison is now between the allurement and delight of God's judgments and honey, finding that satisfying the palate with the most desirable food is less alluring and pleasant for the saint than the certainty that God's judgments will never be overturned or reversed. Once again the notions of quantity and quality are excluded from compromising the comparison by intensifying honey to *virgin honey flowing from the comb* (i.e., the delicacy of bee's honey, not the more common date honey). Its overflowing quantity is indicated by endlessly "flowing" and its superior quality by its being virgin honey, not oxygenated by the air. Honey also has medicinal, healing properties (Prov. 16:24), but that property is not mentioned and so presumably not in view. Adam and Eve found the tree of the knowledge of good and evil, which offered them autonomy to make them wise, more desirable than God's word that offered them life (Gen. 3:6). But people who trust God and his covenant find the law ranks higher than all earthly values and pleasures.

D. Psalmist's Petitions for Salvation vv. 11-13 [12-14]

"Moreover" (*gam*) conceptually links the king's petitions to his praise of Torah, and *by them* (*bāhem*, masc. pl.) grammatically binds them. The stanza consists of two strophes, each having two quatrains (vv. 11 and 12, vv. 13A and B). The first petitions God to forgive the king's hidden sins, and the second, to restrain him from joining proud mockers. Each strophe is introduced by *gam* and by the metaphor of "your slave." *Gam* introduces a related new thought *(also)*, not to emphasize a point ("yea"). The first *gam* unites the petition to the hymn of Torah praise, for it adds an additional benefit — this time personal — to be acquitted of *I AM*'s judgments. The second *gam* introduces a second petition: to be kept from apostates, which in turn will deliver him from guilt of the great transgression. His two petitions express his humility. By requesting to be acquitted of hidden sins and to be kept from apostates he implicitly confesses his own moral weakness.

1. Pardon for Hidden Guilt vv. 11-12 [12-13]

The petition to be free from the guilt and punishment of hidden error is prompted by his teaching about God's judgments: sin is punished and righteousness is rewarded (v. 11). But what about unwitting sin? David's petition answers that nagging question (v. 12).

a. Judgments Threaten Punishment and Promise Reward v. 11 [12]

David speaks of himself as *your slave* (*ʿabdᵉkā,* cf. Ps. 18 superscript [Heb. 18:1]). The nuances of *ʿebed* range from an indentured slave contracted for a specified time to others in positions of trust of varying rank. In other words, it is a metaphor for covenant keeping. (Kidnap slavery was a capital offense [Exod. 21:16] and so that kind of slave is not otherwise in view in the Old Testament legislation.) The metaphor of an indentured slave signifies: 1) responsible obedience to *I AM*'s direction; 2) faithful dependence on his care; 3) personal intimacy of trust of payment; and 4) humility. God's judgments caution the king to take heed. The root of *is warned* (*nizhār,* see n. 38), *zāhar* in *Hiphil,* may mean "instruct," or "admonish" in Exodus 18:20, but otherwise (2 Kings 6:10 [*Qere*] and in Ezekiel 3 and 33 [10 times]) it means "to caution" "to warn [of danger]," a meaning that agrees with the sense in *Niphal,* "to take heed to a warning/a threat." In short, *nizhār* means to be instructed about danger and to take heed. Moreover, "is warned" is a metonymy of effect, assuming the judgments exact punishments.

As for *by keeping them (bᵉšomrām), šāmar* with objects in the semantic domain of concrete persons or things (e.g., a garden [Gen. 2:15], tree [Gen. 3:24], son [Prov. 2:8]), it signifies to keep from danger so as to preserve; but with objects in the semantic domain of wisdom, commands, and judgments, it signifies to preserve them carefully by faithful obedience and compliance (Prov. 3:1, 21). By taking heed to the warnings entailed in the judgments the king is kept from punishment; by his carefully keeping the judgments *comes . . . reward (ʿēqeb).* According to *HALOT, ʿēqeb* originally meant "the very back," "the end" (Ps. 119:33, 112), leading to the derivative meaning of "wages" (Ps. 19:11 [12]).[94] The recompense is unstated but certainly as great as the value of gold and honey (v. 10). The adjective *rab* ("great," "much"), the last Hebrew word of 10 [11]a and 11 [12]b, may signal the connection between "gold" and "reward." God's grace adds a hundredfold to the investment of complying with his judgments (Matt. 19:29; cf. Mark 9:41; Luke 6:23, 35; Rom. 2:6; 2 Cor. 4:17-18; 5:10).

b. Do Not Punish Unwitting Errors v. 12 [13]

As for emphatically glosses the topic. The question "Who can discern" is the predicate. *Errors* (*šᵉnîʾot,* fem. pl.) occurs in the Bible only in this verse, making the

94. *HALOT* 92:873, s.v. *ʿēqeb.*

gloss tentative. Nevertheless, its cognate in Mandean *šugiana* means mistake, oversight, error. And when this meaning is combined with its parallel *nistārôt* (hidden things), the collocation yields the semantically pertinent notion: "hidden faults." *Who (mî)* is a rhetorical question to negate with passion the notion of the verb "discern." This use of the personal, interrogative pronoun involves self-abasement or insult, and "a generalized use of this pattern involves abasing all people, including the speaker, usually in implicit contrast to God."[95] The root of *can discern (yābîn, bîn)* in *Hiphil* with a direct object denotes the act of giving heed and considering something with the senses (e.g., the eyes and ears) in such a way that understanding about the object takes place within oneself (i.e., one acquires and possesses its object).[96] By definition, no person can discern their hidden errors. Semantic pertinence favors construing the preposition *min* in the phrase *minnistārôt* as causal (of the situation),[97] glossed *for* to serve the English idiom. *Hidden* (*nistārôt,* n. 40) syntactically modifies "errors," and "What is hidden" parallels "none can discern error." To facilitate the sense *faults* is added. Freud may have been the first to have named the hidden abnormal psychological impulses that rule our lives as the "id," but David is well aware that none rules his own house and can free him from errors. So he prays: *declare me free from punishment* (*naqqênî, Piel* of *nqh*). *HALOT* defines the verb: "to declare to be free from punishment (with *min* regarding) Ps 19:13; Job 9:28; 10:14."[98] In his forbearance, kindness, and mercy God will not judge us for sins of which we are unaware and so cannot confess and renounce, because Christ made atonement for all sin.

2. *Preserve from Guilt of Apostasy v. 13 [14]AB*

The quatrain expressing the second petition consists of the petition to be restrained from joining mockers (13A) with the expectation that then he will not apostatize.

a. Hold Back from Rule of Insolent Men v. 13 [14]A

None is free from the danger of apostasy. Even King David recognizes that without God's gracious spiritual protection mockers could rule him. So he prays: *hold back (ḥᵃśōk)* your servant, like a horse with a bit, from their sway. The petition entails the work of the Holy Spirit on David's spirit (Rom. 8:2-4;

95. *IBHS,* p. 322, P. 18.2.g.
96. Waltke, *Proverbs 1–15,* p. 176.
97. *IBHS,* p. 213, P. 11.2.11d.
98. *HALOT,* 2:720, s.v. *nqh.*

Gal. 5:16). *Moreover* (*gam*, see v. 12) joins this second petition to the first. *From (min)* with "hold back" now has its ablative sense. The root of *insolent men (zēdîm), zēd,* occurs thirteen times, always in plural apart from Proverbs 21:24. This masculine substantival adjective does not have as its antecedent the feminine noun "errors" *(šᵉnîʾôt). Zēdîm* elsewhere refers to those who: challenge God (Mal. 3:15), attack the psalmist (Ps. 86:14), mock the pious without restraint (119:51), forge lies (119:69), and dig pits (119:85); the psalmist prays that God will put them to shame (119:78) and not let them oppress him (119:122). Jeremiah (43:2) uses it of those who reject his prophecy. *I AM* is said to rebuke them (Ps. 119:21), and he will cause their arrogance to cease (Isa. 13:11; cf. Mal. 4:1 [3:19]). In light of these eleven other occurrences of *zēdîm,* the conclusion may be drawn that *zēdîm* refers to men who, from their prideful exaggerated opinion of their self-importance, disregard *I AM,* the wise and revealed truth. "Mocker" is his name (Prov. 27). From joining such men David prays: *hold back (ḥᵃśōk) your servant* (*ʿabdᵉkā,* see v. 11). *Ḥśk* here means to "restrain," "keep back" your servant from joining them in their impiety and moral impudence.

David does not pray for salvation from within — the cachet that he is a member of the new covenant is the law written on his heart — but for salvation from outside satanic forces that assail him. That is to say, *let them [insolent men] not rule over me (ʾal-yimšol bî). Māšal* means to govern the conduct of a subordinate. If insolent men rule over David, he too will disregard God, the godly, and *Torah.* Without God's help the human spirit alone is no match for Satan, who energizes insolent men, as the failure of Adam and Eve to resist the Satan's rule instructs us (cf. Eph. 6:12). This is probably what John means by "sin unto death" (1 John 5:16-17).

b. To Be Free from the Guilt of Apostasy v. 13 [14]B

Then (ʾaz) signifies a future consequence (with some emphasis intended) and with an accompanying logical force, implying the fulfillment of a condition: "*then = if* or *when this has been done* (with the impf.) . . . Ps. 19:14."[99] *I will retain integrity* (*ʾêtām,* lit. "I will be complete, sound, unimpaired," see v. 7). *And I will be kept free from punishment (wᵉniqqêtî)* construes *Piel nqh* as resultative, not declarative. Whereas David could scarcely avoid committing hidden faults and so had to be declared innocent, now by being saved from insolent men, he is kept free from a justly deserved punishment. This punishment is just *because* (*min,* see v. 13) they are guilty of *great* (*rab,* see v. 10) *transgression (pešaʿ). Pešaʿ* denotes offenses against property and/or person. It may pertain to theft (Gen.

99. BDB, p. 23, s.v. *ʾaz.*

31:36) or killing (1 Sam. 24:10-14). So *pš'* designates a formal category encompassing the various types of material and personal crimes. R. Knierim writes: "a legal technical term for crimes that were subject to legal penalties." He also notes "*peša'* is a theological term because the deeds it describes affect Yahweh or his sovereignty and consequently require his judgment or forgiveness." Furthermore, "Whoever commits *peša'* does not merely rebel or protest against Yahweh but breaks with him."[100] The singular could be collective, covering all kinds of crimes, but its specification by singular "great" suggests that a particularly serious crime is in view. According to the parallel verset, "to let insolent men rule over me," apostasy against God is meant. If God holds him back from such apostates, he will never be guilty of that great crime against God — of breaking faith with him.

Epilogue: Dedicatory Prayer v. 14 [15]

The epilogue is united with the petitions by yet another petition: that his poem be accepted by *I AM.* Since it pertains not to personal pardon but to the "protocol of the royal court, asking for the favor of acceptance,"[101] his final petition is best construed as an epilogue to his poem, not just another in a sequence of petitions, and as a dedication of his song to *I AM.* Accordingly, ambiguous *yihyû* is best construed as a jussive, *let be,* not as an imperfect, "it will be." The root meaning of *rāṣôn* in *lᵉrāṣôn, pleasing* (see n. 42), according to N. Walker, "is two-sided, namely *will* and *pleasure,* whether oneself or another. Doing one's own will and pleasure involves one's desire, but doing the will and pleasure of another results in *acceptance, approval,* delight of another, and his returning *favor* and *blessing*"[102] (cf. Ps. 104:34; 119:108). In Malachi 2:13 the parallel to not finding favor is "he no longer looks at the gift." *I AM* looked with favor on David's psalm, for he included it in the canon of Holy Scripture. *The words of my mouth* (*'imrê-pî,* see v. 2) *and the meditation of my heart (wᵉhegyôn libbî)* are metonymies for his cognitive reflections on *I AM*'s firmament and on his Torah and his unique petitions of salvation. *Meditation (hegyôn)* is the nominal derivate of *hgh* (etymologically "to utter inarticulate sounds" (see Ps. 1:2). David has pondered long and hard on what to say and how to say it (see Prov. 15:28). *Before you (lĕpāneykā)* means "in your eyes, in your estimation, according to your viewpoint").[103]

100. Knierim, *TLOT,* 2:1034-36, s.v. *pš'.*

101. Clifford, *Psalms 1–72,* p. 115.

102. N. Walker, "The Renderings of *Rāṣôn,*" *JBL* 81 (1962): 184.

103. *TLOT,* 2:1012, s.v. *pnym.*

I AM in verse 14 is the seventh occurrence of the divine name in this psalm (see the other six in vv. 7-9), and first imaged as *My Rock (sûrî),* an image of God's protection and majestic strength: The firm, unshakable rock is a stereotypical image for God's help (Ps. 18:46), the protection that he offers (Isa. 17:10), the refuge found in him (Ps. 18:2), his saving activity (Ps. 19:14), and his unshakable faithfulness (Isa. 26:4). No wonder that David wants God's approval. If "rock" images God's mighty power, then **and my Redeemer** *(w^{e}gō'^{a}lî)* images *I AM* as the king's legal family protector from an outside jurisdiction: Psalm 19:14 [15], like Proverbs 23:10f. and Jeremiah 50:34, applies to Yahweh the status of the *gōēl* in a family as the helper of the relative fallen into distress, calling him *gōēl* as protector of the weak over against a mighty opponent. In sum, *I AM* is both able and has obliged himself to protect and to save the king.

Subscript: Psalm 20:superscript [1]A

To the chief musician in Psalm 20:superscript is a subscript to Psalm 19 (see p. 88). Under the leadership of the chief musician all Israel is to join their exemplary king in listening to the heavens' praise of God as Creator and to celebrate *I AM*'s Torah that enlightens and delights the godly, and in humility to petition God for their spiritual salvation. And let them seek *I AM*'s favor in singing this song, for he alone is their mighty Savior.

Part IV: Conclusion

In the introduction we argued that the psalm is a mixture of literary genres: praise, penitential petition, and instruction. Finally, within the canon of the Bible it is a mystery — that is to say, it contains hidden truth.

The sun's universal witness to the knowledge of God, in Paul's argument regarding the salvation of ethnic Israel, illustrates Christ and his apostles' universal witness of the word of Christ to all Israel. They are without excuse, for they heard the good news that Christ died for sins, was buried, and rose again from the dead on the third day (Rom. 10:18). The apostle is using an intertextual allusion to support his argument; he is not saying, however, this was the psalmist's meaning. For him, and so for the church, the universal proclamation of the heavens and the rising of the sun typifies the Dayspring from on high who reveals all the fullness of the Godhead bodily. He is the Sun of righteousness who was raised from the dead to marry his bride, and whose gospel is proclaimed by his church from one horizon to another (cf. Mal. 4:2; Luke 1:78; Rom. 7:4; Eph. 5:32).

As for the praise of Torah, the Law expresses the moral purity, the holiness of God and its benefits to the members of God's covenant community. But Jesus Christ, who is the incarnate Son of God, fully manifests his character. Therefore, Christians use David's praise of Torah to praise the sinless Lamb of God who became righteousness for them and gives them his Spirit, enabling them to enjoy its value and delight. In every dispensation — whether the covenant people are administered by the Old or by the New covenants — those who delight in the Law and find it reviving and enlightening have new hearts, for the natural heart is foolish, bound in sin, and does not welcome the truth of Jesus Christ. Regenerated Christians belong to that covenant community (Luke 22:20; Heb. 8). The Holy Spirit, who gave the Law, has written the message of Christ on their hearts (2 Cor. 3:1-3). For them it is the perfect law that gives freedom, for they are free from their bondage to sin (James 1:25). These truths are pregnant in the psalm, but the New Testament births them.

As for David's humble penitential prayer (vv. 11-14), the New Testament brings out into the full light of day the function of the Law to condemn sinners by its commandments (Rom. 5:13; 1 Tim. 1:8-11). As noted, David thinks and teaches as a sage. Wisdom literature otherwise never gives voice to the student's response to the sage's catechetical teaching. The father's lecture in Proverbs 4:1-9 represents a son's passing his father's teachings to the next generation, but does not represent his spiritual response other than that of acceptance. David's response exemplifies the appropriate response: prayer for salvation, not a resolve to obey, as one might expect. David's response is that of the tax collector: "God, be merciful to me, a sinner."

The Old Testament, like Jesus' parables, is a masterpiece of indirection (cf. Matt. 13:13). On the surface the Old Testament Torah in its broadest sense misleads the proud into presumptuous resolutions to obey, but in fact the Torah proves humankind's inability to obey and so condemns them (cf. Deut. 30:6; Josh. 24:14-27). This is the error of Jews who boasted in themselves, the error against which Paul protects the church. In short, David, like Paul, uses the Law to condemn sin and in its light repents of sin.

Finally, in his dedicatory prayer David addresses God as his Redeemer, the family Brother who saves the family from foreign jurisdiction (see below). That faith is justified because Christ by his death provided redemption from the realm of sin and death. In other words, the psalm is pregnant with the gospel.

In sum, the meek, the righteous, have always lived by faith in *I AM*, not by human resolve.

CHAPTER 12

Psalm 22: Prophetic Psalm of Christ's Passion

Part I: Voice of the Church

Like Psalm 19, Psalm 22 provides an example of how many modern commentators have distanced themselves from the tradition of the Christian Fathers. The spectrum has widened to include both Jewish and Christian commentators who have embraced secularism and those whose religious faith has been trumped by the authority of the academy. These contrast with those who seek continuity with the traditional rabbis or fathers of the church.

As an example of the former, Rabbi Martin Samuel Cohen in his recent translation and commentary on the Psalms interprets the ode of Psalm 22 as that of a Kafkaesque poet. He portrays him suffering from violent diarrhea and a fibrillating heart, lying as he thinks he is on his deathbed, comforted only by a genetic disposition to believe in God. For him, the sole lesson is "for all to learn from contemplating the 22nd psalm . . . that the human personality is nowhere near as malleable as moderns tend to think. Indeed, there is nothing as impermeable as the various barriers life itself erects around the great goals of human spiritual development, making them elusive in the extreme for most people. . . . The poet, however, has learned to look askance at nothing — not even at despair."[1] In his introduction Rabbi Cohen concludes that "with every passing year, the Book of Psalms becomes more central to my understanding both of what it means to be a Jew and what it means to be a human being."[2] It is an existential, inexplicable, non-doctrinal identification of the self with David, real or mythical.

1. Martin Samuel Cohen, *Our Haven and Our Strength: The Book of Psalms* (New York: Aviv Press, 2004), p. 62.

2. Cohen, *Our Haven and Our Strength,* p. xvii.

Rather than being inspired by the spirituality of the Psalter, critical "moderns" despiritualize the psalms. If Psalm 22 cannot be recognized as a personal lament, and its enemies are no longer identifiable, then one's personal identification with the psalm evaporates. Then faith in one's Savior, whom the New Testament apostles identified salvifically with this specific psalm, becomes questionable also. To explore, then, how far the contemporary study of the psalms has strayed from the tradition of the early church, we begin this survey with the New Testament and the early Fathers.

I. Apostolic Interpretation of Psalm 22

The four gospels incorporate texts from the Psalms more than from any other Old Testament book in their presentation of the gospel of Jesus Christ. No psalm is quoted more in the gospels than Psalm 22, suggesting that it shaped the Passion Narratives of the Synoptic Gospels. Adopting a Midrashic style, Matthew more than Mark weaves elements from his Old Testament sources into the texture of his narrative. The strong allusions to Psalm 22 in all three gospels on the lips of the dying Lord may have been intended to portray Jesus as praying the whole psalm on the cross. The Lord Jesus took this psalm upon his lips as his first words on the cross (Matt. 27:46 and parallels).[3] Hebrews places verse 22 [23] on the lips of the resurrected Christ (Heb. 2:12).

The many references to the psalm in the passion narratives are used as Jesus' active fulfillment of the psalms. It appears the apostles' main purpose is to identify Jesus with the witness of David in his humiliation. Christ's *persona,* like that of the psalmist, is manifested by total trust in God's ultimate vindication of him. Hence his kingdom will be an everlasting kingdom, as the end of the psalm celebrates.

For the writers of the gospels, Christ's quotations from Psalm 22 are not just David's "autobiographical" outpourings now being applied in a different literary age; they are inspired pointers actually being fulfilled in the Incarnation. It is the God-breathed witness to Immanuel, God-with-us. For the disciples, faith in Jesus might mean alienation from Judaism, but never alienation from the Scriptures of Israel's God.[4]

3. Here's a listing of citations of Psalm 22 in the narratives of Christ's passion: 1) casting lots for his garments (v. 18; Mark 15:24; John 19:23-24); 2) parching thirst (v. 15; John 19:28-29); 3) agony of the stretched bones (v. 14); 4) digging holes into the hands and feet (v. 16; John 20:27); and 5) mocking by his enemies (v. 8; Matt. 27:43; Luke 23:35).

4. Margaret Daly-Denton, *David in the Fourth Gospel: The Johannine Reception of the Psalms* (Leiden-Boston-Cologne: Brill, 2000), p. 24.

II. Early Christian Apologists

Like other Messianic psalms, such as Psalms 2 and 110, the individual lament of Psalm 22 has always been a crucible for Christian-Jewish relations. After the aural tradition of the first Christian martyrs such as Polycarp, who claimed to remember the words of the aged apostle John, second-century Christianity entered a new phase of confuting heresies, now based on texts — not aural tradition — all claiming to be "authentic" in a literary sense. The growing use of codices in place of scrolls opened the way for a more literate society.[5] Already pursued by classical literary scholars, the early Christian apologists now adopted the canons of their own classical literary criticism to justify what were the valid Christian texts of both Old and New Testaments.

The Epistle of Barnabas (c. 70-131?), perhaps the first post-apostolic Christian writing, given almost canonical status, notes the prophetic character of the sufferings of Christ, quoting from both Isaiah and Psalm 22:17, 19, 23 [18, 20, 24]. Barnabas writes his epistle to defend the Christian faith by the numerous prophecies of this psalm because of his concern about the number of Christians being proselytized by the Jews,[6] whose national revival was marked by the revolt of 66-70, and by the further revolts of 115-18 and 132-35. As a result of this proselytizing in connection with Jewish nationalism and Barnabas's attempt to stem the tide, Psalm 22 early on became a critical text.[7]

Justin Martyr (c. 100-165), who continues the Christian apologia against the proselytizing of the Jews, is the first known Christian apologist to comment fully on the text of Psalm 22. He does so in his *Dialogue with Trypho,* where he narrates his conversations with Rabbi Trypho, who had tried to convert Justin. Like Pascal, a brilliant defender of the Christian faith in the seventeenth century, Justin recognized that "the prophecies [of the Psalmist David] are the clearest about Jesus Christ."[8] As a defense of Christianity against Judaism, Justin begins his literary debate in the *Dialogue* by observing other passages where "David also speaks of the Passion and the Cross, in a mysterious parable; but it is in Ps. 22 . . . [that] the psalmist him-

5. See the survey of this history in Anthony Grafton and Megan Williams, *Christianity and the Transformation of the Book* (Cambridge, MA, and London: The Belknap Press of Harvard University Press, 2006).

6. William Horbury, *Jews and Christians in Contact and Controversy* (Edinburgh: T. & T. Clark, 1998), pp. 136-40.

7. G. N. Stanton, "Aspects of Early Christian-Jewish Polemic and Apologetic," *NTS* 31 (1985): 377-92 (378).

8. Quoted by Louis Jacquet, *Les Psaumes et le Coeur de l'Homme* (Brussels: Duculot, 1975), vol. 1, p. 523.

self is none other than Christ addressing us, as he speaks to the Father." He also focuses extensively on Psalm 22 in his second Dialogue with Trypho (chapters xcvii-cvi):

> David in the twenty-first Psalm [sic, LXX] thus refers to the suffering and to the cross in a parable of mystery . . . and yet this very Psalm you maintain does not refer to Christ; for you are in all respects blind, and you do not understand that no one in your nation who has been called King or Christ has ever had his hands or feet pierced while alive, or has died in this mysterious fashion — to wit, by the cross — save this Jesus alone.[9]

Justin then recites his commentary, verse by verse, on the whole psalm.

In response to the Christian apologists, who claimed that Christ fulfilled the role of suffering Messiah predicted in the Old Testament, rabbinical scholars, who had a nationalistic penchant, eschewed their own earlier interpretations of Biblical texts as references to a suffering Messiah and reinterpreted the same Biblical references as referring to the sufferings of the nation Israel.[10] *Midrash Tehillim* claimed Queen Esther was the subject of Psalm 22.[11] Whether this was a polemic against the Christian interpretation of Psalm 22 or had been developed earlier is uncertain, but *Midrash Tehillim* 22.18-32 is similar to Justin's commentary, a verse-by-verse exposition of the entire psalm, in which the incidents of Esther's life at the Persian court are related to the text.[12] Later Judaism did not preclude other Biblical figures from acting out the psalm. From the eleventh century onwards, the reading of the psalm was allocated to Purim, while from very early on, Christians read Psalm 22 as the great passion psalm during Holy Week, especially on Good Friday.

Hippolytus (c. 170-235), bishop of Rome, as a Jewish convert to Christianity naturally makes extensive use of the psalms in his apologetic against various heresies. In place of the daily sacrifices on the temple altar, Hippolytus

9. Alexander Roberts and James Anderson, eds., *Justin Martyr and Athenagoras*, vol. 2, *Ante-Nicene Christian Library* (Edinburgh: T. & T. Clark, 1867), pp. 221-22.

10. Paul M. Blowers, trans., *The Bible in Greek Christian Antiquity* (Notre Dame: University of Notre Dame Press, 1997), p. 60.

11. Esther M. Menn, "No Ordinary Lament: Relecture and the Identity of the Distressed in Psalm 22," *HTR* 93, no. 4 (2000): 301-41.

12. For example, Esther begins with three long days of fasting and praying, which the *midrash* correlates with the three cries of the Psalmist, "My God," "My God," and then the third day, "why have you forsaken me?" (Esther 4:16; 4:1). When Esther enters daringly into the inner court to confront the king, her prayer is "save me from the sword, my soul from the hand of the dog" (Ps. 22:20).

sees the psalms as now substituting for the temple sacrifices, with "a new style of jubilant praise in the worship of God."[13] The psalms now replace sacrificial animals in the continual praise of God.

Clement of Alexandria (150-215) in his First Epistle (ch. vi) speaks of Christ as the example of humility, quoting from the Isaiah passages of the Suffering Servant. He then adds reference to Psalm 22:6-8 [7-9], but it is not a sustained commentary. In his *Paidagogos* he observes that it requires an effort of moral life to become worthy to receive the teachings of the *Logos.*[14] It is like stating that Psalm 1 has to be lived first, before the rest of the Psalter can ever begin to be exegeted, whereas today, in academic pursuit of Biblical studies, it is commonly assumed that there is *no* moral dimension to such study.

The apologists also addressed heresies within the church. Beginning in the second century, the challenge of literary forgeries and the proliferation of Gnostic texts prompted a more specialized use of exegesis to defend the faith. **Irenaeus** (born 2nd century, died c. 200), for example, employs literary criticism for the sake of Biblical exegesis. This is so because he aims to counter the prevalence of pseudo-exegesis and its attempt to explain obscure passages by yet more obscure explanation.[15] Nevertheless, even he, as well as Clement of Alexandria, quotes apocryphal texts unwittingly.[16]

Other exegetical practices, aside from apologetics, were also developing in the first centuries. The first great commentator on the Scriptures, **Origen** (184-254), is also the first serious exponent of the prosopological exegesis of the Psalms (see pp. 9-10). He adopts a method, observes Marie-Josèphe Rondeau, which was also used in interpreting classical texts such as Homer and Plato.[17] Different persons could be seen as the "speaker," but above all, it is now possible to express clearly the idea that it is Christ himself who communicates in solidarity with all humanity.[18] So from his method, the emergence of a new emphasis on Christ speaking through all the Scriptures is developed: *totus Christi.*

13. Hippolytus, Bishop of Rome, *Fragments from Commentaries on Various Books of Scripture,* in Alexander Robertson and James Donaldson, eds., *The Ante-Nicene Fathers,* vol. 6, part 1 (Edinburgh: T. & T. Clark, 1868), pp. 424-25.

14. *The Writings of Clement of Alexander,* trans. William Wilson (Edinburgh: T. & T. Clark, 1897), *Paidagogos,* p. 114.

15. Robert M. Grant, *Heresy and Criticism: The Search for Authenticity in Early Christian Literature* (Louisville: Westminster/John Knox Press, 1993), p. 91.

16. For example, *Irenaeus, Against Heresies,* in Alexander Roberts and James Donaldson, eds., *Ante-Nicene Christian Library* (Edinburgh: T. & T. Clark, 1886), p. 427 and note 4.

17. Marie-Josèphe Rondeau, *Les Commentaires Patristiques du Psautier (III-Ve siècles),* vol. 2, *Exégèse Prosopologique et Théologique* (Rome: Pontificium Institutum Studiorum Orientalium, 1985), p. 39.

18. Rondeau, *Les Commentaires Patristiques du Psautier,* p. 42.

From century to century it will be reiterated that "the spiritual sense of the Old Testament is the New Testament," and "Christ is the hermeneutical key to the Psalter." This exegetical device becomes more characteristic in the commentators' handling of the Psalms than any other book of the Bible. This is called "the spiritual sense" of the Scriptures. For Origen, the sense of Scripture is not an impersonal thought; it is Christ, the secret, hidden, but living sense of his abiding presence. Later Bernard of Clairvaux, following on Origen's "bridal mysticism," affirms in a sermon on the Song of Songs that Christ appears three times for the believer: in his Incarnation, in his final or "second coming," and in our daily opening the Scriptures.

Origen's (184-254) prosopological exegesis allows him to interpret Psalm 22 as "regarding Christ — for it is certain, as the Gospel bears witness, that this Psalm is spoken of Him in the following words: 'O Lord, be not far from helping me; look to my defense; O God, deliver my soul from the sword, and my beloved one from the hand of the dog' (Ps. 22:19-20)."[19] Significantly, Origen's "spiritual sense of scripture," with its neo-Platonic cultural background, was developing just as the first monastic communities were being founded. Consequently, this influenced significantly how these communities were to treat the Psalter in their daily round of prayer. When one of the early Desert Fathers, **Philimon**, was asked why he preferred the psalms above all the other Scriptures, he responded: "God has impressed the power of the psalms on my poor soul as He did on the soul of the prophet David. I cannot be separated from the sweetness of the visions about which they speak: they embrace all Scripture."[20] Since **Evagrius of Ponticus** (345-99) identifies Christ in Psalms 107 and 149 (LXX), it is not surprising that Psalm 22 was central to such identification.[21] So it became widespread in the third century to use the Psalms in a threefold way, according to the practice of Evagrius of Ponticus: to tranquillize "the passions," as a spiritual remedy; to battle demonic temptations, as a spiritual weapon (*antirrhesis* or "contradiction"); and as a training-ground for *theoria* or contemplation, to gain spiritual vision. In his work *De Oratione,* Evagrius states: "Psalmody calms the passions and quietens the body's intemperance; prayer arouses the intellect to activate its own proper powers," that is, of contemplation.

19. Origen, *De Principiis.*

20. G. E. H. Palmer, P. Sherrard, K. Ware, *The Philokalia* (London: Faber & Faber, 1979), vol. 2, p. 237.

21. See Luke Dysinger, O.S.B., *Psalmody and Prayer in the Writings of Evagrius Ponticus* (Oxford: Oxford University Press, 2005), p. 152.

III. Polemical Interpretation of Psalm 22 in the Third to Sixth Centuries

The official adoption of Christianity by Constantine, following the previous fierce persecution of its martyrs, generated internal dissension in the churches. Why should compromisers prosper in church offices, when "the faithful" had suffered so much by martyrdom? And where are the sufferings of Christ more poignantly expressed than in Psalm 22? Psalm 22 now became a battleground not between Christians and Jews or heretics, but between purists and inclusivists. Nevertheless, the orthodox agreed that Psalm 22 prophesied Christ's Passion and Cross. For **Eusebius of Caesarea** (260-340) it is a prophecy of the Passion of Christ and of the vocation of all Gentiles.[22] Writing on Psalm 22, **Jerome** asserts that the entire psalm sets forth Christ in all his sufferings. **Athanasius** (260-340) argues that when the psalm "speaks of the piercing of the hands and feet, what else than a cross does it signify? After teaching us all these things, it adds that the Lord suffers these things not for his own sake, but for ours."[23] We have only fragments of references to Psalm 22 until **Novatian's** (c. third century) commentary on Psalm 22,[24] which links the prophecy of the suffering Servant of Isaiah with the prophecy of Psalm 22: "For divine Scripture, which foresees all, speaks of things which it knows will take place in the future, as already done. And it speaks of things as already accomplished which it regards as future, because they shall undoubtedly come to pass."

The predictive element of prophecy, however, is not the focus of the early fathers. Rather, the unity of the Old and New Testaments is found in the division between the "literal" or historical in the Old Testament and its "spiritual" or further application in the New Testament. They see "two economies," or "two covenants." In the former the present has a future perspective, while in the latter the present also has a past significance. The latter does not destroy the first, but gives it a fuller meaning; the "spiritual" may be said to give the "literal"

22. Like Origen, Eusebius created a vast library, and under the patronage of Constantine, promoted a new style of scholarship that was essentially the creation of an anthology of other writers. He also consulted Hebrew scholars, so that his knowledge of Biblical authorities was uniquely wide-ranging for his time.

23. Athanasius, *The Life of Anthony and the Letter to Marcellinus,* Classics of Western Spirituality, trans. Robert C. Gregg (New York, Ramsey, Toronto: Paulist Press, 1980), p. 105.

24. Novatian (Novatus) had been a Stoic philosopher, remained a prolific writer, and was heavily influenced by Tertullian. As a "rigorist" he eventually separated his churches from the see of Rome; they survived until the end of the seventh century. (See *Novatian, the Writings,* Russell J. de Simone, O.S.A., trans., *The Fathers of the Church* [Washington, DC: Catholic University of America Press, 1974], p. 9.) He created his great work *On the Trinity* as a Rule of Faith; in this he was a hundred years ahead of his contemporaries.

a greater depth. The Cross of Christ is this hinge, and thus Psalm 22 is critical for this "double meaning" of the "literal" and the "spiritual."

From **Augustine of Hippo** we have two expository sermons on Psalm 22. The fuller version was preached on Good Friday, March 23, 395. Among other complaints against the Donatists, he preaches:

> It is amazing, brothers and sisters, to think that this psalm is also being sung today by the Donatists. Well, I ask you, brothers and sisters, what do you make of it? I confess I don't know, but Christ in his mercy knows that I am astonished that they are no more capable of hearing it than if they were stone-deaf. Could anything be put more plainly to such deaf people? The passion of Christ is recounted in this psalm as clearly as in the gospel, yet the psalm was composed goodness knows how many years before the Lord was born of the virgin Mary. It was a herald, giving advance notice of the coming of the Judge.[25]

Augustine preaches again on Psalm 22 in an Easter sermon, and notes that this annual liturgical commemoration "in a sense makes present what took place in time past, and in this way it moves us as if we were actually watching our Lord hanging on the cross, but watching as believers, not mockers."[26] Augustine also implies that it is our cry with which Christ identifies, "My God, my God, why have you forsaken me?" It is sin that alienates us from God. So argues Augustine, "*This psalm is* written about me." Christ has interceded on my behalf, "and has made my sins his own, in order to make his righteousness ours."[27]

As a test case of orthodoxy (i.e., that the Psalm refers to Christ), **Theodore of Mopsuestia's** exposition of Psalm 22 was used to condemn him of heresy. Rarely have commentators been condemned for heresy on the basis of their interpretation of psalms. But part of the case against Theodore of Mopsuestia at the fifth Ecumenical Council of Constantinople in 553 was his commentary on Psalm 22. Theodore argued that "it behooves all pious people to recite something of this kind. . . . [T]he Jews crucified him on the grounds that he was undermining the law. This was the reason, then, that he quoted this verse, not that an oracle was given him about himself in prophecy, and certainly not that this psalm was composed in reference to him."[28] With such statements that seemed

25. *Expositions on the Psalms,* ed. John E. Rotelle, trans. Maria Boulding (Hyde Park, NY: New City Press, 2000), pp. 228-29.

26. Rotelle, ed., *Expositions on the Psalms,* p. 227.

27. Rotelle, ed., *Expositions on the Psalms,* p. 229.

28. Robert C. Hill, trans., *Theodore of Mopsuestia, Commentary on Psalms 1-81* (Atlanta: Society of Biblical Literature, 2006), p. 243.

to associate him with Sabellianism, Theodore of Mopsuestia was condemned a century after his death. (Later, in the thirteenth century, Thomas Aquinas again cited the error of Theodore of Mopsuestia — that of interpreting the psalm with reference only to David, and not to Christ.) In sharp contrast to Theodore of Mopsuestia, his scholarly contemporary **Theodoret,** bishop of Cyrrhus (393-460), opens his commentary with the clear statement: "This psalm foretells the events of Christ the Lord's Passion and Resurrection, the calling of the nations and the salvation of the world. . . . [M]ore faith is to be placed in the sacred apostles' and the Savior's own clear adoption of the psalm's opening than on those essaying a contrary interpretation."[29]

Prophecy played a vital role within an oracular, popular culture, as a source of divine power, so the identification of the Old Testament prophets was crucial.[30] Oracular power was long associated with the Greek Delphic culture, and the Chaldean oracles also still persisted. Hence the roles of the Biblical prophets, with David in the Psalter as the great archetype of Christ, were all factors in favor of such psalm commentaries, as that of Theodoret. At the same time, Theodoret seeks a balance between the strongly allegorical bent of the Latin fathers, and the more "literal" or historical bias of the Antiochene school of Eusebius,[31] to sustain his "prophetic interpretation."

Unlike the earlier preference for "the spiritual meaning," **Cassiodorus** (c. 490–c. 583) interprets the centrality of prophecy in the Psalms as "the divine breath which proclaims with unshakeable truth the outcome of events through the deeds or words of certain persons." By this, he means a conjunction of divine inspiration, the almost unrestrained use of allegory, free interpretation of the psalm-headings, the central role of Christology in the psalms, and the praise of the church. Cassiodorus begins by affirming: "Though many of the psalms briefly recall the Lord's passion, none has described it in such apt terms, so that it appears not so much as prophecy, but as history."[32] "Why hast Thou forsaken Me?" This is surely the crucial theological question of the church, which even Ambrose answered somewhat shakily when he stated: "The Man Christ thus exclaims when about to die by the separation of the Divinity."

More carefully, Cassiodorus ascribes his abandonment to "the undertak-

29. Thomas Aquinas, Stephen Loughlin, *The Aquinas Translation Project,* p. 145.

30. It appears a Messianic movement adopting a "Zerubbabel," who would restore the temple once more in the re-establishment of Jerusalem, was current in the early fifth century. C. Thomas McCullough, "Theodoret of Cyrus as Biblical Interpreter and the Presence of Judaism in the Later Roman Empire," *Studia Patristica* 1 (1983): 331-32.

31. Jean-Nöel Guinot, "Les Sources de l'Exégèse de Théodoret de Cyr," *Studia Patristica* 25 (1993): 72-94.

32. Guinot, "Les Sources de l'Exégèse de Théodoret," p. 217.

ing of the passion assigned to him."[33] In nearly every paragraph, he identifies a figure of speech both to define it grammatically and to explain its meaning. For example, he observes that in verse 6 [7] "I am a worm and no man" is "to embody the figure of *tapeinōsis* which in Latin is called *humiliatio,* employed whenever wondrous greatness is compared with the most lowly things." In verse 8 [9], "'he hoped in the Lord, let Him deliver him' — this he says is spoken by the Jews as *ironia* and in Latin *irrisio,* its surface-meaning being at variance with what it seeks to say."[34] Since so much of the text is incorporated into the detailed events of Christ on the Cross, Cassiodorus comments: "We surely seem to be reviewing the gospel here rather than a psalm, since these things were fulfilled so authentically that they seem already enacted rather than still to come."[35]

IV. Jewish-Christian Dialogue in the Twelfth Century

Although early apologists such as Justin, and especially Origen, debated with Jewish scholars in the second and early third centuries, the major periods of debate were much later, particularly in the twelfth century and at the time of the Reformation.

The debate in the twelfth century was over the need to make a distinction between what the Hebrew Scripture itself has to say *(pesuto)* and what traditional lore has said about Scripture *(midraso).* For Biblical studies this meant that one focused upon the figural or allegorical/spiritual meaning of the text, in what medieval philosophy had called the category of *realism.* Or else in *nominalism,* one should only be interested in the objective meaning of a word or text in its specific context. The divide between these two positions is also cultural and environmental. For on the one hand, the cloistered monks traditionally applied the Psalms in their daily exercise of *lectio divina* with their fourfold use of literal, allegorical, tropological, and anagogical application. The seventeen Lenten sermons of **Bernard of Clairvaux** (1090?-1153) on Psalm 91 illustrate this strongly figural approach with its rich, memorized allusions to many other psalms and scriptures. The extraordinary richness of scriptural memorization that he exercised in his use of *lectio divina* is reflected in the quotations or allusions **Bernard** gives in these seventeen homilies; over 230 references to the other psalms, and a further 511 other Biblical references.[36]

33. Guinot, "Les Sources de l'Exégèse de Théodoret," p. 216.

34. Guinot, "Les Sources de l'Exégèse de Théodoret," p. 219.

35. Guinot, "Les Sources de l'Exégèse de Théodoret," p. 221.

36. Based on a calculation I have made in the annotated text, Bernard of Clairvaux, *Ser-*

In his commentary on the psalms, **Rashi** (1040-1105; the name is an acronym for Rabbi Solomon Yizhaqi) attempted to defuse or neutralize Christian teaching.[37] For example, Rashi interprets Psalm 22:2 as the abandonment of the nation of Israel in exile to suffer at the hand of the Gentiles.[38] Further, in Psalm 22:28 it is the Gentiles who will pay heed to the evil they have done to the Jews and will repent in the Messianic age, when they see the renewed kingship of Israel.[39]

In the other metaphysical system, the new secular studies now taught their commentaries of the Psalms in the lecture room, where Jewish-Christian debate opened up new horizons, in schools such as **St. Victor** in Paris, in Laon, and in Chartres.

Gilbert, bishop of Poitiers (c. 1080-1154), student of Anselm, develops his psalm commentary in an unprecedented manner. First, he writes his commentary side by side with the text of Scripture. This had been done with classical pagan texts, but never with the Bible. It indicates the shift from the contemplative environment of the cloister, to the new discursive atmosphere of the classroom. Second, whereas Cassiodorus had divided the Psalter into twelve categories, more or less as an afterthought, Gilbert redefines his categories, spotlights them, and makes provision to use them by means of a cross-index.[40] Third, Gilbert uses the psalms as an active or practical philosophy in improving the interior life. Their intent is to help believers live out the economy of salvation.[41] Once lived out in the synagogue, the Psalter is now being lived out richly by the church, as expressive of poetry, music, stimulating language, and affective desires, as well as being philosophical and intellectual. It is education for the whole person. The great popularity of Gilbert's commentary in the twelfth century is evidence of its fresh and integrative character.[42]

While Gilbert and later Peter Lombard were in contact with Jewish schol-

---

mons on Conversion, trans. Marie-Bernard Said (Kalamazoo, MI and Spencer, MA: Cistercian Publications, 1981), pp. 115-261.

37. He failed to comment on Psalms 121, 128, and 134. See Mayer I. Gruber, *Rashi's Commentary on Psalms 1–89,* with English translation, introduction, and notes (Atlanta: Scholars Press, 1998).

38. E. I. J. Rosenthal, "Anti-Christian Polemic in Medieval Bible Commentaries," *JJS* 11 (1960): 125.

39. Rashi, quoted in Rosenthal, "Anti-Christian Polemic," p. 128.

40. For example, he notes in the margin of Psalm 22 that this psalm is the first explicit prophecy about the Passion and Resurrection of Christ, and that the next one is Psalm 34, and so the finding device proceeds forward.

41. Theresa Gross-Diaz, *The Psalms Commentary of Gilbert of Poitiers* (Leiden, New York, Cologne: Brill, 1996), p. 83.

42. Gross-Diaz, *The Psalms Commentary of Gilbert of Poitiers,* pp. 149-55.

ars only indirectly, the remarkable **Herbert of Bosham** (died c. 1194), student of Peter Lombard in Paris (c. 1150), actually used and responded to Rashi's commentary. Herbert became the scholarly advisor of Thomas à Becket after he became Lord Chancellor and before he was Archbishop of Canterbury. His *Psalterium cum commento* (the only copy in existence being in the library of St. Paul's Cathedral) broke new ground.[43] He wrote a running literal commentary on Jerome's last Psalter, the *Hebraica,* which even Jerome had not commented upon. Even more than Gilbert, he turned away from all the patristic sources and liturgical practices, to provide a fresh translation, in which commentary and text flow together, with occasional interlinear glosses.[44] He names his Jewish sources as *litterator,* who in antiquity was simply an instructor in grammar. For Herbert this was a mark of scholarly esteem of Rashi and other Jewish sources, who provided "plain meaning" of the text.[45] For like his associates, Hugh and Richard of St. Victor, Herbert sought textual and therefore "literal" grounds for his Messianism, not allegory. So the basis for Christian-Jewish dialogue was textual rather than theological and figural. In this regard he was centuries ahead of his times.

As Raphael Loewe has pointed out, such twelfth-century Christian Hebraism had a threefold purpose: the establishment of an accurate translation of the Hebrew Bible into Latin; the refutation of Jewish objections to the Latin text; and the development of an authoritative text on which to base the validity of Christianity's eclipse of Judaism. These were of course polemical concerns, which could be interpreted as both positive and negative relationships. Aryeh Grabois suggested that this fostered irenic relations between Jewish and Christian scholars,[46] while other scholars such as Amos Funkenstein and Jeremy Cohen contrast the genial dialogue of scholars with the "mass riots" of crowd violence exerted against the Jews in the late twelfth and thirteenth centuries.[47]

43. Alas, this manuscript has still not been copied or edited, other than in a few small quotations.

44. Deborah L. Goodwin, *"Take Hold of the Robe of a Jew," Herbert of Bosham's Christian Hebraism* (Leiden and Boston: Brill, 2006), p. 66.

45. Ephraim Kanarfogel, *Jewish Education and Society in the High Middle Ages* (Detroit: Wayne State University Press, 1993), pp. 80-85.

46. Aryeh Grabois, "The *Hebraica Veritas* and Jewish-Christian Intellectual Relations in the Twelfth Century," *Speculum* 50 (1975): 613-34.

47. Amos Funkenstein, "Basic Types of Christian Anti-Jewish Polemic in the Later Middle Ages," *Viator* 2 (1971): 373-82; Jeremy Cohen, *Living Letters of the Law: The Idea of the Jew in Medieval Christianity* (Berkeley: University of California Press: 1999).

V. Late Medieval Scholastic Commentaries

More than any of his predecessors, **Thomas Aquinas** (died 1274) united philosophy with Christian doctrine through revision of Aristotelian thought. Etienne Gilson puts it succinctly: "He changed the water of philosophy into the wine of theology."[48] Aquinas relied less on previous authorities, and more on reasoned thought. So unlike the effusiveness of Franciscans like Bonaventura, his work purged symbolic language with its figures of speech; instead, his vocabulary is spare, precise, and definitive.[49] Compared to the effusive language of many previous devotees of the Psalter, Aquinas, a Dominican, was detached and emotionally disciplined.

Aquinas wrote an extensive thirty-three-page summary of traditional commentary on Psalm 22. Whereas other earlier psalms historically reflect on what David suffered from his son's rebellion and from Saul, now we have the sufferings of all Israel from these events, observes Aquinas. This psalm "treats of the passion of Christ in a spiritual manner," and yet also "it is its literal sense," so "the discussion in this psalm is principally about Christ's passion. It touches, secondarily, on the resurrection." Aquinas notes that the psalm is in three parts: a complaint, followed by the story of his passion, then his joyous freedom.[50] Following Augustine's theme of the whole Christ, the psalm expresses Christ and his church as one mystical body. For his "forsakenness" is as the sin-bearer of humanity, so he voices his complaint and confusion on behalf of humanity.

In the central section, he treats of the things that were done to Jesus before the crucifixion, during, and after it. Thomas Aquinas identifies Christ's enemies figuratively as animals: Pilate as the lion; the pride of the High Priest and Scribes as the unicorn, and the Jews as a dog. In the suffering of his body — his bones out of joint, his heart melting as wax, his thirst — Thomas interprets this more corporately about the flight and disarray of his disciples, about the state of the church, its persecution by its enemies, etc. Even the description of the parting of his garments he signifies as being the disunity of the church.

Likewise, the third section of the psalm, which Aquinas identifies with the resurrection, as the fruit of liberation has a manifold effect upon the body

48. Etienne Gilson, *History of Christian Philosophy in the Middle Ages* (New York: Random House, 1955), p. 365.

49. Marcia L. Colish, *Medieval Foundations of the Western Intellectual Tradition, 400-1400* (New Haven and London: Yale University Press, 1998), pp. 296-97.

50. Thomas Aquinas, *In psalmos Davidis expositio,* in Sancti Thomas Aquinatis Opera Omnia (Parmae: Typis Petri Fiaccadori, 1863), vol. 14, pp. 148-312. An English translation of selected Psalms is by Stephen Loughlin, *The Aquinas Translation Project.* This is available at http://www4.desales.edu/- philtheo/loughlin/ATP/index.html.

of the church. First, it opens their minds to understand the prophetic scriptures, as it did for the two disciples walking with the Risen Lord. Second, it releases the divine praise of the church. Indeed, now the whole of the New Testament expresses such praise of God. Third, it prompts them to fear the Lord — not in fear itself — but fear in the love of Lord, who will now be remembered continually. All "this will now be announced to them, as to a People who are born, by a spiritual generation."

Nicholas of Lyra (died 1349) is one of the foremost medieval exegetes; he printed the first Bible commentary (in fifty volumes). As a Franciscan scholar at the Sorbonne in Paris, he emphasized a more literal, less allegorical approach, which later greatly influenced Luther. He was the first Christian scholar to quote Ben Solomon or Rashi by name.[51] Rashi's defense against Christian scholars had been to downplay the "Messianic" component, avoiding allegory, with a defensible, more literal study of the text. Daringly now Nicholas does the same in engaging directly with Rashi's text. He shows a remarkable lack of Christological emphasis, unlike his predecessors, even Gilbert of Poitiers, and explains in his introduction he will only discuss literal/historical meaning to the psalms. Unlike Gilbert and Thomas, who follow Augustine/Cassiodorus to see "the whole Christ/Church" expressive of the Psalter, Nicholas is content to deal more with the individual's spiritual life.[52]

As we saw in the case of the use of Psalm 15, there is increasing awareness of the decadence of a "Christian" society in the thirteenth century onwards. Christians are stung by the Jewish critique of Christian *mores* in this present world, whose kingdom is not "Christian," nor indeed "Messianic." "The Evangelical Awakening" of the thirteenth century begins then with reforming voices such as **Stephen of Muret**, and especially **Francis of Assisi** (1181 or 1182/83-1226), to call the church back to the original humility and poverty of its primitive beginnings. **Otto of Freising** (born c. 1114, died 1158) asks what is preferable, the simplicity of the early church or the grandeur and corruption of the contemporary status?[53] Perhaps consciously for the first time, these reformers — Franciscan and Dominican — avoid the use of the term *Christianitas*, for Christendom is no part of their apostolic business.[54] The preaching of the

51. Beryl Smalley, *The Study of the Bible in the Middle Ages* (Notre Dame: Notre Dame University Press, 1964), p. 190.

52. Theresa Gross-Diaz, "What's a Good Soldier to Do? Scholarship and Revelation in the Postils on the Psalms," in Philip D. W. Krey and Lesley Smith, eds., *Nicholas of Lyra: The Senses of Scriptures* (Leiden, Boston, Cologne: Brill, 2000), p. 119.

53. M.-D. Chenu, O.P., *Man, Nature and Society in the Twelfth Century*, trans. Jerome Taylor and Lester K. Little (Chicago and London: University of Chicago Press, 1979), p. 240.

54. Chenu, *Man, Nature and Society in the Twelfth Century*, p. 263.

Word takes on a new earnestness, and as scholarship leaves behind the old allegories, so this evangelical fervor of reform takes on the practical expression of becoming the *pauperes Christi,* the poor ones of Christ.

With a Franciscan spirit, **Richard Rolle** (1290-1349) sees Jesus throughout the Psalms as identifying with the poor and the humble. For it is not with the lofty Christology of the early Fathers that he follows Christ. Of his life and works, he has given us his own epitaph: "All for Jesus." He begins his commentary on Psalm 22 by stating clearly that this is the voice of Christ in his passion, so that the psalm was written for him as he was nailed on the cross, taking our sins in his own body. We are warned that the purpose of accepting the psalm is to be partakers of Christ's salvation, so that his blood was not shed in vain. Rolle ends his commentary by noting that a profitable reception of the psalm is to be poor in spirit and to despise this world, for "poor men love God, but the rich love themselves."[55] But the sufferings Richard comments upon are not corporately expressive of the "Body of Christ," which Thomas Aquinas focuses upon, but the actual sufferings of Jesus upon his cross. For his focus is upon Jesus' own cross. His commentary is "evangelical," as addressed to "lovers of Jesus," who are blessed in his vicarious death and resurrection. Such "future generations who will proclaim the righteousness of the Lord" are indeed a Messianic fulfillment, as "those who, as a generation yet unborn, will honor our Lord in good will and good deed."[56]

VI. Late Medieval Commentaries: Psalm 22 as "Prophetic"

A cultural awareness of apocalyptic crisis deepens in the thirteenth and fourteenth centuries in association with the evangelical preaching of the friars. The Cistercian **Joachim de Fiore** (died 1202) began to teach a millenarianism that predicted beyond both Judaism *and* Christianity there lay a better charismatic future. In the late Middle Ages apocalypticism, mysticism, and the waning of scholasticism were rechallenging the church about fresh ways of understanding the Scriptural role of prophecy.

Denys the Carthusian (died 1471) is linked with Cardinal Cusa in the cause of church reform in Germany, spending time with him there. Aquinas had concluded, as we have noted, that Moses was the greatest of the Old Testa-

55. H. R. Bramley, ed., *The Psalter or Psalms of David and Certain Canticles, with a Translation and Exposition in English by Richard Rolle of Hampole* (Oxford: Clarendon Press, 1884), p. 82.

56. Bramley, ed., *The Psalter or Psalms of David,* p. 83.

ment prophets, for he saw the glory of God as the great "I AM." But Nicholas of Cusa questions this, according to Denys, "for the reason he saw God through his essence in the present life — because such a vision pertains to prophecy in no way . . . that David is called the most extraordinary of the prophets ought to be understood, so far as concerns this, that he prophesied most excellently and evidently concerning the mysteries of Christ."[57] Yet Denys interprets Psalm 22 as more "history" than "prophecy," for it describes what actually happened at the cross of Jesus. It is the voice of the prophet Christ, who is revealing in himself the fulfillment of the Old Testament predictions of the Messiah. Its expression is the model of how the Christian should express devotionally such words. In contradiction to Theodore who interpreted the abandonment of the human by the divine, the "forsakenness of Christ" was momentary, while conveying indeed bitter sorrow. Denys then conflates the narrative of the passion in the gospels with the words of the psalm. As others had noted, "they numbered all my bones" implies that his stretched, naked, and suffering body did reveal all his bones. But the malice of the persecutors blinded them, observes Denys, to recognize who he was, their Messiah, the Christ.

Again in distinction from the corporate Christ of Thomas Aquinas, Denys now calls us to "let the imprint of the crucified Jesus firmly take place on our hearts, let us fasten his individual torments indelibly in our minds, so that we would be able to say individually with the Apostle: 'I have been crucified with Christ; but it is no longer I who live, but Christ lives in me.'" There is no more efficacious way to overcome temptations and to grow with Christ than to bear his cross. Here we hear echoed the great classic of Thomas à Kempis, *The Imitation of Christ,* likewise a member of the *Devotio Moderna.*

At the end of the psalm, Denys can speak of resurrection, and in doing so, move from the individual to all of God's people. The experience of the cross can only be personally chosen, but the fruit of Christ's passion is now shared. In verse 28 [29], Denys interprets "David announcing the whole world's conversion to Christ" through preaching.[58] Denys concludes that "the Church's life . . . must be cruciformly following the footsteps of Christ." He now gives "a moral exposition" of Psalm 22, going through it once more to apply it wholly to the church of God. The conciliar efforts to reform the church, both Nicholas of Cusa and his associate Denys the Carthusian now realized, had failed. The next chapter will be the Reformation itself, an appropriate place to put closure on this particular history.

57. Denys the Carthusian, *D. Dionysii Cartusiani insigne opus commentariorum in psalmos omnes Davidicos,* in *Doctoris Ecstatici D. Dionysii Cartusiani Opera Omnia* (Monstrolii: Typis Cartusiae S. M. De Pratis, 1898), vols. 5-6; 5.529-543; Article 3, conclusion.

58. Denys the Carthusian, 51.33.27.

Part II: Voice of the Psalmist: Translation

A psalm of David.

1 My God, my God, why have you abandoned me?
So far from saving me, from the words of my roaring?
2 My God, I cry out by day, but you do not answer,
By night, and am not silent.[59]
3 Yet you are the Holy One;
Enthroned on the praises of Israel.
4 In you our fathers put their trust;
They trusted and you delivered them.
5 To you they cried out and were saved;
In you they trusted and were not put to shame.
6 But I am a worm and not a man,
Scorned by mortals[60] and despised by the people.
7 All who see me mock me;
They split open their lips; they shake their heads:
8 "Commit[61] [yourself] to *I AM;* let *I AM* rescue him.
Let him deliver him, since he delights in him."
9 Surely you are the one who brought me out of the womb;
Who caused me to trust[62] at my mother's breast.
10 From the womb I was cast upon you;
From my mother's belly you are my God.
11 Do not be far from me, for trouble is near;
Surely there is none to help.
12 Many bulls surround me;
Strong bulls of Bashan encircle me.
13 Lions, tearing their prey and roaring,
Open their mouths wide against me.
14 I am poured out like water,
and all my bones are out of joint.
My heart has become like wax;
It has melted away within me.

59. Literally, "And there is no rest/silence to/for me."

60. Literally, "a reproach of mortals," construing *'ādām* as a subjective genitive.

61. LXX (cf. Syr. Matt. 27:43) read *gal,* "he committed/trusted," a facilitating pointing of the consonants to harmonize with the rest of the verse. Our poet, however, mixes a mélange of vivid scenes.

62. A few Heb. Mss, LXX, Syr. Jer. read *mibṭaḥî,* "my hope/trust."

15 My strength[63] is dried up like potsherd,
And my tongue is made to stick to the roof of my mouth;
And you lay me[64] in the dust of death.
16 Surely, dogs[65] surround me,
A band of evil men encircle me;
They bore holes[66] in my hands and my feet.

63. The conjecture to read *ḥky* ("my palate"), not *kḥy,* is attractive because of the parallel *lqḥ* ("jaw").

64. A fifth- or sixth-century codex reads *deduxerunt* (*špātūnî* [?]), a poorly attested facilitating reading. Precisely because it is simpler and more natural it is probably secondary.

65. Aquila, Symmachus (Jerome) read *tēratai* ("hunters"); LXX adds *polloi* ("many").

66. Gregory Vall ("Psalm 22:17B: 'The Old Guess,'" *JBL* 116, no. 1 [1997]: 45-56), to whom along with Delitzsch I am indebted in this footnote, comments: "In terms of textual criticism, few verses in the Hebrew Bible have been more hotly contested down through the centuries than Ps 22:17" (p. 45). The MT, normally the most reliable textual tradition, vocalizes the first word of 22:16Bb as *kāʾ*^{a}*rî* (= "like the lion"), giving the improbable sense: "my hands and my feet are like a lion." *ʾry* is not used elsewhere in the Psalter for "lion," casting more suspicion on the text. JPS tries to salvage MT by "they are at my hands and my feet," but an adverbial accusative is not possible in a nominal clause. By revising the received accents and making *hiqqîpûnî* the predicate, one could make some sense of: "they surround me like a lion as to my hands and feet." But as the translation shows, the grammar is awkward and unlikely. The Greek version (c. 2nd cent. BCE) reads *ōruxan* ("they dug [my hands and my feet])," which makes excellent sense with scavenger dogs as the subject. The retroverted Hebrew text for that reading would probably be *kārû* from *krh* or its bi-form, though otherwise unattested, *kwr.* This retroverted reading is actually found in several Hebrew manuscripts, which read *kākʾ*^{a}*rû* and *kōʾ*^{a}*rê* ("diggers of"). The reading is also found in the Masora — textual traditions that accompanied the received text — of Numbers 24:9 and in Jacob ben Chajim's *Masora finalis.* The LXX reading is now attested in the 5/6 HevPsalms scroll (c. 50 to 68 CE) (see *The Dead Sea Scrolls Bible: The Oldest Known Bible,* trans. Martin Abegg, Peter Flint, Eugene Ulrich [San Francisco: Harper, 1999], p. 509). The Jewish translators, Aquila and Symmachus, also probably read *kʾrw,* but invested it with the meaning of the Arabic root *krr,* "they bound [in a ball]." In the Gallican Psalter (c. 387) Jerome rendered *kʾrw* by "foderunt" ("they dug"), but seems to have followed Aquila in his *Psalterium iuxta Hebraeos* (c. 391), where he renders *vinxerunt* ("they have bound"). In much later printed additions of *Psalterium iuxta Hebraeos, vinxerunt* was changed to *fixerunt* ("they fixed my hands and my feet [to the cross]"). But if the original meaning was "to bind," why did the poet use an Arabic word "to bind up a ball" instead of one of the common Hebrew words meaning "to bind"? The reading *kʾry* is first attested in a sixth-century CE Cairo Geniza palimpsest of the *Hexapla.* H. Leštre (*Le Livre des Psaumes* [Paris: Lethielleux, 1897], p. 99) argues that, since Justin was in the habit of reproaching the Jews for introducing textual changes but makes no such mention of Psalm 22:16, the reading *kʾrw* must have been *encore intacte et reconnue de tous* in the middle of the second century. Assuming the root is *kûr,* a bi-form of *krh,* Delitzsch (*Psalms,* p. 200) documents medial *ʾaleph* in so-called hollow roots like *kûr* in Zechariah 14:10 *(rwm)* and Daniel 7:16 *(qwm).* In Psalm 40:7 *krh* "dug" is used to describe forming the ear, so the figure of scavenging dogs boring holes in hands and feet is not farfetched. Syriac-speaking Christians read "they pierced." Some scholars have sought to find a meaning for *krʾy* other than

17 I can count all my bones;
People stare; they gloat over me.
18 They distribute my garments among them,[67]
And cast lots for my clothing.
19 But you, *I AM,* do not be far off;
My Help,[68] come quickly to help me.
20 Deliver my life from the sword,
My precious life from the power[69] of the dogs.
21 Save me from the mouth of lions;
Answer[70] me from the horns of the wild oxen.

"like a lion"; e.g., Dahood revocalized the text as *kī 'ārᵉyū* ("because they picked clean"). Vall, however, rightly opines that as these proposed conjectural emendations "compound various textual, syntactic, orthographical, and contextual improbabilities, they have little to recommend them" (p. 51). Other scholars, reading *k'rw,* have conjectured several different roots for *k'r;* e.g., P. Cappelle sought the root in Akkadian *karû* (the D-stem *kurrû* means "to cut short, shorten"), leading to "as if to hack off my hands and my feet" (NEB, NJB) and the non-sensible "they shriveled my hands and my feet" (NRSV). These suggestions likewise rest on shaky philological ground and so none has won a consensus. Vall thinks the original reading was *'srw* "they bound," but his explanation that *'srw* was corrupted into *s'rw* and that in turn into *k'rw* strains credulity, for there is no root *s'r,* and scribes do not normally confuse /s/ and /k/. We are left then with the LXX as the best text and interpretation of this *crux interpretum.* While interpreting the psalm in the light of Christ's crucifixion, the apostles do not appeal to this verse, even though Jesus' piercing is integral to John's hermeneutic (John 19:32-37; 20:25-27; Rev. 1:7; cf. Isa. 53). But the piercing occurred in his side after his death, not in his hands and feet before his death. Beginning as early as Justin Martyr (c. 100-165), however, Christian writers commonly appealed to "dug/pierced" for a Christian interpretation.

67. *Lamedh* of interest *(dativus commodi)* (*IBHS,* p. 207, P. 11.2.10d).

68. Or "my strength." The English versions and commentaries are about evenly divided in interpreting the hapax legomenon *'ᵉyālût* by "strength" or "help" (see Robin Wakely, *NIDOTTE,* 1:377f., s.v. *'ayil*). *HALOT* gives both options, favoring "strength," and BDB, unaware of Ugaritic, gives only "help." LXX, Syr., and Vulg. read "help," but Targum reads "strength." Aramaic *'yl* means "help," so that *'ᵉyālût* may be an Aramaic loan word. According to Dahood (*AB,* p. 303), Ugaritic *ul (Krt* 68 and 178) means "troop," on which he makes an unconvincing leap to "strength." Moreover, the meaning of *ulny* is uncertain, and the line may mean "troops [a mighty force]" (see Gordon, *UT,* entry 164 and *ANET,* p. 144). *HALOT* curiously does not cite Dahood. In Psalm 88:4 [5] one who goes down to the pit is said to be *geber 'ên-ᵉyāl,* "a man without strength/help." Perhaps the appeal that *ᵉly/ûtî* is asked to "to help me" favors the Aramaic derivation. In sum, though no firm conclusion can be drawn between these two options, that data favors "help."

69. Literally, "hand."

70. *ʿᵃnîtānî* is construed as a precative perfective (see *IBHS,* p. 494, P. 30.5.4c, d). See also I. W. Provan, "Past, Present and Future in Lamentations iii 52-56: The Case for the Precative Perfect Re-examined," *VT* 41 (1991): 164-75.

22 I will declare[71] your name to my brothers;
In the congregation I will praise you.
23 You who fear *I AM,* praise him!
All the seed of Jacob, honor him!
Revere him,[72] all the seed of Israel!
24 For he has not despised or abhorred the suffering[73] of the afflicted one;
He has not hidden his face from him,[74]
But, when he cried to him[75] for help, listened.
25 From you comes[76] my praising you[77] in the great assembly;
I will fulfill my vows before those who fear you.
26 Let the poor eat and be sated; let those who seek *I AM* praise him —
Let your[78] hearts live forever!
27 All the ends of the earth will remember and turn to the LORD,
And all the clans of the nations will bow down before you.[79]
28 For dominion belongs to *I AM*
As ruler over the nations.
29 Surely to him[80] all the rich[81] of the earth will bow down,

71. The cohortative expresses resolve. Unfortunately English lost the distinction between "I shall" (referring to a future situation) and "I will" (referring to resolve to do something).

72. Literally, "Be afraid of." *Min* expresses the cause or agent (*IBHS,* p. 213, P. 11.2.11d). Targ., LXX, and a few Heb. Mss. read *yāgūrû* "they will fear," not *wgwrw. Waw* and *yodh* are easily confused.

73. Bardtke *(BHS)* thinks LXX, Syr., Targ. read *ṣʿqh,* "crying out." But those consonants are not readily confused for *ʿnwt.* C. A. Briggs, *A Critical and Exegetical Commentary of the Book of Psalms* (ICC; Edinburgh: T. & T. Clark, 1906), pp. 199, 205, thinks they pointed *ʿnwt* as an inf. cstr. of *ʿnh* (*ʿănôt,* "to answer"), but he has to supply "he heard." Jerome (*modestiam,* "humility") read *ʿanwat.*

74. LXX and Vulgate read *mimmennî,* a smoother reading, but Semitic literature commonly confounds pronouns (see B. K. Waltke, *Micah* [Grand Rapids: Eerdmans, 2007], p. 74).

75. Some ancient versions gloss "unto him" by "before him."

76. Literally, "from with." The compound preposition demands a verb of motion be supplied (*IBHS,* p. 224, P. 11.4.33d).

77. Hebrew *tᵉhillātî* ("my praising"). The /*t*/ prefix to the noun designates the action of the verb *hll* from which it is derived (*IBHS,* p. 90, P. 5.6c).

78. LXX, Syr., and two Heb. mss. read "their" (see n. 74).

79. Syr., Jer., and one Heb. ms. gloss "before him" (cf. v. 29 [30]; see n. 74).

80. The emendation of MT's *ʾklw wyšthww* [*ʾākᵉlû wayyiš . . .*] ("they will eat and worship") to *ʾk lô yiš . . .* [*ʾēk lô yiš . . .*] is preferred because construing suffix conjugation as a prophetic perfective (*IBHS,* pp. 489-90, P. 30.5.1e) is unnatural.

81. Literally, "fat ones." Some (e.g., NRSV) emend MT's *dšny* to *yšny* [*yᵉšēnê,* "who sleep"] to make a better parallelism with "who go down to the dust," but a merism contrasting fat and dying is just as good. More importantly, the notion that the dead praise God is foreign to Old Testament theology (cf. Ps. 6:5; 88:10; 115:17).

Before him all who go down to the dust will kneel,
Those[82] who did not preserve their lives.[83]
30 Their seed will serve him;[84]
It will be told to their generations about the Lord of all.[85]
31 They will come[86] and proclaim his righteousness;
To a people yet unborn[87] [they will say]: "Surely, he has acted."

Part III. Commentary

I. Form, Structure, and Message

Psalm 22 contains the typical motifs of a petition psalm: direct address (vv. 1a, 19a), complaint/lament (vv. 1b-2, 6-8, 11b-18), confidence (vv. 3-5, 9-10), petition (vv. 11a, 19-21), and praise (vv. 22-31). The following outline unravels the mixture of verses.

I. Complaint and Confidence	vv. 1-10 [2-11]
A. First Strophe:	vv. 1-5 [2-6]
1. Complaint: Abandoned by God	vv. 1-2 [2-3]
2. Confidence: God kept covenant fidelity with fathers	vv. 3-5 [4-6]
B. Second Strophe:	vv. 6-10 [7-11]
1. Complaint: Abandoned by people	vv. 6-8 [7-9]
2. Confidence: God chose psalmist for covenant fidelity	vv. 9-10 [10-11]
II. Lament and Petition	vv. 11-21 [12-22]
Transition:	v. 11 [12]
A. Lament	vv. 12-18 [13-19]

82. Construing *waw* as epexegetical.

83. Literally, "his life" (see n. 74), individualizing "all." Briggs (*Psalms,* p. 200) rightly comments: "The versions and interpreters have many suggestions here [v. 20 (30)B], but none of them are so simple as MT, which gives an explanatory complement to the previous clause."

84. LXX combines 29B and 30A: *hē psychē mou autǭ zȩ̄, kai to sperma mou douleusei* . . . : "my soul will live for him, and my seed will serve . . ." [*napšî lō' ḥayyâ . . . l*]. The switch to first person is unlikely.

85. *IBHS,* p. 124, P. 7.4.3f.

86. LXX confounds the verses: *anangelēsetai tǭ kuriǭ genea hē erchomenē; yspr l'dny ldwr yb'w* (?): "A generation that is coming shall be reported to the Lord." For the inferiority of the LXX's creative vocalizations see *IBHS,* pp. 26-28, P. 1. 6.3j.

87. Literally, "to a people to be born." Gerundive Niphal participle (*IBHS,* p. 387, P. 23.3d).

1. First unit: zoomorphic enemies and self	vv. 12-15 [13-16]
a. Enemy lament: bulls and lions	vv. 12-13 [13-14]
b. Personal lament: bones, heart, tongue	vv. 14-15 [15-16]
2. Second unit: zoomorphic enemies and self	vv. 16-18 [17-19]
a. Enemy lament: dogs	v. 16 [17]
b. Personal lament: bones and garments	vv. 17-18 [18-19]
B. Petition	vv. 19-21 [20-22]
1. Be not far off	v. 19 [20]
2. Deliver from sword, dogs, lion, and oxen	vv. 20-21 [21-22]
III. Psalmist's Praise	vv. 22-31 [23-32]
A. Let Covenant Community Praise *I AM*	vv. 22-26 [23-27]
1. First unit: word of praise	vv. 22-24 [23-25]
a. Psalmist's praise and Israel called to praise	vv. 22-23 [23-24]
b. Cause for praise: God answered prayer	v. 24 [25]
2. Second unit: sacrifice of praise	vv. 25-26 [26-27]
a. Psalmist pays vows	v. 25 [26]
b. Let afflicted eat	v. 26 [27]
B. Nations Will Praise *I AM* Forever	vv. 27-31 [28-32]
1. First unit	vv. 27-28 [28-29]
a. Promise of spatial universal praise	v. 27 [28]
b. Cause for praise: *I AM* rules	v. 28 [29]
2. Second unit	vv. 29-31 [30-32]
a. Promise of social praise	vv. 29-30 [30-31]
b. Cause for praise: *I AM* does right	v. 31 [32]

In sum, the psalm consists of three stanzas of ten verses each: 1-10, 12-21, 22-31 [2-11, 13-22, 23-32], moving from torment to turmoil to triumph.[88] Verse 11 stands apart, functioning as a janus linking the first two stanzas by the key word "far off" (vv. 1, 11, 19 [2, 12, 20]). The first and last stanzas consist of two strophes of five verses each: verses 1-5, 6-10, 22-26, 27-31 [2-6, 7-11, 23-27, 28-32]. Stanza II also consists of two strophes: lament of seven verses (vv. 12-18) and petition of three verses (vv. 19-21 [20-22]), each number representing completeness. The petition is also linked with the lament by reversing the images: "dogs" (v. 16 [17]), "lions" (v. 13 [14]), "wild oxen" (v. 12 [13]). Further symmetries will be noted in the exegesis. Although this cold analysis of the psalm's structure obscures the psalmist's anguish and fervency, its symmetry reveals his spiritual composure, even as he imagines himself enduring a cruel and unjust death. Im-

88. Cf. R. D. Patterson, "Psalm 22: From Trial to Triumph," *JETS* 47 (2004): 213-33.

perative petitions, such as "hasten," and a montage of horrific scenes and nightmarish images express his fervency.

The song's essential message is summarized in verse 24 [25]. In a word, in spite of God's awful delay in answering prayer, he answers and upholds ultimate justice. Samuel Eliot Morrison said: "The wheels of God grind slowly, but they grind exceedingly fine." Two worldviews are represented: the psalmist's versus his murderers' (vv. 7-8 [8-9]). The murderers testify that the psalmist is blameless and trusts God but mock his faith. To destroy his worldview they hound him to death. Nevertheless, the psalmist emerges on the other side of death praising God for hearing his prayer and rescuing him. His gospel message is so wonderful that eventually it reaches the ends of the earth, and all the world joins together in the worship of *I AM* forever. Broyles notes: "It develops from an individual in the dust of death (v. 15 [16]) to universal acknowledgement of the kingdom of God."[89]

After the exegesis, we return to discuss further its form and message in its canonical context.

II. Exegesis

A. Superscript: A Psalm by David (see pp. 87-90)

B. Confidence in Complaint vv. 1-10 [2-11]

The inclusio "my God" frames the first stanza (vv. 1, 10 [2, 11]). Within it his moods restlessly fluctuate to and fro between complaint and confidence. By this fluctuation he profiles against his black complaints (vv. 1-2, 6-8 [2-3, 7-9]) his bright confidence (vv. 3-5, 9-10 [4-6, 10-11]), yet the contrast between the past and present heightens his present pathos. The complaint in the first strophe of God's absence escalates in the second to mockers moving into the spiritual space God vacates. His source of confidence intensifies from the rewarded faith of Israel's fathers to his own faith from birth. The two restless moods are held together by his persevering faith in seeking God's reality.

1. Complaint and Confidence vv. 1-5 [2-6]

The so-called laments of the first stanza are in fact complaints, implicitly to arouse God to do what is right. The laments of the second stanza are in fact la-

89. C. Broyles, *Psalms* (NIBC; Peabody, MA: Hendrickson, 1999), p. 115.

ments, implicitly to move *I AM* to pity. Regarding such complaints within the life of faith, R. W. L. Moberly writes:

> Although the OT constantly stresses the importance of trust . . . as characterizing the true human response to God, the general canonical presentation is such that these are not to be conceived in any simplistic way, as though life were simply a matter of "obeying orders." Rather, there is a recurrent portrayal of life under God as containing space for dialogue with God, with room for question and answer. Obedience to God is to be set in the context of an intelligent relationship and not be mindless.[90]

The first and emphatic word of each verse of the strophe refers to God: "my God" (vv. 1-2 [2-3]) and "you" (vv. 3-5 [4-6]).

a. Complaint vv. 1-2 [2-3]

1 *My God, My God* (*'ēlî 'ēlî,* see 3:2 [3]) combines God's transcendence, indicated by *'ēl,* with personal intimacy of a covenant relationship, indicated by "my." The wicked identify his God as *I AM* (v. 8). In the covenant relationship the human partner obliges himself to commit his life to *I AM,* and *I AM* graciously obliges himself to be the covenant keeper's Provider and Protector. None accuses the psalmist of failing to fulfill his covenant obligation, but the psalmist accuses God of thus far not keeping covenant. A rhetorical and somewhat deprecatory *why* (*lāmâ,* see 2:1) vents his feeling of anger and indignation, not seeking an answer. Goldingay says: "What the suppliant actually wants is action, not explanation."[91] *Have you abandoned me (ʿᵃzabtānî): ʿāzab* is used numerous times in the Law and the prophets to express Israel's apostasy (Deut. 28:20; 29:24 [23]; 31:16; Jer. 1:16; 9:12 [11]); the psalmist turns the tables. God's silence makes him existentially to be *so far off (rāḥôq),* not a very present help in trouble. According to Israel's confession *I AM* is far off from the wicked (Prov. 15:29), but the suppliant complains: "you are far off *from saving me*" (*yᵉšûʿātî,* see 3:2, 8 [3, 9]). *From the words* (*dibrê,* see Ps. 19:3 [4]) *of my roaring (šaʾᵃgātî)*[92] shows his cries, like those of a wounded animal, as pleas for salvation.[93] Albert

90. R. W. L. Moberly, *NIDOTTE,* 4:876.

91. J. Goldingay, *Psalms: Volume 1: Psalms 1–41* (Grand Rapids: Baker Academic, 2006), p. 325.

92. Note the assonance between *yᵉšûʿātî* and *šaʾᵃgātî.*

93. Of the seven occurrences of *šʾg,* four refer to the roaring of an attacking lion (Isa. 5:29; Ezek. 19:7; Zech. 11:3; Job 4:10). Presumably the other three refer to the roar of a lion in pain (Job 3:24; Ps. 22:2; 32:3).

Schweitzer averred that Jesus' cry "My God, my God, why hast Thou forsaken me" indicated that Jesus died as a "deluded apocalyptic," his messianic expectations unfulfilled. But Schweitzer failed to understand that the psalmist's rhetorical cry aims to move God to action. Also, the suppliant's three calls to God demonstrate his persistence in faith, not a deluded defeatist. Calvin says: "The long duration of calamities could neither overthrow it [his faith], nor interrupt its exercise."[94] In the crisis he does not apostatize by turning to false gods (cf. Ps. 4:2 [3]). Schweitzer also failed to interpret the psalm holistically; the psalmist's prayer ends in a triumphant vision of the salvation of the world through his sufferings and deliverance. Until God trumps evil, the afflicted gives voice to his feelings of agony.

2 *My God* (*ʾᵉlōhay,* see v. 1) *I cry out (ʾeqrāʾ)* confirms that his words are petitions. The merism *by day* . . . and *by night* signifies all the time (see Ps. 1:2). *And you do not answer me (taʿᵃneh,* see 3:4 [5]) clarifies the figure of being "far off." *And I am not silent* (*wᵉlōʾ dûmîyâ lî,* see n. 59) shows that the psalmist does not lose hope.

b. Confidence vv. 3-5 [4-6]

The psalmist's memory of God's past saving acts serves as a handmaid to faith.

3 *But you are* (*wᵉʾattâ,* see Ps. 3:3 [4]) typically transforms complaint to confidence. *The Holy One (qādôš)* is an epithet that underscores God's numinous, dynamistic "otherness." Briggs explains *Enthroned* (*yōšēb,* see Ps. 2:4) *on the praises (tᵉhillôt yiśrāʾēl):* "Thither [to the Holy of Holies] the prayers of Israel were directed in temple worship; thither they were conceived as entering, with the clouds of incense from the altar of incense. . . . This incense . . . goes up and envelops the cherubic throne so that the throne of Yahweh is conceived as sustained by them."[95] As rational beings, with faculties of judgment and conviction, true Israel recognizes that her existence depends upon *I AM* and so soberly extols him as the dynamic One. Praise occurs in community, not in isolation. The Holy One is qualified by *of Israel (yiśrāʾēl),* Jacob's new name, when God wrenches Jacob's hip and Jacob responds by clinging to God and praying for blessing, not by quitting. Jacob becomes "One Who Prevails with God and People" by pleading with God, not by his natural strength. "Jacob

94. John Calvin, *A Commentary on the Psalms,* vol. 1, rev. and ed. T. H. L. Parker (London: James Clarke & Co. Ltd., 1965), p. 358.

95. Briggs, *Psalms,* p. 193.

struggled with the angel and overcame him; he wept and begged his favor" (Hos. 12:4).

4 *In you (b^ekā,* emphatic) *our fathers ('^{a}bōtênû)* refers to true, spiritual Israel. Nominal Israel was connected by circumcision, history, memory, and usually blood to their fathers, but true Israel was connected by faith: *they trusted (bāṭ^{e}ḥû).* Israel's true fathers became the church's fathers by her baptism into Jesus Christ (Gal. 3:29; 1 Cor. 10:1). "To trust" means "to rely on someone out of a sense of security" (see Heb. 11:1) This faith is a gift of God, not of human invention (John 1:13; Eph. 1:8-9; Titus 3:5; James 1:17). Repeated, **they trusted** functions as a circumstantial clause (i.e., "because they trusted"). *And [so] you delivered them (watt^{e}pall^{e}ṭēmô)* more precisely means "to bring into a state of security."[96]

5 *Unto you ('eleykā) they cried out (zā'^{a}qû),* an important word for prayer, transforms their internal, invisible faith into an outward, audible form that enters the throne of God. *And they escaped (w^{e}nim^{e}lāṭû): mlṭ,* unlike *plṭ,* refers mainly to escape from imminent death (Gen. 19:17-22) or to get away from it to tell the tale (Job 1:15ff.).[97] The threefold repetition, *in you they trusted (b^ekā bāṭ^{e}ḥû),* emphasizes that the ancestors prevailed by faith, not by human strength. *And they were not put to shame (w^{e}lō' bôšû)* expresses the notion that one has risked his fortune on someone or something, hoping that the power on which he depended would advance his honor, but as it turned out it proved false and so brought the person to ridicule.[98]

2. *Complaint and Confidence vv. 6-10 [7-11]*

a. Complaint vv. 6-8 [7-9]

6 *But I (w^e'ānōkî)* reverses the mood back to complaint. Picking up on "shame" (v. 5), the suppliant contrasts his shame with the fathers' honor. *Am a worm (tôla'at)* contrasts sharply with "you are the Holy One."[99] Cassiodorus

96. Several Biblical texts list and expand the mighty heroes of faith (e.g., 2 Sam. 23:8-39; 1 Chron. 11:20-47; Hebrews 11), but Christ's perseverance to the final goal is so great that he is called "the Pioneer and Perfecter of faith" (Heb. 12:2).

97. G. Fohrer, *TDNT,* 7:979, s.v. *sōzō.*

98. Cf. H. Seebass, *bôsh,* TDOT, 2:52.

99. *Tôla'at* is used for the worm that kills a castor-oil plant (Jonah 4:7), the fruit-grub that attacks the grapes in a vineyard (Deut. 28:39), the worm that infests manna and makes it stink (Exod. 16:20) and that feeds on cadavers in the grave (Isa. 14:11; 66:24). Its parallel is "maggot" (Job 25:6).

rightly interpreted the metaphor as a *tapeinōsis* (see pp. 384-85). The psalmist is regarded as a creature so despicable and threatening to social well-being that he should be destroyed. *Not a man* (*wᵉlōʾ ʾîš*, see Ps. 1:1) means he lacks human dignity. *Scorned by mortals* (*ḥerpat ʾādām*, see n. 60; Ps. 8:5 [6]): His trust in God threatens the basis, the consensus, of a godless society. *And despised* (*ûbᵉzûy*, see Ps. 15:4) *by people* (*ʿām*, see Ps. 3:6 [7]; cf. Ps. 15:4). A spiritual line runs through the hearts of all people, not political or ethnic lines. The city of God and the city of Satan transcend nationalities. The latter seeks to destroy the former; the former seeks to save the latter.

7 The believer's cry to God is matched by the sarcastic blasphemy of the wicked. *All (kol) who see me* (*rōʾay*, see Ps. 8:3 [4]) is relative to the group that regards him as a worm, not his friends (vv. 22-26). *Deride me (yalʿēgû)* expresses a victor's inward joy and disdain (see Ps. 2:4). Their glee expresses itself bodily. *They break open their lips* (*yapṭîrû bᵉśāpâ*, literally, "they make an opening with the lip") is a metonymy for "they deride." *Pṭr* has the essential meaning to split open with the connotation to escape; they cannot hold their vitriol in.[100] *They shake their heads (yānîʿû rōʾš)* expresses disparaging derision (2 Kings 19:21 = Isa. 37:22; Job 16:4; Ps. 109:25; Lam. 2:15).

8 Sarcastically, as Cassiodorus recognized (see p. 385), his deriders admonish: *Commit [yourself] to* I AM (*gōl ʾel yhwh*, literally, "roll unto *I AM*). *Gōl ʾel* is onomatopoetic; one hears the rolling sound of a stone. The metaphor connotes a sense of finality; roll your agony and reproach unto *I AM* and leave it there. Addressing themselves, they indirectly command *I AM: Let him deliver him* (*yᵉpallᵉṭēhû*, see v. 4 [5]), *let him rescue him (yaṣṣîlēhû). Nāṣal* means "to snatch away, to remove, to liberate out of any kind of being held fast."[101] Their taunt, *surely he delights in him* (*kî ḥāpēṣ bô*, see Ps. 1:2) condemns them as murderers, sons of the Devil (John 8:44), for they admit the psalmist is innocent.

b. Confidence vv. 9-10 [10-11]

David now connects the enemies' taunt that he trusts in God and that God delights in him with the truth that he has enjoyed covenant solidarity with *I AM* from birth until the present crisis. Within an inclusio "you," verses 9-10 are cou-

100. Its eight other occurrences refer to open flowers (1 Kings 6:18, 29, 32, 35), breaking open a dam (Prov. 17:14), eluding a hurled javelin (1 Sam. 19:10), and being released/exempted from duty (1 Chron. 9:33; 2 Chron. 33:8). Its nominal derivative *peṭer* denotes the "firstborn" (what first opens and passes through the womb).

101. U. Bergmann, *TLOT*, 2:760, s.v. *nṣl*.

pled together in an ab//b′a′ pattern: "From the womb/belly (*beṭen,* 9A, 10B)" "you made me to trust upon . . ." (active Hiphil, 9B)/"upon you I was cast" (10A, passive Hophal).

9 He meets the mockers' assertive "surely" with his own *surely (kî). You (ʼattâ,* see v. 4) takes his sight off their denigration of him as a worm to God's high calling on his life: you are *the one who brought me out of the womb* (*gōḥî mibbāṭen,* see Pss. 71:17; 139:15-16; Isa. 49:1-2; Jer. 1:5). His confession is particularly apt for Jesus Christ. As a midwife God delivered him from his mother's womb. Moreover, before he knew to choose good and evil, God granted him, as a covenant child, the gift of faith: *the one who caused me to trust* (*mabᵉṭîḥî,* see vv. 5-6). His covenant faith was already present in the milk of his mother; he drank her faith as he nursed *upon [his] mother's breasts (ʻal-šᵉdê ʼimmî).* What a difference it would have made if Jesus' mother was not a Mary!

10 *Upon you* (*ʻāleykā,* emphatic) connects his faith with "upon my mother's breast." The parallel, "you caused me to trust" (Hiphil) shows the incomplete passive *I was cast* (*hošlaktî,* Hophal) as the typical divine passive: God is the agent. The repetition by parallelism, *from the womb (mērāḥem)* and *from the belly of my mother* (*mibbeṭen ʼimmî,* see vv. 9A and B), emphasizes his election at birth to a life of faith. *You are my God* (*ʼēlî,* see v. 1).

C. Lament and Petition vv. 11-21 [12-22]

1. Transition v. 11 [12]

Encouraged by the faith of his fathers and his election, he perseveres in prayer. *Be not far off* (*ʼal-tirḥaq,* see v. 1) *from me (mimmennî)* retains the mood of covenant intimacy. *Surely* (*kî,* see v. 9) *trouble* (*ṣārâ,* see Ps. 4:1 [2][102]) *is near (qᵉrôbâ)* refers to temporal closeness: death is imminent.[103] *Surely there is no helper (ʼên ʻôzēr)* displays that no mortal can save him; only God can.

2. Lament vv. 12-18 [13-19]

His lament has two cycles, each beginning with nightmarish zoomorphic images of murderers surrounding (*sbb,* "to encircle/surround") their helpless vic-

102. *IBHS,* p. 106, P. 6.4.3.
103. J. Kühlewein, *TLOT,* 3:1168.

tim. Kraus thinks on the analogy of Sumerian and Babylonian texts of incantations that the animal images portray demons. But animals are also associated with rulers.[104] These images are followed by his sense of powerlessness under their fierce attacks: first, his inward physiological and psychological disintegration, and, second, his outward social disgrace. In the first his bones are out of joint; in the second they are on display.

a. First Cycle vv. 12-15 [13-16]

He portrays the enemy as bulls surrounding their victim, allowing him no escape, and then as rapacious lions about to devour him. The cycle ends with the psalmist submitting himself to *I AM,* who lays him in the dust of death.

(1) Enemy Lament vv. 12-13 [13-14]

12 The chiastic parallels, A (surround) B (bulls)//B′ (strong bulls) A′ (encircle me) matches his encircled circumstance. The *many* [*rabbîm,* Ps. 3:2] *bulls (pārîm)* are the adult *strong bulls* (*'abbîrê,* lit., "strong"/"powerful"[105]). *Of Bashan (bāšān)* refers to the fertile country bounded by the Jabbok River on the south, the Sea of Galilee on the west, a line from Mount Hermon eastward on the north, and the Hauran range on the east. It was well known for its stately trees (Isa. 2:13; Zech. 11:2) and its well-fed domesticated animals (Deut. 32:14; Ezek. 39:18; Amos 4:1). The parallels *surround (sᵉbābûnî)* and *encircle (kittᵉrûnî)* picture him as shut in on every side with their horns, with no hope of escape.[106]

13 Having captured their victim, they appear as roaring lions. *They open their mouths wide against me (pāṣû ʿālay pîhem)* pictures them as aiming to devour him as quickly as possible (Deut. 11:6; Num. 16:30). As pastoralists, Israelites encountered *lions ('aryēh)*[107] "as a ruthless, almost unstoppable killer, taking from the flock at will."[108] *Tearing (ṭōrēp)* intensifies the victim's pathos. And if a

104. See O. Keel, *Symbolism of the Biblical World: Ancient Near Eastern Iconography and the Book of Psalms,* trans. T. J. Hallett (New York: Seabury Press, 1978), pp. 84-86.

105. The substantival adjective is used of: a chief (1 Sam. 21:8), despots (Isa. 10:13; Job 24:22; 34:20), angels (Ps. 78:25), stallions (Judg. 5:22; Jer. 8:16; 47:3; 50:11), and bulls (Isa. 34:7; Jer. 46:15), seat of government.

106. *Sbb* means "to go in a circle"; *ktr* is used in Judges 20:43 in the military sense of encircling the enemy, as the king in a chess game, so that it cannot escape.

107. An Aramaic loan word equivalent to Heb. *'rî* that indicates the grown (male or female) lion.

108. *Dictionary of Biblical Imagery,* p. 514.

lion's *roaring (wᵉšōʾēg),* which is audible for miles away, spreads its fear abroad, how much more when it is that of many lions in his ears.

(2) **Personal Lament** vv. 14-15 [15-16]

14 The outward terror is matched by his inward physical and psychological state: his bones (v. 14A), heart (v. 14b), and tongue (15). The simile *like water I am poured out (kammayim nišpaktî)* is interpreted by *and all my bones are out of joint (wᵉhitpār ᵉdû kol-ʿaṣmôtay).* The suggestion of many commentators that extreme physical reactions are depicted in verses 14-15 is unlikely. Does distress shake bones out of joint?[109] Death on a cross occurs by asphyxiation; the body's lack of form causes the victim to gasp for air. *HALOT* and BDB interpret *my heart (libbî* see Ps. 4:5, 8) in connection with the simile, *has become like wax (kaddônāg),* clarified by *it has melted within my inward parts* (*nāmēs bᵉtôk mēʿāy,* i.e., internal organs), as a metaphor for loss of courage, as elsewhere in the Old Testament. But more probably the heart is also physical, for its parallels, "bones out of joint," and "tongue sticks to my palate," most naturally describe physical realities. The simile of melting wax, which has a low melting point, is chosen because it is familiar to everyone. As when wax melts and its form disappears, so the beat of his heart fades until felt no longer; the loss of pulse signals death.

15 The image of extreme desiccation holds this tri-colon together. First, *my strength is dried up like a potsherd (yābēš kaḥereś kōḥî). Kōaḥ* refers to his vital powers to produce. *Ḥereś* refers to a piece of earthenware whose existence depends upon a lack of moisture. The simile connotes his strength withers like vegetation without water. Second, *and my tongue (ûlᵉšônî) is caused to stick (mudbāq) to my gums (malqôḥay).* The B verset points to a divine passive (see v. 10). When I (Bruce) was lecturing at Parthian Hatra on a day in July, the heat was so great that I could talk for no more than a minute because my tongue stuck to my gums and palate. Third, the psalmist identifies God as the ultimate agent of his death: *and you put me down (tišpᵉtēnî).*[110] *Into the dust of death (laʿᵃpar māwet,* cf. Job 7:21; 20:11; 21:26; Ps. 22:29 [30]; Dan. 12:2) is an apt metaphor for his desiccation and his ignominy (Gen. 3:14; 1 Sam. 2:8; 1 Kings 16:2; Isa. 47:1; Ps. 7:5 [6]; 44:25 [26]; 119:25).

109. A. Weiser, *The Psalms: A Commentary,* trans. Herbert Hartwell (Philadelphia: Westminster Press, 1962), p. 223.

110. *špt* in two of its three other occurrences refers to putting a cooking pot on a fire (2 Kings 4:38; Ezek. 24:3).

b. Second Cycle vv. 16-18 [17-19]

Though chronologically the second cycle begins before the end of the first, conceptually the images appropriately develop from encircling bulls to devouring lions to scavenging dogs (cf. 1 Kings 21:19). Likewise, the psalmist's fate develops from death to gambling for the garments he leaves behind after death.

(1) Enemy Lament v. 16 [17]

16 *Surely dogs surround me (kî sᵉbābûnî kᵉlābîm);* these are probably contemptible, unclean scavenging dogs (Exod. 11:7; Ps. 59:6, 14 [7, 15]), not hunting dogs.[111] People regard them as particularly disgusting because they devour what is left over after humans are finished eating (Matt. 7:6; 15:26-27; Mark 7:27-28), and, since what they manage to scavenge is inadequate, they eat what is repulsive (Exod. 22:31; Prov. 26:11; 2 Peter 2:22), even human corpses (1 Kings 14:11; 16:4; 21:23, 25; 2 Kings 9:10, 36; Ps. 59:14-15 [15-16]). He expands the dog imagery: *a band* (*ʿᵃdat,* see Ps. 1:5) *of evildoers (mᵉrēʿîm) encircle me* (*hiqqipûnî,* "complete the circle"). In the psalms *mᵉrēʿîm* is a fixed expression for those who cause injury and harm and who stand in contrast to those who wait on God (Ps. 37:9). The scavengers *bore holes in my hands and my feet* (see n. 66) retains the dog imagery.

(2) Personal Lament vv. 17-18 [18-19]

17 The scavengers have little to feed upon: *I can count* (*ʾᵃsappēr,* see Ps. 19:1 [2]) *all my bones* (*kol- ʿaṣmôtay* see v. 14 [15]). *They* (*hēmmâ,* masc. pl.) refers to the congregation of evildoers (masc. pl.), not bones (fem. pl.), who *look at me* in my emaciated condition with pleasure *(yabbîṭû) and gloat over me* (*yirʾû bî,* see Obadiah 12; Ps. 37:34; 54:7 [9]; 112:8).

18 Like scavenging grave robbers the wicked band gamble for his left-behind garments. As victors *they distribute (yᵉhallᵉqû),* better than "divide," *my garments (bᵉgāday),* made of cloth but otherwise unspecified.[112] *Among themselves (lāhem)* entails for their benefit (see n. 67). They are as heartless as Joseph's

111. R. J. Clifford (*Psalm 1–72* [AOTC; Nashville: Abingdon Press, 2002], p. 126) thinks they are hunting dogs because ancient seals portray dogs attacking humans (see Keel, *Symbolism,* p. 87). The evidence of the Old Testament, however, is more compelling.

112. Cf. rich robes, Genesis 37:3; widow's robes, Genesis 38:14; cultic robes, Exodus 28:2; or rags, Isaiah 64:6 [5]. They may be dyed (Isa. 63:1), braided (Ezek. 26:16), torn (Gen. 37:29), washed (Lev. 11:25), eaten by moths (Job 13:28), or burned (Lev. 13:52).

brothers, who coldly ate their lunch while he cried out for salvation from the pit (Gen. 37:24f.; 42:21). *And for my clothing (w^{e}'al l^{e}bûšî)* is the most common Hebrew word for apparel, and since it was often a collective singular, no certain distinction can be made between the plural "my garments" and the singular "my clothing." *They cast (yappîlû,* literally, "they throw") *lots (gôrāl),* a small stone of some sort[113] and often used in connection with "plunder."[114]

3. Petition vv. 19-21 [20-22]

His petition has two parts: "not to delay" (v. 19) and "to save him" (vv. 20-21).

a. Not to Delay v. 19 [20]

But you (*w^{e}'attâ,* see v. 4) plus the imperative mood in connection with the key word, *do not be far off* (*'al-tirḥāq,* see v. 11 [12]), shifts the motifs from lament to petition. He uses God's personal name, I AM *(yhwh),* for the first time. As the second vignette of the lament returned to a time shortly before death, so his petition occurs shortly before his imagined death. His petition confirms that he has persevered in faith. The epithet, *My Strength* or *My Helper* (*'^{e}yālûtî,* see n. 68), counteracts the reality that he has no human helper (v. 11). *Hasten (ḥûšâ)* assumes *I AM* is tarrying in an emergency situation (cf. Isa. 60:22). *To help me ('ezrātî),* like the English term "to help," assumes a subject who has sufficient strength to come to the aid of/to support an object with insufficient strength.

b. To Save from Death vv. 20-21 [21-22]

20 Such is the case here, for after lamenting that he cannot escape death, he prays, *deliver (haṣṣîlâ) . . . me (nepeš,* see Ps. 3:3 [4]; 19:7 [8]). *Nāṣal* essentially means "to snatch away, to remove, to liberate out of any kind of being held fast."[115] *From the sword (mēḥereb)* refers to the most important weapon of warfare in the ancient Near East, consisting of a hilt and blade, ranging from sixteen inches to three feet in length. One or both edges of the blade were sharpened or whetted so as to slay effectively and so kept in a sheath (1 Sam. 17:51; 2 Sam. 20:8). The animal images of the enemy are replaced by the literal reality

113. W. Dommershausen, *TDOT,* 2:450, s.v. *gôrāl.*

114. H.-J. Kraus (*Psalms 1–59: A Commentary* [Minneapolis: Augsburg Press, 1988], 1:298) quotes a Mesopotamian song: "The coffin lay open, and people already helped themselves to my valuables; before I was even dead, the mourning was already done."

115. U. Bergmann, *TLOT,* 2:760, s.v. *nṣl.*

of their swords; otherwise the instrument of their killing is unstated. In the parallel, "deliver" is gapped and "from the sword" is morphed into the image of *from the power of the dogs* (*miyad-keleb,* see v. 17, n. 69). "Power" glosses the metonymy "hand," which stands for "power and strength," and/or "authority, control, or possession."[116] *My precious life* glosses *yᵉḥîdātî* (literally, "my only one"), an adjective that brings out prominently what is unique and beloved. "Life" is certified by the parallel, *naphšî,* glossed by "me."

21 Verse 21 is essentially an emphatic parallel to verse 20. *Save me* (*hôšîʿēnî,* see Ps. 3:7 [8]) matches "deliver my life," and *from the mouth of the lion* (*mippî ʾaryêh,* see v. 14) to "*and from the horns (miqqarnê rēmîm)* of the wild oxen" matches "from the power of the dogs." The bony pointed horns or antlers on the animal's head give the animal a regal look and provide it with an impressive goring weapon. The size and condition of an animal's horns are indicative of its power, status, and health. For these reasons the horns are qualified by *of the wild oxen (Bos primigenius boianus)* or auroch, ancestor of domestic animals. The auroch, now hunted to extinction, captured the imagination of ancient Mediterranean cultures as seen already in Paleolithic cave art. "In Scripture the ox represents the pinnacle of created strength and ability in the then-known world, and the wild ox was the largest and most powerful of them. It became . . . a symbol of brute strength."[117] The gored psalmist's cry *answer me* (*ʿᵃnîtānî,* see n. 70 and v. 2) shows that even in death he perseveres in faith (Prov. 14:32).

D. Praise vv. 22-31 [23-32]

As suddenly as resurrection, in this scene the psalmist is in the house of God surrounded by saints, not on the horns of wild oxen surrounded by wild animals. How to understand this radical change within some psalms, like Psalms 6 and 22, has been much discussed but with no definitive answer, for the psalms themselves give no direct indication. Of these psalms Moberly writes: "Although pain and puzzlement must be expressed in worship, they are not incompatible with praise; but praise rather makes explicit the context of faith and hope within which the lament is sounded."[118] David praises God out of faith that God will save him from his imagined death. The key word *zeraʿ* ("seed")

116. *Dictionary of Biblical Imagery,* p. 361.
117. *Dictionary of Biblical Imagery,* p. 620.
118. Moberly, *NIDOTTE,* 4:880.

holds the two strophes together: the "seed" of Jacob and the "seed" of the nations become one in their praise.

Praise for the saving act is expanded in ever wider horizons through space and time: his personal praise to his brothers (v. 22), to a call for the seed of Jacob to join him (v. 23), to the vision of all the nations worshiping *I AM* forever (vv. 27-31). In death the psalmist bridged the gulf between himself and God by faith; God bridged the gulf by his saving act.

1. *Let the Covenant Community Praise I AM vv. 22-26 [23-27]*

Typically, as here, praise has two parts: the individual's word of praise (vv. 22-24) and an accompanying sacramental animal for the community (vv. 25-26). Each of these units consists of a resolve to praise/sacrifice and of the cause. Only a king could provide a feast as great as this one.

a. Word of Praise vv. 22-24

His word of praise begins with telling *I AM* of his resolve to celebrate his name by faith (v. 22), and not to explain it in any other way. His own resolve to praise his deliverance supports his imperative to his "brothers" to join him in praise (v. 23).

22 *I will recount* or declare (*'ᵃsappᵉrâ*, Ps. 19:1 [2], see n. 71) shifts the motif to praise. *Your name (šimkâ), I AM,* is the name God revealed to Moses (Exod. 3:13-22) in response to his request to know the name the Israelites should invoke for their deliverance. Moses' intention becomes clear in God's answer: "This is my name forever, the name by which I am to be remembered/invoked *(zikrî)* from generation to generation" (v. 15).[119] Proverbs 10:7 is instructive: "The righteous are invoked/remembered" *(zeker),* denoting the active cognitive occupation with a person or situation by retaining and reviving impressions of them and *proclaiming them* to others.[120] One cannot invoke without remembering, and one cannot remember well without invoking/proclaiming. Moreover, the name stands as a surrogate for the character and behavior of a person. *I AM* or *HE IS* transcends time and the vicissitudes of humanity's checkered

119. The root *zkr* means "to remember" and/or "to mention." In the derived stems, especially the *Hiphil,* it means "to mention, name." The noun *zeker* means "memory" and/or "mention" and/or "name." Here and in Isaiah 26:8; Psalm 135:13; Job 18:17; Proverbs 10:7; *passim* it is used interchangeably with *šēm,* the Hebrew word for "name."

120. H. Eising, *Theological Dictionary of the Old Testament* vol. 4, ed. G. Johannes Botterweck, trans. D. E. Green (Grand Rapids: Eerdmans, 1974), p. 66, s.v. *zākar.*

history. As James Russell Lowell put it in his famous stanza: "Careless seems the great Avenger, history's pages but record / One death grapple in the darkness 'twixt old systems and the Word; / Truth forever on the scaffold, Wrong forever on the throne, — Yet that scaffold sways the future, and, behind the dim unknown, / Standeth God within the shadow, keeping watch above his own." *To my brothers (l^{e}'eḥāy)* refers to true Israel who are related by God's covenants to them: through Abraham (Genesis 15, 17), Moses (Exodus 19–24), David (2 Samuel 7), and the New Covenant (Jer. 31:31-34). *I will praise you ('^{a}halleka,* see n. 71), the chiastic parallel to "I will recount your name," refers to public acclamation bestowing social honor on *I AM.* The counterpart to "my brothers" is *in the midst (b^{e}tôk) of the assembly (qāhāl). Qāhāl* refers to a number of persons gathered together for a particular purpose. Here it refers to the faithful gathered together at the house of God (see Ps. 15:1).

23 Addressing the congregation of true Israel, the king labels them as *those who fear **I AM** (yir'ê yhwh,* see Ps. 19:9 [10]). Matching his resolve to praise (v. 22), he commands them: *praise him (hal^{e}lûhû). All the seed of Jacob (kol-zera' ya'^{a}qōb)* qualifies the "fearers of *I AM*" as heirs of Israel's covenants. "Seed" preeminently images the potential for life and generation. "From Genesis 1 on, seeds are generically determined, pronounced and absolute in their individual identities."[121] That identity is their covenant relationship with *I AM.* Parallel to "praise him" is the metonymy of its effect, *honor him (kabb^{e}dûhû,* see Ps. 15:4). *And revere him (w^{e}gûrû,* see n. 72), the parallel to "those who fear *I AM* praise him" (verset Aa), highlights the aspect of the fear, awe, and reverence of him who holds their life and death in his hands (see Ps. 2:11). *All the seed of Israel (kol-zera' yiśrāēl)* escalates the dignity of "all the seed of Jacob."

24 *For (kî,* see vv. 9, 16) introduces the three negative (24A) and one positive (24B) causes for praise. *He did not despise (lō' bāzâ,* see Ps. 15:4) is intensified to *and he did not abhor (w^{e}lō' šiqqaṣ). šqṣ* is a technical term for that which violates the practices of *I AM*'s worship. The verb means to "contaminate" (e.g., Lev. 11:43) or, as here, "to abominate." *Affliction ('^{e}nût)* is a hapax legomenon whose root is probably II. *'ānâ.*[122] This is also the root of *the afflicted one ('ānî),* which in a general sense means "poor, wretched, in a needy condition," and so his spiritual attitude cries out to *I AM,* especially in Psalms (e.g., Ps. 34:6 [7]; 102:1 [2]).[123]

121. *Dictionary of Biblical Imagery,* p. 771.

122. In Qal, "to be destitute, wretched," in Piel "to oppress, to do violence to," in Hiphil "to humiliate."

123. *HALOT,* 2:856.

"The *ʿānî* belongs to the people of Israel, Yahweh's people, and thus to Yahweh himself (Exod. 22:24 . . .)."[124] The third negative, *I AM did not hide his face from him* (*wᵉloʾ-histîr pānāyw mimmenû;* for *str* "to hide," see Ps. 19:6, and for *pnh* "face," see 4:6; 19:14 [15]) is a litotes signifying that in his passions he found favor, not abhorrence, with *I AM,* and figuratively proves "God conceals his countenance from a person as an expression of wrath," and that entails "concrete acts of divine punishment."[125] The positive assertion, *but when he cried out, he listened to his cry for help* (*ûbᵉšawwᵉʿô ʾēlāyw šāmeaʿ,* for *šmʿ* see 4:1, 3 [2, 4]), validates the interpretation.[126]

b. Sacrifice of Praise vv. 25-26 [26-27]

25 *From you* (*mēʾittᵉkā,* see n. 76) *my praising you* (see n. 77) elides the full thought: "from you comes [my salvation and so from you comes] my [act] of praising you." *In the great assembly* (*bᵉqāhāl rāb,* see v. 22) escalates the "assembly" to a large number. Elsewhere TNIV renders *qāhāl rāb* by "great horde" (Ezek. 17:17; 38:4). His act of praising is clarified by the parallel, *I will pay my vows* (*nᵉdāray ʾᵃšallēm,* Lev. 7:11-34). The *neder* designates the payment of a promissory vow to *I AM* in order to gain his help in a difficult or troubling situation,[127] one of the functions of a "peace/fellowship offering" (*šᵉlāmîm,* cf. Lev. 7:11-34) that facilitates communion.[128] His vows included offering a number of sacrifices to feed the great number of people assembled for the meal. The parallel *before those who fear him* (*neged yᵉrēʾāyw,* see v. 24) shows the worshipers participating in the new covenant.

124. R. Martin-Achard, *TLOT,* 2:933, s.v. *ʿnh* II.

125. G. Wehmeier, *TLOT,* 2:817, s.v. *str.*

126. Note the alliteration of *šwʿ* and *šmʿ.*

127. The fact that God dwelt among the people in the Tabernacle/Temple and wanted to have a relationship with them was basic to the Sinai prescriptions. Although the peace offering fat was offered to *I AM* (Lev. 3:16b-17; 7:22-27), its distinctive feature was that all the people had opportunity of this close communion (Lev. 3:1-2; 7:1-21). Since it signified that all is well, it always came last in any series of offerings (see 9:8, 12, 15-17). The priest splashed its blood against the altar on all sides, and it had atoning efficacy. Leviticus 17:11 gives the rationale of blood atonement specifically in the context of peace offerings: "For the life of a creature is in the blood, and I have given it to you to make atonement for yourselves on the altar; it is the blood that makes atonement for one's life" (cf. 14; Gen. 9:4-5).

128. R. E. Averbeck (*NIDOTTE,* 4:135, s.v. *shelem*) says, "The primary focus of this particular offering seems to be the communal celebration supplied by the meat of the offering. It was fellowship or communion offering that indicated and enacted the fact that there was peace between God and his people and that the person, family, or community was, therefore, in a state of well-being."

26 Let the humble eat *(yōʾkᵉlû ʿᵃnāwîm)* fits this interpretation of paying vows. Ambiguous *yōʾkᵉlû* is construed as a cohortative ("let them"), not as a specific future ("they will," TNIV), because the parallel in verse 24 is in the imperative mood and the parallel *yᵉḥî* ("let live") is volitional. The *ʿᵃnāwîm,* the original plural of *ʿānî* (see v. 24), are bowed, both in a circumstance of diminished capacity, power, and worth and in humility before God. *And let them be sated (wᵉyiśbāʿû)* — that is, let them eat to the full and consummate measure — with the sacrament that by its meat fills and nourishes their body and by accompanying words fills and nourishes their spirit. *Those who seek him (dōrᵉšāyw),* the parallel to "bowed under affliction," completes their identity with the psalmist. *Dōrᵉšāyw* denotes persons who carefully[129] and energetically[130] strive to fulfill a passion; they strive to please *I AM* and fervently pray for his favor and to save them from their oppression. *Let . . . praise* I AM (*yᵉhalᵉlû yhwh,* see vv. 22, 23) by eating the sacrament to the full. The praise ends with a focus on the sacrament's spiritual aspect: *Let your hearts* (*lᵉbabᵉkem,* see Ps. 4:4, 7 [5, 8]) *live (yᵉḥî).* The heart "lives," bubbles over with life, when the interplay of intellect, sensibility, and volition finds its source of life in the living God, as expressed by eating the sacrament (see Ps. 69:32 [33]). Such people enjoy every sort of prosperity and self-esteem *forever* (*lāʿad,* see 19:9 [10]). The sacrament replaces the tree of life in the Garden of Eden.

2. *All Nations Praise I AM Forever vv. 27-31 [28-32]*

a. First Unit vv. 27-28 [28-29]

(1) **Promise of Spatial Universal Praise v. 27 [28]**

All the ends of the earth (kol-ʾapsê ʾāreṣ) in David's flat, restricted world extended from lands east of the Euphrates to lands on the Mediterranean Sea in the west, and from the Peloponnesian Islands in the north to Ethiopia in the south. In our worldview it encompasses the seven continents. *All the clans of the nations (kol-mišpᵉḥôt gôyīm)* also assumes a different social structure than ours. In David's world the king was over the nation, the patriarch over the clan, and the father over the tribe. *They will remember (yizkᵉrû)* means that by faith they will bring to mind, accept, and participate in God's saving act of delivering his anointed king from death. *And they will turn* (*yāšūbû,* see 19:7 [8]) *to* I AM, a notion that involves conversion, which is unique in the Old Testament with regard to the nations. Its parallel (Ba) implies their conversion: *and they will wor*

129. Coppes, *TWOT,* 1:198, s.v. *dāraš.*
130. S. Wagner, *TDOT,* 3:294f, s.v. *dāraš.*

ship before you (*w^{e}yištaḥ^{a}wû*), not their old gods. *šḥy* or *ḥwy* means "to bow oneself/to prostrate oneself."

(2) **Cause for Praise v. 28 [29]**

28 *Because* (*kî*, see v. 24) *dominion* or kingship *(hamm^{e}lûkâ) belongs to* I AM *(layhwh)*. The parallel, *as ruler over the nations* (*ûmōšēl baggôyīm*, see v. 27 and Ps. 8:6 [7]), interprets his kingship as over all the nations. The vision of the universal conversion is based on the reality that *I AM* rules all space and time. Israel's eschatological hope of *I AM*'s universal rule is a major theme of the book of Psalms.[131] What is unique to this psalm is the claim that God's saving act of the psalmist is the immediate cause of their conversion.

b. Second Unit: Promise of Future Universal Praise vv. 29-31 [30-32]

(1) **Promise of Universal Social Praise v. 29 [30]**

Surely to him . . . will bow down (*ʾāklô*, see n. 80,[132] *yištaḥ^{e}wû*, see v. 27) asserts the certainty of this vision's fulfillment. The scope of the universal praise includes, on the one hand, *all the rich of the earth* (*kol-dišnê ʾereṣ*, literally, ". . . the fat ones . . . ," see n. 81). Since fat was regarded as particularly nourishing food, "fat ones" is a metonymy for people who are healthy and who enjoy life optimally. On the other hand, it also encompasses *all who descend to the dust* (*kol-yôr^{e}dê ʿāpār*, see v. 15 [16]); viz.: those confronting imminent death, as the weak regularly are. The parallels constitute a merism (see v. 1B). *Before him* (*l^{e}pānyw*, see v. 28) is emphatic, like its parallel "to him," and *they will kneel (yikr^{e}ʿû)* articulates what is meant by its parallel, *yištaḥ^{a}wû* ("worship"). *And none* is added to individualize the "all." *Preserved* (*ḥîyâ*, literally, "made live," see v. 26) *his life* (*w^{e}napšô*, see v. 20) certifies that they died. Though facing certain death, the elect worship *I AM*, for they look for a salvation that lies beyond clinical death (Prov. 14:32).

(2) **Promise of Endless Future Praise v. 30 [31]**

As a result of their recounting of previous generations' telling of God's saving act, *their seed* (*zeraʿ*, v. 23) *will serve him* (*yaʿab^{e}dennû*, see Ps. 19:13 [14]).

131. M. Futato (*Interpreting the Psalms: An Exegetical Handbook*, Handbook for Old Testament Exegesis [Grand Rapids: Kregel, 2007], pp. 69-73) argues that the kingship of God is *the* dominant theme of the book.

132. If MT, "they will eat," is correct, the thought is that nations will join the Eucharistic feast.

"Their" was added to clarify the sense. Concerning "serve" *(ʿbd),* Westermann says: "The question is never whether a person (or a group) serves a god; the only question is which god one serves. Since 'serving God' indicates one's relationship as a whole to God, it cannot mean 'to do God a service.' Instead it signifies acknowledgement of God as Lord, an acknowledgment that requires one's entire existence."[133] *It will be related* (*yᵉsuppar,* see v. 22) *about the Lord* or master *(la'dōnāy)* parallels "they will serve him." *To their generations (laddôr)* explains why their seed will serve *I AM. Dôr* denotes "cycles of time," "life spans." As a parallel to "seed" it denotes the generations descended from the first generation of the nations.

(3) Cause for Praise v. 31 [32]

The plural *they will come (yābōʾû)* validates that the "seed" and "generation" are collective singulars. The subject is the coming generations who come to other nations, even to the ends of the earth, with their gospel story. *And they will declare* (*wᵉyaggîdû,* see Ps. 19:1 [2]) the important message of *his righteousness* (*ṣidqātô,* see Ps. 4:1 [2]) — that is to say, *I AM* did what is right by saving his innocent covenant partner from death. The message will be declared *to people* (*lᵉʿam,* Ps. 3:6, 8 [7, 9]) *yet to be born (nôlād).* Since the praise of the Gentiles will extend to all the earth, the testimony of the worshiping generation extends beyond their own seed to include other nations. What they tell is: *Surely* (*kî,* see v. 9) *he acted* (*ʿāśâ,* see 1:3; 15:3, 5). This emphatic absolute use of *ʿśh* means "to act, intervene, accomplish"[134] (Ps. 37:5; 39:9 [10]; 52:9 [11]; 109:27; 111:8; 115:8; 119:126; 135:6; 147:20).

Part IV. Canonical Context

In the light of the canon, Franz Delitzsch classified Psalm 22 as typico-prophetic (see p. 112). As a type, innocent David's suffering at the hands of the likes of Saul and God's deliverance of him is a divinely intended type of the antitype: the passion and glorification of Christ. David's rare failure to call for redress against his enemies matches the prayer of Christ. Tostengard's claim that the New Testament interpretation "wrenches it out of its setting" ignores Biblical typology.[135] As a prophecy, David uses the language of his culture (e.g., his offering of an animal sacrifice in the liturgy), but he expresses his passions and glorification in

133. C. Westermann, *TLOT,* 2:829, s.v. *ʿebed.*

134. J. Vollmer, *TLOT,* 2:947, s.v. *ʿśh.*

135. S. Tostengard, "Psalm 22," *Int* 46 (1992): 167-70.

terms that find unique fulfillment in Christ's death and resurrection. The Lord Jesus took this psalm upon his lips as his first words on the cross (Matt. 27:46 and parallels), and the gospel writers, especially Matthew and John, frequently allude to the psalm in their accounts of Christ's passion (see above, p. 377). Hebrews places verse 22 on the lips of the resurrected Christ (Heb. 2:12). David prayed to be delivered from the experience of death; Christ prayed to be delivered from real death. The vision of universal salvation is fulfilled uniquely in the church. Significantly, this psalm is *not* handed over in a postscript to the chief musician for all God's people to sing; it is no ordinary lament.

CHAPTER 13

Psalm 23: The Good Shepherd

Part I: Voice of the Church

When a senior Scot thinks of Psalm 23, he or she is transported to the singing of it by the Orpheus choir, to the tune "Crimond," under the direction of Sir Hugh Robertson. Its Gaelic *pathos,* in haunting lyricism, "stirs the blood." But if we are to be historically faithful to the role played by the Psalter in the life of the church, we find that Reformed hymnody of the Psalms has been vulnerable to its misuse also; popular expressions are more vulnerable to misuse than scholarly commentaries, and no psalm has been more popularized than Psalm 23. Since the psalm is not quoted by the New Testament writers, the early worshipers probably did not give it as much Christological attention as other psalms, other than as a Eucharistic hymn.

I. Early Fathers' Use

R. E. Prothero (1851-1937), late fellow of All Souls College, Oxford, assures us that Augustine chose Psalm 23 as "the hymn of the martyrs," but Augustine's own brief notes tell us nothing.[1] **Athanasius** (c. 296-c. 373) provides the earliest reference: "Should you become aware that you are being shepherded and led in the right path by the Lord, sing Psalm 22 [i.e., 23] rejoicing in this."[2] He sug-

1. Rowland E. Prothero, *The Psalms in Human Life* (New York: E. P. Dutton & Company, 1905), p. 12.

2. *Athanasius — The Life of Antony and the Letter to Marcellinus,* trans. Robert C. Gregg (Ramsey, NY: Paulist Press, 1980), p. 116.

gests: "He leads me beside still waters" is "perhaps to be understood as holy baptism"; "you anoint my head with oil" means "the mystic chrism [the consecrated oil used in baptism, confirmation, ordination]"; and "you prepare a table before me" means "the mystic table."[3] **Cyril of Alexandria** (c. 370-444) suggests: "The table is set for the faithful . . . so that by eating and being strengthened we will be able to face our persecutors at any time. For spiritual food, by encouraging the soul, enables it to resist impure spirits and teachers of errors. But the mystic table, the flesh of our Lord, also makes us strong against passions and demons. For Satan fears those who become pious participants in the mysteries."[4] Possibly then, an early use of the psalm was its being sung at the communion service.

Later, **Theodore of Cyrrhus** (c. 393–c. 457) reads the psalm as a prophetic pronouncement of Israel's renewal, even though it is sung eucharistically in the church service. We have nothing from Hilary of Poitiers, nor from John Chrysostom, very little from Theodore of Mopsuestia, and only a slight response from **Jerome**, who indicates that his text in the Vulgate reads, "The Lord is my Ruler," while his *Hebraica* translates it as "the Lord is my Shepherd," but in his commentary he opts for the former liturgical version. **Cassiodorus** repeats the Latin form and summarizes it very briefly because it has "no new information," although he says: "Through the whole psalm it is the most faithful Christian, reborn of water and of the Holy Spirit, who speaks: he has laid aside the old age of the first man [i.e., Adam] . . . led through the desert of sin to the region of re-birth and the water of re-birth."[5] The theme then is the blessed state of being converted, baptized, and now "ruled" by God. This may indicate that it had acquired significance as a baptismal hymn by the fourth century, if not before, as Cyril of Alexandria first suggested. As far as we can trace, **Rupert of Deutz** was the first medieval scholar to distinguish the unique authority of the Biblically inspired writers from that of the subsequent fathers of the church.[6]

3. Athanasius, PG 27:col. 140, cited by William L. Holladay, *The Psalms through Three Thousand Years: Prayerbook of a Cloud of Witnesses* (Minneapolis: Fortress Press, 1996), p. 13.

4. Cyril of Alexandria, PG 69:841-42, cited by William L. Holladay, *The Psalms through Three Thousand Years*, p. 13.

5. *Cassiodorus: Explanation of the Psalms*, in P. G. Walsh, ed. and trans., *Ancient Christian Writers* (New York and Mahwah, NJ: Paulist Press, 1990), vol. 1, p. 235.

6. Ceslas Spicq, *Esquisse d'une Histoire de l'Exégèse Latine au Moyen Âge* (Paris: Vrin, 1944), p. 74.

II. Transition from Monastic to Scholastic Commentary

A. Geroch of Reichersberg

Geroch of Reichersberg (1093-1169), a Benedictine abbot, is a fine example of a theological exegete, whose monastic scholarship was original; his commentary on Psalm 23 is one of the best commentaries of the twelfth century.[7] "The Lord rules me . . . he has converted my soul" is his summary of the psalm.[8] He knows that Jerome has alternate Hebrew renderings, and he integrates them by observing: "Since the Lord rules me, he shepherds by ruling, or he rules by shepherding; he himself is my Lord, he himself is my shepherd and my king. He is Lord, since he gave me being by creating me; he is shepherd and ruler, since by shepherding and ruling he gives me being in a blessed way."[9] He interprets "the pastures" to be the Scriptures, where he was established as a catechumen. His "leading" is his *educante* through the waters of baptism. Here he follows the earlier interpretation of Psalm 23 as a baptismal hymn. "Converting my soul" implies the presence of the Holy Spirit in one's life. This mélange of dissimilar things is an echo of Cassiodorus, who explains the rhetorical use of *sunathroismos* ("when many things are gathered into one") to signify that one wants nothing when one is given everything.[10]

In this context he contrasts "the sheep going astray" with true Christian living by grace. For Geroch the psalm essentially describes the effects of the graces of God upon the life of the Christian, so that at the end of life there will be no fear of death. He allegorizes "thy rod" as light discipline for the child of God, and the "staff" as heavy discipline necessary to knock down the pride of the sinner. He enumerates each assurance of the psalm as "a grace [i.e., blessing]." The seventh blessing is "the communion of the blood and body of our Lord." An eighth blessing is "the oil and gladness anointing one in the resurrected life."[11]

It is actually in the Prelude to this remarkably long commentary (23 pages) that Geroch discusses "David the Shepherd." As "the Shepherd King," "this excellent shepherd feeds the intelligent sheep in one hundred-fifty psalms,

7. Robert L. Benson and Giles Constable with Carol D. Lanham, ed., *Renaissance and Renewal in the Twelfth Century* (Toronto, Buffalo, London: University of Toronto Press, 1991), pp. 409-11.

8. Geroch of Reichersberg, *Commentarius aureus in psalmos et cantica ferialia* (PL 193-194, 193:1040-1062).

9. Geroch of Reichersberg, *Commentarius aureus*, 1042B.

10. *Cassiodorus: Explanation of the Psalms*, vol. 1, pp. 235-36.

11. Geroch of Reichersberg, *Commentarius aureus*, 1061A.

and he will feed them to the end of the age." He does this on "the fruitful pastures . . . of the name of the glorious Trinity."[12] But as the shepherd, David is honored "as the most eminent of the prophets, the foremost of them all . . . not in the act of foretelling of future things . . . but because he has spoken sublimely about the kingdom of God, about the kingdom of Christ and the Church." "This foremost of the prophets, this eminent shepherd, has splendidly declared, he whom history narrates to have fed the sheep of his father, and he himself sings with words of this kind: 'And he chose his servant David, and took him from the flocks of sheep: he brought him from following the ewes great and young'" (Ps. 78:70-71).[13]

Geroch attributes the spiritual power of David to his being a singing minstrel, who "willed to be a child-string-player or cytharoedum . . . progressing little by little in order that he would become a Psalmist; so that with a sweet mixture of music by singing he would prophesy, and by prophesying he would sing the business of the salvation of souls. So that . . . by running the words with poetic steps and by strumming the ringing strings of the Psalter, they might come through the ears into the soul, and sweetly implant the faith, hope and charity of God."[14] Geroch also finds spiritual significance in the musical instrument itself: its triangular shape represents of the Holy Trinity; its ten strings reflect the Decalogue, and the diverse fingers used to play it reflect the diverse gifts given us by the Holy Spirit. Thus David as Ruler is conceived of as the "extraordinary instrumentalist, for whom the Psalms were made pleasant with the harp. When he reigned with favor, wishing to magnify the worship of God, he chose four thousand men who would sing the psalms not only with the voice but with musical instruments, over whom he placed Asaph, Idithun [Vulgate; EVV Jeduthun], Heman, Ethan, or the sons of Korah" (1 Chron. 15:19: 23:5; 25:1).

Geroch defines the terms used in the Psalter: "a 'psalm' *(psalmus)* is the sound of an instrument; a 'song' *(psalmus canticum)* is the chant of the human voice in praise of God; a 'psalm-song' *(psalmi canticum)* is the voice accompanied with the instrument; and a 'song-psalm' *(cantici psalmus)* is the instrument with the occasional use of the voice." Differing psalms reflect the various genres, such as lament, wedding song, certain other dramas, and these in turn are used by the Holy Spirit to reshape and transform our souls, just as "the Spirit of the Lord came upon David" (1 Kings [LXX = 1 Sam.] 16:13 [sic!]).[15]

12. Geroch of Reichersberg, *Commentarius aureus, Preface,* 623C, 624A.
13. Geroch of Reichersberg, *Commentarius aureus, Preface,* 624C.
14. Geroch of Reichersberg, *Commentarius aureus, Preface* 629A.
15. Geroch of Reichersberg, *Commentarius aureus,* 638A.

B. Nicholas of Lyra

Nicholas of Lyra (1270-1349), the Franciscan from Paris, unites several interpretive traditions including the Victorine school and Stephen Langton, among other scholars. He uses Jewish resources, quoting Jewish authorities, especially Rashi, and has some knowledge of Hebrew. He consistently keeps to the literal level, with extended notes, giving his Biblical commentary the title, *Postilla super psalterium . . .*[16] *et cantica canticorum,* as part of a major Old Testament commentary. It has the distinction of being the first printed Biblical commentary (Lyons, 1488). On the printed page, the commentary in large print is on the center of the page, with the glosses around it in smaller text. He accepts Jerome's text, "the Lord rules me," and repeats that "some say that David composed this psalm foreseeing in the Spirit the return from the Babylonian captivity." Because "'the Lord rules me,' . . . 'he has brought me to a place of pasture,' that is into the land of Israel." But he notes Rashi's alternative historical context based on 1 Samuel 22 (David's fleeing from Saul, flight to Moab, and subsequent return to Judah in response to the prophet Gad's directive).[17] Rashi thus interpreted "the Lord rules me," because David returned to Judah in obedience to the word of the prophet, to be wonderfully replenished. Following Rashi, Nicholas makes no reference then to the Eucharistic meal, instead interpreting it in reference to 1 Samuel 22. His desire is to "dwell in the house of the Lord," that is, "in a land where the worship of God thrives." Nicholas then concludes: "This psalm can be explained morally, concerning a devout man fleeing from the world, as if from a place of peril, and finding refuge in a place of religion [i.e., a monastic order], especially of a mendicant [like Nicholas, a Franciscan] trusting in divine provision and defense from adversaries, not only of the body but also of the mind."[18] It is not surprising that later commentators were critical of a "Christian Hebraist," as having given away too much of the spiritual depth of Scripture for the sake of textual scholarship.[19]

16. Nicholas of Lyra, *Postilla in psalterium et cantica canticorum* (Lyons, 1488).

17. 1 Samuel 22:1-5.

18. Nicholas of Lyra, *Postilla* Cs.

19. For an assessment of Nicholas of Lyra's linguistic abilities see Gilbert Dahan, *Les Intellectuals Chrétiens et les Juifs au Moyen Âge* (Paris: Les Editions du Cerf, 2007), pp. 268-70, 303-6, 452-54, 466-68, 556-57.

III. Fifteenth-Century Reforming Commentators

A. Denys the Carthusian

An associate of Nicholas of Cusa, **Denys the Carthusian** (1408-71) is more Augustinian and so maintains a strong Christological focus on the psalms. He ignores the historical David, and maintains the traditional rendering of Psalm 23, "The Lord is my Ruler,"[20] while "the pastures" are identified with "the house of the Church militant, in which there are the most healthy sacraments, the divine Scriptures, and diverse virtues." While beginning with the Gallican version, he then draws upon all three Latin versions (see p. 313).[21] His encompassing view of the psalm is one of gratitude for being given sound doctrine as a churchman to convert his soul, for receiving the sacrament of baptism, as well as being given spiritual direction.[22]

As we saw in the historical survey on Psalm 22, at the end of the fifteenth century Denys the Carthusian is directing our attention once more towards the importance of singing the psalms to reform the church in popular devotional culture, as also Geroch had done. Denys still translates the first line "the Lord is my Ruler," with all the metaphors of the Psalm reflecting upon "spiritual nourishment," for "the Church, a faithful people . . . led in the Spirit . . . who has converted my soul from Judaism, or from foreignness to himself. And He has refreshed my soul with the knowledge of God and Savior. . . . You will be kind to me through the sacrament of reconciliation and penance." He thus celebrates the Eucharist, and now mentions "the good Shepherd" who has led him not through "the shadow of the valley of death" but the shadowy realm of "this world and of worldly things." "You have anointed my head in oil" becomes "you have made me a royal priesthood with the oil of your confirmation." In other words, his is an ecclesial commentary on the benefits of what the church provides with good leadership, right doctrine, and exercise of the proper sacraments. All of this while knowing "God's mercy accompanies me through the whole time of my mortal pilgrimage, according to my steps . . . that I might possess these things in Your heavenly dwelling: . . . that eternity of immortality where there is no end of duration and no end."

Instead of Geroch's "graces," Denys enumerates upon nine "benefits" of Psalm 23. He appears to be one of the earliest reformers to speak of "the benefits

20. Denys the Carthusian, *D. Dionysii Cartusiani insigne opus commentariorum in psalmos omnes Davidicos*, in *Doctoris Ecstatici D. Dionysii Cartusiani Opera Omnia* (Monstrolii: Typis Cartusiae S. M. de Pratis, 1898), vols. 5-6; 5:543-47.

21. Denys the Carthusian, *D. Dionysii Cartusiani*, art. 54, 5:543-47.

22. Denys the Carthusian, *D. Dionysii Cartusiani*, art. 54, 5:544.

of Christ," which a century later John Calvin is to use frequently, and which became the central theme of the Italian reformers.[23] The first benefit is living under the rule of Christ. The second is "the water of salutary wisdom," as illuminated by the Holy Spirit. The third is that "he converts my soul," setting my soul aflame in devotion to him. The fourth is that "He leads me in the paths of righteousness." The fifth is freedom from fear, even close to the perils of death. Like Geroch, the sixth and the seventh benefits are the Eucharist meal, and being anointed with spiritual joy. A ninth benefit is to dwell eternally with our wondrous Ruler.

Denys adds an original, anagogical interpretation of Psalm 23 — the celebration of this psalm's benefit in the heavenly or eternal state. Now the saints are "ruled" eternally, wanting nothing. The contemplative enjoys the eternal vision of God, unchangeably united with God. So as he recites the benefits once enjoyed on earth, now in the state of being *comprehensores,* that is, enjoying fullness of perfection with, in, and for Christ, Denys gives us a glimpse of the heavenly kingdom into which we shall be fully translated. He takes then the theme "The Lord is my Ruler" to its ultimate expression.[24]

B. Jacques Lefèvre D'Étaples

Known as Faber Stapulensis, **Jacques Lefèvre D'Étaples** (c. 1455-1536; see pp. 59-60) describes Psalm 23 as "a Psalm concerning Christ the Lord. In the Spirit the prophet speaks in the person of the Church, the faithful people, and the Elect." The reversal from the alleged "Judaizing" and scholasticism of the preceding epoch is breathtaking. To understand this reversal a brief background history of this important figure is in order. We say "important," because he is an important transitional figure to the Reformation that began in 1517, when he was sixty-two years old.

Lefèvre attempts to liberate theology from the older scholasticism. Personally, he seems to have gone through a religious crisis in 1505, and published his psalm commentary, *Quincuplex Psalterium,* in 1509. This text is a medieval triple Psalter (*Hebraica, Gallicanum,* and *Romanum,* see pp. 8-9),[25] with the three versions set in parallel columns. To these Lefèvre adds both a *Psalterium vetus* (the version used by the churches before Jerome's three revisions) and a

23. Juan de Valdés, Don Benedetto, *Because of Christ,* ed. James M. Houston (Colorado Springs, CO: Cook Communications Ministries, Victor, 2005), p. 22.

24. Denys the Carthusian, *D. Dionysii Cartusiani,* art. 54, 5:545-47.

25. Jacques Lefèvre d'Étaples (Faber Stapulensis), *Quincuplex Psalterium,* Facsimile de l'Édition de 1513 (Geneva: Librairie Droz, 1979), folios 35v-r.

Psalterium conciliatum (the Vulgate version corrected from Jerome's *Psalterium iuxta Hebraeos*). Because of his critical Biblical studies, he has often been seen as a reformer before the Reformation.[26] In 1521, Lefèvre joins his former pupil, Guillaume Briçonnet, now Bishop of Meaux, in reforming the clergy of his diocese. Other reforming scholars, including Guillaume Farel, join them, to revitalize the spiritual life of their flock. Understanding the new need of the vernacular, he translates the whole Bible from the Vulgate into French in 1530. In his preface he tells us he has visited several monasteries, only to find the monks of Saint-Germain and the larger lay community of Meaux no longer in love with the "sweetness" that comes from such studies of the Word of God, and so "when devotion dies out, the flame of religion is extinguished; spiritual things are traded for earthly goods, heaven is given up and earth is accepted — the most disastrous transaction conceivable!"[27]

Lefèvre further explains that this degeneration of Christians' religious sensibility has been caused by their attempts to discover the psalms literally and historically — as Nicholas of Lyra had done (see above) — and thus their failure to taste the sweetness of the Psalter, with their loss of heart and then their consequent disconsolation. Yet even more critical of the mystical sense of Nicholas of Cusa, he argues that to make David a model to imitate leaves out the central role of the Holy Spirit and of Christ from the use of the Psalter.

Lefèvre, once again, tries to use the psalms as a vital instrument of reform and so publishes a further study, *Psaultier de David,* in 1525. But there is a significant change in the manner in which Lefèvre conveys the prophetic meaning of the Psalms. He now introduces another hermeneutic, which would reintroduce "the *spiritual* meaning" of the Psalms; this he interprets to be "the true literal meaning." The *true* literal meaning is the *prophetic* meaning; it is the Holy Spirit who speaks through David, and He is speaking through his mouthpiece David, who speaks about Christ.

By 1525 Lefèvre has found that the words of the Psalms are not really David's but those of the Holy Spirit. Now he sees the "literal sense" is not just some factual or historical sense of data available, but as it is given and received by the Holy Spirit. "Therefore the literal and the spiritual sense coincide. This true sense is not what is called the allegorical or tropological senses, but rather the

26. Lefèvre, after the Psalter text, has the commentary printed below in small type. He divides this into four parts: 1. discussion of title and a summary of the psalm; 2. a continuous exposition, a verse-by-verse rendering; 3. a concordance of words and themes of the psalm and other scriptures; and 4. a "take note" section which covers other issues, especially regarding the text.

27. Lefèvre, *Quincuplex Psalterium,* p. 134, and Heiko Oberman, *Forerunners of the Reformation,* trans. Paul L. Nyhus (London: Lutterworth Press, 1967), p. 298.

sense the Holy Spirit intends as He speaks through the prophet."[28] Lefèvre is therefore conscious of making a critical break from the commentaries of the medieval and early Fathers: "They worked with various senses; we have been intent on one primarily, that sense which is the intention of both the Holy Spirit and the prophet."[29] This may still be called "Augustinian spirituality," but in reversed form. David has been restored to being the prophetic *typos* of Christ. All the Old Testament stories of David now become the actual events of Jesus' life. It is not Jesus who allegorizes events of David's life, but it is David who allegorizes prophetically the human life of Jesus. Hence his description of Psalm 23 as "a Psalm concerning Christ the Lord. In the Spirit the prophet speaks in the person of the Church, the faithful people, and the Elect."[30]

IV. Reformers' Reinstatement of Historical David

Nicholas of Lyra (1270-1349), a Franciscan exegete, and Lefèvre thus become the opposite exegetical poles for Reformation commentaries. Lefèvre accuses Lyra of being a "Judaizer," of sapping the morale of the "spiritual" and therefore of contributing to the decline of the church. However, in the long run, it is Nicholas of Lyra's appeal to Hebraic scholarship that gives him lasting value to the Reformers' commentaries.[31] Lefèvre even goes further as a neo-Platonist than Augustine in order to "evangelize" the Psalter. For him, the historic David vanishes and the New Testament is interpreted as having already been summarized in the Psalms.

Important as are conciliar reformers such as Pierre d'Ailly and Jean Gerson, we have no psalm commentaries that would illustrate their critiques of scholasticism. But their other works clearly demonstrate how irrevocable the split in theology had become in the fifteenth century between "the two ways": the ancient and Thomist form of scholasticism, more indebted to Aristotle to give a metaphysical ontology, and the new way *(via moderna)* of the renovators or Nominalists. Little is added later to the indictment of Gerson that theology

28. Oberman, *Forerunners of the Reformation,* p. 300.

29. Oberman, *Forerunners of the Reformation,* p. 301.

30. This is well illustrated in the titles of some of Lefèvre's commentaries on the psalms: Ps. 1 Psalm of the Beatitude of Jesus Christ; Ps. 2 The Assembly of the Kings and Princes among the Jews against Jesus Christ; Ps. 3 Persecutions of Jesus Christ, His Death and Resurrection.

31. See Steve Ozment, *The Age of Reform, 1250-1550* (New Haven and London: Yale University Press, 1980), p. 70; Steve Ozment, *Homo Spiritualis* (Leiden: Brill, 1969); J. S. Preus, *From Shadow to Promise* (Cambridge, MA: Harvard University Press, 1969), pp. 226-27, 268.

has its own disciplines of faith, which deny the roles of speculation and curiosity in Biblical scholarship.[32] Had he lived longer, **Girolamo Savonarola** (1452-98), in the heart of the classical Renaissance culture of Florence, might have led the forces for reform more deeply as a professional teacher of logic. Instead, it was left to Martin Luther on the periphery of the world of the Renaissance to take the lead.

A. How Luther Learned to Personalize the Psalms

In **Martin Luther's** (1483-1546) earliest Psalms lectures, with which he started his academic career in 1513-15, he takes the side of Lefèvre, believing the literal sense of Scripture will kill the soul.[33] Another exegete, Jacob Perez of Valencia, is reputed to have said, if David had wanted to talk about his known experiences in the psalms, he would not have needed the Holy Spirit.[34] Unfortunately Luther's first commentary on Psalm 23 is missing, so we cannot trace this "spiritual meaning" that he first gave to the psalm. He begins his commentary with the traditional medieval fourfold interpretation: literal/historical, allegorical, tropological, and anagogical. But as Christ is seen to be the Augustinian key, the allegorical remains the guiding control. Luther gave his students a Latin text with wide margins and generous interlinear spaces, so that they could write in their own glosses on grammatical, philological, and theological notes and comments. He adds a *scholia*, or wider interpretation of verses or passages, from which he can expatiate at length in his lectures. He begins with the guideline, "every prophecy and every prophet must be understood as referring to Christ the Lord, except where it is clear from plain words that someone else is spoken of. For thus He Himself says: 'Search the Scriptures . . . and it is they that bear witness to Me' (John 5:39)."[35]

It is possible to trace a deepening in Luther's faith, perhaps suggesting he was experiencing his own conversion as he progressed through these first studies on the Psalms; this probably occurred in early 1516.[36] In Psalm 75:8 Luther is struck by the phrase, "In the hand of the Lord there is a cup of pure wine." He

32. Etienne Gilson, *History of Christian Philosophy in the Middle Ages* (New York: Random House, 1955), pp. 528-33.

33. See Earl Miner, ed., *Literary Uses of Typology from the Late Middle Ages* (Princeton: Princeton University Press, 1977), pp. 20-48.

34. Scott H. Hendrix, *Interpretation* 37 (1983): 233.

35. *Luther's Works,* ed. Hilton C. Oswald (St. Louis: Concordia), vol. 10, p. 7.

36. This is discussed by Michael A. Mullet, *Martin Luther* (London: Routledge, 2004), pp. 65-66.

comments, "Scripture is not in our power nor in the ability of our mind. Therefore in its study we must in no way rely on our understanding, but we must become humble and pray that He may bring that understanding to us, since it is not given except to those who are bowed down and humble."[37] He then notes how blinded the Jews have been in this regard. The Scriptures are not to be read like the classics, where one intelligent scholar can contradict another one. By the time he reaches Psalm 119 Luther is beginning to practice three daily rules for his study of the Psalms: *oratio, meditatio, and tentatio* — prayer, meditation, and the experience of spiritual absorption.

When Luther addresses his second course on the Psalms in 1519-21, he now can affirm that there is no book in the Bible to which he has devoted so much labor. For he now seeks not only to exegete each psalm, but to make each one personally "his own"; he has experienced each one. This becomes for him "the art of faith," to relate the text to personal experiences with the Word. This acts like a lamp in a dark place; or like a rod of iron inflexible in its rule; or indeed, as an inexhaustible spring of the water of life. "Practice on reading one psalm," says Luther, "even one little verse of the psalm. You will progress enough if you learn to make only one verse a day, or even one a week, live and breathe in your heart. After this beginning is made, everything else will follow, and you will have a rich treasury of understanding and affection."[38] In his letters, Luther constantly reminds his correspondents about David. "What father was ever grieved more than David was, when he learned that his son Absalom, for whom he bore a unique love, would drive him out of his kingdom?"[39] In his *Table Talk,* he once observed: "David does not know that we now have his psalms in Germany and that we find comfort in them even as he did long ago. The Lord helped David, who put his trust in God. So he will also aid us who hope in him, for his word is yea and amen."[40]

Eventually, one evening after grace at the dinner table, in 1536, Luther expounded on Psalm 23. "God as the faithful and diligent Shepherd" becomes a major theme of Luther's Christian experience.[41] *Sola Scriptura,* as a daily experience of grace, and as the full message of the Reformation, is now focused upon this psalm. Luther begins by observing: "whenever God's Word is preached properly and purely, it creates as many good things and results as the

37. Heiko Augustinus Oberman, *Luther: Man between God and the Devil,* trans. Eileen Walliser-Schwarzbart (New York: Doubleday, Image, 1992), pp. 250-51.

38. *Luther's Works,* vol. 10, pp. 157-58.

39. *Luther: Letters of Spiritual Counsel,* ed. and trans. Theodore G. Tappert, reprint (Vancouver: Regent College Press, 1997), p. 69.

40. *Luther: Letters of Spiritual Counsel,* pp. 87-88.

41. *Luther's Works,* vol. 12, Jaroslav Pelikan, ed. (St. Louis: Concordia, 1955), p. 148.

prophet here gives it names." For we "learn from this psalm not to despise God's Word. We should hear and learn it, love and respect it, and join the little flock in which we find it, and on the other hand, flee and avoid those that revile and persecute it." Only those who "hear it diligently and seriously . . . our Lord acknowledges them as His sheep."[42] The imagery of "Spiritual shepherding" follows, now recognized to be the reformed character of true Christianity. Indeed, "shepherding" takes over Luther's consciousness: "God is a thousand times more willing and ready to do everything that is to be done for his sheep than is any faithful human shepherd."[43] "The voice of this Shepherd, with which He speaks to His sheep and calls them, is the Holy Gospel . . . . The pasture with which Christ feeds His sheep is also the dear Gospel."[44] This imagery of the Good Shepherd and his gospel dominates the entire commentary. After Melanchthon's inaugural lecture at the University of Wittenberg (August 29, 1518), Luther comments that the audience forgot Melanchthon's social crudity and "saw in him only the David who was destined to go forth against the Goliath of Scholasticism."[45] Perhaps Luther spoke too soon in likening him to David the shepherd boy.

B. Is Melanchthon a Shepherd Boy Like David?

Philipp Melanchthon (1497-1560), Luther's colleague, was perhaps unwisely admired by Luther, for he had strange contradictions of character and convictions. While Luther has discarded Renaissance philosophy to appreciate gospel faith, Melanchthon later asserts that one could not exercise faith without Aristotle. Faith tends to become for him assent to proposition and doctrine, without the strong personal quality that Luther experiences throughout his life. More a professor of Greek and philosophy, Melanchthon only reluctantly takes up theological studies at the persuasion of Luther.[46] Ironically, his claim to faith, *Loci communes* (1521), is the first systematic statement of Evangelical doctrine. But as assent to doctrine, it is far removed from the personal hermeneutic of Luther.

Melanchthon composes his commentary on the Psalms late in life — c. 1553. He is not a Hebraic scholar, but he has benefited from several Humanist

42. *Luther's Works,* vol. 12, pp. 148-49.

43. *Luther's Works,* vol. 12, p. 154.

44. *Luther's Works,* vol. 12, p. 155.

45. Robert Stupperich, *Melanchthon,* trans. R. H. Fischer (Philadelphia: Westminster Press, 1965), p. 32.

46. See the critical portrait of Melanchthon in David C. Steinmetz, *Reformers in the Wings,* 2nd ed. (Oxford: Oxford University Press, 2001), pp. 49-57.

Hebraic sources. His title, like Luther's, is "The Lord is my Shepherd, I shall want nothing." "There are many sweet metaphors in this Psalm the understanding of which is easy," he notes. "The green and grassy places, the flowing streams, the table, signify nourishment and consolation. The rod and staff signify defense and governance." But he makes no attempt to situate the historical context, other than to state: "David gives thanks to God for nourishment, defense and governance, affirming these to be the benefits of God: and at the same time he seeks that these goods henceforth be attributed to Him." He sees the pivotal issue in verse 3, "that we pray as David does, to preserve and rule us, 'for His name's sake,' as is often repeated in the Psalms and elsewhere. So it is said in Psalm 114, 'Not to us, Lord, not to us, but to your name give glory.'"[47] Melanchthon applies the psalm to the educational purpose he has interpreted the Reformation should be, not defense to idle oneself in pleasures, but protection to "serve in the house of God, that he might learn heavenly doctrine and adorn the Church by means of the propagation of salutary doctrine, that he might make the youth and people accustomed to the knowledge of God. This end is proposed for a pious governor." It is a theological educational objective that he sees David pursuing, a mandate given to any German prince to follow and do likewise. "For these songs are not written for David's sake, but for the sake of the universal Church." As Melanchthon composes his commentary, the Turks advance to the doors of Vienna, so he includes reference to them: "Now the Turks threaten war and the devastation of all Europe and of the universal Church of Christ: let us ask from God that he may protect and defend us against these such great dangers, lest knowledge of him be destroyed." Melanchthon focuses exclusively on the defense of doctrine and the politics of German governance by the princes. It is striking how impersonal his application is compared to that of Luther.

C. Reformed Influence of Bucer

Martin Bucer (1491-1551), the former Dominican monk turned reformed pastor (1521), also writes an important commentary on the Psalms, published in 1529 under the pseudonym Aretius Felinus. The following year his commentary is translated into English by George Joye (already a translator for Tyndale) and later into French. In 1526, Bucer also translates into German the Latin commentary of Bugenhagen. Bucer meanwhile consults the Hebrew texts of the twelfth-century rabbis, Kimchi and Rashi, and the later text of A. Ezra. After being

47. Philipp Melanchthon, *Philippi Melanchthonis Opera quae supersunt omnia,* ed. Carolus Gottlieb Bretschneider, vol. 13, *Corpus Reformatorum* (Halle: Halis Saxonum, 1846), pp. 1050-52.

forced out of Strasbourg, Bucer goes to England where as a liturgist he helps Cranmer formulate the Second Prayer Book of 1551. An effective organizer, he is consulted by German princes to organize their state church on various occasions. Significantly then, his Latin title for Psalm 23 is "The Lord Rules," but it is the English translator who then changes this to "The Lord is my Pastor." Following each title, Bucer provides a short summary of the psalm. "In this psalm David declares and sets forth the marvelous power of truth there is in God, and also how blessed it is [to know it]." It is a brief synopsis, which he does for the entire Psalter, just enough to orient the Evangelical reader in his or her private devotions. Highly popular, several editions follow. However, unlike the other commentaries we have discussed, Bucer's brevity makes it difficult to discern any distinctive theological approach.

D. Calvin's "Plain Sense" of the Psalms

Apparently in the spring of 1534 **John Calvin** (1509-64), already a fugitive from Paris, visited the aged Lefèvre to seek advice on the best course of action, now that persecution of the French Reform movement had started. Calvin must have been deeply disappointed by the impotence of the naïve reform movement of Lefèvre and his associates. For Calvin was now realizing that continuing obedience to the old church was the real obstacle to true reform.[48] Shortly afterwards, Calvin resigned from all his benefices of office and fled from France. Many afflictions, public and private, now beset him for the rest of his life; the Psalter then becomes his daily comfort. However, where Luther has forgotten that the metaphor of the Shepherd and his sheep is figural, Calvin is much more restrained. So he comments on "the Shepherd" as "a persisting metaphor," to describe Christ's benefits for his followers. Psalm 23 is a psalm of thanksgiving, and yet Calvin never allows us to forget that in the first place it is sung by David. He thus keeps the text before him, to elucidate, as well as to use David's own moral rectitude as an exemplar. For David is the archetype who never forgets that the benefits of God remain far greater than all the kingly affluence he might enjoy in material ways. Thus the role of the psalm as propaganda for the Reformation, as Luther tends to use it, is not Calvin's spirit.

At the same time, Calvin identifies himself even more personally with David than Luther does. When he opens his exposition of the Psalms, Calvin confesses to the reader:

48. John T. McNeill, *The History and Character of Calvinism* (New York: Oxford University Press, 1957), pp. 114-15.

> I began to perceive . . . that this was by no means a superfluous undertaking, and I have also felt from my own experience that . . . as David holds the principal place among the writers of the Psalms, it has greatly aided me in understanding more fully the complaints made by him of the internal afflictions which the Church had to sustain through those who gave themselves out to be her members. I suffered the same or similar things from the domestic enemies of the Church. Although I follow David at a great distance, and come short of equaling him . . . I have no hesitation in comparing myself with him. . . . It has . . . been of very great advantage to me to behold him as a mirror, both of the commencement of my calling and in the continued course of my functions; so that I know the more assuredly that whatever the most illustrious king and prophet suffered, was exhibited to me by God as an example of imitation. . . . As he was taken from the sheepfold and elevated to the rank of supreme authority, so God, having taken me from my originally obscure and humble condition, has reckoned me worthy of being invested with the honorable office of a preacher and minister of the Gospel.[49]

This, however, is not so much biographical, as it is confessional. He shares with David the struggles of his soul, but it is given to express a vocation rather than a momentary conversion. For it is the continuity of Christian conversion that illuminates Calvin's use of the Psalter.[50] We are sharing in Calvin's own experience of the Christian life when we read his commentary on the Psalms. Contemporary research is revealing more clearly that Calvin's critique of "theological knowledge" is neither as emotional as Luther's, nor as cognitive as that of Melanchthon. Rather, it is defined "theologically," for it is in "knowing the being of God" — theo-logy — that Calvin seeks to have personal experience of the Psalms.[51] In Psalm 23, Calvin begins, as Luther has done, "The Lord is my Shepherd." He is fond of the metaphor of "sheep," because "wandering about" is characteristic of God's people. This is not only because of their wayward sinfulness, but because of "the hiddenness of God," whose ways are often inscrutable to his people.[52] As our Shepherd too, he sees the provident care with which God leads us into the benefits of the gospel. It is also a metaphor expressive of hu-

49. John Calvin, Preface to the *Commentaries on the Psalms,* in John Dillenberger, ed. and trans., *John Calvin: Selections from His Writings* (Garden City, NY: Anchor Books, 1971), pp. 22-26.

50. Wilhelm H. Neuser, *Calvinus Sacrae Scripturae Professor* (Grand Rapids: Eerdmans, 1994), pp. 3-4.

51. Herman J. Selderhuis, *Calvin's Theology of the Psalms* (Grand Rapids: Baker Academic, 2007), pp. 37-38.

52. Selderhuis, *Calvin's Theology of the Psalms,* p. 184.

mility, which alone provides us with moral vigilance, not the carelessness of pride. The lesson Calvin is taking in the psalm is that prosperity and ease can lead to a moral complacency in which we forget God. So he sees the psalm as God making himself "ladders of His benefits, whereon to climb up nearer to Him. And by this means he not only bridles the wantonness of the flesh, but also spurs [us] on more sharply to thankfulness, and to the exercises of godliness."[53] As a consequence, "I will be afraid of no harm" is because of the protection given by the shepherd's staff. Even the threat of death gives no fears "when God in the person of His only begotten Son has exhibited Himself as our shepherd, much more evidently than to the fathers in the old time under the law."[54]

Calvin continues to repeat his favorite word of the gospel, "[his] benefits." Commenting on "Thou shalt prepare," he says: "The winds of the future tense betoken in this place a continual action.[55] David therefore repeats now without figure, the things which he has shown hitherto by the similitude of a shepherd, concerning the bounteousness of God." "To prepare a table" is a literal provision made by any good father. Even when others are maliciously attacking us, God has set such a "table" in our midst. "God ceases not to show Himself to be liberal and bounteous." As in the custom of a lavish banquet, God anoints us with oil, and provides an overflowing cup, not to be riotous but full of thanksgiving. David, then, exemplifies never to be satiated with earthly riches, but to evaluate all things in the light of the character of God. The lesson of Psalm 23 is thus summed up for Calvin in the words of Psalm 33:12: "Blessed are the people whose God is the Lord."[56] Now we can appreciate the uniqueness of Calvin's hermeneutic: it is his deep awareness of the uniqueness of the God of the Scriptures. In this regard Calvin's commentary is remarkable, perhaps the most remarkable ever composed. This long, central preoccupation of Calvin with the Psalms is because David and other psalmists are for him the exemplars of proper prayer, and of the issues and struggles of the Christian life. Through the psalms he interprets faith as a new *perception*, a transformative way of interpreting human life before God.[57]

53. John Calvin, *Commentary on the Psalms*, vol. 1 (London: John Clarke & Co. Ltd., 1965), p. 269.

54. Calvin, *Commentary on the Psalms*, p. 272.

55. See below pp. 442-43, where Bruce independently discerned the same sense but demonstrates its viability from Hebrew grammar.

56. Calvin, *Commentary on the Psalms*, p. 275.

57. Barbara Pitkin, "Imitation of David: David as a Paradigm for Faith in Calvin's Exegesis of the Psalms," *Sixteenth Century Journal* 24, no. 4 (1993): 850-57.

V. Cultural Popularization of Psalm 23

When Calvin arrived in Geneva in 1537 and drew up articles of worship, he stated: "It is a thing most expedient for the edification of the church to sing some psalms in the form of public prayers . . . so that the hearts of all may be aroused and stimulated to make similar praises and thanks to God with a common love." The ensuing task of versifying the Psalms, setting them into melodies, and singing them congregationally takes nearly twenty-five years,[58] in cooperation with a French court poet/musician Clément Marot.

After Marot's death, Calvin seeks Bucer's assistance to complete the versification of the Psalter. Calvin then issues various editions of the Geneva Psalter, until by 1562 all the Psalter is in metrical arrangement.

Meanwhile in England, **Miles Coverdale** created a collection of metrical psalms in English (c. 1535). This was followed in 1549 by the Psalter of Sternhold and Hopkins, who produced an immensely popular Psalter that saw 78 editions by 1600, and 280 editions by 1640. Since it was known that the Psalms are Hebrew poetry, the first motive for having metrical verse is accuracy. Second, the earlier Primers or Books of Hours (see p. 55) made the psalms available only in prose, but verse could more readily give "life" in easier memorization and more popular worship; Common Meter became the choice. Thomas Sternhold, as a musical tutor of the young Edward VI, knew the psalms' royal appeal. This had been the lifelong wish of Coverdale: "O that men's lips were so opened that their mouths might show the praise of God! Yea, would God that our [court] minstrels had none other thing to play upon, neither our carters nor ploughmen other thing to whistle upon, save psalms, hymns, and such godly songs as David is occupied withal!"[59] After Sternhold's death in 1549 (he had translated forty psalms), John Hopkins then translates sixty more, and others complete the Psalter, composing them all in the "ballad stanza" of 4.3.4.3 beat.

It became popular at the English court to have evening entertainment on the recitation of psalms, such as the small collection composed by Sir Walter Wyatt (1503-42). Helen White has drawn the conclusion: "The passion for singing and the reformer's desire to center even the layman's recreation in Scripture combined to transform the expanded Psalter into the music of Sternhold and Hopkins [and] gave the Psalms a popular vogue beyond anything they had ever known."[60]

58. Barbara Pitkin, "Imitation of David," p. 853.

59. G. Pearson, ed., *Remains of Miles Coverdale* (London: Parker Society, 1846), p. 537.

60. Helen C. White, *The Private Books of Private Devotion* (Westport, CT: Greenwood Press, reprint 1979), pp. 232-33.

However, the nature of the "poetic" is to exercise literary freedom, and blending the Psalter with metrical singing was only the first step backwards. The classical poets of the Tudor and Stuart periods then attempted to "improve" on the poetic diction, regardless of the textual or doctrinal meaning of the psalm. By the beginning of the seventeenth century, secular pastoral poetry has taken over. Francis Davison, editor of *A Pastoral Rhapsody* (1602), one of the most important anthologies of pastoral, composes for himself the following version: ". . . through flow'ry meads, / Where a silver spring, / Gently murmuring, / Doth refresh mine anguish, / When with thirst I languish."[61] By the time the metaphysical poet **Richard Crashaw** (c. 1613-49) has taken over the psalm, the fields and streams have become positively baroque. Now with Crashaw, rather than with David as their guide, the Biblical landscape has been left behind, to enter Arcadia. Such poetic transformation, however, has nothing to do with the Biblical gospel of grace.

This association of classical pastoral, involving the poems of Theocritus's *Idyll XXI,* Virgil's *Fourth Eclogue,* and Ovid's *Metamorphoses,* is all mixed into a fanciful poetic diction. Implied is that "poetry" originates after the creation of the world, but it is the unfallen world of Eden, singing all the time, for life is always happy and shepherding is ruled by tranquility. "Nature" is now its benign ruler, not God.[62] Here Pan's pastoral god of paganism generates dreamlike fantasies, which for Shakespeare become *A Midsummer Night's Dream.* The bucolic life of the pastoral implies a new ethos, whose code prescribes few virtues, but proscribes many vices. Pastoral economy is self-contained, self-sufficient, and self-preoccupied, an idyllic existence arising from Nature, as an inexhaustible resource.[63] But it is all the fantasy of indulgent desire, whose simplicity is naïve, dwelling in another "Eden" that never witnessed the Fall of Man. Courtiers may be exiled by the political events around them, their country estates may be their refuge, and so the environs of "pastoral" may be a way of providing an appropriate consistency to the internal disappointments and frustrations of their personal lives. But it is all far removed from the realism of Biblical faith that "the Lord is my shepherd, I shall not want." It is secular compensation for political disappointment, as Shakespeare suggests in his play *As You Like It:* "Are not these woods / More free from peril than the envious court? / Here feel we not the penalty of Adam . . . / 'This is no flattery: these are counselors / That feelingly persuade me what I am'" (2.1:3-5, 10-11).

61. Quoted by Hannibal Hamlin, *Psalm Culture and Early Modern English Literature* (Cambridge: Cambridge University Press, 2004), p. 151.

62. See article "Pastoral" in *Encyclopaedia Britannica,* vol. 3 (1771), p. 461.

63. For the literary critique of the pastoral ideal, see Renato Poggioli, *The Oaten Flute: Essays on Pastoral Poetry and the Pastoral Ideal* (Cambridge, MA: Harvard University Press, 1975).

Part II. Voice of the Psalmist: Translation

A psalm of David.

I AM is my shepherd,[64]
I do not want.[65]
2 In green pastures he allows[66] me to rest;[67]
by choice watering places[68] he leads[69] me.
3 My vitality[70] he restores;
he leads me in paths of righteousness for his name's sake.
4 Even though I walk in a dark ravine,
I do not fear[71] evil, for you are with me;
Your rod and your staff, they comfort me.
5 You prepare before me a table in the presence of my enemies;
You anoint with oil my head; my cup overflows.
6 Surely goodness and kindness will pursue me all the days of my life,

64. Did Jerome translate *poimainei me* (LXX, "shepherds me") by *reget me* ("rules me") because "shepherd" sometimes is used as a title for a ruler, as in the case of Cyrus (Isa. 44:28)?

65. Construing the prefix conjugation as a progressive present (*IBHS*, p. 504, P. 31.3b).

66. In its other uses — literally of flocks (Isa. 13:20; Jer. 33:12; Song 1:7) and metaphorically of a person (Ezek. 34:15) — the *Hiphil* denotes either toleration or solicitude (*IBHS*, pp. 445f., P. 26,5b, c). Since sheep normally rest themselves at midday, the notion of toleration is more likely. With reference to flocks, NIV renders the verb "to rest."

67. Many emend the Masoretic accentuation, making v. 2A the parallel to v. 1 and v. 2B the parallel to v. 3A. Semantically this makes sense, but syntactically the received tradition is superior. According to the tradition vv. 2A and 2B share an identical syntax: prepositional phrase (preposition + construct pl. noun) and predicate (3rd masc. sing. + verb + verbal suffix, *nî*). In other words, verse 2A is a janus between v. 1B and v. 2B, for it shares the thought of v. 1A and the syntax of v. 2B. Moreover, the notion of food in v. 2A and of drink in v. 2B is felicitous. If one should argue that v. 1B is too short, a good argument can be made that the superscript was originally a part of the psalm, and when it consists of three words or less, the superscript constitutes the A verset of the first verse.

68. GKC construe plural as signifying intensification/amplification (GKC, 124e). This is probably so because other genitives are singular.

69. In grazing lands of Palestine the flocks are usually watered at wells or fountains, not at streams. Thus the verb "to lead" *nhl* probably has its terminative sense (*IBHS*, p. 215, P. 11.2.13b).

70. Traditionally "soul."

71. See n. 65.

and I will return[72] to dwell in[73] the house of *I AM*
for endless days.[74]

Part III: Commentary

I. Introduction: Form and Structure

Psalm 23 is a song of trust in *I AM.* In the corpus of Psalms 15–24 it chiastically matches Psalm 16, also a song of trust (see Psalm 15: "Literary Context"). God's covenantal name for his relationship with Israel frames the psalm (vv. 1a, 6Ba).

The psalm consists of three vignettes (vv. 1-4, 5, 6). The first two are extended metaphors, envisioning *I AM*'s relationship with the individual believer. As in a drama, when the curtain lifts, the stage is set for pastoral scenes, and *I AM* appears as a shepherd. After the curtain is dropped at the end of verse 4, the curtain is lifted a second time in verse 5; this time *I AM* appears as host preparing a banqueting table. Once again the curtain drops and opens in verse 6; this time, as reality replaces imagination, the psalmist is seen returning to *I AM*'s eternal house.

Verse 1 introduces the pastoral setting imagery and the psalm's thesis: As one who trusts and follows *I AM,* I do not lack any good thing. The imagery and summary are then elaborated in what earlier commentators called "grace" or "beneficences": food and rest (v. 2), guidance (v. 3), and protection (v. 4). The metaphor is transmuted into an extended allegory that coheres by following the typical day in the life of a shepherd. In the morning he leads his sheep to green pastures and then, at noon, allows them to rest in the grassy pastures by cool and quiet waters. Renewed, the sheep resume their trek back to their sheepfold. The Shepherd leads his sheep from the sheepfold along safe paths to the green pastures and refreshing water and then back to the sheepfold.[75] Should the Shepherd and his sheep confront an enemy, the Shepherd is fully armed with club and crook to fend them off. Upon return to the sheepfold the shepherd attends to his fevered and/or scratched sheep.

72. LXX (*to katoikein me,* "my dwelling") probably pointed *šbty* as *šiḇtî,* inf. cstr. of *yšb* (see Ps. 27:4). Many emend text to read *wᵉyāšabtî* ("I will dwell"). MT points the root as *šûḇ,* not as *yšb* (see commentary). The *waw* is consecutive because of accent shift (see *IBHS,* pp. 520f., P. 32.1c).

73. The pregnant preposition *b* "in" assumes a verb such as "to dwell" (*IBHS,* p. 224, P. 1.4.3d).

74. Literally, "for length of days."

75. Guidance by *I AM* as shepherd also occurs in Ps. 78:52; Isa. 40:11; 49:10.

The second vignette transforms the healing and protective sheepfold into the imagery of a festive banquet, where a rich host lavishly entertains his guest, while adversaries of the sheep-turned-guest look on helplessly, and so intensifies the "graces" and "beneficences" of provision, restoration, and protection. Better than being likened to a sheep under the care of a shepherd is being likened to a guest with a wealthy host who provides a table so abundantly laden with food and drink that the cup brims over; the host refreshes and heals his guest with oil on his head, and all of this while he protects his guest while enemies look on helplessly.

But better than being a sheep under the care of a shepherd and even better than being a guest wined and dined in a sheik's tent is the reality of being forever in *I AM*'s house. The final vignette abstracts God's attributes conveyed by the two images of Shepherd and Host: his goodness and *ḥesed.* In addition, the poet transmutes the implied tent into God's abode.

In addition to the message, "I do not lack," with its elaboration of not lacking food, refreshing rest, and protection, changes of address also hold together the three vignettes. Verses 1-3 (17 words) are implicitly addressed to the congregation; verses 4-5 (22 words) are explicitly addressed to *I AM.* Verse 4 functions as a transition between the two vignettes, looking back to verses 1-3 with reference to the shepherd imagery and looking ahead to verse 5 by using the direct address to God and the host imagery. The climactic verse 6 returns to addressing the congregation, bringing closure to the song.

II. Exegesis

A. Superscript s/s [1A]

A psalm by David (see pp. 87-90). The comparison of *I AM* to a shepherd fits the early years of Israel's shepherd-king, who was called from leading a flock of sheep to leading the flock of Israel (Ps. 78:70-72), but this does not prove Davidic authorship. Sheep were a central part of the Israelite economy and other famous leaders were also at one time shepherds: Abraham, Isaac, and Jacob, and also Moses.

As ancient Israelites parsed their life experiences in terms of their shepherd-king par excellence, Jihadist Muslims use the prophet Muhammad as their model for world conquest, and Christians look to Jesus as their pattern for their lives. Nevertheless, as Calvin saw, David's psalms serve for all God's covenant children as a paradigm to evaluate and interpret their lives (see below, Conclusion).

B. I AM as Shepherd vv. 1-4

1. Summary Statement v. 1

The bold confession, "I AM *is my shepherd*" *(Yhwh rōʿî),* establishes an intimate I-Thou relationship between *I AM* and the individual Israelite; asserts the individual's total dependence upon God's goodness and kindness to care for him; and entails that his relationship is based on loving trust. "So close is the connection between shepherd and sheep that to this day Middle Eastern shepherds can divide flocks that have mingled at a well or during the night simply by calling their sheep, whereupon they follow their shepherd's voice. Shepherds are inseparable from their flocks, and their work is demanding, solitary and sometimes dangerous (Gen. 31:38-40; 1 Sam. 17:34-35)."[76] If a sheep becomes lost, the faithful shepherd leaves the others in the open country to find it, and when he finds it he calls his friends to celebrate with him because he has found his one lost sheep (Luke 15:3-7).

Conditions of shepherding in ancient Israel, however, differed from most modern practices: "Sheep were not fenced in and left to fend for themselves. Instead they were totally dependent on shepherds for protection, grazing, watering, shelter and tending to injuries. In fact, sheep would not survive long without a shepherd."[77]

The relationship of *I AM* to the individual believer is elaborated by a "catalogue of provisions [that] is both marvelously inclusive and fashioned with loving attention to the literal details of a shepherd's life"[78] in order to explicate that the faithful Israelite does *not want (lōʾ ʾeḥsār).*[79] The lexeme *ḥāsar* is often inchoative for the transition to this condition (i.e., "comes to lack"). The faithful does not lack ample food and renewing water (v. 2), or guidance (v. 3) with assured protection (v. 4). The psalmist validates his trust by his experience. When a person lacks essentials for living, such as rest, food, guidance, and protection, his or her life becomes marginalized and unless remedied dies. The Mosaic catechism teaches that complete harmony reigns between the Giver of every good gift and his covenant partner as long as the human is faithful to his covenant obligations (Lev. 25:19; 26:3-5). A lack of provisions signifies a failed relationship (Deut. 28:48, 57; Jer. 44:18; Ezek. 4:17). However, this absolute judgment applies to a comprehensive view of a believer's eternal life. Before the end

76. *Dictionary of Biblical Imagery,* ed. Leland Ryken, James C. Wilhoit, Tremper Longman III (Downers Grove, IL: IVP Academic, 1998), p. 782.

77. *Dictionary of Biblical Imagery,* p. 782.

78. *Dictionary of Biblical Imagery,* p. 784.

79. Is there an intentional sound play with *ḥesed* in v. 6Aa?

of clinical life people live in an upside-down world, where the wicked are full and the righteous are hungry; Israel, David, and the Lord Jesus all hungered in their wildernesses (Deut. 8:3; Matt. 4:2; 12:1, 3; Mark 2:25; Luke 6:3, 25). A song of trust, like the literary genre of the Book of Proverbs, by faith sees and enjoys the present in light of God's promised blessed end, beyond the time when the wicked prosper and the righteous suffer (1 Sam. 2:5; Ps. 107:5, 9, 36; 146:7; Luke 6:25; 1 Cor. 4:11; Phil. 4:12).[80] "But at that time," says Bridges, "how intolerable will be this conscious want through all eternity, when a drop of water to cool the tormented tongue shall be denied! (Luke xvi. 24)."[81]

In the verse-by-verse exposition that follows, the literal background is emphasized. But readers should apply for themselves the Shepherd's graces (per Geroch) or benefits (per Denys and Calvin). What they as God's flock do not lack needs to be interpreted by the readers themselves, as the tropological sense demands.

2. *Provides Food v. 2A*

The pastoral imagery begins with the shepherd's task to lead sheep from his nighttime protection, probably in a sheepfold, to places of grazing *in green pastures* (*n^{e}'ôṯ deše'*, v. 2A). This chiefly poetic term *nāweh* ("pasture," here a countable plural, *n^{e}'ôṯ*) designates a grazing place and connotes delightful and rich provisions. "Green," a gloss for *deše'*, refers to green vegetation: "to the new fresh grass that sprouts after the rains have fallen on Israel . . . (Isa. 15:6). Grass can sprout in the steppe . . . , which then serves as pastureland . . . for livestock (Joel 2:21-22)."[82] The greenness of vegetation is an aesthetic delight as well as a functional prerequisite to life. The plural suggests the Shepherd never runs out of finding green pastures for his sheep.

3. *Provides Rest v. 2B*

After the morning grazing, sheep typically lie down for several hours at midday in a shady or cool place (Song 1:7). And so the good Shepherd *allows me to rest* (*yarbîṣēnî*, see n. 66; cf. Gen. 33:13), a situation that assumes the sheep is sated. Driven hard for one day, a sheep dies (Gen. 33:13).

The parallel reinforces and expands the first verset. The shepherd's solici-

80. B. K. Waltke, *The Book of Proverbs: Chapters 1–15* (Grand Rapids and Cambridge: Eerdmans, 2004), pp. 107-9.

81. C. Bridges, *An Exposition of Proverbs* (Evansville, IN: Sovereign Grace Book Club, 1959; preface 1846), pp. 169f.

82. M. D. Futato, *NIDOTTE*, 1:999, s.v. *deše'*.

tous care to lead his sheep to grassy pastures is his tender care to lead them *to waters in a choice resting place (ʿal-mê mᵉnūḥô)*. We should probably not think of slaking thirst as a subsequent action but as a coincidental situation with the sheep's taking rest in a cool shady place (Song 1:7). The plural may be a countable, matching "pastures," or an intensive. *He leads me (yᵉnahᵃlēnî)* signifies to "guide to a watering-place or station, and cause to rest there."[83] It is sometimes said that shepherds in the East lead their flock, not drive them as in the West, but an ancient cylinder seal depicts a shepherd driving his flock of sheep.[84]

4. *Provides Guidance vv. 3-4*

My vitality (*napšî*, see n. 70; Ps. 3:1 [2], n. 35; 16:10) *he restores* (*yᵉšôḇēḇ*, 19:7 [8]) functions as a transition between the themes of rest with ample provisions and guidance. By providing his sheep with rich provisions of food and cool drink, the good Shepherd revives the psalmist's spirit, life, and vitality to continue the trek home. The lexeme *he leads me (yanᵉḥēnî)*[85] originated in the shepherd's life and is commonly used in situations of leading one safely through snares and triumphantly to a desired and promised destiny (Exod. 15:13; 32:34; Deut. 32:12; Ps. 5:8 [9]; cf. 78:14, 53; Isa. 40:11; 49:10; Rev. 7:17).[86] That connotation nicely satisfies the context of verses 3Bb-4. *In paths (bᵉmaʿgᵉlê)* refers to "cart tracks," "wagon ruts." While the earth is soft, wagon wheels press the trails that others are obliged to follow after it dries and hardens. *Of righteousness (ṣedeq)* values the divine and human modes of behavior as doing what is communally faithful and beneficial. In some social contexts the word is used of the king, whose task is to create a favorable order for the whole people (2 Sam. 8:15; Jer. 22:3, 15; 33:15; Ezek. 45:9). A righteous (i.e., selfless) ruler has the invigorating effect on the land of the rising sun (2 Sam. 23:3), in contrast to a ruler who is wicked (i.e., selfish). *Ṣdq* is also used in reference to a servant offering faithful assistance to his lord (Gen. 30:33). Third, it is also used to bring about the harmony of a community by its individual members, who may be social equals, of doing what is right and just and fair according to God's standard of acceptable behavior (Gen. 38:26; Ps. 15:2; Prov. 1:3). Since this song of trust celebrates *I AM*'s competence, not the sheep's efforts, the first sense of a leader who selflessly creates a favorable situation for his subject is in view (see Ps. 3:3 [4]). Of course, a king's giving his subject laws to maintain the community's harmony and norm of social be-

83. This is the primary meaning in BDB, p. 624, s.v. *nāhal Piel*.

84. *Dictionary of Biblical Imagery*, p. 783.

85. Note the alliteration of *mᵉnūḥôṯ* and, four words later, *yanᵉḥēnî*, both from the root *nḥh*.

86. Jenni, *TLOT*, 2:730, s.v. *nḥh*.

havior is in the best interest of all, but that notion ill fits the shepherding imagery — sheep do not concern themselves with the social propriety of the Ten Commandments. Turning from the use of the word in varying social relationships, K. Koch observes: "*ṣedeq* never encompasses merely an ethical behavior but . . . a circumstance of sound, unassailed success."[87] In other words "right" and "wrong" ("evil") always have the notions of good and bad ethical behavior and of beneficial or harmful effects. Conduct and consequence in Biblical thinking are inseparable. But this is so because God stands behind retributive justice, not because of an inexorable world order, as Koch suggests.[88]

The good Shepherd does this *for the sake of his name (lᵉmaʿan šᵉmô).* A. S. van der Woude notes: "Because names represent the personality, bearers must be concerned with their names, i.e., their good reputations. One acquires a name in the sense of fame if one increases one's honor . . . through mighty deeds."[89] *I AM*'s fame rests "on faithfulness in keeping his covenants (Ps. 138:2) and displaying his power on behalf of the nation (2 Sam. 7:23; Neh. 9:10; Jer. 16:21 . . .). The idea of acting 'for your name's sake' often, along with the concept of maintaining personal integrity, means acting to uphold this reputation, whether by guiding (Pss. 23:3; 31:3 [4]), pardoning (Pss. 25:11; 79:9), sparing (1 Sam. 12:22; Isa. 48:9; Jer. 14:7, 21; Ezek. 20:44) or delivering (Ps. 106:8; 109:21; 143:11)."[90] Since name and person are inseparable, if one loses his name he fades from memory and ceases to exist on earth. Because Absalom had no son to mention his name after his death, he erected a memorial stone to preserve his social immortality (2 Sam. 18:18). The Old Testament prescribed levirate marriage for the widow of a childless, deceased man so that she through his brother could bear a son to give him immortality (Deut. 25:5-10). The ontological *I AM* cannot die, but epistemologically he could cease to exist in human consciousness. He lives existentially because he acts faithfully and beneficially to those who trust him. Were he to lose one sheep along the path of life due to misadventure, his name would be tarnished in its honor and could not be trusted with all of his subjects' heart. In other words, *I AM*'s existential existence on earth and the psalmist's well-being are inseparably connected. *I AM* will not lose any of his faithful people to Death (Rom. 8:38-39), as the Pioneer and Completer of the Christian pilgrimage demonstrated. We live in a universe wherein God's interests and his people's interest cohere, not compete.

87. K. Koch, *TLOT,* 2:1052, s.v. *ṣdq*.

88. Waltke, *Proverbs 1–15,* pp. 73-76.

89. A. S. van der Woude, *TLOT,* 3:1351, s.v. *šēm*.

90. *Dictionary of Biblical Imagery,* p. 585.

5. Provides Protection v. 4

It was the task of a shepherd to lead sheep on a safe path both to and from the sheepfold. Nevertheless, *even* (*gam,* see Ps. 19:11, 13 [12, 14]) supposing the situation should arise[91] and the saint says that *I walk* (*'ēlēk,* see Ps. 1:1) *in a* dark *ravine* (*bᵉgê'*), he or she feels safe. *G̱ê'* signifies a valley, either wide or narrow. Since it is dark — and shepherds do not lead or drive their sheep at night — a ravine-like valley is imagined. The noun glossed *dark (ṣalmāwet)* is often glossed according to its etymology: "valley *(ṣal) of death (māwet).*" But this gloss may be misleading, for in use *ṣalmāwet* does not signify clinical death. In its other seventeen uses, all poetic, "it refers to literal darkness in opposition to light, usually with an implied sorrow or fear."[92] Job uses *ṣalmāwet* to describe his cursed day of birth in parallel with "darkness" *(ḥōšek),* "cloud" *('ᵃnānâ)* and "blackness" *(kamîr)* (Job 3:4-5; cf. 28:3; 34:22; Amos 5:8). Job says, "deep shadows *(ṣalmāwet)* ring my eyes" (Job 16:16). It connotes terror (Job 24:17, twice), deep gloom (Ps. 107:10, 14), deep distress (Isa. 9:2 [1]; Ps. 44:19[20]), and extreme danger (Ps. 23:4; Jer. 2:6). It is also used figuratively of the realm of the dead (Job 10:20-22; 12:22) in conjunction with other nouns belonging to the semantic domain of darkness. In sum, although the gloss, "shadow of death," connotes the emotional aspect of fear, sorrow, and/or danger, to prevent the common misunderstanding that "shadow of death" has a restricted sense of clinical death, it is better glossed by its sense than by its etymology and connotations. *I will not fear* (*lō' 'îrâ,* see Ps. 3:6 [7]) *evil (ra').* *Ra'* conveys the factual judgment that something is bad, whether it be a concrete physical state (e.g., "ugly" cows, Gen. 41:3; "poor/bad" figs, Jer. 24:2), an abstraction ("calamity/disaster"), or moral behavior that injures others (see Prov. 1:16; 2:12). The value judgment that something is bad depends on the taste of the one making the evaluation; "in one's eyes" is often added to the word (cf. Isa. 5:20). Here it denotes both moral evil and physical damage (i.e., calamity). This is so *for (kî) you ('attâ) are with me ('immādi).* The "you" signals the change of address, and "with me," a poetic word used only with first person pronoun, connotes that "I do not fear because" *I AM*'s protective presence walks beside him.

The Shepherd of the royal and priestly sheep is fully armed to fend off an attack by anything or anyone. The notion of protection is emphasized by the syntax of the nominative absolutes, which focuses attention on the instruments of the shepherd to protect his sheep. The mention of both the rod and staff suggests the shepherd is fully equipped. *Your rod* (*šiḇṭᵉḵā,* see Ps. 2:9) is a club. As for the phrase *and your staff (ûmiš'anteḵā)* — the couplet is held together by the

91. *Kî (if)* followed by the imperfect, as here, has the sense of *even supposing that* (Lat. *ut*).
92. James D. Price, *NIDOTTE,* 3:809, s.v. *ṣll.*

alliteration of initial /š/ and of the dentals /ṭ/ and /t/ with the suffix /ḵā/ — the lexeme *miš'eneṯ* occurs eleven times, literally with reference to a staff or figuratively of a support. The angel of the Lord had one in his hand (Judg. 6:21), and nobles are depicted as having scepters and staffs (Num. 21:18). Staffs were used by the blind (Exod. 21:19) and the aged (Zech. 8:4), and are used figuratively to depict trusting in something (2 Kings 18:21 // Isa. 36:6). Here the literal and figurative uses combine. We should probably think of the shepherd's crook. The resumptive pronoun *they (hēmmâ)* focuses attention on the protecting instruments. *Comfort me (yᵉnaḥᵃmūnî)* "does not mean to sympathize but to encourage."[93] H. J. Stoebe notes: "that comfort, if necessary and possible, includes real assistance. . . . This concrete assistance probably also provides the background for understanding Psa 23:4."[94]

C. I AM as Host v. 5

The poet-playwright understandably replaces the staging of a returned-to-sheepfold with festivities at a banquet table. Center stage is the Host and his welcome guest. The playwright leaves it to his reader's imagination to fill in the kind of housing, although the movement from the shepherd's life suggests a shepherd-king's royal tent. The poem continues in direct address from the trusting covenant partner to his God. Once again the catalogue of *I AM*'s provisions is marvelously inclusive and fashioned with attention to the telling detail. The guest praises his Host: *You prepare* (*ta'ᵃrōḵ*, "arrange") *before me (lᵉp̄ānî) a table (šulḥān),* a metonymy for the bowls and goblets laden with rich food and exquisite elixirs. Archaeological, artistic, and textual evidence indicates that in wealthy homes tables were common (cf. Judg. 1:7; 2 Sam. 9:7-13; 2 Kings 4:10; Job 36:16), but probably not in ordinary houses. The verbal placing together of "you prepare" and "before me" suggests the intimacy of the Host and guest (see v. 1). The theme of provision and rest is conjoined with protection by adding that the feast takes place *in the sight of (neged) my enemies* (*ṣōrᵉrāy,* see Ps. 8:2 [3]) who look on helplessly. So mighty is his Host that the beneficiary conspicuously enjoys a royal banquet right in front of his adversaries who cannot touch him. *You anoint* glosses *dšn* Piel, which means literally "make fat," *with oil (baššemen).* Unlike "to anoint" (*mšḥ,* Ps. 2:2), which signifies being consecrated to an office, *dāšan* Piel signifies the pouring of olive oil on the guest's head, connoting the wealth, generosity, and care of the host to promote the re-

93. *HALOT,* citing Karl Elliger, 3:689, s.v. *nḥm,* Pi.

94. H. J. Stoebe, *TLOT,* 2:736, s.v. *nḥm,* Pi.

newal, joy, and healing of his weary and wounded guest: "In a climate where dry skin was a problem, especially for travelers, anointing with oil was a refreshment (Ps. 23:5), which at a literal level, however, refers to healing oil applied to an injured sheep in the sheepfold at the end of the day."[95] *My cup (kôsî)* is a shell-shaped goblet presumably filled with wine.[96] *Runs over (r^ewâyâ)* glosses literally "is superfluity [of drink]." To judge from "I am prayer" (Ps. 109:4), meaning "I am totally given to prayer," and from Ps. 120:7 "I am peace," meaning "I am wholly given to peace," "my goblet is superfluity" means it is brim-full. The goblet functions as a synecdoche for all the dishes on the table that are filled to overflowing with prepared meats, cereals, and vegetables.

D. I AM as Eternal Omnibenevolence v. 6

The poet leaves the realm of the imaginary and returns to the real world, a world as good as and even better than imagined. The sheepfold and banqueting table are transmuted into the house of God, which, in David's day, was a royal tent (see Ps. 15:1). The loving attention to details to explicate God's gracious benefits is now abstracted into God's two benevolent attributes: "goodness and kindness."

The exclamatory conjunction *surely ('ak)* gives vent to the psalmist's expression of a truth newly perceived. Abimelech used the same particle when he realized Rebekah was Isaac's wife (Gen. 26:9; cf. 29:14; 44:28). In this poem of trust celebrating *I AM, goodness* (*ṭôḇ,* see Ps. 4:7 [8]) *and loving kindness (wāḥesed)* are personified metonymies of God's benevolent attributes. When Moses requests to see the glory of God, *I AM* replies, "I will cause all my goodness to pass in front of you" (Exod. 33:19-20). In a subsequent event of that encounter, "*I AM* passed in front of Moses, proclaiming, '*I AM Who I AM,*' the compassionate and gracious God, slow to anger, abounding in love *(ḥesed)* and faithfulness, maintaining love to thousands, and forgiving wickedness, rebellion and sin" (Exod. 34:6-7). *Ḥesed* essentially means "help to the needy" and has no precise English equivalent. It refers to a situation where a needy partner depends on another for deliverance, and the deliverer does so freely out of all his finer spiritual and sensitive instincts (i.e., kindness, mercy, love, and loyalty). K. D. Sakenfeld defined it as "deliverance or protection as a responsible keeping of faith with another with whom one is in a relationship."[97] *I AM*'s be-

95. *Dictionary of Biblical Imagery,* p. 603.

96. *HALOT,* 2:466, s.v. *kôs.*

97. K. D. Sakenfeld, *The Meaning of Ḥesed in the Hebrew Bible* (Harvard Semitic Museum 17; Missoula, MT: Scholars Press, 1978), p. 233.

nevolences *will pursue me* (*yirdᵉp̱ûnî,* cf. Hos. 2:7 [9]) as in a chase or hunt so as not to allow the beneficiary to escape *I AM*'s unfailing desire and commitment to do him good. What a contrast is the pagan's conceptions of God with the Biblical. Many pagans imagine their gods as demonic, and/or hideous to look at — sometimes dragon-like in form — and demanding apotropaic sacrifices — even child sacrifice — to ward off their hostility. Instead of demanding human sacrifice the God of Israel sacrificed his own Son to satisfy his justice. No religion rivals God's revelation of himself as a God of sacrificial love. The adverbial phrase adds that the chase will last *all the days of my life* or "as long as I live," probably referring to his clinical life until swallowed by the earth (cf. Gen. 3:17; Deut. 17:19; Josh. 1:5). But that is not the climactic end of the drama, as verse 6B shows.

And I will return (wᵉšaḇtî) refers to a chronological and/or a logical subsequent situation (see n. 72). Although the ancient versions probably pointed the verb as belonging to the root *yšb,* "I will dwell," the more difficult received tradition, "I will return," is sensible in light of the psalm's image of a day in the life of a shepherd returning to a royal table at end of the day. The preceding verb "to pursue" also goes well with "to return." As commented above, after leaving the sheepfold in the morning and being guided safely to grazing and watering, the sheep return to the sheepfold where they are healed and tended to. So also in the climactic conclusion, personified goodness and lovingkindness are represented as diligently following their cherished object all the days of his life (v. 6A), and then the mortal returns safely to his true home, *the house of* I AM. For David, God's house referred to the royal tent he pitched for the ark (2 Sam. 6:17). After David's death the house was reinterpreted as a reference to Solomon's temple; and in the canon, which includes the New Testament, it refers to the church triumphant secure in the bosom of the resurrected Jesus Christ (John 2:14; 2:12-23; 1 Cor. 3:16-17; 6:14-20; 1 Peter 2:4-10). *For endless days,* which glosses *lᵉʾōreḵ yāmîm* "for length of days," is ambiguous. On the one hand, sometimes it seems restricted by the limits of a clinical lifetime (Job 12:12; Ps. 91:16); in other contexts it seems unrestricted. For example: "Your statutes, *I AM,* stand firm; holiness adorns your house for endless days" (*lᵉʾōreḵ yāmîm,* Ps. 93:5); in Psalm 21:4 [5] "length of days" is qualified as being "forever and ever." In Lamentations 5:20 the phrase is parallel to *neṣaḥ,* "forever." Isaiah 53:10 prophesies that after the Anonymous Servant pours out his life as a guilt offering "he will prolong his days (*yaʾᵃrîḵ yāmîm,* the verbal equivalent of *lᵉʾōreḵ yāmîm*). The non-restricted sense is probably intended here with reference to the temple where the Eternal lives.

Part IV. Conclusion

Ezekiel predicted Messiah's role as shepherd (Ezek. 37:24), and so did Micah (Mic. 5:2, 4 [1, 3], fulfilled in Matt. 2:6). In the New Testament, Jesus Christ as son of David according to the flesh experiences the shepherding care of his Father in heaven, and as Son of God becomes the good shepherd, providing, restoring, guiding, and protecting his sheep. He is the "Good Shepherd" (John 10:1-16), the "Great Shepherd" (Heb. 13:20), and the "Chief Shepherd" (1 Peter 5:4), forever provisioning them, providing them with rest, restoring their vitality, and safely guiding them to royal festivities at the end of days. He does so through all the means of grace at his disposal: the Holy Spirit, the Scriptures, the holy church, and the holy sacraments. He loses none — even passionately exerting himself to find one lost sheep — except the one doomed to destruction according to the eternal plan of God and so prophesied beforehand. His sheep are not to fear the danger of deceptive attacks from within and overt attacks from without (Matt. 7:15; 10:16), and the certainty of undergoing great tribulation in the future (Mark 14:27). This is so because it is God who is giving them the kingdom (Luke 12:32).

As the church's chief shepherd, Christ appoints under-shepherds who love him, as illustrated by his restoring of Peter to feed his sheep (John 21:15-19), and he administers the Holy Spirit to gift elect saints to be his flock's human pastors and teachers to equip them for "works of service" (Eph. 4:3-13). The apostles use the shepherd metaphor to delineate how pastors and elders should fulfill their gift and office (Acts 20:28-29; 1 Peter 5:3-4).[98]

98. *Dictionary of Biblical Imagery,* p. 783.

CHAPTER 14

Psalm 51: "The Psalm of All Psalms" in Penitential Devotion

Part I: Voice of the Church: Historical Regimes of Penance

"The Psalm of All Psalms" is the title the Anglican liturgist J. M. Neale ascribed to this psalm![1] In the medieval Roman Breviary, Psalm 51 was recited every hour at the conclusion of each monastic service, with the exception of Christmas and the forty-day session of Lent. For some thirteen centuries, it was repeated seven times daily. As *De Misere* it was selected for Ash Wednesday, which began the season of Lent, to become pivotal within the church's calendar. Symbolically, as "the fiftieth psalm" of the Vulgate, it was celebrant of the year of Jubilee, as described in Leviticus 25, when all debts were remitted, all slaves liberated, and all prisoners set free. And just as the ram's horn was uniquely blown on the great Day of Atonement, so we may describe this psalm as "The Ram's Horn of the Church." For it echoes the words of the apostle: "where sin has abounded, grace has much more abounded" (Rom. 5:20). No other psalm has been so central to the complex history of Christian penitential devotion, nor to the great doctrine of atonement.[2] Protestants need reminder that the whole complex history of medieval penitence and penance is interwoven with Psalm 51. A late medieval scholar, Alfonso de Tostado (1410-55), wrote a folio

1. Rev. J. M. Neale and Rev. R. F. Littledale, *A Commentary on the Psalms: From Primitive and Medieval Writers . . .* (London: Joseph Masters & Co., 1879), vol. 3, p. 181.

2. Neale has listed over 150 Catholic commentaries and 27 Lutheran ones on this psalm, guessing that there must be also as many by Calvinists.

volume of 1200 pages, possibly the record in length, for a commentary on this psalm.[3] We shall focus our survey to the period prior to the Reformation, when the Psalm's use was most prominent.

A fourfold historical periodization for external forms of penance can be traced in church history: public confession in the early church; secret or tariff penance in the sixth and seventh centuries (originating in Celtic society); tariff penance along with the revival of public penance in the late eighth and ninth centuries under the Carolingian reformers; and scholastic systematization of penance and the promotion of annual confession to a priest (by decree of the Lateran Council of 1215) in the twelfth and thirteenth centuries. We shall trace commentaries on Psalm 51, within this historical sequence.

I. Public Confession in the Early Church

A. Ante-Nicene Fathers (down to 325 C.E.)

One of the earliest uses of Psalm 51 is in funerary inscriptions, such as is found on a tomb in Cilicia that cites Psalm 51:1.[4] As for the church service, the *Didache* 4.14 demands a public confession of sins preceding the prayer in the church service: "In church confess your sins, and do not come to your prayer with a guilty conscience."[5] As for pastoral use, *The Shepherd of Hermas* early in the second century deals with the pastoral problem of the moral life after baptism. For if baptism initiates a new way of life, is further penitence needed to remedy the continuance of sin within the believer's life? Clearly, it is needed. Though *The Shepherd of Hermas* focuses on penance, the penitential psalms are not used, most likely due to the apocalyptic genre. Thus, along with public penance, personal confession and contrition were also practiced in the early church. The Christian origins of "purity of heart" *(puritas cordis)* probably derive from the Old Testament laws of purification, involving actions taken. In the classical and biblical worlds "pure" *(katharos)* implies the action of "being purified" *(kathairo),* of "taking away what is impure." Likewise, in the Syriac or *Peshitta Old Testament* Psalm 51:12, *lebba dakya* translates dynamically as "a heart to be made pure/clean." Its early association with asceticism and the life

3. Santidrian, Saturnino Lopez, "Tostado," article in *Dictionnaire de Spiritualité Ascetique et Mystique, Doctrine et Histoire* (Paris: G. Beauchesne, 1995), pp. 1070-71.

4. Paul M. Blowers, ed., *The Bible in Greek Christian Antiquity* (Notre Dame: University of Notre Dame Press, 1997), p. 293.

5. Johannes Quasten, *The Beginnings of Patristic Literature,* Christian Classics vol. 1 (Allen, TX: Thomas More Publishing, 1983), p. 33.

of the Desert Fathers involved deep exercise of divine grace:[6] acknowledgment of need — of absolution; of self-limitation — I cannot do it myself; and of dependence on God — only God can forgive sins. This dependence is voiced in constant prayer, and the daily/ceaseless recitation of the psalms; especially Psalm 51.

B. Post-Nicene Fathers

In the post-Constantinian commentaries of the church fathers, there appears a wider personal latitude of instruction. **Augustine of Hippo** appears more generous and realistic about the broad spectrum of morality among Christians or indeed "half-Christians." In a sermon preached in Carthage, possibly in the summer of 411, Augustine is mindful of speaking on Psalm 51 to baptized Christians, who are yet "running off after empty things and lying foolishness, careless of their primary vocation!" "It is one thing when a person who does not know what to avoid goes running after these empty pleasures, but quite another when one disregards the voice of Christ in order to do so."[7] Augustine then argues that as David's sin was done and exposed publicly, Christians too should be dealt with publicly in both confession and forgiveness. This became the standard practice of the church until the Carolingian changes of the late eighth and ninth centuries. Augustine uses Psalm 51 as a public warning "to the unwary; [and] so also it will not leave the fallen in despair."[8] As an ex-sinner, both David and Augustine in turn can assure the reader or listener that "God is so rich in mercy that no sinner who turns to [Christ] *need despair* . . ." (v. 15).[9] In the light of rampant immorality in his society — as also is in ours — argues Augustine, "we must live tolerantly among bad people, because when we were bad ourselves, good people lived tolerantly among us. If we remember what we were, we shall not despair of those who are now what we were then."[10] He links the act of repentance with the desire for spiritual health: "to sin with their eyes open . . . is an extremely dangerous thing."[11] Augustine then notes what was then practiced of public penance: "the sin of this man, great as he was, is not

6. *Purity of Heart in Early Ascetic and Monastic Literature* (Collegeville, MN: Liturgical Press, 1999), p. 11.

7. Augustine, *Exposition of the Psalms,* vol. 2, ed. John E. Rotelle, trans. Maria Boulding (Hyde Park, NY: New City Press, 1999), pp. 410, 411.

8. Augustine, *Exposition of the Psalms,* p. 413.

9. Augustine, *Exposition of the Psalms,* p. 425.

10. Augustine, *Exposition of the Psalms,* p. 429.

11. Augustine, *Exposition of the Psalms,* p. 411.

passed over in silence, but proclaimed in the church,"[12] publicly, in front of the bishop (i.e., the prophet). But in his defense of *sola gratia* Augustine still does not call penance a "sacrament." This developed soon after, when remission of sins to penitents became established on Maundy Thursday.[13] But he does interpret Psalm 51 as giving hope to those in despair of their sinfulness. For he recognizes that "a great misery" requires "a great mercy," and this David seeks from God.[14] Augustine then draws his homily to conclusion with what is so apposite for us today: "at a time when there is so much variation in moral standards and such appalling decadence, keep strict control over your homes. Rule your children, rule your households."[15]

Soon after Augustine, **a North African abbot**, in the midst of the Vandal occupation of Rome, composed 171 prayers as collects to be recited with the penitential psalms, both as moral realism and as evoking the comforting grace of God. This nameless abbot understands six of the penitential psalms to be explicitly referring to human sinfulness, unrighteousness, lack of spiritual health, our need of spiritual guidance, and indeed the need of daily grace — as expressed in these collects.[16]

We do not have a commentary on Psalm 51 by **John Chrysostom**, but his comments on the first penitential psalm, Psalm 6, hint at his much more ascetic tenor on the need of confession: "If we are unwilling to lament in this life, there will be no option at all in the next life but to mourn and lament . . . the person who sheds such tears places no value on the things of the earth. . . . Do you think I am directing these remarks only to monks? In fact, the exhortation is for people in the world as well, and for them more than the others, they after all being in particular need of the remedy of repentance."[17]

Theodoret of Cyrrhus (393-466), a bishop in Syria, appears oblivious to the penitential focus of Psalm 51. He interprets it "prophetically." "The divinely inspired David," and the other Old Testament writers, are all viewed as inspired composers, or *prophētai,* a term that he will not apply to the New Testament apostles. For from these *fountains of Israel* spring all the redemptive hymnody of the New Testament church in their anticipating the Gospel

12. Augustine, *Exposition of the Psalms,* pp. 411-12.

13. Innocent I cites this practice as already established by c. 416. See John T. McNeill and Helen Gamer, *Medieval Handbooks of Penance* (New York: Octagon Books, 1965), p. 17.

14. Augustine, *Exposition of the Psalms,* p. 414.

15. Augustine, *Exposition of the Psalms,* p. 429.

16. Thomas Ferguson, "The Penitential Psalms and North African Psalm Collects: A Liturgical Response," *Studia Patristica* 26 (1993): 14-20.

17. St. John Chrysostom, *Commentary on the Psalms,* vol. 1, trans. Robert Charles Hill (Brookline, MA: Holy Cross Orthodox Press, 1998), p. 103.

teaching.[18] He views Psalm 51 as being prophetic of the gospel and predictive of baptismal regeneration, as well as having been originally a corrective for the people in their Babylonian captivity. He interprets the ministry of the prophet Nathan in the psalm as being prophetic of the apostolic ministry of the New Testament writers. The final prophecy is the anticipation, no longer of priestly sacrifices, but of "the gifts of the all-holy Spirit" that will enable the heavenly Zion to offer the sacrifice of Christ's Once-for-All-Sufficient-Sacrifice of Himself.[19]

II. The Personal Devotion of "Compunction"

What could be overlooked in this fourfold survey is the much more comprehensive, personal, devotional consciousness, exercised from Late Antiquity onwards, as expressed by "compunction" or *compunctio cordis* ("uneasiness of guilt or remorse of the heart"). This we now consider rather than the scholars' second category of penance, the Celtic penalty system, for which we have no commentary data. Compunction leads to the healing and bright sorrow of one's inner, personal sinful status, without which Christianity is merely a formal religion. Originally a medical term for the wound caused by the prick of a thorn or other sharp object, it is expressed metaphorically in Acts 2:37. Luke recounts that when the Jews responded to Peter's charge that as "fellow Israelites" they had crucified "this Jesus whom God has made both Lord and Messiah" (v. 36), "they were *pricked* [Greek lexeme, *katanussomai*] *to the heart*." Integral in the catechetical instruction of candidates for baptism was the teaching of the Lord's Prayer, with an emphasis on the fifth petition: "And forgive us our debts as we also have forgiven our debtors" (Matt. 6:12). Later on, as more public confession became practiced before a bishop in the congregation, the text of Matthew 18:15-20 also became basic.

Origen in the late second century (in his homilies on the book of Jeremiah) sees compunction as underlying all confessional postures.[20] Implicitly, we are all sinners, whether we have anything social to confess or not. So it is a basic premise of the beatific life that we shall always "mourn" and always remain "poor in spirit" (Matt. 5:3-4). As the Desert Fathers realized, we can become tepid in our words of repentance, unless we exercise perpetual compunc-

18. Theodoret of Cyrrhus, *Commentary on the Psalms, 1–72,* trans. Robert C. Hill (Washington, DC: Catholic University of America Press, 2000), p. 295.

19. Theodoret of Cyrrhus, *Commentary on the Psalms, 1–72,* p. 302.

20. Joseph Pegon, *Dictionnaire Catholique,* pp. 1312-21, s.v. "compunction."

tion as evidenced by *penthos* ("the gift of tears"). By the time of Chrysostom "compunction" *(penthos)* or mourning had become more widely practiced. It has three components: shedding tears for one's sins, fear of divine judgment, and concern for the eternal destiny of others. Indeed, observes Chrysostom, "When tears come from the fear of the Lord, they last for ever."[21]

John Climacus (c. 579-649) treats repentance *(metanoia)* and compunction separately, in two different chapters.[22] Compunction has become equivalent to the permanent attitude of "the fear of the Lord" — so the godly Israelite would express it — while repentance in association with baptism may be interpreted as a once-for-all event. The Eastern Fathers — Basil, Gregory of Nyssa, Cassian, Evagrius Ponticus, Chrysostom, Ephrem — now all treat compunction as a basic attitude of the true Christian. The Eastern liturgy knows "catanyctic prayers" (Gr. *katanyxis,* derivative of compunction), which aim to bring "tears." Armenian and Syriac monks speak of themselves as *penthountes,* living habitually as penitents, and therefore as mourners.[23] For Symeon the New Theologian, it is the love of God that causes him to live daily in compunction.[24] This led de Guibert to distinguish the compunction of love from the compunction of fear; this double act of devotion persisted throughout the Middle Ages.[25]

Although in popular thought **Gregory the Great** (540-604) is assumed to be the first to identify the "seven penitential psalms," the earlier monastic culture of *compunctio cordis* gave them a much older recognition. The confessional postures of both Hilary of Poitiers and of Augustine already had the seven penitential psalms always before them.[26] Thus from the time of Anthony, the prototype of self-knowledge gained by psalmody, the therapeutic exercise of compunction, and the musical recitation of the psalms have long assimilated the Psalmist and the Prayer as one.[27]

21. Quoted by Tomas Spidlik, S.J., *The Spirituality of the Christian East,* trans. Anthony P. Gythiel (Kalamazoo, MI: Cistercian Publications, 1986), p. 196; *Apologia* 11.8-11; PG 6:463.

22. John Climacus, *The Ladder of Divine Ascent,* trans. Colm Luibheid and Norman Russell (New York: Paulist Press, 1982).

23. Spidlik, *The Spirituality of the Christian East,* p. 194.

24. Spidlik, *The Spirituality of the Christian East,* p. 196.

25. Joseph de Guibert, "La Componction du Coeur," *Revue d'Ascétique et Mystique* 15 (1934): 225-40.

26. The seven are: 6, 32, 38, 51, 102, 130, and 143. As late as Teresa of Avila in the sixteenth century the verse from Psalm 51 was repeated daily: "a broken and a contrite heart, O God, you will not despise." Even in the past generation, Columba Marmion, in his classic *Christ, the Ideal of the Monk,* devotes a whole section to compunction "as the habitual sense of contrition," linking it with self-renunciation, poverty, humility, and obedience.

27. Luke Dysinger, O.S.B., *Psalmody and Prayer in the Writings of Evagrius Ponticus* (Oxford: Oxford University Press, 2005), pp. 58-61.

III. Rupture of Ancient Penance in the Early Middle Ages

In May 589, the bishops of Spain and southern Gaul gathered at the council of Toledo to express their indignation that a new practice of penance had come into some of their churches without their permission. Actually it had infiltrated from the Celtic world, as requiring fines and punishment. Yet by 644-656, the kingdom of Clovis unanimously accepted penal penance, which became a private affair, not a public event, and pardon was taxable, not moral. Catalogues of tariffs were established to create a precise series of punishments. The penitential psalms could no longer serve any purpose, since it was now the confessor who gave absolution. Pardon was received *ipso facto* with the payment of the taxes. It was affirmed that once baptized a "religious" (i.e., a monk) received full remission of sins, since their vows now created an eternal pact with God. In some regions this rupture with traditional penance lasted until the end of the twelfth century.

IV. The Carolingian Personal Reforms Until the Lateran Council of 1215

A. Bede the Venerable (673-735)

Both public penance and privately taxed forms persisted throughout the Carolingian period (eighth to early eleventh century C.E.). But there were notable reformers. Bede the Venerable continued the practice of taxed penance as well as of compunction. He used the daily psalmody of his Abbot Ceolfrith — who is reputed to have recited the Psalter twice daily[28] — and composed his own précis of the Psalms or "Abbreviated Psalter." The latter was his *aide-memoire* to highlight the key themes of each psalm. Under Psalm 51, he quotes as key verses: 1, 2, 3, 4, 9, 11, 12, 14, 15, 17 [3, 4, 5, 6, 11, 13, 14, 16, 17, 19].[29] This précis became the prayer and heart of medieval devotion for laymen and monks alike centuries after Bede. It continued to feed and sustain the spirit of compunction throughout the later Middle Ages.

B. Alcuin of York (c. 735-804)

Alcuin of York, as a leader of the subsequent Carolingian reform, passes on Bede's précis to Bishop Arno, who had queried him about the penitential

28. Benedicta Ward, *Bede and the Psalter* (Fairacres, Oxford: SLG Press, 2002), p. 5.
29. Ward, *Bede and the Psalter,* pp. 33-34.

psalms. Alcuin provides him an *Enchiridion* or moral handbook on the subject, suggesting metaphorically "the universal moral aspects" of these psalms. He teaches the complete remission of sins received in baptism, as well as the continued gift of *penthos* or *compunctio,* which provides a chaste heart, a pure mind, and heavenly joy. He then cites nine uses of the Psalms, the first of which is "to do penance for your sins and to ask pardon by the confession of your sins," using the seven penitential psalms.[30] Later he quotes other psalms, urging the devotee to "sing these psalms with a pierced heart."[31]

Following patristic commentators, Alcuin reflects on the "fiftieth psalm" (Vulgate) as expressive of the year of Jubilee, a theme on which later medieval commentators will elaborate. This "time" is still one of mercy; hence the urgency of penance, but the future will be one of judgment, when repentance may come too late. "Complete repentance is to beware of the future and to lament of the past" (v. 5). Yet the psalm is predictive, as Theodoret had pointed out, and which Alcuin accepts: "foreseeing that sins cannot be redeemed except in the blood of Christ, he [David] praises his [God's] justice." In verse 7 [9], Alcuin interprets "washed with hyssop" to express the humility of Christ that heals the inflammatory disease of human pride. Divine absolution opens our lips to praise God (v. 17), and our inner pride is destroyed by "an afflicted spirit" and "a contrite heart." In his concluding prayer, Alcuin sees again that the essential nature of such contrition is the exercise of a humble spirit. He prepares the way forward for an increasingly personal prayer life. The Council of Chalons-sur-Saône in 813 affirmed that confession alone to God, without the intermission of a priest, was all that was demanded of the penitent. In spite of this, both for further Carolingian ecclesial reform, as well as for royal justice, public penance remained a prominent feature of the ninth to the eleventh centuries.

C. Anselm of Canterbury (1033-1109)

Anselm develops personal contrition even further than Alcuin. His *Prayers and Meditations,* as Sir Richard Southern observes, "stir up [the penitent's] own sense of horror, compunction, humiliation and self-abasement at the recollection of his sins, and then to communicate these feelings to the reader, by arranging his words [poetically] to give them their fullest possible effect. They

30. Alcuin of York, *De psalmorum usu liber cum variis formulis ad res quotidianas accomodatis,* PL 101:465, p. 1.

31. Alcuin of York, *De psalmorum usu liber,* p. 2.

were to be read [he said] 'not cursorily or quickly, but slowly and with profound and deliberate meditation.'"[32] There is more evidence than before that his newly personalized prayers, which he composed for lay persons — notably pious educated women — were to be recited in solitude, to stir up the mind from its inertia, to know oneself thoroughly, and so come to experience contrition and deepened love for God. Some might criticize his prayers as too long, but the concern of Anselm is not aesthetic so that lay persons would like them, but moral so that their hearts might be changed.[33] Likewise in the *Proslogion,* this external withdrawal and inner journey is explicit.[34] This withdrawal into one's self had been the great motive of monasticism. But now in Anselm's private prayers for the laity, he is opening this application wider into the ruling, secular society. Such prayers need also to exercise *excita mentem,* this stirring of the mind, to exercise *compunctio cordis,* moved both by fear of God and love for Him in self-examination. But the end result is the desire *in caelis* (longing for heaven).

Yet the mixed motives for both public and private taxable penance, as well as the cultivation of a more intimate personal prayer life, needed clarification. Baptism is only exercised once and, as a sacrament, is external. But penance is frequent, as we continue to sin, needing both the external sacrament of confession, as well as internally to practice the daily virtue of contrition. This was the motive for the twenty-first decree of the Fourth Lateran Council of 1215: "every Christian, of either sex, after attaining years of discretion, shall faithfully confess all his sins to his own priest at least once a year, and shall endeavor according to his ability to fulfill the penance enjoined on him, reverently receiving the sacrament of the Eucharist at least at Easter. . . ." Then using the metaphorical medical language of the early church, "the priest . . . in the manner of the skillful physician may pour wine and oil upon the wounds of the injured, diligently searching out the circumstances both of the sinner and the sin . . . employing various measures in order to heal the sick."

D. Peter Lombard (1100-1160)

Later medieval commentators build upon this personal devotion, in the context of which we now see how Lombard interpreted penance. For him it was a de-

32. Benedicta Ward, *The Prayers and Meditations of Saint Anselm, with the Proslogion* (London: Penguin, 1973), p. 9.

33. Ward, *The Prayers and Meditations of Saint Anselm,* p. 51.

34. Ward, *The Prayers and Meditations of Saint Anselm,* p. 52.

vice "for those placed far away [from God] so that they may approach him, following upon repentance." He introduces three aspects of penance: compunction of heart; confession of mouth; and satisfaction by means of a "work." He has before him the words of the apostle James: "Confess therefore your sins to one another" (James 5:16). Lombard is clear that it is not the priest who forgives sins; the confessor's role is rather to show God's forgiveness.

Peter Lombard's earliest work is a Gloss on the Psalter, as a revision of the gloss by Anselm of Laon (died 1117). Peter Lombard never intended this gloss to circulate, since it was for his own devotions. It is therefore not easy to trace how Lombard's later treatment on penance, given in the *Sentences*, guided his much earlier reflections on Psalm 51. Peter Lombard has two clear intentions for his Gloss on the Psalter: to teach what the great fathers have already taught, reciting frequently the works of Jerome, Augustine, Cassiodorus, and Alcuin; and to exercise repentance to celebrate the certitude of divine forgiveness. He divides the psalm into five parts: personal entreaty against divine judgment; the confidence of confession before a merciful God; the consequent desire to seek the restoration of others; that such in turn will also "teach" further restoration; and then to anticipate prophetically the building up of Jerusalem. Peter Lombard also interprets the charge of Matthew 16:19, to "bind and loose," as assigned by God to the priests, to show "the people that they are bound or loosed [by God]." But the remorse needed to seek freedom is only created by God's Spirit of love to have "a contrite and humbled heart" (Ps. 51:17 [19]). Alas, Peter Lombard realizes: "It can soundly be said that not all priests have the second of these keys — that is to say, the knowledge to discern [whether God has bound or loosed them], which is to be deplored and lamented." There are many priests who are unworthy confessors, so the penitent needs utmost care to select the right priest.

His contemporary commentator, the German Benedictine **Honorius Augustodunensis** (1075/80-c. 1156), in sharp contrast is much more syncretistic in his misunderstanding of Scripture. Honorius comments: "to be conformed to Christ, comes through imitation, so that through him we might return to the highest glory," which he notes is "the purpose of the whole book" (i.e., the Psalter).[35] "The psalm is written fourth of the penitentials," argues Honorius, "for man is made perfect through the four [Stoic] virtues: prudence, fortitude, justice, temperance. But seven penitential psalms are posited for this reason: sins are remitted through the seven gifts of the Holy Spirit. The first is applied to the spirit of fear, the second to the spirit of piety, the third to the spirit of knowl-

35. Honorius Augustodunensis, *Selectorum psalmorum expositio. Ex inedito ejus ejusdem amplissimo Commentario in Psalmos excerpta*, PL 172:271A, col. 0270.

edge, this fourth to the spirit of fortitude, which one is posited from the four cardinal virtues. In this psalm are particularly noted prayer and humility, through which especially sins are forgiven."[36] Honorius has wholly misunderstood biblical repentance! He is rather a Stoic using a biblical background, who did not think there was any need for the Cistercian movement of reform that occurred during his lifetime.[37]

V. Penance After the Lateran Council of 1215

A. Introduction

At the time of the Lateran Council[38] several new notions of penance begin to influence profoundly the subsequent history of commentaries on Psalm 51. First, already towards 1195-1200, **Raoul L'Ardent** was using the priestly pronouncement: *Ego te absolvo.* This went beyond the teaching of Peter Lombard, even though the gradual development of the priestly role of secret confession between confessor and penitent had been evolving for over more than a century.[39] Second, specific teaching on purgatory is now introduced, becoming a new theological category after 1170.[40] With this arises the self-conscious individual.[41] All of these aspects were expressive of secret individual confession to a priest. Alongside the ancient vocabulary of "compunction," the new term "contrition" *(contritio)* now appears, as a sincere form of individual repentance. This in turn becomes nuanced by the later use of "attrition," as if repentance now will always be expressed insufficiently. These penitential niceties are then elaborated later by Thomas Aquinas, who judges that "attrition" is enough to receive the Eucharist but inadequate to merit justification. Eventually, Duns Scotus (died 1308) introduces the novelty of "the two ways of justification": extra-sacramental, as very difficult to obtain but theoretically pos-

36. Honorius Augustodunensis, *Selectorum psalmorum expositio,* PL 172:282B.

37. Marcia Colish, *Medieval Foundations of the Western Intellectual Tradition, 400-1400* (New Haven and London: Yale University Press, 1998), p. 226.

38. This, the Fourth Lateran Council, is sometimes called "the General Council of Lateran" owing to the attendance by 71 patriarchs and metropolitans, 412 bishops, and 900 abbots and priors.

39. Cyrille Vogel, *Le Pécheur et la Pénitence au Moyen Âge* (Paris: Cerf, 1966), p. 174.

40. Jacques Le Goff, *The Birth of Purgatory,* trans. Arthur Goldhammer (London: Scholar Press, 1984), p. 135.

41. John F. Benton, "Consciousness of Self and Perception of Individuality," in *Renaissance and Renewal in the Twelfth Century,* ed. Robert L. Benson and Giles Constable with Carol D. Lanham (Toronto, Buffalo, London: University of Toronto Press, 1991), p. 284.

sible; and sacramental, which is easier and more certain.[42] These in turn create ecclesial divisions that the long deliberations of the Council of Trent in 1547 could not harmonize.

B. Thomas Aquinas (1225-74)

For the great doctor of the church, Psalm 51 [Vulgate 50] expresses literally "the words spoken of David" of "a universal matter," the forgiveness of sins we all need. "Now the work of God is fourfold: namely of the creation . . . of governance . . . of reparation . . . and of glorification." Following Dionysius, he observes the Psalter treats all four "works," expressed in differing genres. Here in Psalm 51 [50] there is the depreciative or confessional mode.[43] Like Peter Lombard, Thomas begins with the significance of this being the fiftieth psalm and its association with the fiftieth year of Jubilee (Leviticus 25) and the full remission of sins. He notes that David makes a clean break of his acts of adultery and murder with the comprehensive petition: "Have mercy on me!" This in turn reflects upon the divine character of God: to be "merciful." But the twofold effect of sin is both punishment and its stain upon the human heart. David seeks for both to be removed. He expresses this to God alone, for ultimately all sin is judged by God alone, and all sins have their root in original rebellion against God, as in the story of our first parents. Since God loves truth, confession is essential to communicate the sinful state in which we are. In turn, God reveals the secrets of the future through his servants the prophets, and Thomas sees then that this penitential psalm anticipates the cross of Christ and the revelation of the gospel in its later fullness. Like Alcuin, Thomas sees cleansing by hyssop as the remedy of pride, symbolizing a humble and repentant spirit. The effects of grace continue then with a new creation of "being," the healing of the mind, the restoration of God's presence, the experience of divine joy, and the indwelling of God's Spirit. The penitent is now able to make a lifelong commitment, "to teach transgressors God's ways" (v. 13), in the up-building of the church as the Zion of the Lord.[44] In reaction to his non-pastoral explanation, Duns Scotus and later theologians tilted the balance toward new doctrines of absolution and reassurance for the penitent.

42. Pierre Adries, *Dictionnaire de Spiritualité, Ascétique et Mystique* (Paris: Beauchesne, 1995), pp. 973-75, s.v. "penitence."

43. Thomas Aquinas, *Introduction to His Exposition of the Psalms of David,* trans. Hugh McDonald, The Aquinas Translation Project.

44. Aquinas, *Introduction,* Psalm 50 (51), pp. 1-30.

C. Conciliar Reformers

Psalm 51 becomes a focus for reforming movements in the Late Middle Ages. Reforming prelates such as **Ludolph of Saxony** (died 1314) and **Denys the Carthusian** (1402-71) treat penitence more evangelically. Ludolph "personalizes" the role of the penitent David,[45] while later, in tune with the new spirit of the *Devotio Moderna,* Denys would have us imitate the life and spirit of David as the archetype of the true penitent.[46] As a conciliar reformer, however, **Pierre d'Ailly** (1350-1420) more ingeniously interprets all seven penitential psalms as representing "seven steps" in Jacob's ladder, in which Psalm 51 represents the rung of "the love of cleanliness." This analogy might appear at first as more Pelagian than Augustinian, except that Pierre sees "the sixth step as living with mistrust in one's own virtue and confidence in the divine mercy" in his efforts to promote penance "virtuously."[47] It appears that Pierre is making use of Hugh of St. Victor's devotional handbook, *De modo orantis* 8, in his own handbook of the penitential psalms,[48] for in the last two chapters of Hugh's handbook (7 and 8) he enumerates how the spiritual affections are related to the psalms.

The common people, however, probably knew only two prayers: the *Paternoster* and the *Ave Maria.* One commentator, John Mirk, thought the seven petitions of the Lord's Prayer were each intended to contend in penance with the seven deadly sins; the first or Paternoster prayer being against pride.[49] For those with some literacy there was the book of *The Hours,* to enable recitation of the psalms both in singing and praying, and especially the penitential psalms.

D. Educated Lay Devotion: Dame Eleanor Hull (c. 1370–c. 1450)

An educated lay example is **Dame Eleanor Hull**. Born of a diplomatic family attached to John of Gaunt, Eleanor Hull was lady-in-waiting to the second wife

45. Ludolph of Saxony, *In Psalmos V. P. D. Ludolphi Cartusiani enarratio clarissima* (Monstrolii: Typis Cartusiae S. M. De Pratis, 1891), pp. 211-16.

46. Denys the Carthusian, *D. Cartusiani insigne opus commentariorum, in psalmos omnes Davidicos,* in Doctoris Ecstatici D. Dionysii Cartusiani Opera Omnia, vols. 5-6 (Monstrolii: Typis Cartusiae S. M. De Pratis, 1898), 6:39-48.

47. Pierre d'Ailly, *Deuote meditationes circa septe Psalmos penitentiales* (Paris, 1505), fols. A.i.r.-b.v.r 50.

48. Hugh of St. Victor, *De modo orantis,* PL 176:985B.

49. Quoted by John Bossy, "Christian Life in the Later Middle Ages: Prayers," translation of the Royal Historical Society, 1991, pp. 137-38.

of Henry IV. She received a good education, was widowed early, and devoted her later life to a priory of Benedictine nuns at Sopwell, attached to St. Albans.[50] She uses a translation probably made in the 1420s, in Middle English, from a French commentary of "The Seven Psalms," composed c. 1289-1307, possibly by Simon of Tournai, who comments on all seven penitential psalms.[51] The author begins with the historical context of the psalm title and the story of David and Bathsheba. Then the parable of the Publican and the Pharisee is cited, and the posture of Mary Magdalene is described, to illustrate proper attitudes of repentance. David himself is continually quoted as exemplifying all he says in the words of the psalm. So the sense given is that we are listening in on David's own confession before his Lord. Each biblical phrase is cited in Latin, as the language appropriate for worship. It distinguishes three "sacrifices" as appropriate to present to God: the sacrifice of contrition or penance; of justice; and of praise. By the first we are cleansed; by the second, we are justified; and by the third, we are made holy.[52]

E. Penitential Renaissance Reformers

As a Dominican lecturer of the convent of San Marco in Florence, **Girolamo Savonarola** (1452-98) won great popularity preaching boldly against the political corruption of the Medici dynasty in Florence. After the overthrow of the Medicis, Savonarola, the sole leader, attempted to set up a democratic city-republic in Florence. When ordered by Pope Alexander VI to stop preaching for church reform, he refused. Imprisoned and tortured, with dislocated and mangled arms, he wrote his two remarkable prison meditations on Psalms 51 ("Have mercy on me, O God") and 31 ("In you, Lord, have I hoped"), shortly before he died. Luther was inspired by them and published them in 1523.

In his commentary on Psalm 51, Savonarola makes no reference to his own cruel circumstances and no defense of his cause, only praying to God and referring to himself as *homo viator*, a sinner, alongside all of humanity. Finding no refuge on earth, he begins by confessing, "God alone is my refuge . . . he will not cast away his image." But his approach to God is as "the incomprehensible . . . your name is indescribable . . . you are your own wisdom,

50. Alexandra Barrett, ed., *The Seven Psalms: A Commentary on the Penitential Psalms translated from French into English by Dame Eleanor Hull* (Oxford: The Early English Text Society, by the Oxford University Press, 1995), pp. xxiii-xxxiii.

51. These dates refer to the Fall of Jerusalem under the Crusaders and the disbanding of the Knights Templar, both of which are referred to in the text.

52. Barrett, ed., *The Seven Psalms*, p. 132.

your own goodness, your own power, and your own supreme happiness," truly "I AM." "But what am I, except misery itself?"[53] As a dying man, he puts his trust alone in God's mercy and in Christ's resurrection. The popularity of his two texts was such that there were eleven Latin versions, six Italian and Spanish, and eleven German; the English text was reprinted nine times, all in the sixteenth century![54] Devout Christians, Catholic and Protestant alike, could only applaud his passion for purity of life, human helplessness in the face of sin, his appreciation of God's grace and his frequent appeal to the Scriptures. His posture before God is that of the Publican, not the Pharisee. In view of the dire circumstances in which he wrote from prison, tortured in body and mind, this is not a studious commentary, but the outpouring of the heart in distress and in search of comfort before God. It is like his meditations on Psalm 31, a climax to the long tradition of "the art of dying" *(ars moriendi)* in the fifteenth century.[55]

Very different is the cultural context of **John Fisher** (1469-1535), former tutor of Henry VIII. In his time he was regarded "as the most holy and learned prelate in Christendom." Yet two years later he was beheaded because he incurred the wrath of the king. Ordained in 1491, he became confessor of Lady Margaret Beaufort, mother of Henry VII. He persuaded her to found a professorship of divinity at both Oxford and Cambridge, and in 1504 he became Chancellor of Cambridge University and Bishop of Rochester. His focus was on the training of scholarly priests and preachers. Indeed, with his great learning,[56] after 1520 he was a virtual one-man counter-reformation in England, fighting first against Luther, then against the laxity of the clergy, and finally against Henry VIII himself, because of the king's incestuous marriage with Anne Boleyn. As Bishop of Rochester and confessor of Catherine the Queen, Henry's first wife, Fisher refused the dissolution of the marriage by divorce. Indeed he preached publicly against the divorce and acted boldly as a Nathan rebuking David over his Bathsheba. In the light of his fear of the Lord he accepted fearlessly a fate like that of John the Baptist. Anne Boleyn was his equivalent of Salome; Fisher's head was presented to Anne Boleyn right after his execution. Thus his involvement in Psalm 51 was politically deep indeed!

Like Savonarola, Fisher, awaiting his execution in 1535, also composed his

53. Girolamo Savonarola, *Prison Meditations on Psalms 51 and 31,* trans. and ed. John Patrick Donnelly, S.J. (Milwaukee: Marquette University Press, 1994), p. 31.

54. Savonarola, *Prison Meditations,* p. 21.

55. Donald Weinstein, "The Art of Dying Well and Popular Piety and Preaching in the Thought of Girolamo Savonarola," in *Life and Death in Fifteenth-Century Florence,* ed. Marcel Tetel et al. (Durham, NC: Duke University Press, 1989), pp. 89-104.

56. Twenty-six of his manuscripts survive, still unedited in complete form.

meditation on Psalm 51. The popularity of his work (twenty-one editions) indicates Fisher was not alone in his strong sense of moral conscience and devotion. Posthumously, his homilies on all seven penitential psalms were reprinted seven times. His meditations are significant in the history of doctrine, for they indicate a humanist understanding of sin, the sacrament of penance and atonement, all critically questioned at the beginning of the Reformation and rejected by contemporaries such as Luther and other reformers. As a Renaissance humanist, Fisher communicates an optimism that is directed less to the descent into the depths of sin than to the ascent into the blessedness of a merciful God. The wrath of God is redirected to the stupidity of the sinner who either rejects the medicine that will cure him or neglects the remedies he can apply as provided in the sacrament of penance — tears and cleansing purgation, confession to a priest, and charitable acts such as almsgiving and fasting, all receiving efficacy from Christ's blood. Doctrinal confusion is made by the frequent figural ways Fisher describes the plight of the sinner: like Jonah in the whale's belly, or the wounded man set upon by thieves in the parable of the Good Samaritan, or the deep pit in hell full of ravenous beasts.[57] These are depicted more like the horrific paintings of Hieronymus Bosch in the fourteenth century than the Biblical account. For Fisher, nothing brings people more quickly to eternal joy than "the purging of sins."

For him, Psalm 51 demonstrates that the penitent "sheds out of his breast the corrupt blood of sin as if from the cut throat of a beast or from a filthy wound lanced with a lance."[58] With due credit, Fisher never mentions the role of indulgences; instead he distinguishes three stages of penitence: contrition is the bud, confession is the flower, and satisfaction for sins is the fruit, the fulfillment of the other two, which becomes the main focus of his commentary. He links this satisfaction with the gift of the Holy Spirit that the apostles received at Pentecost; namely, "the fire of charity" to embolden them in their testimony. But Fisher reflects also the late medieval apocalyptic figuration of Hieronymus Bosch.

Fisher begins his homily on Psalm 51 with the medieval imagery of the penitential ladder, with its slender cord that hangs over a deep pit full of ferocious animals who eagerly await the fall of the pilgrim. Our only lifeline is our own body, which keeps us alive though it is so fragile. But God is merciful, who exercises mercy upon us inwardly and outwardly. So he can wipe us clean like a dirty tablet; he does this by bestowing on us three gifts: "to be sorry for your

57. Saint John Fisher, *Exposition of the Seven Penitential Psalms,* in modern English with an introduction by Anne Barbeau Gardiner (San Francisco: Ignatius Press, 1998), pp. 96-99.

58. Fisher, *Exposition of the Seven Penitential Psalms,* p. xxviii.

sin"; "to acknowledge your sin by weeping and wailing for it"; and to become "active in good works to do satisfaction."[59] The first step then is "contrition," in "scraping away" the filth of sin. The second step is in "tears that wash away sin." He quotes Chrysostom's treatise on compunction several times. The third step is then to ask God to make us clean by satisfaction. Fisher misquotes Luke 5:32, where Jesus says, "I came into this world not to call righteous people but sinners to penance."[60] Thus Fisher sums up what he understands to be the first part of the psalm: "first, what we as penitents should ask; secondly, what reasons we can make and bring for ourselves for the grant of our petition; and lastly, that we can trust without doubt to obtain what we ask, which our Lord grant us. Amen."

The second part of his homily is on living tentatively in the light of divine forgiveness, with both fear and forgiveness. The doctrine of justification is foreign to Fisher. Rather we must mingle hope and fear in a delicate balance, being neither presumptuous nor despairing.[61] The three uses of the term "Spirit" in the psalm express three stages of the Holy Spirit's presence within us: given us in infant baptism and in our life of Pelagian innocence as children; given with our penitence as adults; and, with the gift of confirmation, given by the growth of the virtuous life in our goal of perfection.[62] In fact, Fisher does not really give us a textual commentary at all, but a pious homily upon contemporary late-fifteenth-century attitudes of "Christian" humanism. As we have seen in other commentaries, Fisher and his pre-Reformation culture are light years away from Calvin's commentary on the Psalms; but to trace penitence from the Reformation is another chapter for another book.

Part II: Voice of the Psalmist: Translation

A psalm of David when the prophet Nathan came to him after David had committed adultery with Bathsheba.

1 Be gracious to me, God, according to your unfailing love;
according to your abundant compassion blot out my transgressions.[63]

59. Fisher, *Exposition of the Seven Penitential Psalms,* pp. 102-3.

60. Fisher, *Exposition of the Seven Penitential Psalms,* p. 109.

61. Fisher, *Exposition of the Seven Penitential Psalms,* pp. 116-17.

62. Fisher, *Exposition of the Seven Penitential Psalms,* p. 122.

63. LXX, followed by *Psalterium Romanum* and the *Psalterium Gallicanum,* read sing. *piš'ī,* but Tg, Peshitta, and *Psalterium iuxta Hebraeos* agree with MT's more difficult pl.; the other words for sin are singular.

2 Thoroughly[64] wash me from[65] my iniquity
  and pronounce me clean[66] from my sin.
3 For my transgressions I know,[67]
  and my sin is always before me.[68]
4 Against[69] you, you only, have I sinned, and what is evil in your sight I did;
  so you are just[70] when you speak,[71] and blameless when you judge.
5 Behold, I was brought forth in iniquity,
  and in sin my mother conceived me.
6 Behold, truth you desired[72] in the covered place;[73]
  And in the bottled-up place you were teaching me wisdom.
7 Purge[74] me with hyssop that[75] I may be clean;
  wash me that I may be whiter than snow.
8 Let me hear[76] joy and gladness;
  let the bones you have crushed rejoice.
9 Hide your face from my sins
  and all my iniquities blot out.
10 A clean heart, God, create for me,
  and a steadfast spirit renew within me.
11 Do not cast me from your presence,
  nor take your spirit of holiness[77] from me.
12 Restore to me the joy of your salvation,

64. Q has an apocopated form, *hereb;* K has its full form *harbēh.*

65. Prep. implies an elided "cleanse" (*IBHS,* p. 224, P. 1.4.3d).

66. *Piel* is construed as delocutive (*IBHS,* p. 403, P. 24.2g).

67. Construed as a progressive impf., expressing a repeated situation, a rare form found elsewhere only in Job 9:21 (*IBHS,* p. 504, P. 31.3b).

68. *Lᵉnegdî* is too weakly supported (in only a few mss.) to be followed.

69. "Against" glosses ambiguous *lameḏ* (*IBHS,* p. 206, P. 11.2.10d).

70. Qal stative form (*IBHS,* pp. 364f., 372, PP. 22.2.2; 22.4c).

71. The unique Qal inf. cstr. *bᵉḏoḇreḵā* was probably created to create an assonance with its parallel *bᵉšop̱ṭeḵā,* causing its pointing as a noun, *biḏ ᵉḇāreḵā* in Heb. mss., LXX, Sym. (cf. Ps. 119:160).

72. Construing the perf. as preterite, interpreting "smeared over" and "bottled up" as a metonymy for the womb.

73. Trad. "the inner parts."

74. Construing the impf. as injunctive (*IBHS,* p. 509, P. 31.5b).

75. *Waw* with the impf. after a volitional form often indicates purpose.

76. Construed as a tolerative Hiphil (*IBHS,* pp. 441, 447, PP. 27.3b; 27.5c).

77. "Your holy spirit" is a valid gloss, but Christian readers mistakenly think it connotes the Holy Spirit's regenerating, indwelling, and sealing believers.

and let a willing[78] spirit sustain[79] me.
13 Let me teach transgressors your ways,
that sinners may turn back to you.
14 Save me from bloodguilt, O God, the God who saves me,
and my tongue will shout out loud your righteousness.
15 O Lord, open my lips,
and my mouth will declare your praise.
16 Surely, you would not desire[80] a sacrifice, or I would offer[81] it;
a burnt offering you would not favor.
17 The sacrifices[82] of God are a broken spirit;
a broken and contrite heart, God, you will not despise.
18 Prosper, in your favor, Zion;
let the walls of Jerusalem be built.[83]
19 Then you will delight in[84] the sacrifices of righteousness,
in burnt offerings offered whole;
then bulls will be offered on your altar.
Psalm 52:1 For the director of music.

Part III: Commentary

I. Introduction

A. Form

From the post-Nicene period to the present, Psalm 51 has been seen as a penitential psalm (cf. Pss. 32, 38, 51, 102, 130, 143), a species of lament/petition psalm

78. LXX opts for the other meaning of *nāḏîḇ*, glossing it by *hēgemonikos*, "noble."

79. Construing *ṯismᵉḵēnî* as jussive due to volitional parallels in (vv. 10-12 [12-14]).

80. Construed as an impf. of obligation (*IBHS*, p. 508, P. 31.4g); in the future God will delight in sacrifices (v. 19 [21]).

81. Cohortative introduces the apodosis after the implicitly conditional clause (*IBHS*, p. 575, P. 34.5.2).

82. MT is commonly emended from *ziḇḥê* ("sacrifices [of God]) to *zibḥi* ("my sacrifice" [God]), because: pl. does not accord well with sing. "broken spirit"; its didactic tone is out of place; it interrupts the "I-Thou" relationship of the psalm, especially with B verset where "God" is vocative. But these very reasons make it difficult to explain away the MT, and a didactic element may occur in testimony (cf. Ps. 34 with its word of testimony [vv. 1-7 (2-8)] followed by teaching [vv. 8-22 (9-23)]).

83. The parallel imperative suggests form is 3rd fem. sing. jussive.

84. Construed as an impf. of specific future in the conceptual apodosis (*IBHS*, pp. 511-13, P. 31.6.2).

(see pp. 197-98); its closest analogies are Psalm 130 and the Prayer of Manasseh. Invariably, in a penitential psalm the psalmist is in distress born out of a consciousness of sin and longs and hopes that the God of mercy will intervene. The foe is spiritual: sin and guilt. As a lament psalm, its motifs are: address to God (v. 1a [3a]), lament (vv. 3-6 [5-8]), petition (vv. 7-12 [9-14]) and praise (vv. 13-19 [15-21]). Verses 1-2 [3-4] introduce his petitions.

B. Structure

These motifs are developed with marvelous symmetries of alternating and chiastic structures. The two-verse introduction of personal petition is matched by a two-verse epilogue of petition for national renewal (vv. 18-19 [20-21]). After the two-verse introduction the lament/confession escalates to four verses (vv. 3-6 [5-8]), the petition, to six verses (vv. 7-12 [9-14]); and praise, to seven — the number of perfection. All the stanzas/motifs have two strophes of mostly equal length. As Aquinas recognized, the prefatory petitions are twofold: for forgiveness and so salvation from punishment (v. 1 [3]) and cleansing from the stain of sin's guilt (v. 2 [4]). The lament consists of confessions of overt sin (vv. 3-4 [5-6]) and of the petitioner's sinful nature (vv. 5-6 [7-8]); the petitions are for forgiveness of sins (vv. 7-9 [9-11], matching vv. 3-4) and for renewal of spirit (vv. 10-12 [12-14], matching vv. 5-6); the praise consists of personal praise (vv. 13-17 [15-19) and of national praise (vv. 18-19 [20-21]). Here's a sketch of this analysis:

I. Superscript	
II. Invocation and Prefatory Petitions (2 verses)	vv. 1-2
A. For forgiveness	v. 1
B. For cleansing	v. 2
III. Confession (4 verses)	vv. 3-6[85]
A. Of sins (2 verses)	vv. 3-4
1. Confession of personal guilt	v. 3
2. Confession of sinning against God	v. 4
B. Of moral impotence (2 verses)	vv. 5-6
1. Of sinful nature	v. 5
2. Of moral nature	v. 6
IV. Petitions (6 verses)	vv. 7-12
A. For forgiveness of sins (3 verses)	vv. 7-9
1. For cleansing from stain of guilt	v. 7

85. Five lines.

2. For word of absolution	v. 8
3. For forgiveness without punishment	v. 9
B. For spiritual renewal (3 verses)	vv. 10-12
1. For steadfast spirit	v. 10
2. For retaining God's spirit of holiness	v. 11
3. For a willing spirit	v. 12
V. Vow of Praise (7 verses)	vv. 13-19
A. Personal praise (5 verses)	vv. 13-17
1. Word of praise	vv. 13-15
2. Sacrifice of praise	vv. 16-17
B. National praise (2 verses)	vv. 18-19
1. Condition: prosperity of Zion	v. 18
2. Consequence: Zion's praise	v. 19
VI. Subscript	Ps. 52 superscript A

Psalms are like pieces of embroidery with overlapping designs. *TNIV Study Bible,* counting lines, not verses, of poetry, analyzes the body of the psalm between the introduction and epilogue, each of two lines, into four stanzas of five lines (3-6, counting vv. 4a and b as two lines), of three lines (vv. 7-9), of three lines (vv. 10-12), and of five lines (vv. 13-17).[86] Note also this chiasm. The first half of eight lines pertains to petitions for forgiveness and cleansing (5 + 3), and the second half of eight lines pertains to petitions for spiritual renewal and praise (3 + 5). In sum, the petitions for forgiveness and cleansing aim to bring God praise both in and from Zion for his benevolent attributes (see Exod. 34:6).[87] Like its ancient Near Eastern parallels the prayer is passionate but probably not spontaneous. The poet consciously structures its symmetries to delight the God of form and beauty and to provide the penitent with a memorable model of theological richness when asking God to be forgiven and restored to the temple.[88]

C. Message

Of all the commentators cited in our survey, Aquinas best traces the psalm's argument. The psalm's teachings on the sinner's penitence and God's forgiveness

86. *TNIV Study Bible* (Grand Rapids: Zondervan, 2003), p. 887.

87. For a somewhat different analysis of the chiasm see David Covington, "Psalm 51: Repenter's Guide," *The Journal of Biblical Counseling* 20 (2001): 21-99.

88. As an example of commentators before the advent of rhetorical criticism, Artur Weiser (*Psalms* [London: SCM, 1962], p. 401) says: "There is no evidence of a homogeneous construction of the strophes"!

are so rich and mingled that they are like the opalescent mixing of colors in a costly pearl. Viewing the psalm holistically, however, one can say that its message to the people of God is that the walls of Zion, a synecdoche and symbol of the kingdom of God, can only be built by penitent sinners. The penitent openly and truly confess their sin and trust their merciful God to forgive their sin through Christ's sacrifice and to cleanse their guilty conscience through his Holy Spirit.

II. Exegesis

A. Superscript

As for genre and authorship, see pages 86-90. Psalm 51 is the first of a collection of eighteen Davidic psalms within the Elohistic Psalter (see p. 101).[89] As for the historical situation (cf. 2 Sam. 11:4; 12:1), the psalm represents David while he awaits God's verdict (between 2 Sam. 12:13a and 12:13b).[90] Several theological reflections are noteworthy. 1) "David's narrative," says E. F. Harrison, confirms that "history has shown that it is easier for men to fight their way to eminence than to retain it. David now possessing absolute power over the realm, faces a test more severe than the sorest battle."[91] 2) His adultery, a sin of passion, and his murder, a coldly calculated, premeditated crime,[92] are both capital offenses (Deut. 22:23-24; Num. 35:19f.), yet David is forgiven and restored to fellowship with God. 3) Moreover, neither Bathsheba's purity nor Uriah's life can be restored. 4) God extends mercy to the sinner who, when confronted with God's word, expresses his faith in God by truly confessing and renouncing sin (Prov. 28:13). 5) True confession, as Augustine saw, is as public as the sin in order to develop a person's spiritual life and to teach others of God's grace. 6) Cleansing is so thorough and forgiveness so great that out of adultery sprang the blessed Solomon. 7) The story of David's forgiveness (2 Sam. 12) is part of the Primary History (Genesis–2 Kings [not Ruth]), which

89. Since the Elohistic psalter is characterized by the number 42 (42 psalms beginning at Ps. 42), it probably was Psalm 51 when the Psalter was finally edited.

90. A Qumran scroll of Samuel has a blank space at the end of 2 Samuel 12:12, according to S. Talmon, "Mizmorîm Hisoniyyum Ba-Lason Ha-Ibrit Mi-Qumran" (*Tarbiz* 35 [1966]: 214-34; cf. *Textus* 5 [1966]: 11-21), to direct the reader to Psalm 51.

91. E. F. Harrison, "A Study of Psalm 51," *BibSac* 92, no. 365 (1935): 26-27.

92. Counting four days to send a messenger from Jerusalem to Ammon-Rabbah to fetch Uriah from the battle, three nights for Uriah to stay in Jerusalem, and four days for Uriah to return to the battle.

includes the Mosaic Law, and so is part of Torah, qualifying the laws of Deuteronomy 22:23; Numbers 35:19f.[93]

B. Address and Prefatory Petitions

David may have originally addressed God by the name *yhwh ("I AM")* in verses 1, 10, 14, and 17 [3, 12, 16, 11] and the editor of the Elohistic Psalter (Ps. 42–83) changed it to *ʾᵉlōhîm* ("God"). In his prefatory petition, David recognizes, as Aquinas rightly interpreted him, "the twofold effect of sin is both punishment and its stain upon the human heart" (see p. 457). David seeks for both forensic or legal forgiveness to escape God's wrath for violating his holiness, and inward purging of his conscience to enable him to praise and worship. He uses three hyponyms for the semantic field of sin: the same triad as in Psalm 32:5. Etymologically, the triad of words for sin (cf. Ps. 32:5) — "transgression" *(pᵉšāʿāî),* "iniquity" *(ʿᵃwōnî),* "sin" *(ḥaṭṭāʾî)* — assume a standard/norm/law that has been fractured.[94] "Transgression" *(pešaʿ),* "a willful, knowledgeable violation of a norm or standard" (*ABD* 6:32), is a willful breach of trust; "the disruption of an alliance through violation of covenant."[95] Picture it as a raised fist against God's standard. "Iniquity" *(ʿāwōn),* the most holistic term, encompasses both religious and/or ethical crimes and the resulting guilt. Picture it as twisting or bending something straight, or of diverging/deviating from a standard.[96] "Sin *(ḥaṭṭâ)* means "miss (mark)," "fall short,"[97] "a disqualifying error,"[98] a disqualifying offense "against someone with whom one stands in an institutionalized community relationship."[99] Since one's relationships to God and to his community are inseparable (cf. Prov. 3:27-35), sin is ultimately against God and his word. Picture it as jumping up to reach a bar and being disqualified for falling short of it.

Standing in the deep, dark hole of his sin, David looks up and sees stars of God's grace that those who stand in the noonday sunlight of their own self-righteousness never see. He matches the triad of terms for sins with a triad of

93. B. K. Waltke with C. Yu, *An Old Testament Theology: An Exegetical, Thematic and Canonical Approach* (Grand Rapids: Zondervan, 2007).

94. The Greek word for sin, *anomia,* means "without law."

95. Eugene Carpenter and Michael A. Grisanti, *NIDOTTE,* 3:707, s.v. *pešaʿ.*

96. R. Knierim, *TLOT,* 2:862, s.v. *ʿāwōn.*

97. For its non-theological sense of missing a standard or way see Judg. 20:16; Job 5:24; Prov. 8:36; 19:2.

98. M. Saebø, *TLOT,* 1:406-8, s.v. *ḥṭʾ.*

99. K. Koch, *TDOT,* 4:311.

terms for grace (cf. Exod. 34:6): "Be gracious to me" (*ḥonnēnî*, "bestow a favor that cannot be claimed," see Ps. 4:1 [2]), "according to your loving kindness" (*kᵉḥasdeḵā*, "help for the helpless," see Ps. 23:6), "according to your abundant mercy" *(kᵉrōḇ raḥᵃmeyḵā)*. "Mercy" denotes the tender yearnings, affections, and love by a superior for a helpless inferior rooted in a "natural" bond by God's common grace, as a mother for her child, or special grace, as the Father for the child he begat through the Holy Spirit. The depth of this love is reflected in its connection with "womb" (*reḥem/raḥam*, cf. Jer. 21:7).[100] "Abounding" *(rōb)* is added to show that God's compassion exceeds natural human compassion. He even extends his mercy to those who spit in his face. By laying hold of the altar, as it were, the penitent's cry for mercy admits his crime and deserved punishment; David throws himself headlong upon the mercy of God, risking everything in the process. If the God of Israel's law does not extend mercy, that law, which a true prophet such as Nathan and a priest such as Zadok will uphold, demands his death.

1. For Forgiveness v. 1

These two triads are matched by a triad of petitions: "blot out," "wash," "launder." *Māḥâ (blot out)* means "to wipe clean" (a dish, mouth, or tears [2 Kings 21:13; Prov. 30:20; Isa. 25:8]); "to blot out" or "obliterate" (a writing or remembrance of some sort [Exod. 32:32; Num. 5:23; Deut. 9:14; Neh. 13:14; Ps. 69:28 (29)]). This imagery draws upon the way kings kept records of the events in their realm (cf. Pss. 56:8 [9]; 87:6; 130:3 [a penitential psalm]; 139:16; cf. 109:13-15; Isa. 44:22). Picture a medieval palimpsest. With a knife, monks erased vellum on which Roman writers had written lascivious literature and rewrote over it texts of Scripture or of a sacred work, such as St. Augustine's *Confessions.*[101]

2. For Cleansing v. 2 [4]

Thoroughly (*harbēh*, see n. 64) derives from the same root as "abundant" *(rbb)* in verse 1. *Wash me* (*kabbᵉsēnî*, literally, "launder me") refers to treading, kneading, or beating to make the garment clean with lye and soap (cf. Jer. 2:22);[102] his guilty conscience is like a soiled garment. *Cleanse me (ṭahᵃrēnî)* refers to physical, ethical, and/or, as here, ritual purification (see v. 7 [9]).[103] This cleansing

100. Coppes, *TWOT*, 2:841, s.v. *raḥam*.

101. For this imagery of God's keeping see pp. 461-62.

102. *Rāḥaṣ* means "to wash by rinsing."

103. H.-J. Hermisson, *Sprache und Ritus im altisraelitischen Kult* (Neukirchen-Vluyn: Neukirchener Verlag, 1965), pp. 84-99.

will purge his stained conscience (see v. 7 [9]). The penitent feels like a stinking garment, unfit for worship with other saints before the holy God.

C. Confessions vv. 3-6 [5-8]

The true penitent does not recall his past good works to lessen the weight of guilt or blame others. David, probably intentionally, says nothing of Bathsheba's possible complicity. Tamar cried out against Amnon's wrong (cf. 2 Sam. 13:9-19), but there is no indication that Bathsheba cried out against David (2 Sam. 11:4-5; cf. Deut. 22:22-24).

1. Of Sins vv. 3-4 [5-6]

a. Consciousness of sin v. 3 [5]

"For" *(kî)* explains his prefatory petitions. Emphatic "I" *(ʾᵃnî)* sounds the note of personal confession, becoming louder and louder by the repetition of "my,"[104] and with a clashing cymbal: *I know* (*ʾēḏāʿ*, see n. 67; Pss. 1:6; 4:4 [5]) and *before me continually* (*negdî tāmîḏ*, see Ps. 16:8). True repentance is not a dead knowledge of sin committed, but a living, never-at-rest, painful consciousness of it (Isa. 59:12 [see also Pss. 32:4; 40:12] [13, aB, b]).[105]

b. Confession Proper v. 4 [6]

Since by definition the terms for sin imply God's standard (see above), all sin is ultimately against God, though it involves his community as well.[106] So only God can judge and forgive sin (cf. Gen. 20:6; 39:9; Mark 2:2-7), as Aquinas understood (p. 457).[107] David does not deny he sinned against God's community (see "save me from bloodguilt, God" [v. 14]), but the community separates itself from God if it refuses to unite with God to extend mercy and to pardon the

104. The first and last words also resonant with the *î* sound of the pronoun.

105. F. Delitzsch, *Psalms*, vol. 5 in C. F. Keil and F. Delitzsch, *Commentary on the Old Testament*, trans. Francis Bolton (Peabody, MA: Hendrickson, 1996), p. 366.

106. As a boy, Mother allowed me to play touch football on a city sidewalk with one restriction: "Do not kick the ball." Unable to resist the temptation, I booted the ball — right through my neighbor's window. I sinned against her, and she dished out the punishment, obliging me to make restitution for the damage I did my neighbor.

107. The teachers of the Law recognized that when Jesus forgave the paralyzed man his sin, he assumed the role of God (Mark 2:2-7).

most guilty penitent.[108] Nathan's rebuke subordinates David's wrong against Uriah to his sin against God for despising his word (see 2 Sam. 12:9, 10). David responded: "I sinned against *I AM*" (2 Sam. 12:13). Initial *against you (l^{e}ḵā),* underscored by *you only (l^{e}ḇadd^{e}ḵā),* emphatically makes the point. *L^{e}ḇadd^{e}ḵā,* from the root I. *bdd* ("to separate, isolate"), disassociates God from other social connections (cf. Rom. 3:4). *And what is evil in your sight* (*w^{e}hāraʿ,* see Ps. 23:4) *I did* (*ʿāśîṯî,* see Ps. 1:3; cf. 2 Sam. 11:27; 12:9) clarifies the point. *So that* (*l^{e}maʿan,* Ps. 23:3) elides the full thought: "I say this so that" (see n. 70).[109] Whatever your sentence, God, *you are just* for only you have the right to make that judgment. *You are blameless (tizkeh) when you judge (b^{e}šop̱ṭeḵā)* further clarifies the thought (cf. Job 15:14; 25:4). *Zakâ* means simply "be (morally) clear, clean, pure." *When you speak,* as the parallel shows, refers to God's verdict.[110] "When you speak" and "when you judge" *(bdbrk//bšpṭk)* breaks up a stereotyped phrase that means "you are just and blameless in pronouncing sentence."[111]

2. *Of Moral Impotence vv. 5-6 [7-8]*

The second confession sets in sharp relief the human contradiction: congenitally sinful (v. 5 [7]) and morally aware (v. 6 [8]). The paradox is held together by four features: the introductory interjections, "behold"; synonyms for gestation ("brought forth," "conceived") and metonymies for the womb: "smeared-over-place" and "bottled-up-place"; and the sharp contrast between what "I am" and "you desire."[112]

108. Bathsheba probably was Ahithophel the Gileonite's granddaughter, for she was the daughter of the famous war hero Eliam son of Ahithophel and wife of the equally famous war hero Uriah (cf. 2 Sam. 11:3; 23:34). If so, Ahithophel probably never forgave David and counseled Absalom to defile his father's wives (2 Sam. 16:21). Probably many in the nation, not only Eliam, never forgave David and fought for Absalom against David.

109. The full expression is *l^{e}maʿan ʾašer* ("to the end that," GKC, 165b). Some think the telic force means — to paraphrase this point of view — "I now realize I sinned in order to apprehend the absoluteness of your law, God." The notion, however, that his sin brings glory to God mitigates the confession and seems unlikely. Others think it expresses a logical consequence: "so that, wherefore, since," but that notion is questionable.

110. H.-J. Krause, *Psalmen* (BKAT 15:1; Neukirchen-Vluyn: Neukirchener Verlag, 1966), p. 386.

111. J. S. Kselman, "A Note on Ps 51:6," *CBQ* 39 (1977): 251-53.

112. Verses 4B-6 are linked by adverbial phases involving *ḇ*: terminally in 4Ba and 4Bb; initially in 5A and 5B and chiastically in 6A (word final) and 6B (word initial).

a. Of Sinful Nature v. 5 [7]

David represents his gestation by the temporal merism of his parturition from the womb (v. 5a) and his conception within it (v. 5b). *Behold (hēn)* invites the audience to join the poet in observing the sonar graph of the unborn's spiritual state: *in iniquity* (*bᵉʿāwôn,* see v. 2 [4]a) *I was brought forth (ḥôlāltî).* His findings anticipate Freud by almost two millennia. *Ḥûl* ("to writhe in childbirth") begins with first contractions of childbirth and ceases with the baby's parturition from the mother's body (cf. Prov. 25:23; 26:10; John 16:21).[113] The divine passive assumes *I AM* is the agent. *And in sin* (*ûbᵉḥēṭʾ,* see v. 4 [6]b) *my mother conceived me (yeḥᵉmaṯᵉnî ʾimmî).* Dalglish rightly comments: "*bᵉḥēṭʾ* ["in sin"] should properly be taken either to describe the status of the generating mother or else be referred generally to the embryological development resulting in transplanting the predicate of sinfulness to the child."[114] *Yḥm* (literally, "to be hot") for human conception, instead of the normal word *hārâ,* is extraordinary, for it is otherwise used only of animals: "to rut and conceive" (Gen. 30:38; 30:41 [2x]; 31:10), and so supports the monastic notion that a mother's activity in conceiving is sinful. But that notion contradicts the positive values that the Old Testament otherwise puts upon bearing children (Gen. 1:28; 9:1, 7; Ps. 127:3, 5, passim). The most holy — the high priest, by birth, and the Nazirite, by choice — were not celibate. Moreover, David is confessing his sin, not his mother's. Zink, however, plausibly suggests that the Old Testament does not make a clear distinction between ritual uncleanness and moral sin, and that since conception in connection with the emission of semen and childbirth in connection with blood make the married partners unclean, the psalmist associates the human propensity toward sin with the ritual uncleanness of childbirth (Lev. 12; 15:18 and 16:18). He argues that moral sin and ritual uncleanness both require a sin offering.[115] Moreover, David is asking for both forgiveness for his sin and for cultic cleansing from the stain of sin. One must be careful, however, not to confound moral guilt with ceremonial uncleanness. In sum, the need for ritual cleansing symbolizes humanity's original sin due to their rebellion in Adam against God's word.[116] With David the penitent live a life of dependence upon

113. A. Baumann, *TDOT,* 4:345, s.v. *ḥûl.*

114. Edward R. Dalglish, *Psalm 51 in the Light of Ancient Near Eastern Patternism* (Leiden: E. J. Brill, 1962), p. 121.

115. J. K. Zink, "Uncleanness and Sin: A Study of Job 14:4 and Psalm 51:7," *VT* 17, no. 3 (1967): 34-60.

116. OT texts pertaining to humanity's original sinfulness include: 1 Kings 8:46; Job 4:17; Pss. 130:3; 143:2; Prov. 20:9; Eccl. 7:20; Jer. 7:9; from birth, Gen. 6:5; 8:21; Ps. 58:3 [4]; Job 14:4; 15:14; 25:4.

God's favor to save them from their original sin that contaminates every aspect of their being. The New Testament also teaches original sin.[117] David applies this doctrine to himself; his full thought is: "When my mother conceived me she was ritually unclean and I was in a state of moral sin."

b. Of Moral Impotence v. 6 [8]

David continues his spiritual sonar graph, repeating *behold (hēn)*. Observe the awful antithesis: *truth you desired (ʾᵉmeṯ ḥāp̄aṣtā)*. The prominent position of truth (*ʾemeṯ*, see 19:9 [10]) strikingly contrasts with the prominent "iniquity" (*ʿāwôn*, v. 5 [7]). *Ḥāp̄ēṣ* ("delight in," see Ps. 1:2; 22:8 [9]) speaks of "desire." The phrase *baṭṭūḥôṯ* ("in the covered place") derives from *ṭûaḥ*, "to plaster or to coat something." Its Arabic and Ethiopic cognates mean respectively to "to smear over" and "to spread, cover." English versions commonly gloss it by "inward parts." But what inward parts: entrails, kidneys, conscience,[118] or womb? The context of verse 6 [8] and its parallel *ûbᵉsāṯūm* ("in the bottled up/shut up place") suggests these adjectival substantives are metonymies for the closed chamber of the womb.[119] There *you were causing me to know (tôḏîʿēnî) wisdom (ḥoḵmâ)*. "Wisdom" means "social skill," which entails religious and ethical knowledge that is rooted in the fear of *I AM*.[120] Both David's sin and his knowledge of truth/wisdom are ever before him; this is the dilemma of every person. Like Israel at Sinai, he did what he resolved not to do and he did not do and what he wanted to do.[121] He sinned against the God-given moral knowledge of conscience, as well as despising God's word (2 Sam. 12:14).[122] In conclusion, note that the spiritual sonar graph shows the unborn is a spiritual being, not just fetal tissue.

117. NT texts include: John 9:34; Rom. 3:9-20; 5:12; Eph. 2:3.

118. So *HALOT*, 2:372f., s.v. *ṭwḥ* and *ṭūḥôṯ*.

119. Dalglish, *Psalm 51*, p. 124.

120. B. Waltke, *The Book of Proverbs: Chapters 1–15* (NICOT; Grand Rapids: Eerdmans, 2004), pp. 76-78.

121. See Dennis E. Johnson, "The Function of Romans 7:13-25 in Paul's Argument for the Law's Impotence and the Spirit's Power, and Its Bearing on the Identity of the Schizophrenic 'I,'" in *Resurrection and Eschatology: Essays in Honor of Richard B. Gaffin, Jr.*, ed. Lane G. Tipton and Jeffrey C. Waddington (Phillipsburg, NJ: P. & R. Publishing, 2008), pp. 3-59.

122. Dalglish, *Psalm 51*, p. 127.

D. Petitions vv. 7-11 [9-13]

1. For Forgiveness and Cleansing vv. 7-9 [9-11]

The introductory petitions for forgiveness (v. 1) and cleansing (v. 2) are now reversed: cleansing (v. 7 [9]), forgiveness (v. 9 [11]). The petition for absolution unites them (v. 8). Whether the language is literal or metaphorical, the liturgy envisioned included the priest's ablution ritual with hyssop (v. 7) and the prophet's word of absolution (v. 8).

a. Cleanse v. 7 [9]

Purge me (*tᵉḥaṭṭᵉʾēnî,* literally, "de-sin me";[123] see v. 2 [4]) means "take away the mass of sin." *With hyssop (ḇᵉʾēzôḇ)*[124] alludes to two liturgical rituals that cleanse by sprinkling blood: of the leper's house (Lev. 14:49, 52) and of a person defiled by a corpse (Num. 19:19).[125] Alcuin of York insightfully suggests that these two rituals, which signify cleansing from defilement, are chosen to express the humility of Christ that heals the inflammatory disease of human pride (see p. 453). The Targum paraphrases: "Sprinkle on me as the priest who sprinkles with hyssop *the blood of the sacrifice* on the leper or the water of the ashes of the red heifer on the person defiled."[126] Atonement by death must be made to remove the guilt. These atoning sacrifices foreshadow the sacrifice of Christ (Heb. 9:11-12), as Aquinas also taught (see p. 457).[127] Expressing his faith in God's sacrificial system, he says: *and I will be clean* (*wᵉʾeṭhār,* see v. 4 [6]b). The parallel adds the notion of lavation: *wash me* (*tᵉḵabbᵉsēnî,* see v. 2 [4]a) *and I will be whiter than snow (ûmiššeleg ʾalbîn).* "Color symbolism seizes upon red as the color of sin probably by its association with bloodshed (cf. Ps. 51:14 [16]; Isa. 1:18)."[128]

123. A Piel privative denominative (*IBHS,* p. 412, P. 24.4f).

124. Hyssop is the *origanum syriacum, aegyptiacum,* also known as marjoram. Its leaves were used as a spice and medicinally as a tonic, carminative (i.e., to expel gas from the alimentary tract), and digestive aid. Its hairy leaves, which can absorb liquids, were tied into bunches and used as sprinklers.

125. Seven of the ten occurrences of hyssop occur in these rituals, and of the few incidences of *ḥṭʾ,* five occur in Numbers 19 and half of these in cleansing the defiled person.

126. Cited by M. Buttenwieser, *The Psalms Chronically Treated with a New Translation* (New York: Ktav, 1969), p. 193.

127. David did not offer a sin offering because his crimes were not unintentional (see Lev. 4).

128. *Dictionary of Biblical Imagery,* ed. L. Ryken, J. C. Wilhoit, and T. Longman III (Downers Grove, IL: IVP Academic, 1998), p. 302. Dalglish (*Psalm 51,* pp. 138f.) thinks it stands opposite to black for mourning, but his data is not convincing.

b. Absolve v. 8 [10]

Let me hear (*tašmîʿēnî,* see 4:1 [2], 3 [4]) *joy* (*śāśôn*) *and gladness* (*wᵉśimḥâ*). The collocation of joy and gladness denotes enthusiastic celebration (Esther 8:16-17; cf. Ps. 105:43; Jer. 7:34; 16:9; 25:10; 33:11). The inapposite juxtaposition of physical "cause to hear," with the psychological "joy and gladness," signals a metonymy of effect; the cause is the prophet's and or priest's word of absolution. The parallel injunction, *Let . . . rejoice* (*tāg̱ēlnâ,* see Ps. 2:11; 16:9) like "divide and conquer," conceptually expresses a purpose clause (i.e., "purge me . . . that bones may rejoice"). *Bones* (*ʿaṣāmôṯ,* see Ps. 22:14) commonly refer to psyche (Ps. 34:20 [21]; 35:10; Prov. 3:8; 12:4; passim). *You have crushed* (*dikkîṯā*) completes and intensifies the metaphor. In Job 4:19 the bi-form *dkʾ* is used of a crushed moth. Psychologically crushed signifies "a high degree of dehumanization and depersonalization"[129] (cf. Ps. 38:8-10 [9-11]).

c. Forgive v. 9 [11]

Hide (*hastēr,* see Ps. 19:6, 12 [7, 13]) *your face* (*pāneyḵâ,* see Ps. 4:6 [7]) *from my sins* (*mēḥᵃṭāʾāy,* vv. 2, 7 [4, 9])[130] asks God to avert his gaze, dissolving his relationship to sin (Isa. 59:2)[131] and so not punishing it. It is one of the twenty images of forgiveness and cleansing in this psalm. The parallel, by repeating the imagery of verse 1, [3]B *and all* (*wᵉkol*) *my iniquities* (*ʿᵃwōnōtāy,* see v. 2 [4]) *blot out* (*mᵉḥēh*) brings closure to the petitions for forgiveness, heightened and reinforced by the closure technique of adding "all."[132]

2. For Spiritual Enablement vv. 10-12 [12-14]

The priestly and/or prophetic absolution is insufficient to purge his deeply stained conscience to fortify him to soldier on as king. He needs from God an inward spiritual grace spirit to accept his forgiveness and to build on it. And so he petitions God to give him that spirit. In the Hebrew text each of the B versets of verses 10-12 [12-14] begins emphatically with initial *wᵉrûaḥ* ("and a spirit") and ends with "me." The two petition strophes, for cleansing and spiritual renewal, are linked by the catchword *ṭhr,* "clean, pure" — from past sin and for future spiritual enablement (vv. 7 [9]a, 10 [12]a) — and by *śāśôn,* "joy" (vv. 8 [10]a,

129. J. Swart/C. Van Dam, *NIDOTTE,* 1:946, s.v. *dkh.*

130. Israel's poets use many images for the riddance of sin; e.g., "cast away into the depths of the sea" (Mic. 7:19), "swept away . . . like a cloud" (Isa. 44:22).

131. A. S. vander Woude, *TLOT,* 2:1008, s.v. *pānîm.*

132. B. Smith, *Poetic Closure* (Chicago: University of Chicago Press, 1968), pp. 182-86.

12 [14]a). The penitential psalm asks for inner transformation; other laments ask for outward transformation.

a. Renew Spirit v. 10 [12]

Heart (lēḇ) is word-initial in the Hebrew text and here refers to entire psychic disposition (see Ps. 4:4). The metaphor, *a clean* (*ṭāhôr,* see vv. 2, 7 [4, 9]) heart, refers to an inclination to regard oneself to be purged and made as white as snow. With that disposition he will not throw his past failures ahead of him and so walk through them again and again, making spiritual progress impossible. *Create (bᵉrāʾ)* refers to God's activity to bring something new into existence; only *God* (*ʾᵉlōhîm,* see v. 1 [3]) can fashion a renewed heart. David is asking for the gift of faith to accept the word of forgiveness. *For me (lî)* emphasizes his dependency.

And introduces the related petition for a steadfast spirit to preserve the new creation. *Spirit (rûaḥ)* concretely denotes "wind" (see Ps. 1:4), "breath," and connotes the power encountered in them. In Israel's psychosomatic thinking the manner of breathing indicates a person's frame of mind: if short, nervousness; if long, patience. Unqualified "spirit" signifies psychic vitality. When broken, one's vitality to promote life is destroyed.[133] To remedy this psychic dissolution David petitions God to restore his former *steadfast* (*nāḵôn,* passive stem) spirit. *Kûn* means intransitively, "to stand firm"; transitively, "to establish, found, anchor"; passively, "to be firm, true, certain." David was a "man after God's own heart" (*coram deo,* i.e., one completely surrendered to God's will), but in his sin with Bathsheba his spirit of complete surrender to God's purpose became conflicted, undermined (2 Sam. 10–12), and so he petitions God to *renew (ḥaddēš)* his former firmness of purpose. *Ḥāḏaš* Qal means to "craft something new," and in Piel, as here, to "make anew, repair, renew, restore."[134] David is not asking God to craft a new spirit to regenerate his heart (cf. Jer. 31:34; 32:39; Ezek. 11:19; 36:26); he was regenerated as shown by his life before his "Bathsheba Gate" and now by his repentance. What he needs is restoration of his former steadfast disposition (cf. 1 Sam. 16–2 Sam. 8). These graces must be *within me (bᵉqirbî).*

133. "Sin is the negative, that which preys upon the positive forces of life. . . . Sin is the very dissolution of the totality. . . . The sinner lacks the firm centre of action; his soul is not a pure and firm organism, but full of inner strife, a dissolved mass." J. Pedersen, *Israel: Its Life and Culture,* 4 vols. (London: Milford, 1926-1940).

134. BDB, p. 293, s.v. *ḥādaš.*

b. Retain God's Holy Spirit v. 11 [13]

Though David's spirit is conflicted and lacks firmness, God has not yet rejected him from kingship. And so he prays urgently: *Cast me not away* (*'al-tašlîḵēnî,* see Ps. 2:3) *from before you* (*millᵉp̄āneykâ,* literally, "from before your face"). To be cast out from *I AM*'s presence is to end a relationship with him. If God had cast him out, he would not have heard his psalm. Broyles notes that Psalm 51 "reflects an intimacy with God few psalms can rival."[135] "Face of *I AM*" speaks of God's presence (cf. v. 9 [11]). Humans survive only by the grace of the attentive presence of God. *Before you* may refer to God's unique presence at the sanctuary. In ancient Near Eastern courts, one who displeases the king is banished from the king's presence.

Matching his petition to sustain intimacy with God, he prays: "*nor your spirit . . . (wᵉrûaḥ)* take from me." God's spirit in the Old Testament, unlike the New Testament, is *qualitatively* (i.e., superhuman power) an aspect of his person, like the spirit of every human being — not *quantitatively* (i.e., a separate person). As a spiritual living Being, God can impart his spirit to human beings. God gave his special empowering spirit in the old dispensation to elected individuals, such as prophets and warriors, to establish his kingdom, but not to all Israelites (cf. Num. 11:18-30).[136] Beginning at Pentecost he gave his empowering spirit to all his covenant people. David is asking God not to take away his empowering spirit that made him king.[137] Compelled by God's spirit, Israel's warlords fought valiantly, while lacking spiritual virtue (cf. Judg. 6:34; Judg. 11:29-31; 14:6; 1 Sam. 11:6). God's empowering spirit came on David at his anointing, but he was already a man after God's heart (1 Sam. 15:28; 16:13). The addition *of your holiness (qoḏšᵉḵâ)* is unique, aside from Isa. 63:10-11 (2x). "Holiness" means "separation," "otherness" and with reference to God designates the sum of God's attributes that separate him from human limitations, especially their infirmity and impurity. *Do not take from me ('al-tiqqaḥ mimmenî)* implies God had not

135. Craig C. Broyles, *Psalms* (NIBC; Peabody, MA: Hendrickson, 1999), p. 226.

136. With regard to function God's super-powerful spirit effects creation (Job 33:4; Ps. 104:30) and redemption (see Isa. 32:15; 44:3; 63:11, 14; Hag. 2:5); equips his servants for their appointed tasks (see Exod. 31:3; Num. 11:29; Judg. 3:10; 1 Sam. 10:6; 16:13; Isa. 11:2; 42:1); inspires his prophets (see Num. 24:2-3; 2 Sam. 23:2; Neh. 9:30; Isa. 59:21; 61:1; Ezek. 11:5; Mic. 3:8; Zech. 7:12); and directs their ministries (see 1 Kings 18:12; 2 Kings 2:16; Isa. 48:16; Ezek. 2:2; 3:14); and will give the whole nation a "new heart and new spirit" to live by his will (see Jer. 24:7; 32:39; Ezek. 11:19; 18:31; 36:26-27).

137. Basing himself on Ezekiel 39 and denying the historicity of the superscription L. Neve ("Realized Eschatology in Psalm 51," *ET* 80 [1969]: 264-66) thinks he is praying that God's guiding, not gifting, spirit not be taken from him. His gifting spirit includes guidance as part of the king's empowering.

yet taken away his empowering presence for purity and rulership. *Nor take (ʾal tiqqaḥ)* means "to take, grasp, seize manually," and with *from me,* "to take away this gripping power," as God had done in the cases of Samson and Saul (Judg. 16:20; 1 Sam. 16:1, 14; 2 Sam. 23:1-2; cf. Isa. 63:10-11).

c. Sustain with a Willing Spirit v. 12 [14]

The king next needs a willing spirit to keep him from quitting. The spiritual condition to promote a persevering spirit is the joy that comes from experiencing God's salvation. Before his moral lapse David knew this joy, and so he prays *restore* (*hāšîbâ,* Ps. 19:7 [8]) *to me (lî) the joy* (*śᵉśôn,* see v. 8 [10]) *of your salvation* (*yišʿeḵā,* see v. 14 [16]; Ps. 3:2 [3]), which is based on God's character to show compassion to those who accept his favor (v. 1 [3], Exod. 34:6-7; 1 John 1:9). Restored joy is the necessary condition for *and with a willing spirit (wᵉrûaḥ nᵉḏîḇâ) sustain me* (*ṯismᵉḵēnî,* see Ps. 3:5 [6]). "Willing" *(nāḏîḇ)* means "to volunteer, to serve without compulsion" (cf. Exod. 35:21; Judg. 5:2; 2 Chron. 17:16; 29:31). This is "a prayer for divine support channeled through a willing spirit, dynamically and morally capable to meet the challenge of his future experience."[138]

E. Testimony of Praise vv. 13-17 [15-19]

In Israel's liturgy the *tôḏâ* ("confession of praise"; see p. 92) consists of a word of praise and a sacrifice of praise in which the celebrants eat with God (see Ps. 22:22-24 [23-25], 25-26 [26-27]; 40:1-6 [2-7], 7-8 [8-9]; 116:1-16, 17-19). The petition and praise stanzas are connected by the catchword "return" *(šûḇ),* the first and last words respectively in the Hebrew text of verses 12 [14] and 13 [15], and by the root *yāšaʿ* ("to save/deliver") in its nominal bi-form derivatives *yēšaʿ* and *tᵉšûʿāṯî* (vv. 12, 14 [14, 16]). Praise transforms petition from self-absorption to God's exaltation. True repentance concerns itself with God's reputation, not the penitent's.

1. Word of Praise vv. 13-15 [15-17]

Not presuming on God's grace, the promises to praise God in the B versets of verses 13-15 are conditioned by the hope of forgiveness in the A versets. By his testimony to God's grace to even a murderer he aims to convert all sinners to

138. Dalglish, *Psalm 51,* p. 162.

become a part of God's covenant community (vv. 13-14). The synonymous repetitions to praise almost make his promise a vow (v. 15).

a. Cause to Praise v. 13 [15]

The Psalter's public praises of answered petitions (i.e., testimony) typically consist of a preparatory resolve to praise, followed by reflection on past need and a report of deliverance and verbal praise — sometimes with instruction (cf. Ps. 32:8-10; 34; 51:13 [15]) — and communal feasting with God (see Ps. 22:26 [27]). Here David addresses *transgressors* and *sinners* (*pōšᵉʿîm, ḥaṭṭāʾîm,* see vv. 1, 2 [3, 4]). Although Hebrew grammar allows the translations "I will [am resolved to] teach" or *let me teach* (*ʾălammᵉḏâ),* the former is ruled out because David cannot fulfill the answers to his petitions in verses 14-15 [16-17]. *Your ways* (*dᵉrāḵeyḵâ,* Ps. 1:1, 6; 2:12) has an intertextual connection with Moses' prayer "show me your ways" (Exod. 33:13), in response to which *I AM* proclaimed his grace in terms found in Psalm 51:1-2 [3-4] (Exod. 34:6). *And sinners will return to you* (*yāšûḇû ʾēlêḵâ,* see above).

b. Condition and Certainty to Praise vv. 14-15 [16-17]

Save me (*haṣṣîlēnî,* Ps. 22:8, 21 [9,22]) *from bloodguilt* (*middāmîm*)[139] implies an *a fortiori* argument: If God pardons a murder, how much more will he forgive less venial crimes, such as adultery?[140] Before the Bathsheba incident David had studiously avoided incurring the guilt of shedding innocent blood (1 Sam. 25:26, 31, 33), for he knew God committed himself irrevocably to vindicate the unjust destruction of his human image-bearer by demanding the murderer's compensatory death (Gen. 9:5-6; 2 Sam. 1:16; 16:7-8; 2 Sam. 3:28-29; 1 Kings 2:5, 9, 31-33; Ps. 9:12 [13]; 2 Kings 9:26; Ezek. 3:18, 20; 24:8).[141] God extended mercy to David and cleared him of his capital offenses of adultery and murder (Lev. 20:10; 24:17, 21) because whoever confesses and renounces sin obtains mercy (Prov. 28:13). His confession lays his sins on the scapegoat that symbolically carried Israel's sin away from the land into the wilderness.

139. So BDB, p. 197, entry g, s.v. *dām.* For this sense *HALOT* 225 cites Exod. 22:1; Lev. 20:9; Num. 35:27; Deut. 19:10; 22:8; Judg. 9:24; 1 Sam. 25:26, 33; 2 Sam. 21:1; Isa. 33:15; Ezek. 9:9.

140. J. Goldingay, "Psalm 51:16a (English 51:14a)," *CBQ* 40 (1978): 388-90, suggests on the basis of Ezek. 3:17-19 and 33:7-9 that the psalmist is praying "to be kept from becoming answerable for the death of other sinners by failing to challenge and invite them to return to God." But this interpretation bypasses the superscription, as Goldingay recognizes, and besides that does not fit the psalm's message: to instruct sinners of God's grace, not of his wrath.

141. Waltke, *An Old Testament Theology,* pp. 303f.

The vocative *God* (*'ᵉlōhîm*) recalls that David's sin was against God alone and so he is the *God of my salvation* (*'ᵉlōhê tᵉšû'āṯî*, see v. 12 [14]). His concern for deliverance is God-centered: *my tongue* (*lišônî*, see 15:3), a synecdoche for his mouth, *will shout out loud* (*tᵉrannēn*) *your righteousness* (*ṣiḏqāṯeḵâ*, see Ps. 4:1 [2]; 15:2), which here is a metonymy for the effect, namely, salvation. *Rnn* signifies a loud expression, usually of joy.

Verse 15 emphatically restates verse 14. The new vocative emphasizes God's sovereignty: *Lord of All* (*'ᵃdōnāy*, see 2:4). The stock-in-trade metonymies for speech, *my lips* (*śip̄āṯî*, see 22:7 [8]) and *my mouth* (*pî*, see 19:14 [15]), vividly portray shaping public opinion by speech. *Open* (*tip̄tāḥ*, "would you would open," as in vv. 7-8 [9-10]) *my mouth* (see 19:14 [15]) — a metonymy for "to pardon" and "to purge" — so that it *will declare* (*yaggîḏ*, see Ps. 19:1 [2]; 22:31 [32]) *your praise* (*tᵉhillāṯeḵâ*). The parallels, "your deliverance" (v. 12 [14]a), "your ways" (v. 13 [15]a), "your righteousness" (v. 14 [16]b), suggest that "my praise" (v. 15 [17]b) celebrates God's benevolent attributes.

2. *Sacrifice of Praise vv. 16-17 [18-19]*

Typically a festive sacrifice with those assembled at the altar accompanies verbal praise. David does not disappoint the expectation of a festive sacrifice but surprises us with its substance. Instead of burning and feasting on a sacrificial bull, he offers the offended covenant community his broken and contrite spirit to feed upon. Neither God nor the nation, shocked and grieving over their king's defiling a loyal soldier's wife and his killing her famous war-hero husband, could stomach such a feast (v. 17 [19]).

a. Unacceptable Sacrifice v. 16 [18]

Surely (*kî*) is always medial, showing that verse 16 [18] continues to speak of his praise sacrifice.[142] *You would not delight* (*lō' taḥpōṣ*, see n. 80; Ps. 1:2) *in a sacrifice* (*zebaḥ*). *HALOT*, with R. Averbeck's approval,[143] defines *zeḇaḥ* as "a sacrifice of slaughtered sheep, goat or cattle to create communion between God to whom the sacrifice is made and the partners of the sacrifice, and communion between the partners themselves as they eat together."[144] *Or I would offer it* (*wᵉ'ettēnâ*, Ps. 1:3) is elliptical for "and if you would delight in it, I would give it."

142. *IBHS*, p. 665, P. 39.3.4e.

143. R. Averbeck, *NIDOTTE*, 1:1068, s.v. *zeḇaḥ*.

144. It can be qualified as a "fellowship offering" (*zeḇaḥ šᵉlāmîm*, trad. "peace offering") and more narrowly as a "testimony offering" (*zeḇaḥ tôḏâ*, trad. "thank offering"); in fact, it is generally synonymous with fellowship offering.

The B verset reinforces his spiritual discernment: *you would not be pleased with a burnt offering* (*ʿōlâ lōʾ tirṣeh*). *Rṣh* in Israel's liturgy is a technical expression to declare the sacrifice as "well-pleasing."[145] The parallel *ḥpṣ* moves "in the direction of 'to want, have interest' through a mitigation of the emotional element."[146] *Burnt offering* (*ʿōlâ* from the verb "to go up"/"ascend") indicates the complete burning up of an animal from the herd or flock (including the entrails) except for its hide, which went to the priest as a stipend for his service. In the case of a bird, offered by the poor, the priest removed the crop with its contents and there was no stipend. *ʿōlâ* is glossed "burnt offering," because it refers to the "ascending of the offering" to *I AM* in smoke by means of its incineration on the altar. The difference between the *zebaḥ* and the *ʿōlâ* "led to their frequent association in one ceremony, and made the two words together a fitting expression of sacrifice in general."[147]

b. Acceptable Sacrifices v. 17 [19]

Turning to the congregation, who are not expecting his resolution, he teaches: *the sacrifices* (*zebḥê,* see n. 82; v. 16 [18]) *of God* (*ʾelōhîm,* see v. 1 [3]) *are a broken spirit* (*rûaḥ,* see v. 12 [14] *nišbārâ,* see Ps. 3:7 [8]). A person having a broken spirit loses his vital life energy (see above); his entire disposition has been humbled under the mighty hand of God (v. 10 [12]). A humble spirit — knowing it is helpless without God's grace — is an essential oil poured on sacrifice offered on the high altar of God. "A brokenhearted person is the opposite of the self-made, hardhearted person, as seen in the contrast between David's and Saul's confession when confronted with their sin."[148] Now addressing *God* (see v. 14 [16]), he implicitly offers his own contrite heart on the high altar, confident that God will accept, not despise, it. *A broken and contrite heart (lēb nišbār wenidkeh)* once again sets in play the parallels "spirit" and "heart" (v. 10 [12]). *Dkh* "contrite" (literally, "crushed"; Latin *contrition* means "grinding, bruising, crushed");[149] his self-will is so broken it is pulverized. *You will not despise (lōʾ tibzeh,* see Ps. 15:4), an antonym to the synonyms "desire/delight" and "accept gladly" (v. 19 [21]).

145. R. Rendtorff, *Die Gesetze in der Priesterschrift: Eine gattungsgeschichtliche Untersuchung* (Göttingen: Vandenhoeck & Ruprecht, 1954), pp. 74f. E. Würtwein, *TLZ* 72 (1947): 147f.

146. G. Gerleman, *TLOT,* 2:466, s.v. *ḥpṣ.*

147. W. B. Stevenson, "Hebrew *ʿOlah and Zebach* Sacrifices," *Festschrift für Alfred Bertholet,* ed. W. Baumgartner (Tübingen: J. C. B. Mohr, 1950), p. 489.

148. *Dictionary of Biblical Imagery,* p. 163.

149. *Dictionary of Biblical Imagery,* p. 163.

F. Epilogue: Nation's Praise vv. 18-19 [20-21]

The king's personal praise is linked with that of his nation by: 1) covenant theology: if the king is restored to favor his nation will prosper; 2) topics: both move from verbal praise (vv. 14-15 [16-17], 18-19 [20-21]) to a sacrifice of praise (vv. 16-17 [18-19], 19 [21]); 3) syntax: they move from the volitional to the declarative mood; 4) catchwords: *ḥpṣ* ("desire") and *rṣh* ("favor") in verse 16 [18] are chiastically repeated in verses 18, 19 [20, 21]; and "sacrifice" *zeḇaḥ* (vv. 16 [18]a, 19 [21]a) and burnt offering (*ʿôlâ*, v. 16) in v. 19 ([21]b).

1. Condition: Build Jerusalem v. 18 [20]

Verset A calls for the prosperity of Jerusalem; verset B specifies the building of its walls. *Prosper* (*hêṭîḇâ*, literally, "cause to be good [delightful and useful])" designates a physical, not moral, quality with an impersonal object like *Zion* (*ʾeṯ-ṣîyôn*, see Ps. 2:6) and its synonym Jerusalem *(yᵉrûšālāyim),* metonymies and synecdoches for the nation. *In your favor* (*birṣôneḵâ*, see Ps. 19:14 [15]) subordinates the king's will to God's will and favor (cf. Mark 14:35). Walker defines *rāṣôn* as two-sided: will and pleasure.[150] The parallel B verset specifies what is meant by "prosper." *Let be built (tiḇneh)* here means "to bring walls into existence through the creative craftsmanship of stone masons."[151] *Walls (ḥômôṯ)* designate a city's large fortification walls, the decisive characteristic of a city. The plural *walls (ḥômôṯ)* anticipates the city's expansion beyond the sugarloaf southern hill, called "City of David," to the northern hill of Zion, where David pitched the tent for the ark. Solomon built the wall around the whole city and perhaps Hezekiah expanded it to the western ridge (1 Kings 3:1; 6:1–7:51; 1 Chron. 21:18–22:19). The holy city's expansion entails its increasing world influence and so of God's glory.

2. Consequence: National Praise v. 19 [21]

Verset A anticipates God's acceptance of burnt offerings; verset B specifies them as the best: "bulls/bullocks." Temporal *then ('az)* introduces the logical/temporal future consequences of covenant theology: the king's moral good leads to the city's material good, leading to praise of God for keeping his covenant promises. When that happens, David says, *you will delight in* (*taḥpōṣ*, n. 84; see v. 16 [18]) *sacrifices of righteousness (ziḇḥê ṣedeq).* "Righteousness" is a

150. N. Walker, "The Renderings of *Rāṣôn*," *JBL* 81 (1962): 184.

151. S. Wagner, *TDOT*, 2:168, s.v. *bānāh*.

metonymy for righteous people who offer the burnt offering (*ʿôlâ,* see Ps. 4:5 [6]). *And* they will be *offered whole* (*wᵉḵālîl,* "whole," "complete"). *ʿôlâ* and *ḵālîl* are complementary terms, the former referring to the manner of offering and the latter to the extent of it.

Then (*ʾaz,* see A verset) now conditions the action of the worshipers on God's acceptance of their offerings. *They will offer* glosses *yaʿᵃlû,* meaning "to move from a lower to a higher place." *Upon your altar* (*ʿal mizbaḥᵃkā,* a derivative of *zbḥ* [see v. 17]), etymologically means "the place of sacrifice" and refers to the bronze altar in front of the house of God. *The altar (mizbēaḥ)* is, conceptually, the altar with its fire, representing the mouth of God who feasts with his people. *Bullocks* (*pārîm,* see Ps. 22:12 [13]) represent the best and imply the nation's prosperity.

G. Postscript

For "to the chief musician" see p. 88. David's public confession of sin and his handing it over to the covenant people supports the early church's understanding that confession should be public — more particularly, when the sin is public knowledge. Moreover, the postscript also supports Denys, who "would have us imitate the life and spirit of David as the archetype of the true penitent" (see p. 458).

CHAPTER 15

Psalm 110: "Sit at My Right Hand"

Part I. Voice of the Church

I. In the New Testament

Psalm 110 has played the most important role in the history of Christian doctrine because of its profound Christology. It is quoted in the New Testament more than any other psalm (twenty-four times) and is the sixth article of the Apostles' Creed.[1] In the devotion of the church it was celebrated on Ascension Thursday.

A. In the Gospels

Five partial or complete quotations of Psalm 110:1 occur in the New Testament (Mark 12:36; Matt. 22:44; Luke 20:42-43; Acts 2:34-35; Heb. 1:13). Together with 1 Clement 36:5 and the Epistle of Barnabas 12:10, they all have the same formulae, the same vocabulary, or later the same textual variations.[2] Central to these recitations is the event of Jesus' trial before the high priest, who asks Jesus, "Are you the Messiah, the son of the Blessed One?" — to which Jesus replies: "I am," adding "you will see the Son of Man seated at the right hand of power, and coming with the clouds of heaven." To this confession, the High Priest responds: "You have heard his blasphemy" (Mark 14:61-64). This testimony is piv-

1. Bruce K. Waltke, "He Ascended and Sitteth . . . Reflections on the Sixth Article of the Apostles' Creed," *Crux* 30, no. 2 (June 1994): 2-8.

2. David M. Hay, *Glory at the Right Hand: Psalm 110 in Early Christianity* (Atlanta: Society of Biblical Literature, 1973), pp. 38-45.

otal to the ensuing death of Jesus by the Jewish authorities. Christianity hangs or falls on this testimony of Jesus in which he quotes Psalm 110. Christ's self-understanding based on his own exegesis gave the early fathers, notably Augustine, a strong Christological interpretation of this Psalm.

B. In the Epistles

Each of the apostolic references in early Christianity has its distinct polemical application of the Psalm. The frequent use of the text made by the writer to the Hebrews may downplay the cult of Melchizedek as used by Jewish, Samaritan, and Qumran sects. As David Hay observes: "Plainly he [Melchizedek] has no independent significance in Hebrews: the author's description of his office and actions makes him not so much a parallel or prototype as simply a witness to Jesus' unique office."[3] In the Pauline corpus, reference to "the right hand of God" (i.e., Rom. 8:34) appears as an early hymn celebrating the continually present intercession of Christ.[4] In Colossians 3:1 it appears as a baptismal formula, reflecting on the heavenly destiny of those who now share in Christ's death. Ephesians 1:20 appeals to the universal kingdom of the Risen Christ in a hymnic acclaim of worship.[5] In the midst of persecution the psalm is given the creedal confidence of 1 Peter 3:22, within a baptismal context, for believers trusting in the risen Christ.[6]

II. Musical Heritage of the Early Christian Confessions

The hymnic quality of these quotations from Psalm 110 suggests they were sung, but what is unknown is how early these hymns were composed. What appears certain is that the earliest Christians adopted the Jewish custom of praying at fixed hours daily, usually three times, possibly with the singing of psalms.[7] It seems likely, then, that most of the New Testament epistolary quotations and later Christian recitations are from hymnic sources, sung at baptismal and other worship services of the early Christian communities.

3. Hay, *Glory at the Right Hand,* p. 153.

4. M. Gourgues, *À la droite de Dieu, Résurrection de Jésus et actualisation du Psaume 110 dans le Nouveau Testament* (Paris: Librairie Lecoffre, 1978), pp. 45-57.

5. Gourgues, *À la droite de Dieu,* pp. 63-73.

6. Gourgues, *À la droite de Dieu,* pp. 75-87.

7. Robert Taft, S.J., *The Liturgy of the Hours in East and West* (Collegeville, MN: Liturgical Press, 1985), p. 11.

In his scholarly study, *Lord Jesus Christ: Devotion to Jesus in Earliest Christianity,*[8] Larry Hurtado is impressed by the remarkably early, rapid, and widespread recognition of the divinity of Christ, of his Messianic death, resurrection, and ascension. His evidences are exhaustive, except for the surprising lacuna of any reference to their hymnic and liturgical character. Hurtado is wholly silent concerning the role music must have played in the early confessional statements. Perhaps this "sudden recognition" was made possible by a tradition already established within the psalm-singing communities of the synagogues. Following Christ's own interpretation of Psalm 110:1, were they not already using the psalms themselves as the premise for worshiping Christ's human-divine nature?[9] By now the Psalter was no longer the hymnbook of the Jews exclusively, for it had become prophetically the hymnal of the earliest Christians.

Johannes Quasten describes the significant role music played in the pagan culture surrounding the early Christians. For "as pleasing to the gods, the magical powers of music were used to drive away demons, and to call down the good gods. . . ."[10] In the mystery cults, music was used in the rites of initiation and the cultic bath, to incite ecstasy for religious catharsis, and to induce prophecy. Greek philosophy first directed that "spiritual sacrifice" be made with music, but eventually repudiated musical instruments also. In contrast, the apostle Paul called on Christians to "Be filled with the Spirit, speaking to one another with psalms, hymns and songs from the Spirit" (TNIV; Eph. 5:19). To the Colossians, Paul adds that this singing must occur "with gratitude in your hearts." Paul's qualification suggests that pleasing music is not dependent on musical instruments but upon the motive of "the heart."

In the *Oracula Sibyllina* (c. before 180 C.E.) Christians are distinguished by "restraining from the wild music of pagans."[11] Instead, states Tertullian, Christians should accompany their singing of psalms and hymns with good works.[12]

8. Larry W. Hurtado, *Lord Jesus Christ: Devotion to Jesus in Earliest Christianity* (Grand Rapids: Eerdmans, 2003).

9. N. T. Wright (*Jesus and the Victory of God,* vol. 2 [Minneapolis: Fortress Press, 1996], pp. 477-653) makes strong claims for Jesus' Messianic self-awareness.

10. Johannes Quasten, *Music and Worship in Pagan and Christian Antiquity,* trans. Boniface Ramsey, O.P. (Washington, DC: National Association of Pastoral Musicians, 1983), pp. 1-19.

11. "In libation on the altar the blood of the victims; no kettle drum is heard, no cymbal, no many-holed flute, instruments full of the senseless sounds, nor the tone of the shepherd's pipe, which is like the curled snake, nor the trumpet, with its wild clamor." Quoted by Quasten, *Music and Worship in Pagan and Christian Antiquity,* p. 60.

12. "Accompanied by a procession of good works, singing psalms and hymns . . . ought to lead this [victim] to the altar of God. Fully devoted from the heart, nourished on faith, guarded

Clement of Alexandria also struggled against "the music of idols."[13] Just as the early Christian churches were built frequently on the ruins of a pre-existing pagan temple, so too, Christian confessional hymns, quoting the psalms, radically changed the pagan role and character of liturgical singing and instrumental music.

III. Messianic Polemics of Justin Martyr

Justin Martyr still belonged to a generation in touch with those who had known our Lord's apostles.[14] Apparently, in his debates and dialogues with Jewish scholars Justin engages more directly with Jewish Messianic expectations based on rabbinical sources than with the Old Testament texts themselves. Possibly this is in order to fill out the universal claims of the risen Savior of the world as depicted by Luke. For example, in *Dialogue* 8:3 Justin suggests that the Jewish teachers had argued that in Psalm 110:1 David's "lord" refers to Hezekiah, and that in verse 2 David's command to his lord that he rule the earth refers to Jerusalem's salvation in Hezekiah's day: "as though he was bidden be seated on the right hand of the temple when the king of Assyria sent to him with threats, and it was signified to him by Isaiah that he should not be afraid of him." Rabbi Hillel interprets this: "There shall be no messiah for Israel, because they have already enjoyed him in the days of Hezekiah." Justin then continues his anti-Hezekiah polemic that Hezekiah was not a priest forever, but Jesus Christ is.[15]

---

by truth, inviolate in innocence, pure in chastity, garlanded with love" . . . [such] "will obtain all things for us from God" (Tertullian, *De oratione,* 28, CSEL 20:198).

13. "When a man occupies his time with flutes, stringed instruments, choirs, dancing, Egyptian ktrotala and other improper frivolities, he will find that indecency and rudeness are the consequences. . . . We completely forbid the use of these instruments at our temperate banquet" (Clement of Alexander, *Paidagogos* 2.4 *GCS Clem.* 1, 182).

14. L. W. Barnard, *Justin Martyr: His Life and Thought* (Cambridge: Cambridge University Press, 1967), p. 5.

15. "Who does not know that he [Hezekiah] is not the redeemer of Jerusalem? And that he himself did not send a rod of power into Jerusalem, and rule in the midst of his enemies, but that it was God who turned his enemies away from him as he wept and wailed." Quoted by Oskar Skarsaune, *The Proof from Prophecy: A Study in Justin Martyr's Proof-Text Tradition: Text-Type, Provenance, Theological Profile* (Supplements to Novum Testamentum, 56; Leiden: E. J. Brill, 1987), p. 401.

IV. Augustine's Figurative Use of Psalm 110

Augustine's fundamental conviction, based on passages such as Psalm 102:18 [19] ("Let this be for another generation"), was that the psalms represented the prophecy of God's New Covenant for Christians. He couples Psalms 2 and 110 together as Messianic prophecies, which accords with orthodox faith today, albeit not so for many modern scholars as we shall see (see pp. 496-97). Augustine's beautiful epigram: *ut per illum ires regentem te, ambulantem per se* ("it would not be good enough for God only to appoint his Son as a signpost to the way; he made him the Way, that you might walk in him who guides you")[16] is derived from this psalm. Christ is both David's son and David's Lord. Matthew 1:1 begins with the certainty, "A book of the descent of Jesus Christ, the son of David." Then the apostle Paul states twice over: Jesus Christ who "was made for David from David's line[age], according to the flesh" (Rom. 1:3); and writing to Timothy, "Remember Jesus Christ, born of David's lineage, whom my gospel proclaims" (2 Tim. 2:8). Augustine then asks his audience, "Do you find it surprising that Christ is both David's son and yet David's Lord?" Indeed, David is "honored by his son's birth [genealogically] and set free by his son's lordship" [salvifically].[17] But the canons of such understanding are "by knocking at the door by devotion" and "seeking the answer in love."[18]

In his commentary Augustine seeks to inspire and to promote the faith of Christians that Jesus is the Christ, the Son of God. This is still the dynamic purpose of the Psalms: "Jesus Christ brings about the unity of Scripture, because he is the endpoint and fullness of Scripture. Everything in it is related to him." As Henri de Lubac puts it, "Christ is . . . its whole exegesis."[19]

Augustine's aims comport with Christ's own exegesis of the Old Testament. He too challenges the Jews in John 5:39: "You study the Scriptures diligently because you think that in them you possess eternal life. These are the very Scriptures that testify about me." Again, he showed to the two disciples on the way to Emmaus: "And beginning with Moses and all the Prophets, he explained to them what was said in all the Scriptures concerning himself" (Luke 24:27). For Augustine it is an exegesis that acts upon us, not just informs us,

16. Skarsaune, *The Proof from Prophecy,* p. 263.

17. Skarsaune, *The Proof from Prophecy,* p. 268.

18. Skarsaune, *The Proof from Prophecy,* p. 267.

19. For Augustine, this is what is meant by the frequent superscript in the Psalms, which according to the LXX means "with a view to the end" (see pp. 212-13). Likewise Origen exhorts, "When you hear the text of the psalm saying, 'with a view to the end,' let your hearts turn to Christ" (Henri de Lubac, S.J., *Medieval Exegesis: The Four Senses of Scripture,* vol. 1, trans. Mark Sebanc [Grand Rapids: Eerdmans, 1998], p. 237).

which only Jesus Christ himself can bring about. The harmony of the two Testaments, as well as the harmony of symbols and typology taken from them both, is given a "new/spiritual sense" by the Holy Spirit alone.

Commenting on the figurative thrust given by Augustine in his reflections on this psalm, Robert Wilken has observed shrewdly, "figurative speech is the natural clothing of religious thought."[20] For mystery touches upon the ineffable, pointing to reality beyond our comprehension.

V. Jerome's Prophetic Sense

As we have seen (p. 48), Jerome is scornful of Augustine's rhetorical approach to Scripture as theological commentary, yet he himself mixes a critical study of the text with prophetic allegory. He begins, "David is the one who is speaking, prophet, holy man, king. . . . As king and prophet what does he say? 'The LORD said to my Lord.' In the Gospel the Savior explains that passage by saying [in Matt. 22:43]: 'If the Christ is the son of David, how, under the influence of the Spirit, does he call him Lord?'"[21] Immediately Jerome makes clear that "in Hebrew the first word for LORD is written in these letters [i.e., the Tetragrammaton, I AM] by which it is only written about God. But the second word for lord is written in these letters by which humans customarily name a master: just as someone is called 'lord' by a servant." Note also, observes Jerome, "God does not sit; one-who-takes-a-body sits. To the latter Lord therefore, the command that he sit is given; he is a human, who has been taken up. We say this in opposition to the Arians." Jerome connects this with the incident of Matthew 22:43 where the Pharisees were presuming Jesus could only claim to be "a son of David" as a man by natural genealogy, but not by divine Sonship. Yet against the Manicheans his true manhood and his deity are also being affirmed in the psalm. With the symbol of royal power, the scepter of righteousness (Isa. 2:3), the Son rules even in the midst of his enemies (Ps. 68:24), making 110:2 a prayer for this to be so.

Jerome finds verse 3 obscure, for the "day" referred to is God's beginning, which is eternal, not temporal. Jerome connects it with John 1:1. With the Son and with the Father, "the beginning" is eternal, and yet Jesus as the man "is praying for help," in discourse with the Father. Jerome gives the whole psalm a Johannine interpretation.

20. Robert Louis Wilken, *The Spirit of Early Christian Thought* (New Haven and London: Yale University Press, 2003), p. 70.

21. Jerome, *Tractatus in librum Psalmos,* Ps. 110, CCL, 78, 220-30.

Jerome reflects on Hebrews 7 in his handling of the reference to Melchizedek in verse 4: "For as Melchizedek, King of Salem offered bread and wine, so you too [Christ] will offer your body and blood." But in verse 5 Jerome raises the question: If in verse 1 Christ sits at the right hand of the Father, how does the Father sit [sic!] at the Son's right hand in this verse? Surely, "it is said so that the Son is co-equal to the Father." He then links the power of his judgment upon evildoers in verse 6 with Luke 2:34, "He has appointed for the fall and the rising of many and as a sign which will be opposed." Verse 7 Jerome interprets "'from the stream by the wayside he will drink,' meaning that Jesus has entered into the muddy stream of the world, and in drinking its mortality, he entered into death, yet having 'the power to lay aside his life, and the power to take it up again'" (John 10:18). Here his homily breaks off, with the closing words: "To Him be the glory forever and ever, Amen."[22]

VI. Luther's Revolt Against Medieval Exegesis

A. Luther's Hermeneutics Broadly

By way of introduction to Luther's hermeneutics, besides what we presented in chapter 2 (pp. 60-61), we should remind ourselves that traditionally, the literal sense *(literalis/historicus)* may be considered as the "outside view of the text," as to what it actually means plainly within its historical context, where this is known. But for Bible readers the role of God in history has meant that the "historical" explanation is inevitably also a theological interpretation. So the other three methods have to go "inside the text" to apply its truths as moral or tropological *(sensus tropologicus);* or again, as being figurative/allegorical *(sensus allegoricus);* and indeed, as being mystical or anagogical *(sensus mysticus/sensus anagogicus)* in anticipating mystical union with God or to anticipate the future heavenly co-existence with God. Medieval exegetes went much further with the text than modern students, since allegorical and anagogical approaches suggest an innate hiddenness, which was exaggerated by clericalism, suggesting it was a special kind of text that needed to be interpreted as a sort of theological riddle. Moreover, scholarly commentators tended to give preference to one of the three symbolic modes, as if they could ever be separated. Thus Christian scholars in dialogue with Jewish scholarship tended towards "the literal" in the sense of the grammatical interpretation. As we have seen (see p. 58), conciliar reformers were more earnest about "the

22. Jerome, *Tractatus in librum Psalmos,* Ps. 110, CCL, 78, 230.

tropological" or moral application of the Psalms. Those with a mystical or eschatological bent favored "the anagogical" approach.

When Luther did away with this medieval *quadriga* (see pp. 60-61), he had two issues in mind. First, he was rejecting polysemy of the text — that is to say, that a text has multiple senses.[23] Second, under clericalism the *quadriga* divisions implied the Scriptures were not sufficiently clear for lay understanding; they needed to be decoded by ecclesial experts. The "something" behind the text, especially in the allegorical approach, implied there was a code needed to interpret it. (This is not to say that Luther did not accept the use of typology, metaphor, and other figures of speech.) His primary concern was to abolish the medieval understanding of what the "literal sense" meant. For Luther the term "literal" refers not just to the factual sense over against the other three senses, but to the factual sense in connection with an inner personal certainty in reading the Bible, with the clear assurance of salvation itself. This sort of reading is also the desire of the other Reformers. In sum, Luther was making a fresh start in his quest *to experience a deeper existential understanding* of the Biblical text and language. Moreover, he rejects the interpretation of language as a "code" that requires "a key" to have "the right" meaning. This is the nature of "symbols": they require the mediation of interpretation.[24]

Instead, Luther prefers the use of *synecdoche*, literally "co-understanding" (i.e., a part to represent the whole), which comes as the Incarnation itself reveals, as a babe or as a slain little lamb, simple and humble enough for all human understanding, while also expressive of the infinite, ineffable wisdom of God. Certainly it is abbreviated expression, yet it is what Calvin later was to call "the plain sense." It enables us to experience what is being communicated, as in the Eucharistic statement, "this is my body broken/given for you . . . my blood shed for you." So Luther argues, the Biblical text is not meant to conceal but to clarify and to communicate simply and clearly.

This requires more than plain language; it is the work of the Holy Spirit to help the reader experience the reality of what is being communicated. Luther appropriates the implications of the Incarnation for interpreting Scripture (i.e., "for the Word became flesh and dwelt among us" [John 1:14]) — that is to say, the vital unity of the Word and Spirit; they are inseparable. Thus a scholarly literary canon is insufficient to communicate the faith of the psalmist or indeed of any Biblical passage. Erasmus might argue it is the task or *scopus* of the theologian to communicate the Scriptures. Luther for his part maintains that it is

23. Jan Lindhardt, *Martin Luther: Knowledge and Mediation in the Renaissance*, Texts and Studies in Religion, vol. 29 (Lewiston, NY: Edwin Mellen Press, 1986), p. 217.

24. Lindhardt, *Martin Luther*, pp. 199-203.

Christ who does this, through the Holy Spirit, as he communicated to the two disciples on the Emmaus Way, "in all the scriptures concerning himself." Christ's words also imply that the entire fabric of the Scriptures has to be understood holistically, in contextual reading and spiritual understanding. "All parts of the Scriptures are to be understood as if they have to do with Christ, whether directly or metaphorically."[25]

B. Luther's Commentary on Psalm 110

In contrast to his early commentary on Psalm 139 (see p. 529), Luther's commentary on Psalm 110 originated in eight sermons preached in May and June, 1535. This psalm represents for Luther a high point of the Old Testament, as expressive of the exalted Christ, the only King, Lord, and Priest of his people. Unlike Jerome, Luther is unclear about the unique term "I AM," so he translates *Yhwh* as "The LORD," while distinguishing him from the Messiah, as the true seed of Abraham, human yet divine. Luther then cites the significant question of Jesus to the scribes, what they think of Christ. "How is it, then, that David inspired by the Spirit, calls him my Lord?" (Matt. 22:43). The answer lies in the statement, "sit at my right hand," which Luther interprets to mean, "to possess the very majesty and power that is called divine."[26] He explores the mystery that Christ is both God and Man, as Romans 1:4 attests: "regarding his Son, who as to his earthly life was a descendant of David, and who through the Spirit of holiness was declared with power to be the Son of God by his resurrection from the dead: Jesus Christ our Lord" (see also Heb. 1:5). Then Luther expatiates on the uniqueness of his kingdom, unlike all human concepts of kingdoms. Altogether Luther expounds on this psalm in 123 pages, the longest discourse he makes on any one psalm in his writings. He concludes: "This beautiful psalm is the very core and quintessence of the whole Scripture. No other psalm prophesies as abundantly and completely about Christ. It portrays the Lord and his entire Kingdom, and is full of comfort for Christians."[27] Significantly, Luther appears not to have consulted Jerome to give his commentary a Johannine orientation.

25. *Luther's Works,* ed. Jaroslav Pelikan, vol. 15 (St. Louis: Concordia, 1955), p. 413.
26. *Luther's Works,* ed. Jaroslav Pelikan, vol. 13 (St. Louis: Concordia, 1955), p. 233.
27. *Luther's Works,* vol. 13, p. 348.

VII. Calvin's Plain Sense of the Text

A. Calvin's Hermeneutics Broadly

Calvin builds on Luther. He is "modern" in treating each psalm individually, equally indifferent to what is "allegorical" and "spiritual," so that he develops his own approach, what he calls "simple" and "natural." By this he means examining the text carefully and plainly within the broad context of all the Scriptures. His view of history is to recognize God as the sovereign Lord of all human events and to see the place of Israel within the whole Biblical continuum of "the church," as God has ordained, from Abraham through David to Christ. Bruce thus maintains Calvin's usage, in distinguishing Biblical typology from allegory, for "type" is "a unique specie of promise and fulfillment [within the Scriptures]."[28] Or as he quotes from G. W. L. Lampe, a type is "primarily a method of historical interpretation, based on the continuity of God's purpose through the history of his covenant. It seeks to demonstrate the correspondence between the various stages in the fulfillment of that purpose."[29] Calvin accepts this eschatological typology, grounded in the Bible's unique Authorship and unity, and thus understands the events of the Exodus, and the Cross-Resurrection-Ascension as one continuum that determines all interpretation of human history. Additionally, he has prepared himself in scholarly research of the Biblical text, even more than Luther. Benefiting from the Renaissance editions of the Hebrew Bible, Calvin was grounded in the latest textual criticism, and was familiar with the major patristic sources (Jerome, Eusebius, especially Augustine) as well as with numerous Jewish scholars whom Luther had ignored.

He adopts effectively the classical role of "the exemplar," using David as such, in both a positive and a negative sense. He accepts also the classical concept of *prosopopoeia,* of David speaking on behalf of Christ, so that a whole prayer could be interpreted as a prayer of Christ, not just the verses Jesus actually quoted as recorded by the Gospels. Unlike Augustine, who sees Christ allegorically in all the Psalms as both "Head" and "Body" *(totus Christus),* Calvin is selective in typology, to permit the power of Biblical reflection to concentrate upon the "plain" message of the Psalm itself. He takes seriously the Psalm texts selected by the New Testament writers.

Scholars have detected certain tensions in Calvin's exegesis. He is open to

28. Bruce K. Waltke with Charles Yu, *An Old Testament Theology: An Exegetical, Canonical, and Thematic Approach* (Grand Rapids: Zondervan, 2007), p. 136.

29. G. W. H. Lampe, "Typological Exegesis," *Theology* 56 (1953): 202.

Jewish interpreters if their Hebrew text is corrective of that of Christian scholars. Yet he remains independent of both Christians and Jews if it seems appropriate to introduce a "middle voice."[30] He is not a "camp follower," like the modern fads of fitting everything into form criticism, or the latest approach. His primary authority is not from the professional academy but from the uniqueness of God and of his lordship over history, secular and sacred. He sees the "bridge" character of the Psalms as linking the history of God's covenant people, whether of Israel or of the Christian community; to him, all are "the Church of God." The church is the theological unity, undivided by what is B.C.E. or C.E., and the Psalms have served, now serve, and will serve, all of God's people, throughout the ages, past, present, and future.

Unlike many contemporary historical Biblical critics, who only recognize sources in ancient Near Eastern literatures, such as Canaanite myths as known from Ugarit, or deriving from Assyrian rituals, Calvin would agree with Karl Barth, when he asks what is "the source of the Psalter? Where did its authors really derive all that they have given us in these poems by means of confession of their praise, their gratitude, their comfort, their confidence, yet also their penitence, their distress in deepest need, their hope and their defiance? How do they know what they obviously think they know concerning God and themselves, God and the created heaven and earth, God's relationship to them and theirs to Him?"[31] It all lies in the prophetic utterance: "Thus saith the I AM." This is the declaration that past, present, and future all lie in the sovereignty of the Lord who declares himself to be, "The I AM." The unchanging character of the Lord God is what gives unity to the Psalms and to their continuing exposition, both now and in the future. God's covenant with his people, both Israel and the church, is eternally the same. So Calvin introduces the reader into a text so that he or she can share in the communion of saints, from the time of Abraham and Melchizedek, to those who followed Jesus as his disciples, to ourselves today, and indeed to all those who will live beyond our own mortality. This is the missing component of much academic study today; it cannot see beyond its own competence. It has lost sight of the divine transcendence that Psalm 110 celebrates.

Already by the middle of the sixteenth century, Calvin was railing against

30. Calvin was even quite relaxed on the inerrancy of Scripture. Commenting on the attribution of a text to Jeremiah in Matthew 27:9, he comments: "How the name 'Jeremiah' crept in here I must confess I do not know and I do not much care. 'Jeremiah' was certainly put in error for 'Zechariah'" (*Calvin's Old Testament Commentaries,* ed. T. H. L. Parker [Edinburgh: T. & T. Clark, 1986], p. 192).

31. Karl Barth, *Church Dogmatics* III/4, ed. G. W. Bromiley and T. F. Torrance (Edinburgh: T. & T. Clark, 1961), section 1, p. 55.

those who "wanted to fill the world with atheism" *(Concerning Scandals),*[32] or against Epicureans, who were proclaiming the indifference of the gods to the human condition. As Calvin's commentary on the Psalms continues to be studied and appreciated, the more Christians will appreciate the significance of his work as a watershed in the history of interpretation.

B. Calvin's Commentary on Psalm 110

Calvin begins with Matthew 22:42-45, wherein Christ applies this psalm to himself. "The Messianic interpretation of this psalm," he adds, "is also supported by the testimony of the apostle." "The psalm is thus, beyond all controversy, a very clear prediction of the divinity, priesthood, victories, and triumph of the Messiah. We have so many Scriptural helps to its exposition that we can be at no loss as to its meaning."[33] Then, as is his practice, Calvin gives a synopsis of the psalm's content. In the first place, David affirms "that God conferred upon Christ supreme dominion, combined with invincible power, with which he either conquers all his enemies or compels them to submit to him. In the second place, he adds, that God would extend the boundaries of this kingdom far and wide; and, in the third place, that Christ having been installed into the priestly office with all the solemnity of an oath, sustains the honors of that equally with those of his regal office. Finally, this shall be a new order of priesthood, whose introduction shall put an end to the Levitical priesthood, which was temporary, and that it [this new order] shall be everlasting."[34]

Calvin sees a typological connection between the uniqueness of David's kingship (i.e., God's choosing of David, his consecration by Samuel, and the covenantal nature of his kingdom) and Christ's kingship. But Christ's Lordship over David makes his identity all the more remarkable. He accepts the prophetic declaration that Christ's kingdom is extended to be both universal in space and everlasting in time. He treats Melchizedek as a historical person who typologically points forward to Christ. In verse 6, he softens the harshness of the language by making it expressive of the military prowess of Christ, to warn us against any revolt against his sovereignty, as Psalm 2:9 also does.[35] His commentary is short and succinct, and he tends to present his interpretations in a

32. Donald K. McKim, *Calvin and the Bible* (Cambridge: Cambridge University Press, 2006), p. 61.

33. *Calvin's Commentary on the Book of Psalms,* ed. and trans. Rev. James Anderson, vol. 4 (Edinburgh: Calvin Translation Society, 1847), pp. 295, 296.

34. *Calvin's Commentary on the Book of Psalms,* p. 295.

35. *Calvin's Commentary on the Book of Psalms,* pp. 309, 310.

tone of Scriptural authority. For he recognizes it is Jesus Christ himself who claims this psalm to be prophetic of himself. Yet he is aware of those around him who would seek to refute him: Jewish scholars, Humanist skeptics, even Catholic traditionalists. But most of all, he is aware of his pastoral charge, of exiles like himself in Geneva, who might be timid in heart, needing the courage to trust in the kingdom of Christ.[36]

Many doctrinally oriented commentators followed Calvin, including Lutheran commentators such as H. Grotius (died 1645) and H. Venema (died 1787), as well as other Calvinists such as Johannes Cocceius (died 1669) and S. van Til (died 1713). But perhaps unwittingly, they were already directing Calvin's "plain sense" into an exegetical direction more rationalistic than "spiritual."

VIII. Conclusion

The church fathers, like the Apostles, selected Psalm 110 as pivotal to the affirmation of the Christian faith. Subsequent psalms research demonstrates the doctrinal vicissitudes and challenges the faith has had and still is experiencing. (For a broad survey of the history of interpretation of the Psalter from the eighteenth century to modern times see chapters 2 and 3.) Contemporary Biblical scholarship adds more confusion than ever with its well-intentioned efforts to recover multiple layers of meaning to the text, its confusion between typology and allegory,[37] and in its "spiritual" and "historical" references having underlying assumptions that are no longer "the plain sense" Calvin desired to communicate.

In this milieu there is increasingly a more sympathetic appreciation of patristic exegesis. As Brevard Childs comments on the possibility of multi-sense

36. Even in Calvin's day there were classical humanists who scorned the lack of poetic claim of the Psalms, more because of their divine claims than as a literary matter of diction. The scholar of classical antiquity, Henry Stephanus, in his work *Liber Psalmorum Davidis* (Paris, 1562), writes soon after Calvin that such critics "charged the poet Antonius Flaminius with the folly of attempting to reproduce in Roman verse the contents of the Psalter, which they said was nothing else than 'committing seed to the arid sand.'" Calvin's response was: "so far from questioning the poetry of the Psalms of David, there existed no production which could be conceived more poetical, harmonious, and heart-stirring and mostly more ecstatic than just the Psalms." Great scholar as he was, Flaminius felt only his own incompetence to treat the Psalms appropriately (August Tholuck, *A Translation and Commentary of the Book of Psalms for the Use of the Ministry and Laity of the Christian Church,* trans. J. Isidor Mombert [Philadelphia: William S. & Alfred Martien, 1858], pp. 9-10).

37. Jason Byassee, *Praise Seeking Understanding: Reading the Psalms with Augustine* (Grand Rapids: Eerdmans, 2007), is a helpful and fresh study, but he ignores this fundamental distinction between "allegory" and Biblical "typology."

exegesis, he also affirms the recovery of Augustine's commentary: "At the head of any list [of the works of the church fathers] stands the *Enarrationes* of Augustine . . . the prism through which the Psalter was refracted during the greater part of Christian history. The exposition is not easy reading and runs counter to everything that the historical critical method assumes as obvious. Augustine does not interpret the text to discover what the biblical author originally meant, but he replays the chords of the text as one plays an organ in order to orchestrate one's praise to the God and Father of Jesus Christ."[38]

Part II. Voice of the Psalmist: Translation

By David. A psalm.
1 An oracle of *I AM* to my lord:
"'Sit at my right hand
until I make your enemies a footstool for your feet.'
2 *I AM* will extend[39] your mighty scepter from Zion.
'Rule in the midst of your enemies!'
3 Your troops offer themselves freely on the day of your strength.[40]
Arrayed in holy splendor,[41] from the womb of[42] the dawn,
the dew of your youth comes[43] to you.[44]

38. Brevard S. Childs, *Old Testament Books for Pastor and Teacher* (Philadelphia: Fortress, 1977), pp. 62-63.

39. Construed as a specific future, not as a jussive ("may he send") in spite of the parallel imperative "rule," because the rest of the psalm predicts victory.

40. Instead of "Your people are willingness," LXX reads *meta sou hē archē,* retroverted as *ʿimmᵉḵâ nᵉḏîḇôṯ.* MT makes a better parallelism between the first and last words of the verse: "your troops" and "your youths," rather than "with you . . . your youths."

41. Several medieval Hebrew manuscripts, a Cairo Geniza fragment, Symmachus, and Jerome read *hārê* "mountains of." *Daleth* and *rēš* are commonly confounded. With "holy," however, one expects a singular "mountain" (i.e., Zion) as in Psalm 2. Also, this alternative is attractive only with the alternative reading, *yᵉlaḏtîḵâ* ("I brought you forth from the womb before the morning").

42. The Greek translations (LXX, Origen, Theodotion) and Syr. read *miššaḥār* ("from the womb, from the dawn"). The Masoretes probably thought that *miššḥar* was a bi-form of *šaḥar.* More probably neither understood enclitic *mem.* The text should be normalized as *rḥm-m šḥr* (see *IBHS,* pp. 158-60, P. 9.8).

43. Implied in the preposition "to."

44. So MT. Others change MT's accents so that "in holy splendor" modifies the preceding clause and refers "from the womb of the dawn you have the dew of your youth" to the king's youth. The emendation questionably separates the foci of verse 3 from Messiah's troops (3A) to his person (v. 3B).

4 *I AM* swears[45] and will not change his mind:[46]
'You are a priest forever,
like[47] Melchizedek.'
5 The Lord is at your right hand;
he will crush kings on the day of his anger.
6 You[48] will judge the nations, you will fill[49] the valley with corpses,[50]
and smash the heads that are over the whole earth.
7 From the wadi beside the way you will drink;
therefore you will lift up your[51] head."

Part III. Commentary

I. Introduction

A. Form

The similarity between Psalm 110 and Assyrian royal prophecies identifies beyond reasonable doubt that the psalm is a royal prophecy, sung as part of Israel's royal coronation ritual. John Hilber in his 2005 Cambridge doctoral dissertation documents the correspondences between the two.

45. Construed as an instantaneous or performative perfective (*IBHS*, p. 488, P. 30.5.1d).

46. Some EVV gloss *nḥm* Ni. by "repent" (KJV, JPS) or an equivalent like "is not sorry" (C. A. Briggs, *The Book of Psalms* [Edinburgh: T. & T. Clark, 1907], p. 378). These glosses mislead because they connote "to turn from sin," "to feel contrition." Better glosses are "relent," "retract," "waver," "break one's vow."

47. The final *yôdh* of the construct *dibrāṯi*, an unexplained connecting suffix (*IBHS*, pp. 127f., P. 8.2.e), may have been chosen for its assonance with the same suffix in its absolute counterpart, *malkîṣeḏeq*, also composed of the construct *malki* and its absolute *ṣedeq*.

48. See commentary for gloss of "he" by "you."

49. Construing the suffix conjugation as an accidental (traditionally prophetic perfective) (*IBHS*, p. 490, P. 30.5.1e).

50. On the basis of *pharangēs* in Aquila and Symmachus and of *valles* in Jerome, Bardtke rightly emends MT's *mālē' gewîyôṯ* to read (with slight modification on my part) *millē'* (Piel) *ḡē'āyôṯ gᵉwîyôṯ*. The consonance (i.e., similar consonants) and assonance (i.e., similar sounds) of *gē'āyôṯ* and *gᵉwîyôṯ* are fertile soil for haplography (*IBHS*, p. 23, P. 1.6.2c). If the skipped word was *gē'* (valley [singular]) it would be a simple case of homoiarchton. Furthermore, textual corruption in MT may prompt the accompanying oral tradition to adjust to the new reading (*IBHS*, p. 25, P. 1.6.3e). The emended text construes *gē'āyôt gᵉwîyôṯ* as a double accusative (*IBHS*, p. 176, P. 10.2.3e).

51. Added *ad sensum*. The absolute form serves best as a catchword with verse 6.

Both begin with an introduction formula: 110:1.
Subdivision of oracle with a second introduction formula: 110:4.
Change in person, both of the addressee and the divine speaker. 110:4-5, 6-7.
Legitimization of relationship between deity and king ("at the right hand"): 110:1.
Enemies at the king's feet: 110:1.
Promise of the destruction of enemies: 110:2, 5-6.
Promise of universal dominion: 110:1, 6.
Presence of loyal support: 110:3.
Divine promise accompanied by denial of lying: 110:4.
Affirmation of priestly responsibility: 110:4.
Eternality of royal prerogatives: 110:4.[52]

Implicitly, the author is a prophet. Weippert, from his broad study of ancient Near Eastern literatures, defines a prophet(ess) as one who has a cognitive experience by vision, audition, or dream that shares in a revelation from deity, and who has an awareness of a commission from the deity to transmit the revelation.[53] The introduction to Psalm 110 shows the author speaks, as Jesus says, "in the Spirit": "An oracle (inspired utterance) of *I AM*" (see commentary). The Assyrian parallels show that the entire psalm is conceived of as an oracle. As a unified oracle no distinction as to the poem's inspiration should be made between its two divine citations (vv. 1b, 4b) and the prophet's reflections on them (vv. 2-3, 5-7). The prophet mediates both. Its prosopological switching of pronouns from first person to third persons to view a subject from the divine and human perspectives respectively is common to the Old Testament and Assyrian prophetic literature (cf. Isa. 3:1-4; Hos. 5:1-7; Amos 3:1-7; Mic. 1:3-7). Hilber comments: "The Assyrian oracles . . . display a rapid shift between persons within the same relatively short oracle."[54]

52. J. W. Hilber, *Cultic Prophecy in the Psalms* (Beihefte zur Zeitschrift für die alttestamentliche Wissenschaft; Berlin, New York: Walter de Gruyter, 2005), pp. 76-88, esp. pp. 76-80. His work has been of considerable help to me in writing a commentary on this psalm.

53. M. Weippert, "Aspekte israelitischer Prophetie im Lichte verwandter Erscheinungen des Alten Orients," *Ad bene et fideliter seminandum: Festgabe für Karlheinz Deller zum 21. February 1987*, ed. Gerline Mauer und Ursula Magen (AOAT 220; Neukirchen-Vluyn: Neukirchener Verlag), pp. 287-319, esp. 289f.

54. Hilber, *Cultic Prophecy*, p. 81. Scholars have debated Mowinckel's 1922 thesis that certain psalms come from permanent cultic servants with recognized prophetic gifts. He argues: 1) these psalms look in form and style like known prophetic literature (e.g., Ps. 81, 86); 2) the prophets Moses, Deborah, Joel, and Habakkuk combine oracles and hymns into a unified corpus; and 3) priest and prophet mediate the deity's mind (Jer. 23:33-40). Furthermore, we first en-

The evidence suggests that Psalm 110 was delivered at the temple by a prophet, possibly a temple functionary, as a part of Israel's cultus and pertains to the newly minted king. The king extends his scepter from Zion. The divine command "sit at my right hand" can be fitted into an enthronement ritual. One collection of Assyrian prophetic texts is linked to enthronement. Laato (1996) associates the Assyrian corpus with Psalm 110 as follows: 1) legitimating of kingship; 2) destruction of enemies; 3) presence of loyal supporters; and 4) priesthood of the king. Hilber draws the conclusion: "It is likely that Psalm 110 was a prophetic oracle originating and subsequently used in conjunction with cultic celebration of the king's enthronement."[55]

B. Structure, Rhetoric, Message

Psalm 110 has two parts (vv. 1-3, 4-7), and, like Assyrian royal prophecies, a second introduction formula introduces the second part (v. 4). In one Assyrian oracle a scribe bracketed the two parts by scribal divisions and colophons.[56] The psalm's two parts have similar structures: 1) introduction naming *I AM* as the speaker and addressee (vv. 1a, 4a); 2) a divine citation (vv. 1b, 4b); and 3) the prophet's reflections (vv. 2-3, 5-7). The first introduction formula also introduces the whole psalm as an oracle. Note the couplets: verses 1-2, 4-5 pertain to *I AM* and king; verses 6-7 are addressed to the congregation about "heads" (v. 6) and "your [literally, his] head" (v. 7). Isolated verse 3 pertains uniquely to the army. Nevertheless, verses 3 and 4 are uniquely tristichs of 1:2 and 2:1 stichs. Thus, verse 3 is also a janus.

The form profiles the similarity and dissimilarity of the two parts. The first part designates "my lord" as king; the second, as priest. In the first, the lord is at *I AM*'s right hand; in the second, the Lord is at the lord's right hand. The

---

counter a band of prophets coming from a high place (1 Sam. 10:5); prophets located at cultic centers (Num. 11:24-30; 1 Sam. 3:21; 19:19-20; 2 Kings 2:3; Jer. 26:7), serving at the temple under the oversight of priests (Jer. 29:26); and some live there (Jer. 35:4; cf. Jer. 23:11). Finally, prophetic ecstasy is linked with music (2 Kings 3:15; Ps. 49:4 [5]; 2 Chron. 20). This data shows a close connection between the sanctuary and prophets, but does not prove that professional prophets are members of Israel's cultus. Priests and others within the cultus, besides professional prophets, can have prophetic experiences. During the Second Temple epoch Josephus reports two incidents of divine revelations to the high priest, John Hyrcanus, and there are reports of special revelation being given to the high priests Jaddua (Neh. 12:11) and Onias III (early second century B.C.E.). Zechariah, father of John the Baptist, received a revelation while serving at the altar of incense within the temple (Luke 1:5-25).

55. Hilber, *Cultic Prophecy*, p. 85.

56. Hilber, *Cultic Prophecy*, p. 78.

psalm moves from the priest-king's exaltation in the register of heaven to his exaltation in the register of earth. Other word-plays closely link *I AM* and his priest-king: "my lord" [i.e., the priest-king] (*ʾ^{a}dōnî,* v. 1) and Lord [i.e., *I AM*] (*ʾ^{a}dōnāy,* v. 5);[57] the day of the king's power (v. 3); and the day of *I AM*'s anger (v. 5). Both parts prophesy that *I AM* and his king establish from Zion a universal and eternal kingdom by vanquishing their enemies. This is the message of the psalm.

Here is a sketch of the psalm's structure:

I. Superscription: author (David), genre (psalm)	v. 1aA
II. Introduction: genre (prophecy), Author *(I AM),* addressee (lord)	v. 1aB
A. First Part: Lord as King	vv. 1b-3
1. Divine Citation: "Sit at my right hand"	v. 1b
2. Prophetic Reflection: Address to Lord	vv. 2-3
a. Initiate holy war	v. 2
b. Lord's troops willing to fight	v. 3
B. Second Part: Lord as Priest	vv. 4-7
1. Divine Citation	v. 4
a. Introduction: Genre (an irrevocable oath)	v. 4a
b. Citation: An eternal priest like Melchizedek	v. 4b
2. Prophetic Reflections	vv. 5-7
a. Address to Lord: he will smash kings	v. 5
b. Address to congregation	vv. 6-7
(1) Lord judges whole earth	v. 6
(2) Lord consummates victory	v. 7

The two parts consist of seven verses: 3 + 4, the number of perfection. Moreover there are ten lines of poetry, 5 + 5 (see translation), the number of fullness.[58] Both numbers figure prominently in the Davidic covenant, which this oracle supplements.[59] D. N. Freedman strikingly observed that each stanza contains seventy-four syllables.[60] In sum, thematically and structurally the psalm has two equal parts. The prophet may have been in ecstasy, but he is in full control of his thoughts and emotions.

57. Other word plays, noted in the commentary, connect the stanzas and their strophes.

58. Verse 1 is a tetrastich; verses 2, 5, 6, 7 are bistichs and verses 3, 4 tristichs.

59. So *BHS* and *NIV/TNIV.* See Waltke, *An Old Testament Theology,* p. 661.

60. Cited in M. Dahood, *Psalms III: 101–150* (The Anchor Bible; Garden City, NY: Doubleday, 1970), p. 113.

II. Exegesis

A. Superscript v. 1aA

By David a psalm (*l^e^dawîd mizmôr,* see pp. 87-90). Authorship is important for Jesus' argument that he is more than a son of David (see conclusion).[61] Academics who deny that *l^e^dawîd* refers to David as the historical author reach no consensus about the date of Psalm 110.[62] Assyrian prophetic oracles (seventh century B.C.E.) support an oracle from the monarchy, not a post-exilic date. The expectation of a universal dominion finds a parallel as early as the Egyptian Execration Texts (twentieth-eighteenth centuries B.C.E.). If the psalm is pre-exilic, as most scholars think, there is no reason to deny David's authorship. He is the only king in Israel's memory through whom divine communication occurs (2 Sam. 23:1-2). *N^e^'ūm* ("inspired utterance") uniquely occurs in another hymn by David (2 Sam. 23:1). *Mizmôr* indicates that plucking of stringed instrument(s) accompanied the prophecy, a natural connection.

B. Introduction: v. 1aB

The oracle of I AM *(n^e^'ūm yhwh)* better glosses *n^e^'ūm* than "says," because its other 375 occurrences are used exclusively of divine speech.[63] God's name *I AM (yhwh)* is his covenant name with Israel. The Author of the Mosaic Covenant, whose key catechetical teachings are to love the God of justice and salvation and to love the neighbor as oneself, is also the Author of the Davidic covenant, which commissions the House of David to spread that catechetical teaching universally (see Ps. 2). David addresses his oracle to *my lord* (*'^a^ḏōnî,* not *'^a^ḏōnay, I AM*), his

61. His argument, however, does not prove authorship; it assumes, not teaches, the Jewish tradition.

62. Dahood (*Psalms III,* p. 112) locates the psalm in the tenth century because of its similarity to Psalm 2 and Northwest Semitic, not biblical, philology. E. S. Gerstenberger (*Psalms Part 2 and Lamentations* [FOTL XV, Grand Rapids: Eerdmans, 2001], pp. 266f.) locates it in the post-exilic period because of its messianic expectation.

63. Bruce K. Waltke, *The Book of Proverbs: Chapters 15–31* (Grand Rapids: Eerdmans, 2005), p. 454, n. 6. Gerstenberger thinks Prov. 30:1; 2 Sam. 23:1; and Ps. 36:2 are exceptions; they are not. In Prov. 30:1 *n^e^'ūm* parallels *maśśā'* ("prophetic burden") and is used with *haggeḇer* ("the powerful man says") as in Num. 24:3 (of Balaam's oracle). 2 Sam. 23:2 names *I AM* as speaking through David. TNIV glosses the term in Ps. 36:2: "I have a message from God in my heart." For a detailed discussion see R. Rendtorff, "Zum Gebrauch der Formel n'um Jawe im jeremiahbuch," *ZAW* 64 (1954): 27ff.

master, to whom he is a slave.[64] *'Aḏōn* occurs almost exclusively with a genitive of relationship to signify the authority of one over another. The epithet, however, veils the identification of "my lord" (see "conclusion"). The absence of the appellatives "king" and "anointed" does not prove the psalm is post-exilic. An Assyrian royal prophecy from the seventh century B.C.E. also does not use the word "king" or its equivalents.[65]

C. Part I: Lord as King vv. 1b-3

1. Divine Citation to David's "Lord": "Sit at my right hand" v. 1b

The divine invitation *sit* (*šēb,* "enthrone" in Ps. 2:4) *at my right hand (lîmînî)* gives David's lord the highest place of honor (cf. 1 Kings 2:19) and, as Luther recognized, on that exalted throne in heaven he "possesses the very majesty and power that is called divine." At God's right hand assures him of divine protection to occupy honor, power, and majesty forevermore (see Ps. 16:8; cf. 74:11). To sit symbolizes the king's authority in contrast to his attendants who stand to wait upon him, and more than that, to sit on the right hand signifies to serve *I AM* as his viceroy.[66] Some argue plausibly that the language is metaphorical to represent the king's favored position and his inviolable protection (Ps. 16:8; 74:11); its counterpart "*I AM* is at your right hand" is metaphor. Others guess that there is an allusion to a special ceremonial place in the temple (cf. 2 Kings 11:14; 23:3).[67] More probably God's right hand refers to the throne hall, the Hall of Judgment, where the king sits to judge (1 Kings 7:7).[68] The temple housing *I AM*'s earthly throne, the ark (1 Sam. 4:4; Isa. 66:1; cf. Matt. 5:34), faces eastward in the great courtyard.[69] The Hall of Judgment housing the king's throne seems to be on the south side, to the right of God's throne, facing northward in the great courtyard. Recall that the Egyptian coronation ceremony had two parts: first the king was crowned in the temple and thus crowned "he was conducted to his palace where he ascended his throne where in a more or less threatening way he announced *urbi et orbi* the start of his

64. Only once does *'āḏôn* appear in the sense of authority over impersonal spheres (1 Kings 16:24).

65. Hilber, *Cultic Prophecy,* p. 86, n. 26.

66. J. J. Stewart Perowne, *The Book of Psalms* (Grand Rapids: Zondervan, 1977; reprinted from 1878), p. 304.

67. A. Weiser, *The Psalms* (OTL; Philadelphia: Westminster Press, 1962), p. 694.

68. Surprisingly, no one to my knowledge has proposed this *Sitz im Leben.*

69. D. Ussishkin, "King Solomon's Palaces," *Biblical Archaeologist* 36 (1973): 78-105.

rule" (see Ps. 2).[70] David, limited by his sociological knowledge, envisions the ascent of his lord to the throne in the Hall of Judgment as the site of the coming universal kingdom.[71] Its fulfillment in the ascension of Christ shows the temple-palace complex is a type of the heavenly reality that broke into history (see Exod. 25:40; Heb. 8:5; 9:24).[72] What is certain is that "sit at my right hand" is fulfilled in the resurrected-bodily ascension of the Lord Jesus Christ into heaven where today the Son of Man sits at God's right hand and is given a kingdom (Dan. 7:13f.; Acts 2:34-36).

The final triumph of this "lord" is depicted by *until I make* (*'āšîṯ*, Ps. 3:6 [7]) *your enemies* (*'ōyᵉḇeyḵā*, Ps. 3:7 [8]; 8:2 [3]) the footstool *of your feet* (*lᵉraḡleyḵā*, Ps. 8:6 [7]). *Until* (*'aḏ*) here "expresses a limit which is not absolute (terminating the preceding action), but only relative, beyond which the action or state described in the principal clause still continues."[73] *Footstool* (*hᵃḏōm*) always (six times) occurs with "feet." The royal footstool, a part of the throne (2 Chron. 9:18), symbolizes power and authority (Isa. 66:1); a victor making his enemies his footstool depicts the victor's complete power and authority over them (cf. Josh. 10:24; 1 Kings 5:3 [17]). On the young Tutankhamen's footstool are representations of foreign captives, prostrate, with their hands behind their backs, to depict symbolically his enemies as already bound and under his feet.[74] From the victor's perspective it connotes his disdain and judgment; from the victim's perspective it connotes shame and humiliation (cf. 1 Cor. 15:25; Eph. 1:22).

2. *Reflection: Prophetic Address to Lord vv. 2-3*

"Your enemies" links the divine citation and the inspired reflection.

70. G. von Rad, *Old Testament Theology*, 2 vols., trans. D. M. Stalker (New York: Harper & Row, 1965), 1:319. See now Lanny Bell, "Luxor Temple and the Cult of the Royal Ka," *Journal of Near Eastern Studies* 44 (1985): 251-94.

71. See the suggested arrangement of the buildings of Solomon's palace in *New Bible Dictionary*, ed. J. D. Douglas et al. (Leicester: Inter-Varsity Press, 1962), p. 1129.

72. Waltke, *An Old Testament Theology*, pp. 818f.

73. *IBHS*, p. 215, P. 11.2.12b, n. 102. GKC, 164f. A Ugaritic text also refutes this claim: "A throne is placed and he's [Kothar] seated at the right hand of Puissant Baal" (UT, 51:v.108-10; *ANET*, p. 134).

74. F. Gössmann, "Scabellum pedum tuorum," *Divinitas* 11 (1967): 30-53; cf. *Dictionary of Biblical Imagery*, ed. Leland Ryken, James C. Wilhoit, and Tremper Longman III (Downers Grove, IL: IVP Academic, 1998), p. 906. Turning from Egypt to Mesopotamia, a relief shows Sennacherib, king of Assyria, sitting upon his throne held up by twelve Israeli captives (*ANEP*, p. 129, no. 371).

a. *I AM* Initiates Holy War v. 2

The divine command prompts the prophet to commission his king to rule the earth, using the symbol of his scepter. The command and commission to fulfill Israel's covenant mandate to subdue her enemies and to bless respectful nations were given originally to Israel's father, Abraham (Gen. 12:3; 22:18); then to the nation through her founder, Moses (Deut. 20:10-15; 28:10-15); and climactically to David (2 Sam. 7). *Scepter (maṭṭeh)* means stick or staff, but in royal context becomes the king's badge of authority and of power to punish his enemies (Isa. 10:5). *Your strong ('uzzᵉḵā)* connotes wielding his coercive mace forcefully without breaking it and so symbolically losing his kingship (cf. Jer. 48:12). The scepter is usually made of gold or iron; the latter probably is in view (cf. Ps. 2:9). *I AM will stretch out* (*yišlaḥ yhwh,* n. 39) has the specialized sense of "to send" with reference to something attached to something else (1 Chron. 13:10; Isa. 18:2; Ezek. 17:6). The depiction connotes ever-widening circles of dominion *from Zion* (i.e., Jerusalem; see Ps. 1:6), conceptualized as the center of the world (2 Sam. 5:7, 9; Pss. 48; 132:13-18; Acts 1:8).[75] Elsewhere the king's scepter establishes justice (Ps. 45:6 [7]; Heb. 1:8).

The command *rule in the midst of your enemies* (*rᵉḏēh bᵉqereḇ,* Ps. 51:10 [12] *'ōyᵉḇeyḵā* [see v. 1]) initiates the holy war. The imperative also connotes assurance.[76] One time *raḏâ* means "to tread [the wine press]" (Joel 3:13 [4:13]) and many times, *to rule* with the associated meaning to compel obedience by punishing disobedience and so commanding respect (cf. Lev. 25:43; 26:17; Ezek. 34:4).[77]

b. Lord's Troops Willing to Fight v. 3

In Assyrian royal prophecy mention is made of the king's army. To fortify the king and to initiate holy war the prophet assures him of the competence of *your troops* (*'am,* a specialized sense of "people" in this holy war context). His army *freely offers itself (nᵉḏāḇôṯ)* glosses a more literal "is volunteerism," an idiom meaning "wholly/freely volunteers."[78] Holy war is conducted only with dedicated, fearless warriors to support their leader on the battlefield (Deut. 20:1-9; Judg. 5:2; 1 Sam. 25:28; 2 Chron. 13:8, 12; 20:13-21; Isa. 13:3f.), not with mercenar-

75. See Waltke, *An Old Testament Theology,* p. 554.

76. GKC, 110c.

77. *HALOT,* 4:1190, s.v. *rdh.*

78. "I am prayer" means "I am wholly given to prayer" (Ps. 109:4); "I am peace" means "wholly given to peace" (Ps. 120:7) and "I am delights" means "I was wholly delighting" (Prov. 8:30).

ies and/or fearful draftees. The stout-hearted freely volunteer themselves because they love and trust their king, and know God is with them, for their cause is justice. Jesus calls this army to follow him in his church militant (cf. Matt. 10:34; Luke 9:57-62; 2 Cor. 4:7-12; 2 Tim. 2:3). Paul offered himself to God as a "drink offering" (Phil. 2:17).[79]

The collocation, *in the day of (bᵉyôm),* is normally equivalent to "when," but when *yôm* is further defined, as by "of your strength," it specifies a particular period of time. *Of your strength* (*ḥêleḵâ,* cf. Eccl. 12:3; Ps. 33:17; Job 20:18) is a metonymy for the time of holy war. Christ's worldwide conquest to his law of liberty begins when he ascends into heaven and pours out his Spirit. After Pentecost his disciples surrender their lives in service to him, even to martyrdom (Acts 7:57-59).

Verset 3Ba adds two images of these troops. First, *arrayed in holy splendor* (*bᵉhaḏrê* [Ps. 8:5 (6)] *qōḏeš* [see Ps. 2:6], literally, "holy splendors") is a metonymy for their regalia (cf. Ps. 45:3 [4]). "Holy" signifies that their garments mark them as set apart to God and so as a pure army (1 Sam. 21:4f.) of such as the priests, for they are conceptualized as a kingdom of priests (Exod. 19:6). The second image, *from the womb (mēreḥem-m),* pictures the dawn of the final king's rule as giving birth to this dedicated army. *Of the dawn* (*šaḥār,* see n. 42) signals dispelling the night in which people weep and presages the beginning of hope and joy in human experience (Ps. 30:5 [6]). This army, as copious as morning dew, mysteriously appearing and glittering on every blade and leaf, refreshes a languishing earth. *Dew* or "light rain" *(ṭal)* evokes the heavenly origin of the troops, for in the Old Testament dew is thought of as coming from the sky and descending upon the earth (cf. Gen. 27:28, 39; Deut. 33:28; Hag. 1:10; Zech. 8:12; Prov. 3:20). Because its descent is imperceptible, it may evoke the invisible working of God. Also, in Israel's agrarian economy dew is associated with life. In sum, God mysteriously raises this holy army to refresh the earth with justice and love, when "the winter of our discontent made glorious summer by the [Son of Man]" (Shakespeare, *Richard III* [1.1.i-iii]; cf. Zeph. 3:5). *Of your youth (yalḏūṯeyḵâ)* completes the metaphor about the army. *Come to you (lᵉḵâ),* the last word of the verse, is a parallel of the army, the first word of the verse. "Youth" connotes freshness, prime strength, prowess, promise, and endurance (cf. Lam. 4:7).

79. Concerning the church's faith in the resurrection of their Lord, Chesterton wrote: "A real Christian who believes should do two things: dance, out of the sense of sheer joy; and fight, out of the sense of victory" (cited by Samuel Young, *God Makes a Difference* [Holiness Data Ministry, Digital Reproduction, copyright 1993-2006]).

D. Part II: Lord as Priest vv. 4-7

Assyrian royal oracles display two parts, and the second also stands under the umbrella of the first: "An oracle of *I AM*" (v. 1aA).

1. Divine Citation to David's "Lord": vv. 4-5

a. Introduction to Genre of Divine Citation: An Irrevocable Oath v. 4a

I AM's oath, underscored by his denial that he changes his mind, stresses the truthfulness and certainty of a statement or of a testimony. This emphasis is necessary, for *I AM*'s proclamation of his investiture of priesthood on the ruler reverses the old Mosaic dispensation, which radically separated the two theocratic offices symbolized by throne and altar. *I AM swears* (*nišbaʿ yhwh,* see Ps. 15:4) to assure his newly minted king that he is also a priest. Also, perhaps *I AM* uses the oath formula to supplement his original oath to David deeding him an eternal house, throne, and kingdom (2 Sam. 7; Ps. 89:3-4 [4-5]). God changes his prophecies when circumstances change (see Jer. 18:5-10), but never changes his oaths (Heb. 6:13-17).[80] A tautology certifies the oath's inviolability: "and will not change his mind" (*wᵉlōʾ yinnāḥēm,* see n. 46).

b. Citation: An Eternal Priest Like Melchizedek v. 4b

I AM additionally proclaims to David's "lord": *you are a priest (attâ ḵōhēn) . . . like Melchizedek.* The addition "You are a priest *forever* (*ʿôlām,* see Ps. 15:5) *like (ʿal diḇrāṯî) Melchizedek*" distinguishes this high priest from Aaron's high priesthood.[81] *Diḇrâ* in its one absolute usage means "cause" (Job 5:8) and in its five other uses as a collocation with *ʿal* means "for the cause/reason that" (Job 5:8; Eccl. 3:18; 7:14; 8:2; Dan. 2:30; 4:17).[82] David's "lord" is a king and an eternal

80. R. L. Pratt Jr., "Historical Contingencies and Biblical Predictions," in *The Way of Wisdom: Essays in Honor of Bruce K. Waltke,* ed. J. I. Packer and Sven K. Soderlund (Grand Rapids: Zondervan, 2000), pp. 180-203.

81. Unlike the Egyptian and Mesopotamian religions, in the old dispensation the king could not intrude on the altar, as proud Uzziah/Hezekiah learned the hard way (2 Chron. 26:16-21).

82. BDB (p. 184, s.v. *diḇrâ*) gives the meanings "cause, reason, manner," but for this text curiously opts for "in the order of." *HALOT* (1:212, s.v. *diḇrâ*) gives "manner" as the only option for this text. Most EVV gloss *ʿal-diḇrāṯî* — probably following *taxin* of LXX — by "in the order of," "in the succession of" (NEB), "in the line of" (NLT). Those glosses are without parallel and misleading.

priest because, before Aaron's priesthood,[83] Melchizedek was a royal priest who is represented as eternal, having no reference to lineage, a fundamental prerogative to serve as a priest. As the writer of Hebrews perceives, because Melchizedek, priest of *I AM,* El Elyon ("The Most High God"), is represented as an eternal king-priest, so now *I AM* (cf. Heb. 7:3) ordains David's "lord" to be his eternal priest-king in the new age that embraces the eschaton.[84]

The writer of Hebrews summarizes the similarities of Aaron's and Melchizedek's priesthood thus: divine appointment, not self-appointment; serving the people in matters related to God; offering sacrifices for their sins;[85] dealing gently with the ignorant going astray among them (cf. Heb. 5:1-4). More specifically, to judge from Aaron's activities the high priest protects the sanctity of the temple and performs what properly goes on there: offering sacrifices, singing and performing other worship activities (Leviticus; Num. 1:53; 3:28, 32);[86] dispensing oracles (1 Sam. 14:36f.; 23:2; 30:7f.; cf. Judg. 18:5); teaching *Torah* (Deut. 31:9f.; 2 Chron. 17:8f.; Ezek. 44:23; Hag. 2:11ff.; Mal. 2:7); and judging (Deut. 17:8-13; 21:5). Bearing the jewels representing the twelve tribes of Israel upon his shoulders and breast, he represents the people before God and mediates God to the people. For these sacred responsibilities the priest is holy and must be free from physical and moral defects and have no association with death such as a corpse (Lev. 21:10-15). He is rewarded with the best of the land and of the animals. Dommershausen draws the conclusion:

> It would be difficult to overstress the importance of the priesthood for OT religion. The priests represent Israel's relationship with God; in a sense, they are mediators of the covenant. The high priest, bearing the names of the twelve tribes on his breastplate, represents as it were the entire nation. The priests actualize Yahweh's presence in the words of their many liturgi-

83. From the time of David (1000 B.C.E.) to the destruction of the temple (70 C.E.) the high priests were Abiathar and the succeeding Zadokites until 171 B.C.E., when Antiochus IV transferred the office to Menelaus and the Hasmoneans.

84. Bruce discovered after drawing this conclusion that the New American Bible also reads "like."

85. The Teacher of Righteousness and his sect at Qumran separated themselves from the Jerusalem priesthood and its temple and in that context spiritualized the notion of sacrifice. Since atonement could not be effected by sacrifice, prayer and moral conduct served as its substitute (1QS 9:3-6). Albeit there is questionably an altar of incense, not of sacrifice, at Qumran (Torleif Elgvin and Stephen J. Pfann, "An Incense Altar at Qumran?" in *Dead Sea Discoveries* [Leiden: E. J. Brill, 2002], vol. 9, pp. 20-33). The substitution of ethics for sacrifice also occurred in Judaism with the destruction of the temple. In the New Testament, the reality of the symbolic temple with its priesthood appeared in the person of Jesus Christ, rendering the old religion obsolete.

86. Presumably kings offered sacrifices through the priests.

cal functions. The holiness worship demands is symbolized in the priesthood, which makes a visible statement that Yahweh is the lord and master of the nation.[87]

If this is true of the priesthood of Levi, how much is it true of the higher priesthood of Melchizedek, an authority figure in both the political and religious spheres, and so in a position to bless (3x, Heb. 7:4-10). Melchizedek's priesthood is founded on his righteous character — his name means "King of Righteousness," his sound theology that *I AM* is *El Elyon* the only High God, and his being God's agent of peace. In the Abraham narrative his appointment as a king-priest functions as a foil to the king of Sodom, a Satanic pretender to rule the earth. Christ's priesthood is grounded in his sinless perfection, his orthodoxy, his bringing true peace, and in God's appointment in contrast to Satan's usurpers of his rightful rule. Both type and antitype bring bread and wine to the faithful. Above all, the priesthood of Melchizedek is superior to that of Aaron, for unlike Aaron, his is *forever* (*lᵉʿôlām*, see Ps. 15:5).[88]

2. *Prophetic Reflections vv. 5-7*

David now addresses his reflections on this citation to Messiah (v. 5) and the congregation (vv. 6-7). Ancient Near Eastern literature, as in the Tell Fekherye Inscription, shifts pronouns between first, second, and third persons without formally signaling the change of perspectives.[89] The shift of pronouns from "you" (v. 5) to "he" (vv. 6-7) signals the prosopological change of perspective. Although the nearest antecedent of "he" is "Lord [i.e., *I AM*]" (v. 5), semantic pertinence demands an earthly antecedent, namely, David's lord. The two parts of David's reflections are held together by the same subject Messiah, the predicate catch-word "smash" *(māḥaṣ)*, and its common object, "kings" and "nations" (vv. 5, 6; see Ps. 2:1-2). A second catchword, "head" *(rōʾš)*, also links the two halves: the head of the enemy is smashed; the head of the lord rises up in triumph. The reflection represents the lord as smashing the tyrannical kings, and the second half draws his conquest to a climactic conclusion; his is an enduring victory.

87. W. Dommershausen, *TDOT,* 7:72, s.v. *kōhēn.*

88. The impeccable Christ is the perfect sacrifice, and his church offers spiritual sacrifices of prayer and praise (Heb. 13:15); her members, a royal priesthood (1 Peter 2:9), offer themselves as living sacrifices in the service of Jesus Christ, including doing good to and sharing with others (Rom. 12:1-2; Heb. 13:16).

89. A. Abou-Assaf, P. Bordreuil, and Alan Millard, *La Statue de Tell Fekherye et Son Inscription Bilingue Assyro-Arméenne* (Recherche sur les Civilisations, Cahier 7; Paris: ADPF, 1982). An index of the stylistic freedom in this inscription is the fact that the first change of persons does *not* take place at exactly the same point in the Akkadian and Aramaic versions.

a. Address to Messiah: Lord of All Will Smash Pagan Kings v. 5

The epithet Lord *(ʾ^{a}dōnāy)* refers to *I AM* as Lord of lords, the Lord of all,[90] and signifies that *I AM* is Messiah's master and that Messiah is his slave-king (see v. 1). This Lord of all, David says, is at *your right hand (ʿal-y^{e}mîn^{e}ḵâ),* thereby assuring him of divine protection and power (see v. 2). True Strength *smashes (māḥaṣ) kings (m^{e}lākîm),* who are empowered by demonic forces (cf. Ps. 2:1-2, 10; cf. Eph. 6:10-20). Their defeat is certain because their king has been dethroned from heaven (Luke 10:18) and bound in the sense that today Jesus Christ takes captives from nations formerly under the enemy's rule and frees them from sin and death to join him in his battle for truth and justice (Eph. 4:1-13). *Māḥaṣ* ("smash") occurs fourteen times, always in poetry, to signify the victor's absolute power. Its subjects are *I AM* (Deut. 32:39; 33:11; Ps. 68:21, 23 [22, 24]; 110:5, 6; Job 5:18; 26:12; Hab. 3:13), or his "star" from Jacob (Num. 24:17), or Israel (Num. 24:17), or an Israelite warrior such as Jael, who crushed the head of Sisera with a tent-peg (Judg. 5:26), and David (2 Sam. 22:39 [= Ps. 18:38 (39)]).

b. Address to Congregation: vv. 6-7

To better interpret David's second reflection it is important to bear in mind that the representation of the Old Testament prophecies about the spiritual realities of the New Testament dispensation are contingent upon the Old Testament culture. As prophets must foretell the future in their own language to think intelligently and to speak lucidly, so their language also represents their world. An Old Testament prophet *cannot* speak in the terms of present-day culture because prophecy is God's word incarnate, adapted to the intellectual capacity of the speaker and his audience.[91] In other words, their imagination is restricted by what sociologists call the sociology of knowledge. For this reason the language of Psalm 110 must be interpreted spiritually after Pentecost when the Holy Spirit broke spiritual realities into salvation history. Christ introduces this method of interpretation: the temple, Jacob's well, and manna all become symbols of his life and body (John 2, 3, 4, 5 *passim*). His apostles follow suit: military armor becomes spiritual armor; temple becomes heavenly sanctuary; and so forth. This address represents holy war in the political terms of the old dispensation; they must be reinterpreted to refer to the spiritual realities of the new dispensation.

90. *IBHS,* pp. 123f., P. 4.4.3e,f.
91. Waltke, *An Old Testament Theology,* p. 818.

(1) Lord Will Judge the Whole Earth v. 6

He will judge (yāḏîn) means he "gives right and just verdicts," in contrast to "judge" *šapaṭ*, "to right wrongs." The lord rewards the good with good and the evil with evil. *Among the nations (baggôyīm)* replaces the synecdoche "kings" (v. 5). At his first advent Jesus Christ commands his disciples to baptize nations and to teach them, and he foretells that at his second advent he will judge among the nations: rewarding those who showed compassion to the poor and punishing those who oppressed them (Matt. 25:31-46).

His punishing the wicked is instantiated first by *he will fill the valleys with corpses* (*millē'* Piel *gē'āyôṯ gᵉwîyôṯ*, see n. 50; cf. Isa. 66:24; Rev. 19:17-18).[92] Prior to that, presumably with his mighty mace, *he will smash* (*māḥaṣ*, see v. 5 with his mace) *the heads (rō'š). Rō'š* is ambiguous, for it could be either a countable singular for the head over the nations (cf. Exod. 18:25; Num. 1:16; so LXX [*kephalos*, also ambiguous]; JPS) or a collective singular for all the leaders of the nations (i.e., "heads," Ps. 68:21 [22]; so Targ. ["heads of kings"] and most English versions). The latter option is preferable; the collective singular was probably chosen for its play with the countable singular "head" in verse 7. If a countable singular is intended, there could be an intertextual allusion to Genesis 3:15, which foretells a battle of champions in which the Seed of the woman will crush the head of the Serpent, who is unmasked in later revelation to expose Satan/the Devil (Rev. 19:20; 20:2), and the singulars in verses 6-7 would signal the final showdown battle of the two seeds. *Who are over the broad earth* or "a wide land" (*'ereṣ rabbâ*; literally, "much land") is a metonymy for all nations.[93]

(2) Lord Will Consummate His Victory v. 7

The second concrete image *from the wadi (minnaḥal)* refers to a sharply defined depression of a valley or streambed, usually in desert areas, that is bone dry in summer and becomes a gulley washer in the rainy season, forming its sharp contours.[94] The image connotes that even in desert areas of the broad earth God will supply Messiah with an abundant amount of water to quench his

92. Such a valley is Jerusalem's Valley of Hinnom, whose exact location is uncertain; but whichever of three possible valleys is intended, all three include Jerusalem's southeast extremity. This valley was used for burning the corpses of criminals and animals, and indeed refuse of any sort. Although references to this valley occur after the time of David, ancient Jebus and other cities must have had such incinerators. I personally spent several days excavating a garbage dump at Gezer.

93. Cf. *HALOT*, p. 1171, s.v. *raḇ*, entry 1.

94. Wadis are common in southwestern Asia and North Africa, including Israel, especially along the Jordanian rift (Deut. 8:7; Isa. 35:6).

thirst and refresh him (cf. Deut. 8:7; Ps. 36:8 [9]).[95] *Along the way (badderek̲)* adds to this image Messiah's marching triumphantly in his conquest of the whole earth. *He will drink* completes the image. In his hurry, he takes a momentary break to refresh himself but does not linger. Neither desert nor fatigue will stop him in his zeal to end tyranny. *Therefore (ʿal-kēn)* introduces a state of later effects:[96] the priest-king's distinguished and exalted authority and joy. As a result of refreshing himself he pursues his foes until *he will lift up his head* (*yārîm*, Ps. 3:3 [4]), a signal that he has distinguished himself, is worthy of honor and dominion (cf. Gen. 40:13; Judg. 8:28; Ps. 3:3 [4]; 27:6) and is full of joy (Ps. 24:7, 9).[97] In contrast to the abased kings whom he makes his footstool (v. 1), *I AM*'s king holds his head high.

Part IV: Identification of "My Lord"

Returning to the introduction we again address the identity of the psalm's lord. Modern scholarship has supported four candidates and *usually* accepts the dictum of historical criticism: *vaticinium ex eventu* ("proclamation at the time of the event"). Form critics *infer* that this royal psalm was used in a coronation ceremony. If one accepts this hypothesis, as we are inclined to do, the issue is whether when the king ascended his throne he was hailed with messianic enthusiasm,[98] and, more than that, whether the oracle contains predictions this Messiah is superhuman, combines throne and altar under his crown, and achieves a consummate, universal victory over his enemies.

A. A Cultic Servant of a Maccabean or of Joshua

Many historical critics at the turn of the twentieth century thought "lord" refers to a Maccabean prince, especially to Jonathan (1 Macc. 9:30f.; 10:20) or to Simon (1 Macc. 14:35, 38, 41). This theory faces insuperable difficulties. 1) The Maccabees are not of David's posterity; 2) They are priests, but the psalm

95. Some scholars speculate with no evidence that during the royal ritual the king drinks from a brook (the spring of Gihon?) to refresh himself for battle (see A. A. Anderson, *Psalms,* vol. 2: *Psalms 73-150* [New Century Bible; Greenwood, SC: The Attic Press, 1977], p. 772).

96. *ʿal-kēn,* also glossed "therefore," introduces a proposed or anticipated response after a statement of certain conditions.

97. A. Bowling, *TWOT,* 2:838.

98. G. A. F. Knight, *A Christian Theology of the Old Testament* (Richmond: John Knox Press, 1959), p. 300.

crowns a prince; 3) Psalms of Solomon 17:23f. (first century) [and the Talmud and Midrash] look for a son of David as Messiah, not for a son of Aaron;[99] 4) the priesthood of the sons of Aaron did not last forever;[100] 5) the psalm is a prophecy, but the Maccabean age is sadly conscious that the voice of prophecy was silent (1 Macc. 4:46; 9:27);[101] and 6) the language of the Qumran hymnic literature, roughly contemporary with the Maccabean age, "is neo-classical, not classical."[102]

Some contend the psalm is composed for the crowning of the high priest Joshua, because Zechariah (520 B.C.E.) prophesied at the crowning of the high priest Joshua (Zech. 6:11) that the high priest's royal crown would become a memorial of the uniting of the two offices and so foreshadowed the crowning of a Messianic King-Priest (6:12-13). This view obviates the last two objections against a Maccabean referent but not the first four, which pertain to any post-exilic Jewish ruler.

B. A Cultic Servant of Zadok

Some think that during the coronation liturgy the speaker(s) turn(s) and address(es) the high priest Zadok.[103] They argue that Zadok derives from Melchizedek.[104] Others think that Zadok addresses David in verses 1-3, 5-7 and that David addresses Zadok in v. 4.[105] But the prophet addresses his whole oracle to "my lord," whom he consistently addresses as "you" in both parts of the psalm (vv. 2-3, 4-5). The interpretation that the antecedent of "you" changes back and forth between king and priest is arbitrary. Moreover, the poet's lord is a champion warrior that rules universally in time and space. No historian makes such a claim for Zadok.

99. C. A. Briggs and Emilie Grace Briggs, *The Book of Psalms*, vol. 2 (ICC; Edinburgh: T. & T. Clark, 1907), p. 374.

100. 1 Maccabees speaks of Simon as "high priest forever," but immediately qualifies it: "until there should arise a faithful prophet."

101. Did the writer of Maccabees evidently discount Josephus' reports of high priests giving prophecies (see. n. 54)?

102. F. M. Cross, *Ancient Library of Qumran* (Garden City, NY: Doubleday, 1958), p. 166.

103. H. H. Rowley ("Melchizedek and Zadok," in *Festschrift, Alfred Bertholet zum 80. Geburtstag / gewidmet von Kollegen und Freunden; herausgegeben durch Walter Baumgartner et al.* [Tübingen: J. C. B. Mohr, 1950], pp. 467f.) thinks Zadok is the speaker in verses 1-3, 5-7, and the king addresses Zadok in verse 4.

104. C. Broyles, *Psalms* (NIBC; Peabody, MA: Hendrickson; Carlisle, Cumbria: Paternoster, 1999), p. 415.

105. Rowley, "Melchizedek and Zadok."

C. David of Solomon

Several academics accept David as the antecedent of "my" in the term "my lord," but nevertheless historicize the "prophecy" and pre-empt it of true predictions. They argue that the aged David calls Solomon his lord in view of Solomon's new status as king. In so doing, they further argue, David spoke a word far greater than he knew. This interpretation is also not tenable. First, the entire prophecy represents David's "lord" as a warrior-king who harshly subdues the whole earth in holy war, but David expected Solomon (i.e., "Peace") to concentrate that nation's strength and resources to building *I AM*'s temple, not to engage in holy war (2 Sam. 7:10; 1 Kings 5:1-6). Second, the subject of our psalm is a priest; Solomon was not. To rebut this anticipated objection it is argued:

> David and his royal sons, as chief representatives of the rule of God, performed many worship-focused activities, such as overseeing the ark of the covenant (see 2 Sam. 6:1-15, especially v. 14; 1 Kgs. 8:1), building and overseeing the temple (see 1 Kgs. 5–7; 2 Kgs. 12:4-7; 22:3-7; 23:4-7; 2 Chron. 15:8; 24:4-12; 29:3-11; 34:8) and overseeing the work of the priests and Levites and the temple liturgy (1 Chron. 6:31; 15:11-16; 16:4-42; 23:3-31; 25:1; 2 Chron. 17:7-9; 19:8-11; 29:25, 30; 35:15-16; Ezra 3:10; 8:20; Neh. 12:24, 36, 45).[106]

These texts, however, cannot bear the weight of the argument. In the ancient Near East, temple building is a royal responsibility; magistrates oversee it and to some extent the priests' activity. Moses, not Aaron, oversees the building of the tabernacle and legislates the Levitical cultus; David has the inspiration for building the first temple, provides for it, and supplements the Mosaic cultus with musical directions (1 Chron. 22:2-5; 28:2; Ps. 30 title). In post-exilic times Zerubbabel, Ezra, and Nehemiah performed similar duties. Herod the Great significantly expanded the temple. But Moses, the House of David, and the post-exilic reformers are never called priests.[107] Moreover, in contrast to other ancient Near Eastern cultures and Melchizedek's El Elyon cult (see below), in the old dispensation, from Aaron until the Maccabees, Israel kept separate the roles of their kings and priests. Similarly, the president and congress of the

106. TNIV Study Bible, p. 973. Surprisingly, this note does not mention specifically that David was wearing a linen ephod, the garment of a priest, when he accompanied the bringing up of the ark to Jerusalem. Nevertheless, the garment does not qualify him to assume the appellation or duties of a priest; the narrative makes no mention of Melchizedek; and the oracle is about his royal sons, not himself.

107. 2 Samuel 8:17 may be the sole possible exception. In the lists of David's officials, David's sons are labeled *kōh^{a}nîm*, which probably means "chief/court officials" (2 Sam. 8:17 as understood in the Sept. [*aularchai*]; Targ. [*rab̲r^{e}b̲în*]; 1 Chron. 18:17 [*hārīʾšōnîm*]).

United States commission the construction of the Supreme Court building, appoint its chief justice and justices, and oversee the federal judicial system, but they are neither called judges nor allowed to function as judges. Then too, why is a solemn oath needful to permit Solomon to perform what are commonly royal functions with regard to the temple? Finally, taxes, not tithes, are paid to Israel's kings. In sum, the psalm's predicates defining David's lord are not fulfilled in Solomon, nor are they expected to be.

D. A Cultic Servant of the House of David

Most deny Davidic authorship and argue that a cultic servant is addressing an exclusively human son of David as his lord. To explain his priesthood, they use the same flawed arguments as in the preceding interpretation: "David of Solomon." Others argue the oracle grants or assumes that David's House inherits an El Elyon cultus at Jerusalem of which Melchizedek was the priest in the time of Abraham when David conquers Jerusalem and makes it his royal city, "the city of David" (Gen. 14:18-20; 2 Sam. 5:6-8).[108] This interpretation is unlikely.

First, at the time of Joshua a true El Elyon cultus — the one Abraham respects — does not exist in Jerusalem, for *I AM* commands Joshua to exterminate the city, leaving no survivors including its king (Gen. 15:17-21; Deut. 7:1-2; Josh. 10:1-27; Judg. 1:4-8). It is unlikely the house of David desires to resurrect and reckon itself as heirs of a failed and shamed Canaanite cultus and synthesize it with the cult of *I AM.* Second, this alleged priesthood would have a higher rank than Aaron's. Melchizedek's superiority to Abraham and so to his sons Levi and Aaron is inferred by Abraham's paying tribute to Melchizedek and by Melchizedek's blessing Abraham. If this theory has historic substance, the king would trump the high priest and have no need to submit to his rule in the sanctuary. Is this interpretation possible in the old dispensation? "Yes." Evidence? "None."

Third, the theory lacks any external validation. To use this psalm to prove the interpretation commits the logical errors of begging the issue and/or circular reasoning; it substantiates the theory from the psalm itself. The Melchizedek in the Abraham narrative appears out of the blue and just as mysteriously disappears. This is more than an argument from silence. The Bible is all about true religion. Its failure to preserve a tradition that David and his sons inherit

108. A. Weiser, *The Psalms: A Commentary* (Philadelphia: Westminster Press, 1962), p. 695; A. A. Anderson, *Psalms,* vol. 2: *73–150* (New Century Bible; Greenwood, SC: Attic Press, 1977), p. 771.

Melchizedek's priesthood is too glaring to be an oversight or an accident. Fourth, unlike Psalms 89 and 132, this royal prophecy makes no reference to David's sons. In sum, the interpretation is made of whole cloth with no external validation.

Fifth, if one argues that the prophet has in mind only Israel's kings during the monarchy, his prophecy is either false, or, if his audience understands he is using *Hofstil,* courtly hyperbole, his oracle has no real substance. No son of David during the first temple period fulfills it. In contradistinction to this prophetic vision of the universal rule of this "lord," no son of David before Jesus Christ rules beyond those of David's empire. Rather than establishing a universal kingdom, the House of David loses its kingdom until Jesus Christ restores it (Acts 15:12-18).

Sixth and correlatively, the preservation of the psalms argues against this interpretation. If the historic circumstances are thought to falsify a prophecy, the prophecy is not preserved. The notion that post-exilic Judaism reinterpreted royal psalms to refer to Messiah morally tarnishes the tradition that saved it and diminishes the psalm's credibility.

E. David of the Son of Man

The New Testament authors do not accept the historical critic's dictum of *vaticinium ex eventu,* but interpret David's address to his lord as prophetic prediction of Jesus Christ. Their conviction uniquely satisfies the accredited grammatico-historical method of interpretation, provided one accepts the canon that prophecy represents the spiritual realities of the new dispensation in terms of its historical conditioning. Delitzsch rightly labels it a unique prophetico-Messianic psalm: "In dying he [David] seizes the pillars of the divine promise, he lets go the ground of his own present, and looks as a prophet into the future of his seed." Delitzsch's arguments, however, are not equally cogent.[109] We argue, first, that the introduction formula identifies the coming Messiah as superhuman:

> While the Pharisees were gathered together, Jesus asked them, "What do you think about the Messiah? Whose son is he?" "The son of David," they replied. He said to them, "How is it then that David, speaking by the Spirit, calls him 'Lord'? For he says, 'The Lord said to my Lord: "Sit at my right

109. F. Delitzsch, *Commentary on the Old Testament,* vol. 5, trans. Francis Bolton (Peabody, MA: Hendrickson, 1996; reprinted from the English edition originally published by T. & T. Clark, 1866-91), pp. 691-99, esp. p. 693.

> hand. . . ."' If then David calls him 'Lord,' how can he be his son?" No one could say a word in reply, and from that day on no one dared to ask him any more questions. (Matt. 22:41-46)

We agree that: 1) the psalm is inspired, 2) David is the author; 3) a father is superior to the son, who owes his life to his father; and 4) a lord, by definition, has authority over his slave. Accordingly, David's lord must be superhuman in his nature. Jesus Christ uniquely validates these assumptions by his being born son of David and Son of God, by his sinless life, by his bodily resurrection from the dead, and by his ascent into heaven (cf. Matt. 22:44f.; Mark 12:36f.; Luke 1:32; 20:42-44). Some contend, however, that Jesus merely uses these wrong assumptions of Judaism, without endorsing them, for the sake of his argument.[110] But if Christ is using false, Jewish assumptions, his argument for his superhuman nature based on this prediction is no longer cogent for Christian apologetics and doctrine.[111] In short, the theory of false assumptions undermines sound doctrine. Finally, the next two arguments, based on the divine citations (vv. 1b, 4) and the prophet's reflection (vv. 2-3, 5-7), validate that the psalm contains true predictions, and if this is so in verses 1b-7, why not allow that David gives a real prediction in verse 1a?

Turning from the psalm's introduction, its two divine citations (vv. 1b, 4) assert that David's lord sits at God's right hand and that by divine appointment serves as his eternal priest-king, resembling the venerable, pre-Aaronic priesthood of Melchizedek, not a hereditary priest of the line of Aaron. Christ's apostles lay down their lives to bear witness that they saw Jesus Christ ascend into heaven where, the writer of Hebrew teaches, he serves God as his priest-king in the heavenly sanctuary (Acts 2:30-36; 5:31; 7:55-56; Rom. 8:34; Eph. 1:20; 4:7-9; Col. 3:1; Heb. 1:3; 5:6-10; 7:11-28; 8:1; 10:12; 12:2). The apostles frequently mention his ascension in connection with his sitting "at the right hand of God," a term molded and minted by Psalm 110. In other words, the historical temple-palace arrangement discussed above is a type of the heavenly reality.

Turning to the prophet's two reflections (vv. 3, 5-7), the scene shifts from the royal throne to the battlefield. He extends his reign in ever-widening circles throughout the world in a holy war through his dedicated troops. So also in ever-widening circles the ascended Christ and his church militant have raised his flag of the New Covenant on every continent and have won disciples to Jesus Christ in almost every nation by the sword of the Word and the power of the Holy Spirit (Matt. 16; Acts 1:8).

110. A. F. Kirkpatrick, *The Book of Psalms: With Introduction and Notes* (Cambridge: Cambridge University Press, 1897), pp. 662f.

111. Perowne, *Psalms*, pp. 297f.

Part V. Conclusion

Those who support a different candidate than Jesus Christ contend that the New Testament and/or the superscripts in the Book of Psalms reinterpret the oracle's original intention. In truth, no other candidate than Jesus satisfies the plain sense of the predications of this unified oracle addressed to David's lord. Historical critics, not the New Testament, reinterpret the psalm from its plain meaning to fit their dogma. David's lord is Daniel's Son of Man, a term Jesus preferred to the political title Messiah. This is so because he, like Daniel's Son of Man, rides the clouds to the Ancient of Days and brings all nations under his dominion (Dan. 7:13f.; Matt. 24:36; 1 Cor. 15:24).[112]

David probably composes his royal prophecy to be sung by cultic functionaries at the coronation ceremony of his heirs, hoping that in the end of salvation history a final successor of his would fulfill and consummate his prophecy. He is probably unaware, however, that his language is a type of the spiritual reality that his eternal son introduced into salvation history. David's royal prophecy of Psalm 16:11 envisions his uncorrupted body at God's right hand forevermore (see Psalm 16). Psalm 110 adds to that vision the prophecy that his transcendent son, as a type of David redivivus, ascends to his throne of judgment and eliminates his self-serving enemies (Matt. 25:31ff.). His hope is not put to shame.

112. Waltke, *An Old Testament Theology,* p. 568.

CHAPTER 16

Psalm 139: Search Me, God

Part I: Voice of the Church

It has been suggested that in the period from 30 to 250 C.E. the whole of the Old Testament is treated as one large commentary on the Scriptures. It is a period before formal commentaries of individual books of the Bible were initiated; rather, texts are quoted, interpreted, and commented upon. This immediate continuity between the Old and New Testaments is evidenced in **1 Clement** to the point that he seems unaware of a new radical beginning in Christianity. Rather he is concerned about inter-Christian conflicts, and his approach to Psalm 139 is as an exhortation to live morally exemplary lives. He argues that if God "sees all things," quoting verses 7-10, Christians should avoid transgression. "For whither can any of us flee from his mighty hand? Or what world will receive any of those who run away from Him?"[1] Then, in submitting to each other in the local church, he urges: "let us be reminded that God created us and presented us with wonderful gifts." Quoting Psalm 139:15, he urges that his readers should always be thankful and worshipful.[2]

I. The Apologists

In the period, roughly 140-180 C.E., Christian apologists focus upon the One God as the world's Creator. Their polemic is against the pagans, yet it is also against the Jews, for they affirm Christ to be both the *Logos* and the Messiah.

1. 1 Clement, xxviii, p. 27.
2. 1 Clement, xxxviii, p. 34.

Clement of Alexandria (150-215), a philosophical contemplative, focuses upon verses 7-10, "not from fear, nor even from desire of salvation, but from the primary desire to know God himself." In this way he seeks "to honor God Almighty."

Origen (185-253), the apologist *par excellence,* knows how offensive Psalm 139 is to pagan philosophers such as Celsus, with whom he debates. Celsus writes a book against Christianity that he titled *True Doctrine.* He is well-versed in the Scriptures, and thus a dangerous antagonist. Celsus has also read the cosmological argument of Plato in *Timaeus* that "to find the Maker and Father of this universe is difficult, and after finding him it is impossible to declare him to all men." Following upon Plato, in *True Doctrine* (c. 170 C.E.) Celsus scorns the Christians for their claim that God has been revealed in a historical person. Celsus easily derides what he considers "the superstitions" of uneducated simple, Christian believers, and more seriously the illegal "magic" Jesus claims to have in his miracles. But his basic concern is to address educated Christians like Athenagoras, who acclaim God to be "uncreated, eternal, invisible, impassible, incomprehensible, infinite . . . encompassed by light, beauty, spirit, and indescribable power" *(Leg. Pro Christ).*[3] Pagan philosophers fully agree about that! But the composer of Psalm 139, while fully expressing these divine attributes, is also aware of the unique intimacy in deepest personal trust, which he can exercise and express to God. This unification of God's ineffability with his intimacy is the primary cause of offense to the pagan philosophers; for them these two realities of God's persona proclaimed in Psalm 139 are incompatible. These two aspects of God meet in the Person of Jesus Christ. Mockingly, Celsus asks: "What is the point of such a descent on the part of God? Was it in order to learn what was going on among men? Doesn't God know everything (*c. Cels.* 4.2)?"[4] So why did God need to come to live on earth as a human being, at a specific point of history? Challenging the Incarnation at its root, Celsus hoped to topple and destroy all notion of the credibility of the faith of Christian philosophers like Justin Martyr, writing some five years after Justin's martyrdom.

Although Christians apparently ignored Celsus for about fifty years, in 248 Origen responds in his *Against Celsus.* Perhaps with Psalm 139 in mind, he argues: "I admit that Plato's statement quoted by Celsus is noble and impressive. But consider whether the Holy Scripture shows more compassion for humankind when it presents the divine Word (Logos), who was in the beginning with

3. Quoted by Robert L. Wilken, *The Christians as the Romans Saw Them* (New Haven and London: Yale University Press, 1984), p. 103.

4. Origen, *Against Celsus,* trans. Henry Chadwick (Cambridge: Cambridge University Press, 1953).

God . . . , as becoming flesh in order to reach everyone."[5] The knowledge of divinity simply by the mind is ineffective, argues Origen, bringing no confidence in the One God. This is why the pagan philosophers identify and worship many gods instead of being able to identify the unique God. Once the uniqueness, as well as the personal, intimate experience of *I AM* has been identified by the Christians, they can then use the Greek philosophical terms such as *eternal, invisible,* and *unchanging* to describe God. Psalm 139 holds these two aspects in remarkable tension: ineffability and intimacy.

II. The Post-Nicene Fathers

If the earlier fathers were concerned with ousting the many gods who had filled the heaven and earth of the pagan *mundus* ("world"), the later post-Nicene fathers are challenged to fill the religious vacuum with both the exaltation of the One God and the manner in which he descended in Jesus Christ to fill the whole earth by His Spirit, as One God in three Persons.[6]

Athanasius (296-373) refers to the ineffable character of God's knowledge in Psalm 139:6 in his first monastic letter to the monks, which advises them to live contemplatively[7] and to admit their fallibility:[8] "when you think of temptations as a testing for you, if you want to give thanks after the trials, you have the one hundred and thirty-eighth psalm" [Vulgate].[9]

Cyril of Jerusalem (316-86) in his Lenten lectures gives catechetical addresses to catechumens preparing for baptism by total immersion, during the night of Holy Saturday and the early morning of Easter Sunday. The candles burning all night in anticipation of the "Resurrection morning" are for him a vivid illustration of Psalm 139:12, "even darkness is not dark to you; the night is as bright as the day, for darkness is as light to you." Baptism is "enlightenment," the candidates being called *phōtizomenoi,* "those to be enlightened," or "those enlightened."[10] Cyril's second reference to Psalm 139 aims to refute some

5. Origen, *Against Celsus,* 7.42.

6. Peter Brown, *The Rise of Western Christendom,* 2nd ed. (Oxford: Blackwell, 2003), p. 121.

7. M. J. Rondeau, "L'Epitre à Marcellinus sur les Psaumes," *Vigiliae Christianae* 22 (1968): 176-97. She suggests the letter was composed in the mid-fourth century, within the context of "desert monastic spirituality."

8. Athanasius, *The Monastic Letters of Saint Athanasius the Great,* trans. Leslie W. Barnard (Fairacres, Oxford: SLG Press, 1994), p. 10.

9. Athanasius, *The Life of Anthony and the Letter to Marcellinus,* Classics of Western Spirituality, trans. Robert C. Gregg (New York, Ramsey, and Toronto: Paulist Press, 1980), pp. 113, 122.

10. Among those present are already baptized Christians, to whom Cyril's *Catecheses* is a

Greeks, "who have said . . . [God's] power does not extend to earth, but only to heaven, so they pervert the text: 'and Your faithfulness to the skies' [Ps. 108:5], and have dared to circumscribe the providence of God . . . and to alienate from God the things on earth, forgetting the Psalm which says: 'If I go up to the heavens, you are there; if I sink to the nether world, you are present there' [Ps. 139:8]. For, if there is nothing higher than heaven, and the nether world is deeper than the earth, He who rules the lower regions reaches the earth also."[11]

Hilary of Poitiers (315-67), in the light of Psalm 139:7-10, saw that "there is no place without God." For God the Creator has made all things, leading him to enter the life of contemplation. These verses, he confesses, "filled my soul with joy, at the contemplation of this excellent and ineffable knowledge, because it worshipped this infinity of a boundless eternity in this Father and Creator."[12] Hilary reflects further that if the Divine is Infinite and Eternal, then is he not also omniscient and omnipotent?[13]

Augustine of Hippo (354-430), following on Hilary's texts, quotes at least three times from Psalm 139 in his *De Trinitate.* In book xv: 13, he uses Psalm 139:6 to apply the wonder of God's knowledge to his own creation, "seeing I am not even able to comprehend myself whom you have made."[14] Then he quotes 1 Corinthians 13:12, "we now see through a mirror," to suggest we can only speak or know of God allegorically, as likenesses,[15] which implies we can only ever be tentative about our "knowing," in contrast to God's omniscience. Augustine also twice quotes Psalm 139:7, 8 to suggest that the many theophanies of God in the Old Testament indicate his omnipresence, and reflect upon the presence of Christ, who is the image of the invisible God, as well as hint also at the presence of the Holy Spirit (book ii: 7).[16]

---

reminder course of instruction, and some of whom recorded his unwritten words by shorthand, probably about 349 C.E. Jerome is aware that they had been secretly distributed. Cyril, over Lent, gave twenty lectures to his Greek audience and followed up with another twenty lectures to his Syriac audience, forty addresses in all! It is a summary "systematic theology" to deepen faith-understanding.

11. St. Cyril of Jerusalem, *The Works of St. Cyril of Jerusalem,* vol. 1, trans. Leo P. McCauley, S.J. (Washington, DC: Catholic University of America Press, 1969), pp. 81, 180-81.

12. It was Hilary's discontent with paganism's demeaning of God as less or other than "the One alone," "omnipotent," and "eternal" that led him to experience the personal reality of Moses' encounter at the burning bush. St. Hilary of Poitiers, *The Trinity,* trans. Stephen McKenna, C.SS.R., The Fathers of the Church (Washington: The Catholic University of America Press, 1954), pp. 5-6.

13. Hilary of Poitiers, *The Trinity,* p. 8.

14. Saint Augustine, *The Trinity,* trans. Edmund Hill, O.P. (Brooklyn, NY: New City Press, 1990), p. 405.

15. Augustine, *The Trinity,* p. 407.

16. Augustine, *The Trinity,* p. 120.

Augustine is using Psalm 139 to determine his epistemology in a way we have abandoned today. For before the later use of "sacraments" in church practices, Augustine was using "sacramenta" much more widely. For him, they indicate there are "signs" everywhere of the presence of God, whereby we might know him by faith — in symbols, types, and figures.[17]

Saturated in the Psalms, Augustine recites an amusing incident. He was prepared to preach on a shorter psalm, possibly on Psalm 138, but the public reader, flustered by the occasion, read the wrong psalm, which happened to be Psalm 139. Unfazed, Augustine then got up to preach from the read text, saying: "we have chosen to follow the will of God in the reader's mistake, rather than our own will by keeping our purpose."[18] Since it was going to be a much longer psalm, and therefore a longer discourse, he hoped his audience would take all this into account with the necessary patience over the event!

Bear in mind, he begins his sermon, that just as the psalm may speak from differing voices, so too Christ, in taking our humanity, sometimes speaks as the eternal Son of God, at other times with our human voice, and yet again with the voice of the church, his body. For Christ has made himself one with us. Yet he also speaks with the psalmist's prophetic voice. As a rhetorician, Augustine is familiar with the classical device of prosopology, of identifying the diverse voices in the drama.[19] In this regard, more than perhaps any other commentator, Augustine draws upon these *personae dramatis* to explore what he considers to be the multi-dimensional aspects of the text. Thus Augustine interprets the first two verses of Psalm 139 as the voice of the Son in his intimacy with the Father, saying in his humanity: "You have tested me, and you know me." Then Augustine adds: "This does not mean that God did not know him already; it means that he made him known to others through the testing." "You know my sitting down and my rising up," he suggests, means "my passion and my resurrection."

As you know, he reminds his audience, our Lord Jesus Christ speaks through the prophets sometimes with his own voice and at other times with ours, because he makes himself one with us. "Let us now listen to the Lord Jesus Christ speaking in our psalm's prophetic words and remember that, though the psalms were sung long before the Lord was born from Mary, they were not sung before he was Lord,"[20] that is, as the *I AM*.

But in the voice of the *totus Christi,* referring now to Christ's body, the

17. Augustine, *The Trinity,* p. 126, n. 58.

18. Augustine, *Expositions on the Book of Psalms,* trans. Maria Boulding, O.S.B. (Hyde Park, NY: New York City Press, 2004), vol. 6, p. 256.

19. See historical introduction to Psalm 1 for further discussion of "prosopology."

20. Augustine, *Expositions on the Book of Psalms,* p. 635.

church, Augustine argues the text can also mean, "In your sight I have both confessed my sins and have been justified by your grace." Interpreting verses 3 and 4 as the voice of the church, Augustine alludes to the story of the Prodigal Son. Although he was in a far country, he was still an open book to the Father. For can there be "any place where you are not present, you whom I have abandoned?" Augustine suggests this is the question of the Prodigal. For in the omniscience of divine love, the Father could rise up and "while he was still on his way his father ran to meet him" (Luke 15:20). In this way Augustine interweaves the parable with the psalm. "Now, Lord you know everything about me, most recent things and things long ago" (so vv. 5, 6). Applying this to his audience, Augustine reminds them of the omniscience of God, in the context of Romans 11:33-35. Even in the despair of our "night," Christ has descended into our "night," "for darkness is as light to you, O God" (Ps. 139:12).

Verses 13-18 describe the mystery of human conception and birth, which Augustine relates to Paul's awareness of being called by God, as from his mother's womb (Gal. 1:15-16). Yet such confidence in our Creator can become corrupted into self-confidence, as when Peter denied his Lord, although Jesus warned him in advance about his threefold denial (Matt. 26:34). Against the Donatists who sought for a "pure church," Augustine uses verses 18-20 to describe the church as a mixed collection of people, good and bad. While we hate the sins of those who are wicked, yet we always should love those whom God has created. Augustine interprets verses 23-24 as referring to how Christ reads the church's heart, as we cannot, leaving the judgment of both the good and the wicked in God's hands, not ours. The church's prayer should then be, "Test me, O God, and know my heart," and indeed, "Lead me in the way everlasting." This is still "the night" of the church, but it is "all light" to God.

Augustine uses the psalm ecclesiastically to express his view of the comprehensive membership of the "catholic church." This he likens to "the mixed net of fish" that Peter and the other disciples caught after the Resurrection. Let the omniscience of God, who knows us more than we can know ourselves and yet whose love embraces us, give us the largesse of spirit to accept within his Body many we would judge as being our enemy. He tells his listeners, these are profound and holy signs, brothers and sisters. How wonderfully does the Spirit of God speak to us! And what delights he prepares for us in this our night! "You already knew, didn't you, that bad people must be borne with in the Church of God and that schisms are to be avoided?"[21] In this way, Augustine draws a broad sweep in defense of the Constantinian church as it had become by the beginning of the fifth century.

21. Augustine, *Expositions on the Book of Psalms,* pp. 281-82.

John Chrysostom (347-407), gifted preacher and the last of the great urban rhetors, aims to create a wholly "Christian" city of Antioch, which the mixed character of Carthage could never be for Augustine.[22] His commentary on the Psalms is probably *extempore* rather than a scholarly composition. It precedes Augustine's by two or three decades, since Chrysostom was a contemporary of Ambrose. But unlike Augustine's use of extensive allegory, Chrysostom is marked by precision, *akribeia.* This is necessary as an exegetical tool, as well as out of respect for "the Word made flesh" with whom there is no inaccuracy or any unnecessary language. It illustrates the humble restraint of the Incarnate Lord to become human. We may consider "Chrysostom the exegete," then, as a forebear of William Tyndale and John Calvin in providing "a plain text" for a reformed people.

Chrysostom begins his commentary on this psalm with the awareness that God "tests" or "searches" us as our Creator, for no one else can know us so intimately. He thereupon relates the whole psalm to the human condition before God, explaining "by 'sitting down' and 'rising up' (v. 2), [the psalmist] refers to the whole of life." "So if God knows even our thoughts, why does he apply also testing through actions? Not for him to learn personally, but to give the stamp of his approval to those subjected to it. For he even knew Job before his trial. . . ."[23] God's "searching" of us, then, is expressive of his close personal knowledge, and God's predictive ability is grounded upon such knowledge, knowing "everything that has happened and will happen."[24] It is with this awareness and belief that the early Fathers could interpret the Psalms themselves as being "prophetic," in ways modern thought now rules out, or at least questions. Chrysostom thus views God as exercising both creative power — "you formed me" — and providential foreknowledge — "you placed your hand upon me" (v. 5), which he relates to such passages as Hebrews 1:1-3 and Colossians 1:16-17.

God's action in the "night," which is as "light" to him (vv. 11-12), he interprets as evidence of divine providence turning adversity into blessing, as the affliction of the Egyptians led to the glorious Exodus of God's covenant people. It happened beforehand to Joseph, turning his slavery into kingship, shame into honor.[25] "Because you took control of my inner being, Lord; you laid hold of me from my mother's womb" (v. 13), argues Chrysostom, then the whole of who

22. Peter Brown, *The Body and Society* (New York: Columbia University Press, 1988), pp. 306-22.

23. St. John Chrysostom, *Commentary on the Psalms,* vol. 2, trans. Robert Charles Hill (Brookline, MA: Holy Cross Orthodox Press, 1998), p. 241.

24. Chrysostom, *Commentary on the Psalms,* p. 243.

25. Chrysostom, *Commentary on the Psalms,* pp. 246-47.

I am is God's possession, the possessor "who protected me, cared for me, secured me, from my earliest years, from my very cradle, and through actions taught me what I said." Experiencing such divinely marvelous knowledge in a personally existential way makes Scriptural prophecy believable, for "You know the future in advance, and the past, and the secrets of our minds; but not even this can I grasp with my reasoning."

He is certain that the ending of the psalm in reference to "the wicked" can only be God's condemnation of the Jews — a significant population in Antioch — who rejected God's Messianic prophecy of Jesus Christ. "They both received the Law and by the Law were cut off."[26] Solemnly, the psalmist repeats, "Test me, O God, and know my heart: examine me and know my ways, and see if the path of lawlessness is in me, and guide me in the eternal path" (vv. 23-24). But why this repetitive prayer at the end, as at the beginning, if God has such foreknowledge of us? Here he echoes Origen's original question. Because it is we who need to know our own hearts and the intimacy of our ways, argues Chrysostom, not *I AM*. "But how is one guided towards it?" He answers his own question, "by enjoying grace from God and contributing to sound values, rendered superior to [material] things of this life."

Chrysostom realizes that vast theological questions are being raised by the psalm, but they are all dealt with existentially in terms of one's own personal experience, and yet do not deny divine transcendence. He is advocating a delicate balance.

III. Monastic Scholars of the Early Middle Ages

Beginning with Jerome, as a scholar-monk, the long continuity through late Antiquity into the Middle Ages of Biblical scholarship was sustained in the monasteries. The Psalms now become the bridge linking the inward life of the monastery with the outward life of the surrounding countryside and its Christian populace.[27] The motive for psalms commentaries centered on the liturgical practice and memory of the Psalter by the community.

Cassiodorus (490-583) has the most comprehensive commentary of Psalm 139 of the scholar monks in the early Middle Ages. He gives the traditional interpretation of the title of Psalm 139, "Unto the End," as relating "to the perfect

26. Chrysostom, *Commentary on the Psalms*, p. 250.

27. Scholar-monks had more ecclesial independence, while the advantages of institutionalized knowledge, the communal resources of extensive libraries, and the ascetic practices of mind and body for serious studies also provided the opportunities to become scholar-saints.

and eternal End which is the Lord Christ . . . so this entire psalm — and this is the view of the most learned father Hilary — is to be recited by the mouth of the Lord Christ." Whereas Cassiodorus in other psalms is closely dependent upon the commentaries of Augustine, here he has already stated he is following the exegesis of Hilary of Poitiers, in his Trinitarian focus, especially upon the two natures of the God-Man. "The first is that by which He is God, co-eternal with the Father; the second that by which He was born of the virgin Mary, and as one and the same Person deigned in time to become Man for our salvation."[28] The humble tone with which Christ speaks of himself through the words of the psalm "is to be understood in accordance with the mystery of the holy incarnation." Indeed, he sees the Psalm "is brimming with profound mysteries." Within a Trinitarian frame, Cassiodorus interprets the Psalm prosopologically: in the first part the Son recounts to the Father his death and resurrection; in the second, the psalmist expounds on the Father's divinity; in the third, Christ proclaims his role as a Servant; and finally, the psalmist describes the preeminence of the faithful in spite of their enemies. So, similar to Augustine, he sees the first two verses concerning "his sitting down" and "rising up" as referring to the Son's Incarnation. But then he moves into verses 3 to 6, as evidence of the predictive knowledge of the Father to anticipate the Incarnation. Only in verse 7 is the implication that no human being can hide from the omnipresence of the Holy Spirit, who is with the Father and the Son, the One God.[29] In verse 8, where others recognize the omnipresence of God, Cassiodorus sees the mystery of the Incarnation — that Christ descended into hell in his death, but has risen at the Ascension to be at God's right hand in glory. Now no darkness can overcome Christ, even the obscurity of Scripture, which can be a form of "darkness," as the prophets expressed it.[30] The whole purpose of this commentary is a polemic against the Arians, to show "that if a person proclaims Christ as perfect God and perfect Man but denies His two natures, he subverts true teaching and his own admission that Christ is perfect God and perfect man."[31]

Bede (c. 673-735) only gives meditative reference to Psalm 139, and

28. Cassiodorus, *Explanation of the Psalms*, trans. P. G. Walsh (New York and Mahwah, NJ: Paulist Press, 1990), vol. 3, p. 373.

29. Cassiodorus, *Explanation of the Psalms*, vol. 3, p. 375.

30. Cassiodorus uses the statement of verse 13 to refute the Nestorian heresy condemned at Ephesus in 431; namely, that there were two separate Persons in Christ, the divine and the human. His argument is tortuous, but he implies that the begetting of the God-Man makes Christ "fearfully and wonderfully made." But in verse 16, "my imperfect being," he now refers to Christ's Body, the church, which is imperfect.

31. Cassiodorus identifies eight psalms that speak about the two natures of Christ: Pss. 2, 8, 21, 72, 82, 108, 110, and now 139.

Alcuin (734-804) none. Later evangelists, such as **Rabanus Maurus** (776-856) in Germany, use the psalms musically rather than in serious study. **Haimo of Auxerre** (died 856), a Benedictine monk, sees that "what could be terrifying Judgment from the All-Knowing God [in Psalm 139] is also the deepest comfort when going to Heaven. I shall not be lonely and strange there, amidst the angels diverse from me in nature and properties, for Christ My Brother, as bone of my bone, flesh of my flesh, is there also, ascended to the right hand of God to prepare a place for me."

We pass over the scholastic period of the twelfth and thirteenth centuries, which exhibit glossalia as textual use of the Psalms, but where other classical texts are gaining ground also. It is a new academic and secular way of life that has lost the devotional focus of Bede, Alcuin, and even Anselm. **Robert Grosseteste** (1168-1253), a bishop of Lincoln and himself a scholar, protests to no avail at the replacement of the Bible with other texts.[32]

Richard of St. Victor (died 1173), an Augustinian canon in Paris, who became one of the great mystical writers of the Middle Ages, identifies Psalm 139 with the contemplative life, for which he provides some annotations without a full text of commentary. Richard is strongly aware that God sees and knows all of our own imperfections, hidden or public. His focus is upon verse 16, "your eyes have seen my imperfection, and in your book all shall be written, days shall be formed, and no one in them."[33] Richard finds this verse in his Gallican Vulgate a challenge to interpret in his *glossa,* hence his interest is in it alone. He interprets it to mean that all God's saints are written in his book, unlike the wicked, who will be "blotted out of the book of life" (Ps. 69:28 [29]). Even so, one may have perfect form as a child, without the further growth required for the full stature of a mature adult. Likewise, the Christian may grow to become imperfect by having "faith without good work, good work with unfaithfulness, chastity with pride, humility with dissipation, making the whole growth of the Christian monstrous by such inconsistencies." The implication then drawn from the Psalm is as an ethical challenge to grow up spiritually, for all is seen and known by God. Since he was probably the best Biblical scholar of the twelfth century, this brief exposition may be rather disappointing. But Richard has a habit of facing the more difficult texts of Scripture to give them his own interpretation.[34] He strongly re-

32. R. W. Southern, *Scholastic Humanism and the Unification of Europe: Foundations,* vol. 1 (Oxford, UK, and Cambridge, MA: Blackwell, 1997), p. 103.

33. In his earlier *Psalmi Iuxta LXX,* Jerome renders verse 16a by "inperfectum meum . . . et nemo in eis," but, after he learns Hebrew, he corrects this in his *Psalmi Iuxta Hebr.* by "informem adhuc me . . . et non est una in eis."

34. Richard of St. Victor, *Expositio difficultatum suborientium in expositione tabernaculi foederis.*

flects the contemplative tradition of "monastic theology" of Bernard of Clairvaux, and yet he is now also in a secular school of teaching.[35]

IV. Reformation Commentaries

We might wish that **Martin Luther** (1483-1546) had rewritten a second commentary on Psalm 139, after his break with Rome. For in a letter of December 16, 1515, he referred to his first commentary on the Psalms as "trifles, quite worthy of being destroyed."[36] He began a second commentary, *Operationes in Psalmos*, published in 1519-20. But this second attempt stopped with Psalm 22, as he was caught up in the crisis of his excommunication. Later in the 1530s he lectured on a few psalms, but Psalm 139 never figured among them.

John Calvin (1509-64) integrates better than anyone else Augustine's "double knowledge." Psalm 139 shows that we gain appropriate Christian subjectivity in our relationship with God. Since without God we cannot know sin, we can live in ignorance of our inner condition, merely contented and morally complacent with our own endowments, observes Calvin. This is in contrast to Renaissance humanism, which sees "man as the measure of all things." At the beginning of the *Institutes* Calvin affirms: "Our wisdom, in so far as it ought to be deemed true and solid wisdom, consists almost entirely of two parts: the knowledge of God and of ourselves. But as these are connected together by many ties, it is not easy to determine which of the two precedes, and gives birth to the other. For in the first place, no man can survey himself without forthwith turning his thoughts towards the God in whom he lives and moves; because it is perfectly obvious, that the endowments which we possess cannot possibly be from ourselves; nay, that our very being is nothing else than subsistence in God alone." Calvin then defines Christian piety: "by which I mean that union of reverence and love to God which the knowledge of his benefits inspires. For until men feel that they owe everything to God, that they are cherished by his paternal care, and that he is the author of all their blessings, so that nothing is to be looked for away from him, they will never submit to him in voluntary obedience; nay, unless they place their entire happiness in him, they will never yield up their whole selves to him in truth and sincerity."[37]

Calvin would never stop then with the Renaissance humanist pursuit of

35. Ceslas Spicq, *Esquisse d'une Histoire de l'Exégèse Latine au Moyen Âge* (Paris: Vrin, 1944), pp. 130-31.

36. Robert N. Fife, *Young Luther* (New York: AMS Press, 1970).

37. *Calvin's Institutes* (MacDill AFB, FL: MacDonald Publishing Company, 1970), book 1, pp. 7, 9.

self-knowledge; rather, the real goal is the knowledge of God.[38] The individual is then the vehicle for the work of the Holy Spirit in the world. Unlike Erasmian humanism, it is not the church that is the mediator and vehicle for the Spirit, but the inward relatedness of the believer to whom is graciously given the self-disclosure of God, through Christ, by his Spirit. This unites the procession of God as revealer and of man as knower. How this is illustrated in Calvin's commentary on Psalm 139 is illuminating.

Calvin begins with the relation between God as Creator and God's omniscience: "In this Psalm David — that he may dismiss the deceptive coverings under which most men take refuge, and divest himself of hypocrisy — insists at large upon the truth that nothing can elude the divine observation. He illustrates this truth from the original formation of man, since he who fashioned us in our mother's womb, and imparted to every member its particular office and function, cannot possibly be ignorant of our actions. Quickened by this meditation due to a reverential fear of God, he declares himself to have no sympathy with the ungodly and profane and beseeches God, in the confidence of conscious integrity, not to forsake him in this life."[39] This is an excellent example of what Calvin calls "the plain sense" of the text.

God's foreknowledge is the focus Calvin would give us, so that whether we affirm that God knows already what we are about to communicate with the tongue, or whether Psalm 139:4 means that God needs no human language from us since he can read our hearts, independent of human language, it all means the same thing: God "knows" as we do not. Verse 6 then affirms that God's knowledge is incomparable with human understanding. Calvin continues to pursue this central idea, that there is nothing human beings can use to hide themselves from God's omniscience and omnipresence. David is still considering in verse 11, "if only he could find any covert or subterfuge, he would avail himself of the license" . . . even if it could be the darkness.

While the psalmist in Psalm 139 is proclaiming his innocence before God, Calvin interprets this with moderation. For Calvin has an awesome sense of the wonder of "God's thoughts as not lying within the compass of man's judgment."[40]

38. But by the early eighteenth century the pursuit of self-knowledge had become an end in itself. The poet Alexander Pope had already stated: "The proper study of mankind is Man." In the last chapter of John Mason's *A Treatise on Self Knowledge: The Nature and Benefit of That Important Science, and the Way to Attain It* (Haverhill, MA, 1812), the author adds that prayer is a help, but only as a devotional tag-on to his study. The views of the Stoics seem just as important to him.

39. John Calvin, *Commentary on the Book of the Psalms,* vol. 5, trans. Rev. James Anderson (Edinburgh: Calvin Translation Society, 1849), p. 206.

40. Calvin, *Commentary on the Book of the Psalms,* vol. 5, pp. 218-19.

Calvin mourns the reality that "while we may cast a glance at our hands and feet, and occasionally survey the elegance of our shape with complacency, there is scarcely one in a hundred who thinks of his Maker. Or if any recognize their life as coming from God, there is none at least who rises to the great truth that he who formed the ear, and the eye, and the understanding heart, himself hears, sees, and knows everything" [cf. Ps. 94:9].[41] Only at the end of the psalm does Calvin admit that "the Psalmist presents himself before God as a witness of his integrity; as if he had said, that he came freely and ingenuously to God's bar, as not being one of the wicked despisers of his name, nor having connection with them" (vv. 19-24).[42] Now in a renewed way he can pray, "Search me O God!" (v. 23), while still aware he was born in sin. In the closing prayer, "Lead me in the way everlasting" (v. 24), Calvin alludes to the prayer of Joshua, in his closing message before his death: "You know in your hearts that not one thing has failed of all the good things that the Lord your God promised . . . you" (Josh. 23:14).

V. Religious Confusion of the Seventeenth and Eighteenth Centuries

After Calvin, perhaps never again were the nuances of Psalm 139 so fully interpreted until now. Augustine's and Calvin's "self-knowledge" in the seventeenth century became a mere Stoic posture, as we see in the essays of **William Montagu**, courtier of Queen Henrietta (wife of Charles I, now imprisoned after the Civil War). Using "the knowledge of our self, as if it were the compass, whereby we must set our course . . . to navigate our spiritual life," he begins with "a map of human nature," trying to comfort his royal patron in her confused and distressed spiritual condition. With the language of commerce, he proposes to his fellow courtiers the basic need of "humility . . . for their commerce with one another," for "there is no better Accountant" to help us recognize "the greatness of God, the meanness of ourselves and our nearness and relation to our Brother."[43] David is an archetype for his meditations because he too was a king and also exiled for a time. For Montagu the Psalms are now "that spiritual globe," to explore oneself. But everything is left in the air, for he has no Biblical understanding of the Psalms.

While from the sixteenth into the eighteenth centuries impressively numerous musical and poetic interpretations of the psalms promoted an ongoing series of worshiping communities, deep interpretations of the psalms tended to

41. Calvin, *Commentary on the Book of the Psalms,* vol. 5, p. 219.

42. Calvin, *Commentary on the Book of the Psalms,* vol. 5, p. 220.

43. William Montagu, *Miscellanea Spiritualia or Devout Essays* (London, 1648), p. 104.

be overlooked. Thus in the popular Anglican psalmody of **Nicholas Brady** (1659-1726) and **Nahum Tate** (1659-1726), Psalm 139 is paraphrased with pious intent but with some inevitable distortions:

> Thou, Lord, by strictest search has known
> My rising up and lying down;
> My secret thoughts are known to Thee,
> Known long before conceiv'd by me.
> Thine eye my bed and path surveys,
> My public haunts and private ways;
> Thou know'st what 'tis my lips would vent,
> My yet unutter'd words' intent.[44]

Its pious decorum of Sunday worship stands in sharp contrast to the Puritan tradition exemplified by **John Owen** (1616-83).[45] With reference to Psalm 139, he comments: "Men may have a general persuasion that they are under the eye of God" which they obtain by a general apprehension of God's omniscience and presence, as "all things are naked and open before him" (Heb. 4:12). Powerfully it is expressed by the psalmist that God "knows all things — that his understanding is infinite — that nothing can be hid from him — and that there is no flying out of his presence, Ps. 139:7, nor hiding from him, the darkness being light to him."[46] What then? One has to read Owen's treatises on "Sin and Temptation," "Indwelling Sin in the Life of the Believer," and other works to explore more fully his counter-cultural stance.[47]

The various references to **Jonathan Edwards** (1703-58) as "the American Augustine"[48] and satirically as "that moral Newton and second Paul"[49] reflect the strong stance he took against "The Enlightenment." Edwards did not write a commentary on the Psalter, for his interest was more as an apologist than as a Biblical scholar, but he does give a sermon fully devoted to Psalm 139, espe-

44. James Hamilton, *Our Christian Classics: Readings from the Best Divines* (London: James Nisbet, 1868), vol. 3, pp. 143-44.

45. As chaplain to Oliver Cromwell, then Vice-Chancellor of Oxford, and leader of the Congregationalists, John Owen was recognized as "the Calvin of England," who saw the state of religious confusion all around him in the same period.

46. *The Works of John Owen,* ed. William H. Goold (London: Johnstone and Hunter, 1850-), vol. 9, p. 98.

47. John Owen, *Triumph over Temptation: Pursuing a Life of Purity,* ed. James M. Houston (Colorado Springs: Victor/Cook, 2005 reprint).

48. Gerald R. McDermott, *One Holy and Happy Society: The Public Theology of Jonathan Edwards* (University Park, PA: Pennsylvania University Press, 1992).

49. A saying attributed to one of his liberal foes, President Dwight of Yale College.

cially on the concluding verses: "Search me, O God, and know my heart; try me, and know my thoughts; and see if there be any wicked way in me, and lead me in the way everlasting" (vv. 23, 24).[50] In several sermons on selected psalms Edwards writes with passion in his "high seriousness" about the glory and beauty of the true Christian calling and of the radical response Christians should make.[51] In the full range of his sermons he expresses as great a solemnity for the human condition as any other preacher in the history of the church.

He begins his sermon on Psalm 139, in the Puritan form, by the exposition of the text, leading to a statement of "doctrine," various points of discussion and defense of the doctrine and its relation to other scriptures, and then its personal application and reception. "This psalm is a meditation on the omniscience of God, or upon his perfect view and knowledge of everything, which the Psalmist represents by that perfect knowledge which God had of all his actions. . . . 'There is not a word in my tongue' says the Psalmist, 'but thou knowest it altogether.' Then he represents it by the impossibility of fleeing from the divine presence, or of hiding from him." Even in the mother's woman, his fetus was not hid from God. At the conclusion, the psalmist's prayer, "Search me, O God," is interpreted as an act of mercy. It cannot be a challenge for God to learn more about him, for God already knows all. It is to cast himself upon the mercy of God, so that the suppliant is guided forward to avoid "the way of sin." For Edwards, the thrust of Psalm 139 is that human beings, beginning with himself, must learn to know more about the deceitfulness of sin and of our general proclivity to be blind to our own inclination to sin. Even as Christians, we go on sinning for the rest of our lives. We need then the utmost vigilance to watch for the occurrence of sin within us; indeed "to watch and pray." For wherever we sin, we dishonor God, living in self-interest rather than for the glory of God. Edwards is focused on verses 23 and 24, to see ourselves as "sinners." First, we need to learn to know "the way of sin" as dynamic, requiring constant study of the Scriptures in being sensitive to its guile and tendencies. For sin is essentially love of self rather than love of

50. *The Works of President Edwards,* Worcester 8th edition (New York: Leavitt & Allen, 1852), vol. iv, sermon xxxi, pp. 502-28.

51. In one sermon he treats of the trait of "the true Christian life," which is being on "a journey towards Heaven" (sermon xxxvi). The whole purpose of life lies in this future goal. From Psalm 73:25, "Whom have I in heaven but Thee?," he describes how God is the best portion the Christian has to desire or seek after (sermon xxxiii). From Psalm 64:1, "O Thou that hearest prayer," he describes how it is God's character to hear our prayers (sermon xxxv). From Psalm 94:8-11, he preaches on the natural blindness we humans have to the things of God.

God.[52] Second, we need to learn to know one's self more intimately, by examining one's heart and motives of will and desire. This he does at length, perhaps as a rehearsal of the inquiry he is later to address in his great classic, *Religious Affections*.[53] This was set in the cultural context of the Great Revival. Was the Revival genuine for all, or was it mixed with hysteria and even hypocrisy?

Clearly, Edwards is reading Psalm 139 within the social upheavals of his time. He faces the grave threat of Deism and the incipient challenge of the Enlightenment. These are morally more blinding in self-confidence than in any true "enlightening" of the heart.[54] The psalms also are an effective "read" for the emotionally disturbed Christians, more enthusiastic than wise about their faith. With the loss of transcendence today, it suggests we need the Psalmist once more, to lead us through the confusions of postmodernism, to consider how lacking in Biblical integrity is much that purports to be "Christian."

Part II: Voice of the Psalmist: Translation

Of David. A psalm.
1 *I AM*, you search[55] me and you know me.[56]
2 You[57] know when I sit and when I rise;
you consider my thoughts[58] from afar.

52. See Robert W. Jenson, *America's Theologian: A Recommendation of Jonathan Edwards* (New York and Oxford: Oxford University Press, 1988), pp. 79-88.

53. See Jonathan Edwards, *Faith Beyond Feelings: Discerning the Heart of True Spirituality*, ed. James M. Houston (Colorado Springs: Victor/Cook, 2005 reprint).

54. A good summary of these issues is made by Stephen R. Holmes, *God of Grace and God of Glory: An Account of the Theology of Jonathan Edwards* (Grand Rapids: Eerdmans, 2001).

55. Construed as a gnomic perfective because of the unchanging, universal nature of God's relationship to David (*IBHS*, p. 488, P. 30.5.1c). The universality of God's active omniscience informs the whole stanza (see Th. Booij, "Psalm CXXXIX: Text, Syntax, Meaning," *VT* 55 [2005]: 1-2). Some propose reading this as a precative perfective (see 3:7 [8]; 4:1 [2]; 22:21 [22]; *IBHS*, p. 494, P. 30.5.4c), but a precative perfective occurs in parallel with volitional forms. So some argue in a circle by arbitrarily emending *wattēdāʿ* to *wᵉtēdaʿ*.

56. Construing the suffix on *hqrtny* as doing double duty. An initial mono-colon is not unique (cf. Ps. 66:1).

57. Though tempting to read *ʾattâ* with verse 1, thereby yielding lines of 2:2 and 3:3, the suggestion is not compelling enough to overthrow the tradition.

58. Construing the *lamedh* as a sign of the direct object, as in Aramaic, and *rēʿî* as a collective sing. to match *dᵉrāḵay* (v. 3b); LXX (B and S) adds *pantas*. Perhaps poetry's preference for elegant variation explains the plural form in verse 17a.

3 My going out[59] and my lying down[60] you discern;[61]
you are familiar with[62] all my ways.
4 Surely, before a word is on my tongue,
I AM, you know it completely.
5 Behind and before[63] — you hem me in;[64]
you have laid the palm [of your hand][65] upon me.
6 Such[66] knowledge is too wonderful[67] for me,[68]

59. Construed as *Qal* inf. cstr. to match *šbty, qwmy, rbʿy. ʾrḥ* means "to wander, travel," but the merisms in verses 2-3 refer to ingressive situations; hence the gloss "going out," not "journeying."

60. *Rbʿ* means minimally "to lie in position, recline" and may mean specifically "to copulate" as in its three other uses in Leviticus (18:23; 19:19; 20:16). The merisms are ingressive, hence the gloss "lying down."

61. BDB (p. 279) regards *zērîṯâ* as the common Hebrew root *zrh,* which in Qal and Piel means to "winnow," "scatter." If so, the verb signifies to separate one from the other and so distinguish them. *HALOT* (p. 280, s.v. II. *zrh*), following Barth, questionably derives it from II *zrh,* a putative denominative of *zeret,* which means "the little finger," and "span of the hand" as a measure. In that case *HALOT* thinks it means "to measure." If so, the figure may signify to rule.

62. This usual gloss for *skn* Hi. is uncertain because there may be more than one root *skn.* I. *skn* in Aramaic means "to advise of danger" (G stem) and "to endanger" (D stem); Ugaritic substantives, perhaps derived from different roots, mean essentially "danger" (I. *skn*) and "cover" [of the king's palace] (II. *Skn*). In Hebrew I. *skn* Ni. means "to run into danger." In Qal, however, *skn* means "to be of use/service," and the participle substantive, *sōkēn,* denotes "steward, take care of." This seems to be derived from II. *skn. Skn* occurs three times in Hi. and is usually glossed: 1) with inf. "to manage carefully," "to be in the habit of [serving]" (Num. 22:30); 2) with *ʿim* "reconcile yourself [with]" (Job 22:21); and 3) with acc. "to be acquainted with" (Ps. 139:3), in which case it is better to derive *zērîṯâ* from the *zrh* "to winnow" instead of *zrt* "to measure." Though the data is ambiguous and the meaning uncertain, the glosses in the text better fit the context than the other options, "to measure" and "to manage."

63. LXX mistakenly joins *ʾāḥôr wāqeḏem* to verse 4.

64. *Ṣûr* is a homonym: I. *ṣûr* means "to cause to incline, lean"; II. *ṣûr,* "to confine, bind, besiege"; III. *ṣûr,* "to show hostility towards"; IV. *ṣûr,* "to fashion, delineate." None contends for I. or III. *ṣûr.* Older versions preferred IV. *ṣûr,* but most moderns reject it as unlikely. The most apt meaning is II. *ṣûr,* "besiege."

65. Heb. simply "palm"; "of your hand" is added to accommodate the English idiom.

66. Syr. affixes the definite article, and LXX and Sym. read *hēgnōsis sou.* Due to a felt need for a definite article to refer to the antecedent, "such" is added to the translation, but the terse Hebrew poetry, especially in exclamation, does not require it.

67. Q reads *pᵉlîʾâ* (the *qātîl* pattern that shapes an adj. from verbs [*pālā*], similar to some passive participles in Aramaic) and K reads *pilʾîâ,* a suffixing pattern that forms an adj. from noun, *peleʾ*). These bi-forms from the same root have no difference in meaning (*IBHS,* pp. 88, 92, P. 5.3c, 5.7.c).

68. Comparative *min* (*IBHS,* p. 214, P. 11.2.11e) of capability (*IBHS,* p. 266, P. 14.4.f). Here *min* marks the subject (i.e., David) compared with an object or goal to be attained (i.e., God's knowledge), and the subject is less than equal to attaining it.

It is too high;[69] I am unable[70] to scale it.[71]
7 Where[72] can I go to escape[73] your spirit?
Where can I flee from your presence?[74]
8 If I ascend[75] to the heavens, you are there;
if I spread out my bed[76] in the Grave, behold, you!
9 Were I to rise[77] on the wings of the dawn[78]
and alight on the far side of the sea,
10 even there your hand will guide me,[79]
your right hand will hold me fast.

69. The Ni. perfective 3fs, *niśg^eḇâ*, is a simple adjectival Ni., essentially equivalent to the Qal stative (*IBHS*, p. 385, P. 23.3.b). The subject *daʿat* and the prepositional phrase *mimmenî* are gapped.

70. An old Qal passive, not Hophal, because *ykl* occurs in the simple, not causative, stem (*IBHS*, pp. 373-76, P. 22.6).

71. Literally, *'ûḵal lâ* means "I am unable to do it." *Lamedh* is construed as a *lamedh* of disadvantage (*IBHS*, p. 207, P. 11.2.10d).

72. Older and more accurate English: "Whither." For elegant variation, with no difference in meaning, the accent is on the ultima of the first *'nh*, an extended form of *'n*, and on the penult, directional *he* with *'n* (*IBHS*, p. 329, P. 18.4.f).

73. The notion of escape/avoid is pregnant in the preposition "from" (*IBHS*, p. 224, P. 11.4.3d).

74. *'nh* [accent on first syllable] *'lk mrwḥ w'nh* [accent on second syllable] *mpnyk 'ḇrḥ*. Note the rhetoric: each verse half begins with two forms of *'nh*, consists only of words with initial *aleph* and *mem* (aside from *w* "and"), and relates in a chiastic structure of verb + prepositional phrase ("from" X) + pronominal suffix ("your"). A similar play of alliteration, using almost exclusively *aleph* and *shin*, occurs in verse 8.

75. The root is *slq*, not *nsq*, though the latter occurs with similar meaning in post-Biblical Hebrew and in Aramaic (cf. GKC, 66e; cf. G. H. Dalman, *Aramäisch-neuhebräisches Wörterbuch zu Targum, Talmud, und Midrasch*, p. 260). However, it is also attested in the Sefire stele of the eighth century B.C.E. (J. A. Fitzmyer, *The Aramaic Inscriptions of Sefire* [Biblica et Orientalia, 19; Rome: Pontifical Biblical Institute, 1967], p. 31).

76. LXX's *ean katabō* probably is a guess for *'aṣṣîʿâ*, not to represent the root *ṣāʿâ*.

77. Construed as non-perfective of desire (*IBHS*, p. 509, P. 31.4b). The verb could represent the psalmist as borrowing the wings of dawn, but elsewhere *nāśāʾ kānāp* means to move the wings in the act of flying.

78. There is no need to prefer over the MT the inferior text of Syr. (i.e., "I lift up my wings as the dawn") or the inferior oral reading of LXX (i.e., "if I lift up my wings to the dawn," or, "I lift up my wings early in the morning").

79. Some exegetes, following Syr., adopt the reading "shall seize me" and retrovert *tiqqāḥēnî*. But LXX's *hodēgēsei me* supports the superior text type of MT.

11 And I then thought:[80] "Surely if[81] darkness crushes me,[82]
and if light becomes night[83] around me,[84]
12 Even darkness will not be too dark for you,
And the night will shine like the day;
Darkness is as light to you."[85]
13 For you gave birth to my kidneys;
you knit me together in my mother's womb.

80. *Wāʾōmar* functions as an anacrusis to the second strophe, and the *waw consecutive construction* signals a chronological sequence.

81. After the anacrusis, the clause renews the series of conditional sentences begun with *ʾim* in verse 8A (GKC, 111x). Syntax and rhetoric show that the two clauses of verse 11 function as protases to the two clauses of the apodoses (vv. 12aA, B). The implied *ʾim* ("if") is sharpened to *ʾak̲* ("surely," v. 11), which introduces the protasis; it is matched by emphatic *gam* ("even," vv. 10, 12), which signals the apodosis. Moreover, the protases and apodoses are held together by a threefold alternating parallelism involving "darkness" and "night" (11a, b; 12aA, B; 12b) and by the alliteration of the gutturals, palatals, liquids, and a sibilant involving every one of the sentence's 17 words: guttural /ʿ~ʾ/ [6x in six words], palatal /g~k/ (9x in 8 words), liquid /l/ (5x in four words), and sibilant /š/ (5x in 5 words).

82. Sym. *episkepasei* and Psalterium iuxta Hebraeos, *si dixero forte tenebrae operient me,* has led to the emendation *yᵉśukkēni* ("overshadow, screen, cover"; see e.g., Kraus *Ps.* 1091, 1092; BHS), but *HALOT* (1147, s.v. *swp*) rightly says "it is not required." The same can be said of G. R. Driver's suggestion (*JTS* 30 [1929]: 375-77) that the root is *šwp, "sweep* close over," appealing to an Arabic root.

83. The Hebrew syntax is ambiguous: the subject could be *ʾôr* ("light") and the predicate nominative *laylâ* ("night") = "the light is night." The similarity of the syntax between verses 8-10 and verses 11-12 removes the ambiguity. The conditional protases introduced by "if" (*ʾim,* vv. 8-9) are resolved in the apodosis introduced by *gam* ("even," v. 10), so also the conditional protasis of verse 11 introduced by *ʾak̲* ("nevertheless") in connection with *ʾim* (v. 11a) plus conjunctive *waw* ("and," v. 11b) is resolved by the apodosis introduced by *gam* ("even," v. 12). Moreover, as the protases of verse 11A pertain to *ḥōšek̲* ("darkness") and of 11B to *laylâ* ("night") and *ʾôr* ("light"), so in the parallel apodoses, *ḥōšek̲* ("darkness," v. 12a) is matched by the subject *laylâ* ("night"), and the predicate *yāʾîr* ("shine") is from the same root as *ʾôr.* Since in verse 12b night is clearly the subject and light the predicate, we must infer for the sake of semantic pertinence that in verse 11b night is the subject and light is the predicate.

84. The unusual verbal suffix with the preposition *baʿad̲* may be due to assonance with *yᵉšûp̄ēnî.*

85. "To you" in verse 12bB is added as an appropriate equivalent to "for you" in verse 12a in this terse poetry. Verse 12b is commonly assumed to be a gloss (see G. R. Driver, "Glosses in the Hebrew Text of the OT," in *L'Ancien Testament et l'Orient* [Louvain, 1957], pp. 123-61; BHS), but the emendation has no support in ancient texts and versions; and the elegant variations of *ḥᵃšēk̲â* and *ʾôrâ* (see n. 83) would be unlikely in a gloss. Moreover, a so-called tri-cola often ends a stanza, as here (S. Terrien, *The Psalms and Their Meaning for Today* [Indianapolis: Bobbs-Merrill, 1952], p. 893, n. 103).

14 I praise you because[86] I am fearfully[87] extraordinary;[88]
your works are wonderful I know[89] full well.
15 My frame[90] was not hidden from you
when I was wrought[91] in the secret place,
when I was colorfully woven in the depths of the earth.
16 My embryo[92] your eyes saw;
In your book all[93] of them were written;
My[94] days were fashioned[95] before one of them came to be.

86. Literally, "upon that" = "because" (Deut. 31:17; Judg. 3:12; Jer. 4:28; Mal. 2:14). Tautological *ʿal* may have been added to assist the metric count and the assonance of the gutturals *aleph* and *ʿayin,* which occur in seven of the ten words. It is tempting to retrovert *ʿal* into an original *ʿalî* ("my Most High"; see H. S. Nyberg, *Studien zum Hoseabuche* [UUA 6; Uppsala, 1935], 58ff., 90, 120; W. F. Albright, *Archaeology and the Religion of Israel* [Baltimore: Johns Hopkins University Press, 1946], p. 202, n. 18; et al.), but the retroversion is gratuitous.

87. The pl. suffix of *nôrāʾôṯ* reveals the Ni. ptcp. is an adjectival substantive, an acc. of manner, describing the way in which an action is performed (*IBHS,* p. 172, P. 10.2.2e), and has a gerundive function (*IBHS,* p. 387, P. 23.3d).

88. Construed as an adjectival Ni. of *plh* ("to be set apart/distinguished," *IBHS,* p. 385, P. 23.3a,b). LXXB (not LXXA), Jerome, Syr., Targ. read *nipl̂êṯā,* "you are extraordinary," probably a facilitating reading. The same is true of 11QPsa, which reads *nwrʾ ʾth* ("you are awesome") instead of *nôrāʾôṯ.*

89. Predicate ptcp. signifies duration (*IBHS,* p. 624, P. 37.6b). Literally it means "I am one who knows."

90. Translation assumes II. *ʿōṣem* is equivalent to I. *ʿeṣem* ("bone"). I. *ʿōṣem* means "might."

91. M. Dahood (*Psalms III: 101–150* [AB; Garden City, NY: Doubleday, 1970], pp. 284, 294) tentatively suggests the unique Pu. belongs to root II. *ʿśh,* "squeeze" = in Pu. "I was being plucked off," glossed here "nipped off" (cf. Job 33:6) because root I. *ʿśh* ("to do," "to make") occurs in the simple stems and root II. *ʿśh* occurs in the D stems. This is possible, but it is chronologically inapt with the parallel that pertains to his formation. More probably the form is an old Qal passive of I. *ʿśh,* "to make." The more difficult MT is preferable to LXX *epoiēsas* (cf. Vulg., Syr., and Targ.) = *ʿāśîṯā.*

92. Some scholars repoint the hapax as *gᵉmūlay* ("my accomplishments," BHS) or *gîlay* + enclitic *mēm* ("circles, cycles/stages of life," Dahood et al.). These emendations have the advantage of providing an antecedent to *kullām* but are not as semantically plausible as "embryo" (so BDB [p. 166] and *HALOT* [1:194], s.v. *gōlem;* see commentary). For variants in the Latin translations, see n. 33.

93. Although the syntax is exceptional, the pl. pronominal suffix has only pl. *yāmîm* as its prospective antecedent. König thinks both *ʿoṣmî* and *golmî* are the antecedents, but an antecedent that distant would also be exceptional.

94. The pronominal suffix of *golmî,* the first word of verse 16a, is gapped in the first word of MT's verse 16b.

95. Since *yṣr* otherwise exists only in the simple stem, *yuṣṣārû* is probably an old Qal passive.

17 And for me, how precious are[96] your thoughts,[97] God!
How vast is the sum of them!
18 Were I to count them, they would outnumber the grains of sand.
I wake up,[98] I am still[99] with you.
19 If only[100] you, God,[101] would slay the wicked[102] —
Bloodthirsty[103] men, get away[104] from me! —
20 who speak of you[105] with evil intent;

96. *Yqr,* a Qal stative (*IBHS,* p. 364, P. 22.2c), to make statements about quality (Wagner, *TDOT,* 6:280, s.v. *yāqar*).

97. Construing *rēaʿ* as a derivative of II. *rāʿâ,* not as a derivative of I. *rāʿâ,* in which case it would mean "friend," "companion." The ancient versions unanimously construed it as the latter because it is far more frequent than the former, but most moderns construe it as the former because that derivative is found in verse 2 and is more semantically pertinent in this couplet pertaining to quality/quantity. Liudger Sabottka ("*Rēʿeykâ* in Psalm 139, 17: Ein Adverbieller Akkusativ," *Biblica* 63 [1982]: 558-59) proposes to interpret *rēʿeykâ* as an adverbial accusative and to render the verse, "Yea for me, how precious are they (i.e., my days), / because you God have thought of them," but the proposal tortuously strains the Hebrew syntax.

98. *Qîṣ* is a bi-form of *yqṣ,* "to wake up." The Hi. is internal, perhaps meaning "I wake myself up" (*IBHS,* pp. 439-41, PP. 27.2f,g). The suffix conjugation is construed as an instantaneous perfective (*IBHS,* p. 488, P. 30.5.1d). Many gratuitously emend the text to *hᵃqiṣṣôṯî* ("I have come to an end"). *Qṣṣ* does not occur elsewhere in Hi.; and MT is sensible (see commentary).

99. Literally, "the going round/continuance of me." The pronominal suffix is used as a subjective genitive with the verbal noun *ʿôḏ* (*IBHS,* p. 143, P. 9.5.1a).

100. Construing with BDB (p. 50, entry 1.b.[3], s.v. *ʾim*) the hypothetical particle *ʾim* in a rare use of expressing wish ("if only . . . ! Oh that . . . !).

101. *ʾᵉlôah* is the sing. form of the usual honorific pl. *ʾᵉlōhîm.* Aside from Job and his friends (cf. 41 of 57 occurrences), the form is relatively unusual, occurring only in poetry, aside from 3x in post-exilic Hebrew: 2x in Daniel and 1x in 2 Chron. 32:15. In the Psalter the pl. *ʾelōhîm* occurs c. 360x, the sing. c. 4x (18:31 [32]; 50:22; 114:7; 139:19, the only instance of vocative). Pl. and sing. signify the quintessence of all divine, transcendent, or heavenly powers. Their antonym is *ʾadāmâ,* "earthly" (*ʾādām); ʾᵉlôah* is what humanity is not. Thus, the term emphasizes God's inhabitance of the heavenly sphere, focusing on his transcendence over human qualities, namely, his immortality and power.

102. Collective sing. as shown by plural in verses 19b-20.

103. MT reads *wᵉanšê.* The relative clause in verse 20 is addressed to God, matching 19a. Since 19b is addressed to David's would-be murderers, it must be an apostrophe interrupting his address to God. Accordingly the *waw* is disjunctive, "Now," and more effectively can be glossed by omitting it, as is done probably in LXX, Syr. Hier.

104. Instead of impv., six Heb. mss. read *sārû* (perf.) and many exegetes follow Syr. and Targ. to adopt another facilitating reading, *yāsûrû* (imperf.). But transitions to direct speech are attested elsewhere in the Psalter (6:8 [9]; 119:115).

105. *ʾāmar* with a direct acc. is exceptional, prompting many to read with *e'* (i.e., Origen's fifth column) *yamrûḵâ* ("they rebel against you"). But that textual evidence is weak, and other

your adversaries[106] misuse[107] your name.[108]
21 Do I not hate those who hate you, *I AM*,
and loathe those who rise up against you?[109]
22 I hate them with complete hatred;
they have become my enemies.
23 Search me, God, and know my heart;
test me and know my anxious thoughts,[110]
24 and see if there is any offensive[111] way in me,
and lead me in the way everlasting.

Psalm 140:1 For the director of music.

---

verbs occur with exceptional pronominal suffixes (E. König, *Historisch-Comparative Syntax der Hebräischen Sprache,* p. 22b).

106. The versions differ between rendering polysemic *ʿāreyḵâ* as "enemies" (Aq. Sym., Jerome, Targ.) or "cities" (LXX, Syr., Vulg.). G. Rice ("The Integrity of the Text of Psalm 139:20b," *CBQ* 47 [1984]: 28-30) tried to redeem the reference to cities by investing *šw'* with the sense of "calamity, destruction," yielding "They have carried away your cities to destruction." Nevertheless, interpreting *ʿar* as an Aramaism — *ʿar* is the Aramaic equivalent of Heb. *ṣār* ("adversaries") — is semantically more pertinent. The several other Aramaisms in the psalm also make that interpretation plausible.

107. The phrase *nāśū' laššāw'* is unique. *Nś'* has no direct object elsewhere except when the object, such as *qôl,* can readily be inferred from the context. As such, the phrase often refers to taking up words (i.e., upon one's lips). The reminiscence of the third commandment (cf. Exod. 20:7; Deut. 5:11) leads many English versions (ASV, ESV, KJV, NASB, NIB, NIV, NKJ, NLT; cf. Targ.) to read "Who utter Thy name with wicked thought, they take it for falsehood, even Thine enemies." Perhaps an original reading, *nś' šmk lšw',* occasioned a haplography due to homoioteleuton. Or perhaps, with little difference in meaning, the suffix "you" in verse 20a is doing double duty: "Your adversaries use you deceitfully [in their speech]." This explanation finds support in the chiastic structure of the parallelism between versets A and B: subject + predicate (verb + *l* + noun) // predicate (verb + *l* + noun) + subject.

108. Read *nāśᵉ'û* with 11QPs[a] *(nśw), pace* GKC 23i.

109. *ûḇiṯqômmeyḵâ* links the verb with its object via the labial preposition *beth* and at the same time elides the labial *mem* of the Hithpolel participle of *qûṭ.* This Hithpolel expresses a reflexive situation ("raise themselves up"), unlike *'eṯqôṭāṭ,* an estimative reflexive (see *IBHS,* pp. 429-31, PP. 26.2.a-c, f).

110. BDB (p. 972), s.v. *śʿp* supposes an insertion of an *r,* which is common in Aramaic according to GKC (85w).

111. *ʿōṣeb* is a homonym: I. *ʿōṣeb* means "pain"; II. *ʿōṣeb* means "idol." LXX translates it by *anomia* (cf. Vulg. "iniquitas"; Syr. "falsehood").

Part III: Commentary

I. Introduction

A. The Psalm's Unity

A striking caesura of theme, mood, and motifs separates a meditation (vv. 1-18) from urgent petitions (vv. 19-24). The meditation segues into the petition by a concluding reflection as the psalmist awakes from his dreamlike reverie to the realities of his life: "I am still with you [*I AM*]" (v. 18b) and then abruptly and shrilly bursts out: "Bloodthirsty men, get away from me" (v. 19b). The mood of meditation gives way to urgency; declarative assertions about *I AM* abruptly shift to urgent imperatives; and God's name *I AM,* the personal name of Israel's covenant-keeping God (v. 1), is exchanged for names that signify *I AM*'s transcendence: *'ᵉlôah* (v. 19) and *'ēl* (v. 23) around *I AM* (*yhwh,* v. 21). This abrupt and striking change suggests to many commentators that Psalm 139 is in fact two psalms (vv. 1-18, 19-24). Although this could have been the case in the history of its composition, it is now a unity; its unified form, tightly reinforced by rhetoric, leads to a unified message, as we shall see.

B. Rhetoric

The psalmist shows himself a first-rate poet by his allusions to the pagan myths of the solar deity, the Mother Earth goddess, and the Tablet of Destinies; by his studied assonance; and by his rhetorical skill. Verbal inclusions frame the psalm: "search and know" (vv. 1b, 23b), "my thoughts" and "my anxious thoughts" (vv. 2, 23), and "way" (vv. 3, 24). An address to *I AM,* emphasized by its relatively unusual placement as the poem's first word, is followed by three stanzas of six verses each, confessing God's intimate omniscience (vv. 1-6), omnipresence (vv. 7-12), and omnificence (vv. 13-18). The third confession, on God's omnificence, lays faith's foundation for the first two confessions. *I AM* knows the psalmist inside out because he made him from his conception, and the darkness of his mother's womb, where God crafted his magnum opus, is so hidden it might just as well have been in the inaccessible bowels of the earth (vv. 15-16), showing that no darkness is too dark for God (vv. 11-12). Finally, the climactic petition stanza also has six verses (vv. 19-24).

Conceptually, each of the six-verse stanzas consists of two strophes: a quatrain, composed of two couplets (vv. 1f., 3f., 7f., 9f., 13f., 15f., 17f.; 19f., 21f.), and a lone couplet (vv. 5f., 11f., 17f., 23f.). As a counterpoint to this symmetrical pattern the first verse of the each strophe is a summary statement that the following three verses expand, yielding the pattern of one verse (vv. 1, 7, 13, 19) plus three verses (2ff., 8ff., 14ff., 19ff.).[112] These symmetries show that though hounded by ungodly murderers (v. 19), the psalmist is in full control of his rationality and his emotions.

Here is an outline sketch of the psalm:

I. Superscript	v. 1a
II. Meditation: Trust, Anxiety, Praise	vv. 1b-18
A. Confession of *I AM*'s omniscience	vv. 1b-6
1. Confidence	vv. 1-4
2. Anxiety	vv. 5-6
B. Confession of *I AM*'s omnipresence	vv. 7-12
1. Anxiety and summary	v. 7
2. Confidence	vv. 8-12
a. *I AM*'s omnipresence in space	vv. 8-10
(1) Vertical axis	v. 8
(2) Horizontal axis	vv. 9-10
b. *I AM*'s transforming presence in darkness	vv. 11-12
C. Confession of *I AM*'s omnificence	vv. 13-18
1. Praise for how and where *I AM* made him	vv. 13-16
a. How *I AM* made him	vv. 13-14
b. Where *I AM* made him	vv. 15-16
2. Praise for God's rare and innumerable thoughts	vv. 17-18
a. God's thoughts are rare and precious	v. 17a
b. God's thoughts are innumerable	vv. 17b-18a
3. Janus: Psalmist awakens	v. 18b
III. Lament with Petition	vv. 19-24
A. Wicked oppose *I AM*	vv. 19-22
1. Wicked are bloodthirsty	v. 19
2. Wicked are blasphemers	v. 20
B. Psalmist confesses hatred of wicked	vv. 21-22
1. Rhetorical questions asserting his hatred of wicked	v. 21
2. Positive confession of his hatred of wicked	v. 22
C. Petitions: Search, know, and lead me	vv. 23-24
IV. Subscript	140:1a

112. So M. Mannati, "Psaume 139:114-16," *Zeitschrift für die alttestamentliche Wissenschaft* 83 (1971): 257-61.

C. Form and Message

Extrapolating the psalm's message depends on identifying its form. The psalm's whole is greater than its parts and determines their significance. But scholars differ on its form.[113] One can say confidently in the taxonomy of form criticism, Psalm 139 is poetry — restrained, terse, figurative speech — more particularly a psalm (to be sung with the pizzicato of a stringed instrument), and still more particularly a petition psalm, consisting of the typical motifs of a petition psalm, albeit in an unusual sequence: address (v. 1a), confidence (vv. 1b-12), praise (vv. 13-18), lament (vv. 19-22), and petition (vv. 23-24) (see pp. 197-98).[114]

The psalmist's petition, however, is atypical. Instead of petitioning God for deliverance from his enemies, he petitions God to know him and so lead him in the way everlasting. Also atypically, the psalmist mixes the motifs of confidence with anxiety (vv. 1b-12), and his petition combines certainty with uncertainty (vv. 19-24). A convincing interpretation demands a cogent synthesis of these atypical mixtures. We attempt that synthesis in our conclusion.

113. For a thorough critical appraisal of scholarly viewpoints up to 1964 see Harriet Lovitt, "A Critical and Exegetical Study of Psalm 139" (UMI dissertation services, 1964), pp. 238-83. Her Columbia University dissertation helped greatly in preparing our commentary. In a preface she writes: "I extend my thanks especially to Miss Claire Quinnetta Powell for her indefatigable help in reading the material which I compiled in Braille or in recorded form"!

114. For an extended discussion on the many proposals of the psalm's form, without finding it, see L. C. Allen, *Psalms 101–150* (WBC, vol. 21; Waco, TX: Word Books, 1983), pp. 256-50. Allen, along with Duhm, Barnes, Mowinckel, Danell, Würthwein, Kraus, et al., wrongly classifies Psalm 139 as a protest-of-innocence petition psalm. In their reconstructed scenario, the psalmist has been falsely accused of idolatry and so protests his innocence, asking God to know his innocence and so implicitly to rescue him and punish his accusers. This interpretation, however, depends mostly upon the questionable understanding that *ʿōṣeḇ* (v. 24) means "idolatry," not "pain," but their gloss is questionable. 1) The psalmist does not protest his innocence but asks God to test the mettle of his integrity, for he has misgivings about its purity (see vv. 23-24). 2) He does not petition God to rescue him from the wicked, but pleads for integrity and intimacy with *I AM* (vv. 19-24). 3) He mutes his petition to eliminate the enemy to a wish that God purge his detractors who threaten his life. 4) As C. Broyles (*Psalms* [NIBC; Peabody, MA: Hendrickson, 1999], p. 483) notes, "They [the wicked] do not accuse the speaker: 'they speak of you [God] with evil intent' (v. 20)." 5) Why does he seek flight from God (cf. vv. 5-6, 7) if he is protesting his innocence? 6) These objections validate that based on philological evidence alone, *ʿōṣeḇ* probably means "pain," not "idolatry." Others label it as a psalm of trust, but it is unclear how that notion meshes with its being a petition psalm and its mixture of confidence and fear, of certainty and uncertainty.

II. Exegesis

A. Superscript v. 1

See pp. 87-92. This is the second in a collection of eight "David" psalms added to the Psalter during the post-exilic period (see pp. 101-4). These psalms served as models on how to live as exiles. *To the choir director* (*lamnaṣṣēaḥ* 4:1a, see p. 88), according to L. Delekat, who does not recognize it as a postscript, occurs only in pre-exilic psalms, giving, albeit weak, support that *ldwd* means "by David," but relatively strong evidence that the original psalm is pre-exilic, contrary to the common academic viewpoint.[115] The reference, "your left hand will lead me, your right hand will grip me," possibly has regal overtones.[116]

B. Meditation: Trust, Anxiety, Praise vv. 1b-18

An inclusio involving the hapax legomenon *rēaʿ* ("my thoughts" [v. 2] and "your thoughts" [v. 17]) frames the meditation. Other rhetorical features be-

115. L. Delekat, "Probleme der Psalmenüberschriften," *ZAW* 76 (1964): 280-97. Most academics argue for a post-exilic date on the basis of the psalm's several Aramaisms: *rʿ* ("thought," vv. 2, 17), *mlh* ("word," v. 4), *slq* ("ascend," v. 8), *glm* ("embryo," v. 16), *qṭl* ("slay," v. 19). Aramaisms in Biblical Hebrew allegedly reflect the post-exilic epoch when Aramaic was the lingua franca of the Persian Empire. Four factors, however, call into question this method of dating: 1) *Qṭl* occurs in Job 13:15, 24:14 and is known in old Akkadian (c. 1750 B.C.E.). 2) Aramaisms may in fact point to an early stage of Biblical Hebrew. For example, M. Dahood (*Psalms III,* p. 287) says: "*millāh* is more accurately classified as part of the Northwest Semitic vocabulary, and other so-called Aramaisms are known in Northwest Semitic from which both Hebrew and Aramaic spring. They look like Aramaisms because they survived only in Aramaic, but in fact Hebrew may be preserving very old forms (see *IBHS,* p. 12, P. 1.41e). According to W. F. Albright (*Peake's Commentary on the Bible,* ed. Matthew Black and H. H. Rowley [London: Thomas Nelson, 1962], p. 62) the known Hebrew vocabulary cannot represent more than a fifth of the total stock of Northwest Semitic words in use between 1400 and 400 B.C.E. *Baʿaḏ* ("around," v. 11) may be an archaic preposition now attested in Ugaritic. 3) Aramaisms may reflect late editings of the text of the Psalter's fifth book, which was added during the post-exilic period. 4) The poet could be using rare forms for rhetorical reasons, as for example, *slq* (see v. 8). In sum, on the basis of the psalm's internal evidence, A. Weiser (*The Psalms,* p. 802) comments, rightly from this kind of data, "it is not possible to assign a definite date for the composition of the psalm."

116. "The gripping of the hand by God belongs to the royal ritual and signifies divine protection and royal honor; e.g. of Cyrus (Isa. 45:1), of the divine servant (Isa. 42:6) and of Israel (Isa. 41:13)" (K. Grzegorzewski, *Psalmen, Gespräche mit Gott* [Berlin: De Gruyter, 1966], p. 64 to Ps. 73:23).

sides those already mentioned unify the meditation. In addition to "for" that introduces the logical connection between the first two and third stanzas (see above), catchwords and themes also link them: "you know" (vv. 2, 4, 6, 14b); "as light so is darkness to you" and "not hidden" (v. 15); "your eyes saw . . . when I was made in the secret place" (v. 16); "Grave" (v. 8) and "lowest part of the earth" (v. 15); probably "for you" (*mimmeḵā*, v. 12); and "from you" (*mimmeḵā*, v. 15). Verses 4 and 16 seem to have a unique relationship: both use "all" in connection with *I AM*'s foreknowledge. Likewise, "wonderful" and "knowledge" in verse 6 matches "wonderful" and "know" in verse 14.[117] Both the first and third stanzas end with a confession of the psalmist's inabilities (vv. 6, 17-18).

The first two stanzas, composing half of the psalm, are linked by merisms: "sit and rise" (v. 2), "go out and lie down" (v. 3), "behind and before" (v. 4); "go and flee" (v. 7); "heavens" . . . "Grave" (v. 8); "rise and settle," "dawn [east] and sea [west]" (v. 9); and "darkness"/"night" and "light"/"day" (vv. 11-12). God's intimate omniscience and omnipresence are inseparable.

1. Confession of I AM's Omniscient Intimacy vv. 1-6

The first stanza strikes with immediate and sustained power its keynote: "you know me." Hyponyms of the semantic field "to know"/"knowledge" (*yd'*, vv. 1b, 2a, 4b, 6a, 6b) multiply in the stanza's first strophe (vv. 1-4): "consider" (*byn l*, v. 2b), "discern" (*zrh*, 3a), "familiar with" (*skn*). In that light, the metaphors of the stanza's second strophe (vv. 5-6) refer to *I AM*'s knowledge: "your knowledge hems me in"; with your knowledge you set your hand upon me. God's omniscience is an "unscalable" height, one of even David's caliber cannot reach to or escape from (v. 6b). This knowledge pertains to *I AM* (*Yhwh* [vv. 1b, 4b], "you" [vv. 2a, emphatic, b; 3a, b; 4b; 5a, b]) and the psalmist ("David" [v. 1a], "I," "my," "me" [vv. 2a, b; 3a, b; 4a; 5a, b; 6a, b]). Finally, note the sound plays in both strophes: *'orḥî wᵉriḇ'î zērîṯâ* (v. 3a) and *'oḥôr wāqeḏem ṣartānî* (v. 5a).

a. Confidence: Welcoming *I AM*'s Intimate Omniscience vv. 1-4

Verbal and conceptual inclusios frame the first strophe (vv. 1-4): vocative *yhwh* (*I AM*, vv. 1 and 4b),[118] "you know" (*yāda'tā*, vv. 2, 4b); and *I AM*'s "search" that commences his active, intimate knowledge (v. 1A) is crowned with "you know all of it" (v. 4b). Asseverative "surely" and "all" (*kōl*), the last word of verse 4,

117. I am indebted to J. Holman ("The Structure of Psalm cxxxix," *VT* 21 [1971]: 305) for this observation.

118. L. Allen, "Faith on Trial: An Analysis of Psalm 139," *Vox Evangelica* 10 (1977): 11.

bring the strophe to its climactic summary. Verses 2-4 elaborate the strophe's summary statement. The catchword word "know" links together the strophe's first couplet (vv. 1-2), and its second couplet is linked both by inclusive "all" (vv. 3b, 4b) and its antonym "there is not" (4a), and by the logical particle "for" that introduces verse 4, which substantiates the psalmist's confession of God's universal knowledge. The couplets of the first strophe, a quatrain, are linked by merisms representing God's knowledge in time ("sit" and "rise" v. 2a) in connection with his transcendence in space ("from afar," 2b), and his universal knowledge in space ("go out" and "lie down") in connection with God's transcendence in time "when there is not yet" (v. 4a). W. P. Brown comments: "God's encompassing knowledge crosses time [vv. 1-2] and space [vv. 3-4] to find and probe the psalmist."[119] The first strophe welcomes God's intimate knowledge: "you are familiar with all my ways" (v. 3), but hostile military metaphors in the second suggests that David attempts to escape it (vv. 5-6).

(1) Omniscience in Time vv. 1-2

1 Vocative of the address, *I AM* (*yhwh,* Ps. 1:2), which is also emphatic by its pride-of-place as the first word of the psalm, tips the reader off to expect a lament/petition psalm. God's personal name, *I AM,* connotes his active concern with his covenant people. *I AM*'s omniscience is essential for God to shape Israel's history according to their covenant relationship. Knowledge is power, and transcendent knowledge is owned exclusively by Israel's faithful, merciful King. *You search me* (*ḥ*ª*qartannî,* i.e., "to probe me") is a purely cognitive and analytical examination and testing.[120] Lovitt states with extensive documentation: "*HQR* [sic] carries strong meaning, denoting a searching that is penetrating, diligent, and difficult." The psalmist unpacks "me" to refer to his spiritual state, for he cites his "heart," "anxious thoughts," "ways" (character and conduct), and "kidneys" (emotions). "And so you know me *(wattēḏāʿ).*" While the search is cognitive and analytical, the act of knowing in Hebrew thought involves an appropriation by the knower of that which is known (see 1:6; 4:3 [4]), not a collection of information on a database to be accessed and manipulated. On the one hand, *I AM*'s knowing of a person may connote choice and intimacy (Gen. 18:19; Exod. 33:12, 17; 2 Sam. 7:20; Amos 3:2; Hos. 13:5) or care and protection (Exod. 2:25; Nah. 1:7; Ps. 1:6; 144:3). On the other hand, it can connote confrontation and judgment (Ps. 138:6; Jer. 12:3; Hos. 5:3). Omniscience in Psalm 139 pertains to this total intimate knowledge, either for weal or woe. *I AM*'s search, in contrast to

119. W. P. Brown, "Psalm 139: The Pathos of Praise," *Interpretation* (1996): 281.
120. M. Tsevat, *TDOT,* 5:149, s.v. *ḥāqar.*

many human legal searches, is loving, not adversarial. Lovitt notes: "the verb ['and you know'] contains an intimation of Yahweh's love as the true motivation of his judgment, because concern and intimacy are necessarily implied in the act of knowing, and because it is precisely *I AM*, the gracious judge, who knows."[121] Celsus, in his deriding the notion that God comes to earth to search out and to know mortals, thinks as a philosopher only in terms of cognitive knowing and not as a worshiper in terms of knowing in personal intimacy, an active knowing of personal communion. *I AM* is ineffable and intimate!

2 Verse 2 extends God's searching, personal knowledge to universal knowledge through merismus. Paradoxically, *I AM*, who is transcendent in time and space, is also temporally and personally present with his elect. *You (ʾattâ) know (yādaʿtā) when I sit* (*šiḇtî*, see Ps. 1:1; 2:4) *and when I rise* (*wᵉqûmî*, see Ps. 1:5). "Sit and rise" refers to all outward actions (cf. Deut. 6:7; Lam. 3:63).[122] *You consider* (*bantâ*, see Ps. 19:12 [13]) *my thoughts (lᵉrēʿî). Rēaʿ* ("thought") occurs only in Psalm 139:2, 17. In Aramaic, root III. *rʿh* means "take pleasure, desire." *BDB* gloss III. *rēaʿ* by "purpose, aim," and *HALOT* by "want," "purpose," "thought."[123] If so, God knows the psalmist's aims, purposes, and desires (see v. 17). *From afar* (*mērāḥôq*, see Ps. 22:1 [2]) probably has its normal sense of spatial distance (Ps. 138:6; cf. Job 39:29), not its rare sense of temporal distance (cf. 2 Kings 19:25 = Isa. 37:26, where it is parallel to *mîmê qedem* "since days of old").[124] More concretely, "afar" refers to God's local enthronement in the heavens, which symbolizes his transcendent rule (Ps. 11:4f. [5f.]). In sum, verse 2b combines God's transcendent knowledge with his transcendence in space.

(2) Omniscience in Space vv. 3-4

3 Verse 3a segues God's spatial knowledge to his universal intimate spatial knowledge. A chiastic structure links the merisms of verses 2-3: from rest ("sit down") to movement ("rise"); from movement ("my going out," *ʾorḥî*) to rest ("my lying down," *wᵉriḇʿî*). If *rbʿ* has its more specialized notion of coitus, the merism also contrasts public and private space. That contrast may also be intended in the merism "to sit and rise," for they respectively may connote to re-

121. Lovitt, "A Critical and Exegetical Study of Psalm 139," p. 78.

122. A similar merism to refer to all activity is found in Egyptian literature (cf. A. Erman, *Die Literatur der Aegypter, Gedichte, Erzählungen und Lehrbücher aus dem 3. und 2. Jahrtausend v. Chr.* [Leipzig, 1923], p. 100).

123. BDB, p. 946; *HALOT*, 3:1256, s.v. III. *rēaʿ*.

124. Verbs used with *rḥq* in a temporal sense are *ʿśh* ("to make, do, prepare") and *yṣr* ("fashion").

tire from public situations versus to engage in them. Thus verses 2a and 3a respectively embrace within *I AM*'s comprehensive, intimate knowledge the elect's public and private lives. *You discern* (*zērîṯâ,* Pi.) flattens the incomplete Hebrew metaphor "you winnow/scatter/sift." As wind separates wheat and chaff, *I AM* sifts a person's behavior. Broyles comments: "His [God's] knowledge is not static; it too goes through a dynamic process."[125] The figurative merisms for his total behavior are replaced with both abstract *all (kôl)* and the more common figure *my ways (dᵉrāḵay),* which alludes to the whole range of the psalmist's life view (see Ps. 1:1; 2:12). *You are familiar with (hiskantâ)* suggests the psalmist welcomes this knowledge. Lovitt notes: "The verb *šāḵan* regularly implies the presence of favor and concern when it denotes a definite relation between its subject and some object of knowledge or action."[126]

4 Asseverative "surely" *(kî),* the first word, and comprehensive "all" *(kôl),* the last word, bring the strophe to its climax. *Hēn* ("behold") lends further stress to this climactic confession. God's active omniscience extends it to the moment a person begins to think a thought. *Indeed, the word is not yet even on my tongue* (*kî 'ên* [see Ps. 3:3] *millâ* [a poetic equivalent of jejune *dāḇār;* see Ps. 19:4 (5)], *bilšônî* [see Ps. 15:3]). *Behold* I AM *you know it completely* (*hēn* [see Ps. 51:5 (7)] *yhwh yāda'tâ* [see v. 1] *kullāh* [see Ps. 2:12], literally, "the all of it," with reference to "word"). Lovitt notes: "It [*millâ,* "the word"] was the focal point at which the will of the speaker entered concretely into the sphere of action." It does not follow, as Freud has shown, that "a man could fittingly be known and his conduct judged by his words."[127] If God knows the thought wholly when there is "nothingness of a word in my tongue" (literally), then he knows the thought before it exists.[128] The notion of God's foreknowledge of what the human is going to decide is so amazing that he introduces it with *kî,* which combines the notions of "surely!" and "for."[129] The Midrash taught God's foreknowledge on the basis of this verse.[130] In verse 16b the psalmist escalates God's omniscience to his predestination of a person's destiny from the time of conception. "The whole of it" *(kullāh)* functions as a comprehensive closure technique to a unit of literature.[131]

125. Broyles, *Psalms,* p. 485.

126. Lovitt, "A Critical and Exegetical Study of Psalm 139," p. 86.

127. Lovitt, "A Critical and Exegetical Study of Psalm 139," p. 89.

128. Sirach (42:20) expresses a similar thought but not quite as clearly: "No thought escapes him, and not one word is hidden from him."

129. *IBHS,* p. 665, P. 39.3.4e.

130. *The Midrash on the Psalms,* trans. W. G. Braude (New Haven: Yale University Press, 1976), vol. 2, p. 343.

131. Cf. B. Smith, *Poetic Closure* (Chicago: University of Chicago Press, 1968), pp. 182-86.

Incredibly, adherents of "Open Theology," who are consistent Pelagian theologians, deny that Scripture teaches God's personal omniscience.

b. Anxiety: Escaping *I AM*'s Intimate Omniscience vv. 5-6

I AM's active omniscience is also frightening, as seen in the second strophe's hostile military terms on the horizontal and vertical axes.

5 *Behind and before ('āḥôr wāqeḏem)* refers to complete horizontal space (i.e., complete enclosure). *Hem me in* (*ṣartānî*, see n. 64) has a chilling tone. Some think "besiege" refers to God's protective care and appeal to Song 8:9. But the metaphor predominantly implies hostility, and even "to lock up" a woman from intercourse in Song 8:9 is ambiguous. Had the poet not meant to connote the predominant sense of I. *ṣûr*, he could have used a neutral term like *sbb* ("to go around in circles"). Calvin comments: "they [people] cannot move a hair's breadth without his knowledge."[132] *You lay the palm of your hand upon me (wattāšeṯ ʿālay kappeḵâ)* also probably connotes hostility. "The hand" *(yaḏ)* and *palm (kap̱)* represent active power (Exod. 14:31; Deut. 32:36; 34:12; Josh. 8:20).[133] When one rests his hand on another, the object is decisively under the subject's control, not his own. On the one hand, God's hand can shelter a person (Exod. 33:22) or graciously impart power and benefit (Ezra 7:6; Neh. 2:8). On the other hand, more often the figure signifies the imposition of a will opposed in some way to another's own. When used with *šîṯ* ("set, place"), the gesture of laying one's hand on another exhibits full authority. The gesture crushes people or destroys the person in judgment (Exod. 7:4; Ezek. 39:21). Job pleads for the removal of God's hand upon him (Job 13:21; see also 41:8 [40:32]).

6 Verse 6b adds from the vertical axis a third military figure, which he introduces with an abstraction in verse 6a. *Such knowledge* (*daʿaṯ*, the nominal form of *yādaʿ* [vv. 1, 2, 4; see n. 66]) is *wonderful* (*pil'îyâ*, see 4:3 [4]), which in this context connotes awe, respect, and fear, *for me* (*mimmenî*, see n. 68). Regarding the root *pl'*, Albertz says: "In the large, major category of its usage, the root *pl'*/*plh* indicates an event that a person, judging by the customary and the expected, finds extraordinary, impossible, even wonderful. *Pele'* never hinges on the phenomenon as such but includes both the unexpected event as well as

132. John Calvin, *Commentary on the Book of Psalms*, vol. 4, trans. J. Anderson (Grand Rapids: Baker Books, 2003), p. 210.

133. L. Brockington, "The Hand of Man and the Hand of God," *BQ* N.S., 10 (1940-41): 191ff.

one's astonished reaction to it (cf. Eng. 'wonder' and 'wonder [at]')."[134] In its comparative use the element of human finitude assumes the foreground, e.g., of the local judge for whom "a legal case is too difficult" (Deut. 17:8); of phenomena in the creation that are too incomprehensible for Agur to mentally grasp (Prov. 30:18). Since he is unable to comprehend such knowledge, obviously he cannot match this omniscience and so outthink or escape from it.

"Such knowledge *is* too *high* for me" (see n. 69). *Śāga̱ḇ* means "to be (inaccessibly) high," and is used most often as a military term, carrying connotations of impregnability and/or security (cf. Deut. 2:36; Prov. 18:11; Isa. 9:10).[135] Though the three metaphors of this strophe could be interpreted as beneficial, their predominant usage connotes hostility. The qualifier, *I do not have the power* (*'ûḵal,* see n. 70)[136] *to scale it (lâ)* completes the thought. Ringgren says that usually *ykl* is negated and human impotence before God is stressed. Without an infinitive complement *ykl* means to "prevail," "overcome" (Gen. 30:8; 32:25 [26]; passim).[137] God's knowledge is being imaged as a cliff that even a warrior of David's caliber is no match for. Lovitt draws the conclusion: "He can but bow beneath its mystery and power, amazed and overwhelmed, yet somehow restless of heart."[138] This aspect of the psalm has been fittingly entitled "The Hound of Heaven" by *The Grail Psalms.*[139] The psalmist's felt need to escape anticipates the concluding strophe: "You know my disquieting thoughts" and "a painful [i.e., sinful] way in me" (vv. 23-24).

2. *Confession of I AM's Intimate Omnipresence vv. 7-12*

Still more rhetorical features unify the first two stanzas. After summary lines (vv. 1 and 7), both continue with two verses employing merismus: "sit" and "rise" (v. 2); "going out" and "lying down" (v. 3); "go up to heaven" and "make my bed in the depths" (v. 8); and "rise on the wings of the dawn" (i.e., the east) and "alight on the far side of the sea" (i.e., the west) (v. 9). These images shuttle back and forth between those on the vertical and horizontal axes: vertical (vv. 2, 6, 8); horizontal (vv. 3, 5, 9). Both follow their merisms with a reference to God's "palm" (v. 5) and "left hand" and "right hand" (v. 10). Their strophes are ar-

134. R. Albertz, *TLOT,* 2:982, s.v. *pl'* ni.

135. Its nominal derivative, *miśgāḇ,* means fortress or "secure height" (2 Sam. 22:3; Isa. 25:12). *Niśgāḇ* is used in a local sense with reference to a lofty city (Isa. 26:5), walls and towers (Prov. 18:11), and the like — also in the Amarna correspondence — that are too high to scale.

136. *HALOT* (p. 411, s.v. *ykl,* entry 3): "to prevail."

137. Ringgren, *TDOT,* 2:72-74, s.v. *yāḵōl.*

138. Lovitt, "A Critical and Exegetical Study of Psalm 139," p. 97.

139. Dahood, *Psalms III,* p. 289.

ranged chiastically. In the first stanza, its first strophe (vv. 1-4) refers to the psalmist's situation of being known by God, and the second (vv. 5-6) to God's active knowledge that restricts him; in the second stanza, the first strophe (vv. 7-10) refers to his restricted location within God's omnipresence, and the second (vv. 11-12) to his situation in light and darkness. The psalmist's incapability with respect to God's personal omniscience (vv. 5-6) is matched by his incapability with respect to God's presence (vv. 11-12), using a comparative of capability with respect to the psalmist and to *I AM* respectively: "too wonderful" and "too high" "for me" (*mimmenî,* vv. 6a, b) and "too dark" "for you" (*mimmeḵā,* v. 12). Finally, in yet another chiasm with reference to tone, the first stanza moves from warmth and assurance (vv. 1-4) to coolness and fright (vv. 5-6), and the second stanza from flight in danger (see "flee," v. 7b) to warmth and assurance (vv. 8-12). This change is signaled by a reference to God's presumably hostile palm upon the psalmist (v. 5) to God's guiding and protecting right hand upon him (vv. 10a, b).

The key word "to know" (vv. 1-6) disappears entirely and gives way to hyponyms of space (vv. 7-12): "where" (v. 7a), "presence" (v. 7b), presentative "behold" (v. 8b), "there" (v. 10). These terms occur with verbs of spatial motion: "go up to" (v. 7a), "flee from" (v. 7b), and the merisms "ascend to heaven" (v. 8a) and "spread out my bed in the grave" (v. 8b); "lift up" (v. 9a) and "alight" (v. 9b).

After the opening two rhetorical questions, "Where," the poet figuratively depicts on the two axes of space, the vertical and the horizontal, God's intimate, unrelenting presence. However he segues from flight into a confession that God's universal intimate presence protects and guides him.

a. Anxiety: Escaping *AM*'s Intimate Omnipresence v. 7

The summary statement of God's intimate omnipresence is stated as a rhetorical question: "Where?" (*'ānâ,* vv. 7a, b, n. 72). The semantic pertinence of the rest of the strophe demands the answer: "No place." Neutral *can I go* (*'ēleḵ,* see Ps. 1:1; 15:2; 23:4) is sharpened by its parallel "can I flee." From *I AM*'s spirit and presence define afresh God's relationship with his covenant partner. *From* indicates the point of view of the one who remained behind.[140] And *your spirit (mērûḥeḵâ,* see Ps. 51:11 [13]) refers to God's spirit, so superhuman that the psalmist cannot get away from it, and so holy that he wants to escape its danger. *From your presence (mippāneḵâ)* is literally, "from your face" (see Ps. 4:6 [7]; 51:11 [13]). The root *bāraḥ* in *can I flee ('ebᵉrāḥ)* in the great majority of its oc-

140. As early as 1 Clement commentators felt the implicit threat of God's presence (see p. 519).

currences refers to flight from grave danger (Gen. 27:43: 31:20; Exod. 14:5), especially with "from" (*min;* Gen. 16:6, 8; 31:27; Exod. 2:15; cf. Jonah 1:3, 10; 4:2; and Job 27:22). Lovitt draws the conclusion from verses 6 and 7: "The psalmist, far from rejoicing in Yahweh's nearness, alludes by studied implication to hostile pressures pervading their confrontation."[141] Presumably, the mortal wants to flee, for otherwise they run the peril of death as the wages of unconscious sins that *I AM*'s search may dig out.

b. Welcoming God's Intimate Omnipresence vv. 8-12

The psalmist's imagined flight of escape from *I AM* paradoxically leads him to more intimacy with God. Presumably, his faith that *I AM* is good enables him to break decisively from a posture of hostility and fear.

(1) *I AM*'s Intimate Omnipresence in Space vv. 8-10

The summary statement of God's universal presence is now developed with references to the vertical (v. 8) and horizontal axes (vv. 9-10), to the tripartite cosmos ("heaven," "sea," "land"), and to the four cardinals of the compass (east, west, north, south). Verse 10 functions as a centerline of this strophe. Jan Holman notes that *gam šām* ("also there," v. 10) is equidistant from *šām* ("there," v. 8) and *gam* ("also," v. 12), holding the two axes together.[142] This verse is also the relative centerline of the entire meditation (vv. 1-18) and features the key word *nḥh* ("lead"), also found in the final verse of the psalm.

(a) Vertical Axis v. 8

The extremes of "heaven" and "Grave" on the vertical axis are inaccessible to living mortals and represent the Immortal's omnipresence (cf. Job. 26:6; Ps. 95:4; Prov. 15:11; Amos 9:2). The merismus is qualitative as well as quantitative. Quantitatively, "heaven" and "Grave" are the highest and lowest points in the psalmist's cosmos (cf. Amos 9:2). Qualitatively, the former is the most desirable space, the place of God's unique presence (1 Kings 8:30), and the latter is the least desirable, the place of the dead (Pss. 16:9f.; 18:5 [6]; 88:3-6). Jonah also tried to flee from God and found his saving presence in the belly of the fish, which he likened to the belly of the Grave (Jonah 1:3; 2:2). *If ('im) I ascend ('essaq,* see n. 75) may have been chosen over more common words for aesthetic reasons.[143] *To the*

141. Lovitt, "A Critical and Exegetical Study of Psalm 139," p. 107.

142. J. Holman, "The Structure of Psalm cxxxix," *VT* 21 (1971): 298-310, esp. 303.

143. Its sibilant consonance is: ś [2x], š [3x], ṣ [2x], for a total of seven in a verse with seven accented words, and especially its parallel, *'aṣṣî'â*. The consonance *aleph* occurs in five of

heavens (*šāmayim,* see Ps. 2:4; 8:1, 3 [2, 4]; 19:6 [7]) denotes the transcendental realm of the divine beings. *You (ʾattâ) are there (šām); šām* refers to a place relative to the situation of the speaking, namely "the heavens."[144] Conjunctive *and (wᵉ)* segues into the opposite pole of the merism. The second *if* is gapped. *I spread out my bed (ʾaṣṣîʿâ)* is also found in Isaiah 14:11; 58:5; Esther 4:3; and in Aramaic and other Semitic cognates. The cohortative expresses self-inclination with the mood of dubiety in connection with bedding down in the grave! In its three other uses the verb refers to making one's bed in degraded circumstances: the grave (Ps. 139:8; Isa. 14:11) and dust and ashes (Isa. 58:5; Esther 4:3). It may have been chosen instead of *yrd* ("to descend") because of its sibilant consonance. Perhaps the common word *škb* "to lie down" was rejected in verse 8B for elegant variation, but more certainly, because the grave is thought of as a place of beds (cf. 2 Kings 15:7;[145] Job 17:13; 21:26; Isa. 14:11; Ezek. 32:25).[146] Even in the *Grave* (*šᵉʾôl,* see Ps. 16:10) *I AM* gives life (1 Sam. 2:6; Ps. 16:10; 30:3 [4]; 49:15 [16]), sometimes to execute justice and judgment (Amos 9:2). *Lo, you*! (*hinnekâ,* see above) expresses vivid and dramatic surprise. *I AM* is actively present in the realm of the dead, albeit they are not aware of it.

(b) Horizontal Axis vv. 9-10

The breaking dawn is imaged as flying across the sky from east to west, representing God's omnipresence on the horizontal axis. No matter how far and how fast the psalmist flies on that axis, God is present. *Were I to rise* (*ʾeśśāʾ,* cf. Ps. 4:6 [7]; 15:3; 16:4) *on the wings of the dawn (kanpê šāḥar)* — note the continued alliteration of aleph and sibilants of verse 8 — is best construed with both the LXX and the Vulgate as an adjunct of place, not of time. *šāḥar* denotes "daybreak, the light of dawn" (Ps. 110:3) in the east. The metaphorical wings of the dawn are a well-known picture in the ancient Near East of the beneficial rising sun (cf. Job 38:12-13; Mal. 4:2 [3:20]).[147] The psalmist pictures himself as taking the sun's

---

the words. The normal Hebrew word for "to go up," *ʿlh,* lacks this assonance. He reserves *nśʾ,* another common term having this assonance, for verse 9a.

144. *IBHS,* p. 657, P. 39.31g.

145. Literally, "he dwelt in a house of beds" (i.e., he died).

146. A Ugaritic text (UT 51:VIII:7-9) reads: "And go down to the house of beds [i.e., the netherworld], be counted among those who go down to the netherworld" (cf. N. J. Tromp, *Primitive Conceptions of Death and Nether World in the Old Testament* [Rome: Pontifical Biblical Institute, 1969], p. 157).

147. A "Universalist Hymn to the Sun" (i.8, *ANET,* p. 368) reads: "Hail to thee, sun disc of the daytime, creator of all and maker of the living! Great falcon, bright of plumage." See representations of winged sun discs in the Northwest Semitic area in *ANEP,* nos. 486, 493; the winged sun disk spans the entire scene. The image may also be seen in the Greeks' winged goddess of dawn, Eos.

plumage and flying with the speed of light at the day's dawning. *I alight* (*'ešk^e^nâ*, see 15:1; 16:9; with reference to flight see Ps. 55:6 [7]) — note yet another aleph and sibilant — also expresses dubiety (see v. 8), for, in the Biblical world, his undesirable destination in the Occident is as intimidating as the Grave. *On the far side* (*b^e^'aḥ^a^rît*) refers to after-part and so the most remote part *of the sea* (*yām*, Ps. 8:8 [9]; i.e., the western Mediterranean Sea [Judg. 5:17]). In Israel's cosmography the land was surrounded by the primeval abyss that existed before the creation of land. Although it can be spoken of neutrally as a part of the cosmos (Gen. 1:2), normally sea represents chaotic power hostile to God and the world (Job 26:12f.; 38:8-10; Pss. 46:2f. [3f.]; 104:6f.).[148] The Occident is where the last light of the day is swallowed up by darkness. In sum, east and west represent extremes on the horizontal axis, both quantitatively and qualitatively.

10 Emphatic *even (gam)* signals this final climax in the exposition and draws its two protases of verse 8 to their resolution.[149] *There (šām)* refers to the intimidating hostile sea. Steady flight would carry the psalmist away beyond the habitable world to places where he expected to find chaos and death, but he found instead the Creator of order and life.[150] Again, ironically his flight from God leads him to awareness of God's presence with him and his need of responsible existence; his discovery of God in symbols of death transforms his anxiety to hope. *Your . . . hand* (*yāḏ^e^ḵâ*, "hand," see v. 5B) and *your right hand* (*y^e^mîneḵâ*, Ps. 110:1, 5) are a broken stereotype phrase[151] for left and right hands (Judg. 5:26; 2 Sam. 20:9-10; Pss. 26:10; 89:25 [26]; 138:7). Israel's eastern orientation associates the left with the north, the right with the south, the other two cardinal points of the compass in contrast to his flight from east to west. Separately, the right hand connotes strength (cf. Pss. 45:4 [5]; 89:42 [43]; 110:1), and the left hand what is sinister; but together they signify total power.[152] *Leads me* (*tanḥēnî*, see Ps. 23:3) is commonly used in situations of God's leading his people safely through snares and dangers and triumphantly to a desired and promised destiny (see Exod. 13:17, 21; 15:13; Deut. 32:12; Pss. 5:8 [9]; 27:11), an apt notion here for being led through the symbols of dread and death. In the parallel, *and . . . will grasp me* (*w^e^tō'ḥ^a^zēnî* — note the alliteration with *tanḥēnî*) — refers to "seize," "grasp," and/or to "hold on to" with a firm and strong grip. Were the

148. Arent Jan Wensinck, *The Ocean in the Literature of the Western Semites* (Amsterdam: J. Müller, 1918), p. 20.

149. *IBHS*, p. 663, P. 39.3.4d.

150. *ś^e^môl*, "left hand," never occurs in the Psalter.

151. Bruce K. Waltke, *The Book of Proverbs: Chapters 1–15* (Grand Rapids and Cambridge: Eerdmans, 2004), p. 43.

152. Ackroyd, *TDOT*, 5:419, s.v. *yāḏ*.

psalmist to slip into the grave or fall off the western edge of the earth into pitch darkness, God would seize him, grasp him, and hold him fast — *'ḥz* means all three — saving him from the snares of dangerous space.[153] In Psalm 73:23f., where *'āḥaz* and *nāḥâ* appear in close conjunction, as here, *'ḥz* also refers to God's care.

(2) *I AM's* Transforming Presence in Darkness vv. 11-12

In the first strophe (vv. 7-10) two protases representing two threatening situations to existence in terms of space are transformed in two apodoses into two reassuring confessions of faith. So also in the second strophe two protases (cf. vv. 11-12) representing two threatening situations (crushing darkness and light turning to night) are transformed in the apodoses into two reassuring confessions of faith, stated first weakly in the negative ("darkness is not too dark," v. 12a), then strongly in a positive confession ("night shines as the day," v. 12b), and climactically ("as light so is darkness to you," v. 12c).

"Then I thought," an anacrusis, introduces the new strophe. Nevertheless, in addition to their similar syntax, the two strophes are linked conceptually and logically. In ancient iconography some figures of the sun disk represent its rays as ending in hands or wings that become the arms of the throne.[154] This representation may suggest the conceptual connection of the sun's rays and wings in verse 9 with hands in verse 10. The psalmist's reflections on the wings of the dawn and its relationship to hands segue into the contrast of light eliminating darkness. In ancient thought all three — wings of dawn, hands, and light — are associated with the solar deity (see above). Also, Grave (*šᵉ'ôl,* v. 8) and Sea (v. 9) are associated with darkness (vv. 11a, 12a; cf. Job 17:13; Ps. 88:12 [13]).[155] Night (*layᵉlâ,* vv. 11b, 12b) is also associated with terror (Job 27:20). As for the strophes' logical connection, *then* (n. 80) rhetorically signals the psalmist's subsequent but always subordinate situation to a preceding situation.[156] *I thought ('ōmar),* the common word for "to say," can mean "to think" (cf. *'āmar 'el libbo,* "to speak to his heart"). Wagner explains: "In the ancient Near East 'thinking processes' and 'intellectual processes' often transpire as phonetically intelligible expressions." In Genesis 26:7, 9, "*'āmar* means to accept something as a fact after careful reflection, and in Pss. 10:6 and 14:1 it expresses the conviction at which a person arrives after grappling with a phenomenon intellectually for a long

153. According to A. L. Oppenheim ("Idiomatic Accadian," *JAOS* 61 [1941]: 251-71, esp. 270), "*qâtâ ṣabâtu* can mean 'to seize the hand of somebody to assist, to help' . . . and can be replaced with that [lit., the first] meaning by *aḥâzu.*"

154. *ANEP,* nos. 400, 405, 408, 409, 411, 415-17.

155. N. J. Tromp, *Primitive Conceptions of Death,* p. 95ff.

156. *IBHS,* p. 547, P. 33.2a.

time."[157] The psalmist's imagination now conjures up unnamed agents who radically change his state to bruising darkness (v. 11). He resolves that foreboding situation by confessing darkness matters not a fig to *I AM;* God transforms darkness to light, chaos to order, death to life (v. 12). Emphatic *surely ('ak)* is most apt for his confronting the horror of darkness.[158] In the Biblical world *ḥōšek̠* ("darkness") is associated with the primeval ocean covered in darkness (see Gen. 1:2; Job 38:8-9) and is usually seen as a negative power of chaos threatening life and human existence.[159] The psalmist personifies the darkness: *will crush me (ḥšk yᵉšûp̄ēnî). šûp̄* is well known from Genesis 3:15: "The Seed of the woman will crush/bruise [*šûp̠*] your head, and the Serpent will crush/bruise [*šûp̠*] his heel."[160] Darkness in the Bible is more than the absence of light: "It possesses a quality of its own, which unmitigated makes it inimical to life."[161] It is a realm that is cut off from light, hostile to that which provides safety, freedom, and success; it is the realm of evil and of the wicked (Job 24:13-17; Isa. 29:15; Ezek. 8:12), of disaster (Job 3:4; 15:22; 22:11) and of death (Job 17:13; 18:18; Ps. 88:18 [19]), and used in cursing (Job 3:4; Pss. 35:6; 69:23 [24]). The Grave, with its prevailing isolation from *I AM*'s life-giving presence, is a place of darkness (1 Sam. 2:9; Ps. 88:6, 12 [7, 13]; 143:3; Job 10:21f.; Lam. 3:6). In the eschaton, when there will be no sea, light will totally eliminate night's darkness (Zech. 14:7; Rev. 21:1, 25), and for the wicked at that time, cosmic light will cease (Ezek. 32:7f.).[162] In verse 11b "darkness" is replaced with "night." *Light ('ôr),* in contrast to darkness, represents the good will of God toward his creation. Bringing light into existence constitutes God's first act in transforming chaos into cosmos (Gen. 1:3ff.; Job 26:10). The light of day is foundational to life and represents the time when the realms of life, freedom and success rule; the wicked rule the night. Light represents the organized power of life and order (Job 33:28, 30; Ps.

157. Wagner, *TDOT,* 1:333, s.v. *'āmar.*

158. BDB, p. 36b. Contra N. H. Snaith, *VT* 14 (1964): 224f.

159. In its proper place bounded by light the two together can be called "good." Bounded darkness can be used by God as an element in his self-revelation (Exod. 19:16, 18; 24:15ff.; Ezek. 1:4; Ps. 18:11 [12]). God uses its negative quality as a vehicle of judgment (Amos 5:18; 8:9; Isa. 5:30; Mic. 3:6).

160. Some ancient and modern versions corrupt the meaning in Psalm 139:11 by either emending *šûp̠* or by betraying it with glosses "to cover," "to hide" (see n. 82). BDB (p. 1003, s.v. *šûp̠*) in a rare faux pas asserts "mg. unsuitable, read perh. *yᵉšûkkēnî cover, screen, me.*"

161. Ringgren, Mitchel, *TDOT,* 5:248.

162. Verbs used with darkness, the wretched realm of the "organized power of chaos" (H. Ringgren, *The Faith of the Psalmists* [1963], pp. 119ff., on Ps. 104:19-23), include "falling" (*nāp̠al,* Gen. 15:12) and "silencing" (*ṣmt,* Job 23:17). One may be "thrust" (*hdp,* Job 18:18) into darkness or "perish" (*dmm,* 1 Sam. 2:9) in it. The darkness of the ninth plague was "to be felt" (*wᵉyāmēš ḥōšek̠,* Exod. 10:21). Translators ought not to flinch in glossing *šûp̠* by "crush."

43:3). To see the light is to live (Job 33:28); the dead see it no more (Ps. 49:19 [20]). Lovitt comments: "In the light, life can be properly oriented, and properly directed action can be taken [Isa. 2:5; Job 29:3; Ps. 43:3; cf. Ps. 36:10); hence light can express the quality of a life of righteousness [Prov. 4:18; cf. Ps. 37:6]."[163] A common Hebrew idiom is "the light of life" (Ps. 56:13 [14]). Light is the time of salvation (Isa. 30:26), prosperity, well-being, and success (Job 17:12; 18:5f.; 22:28; Prov. 13:9; Lam. 3:2; Esther 8:16). *Night (layᵉlâ)* here is not merely a temporal period (as in Ps. 1:2; 16:7), but a conceptual equivalent of "darkness" — the time when darkness with all its negativity rules.[164] In the psalmist's nightmare he experiences the doom of the wicked as night swallows up the light *round about me (baʿᵃḏēnî).*[165] In the apodosis, the psalmist's confession of faith transforms hell into heaven. Darkness, he realizes, not to mention crushing darkness from which he cannot escape, does not exist in God's presence. *Even* (*gam,* see v. 10) *that darkness* (*ḥōšeḵ,* see v. 11A) *is not too dark (lōʾ-yaḥšîk)* for *you (mimeḵâ).* In fact, in God's presence *night (layᵉlâ) shines* (*yāʾîr,* denominative of *ʾôr*). *Darkness (kaḥᵃšēḵâ) is as light (kāʾôrâ).*[166]

3. *Confession of I AM's Intimate Omnificence vv. 13-18*

The confessions segue from God's transforming night/darkness to day/light to God's fashioning the mortal in the darkness of the womb. The stanza represents God as a skillful weaver of embroidered cloth dedicated to creating his magnum opus. His studio is the dark chamber of a mother's womb. Introductory *for (kî)* logically connects the third stanza with the first two; God's personal omnificence, "*I AM* created me," lays faith's foundation for God's active omnicompetence (cf. Ps. 33:15). Each of the stanzas' two strophes, again of four and two verses respectively, present striking oxymorons: the hidden lies open and the innumerable is rare. In the first (vv. 13-16), with God the womb's darkness is light, and its hiddenness lies open. In the second (vv. 17-18), God's intimate activity with the psalmist is represented in an ironic economic paradox: against the law of supply and demand, each of the Creator's thoughts toward him is rare and precious (v. 17a) and yet God's thoughts are so many, they are innumerable (vv. 17b-18a). The two units of the first strophe are both quatrains

163. Lovitt, "A Critical and Exegetical Study of Psalm 139," p. 128.

164. Shakespeare in his descriptive scene of Tarquin's rape of Lucrece writes: "This said, he [Tarquin] sets his foot upon the light, / For light and lust are deadly enemies: / Shame folded up in blind concealing night, / When most unseen, then most doth tyrannize."

165. *HALOT,* p. 141, s.v., *baʿaḏ.*

166. Compare the "Hymn to the Sun-God" (iv.8-9): "O brightener of gloom, who makes darkness to shine, / O opener of darkness, who makes the broad earth to shine" (*ANET,* p. 389).

(vv. 13-14, 15-16), and so is the last strophe (vv. 17-18). The first and last of these quatrains (vv. 13-14 and 17-18) are bi-cola, and the center one consists of two tri-cola. In sum, like the other three stanzas this one also consists of six lines of Hebrew poetry. The stanza fades away as the psalmist awakens from his reverie to confront the realities of his enemies and his own identity (v. 18b).

a. Praise for How and Where *I AM* Made Him vv. 13-16

The first strophe pertains to his gestation, when God formed him in his mother's womb and predestined his future. In its first quatrain (vv. 13-14), in connection with an introductory summary of the stanza, the psalmist confesses *I AM* formed everything about him, so that God knows him exhaustively (vv. 13-14); the second quatrain pertains to where God fashioned him (vv. 15-16); his mother's womb — like the darkest and most remote bowels of the earth — does not restrict God's activity. He ends the quatrain with the amazing confession that *I AM* predestined his existence (v. 16b). Catchwords link the two quatrains: the verbs "gave birth" and "knit" (v. 13), "fearfully and wonderfully made" and "works are wonderful" (v. 14), "wrought" and "colorfully woven" (v. 15). All of these are associated with nouns for womb: "womb" (v. 13), "secret place" and "depths of the earth" (v. 15), "embryo" (v. 16). A chiastic structure also wraps the two quatrains into one strophe: two clauses (v. 13) + three clauses (v. 14) versus three clauses (v. 15) + two clauses (v. 16).

(1) How *I AM* Made Him vv. 13-14

His confession that God formed him, doubly expressed in verse 13, expands into enthusiastic praise from a new perspective in verse 14, and reflections on the marvel of his conception (v. 13) escalate to his being wonderfully fashioned (v. 14). As verses 1 and 7 summarize their stanzas, verse 13 also lays the third stanza's foundational line.

13 *For* (*kî*, "surely," see v. 4) logically connects the first three stanzas. Initial *you ('attâ)* emphasizes that he continues to address *I AM* (vv. 1, 2). The well-attested gloss *gave birth (qānîṯā)* for polysemic *qānâ* is most sensible in this context (Gen. 4:1; Deut. 32:6; Prov. 8:22).[167] *My kidneys* (*kilyōṯāy,* see Ps. 16:7) is a synecdoche, a *pars pro toto,* for the person. Verset 13B advances the reflection from conception to gestation: *you knit me together (tᵉsukkēnî)*[168] *in my mother's*

167. Waltke, *Proverbs 1–15,* p. 409.

168. II. *skk* is a bi-form of *nsk,* which in Middle Hebrew and Aramaic means "to weave, plait," a metaphor that connotes the care, skill, industry, and intimacy of an artist, and is as old

womb (*beṭen 'immî,* see Ps. 22:9-10 [10-11]). That notion is expanded in the next quatrain (vv. 15-16).

14 All texts about God's fashioning in the womb imply God's loving care (Job 31:15; Isa. 44:2; 49:5; Jer. 1:5) — recall that the Hebrew word for "mercy" derives from "womb" — helping to explain David's outburst of praise. In contrast Job, sick in body and bitter in spirit, accused God of not loving him and so cursed his birth. As in verse 6, the psalmist stops at the end of a couplet to reflect upon God's wonders *(pl').* *I* [publicly] *praise you* (*'ôḏᵉḵâ,) because* (*'al kî,* see n. 86) *I am fearfully extraordinary* (*nôr'ôṯ niplê'ṯî,* see v. 6 and nn. 87, 88).[169] *Yr'* ("to fear") connotes the "fear of *I AM*" (see Ps. 22:23 [24]).[170] Lest one think the psalmist's formation is uniquely wonderful, he generalizes the truth in verse 14b: [all] *your works* (*ma'ᵃśeyḵâ,* see Ps. 8:3, 6 [4, 7]) *are wonderful* (*niplā'îm,* "to be wondered at"), both in creation (Ps. 8:3, 6 [4, 7]; 103:21-22; 104:13) and in salvation history (Exod. 34:10; Deut. 3:24; Judg. 2:7, 10). *I* (*napšî,* see Ps. 3:2 [3])[171] *know* (*yōda'at,* see v. 1) all the time (see n. 89) *full well* (*mᵉ'oḏ,* "abundantly," "exceedingly"); his awe is beyond reasonable doubt.

(2) Where *I AM* Made Him vv. 15-16

15 *My frame* (*'oṣmî,* see n. 90; Ps. 22:17 [18]), both skeletal and psychic (see Ps. 51:8 [10]), *was not hidden (lō'-niḵḥaḏ) from you* (*mimmeḵa,* see v. 12). Of the four occurrences of Ni. *kḥd,* three pertain to God's omniscience (Ps. 69:5 [6]; 139:15; Hos. 5:3; cf. 1 Kings 8:39; Ps. 44:21; Isa. 40:28; 42:9). *When* (*'ᵃšer* (see Ps. 8:3 [4])[172] *I was wrought* (*'uśśêṯî,* see n. 91 and *m'śh,* v. 14) *in the secret place (bassēṯer).* Al-

---

as the Babylonian cosmogony, *Enuma Elish* (6:5) (c. 1750 B.C.E.). This ancient account of creation celebrates Marduk, the patron deity of Babylon in various extant versions. The version from Ashurbanipal's library dates to the seventh century B.C.E., but most scholars date the story's composition to the eighteenth century B.C.E., when the god Marduk had a prominent status; some, however, date its composition as late as the fourteenth to twelfth centuries B.C.E.

169. J. C. Collins ("*Plh* in Psalm 139:14 in Light of the Context," *Presbyterian Covenant Seminary Review* 25 [1999]: 117) rightly distinguishes *plh* ("to be distinct") from *pl'* ("to be wonderful"), but he over-reads the text when he specifies this distinction to be the psalmist's membership in the covenant community. It could just as well be his distinction as a king (Ps. 4:2 [3]). In this context it probably refers to his distinction as a human being.

170. For a fuller discussion see B. Waltke, "The Fear of the LORD," in *Alive to God: Studies in Spirituality,* ed. J. I. Packer and Loren Wilkinson (Downers Grove, IL: InterVarsity, 1992), pp. 17-33.

171. *Napšî* is required because the subject of a participle is normally expressed (*IBHS,* p. 623, P. 37.6a).

172. GKC, 164d.

though *bassēṯer* means "in secret/secretly" (Deut. 13:6 [7]; 27:15, 24; 28:57; 2 Sam. 12:12; Isa. 45:19; 48:16; Jer. 37:17; 38:16; 40:15; Pss. 101:5; 139:15; Job 13:10; 31:27), its parallel "in the depths of the earth" suggests it retains its nominal sense, a metonymy for the womb (see above; Ps. 51:5 [7]; cf. Deut. 29:29 [28]; Hos. 13:14). *When,* gapped in verse 15bB, *I was colorfully wrought (ruqqamtî). Rōqēm* signifies a weaver of colored cloth or embroiderer of colored thread, a craftsman who decorates cloth with colorful patterns using a needle, and so revives and intensifies the same connotations as those of "you knit me" (*t^esukkēnî,* v. 13). Another metonymy, *in the depths (b^eṯaḥtîyôṯ) of the earth (ʾereṣ)* refers to the Grave, the place of the dead (Isa. 44:23; cf. Ezek. 26:20; 31:14, 16, 18; 32:18, 24). The figure may derive from another ancient myth of Mother Earth in whose womb, often identified with the abode of the dead (cf. v. 8), human beings were thought to be formed before their birth (cf. Sir. 40:1).[173] If so, the poet is again using mythological imagery, not theology, for he confesses God as his personal Creator in his mother's womb.

16 *My embryo (golmî) your eyes (ʿêneyḵâ,* Ps. 51:4 [6]) *saw (rāʾû). Gōlem* is a hapax, but its Aramaic cognate may refer to a "formless mass" or an "incomplete vessel"; in this context it refers to the embryo, not to his unfinished spiritual state, as Richard of St. Victor thought due to Jerome's original error (see n. 33). Scientists who now better understand the immediate cause of embryonic development through stem cell research rarely praise the Ultimate Creator of the stem cell because God has no place in their epistemology. To "see with eyes" denotes the locus of personal activity (1 Kings 8:29; Isa. 37:17; Ps. 32:8) and of the appropriation of what is seen through attention and evaluation (see Ps. 16:10). *And (w^e)* links God's involvement in the mortal's creation with his predetermining its fate. God does not passively observe the developing embryo but actively programs its future. *All of them (kullām)* anticipates "the days that were fashioned beforehand."[174] The psalmist was unaware of the genome,[175] which contains all of the hereditary information, but he was aware of the concept of "seed," which carries in itself hereditary characteristics causing the begetter to beget its likeness.[176]

173. In a myth that theoretically developed in the Neolithic and Chalcolithic periods, before the beginning of the historical period, ancients conceived of Mother Earth as made pregnant by the god of heaven and supplying the material for the human body.

174. The personal pronoun can precede its antecedent for emphasis: Genesis 27:34 ("bless me, even I").

175. Genome is a portmanteau of "gene" and "chromosome."

176. B. K. Waltke with C. Yu, *An Old Testament Theology: An Exegetical, Thematic and Canonical Approach* (Grand Rapids: Zondervan, 2007), p. 321.

In addition to shaping human personality, God predestined the psalmist's destiny by writing the mortal's personal diary beforehand: *upon your book they* [all my days] *were written (ʿal sipr^eḵâ . . . yikkāṯēḇû).*[177] This imagery derives from yet another myth, the "Tablet of Destinies,"[178] envisaged as a clay tablet inscribed in cuneiform. Whoever holds or owns the tablet has supreme authority as ruler of the universe. God knows the psalmist's full thoughts before he expresses them (v. 3) because God rules them (v. 16). In verse 16b he clarifies his figure: God predestines a person's future,[179] that is, *days (yāmîm)* — the meaning is "all my days," without emending the text (pace BHS). Standing emphatically before *yāmîm ("days"), kullām (all of them,* see n. 93) boldly stresses the inclusiveness of this predestination. *Were fashioned (yuṣṣārû),* a figure for "were created," is used for forming a clay pot or form or for casting or forming metal (cf. Gen. 2:7, 19; Isa. 45:18; Jer. 10:16; Amos 7:1).[180] Here *yāṣar* designates the mental act of forming a plan prior to its enactment (Isa. 22:11; 37:26; Jer. 18:11; 33:2; cf. *yēṣer,* "framing," "purpose"; Gen. 6:5; Deut. 31:21). *I AM* did more than number the psalmist's days beforehand (cf. Job 14:5); he formed his future by foreordaining the fundamental character that gives concrete shape to that future, as in the case of Jeremiah (Jer. 1:5). Emphatically, *when not one* [i.e., of the days fashioned] *is* [i.e., yet exists] *among them.* Corresponding to the potter's superiority over his material, the Book of Destiny represents God's might and freedom in his involvement with that which he fashions and the powerlessness

177. The Bible distinguishes at least three books of God: 1) Book of Life (Exod. 32:32f; Ps. 69:28 [29]; Isa. 4:3; Dan. 12:1; Mal. 3:16; cf. Phil. 4:3); 2) Book of Good and Bad Deeds (Neh. 13:14; Isa. 65:6; Dan. 7:10; cf. Rev. 20:12); and 3) Book of Destiny, which is in view here (Rev. 5:1). Bible students have suggested a wide variety of classifications, which Gary Smith ("The Book of Life," *Grace Theological Journal* 6 [1985]: 219-30) summarizes as the nine interpretative options. He agrees that the book in Psalm 139:16 is a Book of Destiny, which contains records of decreed events.

178. The Gilgamesh epic also connects the motif of creation with the theme of predestination. Before the soul ascends from the underworld to the light, the Anunnaki, the great gods, meet with Mammetum, "maker of fate," and determine the fate/destiny of each human being (ANET, 93, tablet X, vi). A similar connection of creation and predestination is found in the creation epic *Enuma Elish,* ANET 62, tablet I, 79-80.

179. M. Buttenwieser (*The Psalms Chronologically Treated with a New Translation* [The Library of Biblical Studies; New York: Ktav, 1969; first published 1938], p. 545, n. 16) glosses *ysr* by "preordain" or "order" (2 Kings 19:25; Isa. 22:11; 46:11). Schmidt says: "He [God] forms 'from the womb' individuals, prophets (Jer. 1:5), and the servant of Yahweh (Isa. 49:5; cf. 49:8), as well as Israel (. . . 44:2, 24 . . .). Election or selection for a mission occurs, accordingly, with one's involvement. Similarly, 'formation' has priority over events of which God had foreknowledge and which he brought about (2 Kings 19:25 = Isa. 37:26; Isa. 22:11; 46:11)" (W. H. Schmidt, *TLOT,* 2:586, s.v. *yṣr*).

180. W. H. Schmidt, *TLOT,* 2:585f., s.v. *yṣr.*

of the thing fashioned.[181] God foreordains a person's narrative as one swift movement and unity. Recall, Calvin commented: "The mighty gifts with which we are endowed are hardly from ourselves; indeed, our very being is nothing but subsistence in the one God."[182] This doctrine, however, must be held in tension with the doctrine of human accountability.[183]

b. Praise for God's Rare and Innumerable Thoughts vv. 17-18

1. God's Kind Thoughts Are Rare Yet Numerous v. 17

Verset 17a sets up the first half of the economic paradox, and verset 17b, its counterpart. *And for me (wᵉlî)* is best construed as a benefactive *lameḏ* (i.e., "for my advantage"), not as *lameḏ* of specification (i.e., "as for me" = "in my opinion").[184] Rhetorical *how (mah,* literally, "what," see Ps. 8:1 [2]) expresses amazement and admiration. *Precious are* (*yāqᵉrû,* see n. 96) invests the verb's broad meaning, "valuable are" (see Dan. 2:11), with its more specific notion of being rare (1 Sam. 26:21; 2 Kings 1:13; Ps. 72:14; Isa. 43:4). Wagner explains the connection: "This notion of value leads to nuances reflecting quantity rather than quality, always in the sense of a smaller quantity: '(be) rare, scarce'"[185] (cf. 1 Sam. 3:1; Ps. 40:5 [6]). *Your thoughts* (*rēʿeyḵâ,* see v. 2) refers God's purpose to benefit the psalmist when he wrote his Tablet of Destiny. The title *God ('ēl)*[186] is most appropriate in connection with the Creator's writing a Tablet of Destiny.

Emphatically repeated, *how (meh)* sets up the second part of the oxymoron: rare and innumerable. Though the verb glossed *vast are ('āṣᵉmû)* in contexts that speak of threats means "to be strong," its parallel here speaks of quantity, "to be vast" (of enemies, widows, iniquities, apostasies, sins, God's wondrous deeds, including God's thoughts [Isa. 31:1; Jer. 5:6; 15:8; 30:14f.; Pss. 38:19 [20]; 40:5 [6]; 69:4 [5]). The parallel *the sum of them (rā'šēhem)* assumes *ro'š* ("head") here abstractly refers to a total amount/number (Num. 1:2; 4:2; 31:26, 49; Ps. 119:160).[187] The next couplet expands the notion of being numerous to their being innumerable.

181. This usage of *yṣr* precludes A. Weiser's (*The Psalms* [E.T., 1962]) contention that God only predetermines one's length of life.

182. *Institutes of the Christian Religion,* ed. John T. McNeill, trans. Ford Lewis Battles (Philadelphia: Westminster, 1960), p. 35.

183. E. J. Young, *Psalm 139: A Study in the Omniscience of God* (London: Banner of Truth Trust, 1965), p. 83.

184. *IBHS,* p. 207, P. 11.2.10d.

185. Wagner, *TDOT,* 6:280, s.v. *yāqar.*

186. It could be transliterated as a Proper Name, but more probably since *I AM* is God's proper name, it is better construed as a title, "God."

187. HALOT, 3:1167, entry 10b, s.v. *r'š.*

(2) God's Thoughts Are Innumerable v. 18a

Having spoken of the sum of God's blessed thoughts, the poet immediately disabuses mortals of thinking they can tally them. The pronouns in *were I to count them* (*'espᵉrēm;* i.e., enumerate my thoughts) show that verses 17-18 are a couplet; "them" in versets 17b and 18a both look back to "thoughts" in verse 17a. *They would become more numerous* (*yirbûn,* see Ps. 16:4) invests polysemic *rbh* with its quantitative sense, not qualitative ("to become great"), because *than sand (mēḥôl)* is a traditional figure for that which is vast in number or extent (Gen. 22:17; Josh. 11:4; 1 Sam. 13:5) and is used particularly of God's thoughts and deeds in Psalm 40:6 (cf. Sir. 18:4-7). As the poet has expanded God's creative work in his birth to his works in general (v. 14), so now he extends *I AM*'s thoughts during his gestation to the whole gamut of his predetermined acts in salvation history.

c. Janus: Psalmist Awakens v. 18b

The expression *I wake up* (*hᵉqiṣōṯi,* see n. 98) is used for waking from sleep (Ps. 3:5 [6]), sometimes in connection with other conditions, such as awaking from the stupor of drunkenness (Joel 1:5; Prov. 23:35), from death (Isa. 26:19; Dan. 12:2),[188] from a prophetic vision (Jer. 31:26), or, as here, from a dreamlike reverie. The psalmist's dream of God's sublimities refreshes him to confront boldly the terrible reality of his situation and to commit himself unreservedly to God's scrutiny. *And I am still* (*wᵉʿôḏî,* literally, "the continuing of me, see n. 99) connects the heretofore loyalty and intimacy of God with the psalmist's from-now-on loyalty to God. *With you ('immāḵ)* connotes presence and community. Lovitt says: "it connotes a mutuality based on participation in an inclusive reality or relationship."[189] The motif of God's presence, which manifests itself in power and protection, stems from Israel's early nomadic life and one that gave structure to her existence, not in unique occurrences of God's saving acts (cf. Ps. 73:23). The psalmist nuances that tradition: he hands his life over to *I AM*'s purpose. God formed him and predetermined his destiny to fight God's battle against the wicked.

C. Lament and Petition vv. 19-24

His triadic confession segues into the fourth stanza: a wish with regard to the wicked (vv. 19-22) and a petition with regard to himself (vv. 23-24). The inter-

188. Targ. and Syr. find this sense in Psalm 139:18, but its context offers no support for their interpretation.

189. Lovitt, "A Critical and Exegetical Study of Psalm 139," p. 174.

play of his confession of loyalty to *I AM* against the wicked and his petition to prove his integrity unify the stanza. God's innumerable mighty acts in salvation history must continue to multiply in the present and future until the wicked are eliminated. The fourth stanza, like the first three, also consists of two strophes; the first of two quatrains (vv. 19-22) and the second of a single quatrain (23-24). The first strophe pertains to the wicked and the psalmist (vv. 19-22) namely, these bloodthirsty blasphemers (vv. 19-20) whom he utterly hates (vv. 21-22); the second strophe pertains to God and the psalmist; namely, a petition that God prove the authenticity of his loyalty to him (vv. 23-24).

The psalmist escalates his petitions from a wish that God slay the wicked to his machine-gun-like imperatives that *I AM* know his loyalty in their common battle against the wicked. At the same time, the wicked's false and disingenuous speech (v. 20) contrasts sharply with the psalmist's honest and genuine speech; namely, he realizes his confessed zeal for God's rule must be tempered by the mortal's uncertainty about the purity of his motives.

1. *Lament and Wicked vv. 19-22*

The thematic key to the first strophe is the bloodthirsty and cagy wicked (vv. 19-20) whom he loathes (vv. 21-22). Its couplets are chiastically arranged: enemies of psalmist (v. 19), of God (v. 20); enemies of God (v. 21), of psalmist (v. 22).

a. Wicked Oppose *I AM* vv. 19-20

Relative *who* (*'ᵃšer,* v. 20) qualifies the wicked (v. 19), grammatically binding together verses 19-20 as a couplet. Conceptually, the couplet censures them for breaking God's law: with respect to neighbor — murder (v. 19), and with respect to God — blasphemy (v. 20).

(1) Wicked Are Bloodthirsty v. 19

If only (*'im,* see n. 100; Ps. 4:6 [7]) *you would slay (tiqṭōl), God* (*'ᵉlôah,* see n. 101; Ps. 3:2, 7 [3, 8]; 4:1 [2]), *the wicked* (*rāšāʿ,* see Ps. 1:1, 4, 5, 6; 3:7 [8]), who are especially characterized as proud and oppressive.[190] *Qṭl,* "to kill," occurs elsewhere only in Job 13:15 (with God as subject) and 24:14 (with murderers as subject). Perhaps the poet chose *tiqṭōl* for its assonance with *'ᵉlôah,* also a rare word. His wish that God slay the wicked is most unusual. Typically the prayer in a lament psalm urgently petitions God to deliver him from the wicked and vehemently

190. H. Ringgren, "Eine Bemerkung zum LXXIII Psalm," *VT* 3 (1953): 265-72.

prays that God will punish them (cf. Ps. 59:1-2, 11-13 [2-3, 12-14]).[191] Here, however, as Abner warned Asahel to stop chasing him (2 Sam. 2:18-23), the psalmist, in an apostrophe, shouts at the *bloodthirsty men* (*wᵉʾanšê* [see Ps. 1:1] *dammîm,* see n. 103; cf. Ps. 26:9) to abandon their pursuit of him. The bloodthirsty hate people of integrity (Prov. 29:10) and God hates them (Ps. 5:6 [7]), and so they do not live out half their days (55:23 [24]; cf. 26:9). *Depart (sûrû)* means "to turn aside from the direction one has set out on" (1 Sam. 6:12). *From me* entails that bloodthirsty men are pursuing him.

(2) Wicked Are Blasphemers v. 20

They speak of you (*yōʾmᵉrūḵâ,* see 2:7; 3:2 [3]; n. 105) *deceitfully* (*limᵉzimmâ*). Fox defines *mᵉzimmâ* as "private, unrevealed thinking and the faculty for it."[192] Here their planning is hostile and full of intrigue (Prov. 24:8), and so condemned by God (12:2) and the community (14:17).[193] Their evil schemes include using God's name to make him an accomplice with them. *Your adversaries* (*ʿāreyḵâ*)[194] occurs elsewhere only in 1 Samuel 28:16 (see n. 106); it draws a sharp line between the true covenant community and those outside of it, including the likes of Saul and Absalom in the nominal community.[195] He stigmatizes their speech: they *misuse your name in their speech* (*nāśūʾ laššāwʾ,* see nn. 107, 108). *šawʾ* with reference to speech may refer to any kind of false speech: false witness (Deut. 5:20), false report or rumor (Exod. 23:1), false worship (Isa. 1:13), or false prophecy (Ezek. 13:3-7), and so forth.

b. Psalmist Confesses Hatred of Wicked vv. 21-22

In the strophe's second quatrain David spiritually counterattacks: he hates those who hate God, not with malevolence and vindictiveness, but because in the covenant community God's enemies are Israel's enemies. In this spiritual battle "there can be no middle position."[196] The psalmist's identification with Israel's holy God prompts him to express his aversion to the impious and wicked in-

191. The psalmist's wish for the death of the wicked springs from the conviction that *I AM* is a moral God who administers judgment (Luke 18:1-8; 2 Tim. 4:14; Rev. 6–9:11). At the same time saints pray that their tormenters repent and find God's forgiveness (Prov. 25:21-22; Luke 23:34; Acts 7:60; see pp. 95-98).

192. Waltke, *Proverbs 1–15,* p. 95.

193. Waltke, *Proverbs 1–15,* p. 95.

194. Note the anagram of *rʿyḵâ* (v. 17, n. 97) and *ʿryḵâ.*

195. If Dahood is right that *ʿārîm* in Psalm 9:7 means "adversaries" — I think there is a pun — the same three hyponyms, *rāšaʿ, ʿārîm, ʾōyēḇ,* occur in Psalm 9:5-6 [6-7].

196. T. A. Lenchak, "Puzzling Passages," *Bible Today,* p. 320.

tensely. David's rhetorical and grammatical maneuvers show that by "hate" he means the strongest possible aversion to someone or something, not merely a dislike of them. His zeal for God could not be stated more emphatically than within these dozen words; unrestrained zeal is necessary to counter effectively the enemy in the battle of religious affections.

A question again signals a new unit (cf. vv. 7, 21). An exceptional fourfold repetition of "to hate" plus its hyponym "to loathe" loudly gongs with continued reverberations the strophe's keynote. His spiritual counterattack has two parts: rhetorical questions to assert emphatically his hatred of those who hate God (v. 21) and a zealous affirmation of his complete hatred for them (v. 22).

(1) Rhetorical Questions Asserting His Hatred v. 21

Do not I hate those who hate you, God *(hᵃlô' mᵉśan'eyḵâ yhwh 'eśnā'),* with its expectation of an affirmative answer, emphasizes the writer's zeal.[197] Putting the objects, "those who hate you" and "those who rise up against you," in the foreground stresses their opposition to *I AM. Śn'* occurs four times with elegant variation (2x in 21a [ptcp. and verb in prefix cj.] and 2x in 22a [noun and verb in suffix cj.]); it is reinforced by *qûṭ,* "loathe." "No other verbs," says Jenni, "compete seriously with *śn'* in its general meaning 'to hate,' usually with a personal object." His rhetorical question is equivalent to an abjuration — he swears, as it were, and will not withdraw one word of it. His spiritual counterattack to overcome the enemy must be stronger than their animosity.

And (û) implies a second rhetorical question, though gapped: "Do . . . not? *(hᵃlô').* The radical antithesis between God's friend and foe finds fresh expression: *I loathe those who rise up against you* (*ûḇiṯqômᵉmeyḵâ 'eṯqôṭāṭ* — note the assonance of *qô*). *I loathe/detest* (*'eṯqôṭāṭ,* Hith.) intensifies the psalmist's hate: he regards them with extreme disgust and/or shows himself to be a person who feels utter disgust for them.[198] *Those who raise themselves against you* (i.e., they attack and the battle is engaged; n. 109; Ps. 3:1[2]; cf. Ps. 26:5; 31:6 [7]) implies he counts on *I AM* to exact vengeance against those who fight against *I AM* (Exod. 20:5; Deut 5:9; 7:10; 32:41; 2 Chron. 19:2).

(2) Positive Confession of His Hatred of the Wicked v. 22

Several grammatical maneuvers give him the spiritual advantage in this battle of hates. 1) The two negative questions, implying an affirmative answer in verse

197. Commenting on this strong statement, Theodoret remarks, "As sinners I hate them, but as human beings I pity them" (Theodoret of Cyrus, *Commentary on the Psalms: Psalms 73–150,* trans. Robert C. Hill [Washington, DC: Catholic University of America Press, 2001]).

198. *IBHS,* p. 430f., P. 265.2f.

21, are morphed into two vehement positive affirmations in verse 22.[199] 2) The first of these employs a term for "perfect" (literally, "complete") hatred: *I hate them with a perfect hatred (taḵlîṯ śin'â śᵉnē'tîm);* the qualitative fullness of his hatred is escalated to pure hatred. 3) A cognate accusative, "hate with . . . hatred," intensifies his hatred to seething hatred.[200] 4) This completeness is expressed by a genitive of genus ("the completeness of hatred") instead of the expected attributive genitive ("hatred of completeness"), so that it functions as an absolute superlative — there can be no hatred more pure than his. 5) Placing the cognate accusative, "hatred," first, means that together with "completeness" it becomes the first and foremost word of the verse. Calvin commented: "Our attachment to godliness must be inwardly defective, if it do [sic!] not generate an abhorrence of sin, such as David here speaks of" (cf. Ps. 69:9 [10]).

In this battle verse 22a matches verse 21a, pitting the wicked's hatred against God with his hatred of them; and verse 22b matches 21b, pitting their attack against God with their becoming David's enemies:[201] *they have become my enemies* (*lᵉ'ôyᵉḇîm* [see Ps. 3:7 (8)] *hāyû lî,* investing *hāyâ* with its active force of "happen," "come to pass," not its passive sense of "was"). The verb may suggest that they were not always his enemies, but in a crisis moment they became such, as happened in the case of Saul (1 Sam. 18:16; 22:6-8) and Absalom (2 Sam. 15–18).

2. *Petition: Search and Know, Test and Know, See and Lead vv. 23-24*

David's appeal for honesty in his confession will rout the wicked. His abrupt shift from hot indignation against others turns to an urgent plea that God assess the truth of this confession. Instead of irrationally fighting God's active omniscience, he lays his heart bare to *I AM*'s X-ray of his hidden self to assure both covenant partners of the reality of the mortal's confession of loyalty to God. Conflicted as mortals are, they have both a clean conscience and the disquieting realization that they are not able to fathom their own motives (Jer. 17:9; Prov. 18:4). Richard of St. Victor, recall, recognized the mortal flaw: "faith without good works, good works with unfaithfulness, chastity with pride, humility with dissipation" (see p. 528). David's petitions aim to overcome his realization of that debilitating spiritual reality by his petition to arm him fully in his spiritual battle against the wicked. Paradoxically, God's judgment of the psalmist is a coveted gift.

This climactic strophe (vv. 23 and 24) is linked grammatically by a con-

199. *IBHS,* p. 684, n. 48.

200. *IBHS,* p. 167, P. 10.2.1g.

201. The brace *miṯqômᵉmîm* and *'ôyᵉḇîm* occurs in Job 27:7.

junction "and" (v. 24a) and by an escalating and unrelenting flow of six petitions. The first five ask *I AM* to judge him, and the climactic sixth asks God to lead him in the everlasting way.

23 The connoisseur of petition psalms has been anticipating imperatives addressed to God but not the unexpected plea: *search me* (*hoqrēnî,* see v. 1), *God* (*'ēl,* see vv. 17, 19), and *test me (bᵉḥānēnî,* v. 23B). Remarkably, the object of his petition is not God's judgment of the enemy but of himself. *Bḥn* concretely denotes testing and purifying metal by fire (Job 23:10; Prov. 17:3; Zech. 13:9), but with God as subject and a human being as object it denotes an intense divine examination in which *I AM* does not acquire the knowledge of his testing by any normal human activity; it is a spiritual search of which only God is capable (cf. Prov. 16:2; 27:21). The purpose and result of "search" and "test" is expressed in the second imperative, *and know* intimately (*wᵉda',* vv. 23a, b, see vv. 1-2), which is exceptionally repeated, and so emphasized, in verset b. The object of the search to know is the psalmist's *heart* (*lᵉḇāḇî* [v. 23a], see Pss. 4:4, 7 [5, 8]; 16:9; 19:8, 14 [9, 15]) — his whole spiritual orientation,[202] including his thoughts (cf. *rēa'* [v. 2]), emotions, and motives. He qualifies his heart in the parallel by *anxious thoughts* (*śar'appây,* v. 23b, see n. 110; cf. Ps. 94:19).[203] Apparently, he is uncertain that his heart is as wholly devoted to God as he confesses and wants it to be.

24 The third set of anthropomorphic imperatives again combine active knowing with spiritual leading. *And see* (*rᵉ'ēh,* see Ps. 16:10) "if a painful way is in me." *If ('im)* also implies an uncertainty about the purity of his heart: "The heart is deceitful above all things and beyond cure. Who can understand it?" (Jer. 17:9). Without admitting the reality of sin's presence, he knows the pervasive and subtle reality of sin. Lovitt comments: "The poet acknowledges that he is, in the last analysis, unable fully to know and judge himself. There are depths and directions in his motivation and action which he cannot assess."[204] To search another person's interior spiritual life is impossible (Prov. 14:10), and individuals cannot be certain even of their own motives (1 Cor. 4:4-5). Only God knows the reality (1 Sam. 16:7). Although way *(dereḵ),* which in the Hebrew text occurs before "painful," denotes an outward way of life, here the addition of *in me (bî)* shows that the psalmist continues to think of his inner spiritual state: of his mental, emotional, and moral processes. The gloss *offensive* (*'ōṣeb,* literally,

202. J. Pedersen (*Israel: Its Life and Culture,* vols. 1-2 [London: Oxford University Press, 1926], p. 102) says: "When special emphasis is put on the tendency of the soul, the word *heart* is often used."

203. Its dialectical variant *śᵉ'ippîm* also means "anxious thoughts" (Job 4:13; 20:2).

204. Lovitt, "A Critical and Exegetical Study of Psalm 139," p. 213.

"painful") interprets the noun as a derivative of II. *ʿṣb* ("to hurt, pain"), not of I. *ʿṣb* ("to shape"). If it derives from the latter, it means "idol" (Isa. 48:5), not "hurt, pain" (Isa. 14:3; 1 Chron. 4:9). Either is a possibility, but II. *ʿṣb* is more probable in light of the psalm's argument (see n. 111) and of its parallel, "anxious thoughts." II. *ʿṣb* may denote the objective cause of pain or the subjective experiencing of it. In the latter, it can refer to physical pain or, as here, to psychical pain. Lovitt says: "Frequently . . . it is an inward injury felt as grief or sometimes as vexing offense which provokes anger."[205] In a rare faux pas Lovitt thinks it refers to psychical pain that the psalmist feels, but in that case he would know, not question, whether there was a painful way in him. More probably the painful way in him refers to the pain his sin inflicts upon *I AM,* his covenant partner (Isa. 63:10; Eph. 4:30). Hence the gloss "offensive." What is offensive to God will end in everlasting destruction.

The figure of "way" segues into the second petition: *and lead me* (*ûnᵉḥēnî,* see Ps. 23:3) *in the way* (*ḇᵉḏereḵ,* see v. 24a) *everlasting* (*ʿôlām,* see Ps. 15:5; 110:4). By casting himself upon God to lead him, ironically, as death becomes God's presence and as night becomes day in his presence, his offensive way through openness to him becomes quantitatively and qualitatively his everlasting way. The fixed everlasting way is qualitatively covenant loyalty to God and quantitatively eternal life. This is so because *I AM* himself knows this way and watches over it (Pss. 1:5-6; 15:5b; 16:11; 22:26, 29 [27, 30]). Lovitt comments: "His own integrity is not sufficient for this. His own ways could, in fact, carry him toward pain and destruction. Only if Yahweh will lay his hand on him, to guide, sustain, and control him utterly, can the poet hope that his ways will conform to Yahweh's way."[206] Asaph, conscience stricken, confessed that he slipped into becoming a "brute beast before you" (Ps. 73:22), "yet . . . you hold me fast (Heb. *ʾḥz,* cf. Ps. 139:10) . . . ; you lead/guide (Heb. *nḥh*), and afterward you will take me to glory" (Ps. 73:23-24).

D. Subscript 140:1a

For the director of music (lamᵉnāṣṣēaḥ, see p. 88). Importantly, the subscript extends the message of the psalm to each and all of God's covenant people. Brown comments: "Through all the circling years, the God of all life is present for the sake of one life."[207] Since the petition was from the beginning handed over to be

205. Lovitt, "A Critical and Exegetical Study of Psalm 139," p. 212.
206. Lovitt, "A Critical and Exegetical Study of Psalm 139," p. 217.
207. Brown, "Psalm 139," p. 283.

used in Israel's liturgy, it matters not a whit whether it originally was a private prayer.

Part IV: Conclusion

Literary critics note that in good literature rhetoric and message, style and substance, are inseparable. The key words "know me" and "lead me" in the first and second stanzas respectively form an inclusio with the psalmist's two petitions in the fourth stanza, namely, that God know him and lead him (vv. 23-24). Recall, "lead me" (v. 10) in the second stanza stands at the center, a pivot, of the meditation. A third key word, "way" (vv. 3 and 24), shows his confessions pertain to piety and ethics. These key words involve an oxymoron that informs the whole, including many other oxymorons. Why command *I AM* to know and lead him if God always knows and leads him? Resolving the enigma unlocks the gate to the message of the psalm.

The believers' war with the wicked is first and foremost a spiritual battle to establish an honest, warm, intact personal relationship with God. To achieve the success against the wicked, which they intuitively hope for (cf. Matt. 10:34; Mark 10:29-30; John 15:18; Rom. 8:35; James 4:4), they must first succeed in assuring themselves that no barriers separate them from fellowship with the *I AM,* who alone can guarantee that success and who planned from the beginning for their well-being. The psalmist intertwines his confessions of faith in God's intimate and active omniscience (cf. Matt. 12:25; Mark 2:8; 12:15; Luke 5:22; 6:8; 11:17; John 1:48; 2:24f.; 13:11), omnipresence (Matt. 18:20; 28:20; cf. John 14:16), and omnificence (cf. John 1:3; 1 Cor. 8:6; Col. 1:16; Heb. 1:2) with his pledge of allegiance to God, expressed in climactic pleas that strive for that assurance. This intertwining of confession with petitions in itself shows the genuineness of the psalmist's confession and transforms his confessions into the warmest spiritual relationship between himself and *I AM.* In short, the psalm teaches the covenant people several truths on how to have authenticity and integrity in their relationship with God.

First, the faithful welcome God's intimate scrutiny of their hearts. The mortal can either welcome or resist God's intimate covenant loyalty with his elect. Intuitively mortals resist invasion into their privacy and/or fear others might actually discover their depravity, or that, at the least, they will disappoint others: "For words, like Nature, half reveal and half conceal the Soul within."[208] Brown says:

208. Waltke, *Proverbs 15–31,* p. 72.

> "Impenetrable defenses are developed to protect our knowledge from unwanted intruders." People retreat from relationships, mask their true reality; and "'talk' in anonymity or in disguise." "We vigorously guard ourselves against divulging too much. We entrust ourselves to no one but ourselves. Each home is an enclave, each self, an island."[209]

They irrationally also assume these postures with God, as illustrated by Adam and Eve's cover-up, hiding from God behind trees and a fig leaf and speaking less than truthfully. Isaiah (29:15-16) says: "Woe to those who deeply hide their plans from *I AM*, and whose deeds are done in a dark place, and they say, 'Who sees us?' or 'Who knows us?'" And the psalmist (94:7-11) says of the senseless: "They have said, '*I AM* does not see, nor does the God of Jacob pay heed.' Pay heed, you senseless among the people; and when will you understand, stupid ones? He who planted the ear, does he not hear? He who formed the eye, does he not see? . . . *I AM* knows the thoughts of mortals." To have a relationship with God, we must honestly confess that we cannot elude the Hound of Heaven's active and personal omniscience, omnipresence, and omnificence, and must dismiss the deceptive covers under which most mortals take refuge, divesting ourselves of hypocrisy.[210] To surrender with welcoming praise to *I AM*'s sublime covenant commitment to his saint is the only reasonable posture.

Second, the faithful confess with true praise to God that "God created me at the moment of my conception and that his intentions were good" — that is to say, that he holds his covenant partners and leads them through thick and thin to the blessings he predetermined for them. That confession empowers the faithful to seek intimacy with *I AM*, not merely to welcome his scrutiny.

Third, saints clearly confess their allegiance to the covenant-keeping God. Their zeal against the wicked is for the sake of God's honor, not so much for their own sakes. The zeal for God's house burns in their hearts. They are fully conscious of the gulf that separates them from the wicked.

Fourth, true worshipers come ingenuously to God's bar of justice, confessing that though they are unaware of any condemning sin, they are not unaware of sin's subtlety to delude them — they know that apart from sovereign grace their hearts are desperately wicked (cf. Matt. 26:33-35; Mark 14:29-31; cf. John 13:37f.). Though expecting to be exonerated of guilt, they do not fancy themselves faultless or competent to make a final judgment about their motives (cf. 1 Cor. 4:4). Their only recourse is total honesty about their apprehensions. Commenting on Augustine's notions of penitence, Professor Houston wrote:

209. Brown, "Psalm 139," pp. 281, 283.

210. Calvin, *Commentary on the Book of Psalms,* vol. 4, p. 206.

"Self-defense only shuts the door upon God's mercy, whereas humility opens us to deeper self-knowledge, leading in turn to greater intimacy with the Lover of our souls."[211]

Fifth, from other Scriptures it can be inferred they hope God will make known to them an unconscious, painful/offensive way in them. God makes saints know their painful way by their conscience, as when it smote David when he cut off Saul's garment; and/or by rebuke from a friend, as when Abigail rebuked David when he sought to avenge himself against Nabal; and/or by a prophetic word, as what Nathan delivered to David when he took away Bathsheba's purity and Uriah's life.

Sixth, though innocent ignorance is excusable (Ps. 19:12 [13]; 1 Tim. 1:13), saints want God and themselves to know their integrity to one another. And so, in their final plea[212] they cast themselves on God, petitioning him with the assurance of faith to lead them in the qualitatively and quantitatively everlasting way. Until they themselves know as they are known, they soldier on with a conscience cleansed by the sacrifice of Christ, confessing their sin and seeking the empowerment of the Holy Spirit to enable them to persevere in the faith.

Parenthetically, the psalm plays an important role in the debate on the morality of abortion. A. K. Tangberg summarizes its contribution best: "It is clear that the essential *I* has its origin in conception and this is the beginning of God's miraculous creation. This creation is also the beginning of God's providential care for the individual, which continues throughout the person's lifetime."[213]

211. Supra, Psalm 51 (Augustine).

212. L. C. Allen (see n. 118), interpreting the psalm's form as a protest of innocence, alleges the psalmist's plea that God know him "is remarkably akin — in an expanded form — to Jeremiah's passionate appeal for vindication against his attackers: 'You know me, Yahweh, you see me and test my attitude towards you. Pull them out like sheep for the slaughter' (Jer. 12:3; cf. 15:15)." To be sure, Jeremiah also wants God to know him, but the reason for his appeal is that God will know his innocence and so avenge the injustice being inflicted on him. By contrast the psalmist confesses his anxious thoughts and the possibility of a painful (sinful) way in him.

213. G. F. Hall's abstract (Number: OTA08-1985-Feb-293) of K. A. Tangberg, "Vurderingen av det ufødte liv I det gamie Israel og Orienten," *Tidsskrift for Teologi og Kirke* 55 (1984): 212-21.

Glossary

aggadic interpretation: from the Hebrew root *ngd,* "to explain," "to declare"; refers to Jewish commentary on narrative, non-legal material.

Akitu festival: annual festival observed in Babylon celebrating the supremacy of Marduk during the month of Nisan in which a reenactment of his enthronement is thought to secure success for the upcoming year.

Alexandrian commentators: Christian commentators of the third and fourth centuries who, influenced by Greek culture, read Scripture with an allegorical bias; Origen is their great master.

allegory: from the Gr. *allegoria,* "speaking otherwise," by which another level of meaning is concealed within what is usually a story of some kind. Since its Greek origin is related to myth and fable, we have strongly distinguished this literary device from typology*.

Ambrosian chant (also known as Milanese chant): monophonic chant associated with St. Ambrose, though his precise relationship to these chants is unknown.

anacrusis: unstressed syllables at the beginning of a poem.

anagogic: "elevation," that is, seeking symbolic meaning in the text.

analogy: closely linked with the theory of participation, analogy justifies our knowledge of God. This is controlled by the distinctives of the analogy of attribution and the analogy of proportionality, to avoid distorting the unique revelation of God, the "I AM," from anthropomorphism. Thus analogy does not give us exhaustive knowledge of God nor remove the mystery of his divine being.

anaphora: a literary device in which a word or phrase is repeated at the beginning of successive clauses for the sake of emphasis.

Antiochene commentators: Christian commentators influenced by a more Semitic culture from Syria, who read the Scriptures in a literal and historical way that was self-consciously opposed to the excesses of allegory.

Apocalypse of Baruch: The Syriac work by this title (also known as *2 Baruch*) is to be distinguished from the *Greek Apocalypse of Baruch,* or *3 Baruch.* This pseudepigraphal work, attributed to Jeremiah's secretary by that name, deals with theological issues raised in light of the destruction of the Temple in 70 CE.

Apollinarians: fourth-century sect founded by Apollinarius, Bishop of Laodicea, who argued that the divine Logos took the place of a human soul in Jesus.

apologists: early church fathers who defended Christian doctrines against Jewish and pagan writers.

Arianism: possibly the most dangerous heresy of the Church; following on the teaching of Lucian of Antioch, and later of Arius of Alexander, it denied the divinity of Christ and was condemned by the Councils of Nicea (325), Constantinople (381), and Chalcedon (451).

Book of Hours: medieval illuminated manuscripts with illustrated psalms and prayers to aid public and private devotion.

Book of Jubilees: a pseudepigraphic writing c. 150 BCE that retells the biblical story from Genesis 1 to Exodus 24, purportedly as given through angelic mediation to Moses during his forty-day stay on Mt. Sinai.

books of Maccabees: four books written during the Second Temple period that focus on the Jewish rebellion led by the Maccabees against the Seleucids; only the first book is valued for its historical content.

breviary: medieval liturgical book; a collection of prayers, hymns, psalms, readings, and notations for daily use in Divine Office popular from the eleventh century onward, often developed by a cathedral community.

capitulary: a written ordinance or decree issued by the Carolingian rulers that dealt with administrative or ecclesiastical concerns.

Cappadocian fathers: developed in the fourth century as a monastic scholarly movement from Syria, which explored the compatibility of Christianity with Greek philosophy.

Carolingian Renaissance: the cultural renewal associated with the Frankish king Charlemagne and his successors in the eighth and ninth centuries.

catena (from the Latin for "chain"): the stringing together of various verses based on a common word.

cathedral office: refers to the two liturgical offices daily (morning and evening), in contrast to the monastic offices of seven or eight times a day.

Cistercian order: a Benedictine reform movement established in 1098 by St.

Robert of Molesme; the order emphasized solitude, recruitment of adult monks, and a return to manual labor.

citation: reflects upon a clearly marked path along which the biblical witnesses move forward to the person of Christ in their citing of earlier scriptural passages.

compunction: from the Latin *conpunctio,* a medical term for being pricked as by a thorn; first used in the audience response of Peter's address in Acts 2:37, as "cut to the heart." Thereafter it refers to sorrow over sin, and a state of being in the process of conviction, repentance, and conversion.

contrition: an expression of godly sorrow for one's sinful condition, reflected in the Psalmist's experience of a "broken and a contrite heart" (Ps. 51:17). From the Latin *contritus,* it reflects on the Hebrew *daka'* or "bruised" (Isa. 57:15). For the Fathers, contrition — like compunction — was fundamental to a biblical view of the relations of God and humanity.

Council of Chalcedon: fourth of seven evangelical councils (451 CE); it repudiated Monophysitism* and upheld the nature of Christ as both human and divine.

Council of Constantinople: council that took place in 381 CE and repudiated Arianism.

Council of Ephesus: third of seven evangelical councils (431 CE); it repudiated Nestorianism*.

Council of Sens: council that took place in 1141 and condemned the teachings of Peter Abelard.

Council of Toulouse: Taking place in 1229, this council banned the possession of vernacular Bibles by the laity in response to the Albigensian heresy, but reaffirmed the freedom given to the laity for the vernacular use of the Psalms.

Council of Trent: council convened in 1545-61 to repudiate the Protestant Reformation.

Deism: the philosophical movement arising from Socinianism* in the sixteenth century that became very popular in western Europe by the eighteenth century. It emphasized a non-intervening "God" or divine principle that allowed for "Nature" to be given pseudo-divine autonomy.

Desert fathers: early Christian hermits who, beginning in the third century, lived a life of asceticism in the Egyptian desert.

Devotio Moderna: the Rheno-Flemish spiritual movement of reform that flourished in the Rhineland and Belgium in the thirteenth to early fifteenth centuries. This spontaneous lay movement was strongly influenced by women, the Beguines, who with their male counterparts, the

Beghards, used their homes as a communal movement of piety and charity. There are still Belgian Beguine communities today.

Divine Office ("Divine Liturgy," or "Canonical Hours," or "Cursus"): the practice of reciting monastic hours of prayer, which incorporated specific psalms, sung in response and antiphonally. The earliest western cursus is the Ordo Monasterii, attributed to Alypsius of Thegaste in North Africa, c. 395 CE. Later elaboration followed in Gaul.

Dominican: name of the order founded by St. Dominic in the early thirteenth century in order to combat heretical teaching (such as that of the Albigensians); primarily concerned with preaching.

Donatism: Named after their leader Donatus, this Christian movement in North Africa broke with the Roman church over the election of Caecilian as bishop of Carthage in 312. The Donatists opposed state interference in church life, and possessed a strong ascetic discipline of penance and a willingness for martyrdom if necessary.

eisegesis ("leading into"): a subjective reading of the text, which is more frequent than exegesis* in many commentaries.

empiricism: a philosophical tradition that maintains that most knowledge is gained by experience and ultimately obtained from the senses.

Enlightenment: the intellectual movement rooted in the scientific advances of the seventeenth century that expanded in the eighteenth century to advocate reason as the primary means of advancing knowledge; it was applied to religious, literary, and socioeconomic theories.

1 Enoch (also known as the *Apocalypse of Enoch*): a Second Temple composite work dealing with disparate subjects including future history, God's eschatological judgment, and fallen angels; it is of particular importance to Christians for the light it sheds on Essene theology.

eschatology: the Christian doctrine concerning future events taking place before "the end times." Hence it relates to God's sovereignty over all human history.

exegesis ("drawing out"): the attempt to determine the meaning of a text intended by the author(s) and warranted to be understood by the original audience.

4 Ezra: a Jewish apocalyptic work c. 100 CE.

form criticism: A development from historical criticism, it is an interpretive approach that seeks to identify the literary genre of a text and provide a classification of diverse literary expressions.

Fourth Lateran Council: the twelfth ecumenical council, convened by Pope Innocent III in 1215, with the intent of clerical reform, especially the revival of the Dominican and Franciscan Orders.

Franciscan: name of the order founded by St. Francis in the early thirteenth century; it emphasized simple expository preaching of the Gospels coupled with simple living devoid of excessive possessions.

gloss: a marginal or interlineal note in a text, by which the original language can be explained in a translation of the passage being studied.

Gnosticism: a heretical movement, popular in the second century, that based salvation on acquiring inner knowledge.

hapax legomena ("spoken once"): a word that appears only once in a defined corpus of literature.

haplography: accidental omission by a copyist of a letter, word, or lines due to similarity and close proximity of letters, words, or lines.

Hashem: Hebrew, "the name"; used by Jews to avoid speaking God's personal name (see Tetragrammaton).

Hasidim (from the Hebrew *hsd,* "godly," "pious"): the title given to Jewish pious ascetics in the Maccabean period who resisted Hellenization. The name was later adopted in the twelfth and thirteenth centuries in the Rhineland, and later still in the nineteenth century in eastern Europe.

Hexapla: Following the innovation of "the paged book," Origen created a six-column text of various Hebrew and Greek versions of the Old Testament in an attempt to standardize Greek translations of the Hebrew original. It was a remarkable breakthrough in reducing a vast armarium of scrolls into one text.

historical (biblical) criticism: the scholarly movement that developed from the eighteenth century with a critical use of archaeological, historical, geographical, and cultural data to interpret the biblical text.

humanism: the bias toward the role and scope of human achievements, whether with or without God.

hyponym: a word whose meaning is included as part of the meaning of another word.

inclusio: a literary device used in Hebrew poetry in which key words or phrases are repeated at the beginning and end of a poem as a means of achieving closure.

introit: antiphon or liturgical text, often used with psalms at the beginning of the celebration of the Roman Mass or Lutheran high service.

Janus: a literary device deriving its name from a two-headed Roman god perched on a door and simultaneously looking forward and backward. In literature, it refers to a transitional passage that hearkens back to what precedes it as well as hearkening ahead to what follows, thus linking the passages together.

Kabbalah: from the Hebrew root *kbl,* "to receive"; it refers to Jewish teachings, originally transmitted orally, predominantly of a mystic nature, which focused on the "inner" or mystical meaning of these texts; special methods of interpretation were devised to communicate their mysteries.

lectio divina: the "holy reading" of the Bible as the "sacred page," developed by the early fathers, particularly Origen, and developed later in monasticism, especially between the twelfth and fourteenth centuries. As a thorough assimilation of the Scriptures, *lectio* referred to much more than reading, being associated with prayer, while *meditatio* as "meditation" also included memorization, prayerful rumination, and moral challenge for the daily "conversion" of one's way of life. The revival of *lectio divina* today is a recovery of "participatory exegesis."

literary criticism: as old as literature itself; the explication and evaluation of works of literature. The early fathers adopted various principles of criticism from the classical culture, just as contemporary biblical criticism applies contemporary literary theories, both conservatively and more radically.

litotes: a form of understatement in which something is affirmed by denying its opposite.

Liturgy of the Hours: the practice of set hours for prayer, such as the third, sixth, and ninth. Clement of Alexander first notes the practice of these times in Egypt.

Lollards: late medieval reformers in England who as a lay movement emphasized the authority of Scripture over the clergy; they also engaged in the reform of morals.

LXX: Roman numerals for "seventy," denoting the Septuagint, the oldest known Greek version of the Hebrew Bible, translated between the third and first centuries BCE in Alexandria. "Seventy" is a reference to the claims of the apocryphal *Letter of Aristeas* that 72 scribes took 72 days to complete the translation of the Torah; in common usage the term "LXX" has been extended to refer to the whole OT.

Manichaeans: third-century Gnostic heretics of Persian origin who believed in an evil god as the source of the world and who sought by ascetic practices to overcome evil.

Masoretic Text (MT): the authoritative text of the Hebrew Bible; in the seventh to tenth centuries CE, Jewish traditionalists (Masoretes) added vowel points, textual markers, and annotations in an attempt to preserve how the text was read; the oldest extant manuscript dates to c. 895 CE.

merism: from the Greek *merismos,* "distribution"; a literary device in which totality is expressed by referring to opposites or extremes; an example would be Genesis 1:1 where "heaven and earth" are used to represent the entire cosmos.

metonymy: a figure of speech in which a part is used to refer to the whole of something to which it is closely related.

Midrash(im): from the Hebrew *drsh*, "to seek," "to investigate"; it refers to Jewish exegesis, whether of the Scriptures or of other Jewish writings; the term can also be used as a reference to the literature that arose from this type of study.

Mishnah: from the Hebrew *shnh*, meaning "to repeat," "to learn"; it is the first record of rabbinical oral law, from about 200 CE, in six main categories of laws for daily life.

missal: a liturgical book containing instructions for the celebration of Mass throughout the year. It includes prayers, psalms, other biblical readings, and ceremonial and singing directions.

Monarchianism: the name given to second- and third-century heretical writers who denied the separate persons in God. Differing names were given according to their bias: the Adoptionists held Jesus to be a mere man; the Modalists identified the divine persons as mere modes of being for the one God; eastern modalists were Sabellians.

Monophysites: heretical group who reacted to Nestorianism* in the third and fourth centuries and affirmed that Jesus had one divine nature; condemned in the Council of Chalcedon*.

Montanists: a second-century apocalyptic movement originating in Phrygia and spreading later through North Africa; it valued contemporary outpourings of the Spirit over ancient biblical prophecy.

Neo-Platonism: Influenced by Plotinus's reinterpretation of Plato, from the third century onward this movement opposed the dualistic interpretations of Plato's thought.

Nestorianism: a third- and fourth-century heresy from Syria that affirmed the two separate natures of Christ as two persons, one human, the other divine; condemned at the Council of Ephesus; it led to the schism of the Assyrian and Byzantine churches.

Pelagianism: the fourth-century heresy of Pelagius, a Roman lawyer, who taught that humans have responsibility for their own salvation, thus minimizing the grace of God in human redemption.

penance: from the Latin *poena*, "punishment," it reflects upon both the inner turning toward God as a sinner and the outward discipline of the Church in appropriate punishment in order to reinforce repentance of heart by outward deeds. Later for the Reformers, more emphasis was given to divine mercy than to the pursuit of a penitential way of life.

penitence/penitential: The act and result of penance were celebrated from the early Middle Ages in the recitation of the seven penitential psalms (6, 32, 38, 51 [Miserere] 102, 130 [De Profundis], and 143). They were regularly recited by the Western church on Fridays during Lent. Many vernacular rhyming versions were made of these psalms. For catechetical purposes these psalms were appropriated to "the Seven Deadly Sins": Ps. 6 against wrath; Ps. 32, against pride; Ps. 38 against gluttony; Ps. 51 against lechery; Ps. 102 against avarice; Ps. 130 against envy; Ps. 143 against sloth.

peshat (Hebrew, "spread out"): refers to the plain, simple meaning of a text.

Peshitta: Aramaic for "straight," it denotes versions of the Syriac Bible in Aramaic.

post-exilic: the period initiated by the Persian liberation of the Jews from Babylonian exile under Cyrus beginning in 538 BCE.

proper psalm: specific psalms appointed to be used liturgically at special occasions within the Church's yearly calendar.

prophecy: As a specific citation, prophecy demonstrates God's rule over history and his "openness to the future." It found concrete expression in his covenants with his faithful servants of the Old Testament, including David, and above all in Jesus Christ.

Prymer: thirteenth- to sixteenth-century books of devotion for the laity, which contained psalms for Matins and Lauds, Gradual Psalms (120–134), the Seven Penitential Psalms, together with the "Little Office of Blessed Virgin Mary" and "Office for the Dead" (for Vespers).

Puritans: Calvinist reformers who arose in England at the end of the sixteenth century; they preferred being known as "Precisians" but were nicknamed "Puritans" for their reforming zeal within the Church of England; they spread into New England in the next century.

Qumran: site near the Dead Sea for an ascetic Jewish sect from the second century BCE to the first century CE that held the Dead Sea Scrolls.

Roman breviary: liturgical book setting out regulations for celebration of medieval Mass or other canonical offices; it included readings, hymns, prayers, and the Psalter; divided according to the four seasons of the year.

Romanticism: an intellectual movement that arose in reaction to the rationalistic Newtonian worldview of the eighteenth century; it sought to promote, among other ideas, the "human face of nature."

Sabellianism (also known as Modalism): a third- and fourth-century heresy that denied the existence of the three distinct persons of the Godhead, arguing instead that Father, Son, and Holy Spirit were different modes of the one God.

Scholasticism: the method of learning developed in the twelfth to fourteenth centuries to reconcile the renewal of classical thought with medieval Christian theology.

scholia: grammatical, critical, and explanatory comments inserted in the texts used for teaching.

shofar: the ram's horn used as a musical instrument in ancient Israelite worship, notably on the Day of Atonement.

Socinianism: the Unitarian teachings of the Italian Faustus Socinus (1539-1604), who attacked the doctrine of the Trinity; led to the founding of the Socinian sect that spread significantly into England in the seventeenth century.

Talmud (derived from the Hebrew *lmd,* "to study or learn"): a rabbinic commentary and interpretative writings viewed by Jewish scholars as second in authority only to the Old Testament text; includes both the Mishnah (the oral law put into writing) and the Gemarah (commentary on the Mishnah). The Jerusalem Talmud is also known as the Palestinian Talmud. The reference to "Talmud," when used without qualification, usually refers to the Babylonian Talmud.

Tell Fekherye inscription: a life-sized statue of a man discovered in northern Syria in 1979; the statue contains an engraved bilingual (Assyrian and Aramaic) inscription on both sides of the man's skirt.

Tetragrammaton (Greek, "four letters"): referring to God's name in Hebrew, YHWH, usually translated in English as "LORD," and in this commentary as "I AM."

theism: the view that all limited or finite things are dependent in some way upon one supreme or ultimate being; as a philosophy it includes discussions with other religions concerning the nature of God.

theodicy: the vindication of divine goodness in light of the presence of evil in the world.

Tractarian Movement (also known as the Oxford Movement): nineteenth-century reformers who sought to revive the church in England by presenting their arguments and concerns in published "tracts."

tropological reading: a mode or turn of speech; at first it meant no more than allegory. But for Origen, the "third exposition" of Scripture, after the "literal" and the "allegorical" (as the "edification of faith"), was the "tropological" (for the "edification of morals"). What had been written prophetically ought to be explained morally as well, the medieval commentators argued. In broad terms, this meant that what was understood should be applied in moral behavior.

typology: a unique specie of promise and fulfillment. Whereas prophecy is concerned with prospective words and their fulfillment, typology is concerned with comparative historical events, persons, and institutions recorded in the Bible. Unlike allegory*, which is a loose, literary device, typology is fixed by the biblical canon.

Ugaritic: an ancient Northwest Semitic language of Ugarit (in modern northern Syria), a small but powerful city-state that flourished between 1800 and 1200 BCE; the texts were unearthed in 1928 by a French team of archaeologists and published in 1939. The deciphering of the language of these diverse texts (administrative, literary, and mythological) has helped clarify difficult Hebrew words and illumine parallels between Israelite customs and those of the surrounding cultures.

Unitarian: believer in one God who denies the Trinity and thence the divinity of Christ (see Socinianism*).

Vulgate (from the Latin *editio vulgata,* meaning "the common version"): this version of the Bible was translated primarily by Jerome, c. 383. From the sixth century it became the accepted version of the Western church. In 1546, the Council of Trent decreed that it was the exclusive authority for the Bible.

Index of Authors

COMMENTATORS ON THE PSALMS (up to the end of the sixteenth century)

Aelred of Rievaulx, 154
Alcuin of York, 37, 52-53, 152, 452-53, 455, 457, 474, 528
Ambrose, 37, 151
Andrew of St. Victor, 55
Anselm of Canterbury, 220, 453-54
Anselm of Laon, 455
Anthony the Elder, 44, 451
Aquila, 160, 224, 309, 393
Aquinas, Thomas, 55, 57, 120, 190, 218-19, 313-14, 326, 350-51, 388-89, 390, 391, 456, 457
Athanasius, 43, 117, 118, 245, 382, 416, 521
Augustine of Hippo, 2, 14, 37, 48-50, 56, 116-17, 118, 122-23, 146, 149, 151, 183-84, 212-15, 223, 235, 248-49, 280, 309, 350, 383, 448-49, 451, 455, 469, 488-89, 493, 497, 522, 527
Averbeck, R. E., 411

Bacon, Roger, 124
Barnabas, 182, 378
Basil the Great, 15, 45, 117, 276, 278-79, 451
Bede, the Venerable, 52, 452, 527-28
Benedict of Nursia, 186-87, 276
Bernard of Clairvaux, 50, 54, 55, 154, 281-82, 381, 385
Bruno of Asti/Segni, 54, 187, 217-18
Bruno the Carthusian, 187
Bruno of Segni, 188
Bruno of Wurzburg, 187
Bucer, Martin, 62, 63, 428-29, 432
Bullinger, 63

Calvin, John, 5, 8, 37, 38, 62-64, 74, 85, 101, 112, 125-27, 146, 156-57, 190, 221, 235, 238, 252-53, 263, 288-89, 315-17, 325, 326, 346-48, 400, 422, 429-31, 438, 462, 493-96, 529-31, 549, 562, 567, 571
Cassian, John, 451
Cassiodorus, 51-52, 123, 146, 151-52, 216, 223, 249-50, 280-81, 296, 311, 384-85, 417, 418, 455, 526-27
Chaucer, William, 285-86
Chrysostom, John, 6, 46-47, 51, 63, 150, 210-11, 225, 239, 246-48, 296, 449-50, 451, 462, 525-26
Clement of Alexandria, 40, 145, 308, 380, 487, 520
Clement of Rome, 12, 182, 204
Commodianus, 308
Coverdale, Miles, 432
Cyprian, 308
Cyril of Alexandria, 417
Cyril of Jerusalem, 521-22

d'Ailley, Pierre, 59, 424
Denys the Carthusian (or Dionysius the Carthusian), 59, 190, 286-87, 306, 314-15, 390-91, 421-22, 438, 458, 483
Desert fathers, 43, 450
The Didache, 447
Diodore of Tarsus, 45-46, 88, 120, 131, 308
Duns Scotus, 456-57

Ephrem, 451
Erasmus, Desiderius, 2, 124-25, 146, 154-55, 190-92, 219
Eusebius, 43, 118, 149, 150-51, 308, 382, 493
Evagrius Ponticus, 186, 381, 451

Fisher, John, 60, 460-62
Francis of Assisi, 244-45, 389

Geroch of Reichersburg, 54, 187, 189-90, 312-13, 418-19, 438
Gerson, Jean, 59, 287, 424
Gilbert of Poitiers, 54, 55, 56, 386, 389
Gregory the Great, 6, 187, 451
Gregory of Nyssa, 45, 115, 248, 451
Grosseteste, Robert, 283, 528

Haimo of Auxerre, 187-88, 216-17, 528
Haimo of Halberstadt, 52, 187
Herbert of Bosham, 56, 207, 218, 250-51, 283, 387
Hilary of Poitiers, 6, 44-45, 56, 115-16, 117-18, 121-22, 145-46, 219, 277-78, 417, 451, 522, 527
Hillel, Rabbi, 487
Hippolytus, 41, 146-47, 308, 379-80
Honorius Augustodunensis, 54, 118, 123, 455-56
Honorius of Atun, 187
Hopkins, John, 432
Hugh of St. Victor, 55, 387, 458
Hull, Dame Eleanor, 458-59

Irenaeus of Lyons, 41, 115, 380

Jerome, 6, 46, 56, 61, 118-19, 120, 207, 276, 279-80, 309-11, 312, 324, 327, 417, 434, 489-90, 493, 497, 522
Joachim de Fiore, 390, 492
Justin Martyr, 40, 41, 115, 120, 145, 182, 204, 378-79, 394, 487

Kara, Joseph, 57
Kimchi, David, 179, 428

Langland, William, 283, 286, 287
Langton, Stephen, 420
L'Ardent, Raoul, 456
Lefèvre D'Étaples, Jacques, 59-60, 125, 422-24
Lombard, Peter, 284, 386
Lowth, Robert, 71
Ludolph of Saxony, 315, 458
Luther, Martin, 4, 16, 37, 60-61, 63, 72, 74, 125, 127, 155-56, 190, 220-21, 251-52, 348-50, 425-27, 428, 459, 490-93, 503, 529

Maimonides, 55, 137
Manetti, Giannozzo, 58
Marot, Clement, 74, 315, 432
Martyr, Peter, Vermigli, 157, 254
Melanchthon, Philipp, 62, 315, 427-28
Melchior, 191
Montano, Benito Arias, 58
Moses bar Kepha, 118

Nicholas of Cusa, 58-59, 287, 391, 421
Nicholas of Lyra, 57-58, 60, 124, 219, 389, 420, 423, 424-25
Novatian, 382

Origen, 6, 9, 41-43, 49, 117, 118, 145, 147-48, 183, 187, 308, 380, 381, 450-51, 497, 520-21
Otto of Friesing, 389

Palladius, 184-86
Peter Lombard, 56, 119, 313, 454, 455, 457
Philimon, 381
Pierre d'Ailly, 287, 458
Poach, Andreas, 251
Polanus, Amandus, 257
Polycarp, 378

Pseudo-Bede (Manegold von Lautenbach), 188-89, 217

Sternhold, Thomas, 432
Symmachus, 160, 224, 309, 393, 497

Theodoret of Cyrrhus, 46-48, 120, 150-51, 184, 212, 248, 280, 384, 449-50, 566
Theodore of Mopsuestia, 47, 51-52, 211-12, 223, 245-46, 280, 308-9, 383-84, 417
Theodotion, 224, 309, 497
Tertullian, 145, 486
Thomas à Kempis, 287, 314, 391
Tostado, Alfonso de, 446-47
Trypho, Rabbi, 378
Tyconius, 49-50, 213

William of St. Thierry, 117
Wyatt, Sir Walter, 432
Wyclif, Thomas, 57, 283

Zwingli, Huldrych, 63, 155

MODERN AUTHORS
(since the seventeenth century)

Allen, Leslie C., 357, 543, 545, 572
Anderson, B. W., 96, 224, 238
Archer, Gleason L., 92
Arndt, Johann, 68
Auffret, Pierre, 162, 292
Auwers, J.-M., 118
Averbeck, R. E., 411, 480

Balas, David L., 115
Barnard, L. W., 40
Barr, James, 266, 358
Beckwith, Roger, 21, 22
Behr, John, 115
Bengel, Johann Albrecht, 69
Bernard, Robert W., 49
Blaiklock, E. M., 201, 272
Blowers, Paul, 39, 42, 43
Boston, Bruce, 138
Bowling, A., 201
Branson, R. D., 332
Braude, William G., 102
Brennan, Joseph H., 193-94
Briggs, Charles A., 93, 192, 240, 331, 344-45, 400, 513
Bright, John, 20, 24
Bright, Paula, 48
Brown, Raymond, 325
Brown, William P., 342, 546, 569, 571
Broyles, C. C., 295, 299, 320, 354, 398, 477, 513, 543, 548
Brueggemann, W., 23, 77
Bullinger, E. W., 358
Burnett, Joel S., 101
Burton-Christie, Douglas, 43
Buss, Martin, 129
Buttenwieser, M., 295, 474, 561
Buxtorfs, Johannes, 65
Byasse, Jason, 496

Calmin, Augustin, 67
Cappel, Louis, 65
Cerrato, J. A., 39
Chaney, Marvin L., 368
Charlesworth, James H., 20, 21

Cheyne, Thomas Kelly, 74, 93
Childs, Brevard S., 23, 28, 82-83, 101, 266, 496-97
Clifford, R., 356, 406
Clowney, Edmund P., 139
Cocceius, Johannes, 496
Colish, Marcia, 152, 218, 456
Contreni, John J., 53, 54
Cook, Edward E., 33-34
Cohen, Jeremy, 387
Collins, J. C., 559
Craigie, Peter, 327
Crashaw, Richard, 433
Cross, F. M., 136, 167, 513
Crouzel, Henri, 42

Dahan, Gilbert, 58
Daly-Denton, Margaret, 377
Dahood, M., 90, 164, 192, 224, 225, 235-36, 239, 254, 262, 343, 501, 502, 538, 550, 565
Dalglish, Edward R., 472, 478
Danell, G. A., 207, 543
Darby, J. N. D., 261
Davison, Francis, 433
Delekat, L., 207, 544
Delitzsch, Franz Julius, 74, 75, 87, 170, 236, 238, 240, 319, 342, 345, 346, 414, 470, 516-17
De Wette, W. M. L., 69
Dimant, Devorah, 35
Dodds, C. H., 366
Driver, S. R., 319-20, 335, 338, 339
Duhem, Pierre, 81, 543
Duhm, Bernard, 25, 93, 345
Durr, L., 355

Eaton, John, 78, 91, 100, 131, 143, 182, 203, 225, 226, 341-42, 344
Edwards, Jonathan, 10, 532-34
Ehrlich, A. B., 112
Engnell, I., 99
Ernesti, J. A., 4
Evans, G. R., 154

Falk, Daniel, 27, 35, 36
Finkelstein, J., 305
Fishbane, M. A., 354
Fitzsimmons, F. S., 240
Flaminius, Antonius, 496
Flint, Peter, 26
Fohrer, Georg, 343
Francke, August Hermann, 68-69, 73, 75
Freedman, D. N., 502
Frei, Hans, 70, 71
Funckenstein, Amos, 387
Futato, M., 356, 413, 438

Gabler, Johann Philipp, 69
Gamble, R. C., 63
Gerstenberger, Erhard, 77, 197, 265, 343, 502
Gesenius, Wilhelm, 69-70
Gesenius-Buhl, 268, 270
Gillingham, Susan, 13, 28, 30, 34, 245
Goldingay, John, 320, 342, 399, 479
Goodwin, Deborah L., 56
Gosselin, Edward G., 59
Gourgues, M., 485
Grabois, Aryeh, 387
Grafton, Anthony, 14, 42, 43, 378
Gratz, H., 74
Gross-Diaz, Theresa, 56
Grotius, Hugo, 66, 496
Gunkel, Hermann, 75-76, 91, 93-94, 98-99, 106, 172, 344

Harrison, E. F., 467
Harrisville, R. A., 68
Hay, David M., 484, 485
Hengstenberg, E. W., 87, 235, 318-19
Hilber, J. W., 499-500
Hitzig, Ferdinand, 74, 345
Hobbs, Gerald R., 62
Hofmann, J. C. K., 85
Holladay, W. J., 29, 30, 31, 32, 160
Holman, J., 545, 552
Honker, Louis C., 23
Hooke, S. H., 99
Horbury, William, 378
Horne, Bishop George, 71-72, 253, 317-18, 325
Houston, James M., 303, 422, 534, 571-72
Hupfeld, Hermann, 74, 345

Hurtado, Larry, 486

Jacquet, Louis, 204, 378
Jaki, Stanley, 216
Janzen, W., 133
Jobes, Karen H., 32, 33
Johnson, A. R., 76
Jonker, Louis C., 23

Kayatz, C., 360, 404
Keel, O., 169, 171, 226, 406
Kellermann, D., 333
Kidner, D., 87, 97, 111, 143, 203, 240, 337-38
Kirkpatrick, A. F., 87, 172, 206, 207, 327, 354, 517
Kitchen, Kenneth, 170
Kittel, Rudolph, 344
Knierim, R., 373
Knight, G. A. F., 512
Koch, K., 133, 134, 135, 440
Kraus, Hans-Joachim, 76, 143, 343, 404, 407, 543
Kugel, James L., 3

Ladner, Gerhardt, 15
Lampe, G. W. H., 493
Laplanche, François, 66
Leclercq, Jean, 50, 55, 117
Leighton, Archbishop Robert, 221-22
Lewis, C. S., 95-96, 210, 226, 269, 340, 355
Liedke, G., 141
Lovitt, Harriet, 543, 547, 548, 552, 557, 563, 568-69
Lowth, Robert, 71
Lubac, Henri de, 14, 58, 488

Mannati, M., 542
Martin, Chalmers, 97
May, James L., 77
McCarthy, Michael Cornelius, 50
McKane, W., 134
McKinnon, James, 40
McNamara, M., 52
Meinhold, A., 354
Mendelhall, George E., 96
Michaelis, Johann Heinrich, 69
Miller, P. D., 294
Moberly, R. W. L., 408
Montagu, William, 531
Mowinckel, Sigmund, 24, 25, 76, 98-99, 100, 163, 344, 499
Muilenberg, James, 98

Nasuti, Harry P., 28
Nauroy, G., 45
Neale, J. M., 11, 74, 75, 446
Neuser, W. H., 64

Oden, Thomas C., 12
Oesterley, William O. E., 200, 225
Owen, John, 532

Pascal, Blaise, 378
Patterson, R. D., 397
Perowne, Bishop J. J. Stewart, 75, 87, 240, 319, 503, 517
Plantinga, Alvin, 81
Plumb, John H., 3
Poole, Matthew, 127
Pritchard, J. B., 90
Prothero, Rowland, 12, 119, 416
Purves, George T., 40

Quasten, Johannes, 486

Rambach, Johann Jakob, 70, 71
Reuss, E., 74
Richards, K. H., 133
Ringgren, H., 197, 268, 556, 564
Romaine, William, 78-79
Rondeau, Marie-Josephe, 46, 117, 119, 183, 184, 212, 380, 521
Rordorf, Willy, 39

Saebo, Magne, 13, 45, 46, 47, 49, 50, 52, 57, 61, 63, 65, 66, 67, 68, 120, 124, 125, 130, 140, 141, 182, 468
Sakenfeld, K. D., 233, 443
Sawyer, J., 89, 199-200, 208, 327
Schaper, J., 21, 22
Schroder, O., 355
Schweitzer, Albert, 399-400
Selderhuis, Herman J., 125, 126

Sheppard, Gerald, 32, 97
Silva, Moises, 32, 33
Simon, Uriel, 23
Smalley, Beryl, 218
Sozzini, Fausto, 66
Spieckermann, H., 343
Spurgeon, Charles H., 253-54, 354, 365
Stanley, Christopher, 267
Stanton, G. N., 378
Stead, G. C., 44
Stephanus, Henry, 496
Sternberg, Meir, 83
Stewart, Columba, 186

Taft, Robert, S.J., 185, 485
Terrien, Samuel, 78, 107, 320
Thielman, Frank, 110
Tholuck, Augustus, 73-74
Tomasic, Thomas Michael, 117
Toon, Peter, 79
Tostengard, S., 414
Tournay, Raymond Jacques, 22, 26, 29
Treves, Marco, 179

Vall, Gregory, 393, 394
Van Til, S., 496
Von Hoffmann, J. C. K., 85
Von Rad, G., 170
Von Soden, W., 136

Walker, N., 373
Wallace-Hadrill, D. S., 151, 152
Waltke, Bruce, 4, 19, 21, 24, 66, 80, 82, 83, 84, 85, 86, 88, 98, 102, 128, 131, 132, 133, 149, 167, 168, 174, 176-77, 178, 179, 207, 208, 236, 239, 242, 244, 295, 328, 332, 335, 371, 355, 356, 357, 360, 361, 365, 366, 367, 368, 438, 468, 479, 484, 493, 502, 504, 505, 508, 510, 518, 558, 560, 570
Ward, Benedicta, 52, 184, 454
Watson, Thomas, 127, 139
Watts, Isaac, 78-79
Weick, R. S., 124
Weippert, M., 499
Weiser, Artur, 76, 100, 231, 254, 295, 320, 325, 328, 329, 330, 339, 405, 503, 515, 544

Wellhausen, J., 93
Westermann, Claus, 76, 94, 198, 255, 343, 414
Wette, M. L. de, 73-74
White, Helen, 432
Whitney, G. E., 336
Whybray, R. N., 367
Wickham, Lionel R., 45
Widengren, G., 99
Wilken, Robert Louis, 12, 14, 41, 44, 520
Williams, D. H., 2
Williams, Megan, 14, 42, 43, 378
Willis, John T., 160, 295
Wilson, Gerald, 23, 102, 103, 104
Wilson, H., 90
Workman, Herbert B., 186
Wright, Christopher J. H., 111
Wright, N. K., 486
Wright, R. B., 35

Young, E. J., 562

Zink, J. K., 472

Index of Subjects

Abraham (Abram), 120, 198, 283, 494, 505; children of, 348, 492-94; covenant, 137, 198, 201, 309, 410, 505; household of, 268; as king-priest, and Melchizedek, 509, 515; as shepherd, 436; as sojourner, 296

Absalom, 440; betrayal of David, 88, 97, 184, 188, 190-92, 196-97, 203, 206, 212, 238, 240, 426, 565, 567

Acrostic poem, 29, 179

Adam: and Christ, 119, 183, 190, 249, 312; descendants of, 31, 316, 433, 472; disobedience of, 123, 369, 372, 417, 433, 571

Aide-mémoire, 39, 52, 452

Allegorical: allegorical debate, 38; Calvin's aversion to, 316; Justin as allegorist, 41; and Luther, 350, 490-91; method of interpretation, 5, 6, 7, 8, 47, 54, 64, 218, 385; Origen as allegorist, 42; sense, 325, 423

Allegory, 58, 59, 59, 314, 435; and Augustine, 60, 525; avoidance of, 389-90; literary, 318; mystic, 72, 317; and Paul, 6, 42, 348; and psalm interpretation, 121, 350, 384, 387, 489; and typology, 9, 14, 47, 51, 149, 318, 493, 496

Alliteration, 98, 368, 442, 537, 553-54

Allusions, 31, 32, 34, 62, 191, 308; intertextual, 374, 377, 385; to pagan myths, 541

Altar: of faith, 214; of temple, 29, 129, 331, 379, 400, 464, 469, 480-81, 483, 507, 512

Anagogy (anagogic), 49, 58; anagogical approach, 70, 422, 490-91

Anaphora, 136, 198, 364

Angel, 268, 274; in heaven, 37, 147, 181, 528; humankind as lower than, 246, 249, 252, 254, 273; and music, 184-85, 195, 247, 253, 284; struggle with, 401

Anthropomorphism, 33, 265; anthropomorphic metonymy, 269

Antiochene School, 6, 45, 47, 308, 384

Antitype, 9, 111, 200, 208, 285, 414, 509

Apologist, 40, 67, 115, 145, 182, 378-80, 385, 519-21, 532

Apposition, 265, 269, 271

Archbishop: Anselm, 220, 453-54; of Canterbury, 387; Ebbo of Rheims, 312; Matthew Lang of Salzburg, 349; Robert Leighton of Glasgow, 221; Thomas à Becket, 56

Arianism, 44-45, 51, 310, 489, 527

Ark of the Covenant, 91, 225, 297, 482, 514

Army, 205, 500; Egyptian, 260; royal, 91, 179, 505-6

Ars moriendi, 220-21, 460

Asaph, Asaphites, 26, 89, 101, 146, 208, 419, 569

Ascension, 5, 37, 38, 72, 106, 110, 189, 249,

313, 486, 493, 504, 517, 527; feast day of, 244-45, 253, 484
Ascription, 46, 88, 90, 119, 219, 260
Assonance, 98, 132, 142, 166, 177, 205, 293, 541
Atonement, 106, 371, 446, 474; Day of, 446; as a sacrament, 461

Babylon, 19-20, 141, 296; texts from, 239
Baptism, 150, 181, 276; and Christian living, 447, 451, 453; infant, 462; and morality, 447; preparation for, 521; sacrament of, 421, 454; waters of, 417-18
Battle: divine, 99, 196, 198, 206, 239, 263, 563, 569; eschatological, 30, 109; spiritual, 165, 263, 381, 467, 510-11, 565-67
Benedictine order, 51, 53-54, 215, 313; abbot, 418; monk, 216, 528
Benediction: Aaronic, 239-41; of David, 194-95, 198, 205-9, 292, 306; priestly, 101
Biblical theology, 69, 78, 88
Birth, 202, 417, 472, 506, 529; of Christ, 106, 111, 148, 180, 246; of Job, 441; of king, 103, 159, 162, 171, 398, 403, 488; mystery of, 524, 537, 558, 560
Bishop, 40, 52, 53, 315, 449-50; Arno, 452; Athanasius of Alexandria, 43-44; Augustine, 48, 50; Bossuet, 67; Cappadocian Bishop Basil of Caesarea, 278; Chrysostom, 46; Diodore, bishop of Tarsus, 45; Eusebius of Caesarea, 43, 149; George Horne of Norwich, 71-72, 253, 317, 325; Gilbert of Poitiers, 56, 386; Guillaume Briçonnet of Meaux, 423; Hilary of Poitiers, 44; Hippolytus of Rome, 379; John Fisher of Rochester, 460; Liberius of Rome, 44; Lowthe, 317; Perowne, 75, 87; Robert Grosseteste of Lincoln, 283, 528; Roman Catholic, 358; of Spain and southern Gaul, 452; Theodore of Cyrrhus, 47, 384, 449-50; Theodore of Mopsuestia, 47, 280; Theodoret in Syria, 248
Blessing, 274, 515; bestowed on king, 92, 105, 212, 200, 212, 373; covenantal, 121, 135, 137, 193, 196, 225, 239, 241, 365, 400, 525, 571; definitions of, 120, 133, 206, 207; divine, 212, 225, 339, 418, 529; enjoyed by believers, 34, 248, 314, 418, 331-32, 337, 339
Blood, 38, 87, 401, 416, 472; of Christ, 390, 418, 453, 461, 490-91; libations of, 322, 329-30, 374; shedding of innocent, 479
Breviary, Breviaries, 29, 215, 446

Canonical-messianic approach, 80, 88, 100-101, 112
Cappadocians, 45, 186, 278
Carolingian reform, 52, 53, 151-52, 187-89, 250, 281, 447, 452-53
Catechism: Christian, 204; Geneva, 4; Mosaic, 437
Chaos: cosmic, 99, 169, 554, 556; wilderness as symbol of, 208
Chiasm, 205, 259, 292-94, 304, 358, 466, 551; chiastic complement, 304; chiastic parallel, 177, 265, 404, 410; chiastic pattern or structure, 98, 131, 290, 292, 327, 359, 465, 547, 558
Christology, 35, 57, 251, 384, 390, 484; Calvin's, 64, 316; Johannine, 312
Cistercian order, 37, 51, 54, 282, 390
Communion, 253; with God, 277, 327, 411, 418, 480, 547; sacrament, 220, 417; of saints, 68, 87, 494
Complaint, 229, 273; in lament psalms, 198; in petition psalms, 95, 97, 198, 229, 388, 396, 398-401
Confession, 4, 37, 82, 494, 571; of Augustine, 213, 469; Belgic, 84; of Christ, 484; of David, 264, 326-29, 349, 403, 437, 459, 465, 470-71, 479, 541, 542, 545-46, 548, 550-51, 555, 557-58, 563-64, 566-67, 570-71; early Christian, 485; of Israel, 399, 478; last rites of, 220; private, 447, 449, 453-57, 461; public, 27, 447-48, 450, 467, 483; of Saul, 481; of trust, 237, 290, 326-28
Constantine, 43, 47, 152, 382
Covenant, 63-64; Abrahamic, 107, 173, 180, 211; ark of, 297; Book of, 130; chil-

dren, 436; community, 479-80, 565; continuity of, 70, 71, 493-94; Davidic, 99, 103, 104, 105, 107, 111, 162, 169-70, 173, 194, 201, 226, 295, 319, 339, 501; and faith, 83, 129-30; fidelity, 133, 230, 255, 296, 303, 364, 370, 396, 414, 437, 440, 442, 482, 541, 567, 569-71; fulfillment of, 505; of God, 369, 410; of grace, 85, 318; and hope, 106; Mosaic, 100, 103, 136, 169, 172, 176, 225, 305, 348, 502; name, 502; New, 70, 110, 245, 252, 310, 372, 375, 411, 488, 517; Old, 63, 70, 110, 247, 252, 375; origins of, 76; people, 5, 129, 130, 132, 137-38, 174, 232, 281, 358-59, 365, 375, 477, 570; priests as mediators of, 508; promises of, 21, 329; relationship, 399, 402-3, 482, 569; renewal, 100; theology, 292; two, 382; unity of, 63-64; values of, 291; violation of, 468; and worship, 409; written on the heart, 139

Council: of Chalcedon, 51, 150; of Chalons-sur-Saône, 453; of Constantinople, 150, 383; of Ephesus, 246; Fourth Lateran, 452, 454, 456, 447; of Nicea, 44; Second Council of Nicea, 52; of Sens, 54; of Toledo, 452; of Toulouse, 38, 283; of Trent, 63, 457; of the ungodly, 123

Creation, 62, 100, 274, 310, 433; awe-inspiring phenomena of, 550, 559, 572; doctrine of, 341, 343, 347; general revelation of, 354, 356-59; Genesis account of, 267-72, 341, 553; God's goodwill toward, 556; Haydn's oratorio, 340; of humankind, 253-54, 522, 560, 572; humankind's authority over, 247, 268; *I AM's* glory in, 95, 244-47, 256-59, 290, 340-41, 343, 354, 358, 559; *I AM* as lord of, 162, 167, 169, 173, 229, 234; new, 297, 457, 476; in opposition to "nature," 67, 318, 342-43, 433

Creator, 172; and comprehensive knowledge, 267, 341-43, 356-57, 525, 530; glory of, 357; God as, 37, 44, 78, 116, 127, 133, 172, 173, 189, 191, 210, 229, 255-56, 258, 261, 264-67, 270-71, 346, 361, 374, 519, 522, 524, 554, 560; Jesus as, 112; and redeemer, 253, 291, 341, 342; transcendence of, 229, 291

Cross, 405, 493; anticipated in the psalms, 191, 202, 208, 242-43, 382-83, 385, 390-91, 457; Christ exalted on, 312; Christ praying on, 281, 377, 415; Christ's death on, 143, 220, 310, 377-79

Cross-index system, 56, 386

Cult, cultus: of *I AM*, 225, 227, 236-38, 515; of Melchizedek, 485, 514, 515; pagan, 76, 99, 226, 232, 515; as setting for the psalms, 76, 77, 99-100; temple, 99-100, 295, 500, 514

Cult-functional approach. *See* Liturgical criticism

Curse, 95; conditional, 303; of God, 137, 199, 208, 306, 339; ritual, 174

Dead Sea Scrolls, 27, 28, 102. *See also* Qumran

Death, 3, 28, 38, 65, 79, 108, 118, 197, 214, 236, 285, 307, 309, 384, 410, 432, 440, 554; atonement by, 106, 474; bed, 221; clinical, 133, 143, 314, 318-20, 413-14, 441; confidence in the face of, 295, 325-28, 334, 336-37, 339, 418, 431, 444; of David, 295, 393, 397-98, 444; defeat of, 5, 100, 136, 215, 253, 274-75, 311, 314, 319-20, 324-25, 334, 337, 384, 398, 409, 412, 440, 510, 569; as defilement, 508; evil, 339; freedom from, 136, 215, 510; of God, 164; images of, 99-100, 220, 333, 554; imminent, 401, 403-8, 413-15; of Jesus, 5, 10, 79, 110, 120, 141, 143, 182-83, 190-92, 209, 246, 249, 274, 308-12, 318, 327, 338, 375, 390, 415, 485-86, 490, 527; of Joshua, 531; as judgment, 120, 163, 303, 329, 469, 479, 552; law of, 189; mystery of, 324; peril of, 95, 552, 554, 556; premature, 325; realm of, 338; of the righteous, 242; risk of, 170, 174, 208; sin unto, 372; as sleep, 190, 212, 242, 243, 563; of Suffering Servant, 106; the third, 188; threat of, 431; valley of, 421-22, 441; vicarious, 390; of wicked, 142, 144, 338, 479, 490

Deity: of Christ, 40, 41, 66, 246, 310; and king, 164, 499; pagan, 99-100, 169, 489, 541, 555; and prophet, 499

Deliverance, 100, 400; from foes, 290, 543; by God, 91, 109, 126, 179, 193-95, 199-201, 204-5, 293, 339, 349, 400, 409, 414, 443, 479-80; pleas for, 36, 195, 198, 204, 208, 290, 409, 543; and sleep, 184

Desert fathers, 43, 184-89, 381, 448, 450

Destruction, 122, 236, 445, 479; of enemies, 308, 499-500; everlasting, 569; of the old man, 150; of the temple, 19, 74; of the wicked, 34, 97, 128, 141-42, 179

Devotion, 116, 312, 423, 461; to Christ, 422, 486, 488; of compunction, 450-52; devotional usage of the Psalms, 13, 37-39, 44, 55, 75, 117, 191, 213, 284, 484; *Devotio Moderna,* 220, 286, 314-15, 458; of educated laypeople, 458-59; penitential, 446; private, 429, 454-55; religious life of, 10, 11, 341; waning of, 3, 7, 124, 423

Doctrine, 56, 65, 70, 95, 348, 427, 533; of absolution, 457; of atonement, 446; Augustine's *On Christian Doctrine,* 48, 49; of Christ, 47; Christian, 124, 341, 388, 484, 517; and the church, 428; of creation, 341, 343, 347; doctrinal discussion in commentaries, 55; eschatology, 106; and faith, 427; of God, 44, 100, 125, 346, 562; and hermeneutics, 70; history of, 4, 12, 14, 461, 484; of intermediate state, 335; of justification, 219, 462; of original sin, 473; Origen's *True Doctrine,* 520; of resurrection, 320; rule of *I AM,* 100; sound, 14, 96, 126, 227, 421, 428, 517, 520; of sovereignty and human responsibility, 562; of Trinity, 51, 66, 252; of two kingdoms, 72; of verbal inspiration, 68; wrong, 123

Dominican, 56, 62, 388, 389, 428, 459

Donatist controversy, 48, 49, 51, 213, 250, 383, 524

Doxology, 22, 101, 118, 206

Ear, 7, 162, 371, 393, 405, 419, 531, 571; of God, 229, 230; inner, 344, 358, 361

Earth, 79, 118, 129, 156, 217, 240, 253, 277, 316, 329, 333, 413, 422, 423, 439, 440, 444, 449, 459, 520; in ancient Near eastern cosmology, 225, 261, 355, 359, 521, 541, 560; creation of, 37, 494; divine rule over, 97, 108, 162, 166, 168, 172, 178-79, 191, 194, 230, 246-47, 254-55, 258-62, 333, 358, 487, 501, 505-6, 509, 522, 547; evil kingdoms, 108, 158-59, 161, 164, 166-68, 174-75; humankind's rule over, 226, 255-62, 264-67, 269, 271-74, 505, 509, 514; as inheritance, 103, 142, 159, 162, 171, 173; judgment of, 142-43, 234, 498, 501, 511-12; new, 111-12; remotest parts of, 103, 106, 180, 203, 335, 347, 350-51, 361, 363, 395, 398, 412, 414, 538, 541, 545, 555, 558, 560

Egypt, 20, 163-64, 169, 233, 262; Abraham and Israel in, 296; army of, 260; coronation liturgy in, 163; execration texts, 174; Heliopolis, 360; iconography, 208; and Joseph, 269; kingship, 171, 226; literature, 172; monks of, 184-87; oppression of, 204; pagan religion, 186, 226; river of, 172

Enemy, 562; of Christ, 10, 149, 180, 388, 489, 495, 518; conquest of, 167, 169, 258, 259, 261, 495, 497-501, 504-5, 512; deliverance from, 41, 100, 230, 318, 435-36, 442, 509, 543; destruction of, 108, 109, 167, 261, 518; forgiveness of, 95, 98; of God, 31, 169, 185, 213, 249, 255, 257, 259, 260-61, 264, 274, 540, 564-65; of Israel, 109, 164, 250, 263-64, 308, 565; judgment of, 78, 234, 250, 267, 568; lament of, 405; personal, 188-91, 206, 213, 524; in petition psalms, 94, 97; of psalmist, 87, 91, 95, 99, 103, 153, 188, 193-201, 205-6, 208, 221, 240, 314, 319, 377, 397, 402, 414, 434, 436, 442, 540, 543, 558, 564-67; of saints, 108, 274, 388, 430, 527, 566; zoomorphic portrayal, 397, 404, 406

Enlightenment, 4, 13, 38, 67, 68, 69, 82, 317, 521, 532, 534

Enthronement festival, 99-100, 500
Enthronement psalms, 104, 107, 112
Eschaton, 97, 105, 181, 272, 508, 556
Eternity, 79, 111, 122, 155, 156, 277, 306, 310, 421, 438, 522
Ethics, 100, 103, 122, 230; and piety, 291-94, 300, 302, 570; and worship, 291, 296
Evil, 69, 333, 339, 365, 369, 403; actions, 27, 133, 153, 154, 247, 279, 280, 292-93, 300-301, 386, 440, 463, 471, 565; darkness as the realm of, 556; death, 339; defeated, 32, 108, 400; events, 154, 247; evil-doer(s), 34, 97, 161; fear of, 434, 441; intent, 539; judgment of, 30, 149, 511; power(s), 85, 135, 184, 309, 314; punishment of, 140, 511; thoughts, 185, 186, 189, 190, 217-18; triumph of, 135; way of life, 120, 127, 288, 393; in the world, 248, 253, 311
Exile, 496, 544; Babylonian, 19-20, 23, 45, 47, 92, 102, 104, 107, 169, 180, 280, 345, 346, 386, 389; of David, 92, 221
Exodus, 68, 493, 525

Faith, 73, 75, 166, 189, 214, 235, 288, 308, 330, 339, 373, 431, 443, 534; challenges to, 4, 37, 45, 66, 68, 70, 199, 231, 262, 264, 376-77, 380, 384, 398, 425, 496, 520; and Christ, 61, 139, 156, 274, 275, 309, 377, 488; Christian, 151, 181, 277, 312, 357, 378, 496; commitment, 365; confessions of, 39, 555, 557, 570; covenantal, 83, 100, 139, 329, 403; crisis of, 20, 26, 34; and ethics, 292-94, 306; gift of God, 84, 139, 325, 401, 403, 476; in God, 64, 80, 116, 126, 130, 138, 140, 176, 194, 227, 236-39, 241, 267, 302, 326, 329, 339, 375, 400-401, 412, 433, 438, 467, 523, 572; historical, 15, 38, 75; and joy, 316, 327; of the king, 161, 172, 194, 197, 199-209, 238, 407-9, 474, 552, 555, 572; Luther's, 61, 425-27; and orthodoxy, 5, 488; and practice, 80, 126, 242, 288, 327-28, 399; psalms as source of, 117, 213, 238, 419, 431, 534; righteous live by, 143, 357, 375; rule of, 2, 51, 63, 149, 195; and sacraments, 220; and scholarship, 6, 12, 66, 80-83; and Scripture, 6, 147, 149, 249, 325, 365, 491; and works, 140, 238, 249, 274, 278, 296, 306, 528, 567
Festival, 256; covenant renewal, 100; enthronement (or fall), 99, 100, 343; Jewish, 25-26, 102; New Year, 76
Figure of speech, 62, 216, 262, 281, 355, 385, 388, 491
Flock, 255, 270-71, 404, 419, 436, 437, 439, 481; ecclesial, 45, 124, 148, 423, 427, 438
Forgiveness: of enemies, 98; public, 448; of sins, 188, 207, 220, 230, 237, 291, 306, 329, 373, 455-57, 462, 465-69, 472-78
Form-criticism, 38, 80-82, 98, 227, 494, 512, 543; and deWette, 69, 75; introduction of, 75-77, 93-95; and psalm titles, 86
Fourfold interpretation of Scripture, 6, 49, 54, 59, 60, 61, 64, 124, 187, 251, 385; and Calvin, 252; and Luther, 251, 425

Gallican Psalter, 49, 312, 313, 421, 528
Gattungen, 94, 95
Genre, 11, 16, 44, 61, 64, 94, 98, 287; apocalyptic, 447; *ars moriendi*, 220; divine citation, 501, 507; ignorance of, 79; of individual psalms, 77, 78, 88, 120, 219, 344, 356, 374, 419, 438, 457; of *lectio divina*, 313; and psalm superscriptions, 87, 88, 195, 227, 229, 259, 327, 355, 467, 501
Glory, 217; of Christ, 5, 111, 119, 123, 204, 222, 234, 246, 249, 252, 274, 277-78, 282, 310, 490, 527; of the Christian calling, 533; cloud, 169; of David, 110, 112, 192, 194, 201-3, 208, 223, 228, 231, 233, 238; eternal, 188, 286, 311; of God, 120, 138, 178, 237, 243, 246, 253-54, 257, 259-61, 264, 271, 275, 286, 290, 313, 329, 345, 347, 349, 351, 353, 357-60, 362, 364, 391, 428, 443, 482, 527, 533, 569; heavenly, 121, 257, 188; of humankind, 119, 246, 253, 255, 257, 268-69, 455; of the kingdom, 79; of Messiah, 34, 107-8, 110; of New Covenant, 247

Glossa, 55, 528; glossalia, 528; glossia, 313; *ordinaria,* 55
Gospel, 10, 57; of Christ, 5, 61, 143, 307, 374-75, 377; of John, 148; and law dialectic, 61, 62; living, 57; message, 78, 146, 254, 282, 310, 348-49, 430, 433; minister of, 430; passion narratives, 391; and the Psalter, 156, 375, 377, 381, 383, 385, 398, 414-15, 427, 430-31, 449-50, 457, 488-89, 493
Grace, 147, 174, 287, 421; as benefits, 421, 435-36, 438, 457, 476; of Christ, 245, 248, 314, 445, 524; covenant of, 63, 85, 318; gifts of, 153, 172, 287, 314, 426, 445-46, 475, 526; of God, 5, 63, 130, 138, 176, 198, 220, 229, 237, 253, 274, 284, 286, 306, 311, 317, 347-49, 358, 370, 418, 448, 449, 460, 467-69, 477-79, 481, 526, 571; gospel of, 433; and justification, 524; and law dialectic, 62, 63; living by, 418, 476; and prayer, 172, 228, 231, 426; spirit of, 475
Grammatico-historical interpretation, 5, 50, 88, 112, 516
Guilt, 134, 254, 468; of apostasy, 354, 371, 372; communal, 27; and compunction, 450; confession of, 465, 468, 470; of David, 204; freedom from, 306, 474, 571; judgment of, 237, 264, 273; moral, 472, 479; offering, 106, 444; pardon for, 354, 369

Hades, 309, 312, 318, 320. *See also* Sheol
Headings. *See* Superscriptions; Titles
Heart, 4, 60, 84, 184, 216, 238, 345, 376, 397, 402, 423, 425, 452, 454, 496; become like wax, 388, 392, 405, 486; believing, 155-56, 214, 375, 440; clean, 463; compunction of, 450, 453, 455; contrite, 453, 455, 464, 481; distressed, 460; entire psychic disposition, 476; examination of, 220-21, 223, 234-36, 240, 299, 306, 310, 524, 526, 530-31, 533-34, 540, 546, 567-68, 570; and faith, 236, 299, 316, 339, 412, 440, 477; and fear, 405; and gladness, 210-12, 224-25, 239, 256, 284, 316, 323, 325, 334, 352, 366-67, 412; and God's law, 130, 142-43, 296; and gratitude, 432, 486; hardening of, 127, 135; inscribed on, 139, 309, 372, 375, 391; live forever, 395; loss of, 423; meditations of, 277, 279, 280, 288, 289, 313, 352, 373, 426; need to guard, 204; as organ of hearing, 116, 360; as organ of knowledge, 361, 531, 555; poor in, 314; and psalms 38, 52, 277; pure in, 133, 185, 288, 291, 294, 296, 300, 447, 453; and reason, 85; and rebuke, 310; regenerate, 130, 144, 297, 375, 412; restlessness of, 550; sinfulness of, 125, 198, 217-18, 457, 571; slowness of, 5, 214; sorrow of, 37; timid, 496; truth in, 289, 294
Heaven, 79, 111, 129, 156, 194, 220, 225, 226, 246, 251, 271, 284, 306, 329, 335, 423, 454, 484, 501, 510, 521, 545, 551, 557; and Christ, 143, 220, 246, 249, 503, 504, 506, 517, 551; citizens of, 280; creation of, 246, 258, 494; dwelling place of angels, 37, 181; dwelling place of God, 108, 153, 158, 162, 166, 176, 203, 246, 260, 335, 445, 350, 522, 536, 545, 547, 553; God's rule over, 256, 260, 552-53; "The Hound of," 550, 571; Jesus exalted above, 249; kingdom of, 108, 247, 311; new, 111-12; powers of, 333; rule over, 254-61, 522; Satan dethroned from, 510; testifies of God, 255, 257, 259, 261, 262, 264-65, 342-43, 346, 347, 349, 351, 353-54, 356-62, 374; throne of, 165-66, 172, 503
Heilsgeschichte, 85. *See also* Salvation history
Hell, 319, 557; and Christ, 183, 252, 312, 527; images of, 220, 461; powers of, 253, 311
Heresy, 13, 38, 51, 64, 103, 183, 246, 310, 378-80, 383
Heretic, 145, 247, 249, 286, 382
Hexapla, 42, 46
Hezekiah, 41, 45, 89, 308, 482, 487
High Priest. *See* Priest
Historic biblical criticism (HBC), 101, 325, 338, 497; beginnings of, 15, 65-69,

80-81, 340; effects of, 307, 317-20; and Pentateuch, 73; and study of Psalter, 78, 80-87, 210, 325-26; and *vaticinium ex eventu*, 112, 512, 516
Holy Ghost. *See* Holy Spirit
Holy One, 212, 213, 233, 273, 309, 311, 318-19, 321, 334, 338, 392, 400-401
Holy Spirit, 49, 127, 146, 155, 156, 252, 313, 469, 527; and cleansing of the conscience, 467; gift of, 445, 461; as giver of gifts, 523, 419, 445, 450, 455; as giver of the Law, 375; Holy Ghost, 79; and illumination, 4-5, 42, 59, 82, 84, 317, 417, 422-25, 489, 491-92; indwelling of, 153, 249, 278, 306, 418, 462, 467; and inspiration, 2, 48, 118, 121, 277, 375, 489; and joy, 313; power of, 510, 517, 572; praise of, 127; and transformation, 125, 214, 350, 371, 417, 530
Holy war, 170, 501, 505-6, 510, 514, 517
Hope, 1, 32, 104, 179, 285, 404; as contemplative benefit, 211; dwelling in, 319-20; eschatological, 27, 36, 133, 143, 309-11, 314, 327, 413; of forgiveness, 478; fulfilled in Christ, 63, 180, 319; in God, 419, 426, 554, 572; God as source of, 122, 155, 179, 199, 203, 211-12, 214, 228, 327, 554, 569, 570; of individual, 12, 32, 462, 506; Messianic, 106, 107; of psalmist, 201, 228, 310, 324, 336, 400, 408, 449, 465, 494, 518; of the resurrection, 212, 318-20, 336, 338
Hymn, 45, 74, 78, 79, 104, 120, 177, 219, 432, 486-87; baptismal, 417-18; book of, 119; of creation, 244, 272, 343, 354, 356; of David, 162, 212, 353, 502; Eucharist, 416; of Israel, 136, 246, 256; "of the martyrs," 416; pagan, 90, 94, 342, 345, 353; of petition, 355; of praise, 76, 79, 94, 103, 247, 249-50, 255-56, 353, 355-57; and psalm titles, 79, 89-90, 247, 355; psalms as, 79, 94, 103, 119, 130, 354, 485; and Qumran, 31; of redemption, 245, 249; to Torah, 343-45, 369
Hymnal, hymnbook, 10, 25, 39, 78, 486; hymnic compositions, 31; of Israel, 162, 355
Hymnody, 10, 62, 78, 107, 242, 254, 341; of New Testament, 449; Reformed, 416
Hyperbole, 97, 247, 336, 339, 516

Idols, idolatry, 40, 152, 206, 232, 237, 315, 543, 569; music of, 487
Image, 33, 90, 216, 332, 350, 355, 359, 362, 363, 374, 398, 405, 410, 444, 506, 511-12; of animals, 397, 403-4, 406, 407; arboreal, 131, 140, 143; of Baal, 225; and Christ, 217, 220, 523; of death, sin, and hell, 220; God's, 215, 253, 266-67, 269-70, 346, 374, 459, 479; *Imago dei*, 215, 244, 253; of poet, 355, 550; stereotypical, 374; of Shepherd and Host, 436, 438
Imagery, 33, 188, 331; animal, 405; of festive banquet, 436; of forgiveness, 475; mythological, 166-67, 560-61; of penitential ladder, 461; royal, 469; of "spiritual shepherding," 427, 435, 440
Imprecatory psalms, 95; imprecation, 304
Incarnation, 14, 37, 38, 41, 99, 152, 183, 189, 245, 247-49, 350, 278, 377, 381, 491, 520; mystery of, 527
Inclusio, 98, 160, 238, 258-59, 306, 362, 398, 402, 544, 545, 570
Inheritance: Christ's, 10, 103, 159, 170, 172-73, 310, 312-13; of church, 248, 312-13; from *I AM*, 326, 330-32; of land, 20, 322, 326, 330-32
Inscriptions of Psalms, 45, 93, 221. *See also* Superscriptions; Titles
Instrument, 38, 51, 72, 48, 173, 423, 441-42; musical, 40, 87, 89, 216, 217, 219, 251, 419, 486; stringed, 193, 195, 208, 244, 256, 284, 355, 502, 543

Jerusalem, 26, 35, 39, 280, 329, 365, 521; and absence of imprecatory petitions, 95; building up and exaltation of, 455, 464, 482; heavenly, 202, 277; and king, 41, 154, 164, 168, 180, 191, 202, 208, 505, 515; the Lord, 35; temple location, 21, 26, 109, 280
Joshua, 175, 277, 515, 531; high priest, 107, 512-13

Judaism, 3, 19, 20, 24-26, 107, 377-79, 390; conversion from, 421; eclipse of, 387
Judge, 141, 155-56, 202, 515; bribing of, 278, 305; Christ as, 156, 383; God as, 78, 108, 127, 230, 264, 306, 547; of Israel, 202, 550
Judgment, 74, 154, 284, 291; divine judgment, 27, 30, 36, 121, 176, 178-79, 230, 234, 273, 311, 315, 316, 333, 352, 353, 362, 364, 368-70, 373, 437, 451, 453, 455, 471, 490, 518, 524, 528, 546-47, 549, 553, 567-68; of enemies, 95, 250, 267; final judgment, 27-30, 97, 102, 108, 128, 131-33, 140-43, 161, 262, 571; Hall of, 503-4; humanity's, 169, 364, 368, 400, 530, 571; of nations, 91, 141, 267; psalms of, 277; of rich, 279; threat of, 315; throne of, 518; value, 301, 441; word of, 279, 333
Justice, 72, 118, 206, 177, 285; ark of the covenant as a symbol of, 225; divine, 95-97, 149, 172, 178, 197-200, 205, 225, 228, 230, 398, 440, 444, 453, 502, 505-6, 510, 553, 571; in human affairs, 153, 169, 206, 216, 232, 277, 279-80, 285, 289, 306, 453, 455, 459, 515; sacrifice of, 214, 216, 459

Kingdom, 72, 210, 283, 389, 452, 492; Davidic, 9, 20, 103, 105, 154, 172, 426, 507, 516; evil, 108; glories of, 79; of Heaven, 247, 311; heavenly, 422; of *I AM*, 166, 260, 274, 445, 477, 501, 504; of Jesus Christ, 79, 108, 118, 131, 151, 156, 157, 161-62, 252, 349, 377, 419, 485, 492, 495, 496, 504; northern, 164; Old, of Egypt, 89, 208; of priests, 331, 506; righteous, 97, 103, 108; of Satan, 274; of Solomon, 180. *See also* Kingdom of God
Kingdom of God, 97, 108, 110, 132, 252, 262, 274, 398, 419, 467, 477
Korah, Korahites, 26, 91, 101, 146, 419

Lament, 95, 154, 415, 465; community, 36, 69, 76, 94; individual, 69, 76, 94, 216, 377-78, 397-98, 403-8, 449, 476, 542; of Jesus, 188, 189, 198; and praise, 408, 543; psalms of, 32, 91, 227, 229, 419, 464-65, 546, 564; royal, 99, 191, 194-95, 198, 200-201, 208, 396, 453, 543, 563-64; unwillingness to, 449
Land, 104, 296, 329, 349, 361, 412, 439, 511, 552, 554; animals of, 257, 269-71; of Canaan, 20; creation of, 554; drought, 210, 227; fertility of, 100; inheritance of, 20, 173, 330-31, 362; of Israel, 420; of promise, 34, 63, 205, 225, 241, 309, 321, 331, 479; rewarded to priests, 508; shaking of, 234; and Sheol, 335
Law, 5, 31, 43, 253, 271, 347; benefits of, 439-40; Book of the, 166, 169, 171-72, 181; and Christ, 41, 43, 63, 64, 71, 121, 143, 156, 182, 212, 217, 281, 383, 431, 506, 526; conformity to, 326; of Creator, 271-72; cuneiform, 305; delight in, 136, 375; and fear of *I AM*, 176; and Gospel dialectic, 61, 62, 63, 348; of liberty, 165-66, 506; of the Lord, 121, 123, 128, 130, 142, 155, 161, 166, 326, 342, 340, 346, 348, 349, 350, 352, 354, 356, 368, 369, 469, 564; and love, 225, 346; meditation on, 128, 132, 136; metaphor for, 140; moral beauty of, 364, 367, 368, 369, 375; of Moses, 29, 41, 102, 154, 163, 173, 176, 279, 284, 297, 353, 364, 365, 399, 447, 468; of nature, 81, 273, 342, 347; and Pharisaic practices, 341, 344; praise of, 343-45; in first psalm, 103, 119, 121, 123, 128, 130, 142; and promise, 213; and Qumran, 109; and sacrifices, 237; scope of, 140; of sin and death, 189; as special revelation, 350; spiritual, 71; and sun in ancient Near Eastern religions, 355; of supply and demand, 557; written on heart, 372, 375
Lectio divina, 50, 54, 313, 385
Literal exegesis, interpretation method, 6, 8, 14, 33, 39, 42, 43, 45, 50, 55, 56, 66, 63, 70, 150-51, 314, 317; and Chrysostom, 46, 63, 221; Justin as literalist, 41
Literal meaning, sense of, 45, 49-50, 57, 58, 61, 62, 70-72, 124, 171, 251, 320, 382-89, 420-25, 442, 443, 490-91

Literary-analytical approach, 86, 93, 112
Literary criticism, 4, 378, 380
Liturgical criticism: cult-functional approach, 98, 112
Liturgy, 45, 50, 124, 184; Eastern, 451; liturgical celebrations, 26, 188, 244; as mediator of salvation, 203; monastic, 184; Mosaic, 102, 129-30; pagan, 100, 163; and piety and ethics, 103, 291; sacrifice in, 414, 481; and scholarship, 124; in temple, 103, 107, 161, 179, 208, 295-96, 298, 478, 481, 513-14; and use of psalms, 10, 45, 50, 78, 129-30, 133, 152, 161-62, 177, 188, 216, 244, 256, 474, 478, 570
Love, 49, 138, 183, 284, 318, 365, 367, 488; brotherly, 296; of cleanliness, 458; of David for Absalom, 426; of delusion, 223, 231-33; for enemies, 95, 524; of false worship, 232; for God, 117, 142, 144, 163, 172, 176, 213, 234, 237, 351, 367-69, 389, 390, 432, 445, 454, 502, 506, 529, 533; God's, 138, 200, 229, 230, 234, 237, 253, 443, 444, 451, 455, 462, 469, 506, 524, 547; law of, 225; of law, 346; of learning, 117; of money, 186; of neighbor, 142, 237, 280, 296, 502; of self, 533; for sinners, 97, 524; Spirit of, 455; of God's Word, 126, 155, 423, 427

Meditation, 44, 136, 184; Canaanite, 343; of David, 352, 373, 530, 531, 533, 541, 542, 544-45, 552, 570; medieval, 50, 312, 313, 453-54; at night time, 350; practice of, 139, 184; prison, 459-61; prophetic, 344; and the Psalter, 103, 116, 119, 125, 131, 284, 426; of Robert Leighton, 221-22
Melchizedek, 110, 485, 490, 494-95, 498, 501, 507-9, 513, 517
Merism, 240, 271, 359, 400, 413, 545, 546, 547, 548, 550-53; temporal, 472
Messiah, 182, 266, 484, 492, 519; messianic expectations, 34, 41, 76, 78, 90, 105, 106, 107-8, 120, 180, 183, 196, 221, 267, 287, 317, 379, 391, 487, 492, 509-13, 516, 518; and New Testament, 5, 35, 71, 110-12, 247, 445, 450, 484, 495, 519; rejection of, 154; and resurrection, 315, 318; and suffering, 5, 40, 107, 379
Messianic psalms, 39, 66, 74, 77, 111, 210, 378, 516
Metaphor, 33, 55, 112, 127, 165, 306, 355, 359, 421, 428, 475, 491, 506, 545-46, 550; arboreal, 140; "boundary lines" for favored life, 331-32; "chaff" for wicked, 132; "children and infants" for Israel, 261-62; for Christ's benefits, 429-30, 435, 445; "a clean heart" for inclination to regard oneself as purged, 476; "cordage" for bondage, 165-66; "crushed bones" for psychological defeat, 475; "gushing waters" for speech, 360; "heavens" for firmament and supernal waters, 359; "hem me in" for hostility and God's knowledge, 545-46, 549, 550; "*I AM* is at your right hand" for king's favored position, 503; incomplete, 262, 269; "lift up . . . your face" for prosperity and salvation, 239; "light, sun, and to shine" for prosperity, 239; "measuring cord" for the extent of God's judgment, 362; "melted heart" for loss of courage," 405; "my cup" for the Lord, 331; "never toppled" for stability and durability, 306; pastoral metaphor for Christ's benefits, 435; "path" for actions and outcome, 337; "roll unto *I AM*" for finality, 402; "shepherd" for pastors, 445; "shepherd and sheep" for Christ's benefits for his followers and humility, 429-31; "shield" for God, 201; of travel or pilgrimage, 280; "water" for Law, 140; "way," 131, 134-35, 139, 140, 161, 178, 271, 299, 568; "winnow" for God's knowledge of a person's behavior, 548; "worm" for despicable person, 402; "your slave" for covenant keeping, 369-70; "of your youth" for army, 506
Metonymy, 22, 166, 332, 337, 355, 373; of adjunct, 202; anthropomorphic, 269; of cause, 230, 358; delusions for baseless rumors and accusations, 232; "delu-

sions" for false fertility deities, 232; "depths of the earth" for womb or grave, 560; of effect, 202, 236, 358, 370, 410, 475, 480; empty for false accusations or idols, 232; "fat ones" for those who enjoy life optimally, 413; "fill me with joy" for future blessings beyond death, 337; "firmament" for sun, moon, and stars, 359; "flood" for blue sky, 166; "glory" for king's luster in victory, 202, 231; "glory" for social esteem, 268; "glowing heat" for sun, 364; "godly" for king, 233; "good" for rain, 225; "hand" for power, 408; "heavens" for heavenly hosts in the night sky, 261; "holy splendors" for regalia, 506; "lot" for land, 331; "measuring line" for lot, part, 331; "my lips" for speech, 480; "open my mouth" for to pardon and to purge, 480; personified, 443; "psalter" for "writings" section of Hebrew Bible, 22; "of the righteous," "righteousness" for righteous people, 237, 482-83; "sanctuary of hope" for devout worshiper, 179; "smeared-over-place" and "bottled-up-place" for womb, 471, 473; of source, 359; "table" for rich food and drink, 442; "they make an opening with the lip" for deride, 402; "wide land" for all nations, 511; "of your strength" for the time of holy war, 506; "strength" for bulwark or citadel, 262; "words of my mouth and meditation of my heart" for cognitive reflections, 373; "Zion" and "Jerusalem" for the nation, 168-69, 482

Midrash, 58, 102, 513, 548; *Tehillim*, 250, 379

Miktam, 309, 314, 316, 321, 327

Mizmôr, 87, 195, 228, 256, 355, 502

Monarchy, 20, 23, 24, 27, 70, 76, 104, 169, 342, 502, 516

Monastery, 52, 53, 56, 151, 187, 215, 217, 313, 423, 526

Monasticism, 117, 186, 282; history of, 52; and morality, 124; and self-examination, 454

Monk, 50-54, 280, 423, 449, 452, 469; Aquinas as, 340, 350; Augustine as, 340; Benedictine, 216, 528; cloistered, 385; Dominican, 428; Jerome as, 46, 526; monastic exegesis, 50, 51, 52, 54, 156, 187, 526; monastic formation, 51, 281-82, 449, 451, 521; and prayer, 184-87, 211, 451-52; and repetition of psalms, 276; and singing, 215; and sleep deprivation, 184-86

Moses, 5, 25, 27, 41, 44, 49, 67, 68, 102, 118, 129, 137-38, 154, 156, 201, 277, 409, 488; and apostates, 231; blessing of, 241; and building of tabernacle, 514; covenant of, 410, 505; and Decalogue, 63, 299-300; and God's glory, 443, 479; and God's name, 409; law of, 29, 41, 154, 163, 348, 353, 365; in Midian, 296; and Pentateuch, 102, 488; as prophet, 59, 110, 131, 390-91; and Psalter, 104; as shepherd, 436; and Spirit of God, 348; war cry, 205

Mountain, 34, 168; holy, 166, 169, 178, 192, 203, 277, 279-80, 289, 295-98, 306; shaking of, 234

Mount Zion. *See* Zion

Music, 52, 129, 195, 327, 337, 344, 432; of angels, 247; of David, 419; director of, 88, 193, 212, 224, 242, 464, 540, 569; liturgical, 74, 296; power of, 340; sacred, 26, 227, 270, 272, 386, 419, 432; in temple, 89, 91, 207-8, 242; and worship, 39, 486-87

Mystery, 38, 146, 366, 489; of Christ, 281, 315, 350, 391, 492, 527; of creation, 357, 524; cults, 486; of death, 324; divine, 7, 38, 58, 116, 121, 138, 148, 154, 337, 344, 417, 550; of the Gospel, 310; of the Incarnation, 527; in the psalms, 10, 188, 343, 357, 374, 379; and reason, 82; of Trinity, 38

Myth, 69, 99-100; pagan, 118, 494, 541, 560-61

Nestorian, Nestorianism, 47, 150, 246-47, 249

Night, 135, 200, 323, 521; as bright as day,

521, 524-25, 537, 555, 569; and darkness, 182, 310, 545, 555-57; day and, 31, 119, 121, 128, 139, 277, 343, 359, 400; as fixed time, 347; and prayer, 216, 222, 242, 332-33; sky, 256, 257, 258, 261, 264-65, 350, 351, 360, 362, 392; and shepherding, 437, 441; as time of peril, 184-86, 203, 204, 209, 506, 524, 555

Obedience, 5, 34, 105, 123, 127, 139, 156, 225, 296, 333, 346, 399, 420, 429, 505, 529; of faith, 306, 370

Orthodoxy, 2, 3, 4, 5, 7, 8, 13, 15, 37, 38, 45, 66, 82, 85, 151, 307, 326, 383; of Christ, 509; and Council of Chalcedon, 51; Lutheran, 319; Nicene orthodoxy, 43-44; questioning of, 80-82

Papacy, 59, 155, 252

Parallelism, 90, 142, 205, 258, 268, 294, 336, 355; antithetical, 302; chiastic, 265; and repetition, 403; synonymous, 266, 332

Peace, 19, 35, 118, 142, 204, 209, 284, 285, 514; agent of, 509; granted by God, 293; offering, 411; prayer for, 180, 239; and sleep, 212-13, 220-21, 224, 227, 240-42; wholly given to, 443

Penitential psalm, 55, 61, 93, 106, 187, 356-57, 447, 449, 451-58, 461, 464-65, 469, 476

Pentecost, 38, 307, 461, 477, 506

Peshitta, 47, 447

Petition, 87, 103-4, 161, 225, 263, 274; of children and infants, 258, 261, 262; of Christ, 315, 450, 458; of David, 88, 202, 204-9, 226-36, 238-39, 242, 328, 333, 340, 353, 357, 369-74, 397-98, 400, 403, 407, 457, 465-66, 468-70, 474-79, 541-43, 563-64, 567-70; penitential, 356, 374, 462; psalms of, 94-97, 107, 194-98, 326-27, 340, 355, 356, 396, 464-65, 543, 546; for salvation, 354, 368, 373

Piety, 7, 35, 68, 73, 93, 191, 273, 315, 455, 529; and ethics, 291, 293-94, 302-4, 570; Lutheran, 344

Postmodernism, 3, 129, 273, 534

Postscript. *See* Subscript

Praise, 10, 11, 22, 37, 40, 79, 87, 89, 102, 103, 127, 152, 155, 161, 401; of church, 384, 389; communal, 400; confession of, 494; with confidence, 326; of David, 340, 408-14, 542-44, 558-59, 562; enthroned on, 400; eternal, 126; of God, 253-54, 256, 258, 263, 268, 316, 332, 344, 347, 354, 356-57, 364, 374, 395, 432, 453, 464, 479; hymns of, 76, 94, 247, 250, 255, 353; of Israel, 392, 482; for king's victory, 290; in lament psalm, 227, 231, 242, 356; of Law, 343-45, 359, 367, 375; of Messiah, 253; of nature, 342-43, 358-60; in petition psalms, 95, 197, 201-2, 396-97, 465; of psalmist, 244-45, 247, 261, 277, 341, 357, 497; and purging of conscience, 468; sacrifices of, 126, 380, 397, 466, 478, 480, 482; of saints, 274, 571; singing of, 217; testimony of, 478; vow of, 466

Prayer, 36, 54, 88, 97, 126, 157, 169, 184, 186, 190, 213, 254, 284, 277, 288, 313, 326, 356, 443, 458, 524, 526; of Anselm, 453-54; answered, 95, 104, 226, 232, 262, 397-98; and canonical hours, 185, 187, 216, 381; and Christ, 183, 209, 217, 243, 260, 318, 414, 450, 458, 489, 493; ceaseless, 185, 187, 328, 448; as collects, 449; confession, 27, 349, 447; of David, 27, 91, 97, 101, 161, 170, 200, 202-3, 209, 223, 227-29, 273, 316, 318, 345, 353-54, 373, 375, 398, 400-401, 403, 431, 466, 478, 493, 531, 533, 564, 570; and enemies, 97, 263, 489; evening, 194, 210-11, 216; and interpretation of Scripture, 4, 43, 68, 426; and king, 103, 161, 169, 172, 180, 200, 225-26, 233-34, 238-41, 290; of Manasseh, 465; morning, 182, 185, 186, 194, 196; of Moses, 27, 479; penitential, 278, 375, 451, 453-54; perseverance in, 403, 448; and the Psalms, 27, 56-57, 61, 69, 87, 120, 172, 193-96, 213, 217, 261-64, 326, 343, 349, 432, 451-52, 456, 564; power of, 227, 231, 237, 243; prayer book, 10, 37, 115, 429; wholly given to, 443, 453

Pride, 14, 26, 123, 134, 153-54, 213, 285, 294, 388, 418, 453, 457, 474, 546, 567; and chastity, 528; evil of, 186, 263, 278, 431, 458

Priest, priesthood, 48, 93, 129, 184, 191, 206, 234, 259, 283, 285, 286, 296, 298, 329, 455, 515; Aaronic, 507-8, 513, 515, 517; of all believers, 156; Christ as, 41, 110, 161, 287, 310, 315, 460, 492, 495, 509, 517; confession to, 447, 453-56, 461; Hezekiah as, 487; high priest, 107, 108, 109, 196, 210, 276, 388, 472, 484, 507-8, 512, 513, 515; and king, 105, 171-72, 500-501, 507-9, 512-14, 517; kingdom of, 331, 506; Levitical, 495, 509; Melchizedek, 498, 507-9, 515-17; royal, 103, 161, 208, 421, 509; and sacrifice, 474, 481; in Second Temple Period, 108-9; and temple, 99, 262, 509, 514; training of, 460; wicked, 31, 111, 262, 315; Zadok, 109, 165, 196, 469

Promise, 4, 20, 216, 304; Davidic, 20-21, 24, 27, 104, 108, 172, 226, 482; divine, 63, 121, 165, 172, 175, 201, 213, 217, 225, 242, 277, 315, 318, 346, 348, 370, 493, 499, 506, 516; land of, 205; Messianic, 20, 180; of praise, 256, 397, 412-13, 478-79

Prophecy, 9, 14, 20, 47, 49, 319, 390, 486, 507; Assyrian royal, 497, 498, 500, 502-3, 505, 507; and Christ, 28, 41, 60, 75, 85, 110, 154, 162, 163, 180, 307, 315, 324, 325, 339, 350, 378, 382-83, 425, 450, 488, 510, 523, 526; culturally conditioned, 414, 510, 516; and David, 30, 72, 180, 250, 339, 391, 514, 518; false, 565; psalms as prophecy, 35, 39, 57, 61, 162, 213, 246, 252, 325, 372, 382-84, 391, 414, 450, 498, 501-2, 513, 516, 523; as source of divine power, 384; as *vaticinium ex eventu*, 81

Prosopological approach, prosopoeia, prosopology, 9, 44, 117, 146, 149, 183, 212, 308, 380-81, 493, 509, 523, 527; prosopological language, 147, 499

Providence, 3, 8, 121, 126, 127, 199, 210-12, 254, 330, 347, 522, 525

Psalm heading, 47, 73, 151, 213, 219, 221, 384. *See also* Superscription; Title

Psalms, Book of the, 29, 119; Book I, 29, 102-3; Book II, 29, 103; Book III, 103, 104; Book IV, 23-24, 29, 103, 104, 107; Book V, 23-24, 29, 104, 107

Punishment, 26, 34, 173, 175, 452; divine, 176, 178, 209, 263, 264, 273, 352, 369-72, 411, 457, 465-66, 468-69; of enemy, 194, 230; of ungodly, 122

Qumran, 5, 36, 109, 485; literature, 13, 25-31, 36, 90, 513

Rabbis, 5, 39, 66, 90, 342, 376; Hillel, 487; Kimchi, 180, 240, 438; Rashi, 55-58, 180, 218, 250, 251, 386-87, 389, 420, 438; Trypho, 41, 378-79

Redeemer, 41, 157, 253, 291, 318, 341-42, 350, 352, 354, 374-75

Redemption, 35, 37, 169, 244-45, 249, 257-58, 312, 358, 375

Reign: of David, 74; of Hezekiah, 45, 308; of the Lord, 77; of Messiah, 34, 74, 106, 108, 112, 120, 180, 517; of Pharaoh, 226; of tyranny, 260

Remnant, 29, 30, 108, 329

Repentance, 98, 111, 214, 349, 448, 449, 450, 451, 453, 455, 456, 470, 476, 478; fruit of, 188; Mary Magdalene as example of, 459

Restoration, 24, 26, 47, 111, 230, 362, 436, 455, 457, 476; community, 20, 21; and Messiah, 34, 111

Resurrection, 408; of deity, 99; general, 108, 110, 212-13, 391; of Jesus, 1, 5, 10, 37, 38, 40, 172, 182, 185, 188-89, 191-92, 204, 221, 245, 249, 267, 307-9, 311-15, 318-20, 325, 327, 336, 338, 346, 384, 388, 390, 415, 460, 486, 492-93, 517, 521, 523, 524, 527; of Suffering Servant, 106

Rhetorical: criticism, 80-81, 98, 227, 353; critics, 95; cry, 400; exclamation, 238, 260; features, 98, 341, 544, 550; question, 163, 231, 265, 273, 296, 371, 399, 542, 551, 566; and techniques, 86

Righteousness, 133, 285, 287, 344, 355, 367,

509; and Christ, 79, 143, 375, 383, 390, 489; definition of, 229-30, 482-83; faith as, 61; of God, 97, 200, 211-12, 230, 236, 256, 396, 414, 464, 480; of God's judgments, 97, 108, 368; of king, 105; kingdom of, 97; paths of, 434, 439; rewarded, 369-70; and sacrifices, 222, 237, 464, 482; self-righteousness, 111, 468; and Son of Man, 108; Teacher of, 5, 31, 109; way of life, 32, 139, 288, 292, 300, 422, 434, 439, 557

Royal psalms, 24, 27, 28, 34, 76, 94, 99, 106, 512, 516

Sacrament, 147, 220, 412, 421, 445, 523; of atonement, 461; baptism as, 421, 454; confession as, 454; of the Eucharist, 451; penance as, 421, 449, 461

Sacrifice, 89, 95, 298, 411, 464, 508; animal, 237, 414, 480-81; apotropaic, 444; of blood, 309, 474; child, 210, 225, 444; Christ as, 237, 296, 444, 450, 467, 474, 572; of contrition, penance, and justice, 214, 216, 459; daily, 26, 379; of praise, 126, 380, 397, 409, 411, 459, 466, 478, 480, 482-83; of righteousness, 222, 237, 464, 482; spiritual, 222, 237, 481, 486

Salvation, 4, 26, 118, 201, 242, 287, 325, 386, 419, 487, 491, 520, 557; assurance of, 491; and Christ, 63, 209, 244, 348, 390, 527; economy of, 386; eternal, 155, 333; of ethnic Israel, 374; future, 34, 131-32, 141, 327-28, 413; God's, 139, 179, 228, 239, 267, 296, 298, 306, 311, 341, 346, 362, 411, 463, 478, 480, 502; and king, 196-97, 200-203, 206, 228, 232; in Old Testament, 73, 200; petitions for, 230, 354, 356, 369, 372-75, 399, 407, 465; universal, 173-74, 181, 248, 384, 400, 415; way of, 346

Salvation history, 8-9, 14, 64, 85, 95, 102, 105, 147, 161, 172, 198, 257-58, 335, 510, 518, 559, 563-64

Sanctuary, 88, 143, 179, 285, 288, 291, 292, 296, 477, 515; heavenly, 510, 517

Satan, 30, 107, 199, 274, 372, 402, 417, 511

Saul, 89, 97, 178, 188, 221, 304, 388, 414, 420, 478, 565, 567

Savior, 5, 9, 41, 78, 127, 147, 153, 179, 309-11, 374, 489; faith in, 377; knowledge of, 421; risen, 487

Scholasticism, 38, 54-60, 152, 218, 283, 390, 422, 424, 427

Sea, 137, 203, 260, 404, 412; humankind's rule over, 255, 269, 271-72; *I AM's* dominion over, 234, 260, 536, 545, 550, 552, 554, 556; representing chaotic power, 554-55

Seed, 253, 396, 408, 413-14, 560; of Abraham, 198, 492; of Adam, 31; of David, 108, 319, 516; of Jacob, 395, 409-10; of the woman, 511, 556

Selah, 214, 219

Shame, 31, 126, 199, 202, 222-23, 231, 233, 372, 392, 401, 504, 518, 525

Sheep, 270, 435-45; figural, 427, 429-30, 445; going astray, 418-19; sacrifice of, 237, 480; separated from goats, 50, 141

Sheol, 308, 312, 318-19, 335, 339. *See also* Hades

Shepherd: David as, 418-19; good, 416, 421; human, 427; *I AM* as, 230, 417-18, 426-31, 433-45; *Shepherd of Hermas,* 447

Sin, 97, 123, 130, 417, 460, 562; abhorrence of, 567; abounding of, 314; admonition not to, 223, 234-36, 278; and anger, 235; atonement for, 106, 141, 371; bearer of, 388; in believers, 121, 532, 533; bondage to, 375; born in, 27, 531; and Christ's death, 5, 136, 183, 204, 333, 374, 383, 390; conceived in, 472-73; confession of, 37, 447, 451, 453-55, 479-81, 483, 524, 571, 572; and death, 189, 212, 274-75, 372, 510; deceitfulness of, 533, 568; definition and essence of, 133-34, 197, 273; deliverance from, 136, 204, 417; effects of, 105, 123, 129, 135, 139, 204, 249, 253, 274, 367, 375, 383, 457, 468, 569; forgiveness of, 138, 220, 306, 314, 320, 369, 390, 443, 446, 448-49, 452, 455-57, 463, 465-68, 472, 474, 475; hidden, 355, 369, 371; mourning for, 451, 462-63, 465,

470-71; nature of, 127, 197, 253, 273; penance for, 447, 453-54, 461; punishment of, 36, 178, 369; renunciation of, 479-80; repentance of, 111, 120, 214, 254, 375, 448, 470-75; types of, 130, 278, 280, 370, 372, 458; unknown, 126, 529, 552, 568, 571
Sleep, 10, 166, 184-86, 204, 211, 214, 220, 222; death as, 183, 185, 190, 212; of *I AM,* 235; of king, 200-201, 227, 238, 240-43
Socinianism, 66, 67
Solomon, 57, 146, 164, 165, 171-72, 180, 250, 295, 304, 353, 386, 389, 467, 514-15; deeds of, 169, 175, 282, 482; *Psalms of,* 34-35, 109, 180, 513; Song of, 367; and temple, 225, 277
Son of God, 111, 310, 488, 523
Son of Man, 108, 111, 249, 267, 274, 310, 484, 504, 506, 516, 518
Song, 10, 29, 87, 79, 184, 247, 344, 486; and Moses, 104, 201; of praise, 11, 343, 355; psalms as songs, 40, 53, 75, 77, 79, 87, 101, 129, 130-31, 145, 195, 213, 216-18, 247, 256, 284, 355, 373-74, 419, 428, 432, 436; of Solomon, 204, 261, 269, 335, 364, 367, 549; of Songs, 12, 37, 43, 55, 381; of thanksgiving, 245; of trust, 76, 94, 326, 435-36, 438-39; of Zion, 94
Sovereignty, 64, 151, 191, 252, 373, 480, 494-95
Spirit, 14, 115, 213, 450, 466; came upon, 419; of Christ, 61, 73; filled with, 249, 486; of God, 5, 105, 142, 236, 348, 375, 536, 551; of holiness, 492; indwelling of, 457, 462, 499, 516; pouring out of, 506, 521; power of, 2, 5, 6, 209, 477, 489, 492, 499, 516; and understanding of Scripture, 83, 85, 491; work of, 420-24, 455, 530
Spiritual approach, meaning of, 42, 45, 54, 61, 72, 124, 149, 150, 151, 248, 251, 317-18, 380-85, 423, 425, 489
Subscript, 87, 88, 227, 242, 353, 354, 357, 374, 466, 542, 569; postscript, 88, 194, 207, 209, 415, 483, 544
Suffering, 140, 376; of Christ, 181, 188-91, 202, 204, 246, 249, 309, 311, 378-79, 382, 388, 390-91, 400; of David, 96, 112, 204, 414; of Israel, 379, 388; of saints, 133, 245, 311, 315; Servant, 106, 164, 380, 382
Superscript, superscriptions, 200, 227, 244, 257-58, 353-55, 374, 465-66, 518, 542; Davidic, 25, 27, 90, 92, 228-29, 259, 295, 336-27, 345, 357, 370, 398, 436, 467, 501-2, 544; definition of, 87; historical, 23, 25, 88, 92, 208; lack of, 102; and postscripts, 88, 194; reliability of, 22-23, 25, 28, 86-94; and verse numbering, 16, 195
Symbol, 6, 49, 55, 180, 208, 269, 467, 510, 523; of death, 554; of judgment, 250; nature of, 491; of royal power and strength, 408, 489, 505
Synagogue, 32, 39, 65, 99, 283, 345, 386, 486; and use of psalms, 76, 103
Synecdoche, 169, 443, 467, 480, 482, 491, 511, 558

Talmud, 75, 513
Targum, 22, 33-34, 173, 251, 268, 474, 511
Temple, 90, 109, 237, 290, 328, 335, 466, 503; access to, 290-91; building of, 287, 514-15; and Christ, 71, 110-11, 152, 166, 180, 262, 277-78, 287, 444, 487, 504, 510, 516; creation as, 259; cultus, 99, 237, 379, 400, 500, 508; dedication of, 225; and liturgy, 103, 107, 129, 162-63, 165, 194, 208, 291, 400; location of, 168-69, 226, 280, 503; music, 26, 89, 91, 102, 207-8, 242, 246, 296; pagan, 487; palace complex, 504, 517; rededication of, 25; Second Temple Period, 19-36, 93-94, 108, 180; theology of, 343
Temptation, 125, 381, 391, 153, 216, 521, 521
Thanksgiving, 91, 155, 332, 431; song of, 245
Thanksgiving psalms, 32, 90, 94-95, 249, 340, 429; as genre, 61
Throne, 410, 507, 512, 555; of Assurbanipal, 226; and Christ, 78, 156, 172, 287, 307, 517-18; of David, 105, 107, 163, 165, 172, 180, 194, 203, 205-6, 208,

295, 307; of God, 78, 169, 180-81, 194, 261, 400-401, 507; of heaven, 165, 172, 503-4; of judgment, 518; and Suffering Servant, 106

Title, 22, 111, 119, 167, 181, 191, 211, 229, 245, 248, 250, 251, 297, 314, 345, 420, 428, 429, 446, 514, 526, 562; authorship, 23, 34; headings, 47, 72, 73, 151, 213, 219, 221, 384; historical, 183, 459; musical, 216, 217, 218, 247, 251, 316; reliability of, 47, 67, 72, 74, 79, 87, 459, 526

Torah, 25, 39, 333; and forgiveness of David, 468; and *I AM* as author, 10, 161, 230; *I AM's* glory in, 290, 340-41, 346; meaning of in the psalms, 103, 136, 348; praise of, 353, 356-59, 364-69, 375; psalm, 291, 343; response to, 139, 143, 232, 295, 357, 373-74; teaching on, 24, 32-34, 39, 342-43, 508

Transcendence, 72, 82, 83, 166, 167, 192, 229, 267, 328, 359, 399, 494, 526, 534, 541, 546-47

Trinity, 38, 44, 247, 291, 419; doctrine of, 51, 66, 116, 252; eastern trinitarian thought, 44; in Johannine theology, 181; and Psalter divisions, 118

Tropology, tropological approach, sense, 6, 7, 50, 59, 124, 184, 190, 248, 281-82, 385, 423, 425, 438, 490-91

Type, *typos,* 66, 141, 173, 344, 373, 523; and antitype, 9, 111, 200, 208, 509; David as, 64, 105, 110, 207, 339, 414, 424, 518; in Old Testament, 41, 105, 110, 143, 190, 297, 306, 325, 504, 517; of poetry, 75-76; as promise and fulfillment, 493; of psalms, 69, 76, 93-94; psalms as, 72, 111-12

Typology, 45, 86, 93, 211, 518; and Christ, 85, 123, 183; and discontinuity, 106; distinct from allegory, 9, 14, 51, 149, 318, 493, 496; eastern fathers' use of, 149-51; New Testament, 42, 47, 414, 489; in the psalms, 39, 339; typico-prophetic, 6, 112, 147, 180, 339, 414; typological interpretation, 8, 41, 42, 491

Ugarit, 93, 239, 494; Ugaritic, 3, 90, 236, 239, 333, 334, 343, 367

Voice, 191, 202, 217, 236, 242, 253, 342, 346, 358, 375, 389, 506; of angels, 253; of author(s), 4, 6, 10; of Christ, 9, 388, 390-91, 427, 448, 523; of the church, 1, 2, 10, 49, 115, 145, 182, 189, 210, 213, 216, 244, 276, 307, 340, 376, 416, 446, 484, 519, 524; of conscience, 333; of creation, 351, 358, 361-62; of God, 2, 4; of Holy Spirit, 2, 236; of prophets, 20, 27, 513, 523; of psalmist, 10, 128, 145, 157, 192, 200, 203, 223, 254, 289, 321, 351, 392, 400, 419, 434, 462, 497, 523, 534; of shepherd, 427, 437; of text, 4

Vulgate, 12, 46, 48, 54, 118, 152, 251, 279, 313, 417, 419, 423, 446, 453, 457, 521, 528, 553

Wealth, 120, 140, 206, 231, 232, 237, 279, 283, 368, 442

Wicked, 28, 366, 533; against believers, 36, 274, 563-67, 570; darkness as the realm of, 556-57; deeds of, 96, 103, 127, 153, 206, 242, 257, 406, 439, 524; destruction of, 34, 97, 191, 193, 292, 205-6; exposed, 355; God against, 292, 399, 531, 539, 563-67, 571; and judgment, 28, 97, 102, 123, 128, 131-33, 140-43, 161, 193, 257, 287, 438, 511, 524, 526, 528; oppose *I AM,* 176, 178, 316, 338, 366, 402, 531, 542; Priest, 31; in realm of darkness and death, 338; in Sheol, 335

Wisdom, 32, 134, 175, 286, 314, 357, 370; and Christ, 286; and fear of *I AM,* 357, 367; and God, 4, 78, 79, 217, 236, 310-11, 328, 340-41, 347, 348, 356, 365, 459, 463, 473, 491, 529; growth in, 53; and Holy Spirit, 105, 422; literature, 375; in petition psalms, 328; psalm of, 120, 340, 342, 356; salutary, 422; songs of, 94; of the world, 147

Word of God, 8, 13, 37, 61, 120, 122, 123, 174, 248, 348, 349, 368

Worship, 14, 63, 346, 347, 408; corporate, 2, 8, 24, 29, 39, 53, 79, 130, 187, 277, 432,

470, 485, 532; and ethics, 291; false, 39, 76, 152, 163, 181, 216, 225, 232, 265, 279, 329, 346, 410, 521, 565; orthodoxy as "right worship," 3, 43-44; private, 24, 27; and the Psalter, 10-11, 38, 39, 79, 92, 126, 152, 175-76, 209, 408, 419, 432, 459, 485; in temple, 91, 296, 400, 508-9, 514; true worship, 20, 38, 121, 129, 156, 175-76, 216, 360, 361, 398, 412-13, 419-20, 468
Wrath, 92; of God, 149, 157, 158, 159, 162, 167, 177-79, 197, 411, 461, 468; of the king, 460

Zion, 156, 262; citizens of, 288, 457; heavenly, 285, 306, 450; as holy hill, 196, 226; and king, 90, 99-100, 154, 161-62, 166-69, 172, 180, 203, 297, 482, 497, 500-501, 505; Mount, 90, 161-62, 226, 277-78, 295-98, 335; prosperity of, 464, 466-67, 482; songs of, 94

Index of Scripture References

OLD TESTAMENT

Genesis

1 244, 245, 272, 410
1:2 554, 556
1:3ff. 556
1:6 261
1:8 359
1:14 262
1:15 262
1:16 257
1:17 262
1:22 198
1:26 215, 266, 269
1:26-28 269, 270, 272, 274
1:28 270, 472
2 270
2:7 561
2:15 370
2:19 561
3:6 369
3:14 405
3:15 511, 556
3:17 444
3:19 316, 339
3:24 370
4:1 404, 558
4:8 235
6:5 472, 561
6:7-8 229
8:21 472
9:1 198, 472
9:4-5 411
9:5-6 479
12:1-3 20, 207
12:2 137
12:3 505
12:10 296
14:18-20 515
14:18-22 328
15 410
15:1 201
15:2-3 171
15:12 556
15:17-21 515
16:6 552
16:8 552
16:13 328
17 410
17:1 328
17:8 173
18:11 135
18:19 546
19:9 296
19:17-22 401
19:19 228
20:1 296
20:6 470
21:1 266
21:33 328
22:17 563
22:18 505
24:2 269
26:7 555
26:9 443, 555
27:7 206
27:28 225, 506
27:34 560
27:39 506
27:43 552
28:3 328
29:14 443
30:8 440
30:33 439
30:38 472
30:41 472
31:10 472
31:20 552
31:36 373
31:38-40 437
32:5–33:10 228
32:25 550
33:13 438
33:20 328
35:11 328
37:3 406
37:24f. 407
37:29 406
38:14 406
38:26 439
39:6 335
39:9 470

40:13 202, 512
41:3 301, 441
43:14 328
44:28 443
45:24 234
46:3 254
48:3 328
48:4 173
48:14 333
48:18 333
50:24 266
50:25 266

Exodus

2:4 254
2:10 171
2:15 552
2:17 205
2:25 546
3 137
3:12 176
3:13-22 409
3:14 44, 116, 117, 136-37
3:16 266
4:14 366
4:22 171, 172
4:23 172
7:4 549
7:10 137
8:22 233
9:4 233
10:21 556
11:7 406
12:6 279
13:17 554
13:21 554
14:15 552
14:31 176, 178, 549
15:1 89, 90, 92
15:6 260
15:10 260
15:13 439, 554
15:16 236
16:20 401
18:20 370
18:25 511
19–24 410
19:6 329, 331, 506
19:9–20:21 176
19:16 556
19:18 556
19:25 235
20:3 321
20:5 566
20:7 301, 540
20:17 368
21–23 368
21:6 337
21:16 370
21:19 442
22:1 479
22:20-23 297
22:21 296
22:24 411
22:25 305
22:31 406
23:1 565
23:5 335
23:8 305
23:12 272
24:3-8 130
24:15ff. 556
25:40 277, 504
28:2 406
29:7 105
29:40 330
30:9 330
31:3 477
32–34 130
32:20 231
32:32 469
32:32f. 561
32:34 439
33:7 232
33:11 277
33:12 546
33:13 479
33:17 546
33:19 138
33:19-20 443
33:22 549
34:6 130, 229, 237, 466, 469, 479
34:6-7 138, 237, 443, 478
34:10 559
34:22 363
35:21 478
40:9-11 105

Leviticus

3:1-2 411
3:16b-17 411
4 474
5:4 304
7:1-21 411
7:11-34 411
7:22-27 411
8:10-11 105
9:8 411
9:12 411
9:15-17 411
9:23 206
10:1-2 105
10:3 236
11:10 137
11:25 406
11:43 410
12 472
13:46 242
13:52 406
14:49 474
14:52 474
15:18 472
16:18 472
17:11 411
18:16 60
18:23 535
18:25 267
19:12 304
19:19 535
19:34 296
20:2 297
20:9 479
20:10 479
20:16 535
20:21 60
21:3 302
21:10-15 508
24:16 297
24:17 479
24:17-22 96

24:21 479
24:22 297
25 446, 457
25:6 297
25:19 437
25:36 305
25:37 305
25:43 505
26:3-5 437
26:16 263
26:17 505
26:28 175
26:38 142

Numbers

1:2 562
1:16 511
1:53 508
3:28 508
3:32 508
4:2 562
5:23 469
6:25 239
6:26 224, 239
7:10-11 105
8:11 176
10:35 31, 205
11:18-30 477
11:24-30 500
11:29 477
16:3 329
16:30 404
18:20 310, 331
19 474
19:19 474
21:18 442
22:30 535
23:9 241
23:19f. 268
24:2-3 477
24:3 502
24:9 393
24:17 510
27:7 159, 172
27:23 261
28–29 26
31:26 562
31:49 562
32:32 159
35:2 159
35:6 101
35:15 297
35:19f. 467, 468
35:27 479

Deuteronomy

1:16 297
2:36 550
3:24 559
4:21 173
4:36 175
4:37-38 20
5:9 566
5:11 540
5:20 565
6:7 547
6:13 176
7:1-2 515
7:1-11 20
7:10 566
8:3 438
8:5 175
8:7 511, 512
9:14 469
9:26-29 27
10:9 331
10:17 305
10:18 296
10:19 296, 297
11:6 404
11:11-12 225
11:13-14 225
11:22 232
12 20
13:4 176
13:5 97
13:6 560
14:29 296
16:19 305
17:7 97
17:8 550
17:8-13 508
17:12 97
17:16 206
17:18 172
17:19 444
18:1 331
19:10 479
19:11 198
19:13 97
19:19 97
20:1-9 505
20:10-15 505
20:16 173
21:5 508
21:9 97
21:21 97
21:23 199
22:6f. 272
22:8 479
22:22 97
22:22-24 470
22:23 468
22:23-24 467
22:23-27 199
22:24 97, 203
22:16 198
23:1-4 295
23:19 279
23:20 305
25:5 60
25:5-10 440
26:1-15 295
26:11-13 296
27:5 173
27:15 560
27:24 560
27:25 305
28:10-15 505
28:12 225, 239
28:20 399
28:29 199
28:31 199
28:39 401
28:47 240
28:48 437
28:53 263
28:57 437, 560
28:58 176
29:22 240
29:24 399

29:29 560
30:6 375
30:15-20 119
30:20 232
31:9f. 508
31:16 399
31:17 538
31:21 561
31:30 92
32:6 558
32:8f. 331
32:12 241, 439, 554
32:14 404
32:17 165
32:18 171
32:36 549
32:39 510
32:41 566
32:44 92
32:49 173
33:8 234
33:11 510
33:23 224
33:28 241, 506
33:29 201
34:12 549

Joshua
1:5 444
1:8 128, 140
6:26 262
8:20 549
10:1-27 515
10:12 236
10:13 236
10:24 504
11:4 563
15–19 330
18:10 330
23:14 531
24:14-16 176
24:14-27 375
24:14-28 175

Judges
1:4-8 515
1:7 442
2:7 559
2:10 559
3:10 477
3:12 538
5:1 89, 90, 92
5:2 478, 505
5:16 135
5:17 554
5:22 404
5:26 510
5:31 239
6:21 442
6:34 477
7:15 205
8:28 512
9:18 198
9:24 479
11:29-31 477
12:2 199
12:6 101
14:6 477
16:20 478
17:7-9 296
18:5 508
18:7 241
19:1 296
19:16 296
20:16 133, 468
20:43 404

Ruth
1:2 296
1:6 226
2:20 302
2:10 228
2:13 229
4:7 5
4:15 365
4:16 171

1 Samuel
1:7 91
1:11 202
1:20 363
1:27 199
2:1 90
2:1-10 329
2:5 438
2:6 553
2:8 405
2:9 556
2:10 202
2:21 266
2:35 105
3:1 562
3:21 500
4:4 503
4:5-6 203
6:12 565
9:9 5
10:1 105, 177
10:5 500
10:6 105, 477
10:25 172
11:3 199
11:6 477
12:21 232
12:22 440
13:5 563
14:9 236
14:15 234
14:36f. 508
15:1 105
15:3 262
15:17 105
15:22-23 130, 237, 299
15:28 477
16–31 92, 195
16:1 478
16:1-13 105
16:7 568
16:13 105, 165, 477
16:14 478
16:14-23 89
16:18 331
17:7 201
17:34-35 437
17:41 201
17:44 270
17:51 407
18:5 174
18:7 204
18:14 174
18:15 174

18:16 567
19:6 304
19:10 402
19:19 500
21:4f. 506
21:8 404
22 420
22:1-5 420
22:6-8 567
22:19 262
23:2 508
24:6-11 105
24:10-14 373
25:26 479
25:28 505
25:31 479
25:33 479
26:9-24 105
26:19 20, 319
26:21 562
28:13 268
28:16 565
30:7f. 508

2 Samuel

1–10 92, 195
1:16 479
2:1-4 180
2:4 105
2:7 105
2:18-23 565
3:28-29 479
3:35 304
5:1-3 180
5:3 105
5:6ff. 168
5:6-8 515
5:7 505
5:9 505
5:17 105
5:17-25 180
6:1-15 514
6:17 297, 444
6:18 206
7 410, 505, 507
7:2 297
7:6 297
7:7-16 20
7:10 234, 514
7:12 171
7:14 30, 99, 103, 138, 170, 171, 173
7:14-15 171
7:16 105
7:20 546
7:22 176
7:23 440
8:2 362
8:15 439
8:17 514
9:7-13 442
10–12 476
11–20 92
11:1 74
11:3 471
11:4 467
11:4-5 470
11:20 195
11:27 471
12 467
12:1 467
12:1-7 29
12:9 471
12:10 204, 471
12:12 467, 560
12:13 204, 467, 471
12:14 473
12:20 298
13:9-19 470
14:4 199
14:12 200
14:22 229
15–18 567
15:12-14 196
15:24-35 196
15:25 196, 203
15:30 202
15:31 203, 204
16:4 229
16:5-11 193, 199
16:7-8 479
16:21 196, 471
17:14b 197
18:3 196
18:8 196
18:18 440
18:33 234
19:37 179
20:3 228
20:8 407
20:9-10 554
21–24 92, 195
21 210, 225
21:1 92, 232, 479
21:7 105
22:1 89, 353
22:2-3 201
22:3 550
22:6 335
22:8 234
22:26 233, 234
22:39 510
23 105
23:1 90, 502
23:1-2 478, 502
23:2 477, 502
23:3 74, 439
23:8-39 401
23:16 330
23:17 330
23:34 471
24 197

1 Kings

1:13 304
1:17 304
1:26 180
1:29f. 304
1:39 297
1:43-48 180
1:45 165
2:1-4 295
2:3 353
2:5 479
2:9 479
2:19 333, 503
2:28-30 297
2:31-33 479
3:1 482
3:5 172
5–7 514

5:1-6 514
5:3 504
5:17 262
6–8 277
6:1–7:51 482
6:18 402
6:29 402
6:32 402
6:35 402
7:7 503
8:1 514
8:4 297
8:22 229
8:29 560
8:30 552
8:35-36 225
8:37 263
8:38 229
8:39 559
8:46 472
8:54 229
9:15-19 180
11:1-13 180
11:20 171
11:27 180
12:11 175
14:11 406
16:2 405
16:4 406
16:13 419
16:24 503
16:34 262
18:12 477
18:19-40 231
18:41-46 238
19:18 177, 225
21:19 406
21:23 406
21:25 406
22:24 206

2 Kings

1:13 562
2:3 500
2:16 477
2:24 101
3:15 500
4:10 442
4:38 405
6:8-23 201
6:10 370
6:26 199, 200
9:10 406
9:26 479
10:14 101
11:4-12 165
11:12 172
11:14 503
12:4-7 514
14:25 365
15:7 553
18:17-37 199
18:19-35 196
18:21 442
19:21 402
19:25 547, 561
21:13 469
22:3-7 514
23:3 503
23:4-7 514
25:1-12 19
25:26 20
25:27 202

1 Chronicles

4:9 569
6:31 514
9:22 262
9:23 297
9:25 240
9:33 402
11:18 330
11:20-47 401
13:10 505
15–16 91
15 26
15:1 297
15:11-16 514
15:19 419
15:21 207
15:22ff. 27
16 26
16:1 297
16:4 94
16:4-6 129
16:4-42 514
16:8-9 79
17:5 297
18:17 514
21:18–22:19 482
22:2-5 514
22:9-10 171, 180
23:3-31 514
23:4 207
23:5 89, 208, 419
25:1 208, 419, 514
25:1ff. 27
25:2 208
25:3 208
25:6 208
28 91
28:2 514
28:6 171
29:5 261
29:12 270
29:23 180

2 Chronicles

1:3 297
1:4 297
2:1-17 207
6:41 234
6:41-42 26
9:18 504
13:8 505
13:12 505
14:8 201
15:8 514
17:7-9 514
17:8f. 508
17:16 478
19:2 566
19:8-11 514
20 26, 500
20:13-21 505
20:19 27
23:18 208
23:19 295
24:4-12 514
24:23 363
25:27 240

26:16-21 507
29 91
29:3-11 514
29:25 514
29:25-30 89
29:26 89
29:27 208
29:30 101, 514
29:31 478
32:2-8 206
32:15 539
32:33 201
33:8 402
34:8 514
34:12-13 207
35:15-16 514

Ezra
2:64-65 19
3:8 207
3:10 362, 514
7:6 549
8:20 514
10:1 229

Nehemiah
2:8 549
8:12 240
9 27
9:10 440
9:17 229
9:30 477
9:31 229
12:11 500
12:24 514
12:36 89, 514
12:45 514
13:14 469, 561
13:16 271

Esther
1:8 262
2:7 171
4:1 379
4:3 553
4:16 142, 379
8:16 557
8:16-17 475
9:17-18 240

Job
1:15ff. 401
3:4 556
3:4-5 441
3:16 261, 367
3:17 335
3:18-19 335
3:24 399
4:3 175
4:10 399
4:13 568
4:17 472
4:19 475
5:8 507
5:17 133
5:18 510
5:24 133, 468
7:9 335
7:17 266
7:17-18 272, 273
7:18 192
7:21 405
9:21 463
9:28 371
9:31 324
10:14 371
10:20-22 441
10:21f. 556
11:8 261
12:12 444
12:22 441
13:10 560
13:15 544, 564
13:17 360
13:21 549
13:28 406
14:4 472
14:10 192
14:15 561
15:14 471, 472
15:14-15 273
15:17 360
15:22 556
16:4 402
16:10 206
16:16 441
17:12 239, 557
17:13 553, 555, 556
17:14 324
17:16 335
18:5f. 239, 557
18:10 135
18:17 409
18:18 556
20:2 568
20:11 405
20:18 506
21:9 173
21:13 324
21:18 141
21:26 405, 553
22:11 556
22:12 261
22:21 535
22:28 239, 360, 557
23:10 568
23:17 556
24:13-17 556
24:14 544, 564
24:17 441
24:22 404
25:4 471, 472
25:6 266, 401
26:6 552
26:10 556
26:12 510
26:12f. 554
27:7 567
27:20 555
27:22 552
28:3 441
28:12-24 359
28:28 367
29:3 239, 557
29:13 206
29:17 206
29:21 236
30:27 236
30:28 364
31:15 559
31:27 560

31:34 236
32:6 360
32:10 360
32:17 360
32:22 179, 324
33:4 477
33:6 538
33:23 367
33:28 556, 557
33:30 239, 324, 556
34:20 404
34:22 441
34:24 192
36:2 360
36:16 442
37:13 173
37:21 261
38:8-9 556
38:8-10 554
38:12-13 553
38:12-15 355
38:31-33 261
39:4 160
39:11 335
39:16 164
39:29 547
40:1-11 179
40:10 269
41:8 549

Psalms
1–126 60
1–72 103-4
1–60 62
1–8 102
1–2 102
1 10, 15, 29, 30, 32, 45, 88, 94, 102, 103, 115-44, 145-46, 189, 193, 207, 291, 356, 380
1:1 30, 160, 178, 179, 234, 402, 441, 479, 547, 548, 551, 564, 565
1:2 24, 30, 31, 103, 116, 160, 163, 164, 166, 233, 359, 365, 373, 400, 402, 473, 480, 546, 548, 557
1:3 414, 471, 480
1:4 102-3, 104, 476, 564
1:5 28, 367, 368, 406, 547, 564
1:5-6 335, 569
1:6 32, 116, 161, 178, 233, 306, 337, 470, 479, 505, 546, 564
2 6, 10, 15, 30, 32, 66, 88, 93, 99, 102-4, 112, 145-81, 189, 193, 207, 219, 266, 308, 488, 502, 504
2:1 30, 296, 399
2:1-2 30, 110, 509, 510
2:2 129, 442
2:3 477
2:4 241, 400, 402, 480, 503, 547, 553
2:5 260
2:6 129, 180, 203, 233, 298, 482, 505, 506
2:7 99, 106, 110, 199, 205
2:7-8 103, 106
2:7-11 172
2:8 203, 228, 331
2:9 173, 441, 495, 505
2:10 32, 510
2:10-12 105
2:11 410, 475
2:12 32, 142, 479, 518, 548
3–41 101
3–7 161, 193
3 10, 16, 23, 88, 92, 95, 161, 182-209, 215, 248
3:1 198, 263, 439, 566
3:2 153, 399, 478, 559, 564
3:3 231, 333, 335, 400, 407, 439, 512, 548
3:4 400
3:5 241, 308, 478, 563
3:6 402, 414, 441, 504
3:7 408, 481, 504, 564, 567
3:8 200, 206, 399, 414
4 10, 16, 88, 91, 161, 194, 210-43
4:1 183, 194, 299, 368, 403, 411, 414, 469, 475, 480, 564
4:2 194, 199, 266, 400
4:3 172, 201, 234, 336, 337, 411, 475, 546, 549
4:4 300, 333, 334, 412, 470, 476, 568
4:5 405, 483
4:6 194, 239, 411, 475, 551, 553, 564
4:7 300, 333, 412, 443, 568
4:8 203, 368, 405
5 45, 161
5:3 231
5:6 565
5:8 230, 439, 554
5:12 201
6 30, 408, 449
6:1 175
6:3 111
6:5 335
6:8 96
6:9 229
6:11-13 16, 30
7 23, 92, 244, 256
7:5 405
7:7-8 91
7:8-9 97
7:17 230
8 16, 94, 110, 193, 244-75, 308
8:1 329, 553, 562
8:2 96, 442, 504
8:3 359, 402, 553, 559
8:5 402, 506
8:6 413, 504, 559
8:8 554

8:9-10 88
9–13 193
9 88, 256
9:12 479
10 88, 102
10:4 197
10:6 555
10:11 197
11–13 30
11:4f. 547
12:1 234
12:2 300
12:4-5 153
13:1-2 226
13:3 335
13:4 263
14 45, 193, 276, 280, 291
14:1 197, 555
14:7 203, 281
15–24 102, 276, 435
15 16, 34, 45, 95, 130, 276-306, 389
15:1 334, 362, 410, 443, 554
15:2 365, 439, 480, 551
15:3 301, 414, 548, 553
15:4 282, 301, 367, 402, 410, 481, 507
15:5 414, 507, 509, 569
16 6, 15, 30, 307-39, 518
16:4 553, 563
16:7 175, 310, 557, 558
16:8 89, 90, 470, 503
16:8-11 110
16:9 475, 554, 568
16:9f. 552
16:10 233, 234, 308, 439, 553, 560, 568
16:11 518, 569
17:1 229
18 6-8, 23, 89, 90, 92, 96, 99, 345-46, 353, 370
18:2 201, 203, 374
18:5 552
18:7 178, 234
18:28 239
18:30 201
18:31 33
18:32-45 179
18:35 201
18:38 510
18:43 91
18:46 33, 374
18:49 91, 110
18:50 165, 353
19 94, 290, 291, 340-75
19:1 261, 347, 406, 409, 414, 480
19:2 360
19:3 360, 399
19:4 548
19:6 411, 475, 553
19:7 103, 136, 407, 412, 478
19:8 568
19:9 410, 412
19:10 166
19:11 370, 441
19:12 475, 547, 572
19:13 413, 441
19:14 411, 480, 482, 568
19:19 473
20 45, 91, 99
20:1-4 203
20:1-5 228
20:6 200
20:7 206
20:7-9 197
20:7-10 197
20:9 200
21 45, 91, 99, 107
21:1 200
21:2 203, 228
21:4 228, 444
21:5 202, 203, 268, 269
21:6 261, 268
21:9 179
22 6, 15, 61, 66, 112, 198, 376-415, 529
22:1 547
22:7 480
22:8 473, 479
22:9 222
22:9-10 559
22:9ff. 105
22:12 483
22:14 475
22:16 333
22:17 559
22:18 112
22:21 479
22:22 110
22:22-24 478
22:23 559
22:24 333
22:25-26 478
22:26 479, 569
22:27-31 91
22:29 569
22:31 230, 480
23 15, 326, 416-45
23:3 471, 554, 569
23:3-4 230
23:4 471, 551
23:5-6 292
23:6 239, 298, 469
24 30, 130, 290
24:3 50
24:3-4 291
24:3-5 291
24:3-6 30, 232, 291
24:6 232
24:7 90, 236, 512
24:9 90, 236, 512
25:11 440
25:19 198
26 129
26:5 566
26:9 565
26:10 554
27–30 45
27:3 198
27:4-5 293
27:4-6 298
27:5 297
27:6 201, 202, 297
27:8 232
27:11 554

28 91
28:8 200
29 90, 94
29:10 166, 261
30 25, 91, 92, 514
30:3 183, 308, 553
30:4 233
30:5 506
30:9 183
30:12 236
31 45, 459, 460
31:3 440
31:5 111
31:6 556
31:13 198
31:16 203, 239
31:17 236
31:23 233, 234
32–34 45
32 346, 464
32:4 470
32:5 468
32:8 560
32:8-10 479
33 94, 102
33:2 208
33:10 200
33:12 431
33:15 557
33:16-18 197
33:17 506
34 23, 92, 276, 479
34:6 410
34:12 239
34:12-16 112
34:20 112, 475
35:5 141
35:6 556
35:10 475
35:13 229
35:15 236, 557
35:19 111, 141
35:27-28 97
35:28 230
36:2 176, 178
36:8 512
36:9 239, 357, 359
36:10 557
37 31, 94
37:5 414
37:6 557
37:7 31, 236
37:9 406
37:11 110
37:13 167
37:18-19 31
37:32-33 31
37:34 406
38 464
38:8-10 475
38:11 97
38:19 198, 562
39:9 414
39:12 229
40:1-6 478
40:4 232
40:5 562
40:6 563
40:7-8 478
40:9 230
40:12 470
40:16 232
41 45, 102, 104, 118
41:13 22
42–83 101, 468
42–49 101
42 45, 88
42:3 196, 199
42:4 88
42:6 111
43 45, 88
43:1 234
43:3 239, 556, 557
43:3-4 88
44 35, 91
44:3 239
44:9 199
44:13-16 196
44:19 441
44:21 559
44:25 405
45 50, 66, 99, 308
45:3 179, 261, 269, 506
45:4 268, 554
45:6 99, 110, 505
45:7 104
45:13 201
46 94
46:2f. 554
46:5 306
46:9 263
48 45, 94, 505
48:2 203
48:10 230
49 94
49:2 231
49:4 500
49:15 309, 335, 553
49:19 557
50 101, 118
50:5 233, 234
51–52 23
51 15, 27, 45, 61, 74, 92, 446-83
51:1-2 479
51:4 134, 560
51:5 548, 560
51:8 559
51:10 505
51:11 551
51:13 97, 479
51:14 230, 474
52 92
52:9 233, 414
52:11 360
54 23, 92
54:3 198
54:4 204
54:7 406
55:6 554
55:18 198
55:22 112
55:23 565
56–60 327
56–57 23
56 92, 309
56:1-2 198
56:8 469
56:13 557
57 92, 309
57:2 203

57:4 204
57:9 91
58 309
58:6 206
58:10-11 97
59–60 23
59 92, 309
59:1-2 565
59:4 198
59:8 167
59:11-13 565
59:14 405
59:14-15 405
59:16-17 201
60 91, 92, 309
60:11 200
60:12 200
61 91
61:1 229
61:4 296, 297, 298
61:4-5 293
62:2 31
62:5 236
62:7 202
62:9 231
63 88, 91, 92, 185
65 94
65:2 229
65:11 269
66 91
67 94
67:1 239
67:6 239
68 31, 94
68:2 31
68:11 360
68:15-16 203
68:16 20
68:18 20
68:21 510, 511
68:23 510
68:24 489
68:24-27 129
68:30b 34
69 23
69:4 562
69:5 559
69:6 232
69:7-9 97
69:9 110, 567
69:22-28 97
69:23 556
69:27 230
69:28 469, 528
69:32 412
69:34-36 23
71:15 200
71:17 403
72 74, 97, 99, 103-4, 118, 172
72:4 200
72:5 106, 261
72:6 105
72:7 261
72:8 173
72:14 562
72:16 105
72:17 261
72:19-20 22
72:20 101, 103
73–89 104
73–83 101
73 23, 94
73:13 164
73:21 333
73:22 569
73:23 563
73:23-24 555, 569
73:25 533
73:26 331
74 35
74:10 263
74:11 503
74:18 196, 263
75 91
75:8 425-26
76 94
77:8 360
77:16 234
77:18 234
77:20 104
78 70-71, 419, 436
78:2 110
78:14 439
78:24 110
78:52 435
78:53 439
78:55 331
78:70-71 419
78:70-72 436
79 35
79:2 233, 234
79:2-3 24, 35, 110
79:6 260
79:9 440
79:10 196
80:3 239, 365
80:7 239, 365
80:19 239, 365
81 244
81:3 129
81:14 179
82 97
82:1-2 30
82:6 110
83:17-18 97
83:18 241
84–88 101
84 91, 94, 244
84:2 277
84:8 229
84:10 105, 298
84:11 202
85:8-9 233, 234
85:12 239
86:1 229
86:2 233, 234
86:4 366
86:6 229
86:10 241
86:14 198, 372
86:15 229
87 94
87:6 469
88 88
88:2 229
88:3-6 552
88:6 556
88:11-18 335
88:12 555, 556
88:18 556

89 23, 91, 102, 104, 118, 516
89:3-4 20, 507
89:20 105, 233
89:22-29 172
89:25 554
89:26 171, 228
89:26-27 180
89:26-29 171, 205
89:27 205
89:35-37 20
89:41 196
89:42 554
89:45 263
89:47-52 99
89:48 335
89:52 22
90–106 23, 104
90 112
90:1 104
90:1-2 104
91 94, 107, 282
91:4 201
91:15 203
91:16 444
92:10 91
93–99 104
93:3-4 260
93:5 444
94:2 230
94:7-11 571
94:8-11 97
94:9 531
94:10 174
94:17 335
94:19 568
95 186, 276
95:4 552
96 94
96:1-13 26
96:3 359
96:6 268, 269
97:8 169
97:10 233, 234
98 94
99:3 176
99:6 104
100 94, 118
101 99, 291
101:5 560
102 91, 464
102:1 229, 410
102:18 149, 488
102:25-27 112
103–106 22
103 94
103:4 269
103:7 104
103:8 229
103:18 366
103:21-22 559
104 94, 259, 356
104:6f. 554
104:13 559
104:15 366
104:26 271
104:34 373
105 94
105:1-15 26
105:3 366
105:3-4 232
105:15 105
105:26 104
105:43 475
106 102, 118
106:1 26, 47, 104, 118
106:8 440
106:16 104
106:23 104
106:32 104
106:37 165
106:47 104
106:47-49 26
106:48 22
107–150 104
107 92, 381
107:5 438
107:9 438
107:10 441
107:14 441
107:36 438
108–110 104
108 355
108:5 522
109:4 229, 443
109:13-15 469
109:21 440
109:25 402
109:27 414
109:31 200
110–133 62
110 6, 15, 72, 74, 75, 77, 99, 106, 172, 179, 266, 308, 484-516
110:1 106, 554
110:3 99, 553
110:4 569
110:5 510, 554
110:6 510
110:7 202
111–113 22
111 94
111:6 173
111:7 366
111:8 414
112 94
112:8 406
113 94
114 94, 428
114:4 34
115–117 22
115:8 414
115:16 260
116:1-16 478
116:10 112
116:17-19 478
117 94
118:6-7 197
118:10 91
118:19 237
118:27 239
119 29, 45, 64, 342, 345, 356, 366, 426
119:1 103, 136
119:4 200
119:21 370
119:25 405
119:33 370
119:36 140
119:41 200
119:46 91

119:51 372
119:57 331
119:69 372
119:78 372
119:85 372
119:108 373
119:112 370
119:126 414
119:135 239
119:160 562
120:7 443
121:1-2 169
121:6 203
122 94
122:9 239
126 92
127 94
127:1 309
127:3 472
127:5 472
128 94
129:4 165
130 464, 465, 469
130:3 469
132 99, 129, 516
132:1-9 297
132:2-5 304
132:8-10 26
132:11-12 20
132:11-15 226
132:13-14 20
132:13-16 298
132:13-18 505
132:16 129
132:17 105
133 94
135 22, 94
135:6 414
136 94
137 31, 92, 95, 345
137:4 20
138–145 104
138 523
138:2 440
138:6 546, 547
138:7 554
139 16, 91, 517-72
139:2 547
139:8 335
139:10 569
139:11f. 239
139:13f. 333
139:15 559, 560
139:15-16 403
139:16 331, 469
139:17 547
139:19-22 97
139:20 260
140 185
140:6 203
141 245
141:7 335
142 92
142:1 229
142:5 331
142:7 97
143 464
143:1 229
143:3 556
144 91
144:1-11 99
144:3 546
145–150 94
145:5 268, 269
145:6 176
145:8 229
145:12 268
145:14 204
146–150 22, 102
146:3 197, 200
146:6 112
146:7 438
146:9 296
147:20 414
148 356
148:7 347
148:14 302
149 381
149:5 234
149:6-7 262-63
150 118, 129
151 29, 32, 36
154 29
155 36, 39

Proverbs

1–9 134
1:3 305, 439
1:7 130, 302, 367
1:12 324
1:15 135
1:16 441
1:22 134
1:32 365
2:1 305
2:8 370
2:9 135
2:12 441
2:15 135
2:22 142
3:1 370
3:3 399
3:8 475
3:9 399
3:13 131
3:16 310
3:18 131
3:20 506
3:21 370
3:27-35 468
3:28 301
3:29-30 302
3:34-35 134
4:1-9 375
4:11 135
4:14-15 135
4:18 359, 367, 557
5:16 140
5:17 140
6:23 367
6:34 264
7:20 305
7:25 135
8:2 135
8:12ff. 310
8:17 232
8:20 135
8:22 558
8:30 505
8:36 133, 468
9:7 175, 332
9:7-8 134

9:9 175
9:12 134
10:6 206
10:7 409
10:10 305
10:30 306
11:26 206
12:4 201, 475
13:1 134
13:9 239, 367, 557
13:23-24 173
13:24 173
14:6 134
14:7-8 134
14:10 240, 568
14:32 408, 413
15:11 335, 552
15:12 134
15:24 335
15:27 305
15:28 373
15:29 399
15:30 367
16:2 568
16:15 367
16:24 369
17:3 568
17:14 402
17:17 301
18:4 360, 567
18:11 550
18:24 232
19:2 133, 468
19:18 175
19:25 134
19:29 134
20:1 134
20:9 472
20:16 305
20:28 206
20:29 268
21:11 134
21:24 134, 372
21:31 206
22:10 134
22:15 173
22:27 305
23:10f. 374
23:15f. 333
23:35 563
24:6 206
24:8 565
24:9 134
24:20 239
25:21-22 565
25:23 472
26:3 173
26:8 303
26:10 472
26:11 406
27 372
27:10 302
27:20 335
27:21 568
28:5 232
28:8 305
28:13 467, 479
29:8 134
29:9 235
29:10 565
29:15 173
29:19 175
30:1 502
30:4 171
30:16 335
30:18 550
30:20 469
30:21 234
31:1 175, 332
31:2 177

Ecclesiastes

3:18 507
5:1-7 304
5:4-6 293
7:20 472
9:7 240
12:3 506
12:13 367

Song of Songs

1:7 434, 438, 439
2:6 204
3:11 269
6:10 261, 364, 367
8:6 335
8:9 549

Isaiah

1:2 171
1:10-17 295
1:11ff. 298
1:11-15 130
1:11-17 237
1:13 565
1:18 474
1:23 232
1:27 169
2:2 203
2:2-3 277
2:3 489
2:5 557
2:13 404
3:1-4 499
3:12 135
4:3 561
4:5 363
5:14 335
5:20 441
5:25 234
5:29 399
5:30 556
7:13 266
7:14 106
8:11 30
8:19 268
9:2 239, 441
9:3 240
9:10 550
10:5 505
10:12 169
10:13 404
10:15 173
10:24 169
11:2 477
13:3f. 505
13:11 372
13:20 434
14:3 569
14:9 234
14:11 401, 553

14:18 201
14:22 198
14:32 262
15:6 438
16:10 240
17:10 374
17:13 141
18:2 505
19:21 176
21:5 201
22:7 205
22:11 561
22:13 240
23:2 223, 236
24:11 240
24:19 306
24:23 364
25:8 469
25:12 550
26:4 374
26:5 550
26:8 409
26:19 563
28:14 134
28:16 262
28:21 234
28:26 332-33
29:15 556
29:15-16 571
29:20 134
30:7 164
30:26 364, 557
30:27 179
31:1 206, 562
31:3 268
32:5 303
32:15 477
33:5 169
33:14-16 291, 295
33:15 479
34:7 404
34:11 362
34:17 362
35:6 511
36:6 442
37:12 402
37:17 560
37:26 547, 561
38:9 89, 90, 92
38:10 335
38:18 324, 335
38:20 91
40–48 20
40:9 169
40:11 435, 439
40:12-14 360
40:25-26 261
40:28 559
41:13 544
41:21-29 9
41:22-29 20
42:1 108, 477
42:1-4 164
42:6 544
42:9 559
43:4 562
44:2 559, 561
44:3 477
44:17 229
44:22 469, 475
44:23 560
44:24 561
44:28 434
47:1 405
45:1 544
45:3 233
45:5 233
45:18 561
45:19 560
46:11 561
48:5 569
48:9 440
48:16 240, 477, 560
48:20 20
49:1-2 9, 403
49:1-6 164
49:4 164
49:5 559, 561
49:8 561
50:4-9 164
51:12 266
52:13 106
52:13–53:12 164
53 394
53:11 198
54:10 306
57:5f. 330
57:20 133
58:1-8 295
58:5 553
59:2 475
59:12 470
59:15-19 165
59:21 477
60:22 407
61:1 477
61:1-2 97
61:1-3 105
61:10 363
62:5 363
63:1 406
63:8f. 199
63:10 569
63:10-11 477, 478
63:11 477
63:12 333
63:14 477
63:17 176, 178
64:6 406
65:6 561
65:11 330
66:1 503, 504
66:3 330
66:24 401, 511

Jeremiah
1:5 403, 559, 561
1:16 399
2:6 441
2:11 322
2:19 176, 178
2:20 165
2:22 469
2:25 232
2:27 171
3:14 169
4:28 538
5:2 304
5:5 165
5:6 562
5:24-25 239

7:1-11 295
7:9 304, 472
7:18 330
7:22-23 130
7:23 138
7:34 363, 475
8:14 236
8:16 404
9:6 278
9:12 399
9:23-24 148
10:16 331, 561
10:24 175
12:3 546, 572
12:12-13 29
14:7 440
14:8 199
14:19 169
14:21 440
14:22 231
15:8 562
15:9 239
15:12 173
15:15 572
15:17 242
16:9 363, 475
16:19 173
16:21 440
17:6 239
17:9 567, 568
18:5-10 507
18:11 561
18:15 135
19:5 225
19:13 330
20:14-18 97
20:18 324
21:7 469
22:3 439
22:15 439
22:18 261, 268
22:24 106
22:30 106
23:3 198
23:11 500
23:33-40 499
24:2 301, 441
24:7 477
25:10 240, 363, 475
25:15 331
26:7 500
28 106
29:5-7 19
29:18 302
29:26 500
30–33 20
30:9 198
30:11 175
30:14 263
30:14f. 562
31:2-3 229
31:26 563
31:31-33 297
31:31-34 139, 410
31:34 476
31:39 362
32:39 476, 477
33:2 561
33:11 363, 475
33:11-12 240
33:12 434
33:15 439
35:4 500
35:7-10 297
37:17 560
38:16 560
40:15 560
41:16–43:7 20
42–50 296
42:18 302
43:2 372
44:7 262
44:8 302
44:17 324
44:18 437
46:15 404
47:3 404
47:6 236
48:2 236
48:12 505
49:31 241, 242
50:11 404
50:34 374
51:33 250

Lamentations

1:1 242
1:2 263
1:9 263
1:11 365
1:16 262
2:10 236
2:13 169
2:15 402
2:16 263
2:17 263
3:1 324
3:2 557
3:6 556
3:24 321, 331
3:26 242
3:28 236
3:30 206
3:63 547
4:4 262
4:7 506
4:20 105

Ezekiel

1:4 556
2:2 477
2:10 223
3 370
3:14 477
3:17-19 479
3:18 479
3:20 479
3:48 140
4:10 240
4:11 240
4:17 437
5:13 20
5:20 444
6:7 20
8:12 556
9:9 479
11:5 477
11:19 476, 477
13:3-7 565
16:43 235
17:6 505
17:17 411

18:8 305
18:13 305
18:31 477
19:7 399
20:40 178
20:44 440
22:12 278, 279
22:21 179
24:3 405
24:8 479
24:17 236
26:2 263
26:16 406
26:20 560
28:22 178
31:14 560
31:16 560
31:18 560
32:7f. 556
32:18 560
32:24 560
32:25 553
33 370
33:7-9 479
34:4 505
34:15 434
36:24-32 20
36:26 476
36:26-27 477
37:15-28 20
37:24 445
39:18 404
39:21 549
44:23 508
45:9 439
47:12 143

Daniel

2:11 562
2:30 507
4:17 507
6:6 157
6:10 169
6:11 157
6:15 157
7:9-14 108
7:10 561
7:13f. 504, 518
7:16 393
9:25 365
11:21 261, 268
11:35 367
12:1 561
12:2 405, 563
12:11 240

Hosea

1:7 206
2:7 444
2:8 135
3:4 105
5:1-7 499
5:3 546, 559
6:4-6 295
6:6 130, 237, 298
8:3 263
9:11 254
10:3 176, 178
11:1 171
12:4 401
12:10 297
13:2 177
13:3 141
13:5 546
13:14 335, 560

Joel

1:5 563
1:20 270
2:10 234
2:16 262, 363
2:21-22 438
3:13 250, 505

Amos

2:4 232
3:1-7 499
3:2 546
4:1 404
5:8 441
5:13 236
5:18 239, 556
5:20 239
5:21ff. 298
5:21-24 237, 295
6:1 169
6:5 89
7:1 561
7:17 331
8:9 234, 556
9:2 552, 553
9:11-15 20

Obadiah

12 406
17-21 20

Jonah

1:3 552
1:10 552
2 92
2:2 552
2:9 232
4:2 229, 552
4:7 401

Micah

1:3-7 499
1:13 206
2:2 368
2:5 331
3:6 556
3:8 477
4:1 203
4:2 169
5:1 206
5:2 445
5:2-6 106
5:3 173
5:4 445
5:14 96
5:10-15 206
6:1-8 291
6:6-8 130, 237, 295
6:7 204
7:9 230
7:14 241
7:19 475

Nahum

1:7 546

3:16 261

Habakkuk
1:9-10 192
3 88
3:1 89, 90
3:2 360
3:7 234
3:9 360
3:13 510

Zephaniah
1:6 232
2:4 137
3:5 506

Haggai
1:10 506
2:5 477
2:11ff. 508
2:11-13 295
2:23 106

Zechariah
4:9 262
6:11 513
6:12-13 287, 513
6:13 261, 268
7:12 477
8:4 442
8:12 506
9:10 206
10:8 198
11:2 404
11:3 399
13:9 568
14:7 556
14:10 393

Malachi
2:7 508
2:14 538
3:5 296
3:15 372
3:16 561
3:20 553
4:1 372
4:2 329, 375

INTERTESTAMENTAL WORKS

Sirach
18:4-7 563
40:1 560
42:20 548
47:8-10 90
48:17 140
50:16-17 26
51:13-30 29

Baruch
29:3 108
30:1 108
39:7 108
40:1 108
40:2 108
40:3 108
70:9 108
72:2 108
74:2 108

1 Maccabees
1:36-40 35
2:7-13 35
3:45 35
4:25 26
4:46 513
4:54 26
9:27 513
9:30f. 512
10:20 512
14:35 512
14:38 512
14:41 512

2 Maccabees 108

Book of Jubilees 109

Testament of the Twelve Patriarchs 109

T. Levi
4:4 109
10 109
14–15 109
16 109

Psalms of Solomon 109
8:11 109
17:5-6 109
17:21 109
17:23f. 513
17:32 109
18:5 109
18:7 109

1 Enoch
46:1-3 108
68:3 333

4 Ezra (2 Esdras)
7:30-44 108

NEW TESTAMENT

Matthew
1:1 163, 488
1:12 106
1:18-25 180
2:6 445
4:2 438
5:3-4 450
5:3-12 133
5:5 110, 142
5:16 350
5:17-18 367
5:34 503
5:39-42 98
5:42 278
5:43-48 98
6:6 183
6:9-10 260
6:12 450
6:14 98
6:22-23 367
7:6 406
7:15 445

7:23 96, 116
10:16 445
10:34 506, 570
11:30 147, 166
12:1 438
12:3 438
12:7 130
12:25 570
12:34 360
13:4 139
13:13 375
13:19 139
13:30 97
13:35 110
15:17-19 218
15:26-27 406
16 517
16:19 455
18:3 247
18:15-20 450
18:20 570
19:27-28 181
19:29 370
21:15-16 247
21:16 246, 262
21:42 110
22:21 215
22:41-46 112, 517
22:42-25 495
22:43 90, 489, 492
22:44 110, 484
22:44f. 517
22:45 90
23:33-36 209
24:1-3 208
24:35 121
24:36 518
25:27 287
25:31ff. 518
25:31-46 511
25:46 96, 97, 209
26:30 40
26:33-35 571
26:34 524
26:38 110
26:63 180
27:9 494
27:27-46 208
27:34 110
27:39 110
27:43 377, 392
27:46 110, 198, 208, 377, 415
27:48 110
28:18 253
28:18-20 110, 175, 181
28:20 570

Mark

1:12 208
2:2-7 470
2:8 570
2:25 438
7:27-28 406
9:41 370
10:29-30 570
12:9 209
12:15 570
12:33 130
12:36 484
12:36-37 90, 517
14:26 40
14:27 445
14:29-31 571
14:35 482
14:61-64 484
15:24 377

Luke

1:5-25 500
1:32 517
1:34f. 111
1:78 375
2:11 35
2:13-14 40
2:34 490
2:37 277
4:18-20 97
5:22 570
5:32 462
6:3 438
6:8 570
6:23 370
6:25 438
6:28 98
6:35 98, 370
9:57-62 506
10:18 510
10:21-22 334
10:29-36 301
11:17 570
12:32 445
15:3-7 437
15:20 524
16:24 438
17:2 97
18:1-8 97, 565
18:6-8 96
18:11-14 278
20:42 90
20:42-43 484
20:42-44 517
21:28 202, 209
22:20 375
23:34 209, 565
23:35 377
23:46 110
24:13-49 2
24:25-26 5
24:27 488
24:44 22, 41, 110, 154, 163
24:44-45 338

John

1:1 489
1:1-14 122
1:3 570
1:9 478
1:13 401
1:48 570
1:49 111, 180
2 510
2:9 206
2:12-23 444
2:14 444, 491
2:17 110
2:24f. 570
3 510
3:16 111
4 510
5 204, 510

5:3 166
5:19-28 209
5:39 425, 488
6:31 110
6:38 314
8:25 123
8:31 85
8:44 402
8:47 85
9:34 473
10:1-16 445
10:18 490
10:34 110
11:38f. 336
12:20-36 209
12:27 110, 209
12:47-48 156
13:11 570
13:18 110
13:37f. 571
14:16 570
15:18 570
15:25 110, 208
16:21 472
17 111, 181, 209, 243, 315
17:1-26 209
17:2 110
17:6 312
17:11 314
17:20 312, 315
19:23-24 28, 377
19:24 110
19:28-29 377
19:32-37 394
19:36 110
20:25-27 394
20:27 377
21:15-19 445

Acts of the Apostles

1:8 505, 517
1:16 90
1:20 110, 119
2:5 146
2:25 90, 314, 318
2:25-31 110
2:25-32 338
2:25-36 28
2:26 323
2:27 323
2:29-32 307
2:29-33 309
2:30-36 517
2:31 319
2:34-35 484
2:34-36 504
2:36 450
2:37 450
2:46-47 40
4:23-29 145
4:24 112
4:24-30 150
4:25-26 28, 90, 110
4:25-28 110
4:25-29 147
4:27 147, 164
5:31 517
7:55-56 517
7:57-59 506
7:59 209
7:60 98, 565
13:33 145
13:35 307, 318, 338
14:15 232
15:12-18 516
16:25-26 40
20:28-29 445

Romans

1:3 488
1:4 492
1:17 61
2 354
2:6 370
3:4 471
3:9-18 164
3:9-20 473
4:6 90
4:14 42
5:12 473
5:13 375
5:20 314, 446
6 190
7:4 375
7:7 368
7:24-25 183
8:2-4 371
8:10-11 143
8:17 181
8:17-18 202
8:18 188
8:20-23 198
8:34 485, 517
8:35 570
8:38 165
8:38-39 440
10:4 212, 217
10:17 361
10:18 374
11:9 90
11:33 311
11:33-35 524
12:1-2 509
12:17-21 96
13:9 368
15:5-6 40
15:9 110

1 Corinthians

1:27-29 264
2:6-8 147
2:6-15 83
2:9 148
2:10-11 142
2:10-16 42
2:11 4
2:14 139
3:1-2 249
3:16-17 444
4:4 571
4:4-5 568
4:11 438
5:12-13 181
6:14-20 444
8:6 570
9:9-10 42
10:1 401
10:11 42
10:20f. 165
10:26 112

11:28 291, 295
11:30 291
11:31 295
12:27 183
13:1 40
13:12 522
13:13 139
14:7-8 40
14:26-27 40
15:4 338
15:20-28 180
15:23-28 111
15:24 518
15:25 504
15:27 110, 253
15:35-58 337
15:51-52 40
15:54 215

2 Corinthians

3:1-3 375
3:6 42, 61
4:7 226
4:7-12 506
4:8-9 191
4:13 112
4:16 148
4:17-18 370
5:1-2 280
5:10 370
5:21 183
6:2 97
6:9 191
8:9 278
9:9 112
10:4 165

Galatians

1:15-16 524
3:13 199
3:29 401
4:24 6, 42
5:16 372

Ephesians

1:8-9 401
1:20 485, 517
1:22 504
2:3 473
2:8 139
2:19 297
3:1-13 9
4:1-13 510
4:3-13 445
4:7 313
4:15 183
4:26 112, 235
4:30 569
5:18-20 40
5:19 486
5:32 375
6:10 201
6:10-20 165, 510
6:11-18 97
6:12 165, 372

Philippians

2:7 183
2:8 253
2:9 150
2:9-10 180
2:17 506
4:3 561
4:12 438

Colossians

1:16 165, 570
1:16-17 525
1:24 202
2:8-15 122
2:15 165
3:1 485, 517
3:16-17 40

1 Thessalonians

5:2-3 179
5:17 185

2 Thessalonians

1:5-9 97
1:6-9 96

1 Timothy

1:8-11 375
1:13 572
3:16 40

2 Timothy

1:10 5
2:3 506
2:8 488
3:16 83, 96
4:14 97, 565
4:14-18 97

Titus

3:5 401

Hebrews

1:1-3 525
1:1-14 28
1:2 570
1:3 517
1:5 30, 110, 492
1:8 505
1:8-9 110
1:10-12 112
1:13 484
2:5-10 110
2:5-13 266
2:6 253
2:6-9 246
2:7 252, 268
2:8 274
2:8-9 272
2:9 267, 274
2:10-12 110
2:12 377, 415
2:12-13 209
4:7 90
4:12 532
4:15 333
5:1-4 508
5:5 110
5:6-10 517
5:8-9 333
6:13-17 507
7 490
7:3 508

7:4-10 509
7:11-28 517
8 375
8:1 517
8:5 504
9:11-12 474
9:24 504
10:1 63
10:5-10 110
10:6-9 130
10:7 119
10:12 517
11 401
11:1 401
12:2 401, 415, 517
12:22 277
13:15 40, 509
13:16 509
13:20 445

James
1:13-15 368
1:17 139, 329, 401
1:25 166, 375
3:5-9 323
4:4 570
5:13 40
5:16 195, 455
5:17-18 238

1 Peter
1:13-14 280
2:4-10 444
2:9 103, 161, 208, 243, 509
2:23 200, 209
3:10-12 112
3:22 485
5:3-4 445
5:4 445
5:7 112

2 Peter
2:22 406
3:8 112
3:8-9 179

1 John
1:9 478
5:3 166
5:16-17 372

Revelation
1:7 394
2:27 173, 180
4:8 40
5:1 561
5:9-10 40
6–9:11 565
6:9-10 97
7:17 439
12:5 173
13:5 101
19:15 173
19:17-18 511
19:20 511
20:2 511
20:11-15 97
20:12 561
21:1 556
21:25 556
22:20 179